D0206942

WORLD

FIFTH EDITION

CIVILIZATIONS

FIFTH EDITION

WORLD CIVILIZATIONS

PHILIP J. ADLER
EAST CAROLINA UNIVERSITY

RANDALL L. POUWELS
UNIVERSITY OF CENTRAL ARKANSAS

WADSWORTH
CENGAGE Learning™

Australia • Brazil • Japan • Korea • Mexico • Singapore • Spain • United Kingdom • United States

World Civilizations, Fifth Edition
Volume I: To 1700
Philip J. Adler, Randall L. Pouwels

Publisher: Clark Baxter

Acquisitions Editor: Ashley Dodge

Senior Development Editor: Sue Gleason

Assistant Editor: Ashley Spicer

Editorial Assistant: Heidi Kador

Associate Development Project Manager: Lee McCracken

Executive Marketing Manager: Diane Wenckebach

Marketing Assistant: Aimee Lewis

Marketing Communications Manager: Tami Strang

Senior Content Project Manager: Lauren Wheelock

Senior Art Director: Cate Rickard Barr

Manufacturing Manager: Marcia Locke

Permissions Editor: Roberta Broyer

Production Service: Pre-Press PMG

Cover/Text Designer: Shawn Girsberger

Photo Researcher: Linda Sykes

Cover Image: Pilgrims quarrelling while on their way to Mecca, from the Kulliyyat of Sa'di (manuscript) by Persian School (16th century) ©British Library, London, UK/ © British Library Board. All Rights Reserved/ The Bridgeman Art Library Nationality

Compositor: Pre-Press PMG

© 2008, 2006 Wadsworth, Cengage Learning

ALL RIGHTS RESERVED. No part of this work covered by the copyright herein may be reproduced, transmitted, stored or used in any form or by any means graphic, electronic, or mechanical, including but not limited to photocopying, recording, scanning, digitizing, taping, Web distribution, information networks, or information storage and retrieval systems, except as permitted under Section 107 or 108 of the 1976 United States Copyright Act, without the prior written permission of the publisher.

For product information and technology assistance, contact us at
Cengage Learning Customer & Sales Support, 1-800- 354-9706
For permission to use material from this text or product,
submit all requests online at **cengage.com/permissions**
Further permissions questions can be emailed to
permissionrequest@cengage.com

Library of Congress Control Number: 2007927204

ISBN-13: 978-0-495-50261-6

ISBN-10: 0-495-50261-8

Wadsworth
25 Thomson Place
Boston, MA 02210
USA

ExamView® and ExamView Pro® are registered trademarks of FSCreations, Inc. Windows is a registered trademark of the Microsoft Corporation used herein under license. Macintosh and Power Macintosh are registered trademarks of Apple Computer, Inc. Used herein under license.

Cengage Learning is a leading provider of customized learning solutions with office locations around the globe, including Singapore, the United Kingdom, Australia, Mexico, Brazil, and Japan. Locate your local office at: **international.cengage.com/region**

Cengage Learning products are represented in Canada by Nelson Education, Ltd.

For your course and learning solutions, visit **academic.cengage.com**

Purchase any of our products at your local college store or at our preferred online store **www.ichapters.com**

Printed in Canada
3 4 5 6 7 11 10 09 08

For Gracie, an historical event
—Philip Adler

To Claire Haney Pouwels in
loving memory
—Randall L. Pouwels

BRIEF CONTENTS

CONTENTS

MAPS

PREFACE

WORLD CIVILIZATIONS is a brief history of civilized life since its inceptions some 5,000 years ago. It is meant to be used in conjunction with a lecture course in world history at the introductory level. The authors, who zbring more than fifty total years of classroom experience to its writing, have kept the needs and interests of freshman and sophomore students in two- and four-year colleges and universities constantly in mind.

World Civilizations deals with the history of civilization throughout the globe but attempts to walk a middle line between exhaustive detail and frustrating brevity. Its narrative embraces every major civilized epoch, but the treatment of topics is selective and follows definite patterns and hierarchies. It deliberately tilts toward social and cultural topics, as well as toward the long-term processes that affect the lives of the millions, rather than the acts of "the captains and the kings." The evolution of law and the formative powers of religion upon early government, for example, receive considerably more attention than wars and diplomatic arrangements. The rise of an industrial working class in European cities is accorded more space than the trade policies of European governments. Such selectivity, of course, is forced on any author of any text, but the firm intent to keep this a concise survey necessitated a particularly close review of the material. Dividing a brief narrative into fifty-six short chapters both gives the instructor considerable leeway for additional material or expansion of the topics and makes it likelier that students will read the assigned material. This approach has been relatively successful and has found sufficient favor among many teachers to justify the appearance of this fifth edition.

CHANGE IN THIS EDITION

The following points are among the many changes in this edition:

Part One: Additional material on agrarian and nomadic civilizations, and on trade and exchange.

Chapter 3 New Evidence of the Past box on the Egyptian priesthood.

Chapter 5 Additional coverage of early Indian and Southeast Asian states.

Chapter 6 Added material on early agriculture in ancient China.

Chapter 7 Material on early trade and exchange in the Mediterranean basin added.

Chapter 8 Chapters on Hellenic culture and Hellenistic civilization combined.

Chapter 9 Additional material on trade and exchange within the Roman Empire and via the Silk Road, Indian Ocean, North Africa, and Western Europe.

Chapter 12 Additional material on East Africa and Indian Ocean trade.

Chapter 16 Additional cultural material on neo-Confucianism and the spread of Buddhism into China, and on economic and commercial expansion under the Song.

Chapter 19 Significant changes have been made in the chapter on the Mongol intrusion. The chapter has been moved before the late medieval and Renaissance. New material has been added on the Yuan Dynasty and the significance of the Mongol expansion for Eurasian contacts and exchanges.

Chapter 25 Two chapters combined into one chapter entitled "Foundations of the European States," including Eastern Europe.

Chapter 28 New Society and Economy box, "Recovering Life Stories of the Voiceless: Testimonial Narratives by African Slaves."

ORGANIZATION OF THE FIFTH EDITION

The table of contents in this fifth edition contains a significantly increased amount of non-Western coverage, has been reorganized more chronologically, and shows increased coverage of worldwide trade and exchange.

The organization of *World Civilizations* is chronological. There are six parts, dealing with six chronological eras from ancient civilizations (3500–500 BCE) to recent times (post-1920 CE). The parts have several binding threads of development in common, but the main point of reference is the relative degree of contact among civilizations. This ranges from near-perfect isolation, as, for example, in ancient China, to close and continual interaction, as in the late twentieth-century world.

The second organizing principle is the prioritization of certain topics and processes. We generally emphasize sociocultural and economic affairs, and keep the longer term in perspective, while deliberately minimizing some short-term phenomena. In terms of the space allotted, we emphasize the more recent epochs of history, in line with the recognition of growing global interdependence and cultural contact.

Although this text was, from its inception, meant as a world history and contains proportionately more material on non-Western peoples and cultures than many others currently in print, the Western nations receive attention consonant with their importance to the modern history of the globe. (In this respect, "Western" means not only European but also North American since the eighteenth century.) The treatment adopted in this book should allow any student to find an adequate explanation of the rise of the West to temporary dominion in modern times and the reasons for the reestablishment of worldwide cultural equilibrium in the latter half of the twentieth century.

After an introductory chapter on prehistory, we look first at Mesopotamia, Egypt, India, and China. In these river valley environments, humans were first successful in adapting nature to their needs on a large scale. Between about 2500 BCE and about 1000 BCE, the river valley civilizations matured and developed a culture in most phases of life: a fashion of thinking and acting that would be a model for as long as that civilization was vital and capable of defending itself. Elsewhere, in Africa and in Mesoamerica, similar processes were under way. However, in two noteworthy respects these regions provided exceptions to the pattern by which people learned to produce food for themselves. In Africa's case, people of the Sahara region domesticated livestock, most likely cattle, before they learned to grow and depend on crops. Also unlike the patterns established in the Old World, early Native American farmers of the Western hemisphere developed forms of agriculture that did not depend on the flood waters of major rivers.

By 500 BCE, the Near Eastern civilizations centered in Egypt and Mesopotamia were in decline and had been replaced by Mediterranean-based ones, as well as new ones in Africa, Asia, and the New World, which drew on the older civilizations to some extent but also added some novel and distinctive features of their own. First the Greeks, then the Romans, succeeded in bringing much of the known world under their influence, culminating in the great Roman Empire reaching from Spain to Persia. For Europe, the greatest single addition to civilized life in this era was the combination of Jewish theology and Greco-Roman philosophy and science.

In the millennium between 500 BCE and 500 CE, the entire globe underwent important change. India's Hindu religion and philosophy had been challenged by Buddhism, while China recovered from political dismemberment to become the permanent chief factor in East Asian affairs. Japan emerged slowly from a prehistoric stage under Chinese tutelage, while the southeastern part of the Asian continent attained a high civilization created in part by Indian traders and Buddhist missionaries.

In the Mediterranean starting about 800, an amalgam of Greco-Roman, Germanic, and Jewish-Christian beliefs called Europe, or Western Christianity, had emerged after the collapse of Roman civilization. At the same time, the emergence of Islam created what many scholars believe was the first truly "world" civilization. Rivaling the great civilizations of Asia and considerably surpassing that of Europe, the great empire of the Abbasid caliphs in Baghdad (750–1258 CE) acted as a commercial and intellectual bridge that transcended regional barriers from China to Europe. Therefore, in the many lands and peoples bordering the Indian Ocean, the spread of Islam along the highways of commerce contributed to the emergence of sophisticated maritime civilizations in Southeast Asia, India, and East Africa. In West Africa, the great Sudanic civilizations of Mali and later Songhay likewise were based solidly on an Islamic foundation. Despite isolation, Native Americans of the New World created a series of highly sophisticated civilizations in the high Andes mountains of South America, in Mesoamerica, and in the southwestern and midwestern parts of what now is the United States.

By 1500, Western Christianity began to rise to a position of worldwide domination, marked by the voyages of discovery and ensuing colonization. In the next three centuries, the Europeans and their colonial outposts slowly wove a web of worldwide commercial and technological interests anchored on military force. Our book's treatment of the entire post-1500 age gives much attention to the impacts of Western culture and ideas on non-Western peoples, and vice versa. In particular, it looks at the African civilizations encountered by early European traders and what became of them, and at the Native American civilizations of North and Latin America and their fate under Spanish conquest and rule.

From 1700 through World War I, Europe led the world in practically every field of material human life, including military affairs, science, commerce, and living standards. This was the age of Europe's imperial control of the rest of the world. The Americas, much of Asia, Oceania, and coastal Africa all became formal or informal colonies at one time, and some remained under direct European control until the mid-twentieth century.

In the nineteenth and twentieth centuries, the pendulum of power swung steadily away from Europe and toward what had been the periphery: first, North America; then, Russia, Japan, and the non-Western peoples. As we enter a new millennium, the world not only has shrunk but has again been anchored on multiple power bases, Western and other. A degree of equilibrium is rapidly being restored, this time built on a foundation of Western science and technology that has been adopted throughout the globe.

Our periodization scheme, then, is a sixfold one:

◆ Ancient Civilizations, 3500–500 BCE.
◆ Classical Mediterranean Civilizations, 500 BCE–800 CE
◆ Equilibrium Among Polycentric Civilizations, 500–1500 CE.
◆ Disequilibrium: The Western Encounter with the Non-Western World, 1500–1700 CE
◆ Revolutions, Ideology, and the New Imperialism, 1700–1920
◆ Equilibrium Reestablished: The Twentieth-Century World and Beyond, 1920–Present

PEDAGOGY

An important feature of *World Civilizations* is its division into a number of short chapters. Each of its fifty-six chapters is meant to constitute a unit suitable in scope for a single lecture, short enough to allow easy digestion and with strong logical coherence. Each chapter offers the following features:

◆ Thematic boxes and photographs are keyed to the five broad text themes: Society and Economy, Law and Government, Patterns of Belief, Science and Technology, and Arts and Culture. All chapters have one or more boxed inserts, some of which are based on biography, many others on primary sources. To encourage readers to interact with the material as historians would and to compare themes across chapters, each boxed feature concludes with "Analyze and Interpret" questions. And, to provide readers with access to additional readings, many document excerpts are keyed to the full document or related documents available in the World History Resource Center.

◆ An additional boxed feature, Evidence of the Past, spotlights artifacts, material culture, and oral traditions as source materials for historical study. Once writing became common, of course, some materials that you will see in Evidence of the Past are written primary sources, but we point out to you, where appropriate, their roots in oral traditions. We also include some eyewitness accounts for your analysis.

◆ A chapter outline and a brief chapter chronology help readers focus on the key concepts in the material they are about to encounter.

◆ A chapter summary encapsulates the significance of the chapter's concepts.

◆ A "Test Your Knowledge" section at the end of the chapter provides a brief—and unique—self-test. Reviewers tell us that their students rely on these tests to assess their understanding of each chapter and to prepare for quizzes and exams.

◆ Key terms appear in boldface type and are repeated at chapter end in an "Identification Terms" quiz.

◆ Parenthetical pronunciation guides now appear within the text, facilitating ease of reading unfamiliar names.

◆ A sampling of the documents available in the *CengageNOW™* study system also appear at the end of each chapter.

◆ Color illustrations, many of them new, and abundant maps. We include "Worldview" maps that show global developments. Many maps are keyed with icons to indicate that there is an interactive version of the map in the World History Resource Center. Strong map and photo captions encourage readers to think beyond the mere appearance of each visual and to make connections across chapters, regions, and concepts. And critical thinking questions encourage you to work with and read maps as a historian might.

◆ A world map in the front of the book.

Other features include the following:

◆ An end-of-book Glossary, now with a pronunciation guide, provides explanations of unfamiliar terms and pronunciation guidance for the more difficult among them.

◆ Each period opens with a brief part introduction and a Worldview map highlighting the major civilizations discussed in that part of the text. At the end of each part, there is a Worldview chart comparing the same civilizations, color-coded to the same groups in the part-opening map and affording a nutshell review of their accomplishments according to the text's five major themes. This edition includes a new "Cross-Cultural Connections" section at the end of each Worldview, to encourage thinking beyond regional borders.

SUPPLEMENTS

The following supplements are available for the instructor:

PowerLecture: A Microsoft® PowerPoint® Tool with Instructor's Resource CD-ROM

This all-in-one multimedia resource includes the *Instructor's Manual,* the *Resource Integration Guide,* and Microsoft® PowerPoint® slides with lecture outlines. Most of the map acetates are incorporated into the presentations. Also included is ExamView, an easy-to-use assessment and tutorial system that allows instructors to create, deliver, and customize tests and study guides (both print and online) in minutes. ExamView offers both a Quick Test Wizard and an Online Test Wizard that guide users step by step through the process of creating tests—users can even see the test they are creating on the screen exactly as it will print or display online. Instructors can build tests with as many as 250 questions using up to 12 question types. Using ExamView's complete word-processing capabilities, instructors can add an unlimited number of new questions or edit existing questions.

This CD-ROM contains preloaded, book-specific Response System content (via our exclusive relationship with *TurningPoint®* software) designed to work seamlessly with Microsoft® PowerPoint® and the "clicker" hardware of the instructor's choice.

eBank *Instructor's Manual with Test Bank*

Prepared by Janet Brantley, Texarkana College. One volume serves all three versions of the text. Includes the *Resource Integration Guide,* chapter outlines, lecture topics, definitions of terms to know, and student activities, including journal entry topics. The test bank includes over 3,000 multiple-choice, essay, and fill-in-the-blank questions. Multiple-choice questions have five choices each. Also available in PowerLecture.

Transparency Acetates for World History

Includes over 100 four-color maps from the text and other sources. Packages are three-hole punched and shrinkwrapped. Map commentary is provided by James Harrison, Siena College.

Sights and Sounds of History

Short, focused video clips, photos, artwork, animations, music, and dramatic readings are used to bring life to the historical topics and events that are most difficult for students to appreciate from a textbook alone. For example, students will experience the grandeur of Versailles and the defeat felt by a German soldier at Stalingrad. The video segments (averaging four minutes in length) are available on VHS and make excellent lecture launchers.

CengageNOW

Just what you need to know and do NOW! CengageNOW™ is an online teaching and learning resource that gives you more control in less time and delivers the results you want—NOW. For further information, visit academic.cengage.com/cengagenow.

Wadsworth World History Resource Center

World History Resource Center, at academic.cengage.com/history, gives students access to a "virtual reader" with hundreds of primary-source documents, photos, interactive timelines and maps, and more. A map feature including Google Earth coordinates and exercises aids in student comprehension of geography and use of maps. Students can compare a traditional textbook map with an aerial view of the location today. Available within CengageNOW, or for separate purchase. Contact your local representative for ordering details.

Book Companion Website

Both instructors and students will enjoy the chapter-by-chapter resources for *World Civilizations,* with access to the Wadsworth History

Resource Center, at academic.cengage.com/history/adler. Text-specific content for students includes tutorial quizzes, Internet activities, and more. Instructors also have access to the Instructor's Manual, lesson plans, and PowerPoint slides (access code required).

InfoTrac® College Edition with InfoMarks®

Give students access to an entire library's worth of reliable sources with InfoTrac College Edition, an online university library of more than 5,000 academic and popular magazines, newspapers, and journals.

Sources in World History, Fourth Edition

This updated two-volume reader, edited by Mark Kishlansky, includes a diversity of historical documents from world and Western history designed to supplement textbooks and lectures in the teaching of world civilizations. It provides a balance of constitutional documents, political theory, philosophy, imaginative literature, and social description.

Primary Source Reader for World History

Two volumes, edited by Elsa A. Nystrom. This thoughtful, affordable collection of essential primary source documents gives students a broad perspective on the history of the world. The readings are divided by eras and organized according to principal themes such as religion, law and government, and everyday life. Each group of readings has a section describing the significance of subsequent readings and how those readings interrelate.

Document Exercise Workbook for World History, Third Edition

Prepared by Donna Van Raaphorst of Cuyahoga Community College, this two-volume workbook provides a collection of exercises based on primary sources in history.

Map Exercise Workbook, Third Edition

Prepared by Cynthia Kosso of Northern Arizona University, features approximately 30 map exercises in two volumes. Designed to help students feel comfortable with maps by having them work with different kinds of maps to identify places and improve their geographic understanding of world history. Also includes critical thinking questions for each unit.

Magellan World History Atlas

This atlas contains 45 four-color historical maps in a practical 8" x 10" format.

Migration in Modern World History 1500–2000 CD-ROM

An interactive media curriculum on CD-ROM developed by Patrick Manning and the World History Center at Northeastern University. Migration goes beyond the mere chronicling of migratory paths. Over 400 primary source documents in Migration provide a springboard to explore a wide range of global issues in social, cultural, economic, and political history during the period 1500–2000.

Journey of Civilization: The World and Western Traditions CD-ROM

This CD-ROM takes the student on 18 interactive journeys through history. Enhanced with QuickTime™ movies, animations, sound clips, maps, and more, the journeys allow students to engage in history as active participants rather than as readers of past events. Contact your local sales representative for information on packaging this book with the text of your choice.

ACKNOWLEDGMENTS

The authors are happy to acknowledge the sustained aid given them by many individuals during the long incubation period of this text. Phil Adler's colleagues in the history department at East Carolina University, at the annual meetings of the test planners and graders of the Advanced Placement in European History, and in several professional organizations, notably the American Association for the Advancement of Slavic Studies, are particularly to be thanked.

In addition, the following reviewers of past editions were instrumental in the gradual transformation of a manuscript into a book; we remain indebted to all of them and to the students in HIST 1030–1031, who suffered through the early versions of the work.

William S. Arnett, *West Virginia University*

Kenneth C. Barnes, *University of Central Arkansas*

Marsha Beal, *Vincennes University*

Charmarie J. Blaisdell, *Northeastern University*

Laura Blunk, *Cuyahoga Community College*

William Brazill, *Wayne State University*

Alice Catherine Carls, *University of Tennessee–Martin*

Orazio A. Ciccarelli, *University of Southern Mississippi*

Robert Clouse, *Indiana State University*

Sara Crook, *Peru State University*

Sonny Davis, *Texas A&M University at Kingsville*

Joseph Dorinson, *Long Island University, Brooklyn Campus*

Arthur Durand, *Metropolitan Community College*

Frank N. Egerton, *University of Wisconsin–Parkside*

Ken Fenster, *DeKalb College*

Tom Fiddick, *University of Evansville*

David Fischer, *Midlands Technical College*

Jerry Gershenhorn, *North Carolina Central University*

Erwin Grieshaber, *Mankato State University*

Eric Haines, *Bellevue Community College*

Mary Headberg, *Saginaw Valley State University*

Daniel Heimmermann, *University of Northern Arizona*

Charles Holt, *Morehead State University*

Kirk A. Hoppe, *University of Illinois–Chicago*

Raymond Hylton, *Virginia Union University*

Fay Jensen, *DeKalb College–North Campus*

Aman Kabourou, *Dutchess Community College*

Louis Lucas, *West Virginia State College*

Ed Massey, *Bee County College*

Bob McGregor, *University of Illinois–Springfield*

John Mears, *Southern Methodist University*

Will Morris, *Midland College*

Gene Alan Müller, *El Paso Community College*

David T. Murphy, *Anderson University*

Tim Myers, *Butler County Community College*

Elsa A. Nystrom, *Kennesaw State University*

William Paquette, *Tidewater Community College*

Nancy Rachels, *Hillsborough Community College*

Enrique Ramirez, *Tyler Junior College*

Bolivar Ramos, *Mesa Community College*

Robin Rudoff, *East Texas State University*

Anthony R. Santoro, *Christopher Newport University*

Shapur Shahbazi, *Eastern Oregon State University*

John Simpson, *Pierce College*

John S. H. Smith, *Northern Nevada Community College*

Maureen Sowa, *Bristol Community College*

Irvin D. Talbott, *Glenville State College*

Maxine Taylor, *Northwestern State University*

Eugene T. Thompson, *Ricks College*

Susan Tindall, *Georgia State University*

Kate Transchel, *California State University, Chico*

Bill Warren, *Valley City State University*

Robert Welborn, *Clayton State College*

David Wilcox, *Houston Community College*

Steve Wiley, *Anoka-Ramsey Community College*
John Yarnevich, *Truckee Meadows Community College– Old Towne Mall Campus*
John M. Yaura, *University of Redlands*

Many thanks, too, to Lee Congdon, James Madison University; Maia Conrad, Christopher Newport University; Theron E. Corse, Fayetteville State University; Dennis Fiems, Oakland Community College, Highland Lakes; Lauren Heymeher, Texarkana College; Maria Iacullo, CUNY Brooklyn College; Rebecca C. Peterson, Graceland College; Donna Rahel, Peru State College; Thomas J. Roland, University of Wisconsin–Oshkosh; James Stewart, Western State College of Colorado; and Brian E. Strayer, Andrews University.

The fourth and fifth editions, especially thoroughgoing revisions, had especially perceptive groups of reviewers. Our thanks to them for their comments and suggestions.

Patricia M. Ali, *Morris College*
Robin L. Anderson, *Arkansas State University*
Janet Brantley, *Texarkana College*
Stewart Brewer, *Dana College*
Brian Bunk, *Central Connecticut College*
David Cauble, *Western Nebraska Community College*
Janice Dinsmore, *Wayne State College*
Joseph Dorinson, *Long Island University*
Nancy Fitch, *California State University, Fullerton*
Ali Gheissari, *San Diego State University*
Stephen Gosch, *University of Wisconsin, Eau Claire*
Wendell Griffith, *Okaloosa-Walton Community College*
Samuel Hoff, *Delaware State University*
Tamara Hunt, *University of Southern Indiana*
Ellen J. Jenkins, *Arkansas Technical University*
Karen Kimball, *University of Maine, Machias*
Aran S. MacKinnon, *University of West Georgia*
Terrence Monroe, *Darton College*

Elsa Nystrom, *Kennesaw State*
Thomas M. Ricks, *University of Pennsylvania*
Gary Scudder, *Champlain College*
William Seay, *J. Sargeant Reynolds Community College*
Thomas G. Smith, *Nichols College*
Anthony J. Springer, *Dallas Christian College*
Werner Steger, *Dutchess Community College*
Leslie Tischauser, *Prairie State College*
Kate Transchel, *California State University, Chico*
Lloyd Uglow, *Southwestern Assemblies of God University*
Michael Vollbach, *Oakland Community College*
Peter von Sivers, *University of Utah*
Marjorie Walker, *Samford University*
Max E. White, *Piedmont College*
Michael D. Wilson, *Vanguard University*
William Wood, *Point Loma Nazarene University*

But we would like to give special kudos to the following members of our Editorial Review Board, who stood by us throughout this edition's development process, approving every change and every new idea that you see in the text and package. Their involvement has been extraordinarily helpful and much appreciated. Janet Brantley in particular continues to provide invaluable service accuracy-checking as well as preparing the *Instructor's Manual with Test Bank*.

Robin L. Anderson, *Arkansas State University*
Janet Brantley, *Texarkana College*
Stuart Brewer, *Dana College*
Tamara L. Hunt, *University of Southern Indiana*
Ellen J. Jenkins, *Arkansas Technical University*
Elsa A. Nystrom, *Kennesaw State University*
Kate Transchel, *California State University, Chico*
William Wood, *Point Loma Nazarene University*

We would also like to acknowledge Clark Baxter's contribution as publisher; Sue Gleason's as senior development editor; Lauren Wheelock's as project manager, editorial production.

And special thanks go to Joel B. Pouwels, Associate Professor of Spanish, University of Central Arkansas, for her important suggestions and contributions to the chapters on Latin American civilizations.

Note: Throughout the work, the pinyin orthography has been adopted for Chinese names. The older Wade-Giles system has been included in parentheses at the first mention and retained in a few cases where common usage demands it (Chiang Kai-shek, for example).

ABOUT THE AUTHORS

PHILIP J. ADLER taught college courses in world history to undergraduates for almost thirty years prior to his recent retirement. Dr. Adler took his Ph.D. at the University of Vienna following military service overseas in the 1950s. His dissertation was on the activity of the South Slav émigrés during World War I, and his academic specialty was the modern history of Eastern Europe and the Austro-Hungarian empire. His research has been supported by Fulbright and National Endowment for the Humanities grants. Adler has published widely in the historical journals of this country and German-speaking Europe. He is currently Professor Emeritus at East Carolina University, where he spent most of his teaching career.

RANDALL L. POUWELS earned his B.A. in history at the University of Wisconsin and his Ph.D. in history at UCLA in 1979. His Ph.D. dissertation was on the history of Islam in East Africa. His book *Horn and Crescent: Cultural Change and Traditional Islam on the East African Coast, 800–1900* (Cambridge, 1987) has become a standard work in African history. *The History of Islam in Africa* (Athens, Oxford, and Cape Town, 2000) was jointly edited with Nehemia Levtzion of Hebrew University, Jerusalem. Widely praised in reviews, it was selected by *Choice* as an Outstanding Academic Title for 2001 and was made a selection of the History Book Club. In addition, he has written numerous articles and reviews on East African history, the history of Islam in Africa, and historical methodologies. His other research interests include the history of the Middle East and the history and archaeology of Native Americans. Over the years, his work has been supported by grants and fellowships from Fulbright-Hays, the National Endowment for the Humanities, the Social Studies Research Council, the National Geographic Society, and the American Philosophical Society. He has taught African history for over twenty years at LaTrobe University in Melbourne, Australia, and at UCLA. He is presently Professor of African and Middle Eastern History at the University of Central Arkansas.

Introduction to the Student: Why Is History Worth Studying?

HUMAN ACTIONS tend to fall into broad patterns, whether they occurred yesterday or 5,000 years ago. Physical needs, such as the need for food, water, and breathable air, dictate some actions. Others stem from emotional and intellectual needs, such as religious belief or the search for immortality. Human action also results from desires, such as literary ambition or scientific curiosity, or the quest for political power over others, rather than from absolute needs.

History is the record of how people have tried to meet those needs or fulfill those desires. Many generations of our ancestors have found that familiarity with that record can be useful in guiding their own actions. The study of past human acts also encourages us to see our own present possibilities, both individual and collective. This may be history's greatest value.

Many people are naturally attracted to the study of history, but others find it difficult or (even worse) "irrelevant." Some students—perhaps yourself—dread history courses, saying that they can see no point in learning about the past. My life, they say, is here and now; leave the past to the past. What can be said in response to justify the study of history?

People who are ignorant of their past are also ignorant of much of their present, for the one grows directly out of the other. If we ignore or forget the experience of those who have lived before us, we are like an amnesia victim, constantly puzzled by what should be familiar, surprised by what should be predictable. Not only do we not know what we should know, but we cannot perceive our true possibilities, because we have nothing to measure them against. The nonhistorical mind does not know what it is missing—and, contrary to the old saying, what you don't know can definitely hurt you!

A word of caution here: this is not a question of "history repeats itself." This often-quoted cliché is clearly nonsense if taken literally. History does *not* repeat itself exactly, and the difference in details is always important. But history does exhibit general patterns, dictated by common human needs and desires. The French Revolution will not recur just as it did 215 years ago. But, as we know all too well, people still depose their leaders and rise up in arms to change the way they live. Some knowledge of and respect for those patterns has been a vital part of the mental equipment of all human societies.

But there is another, more personal reason to learn about the past. Adults who are historically unconscious are confined within a figurative wooden packing crate, into which they were put by the accident of birth at a given time and in a given place. The boards forming the box restrict their freedom and block their view in all directions. One board of the box might be the prosperity—or lack of it—into which they were born; another, their physical appearance, race, or ethnic group. Other boards could be their religion, whether they were born in a city slum or a small village, or whether they had a chance at formal education (about three-fourths of the world's children never go beyond the third year of school). These and many other boards form the boxes into which we are all born.

If we are to fully realize our potential as human beings, some of the boards must be removed so that we can see out, gain other vistas and visions, and have a chance to measure and compare our experiences with others outside. And the smaller our "global village" becomes, the more important it becomes to learn more about the world beyond the campus, city, state, and country in which we live. An introductory course in world history is an ideal way to learn about life outside the box.

As a good student, your best resource is your own sense of curiosity. Keep it active as you go through these pages. Remember, this and every other textbook is the *beginning*, not the end, of your search for useful knowledge. Good luck!

P. J. A.
R. L. P.

Note: Some of you may at first be confused by dates followed by BCE, meaning "before the common era," and CE, meaning "common era." These terms are used to reflect a global perspective, and they correspond to the Western equivalents BC (before Christ) and AD *(anno Domini).* Also, a caution about the word *century* is in order: the phrase *seventeenth century CE* refers to the years 1601 to 1699 in the common era, and the phrase *first century BCE* refers to the years 99 to 0 BCE With a little practice, these terms become second nature and will increase your fluency in history.

Part ONE

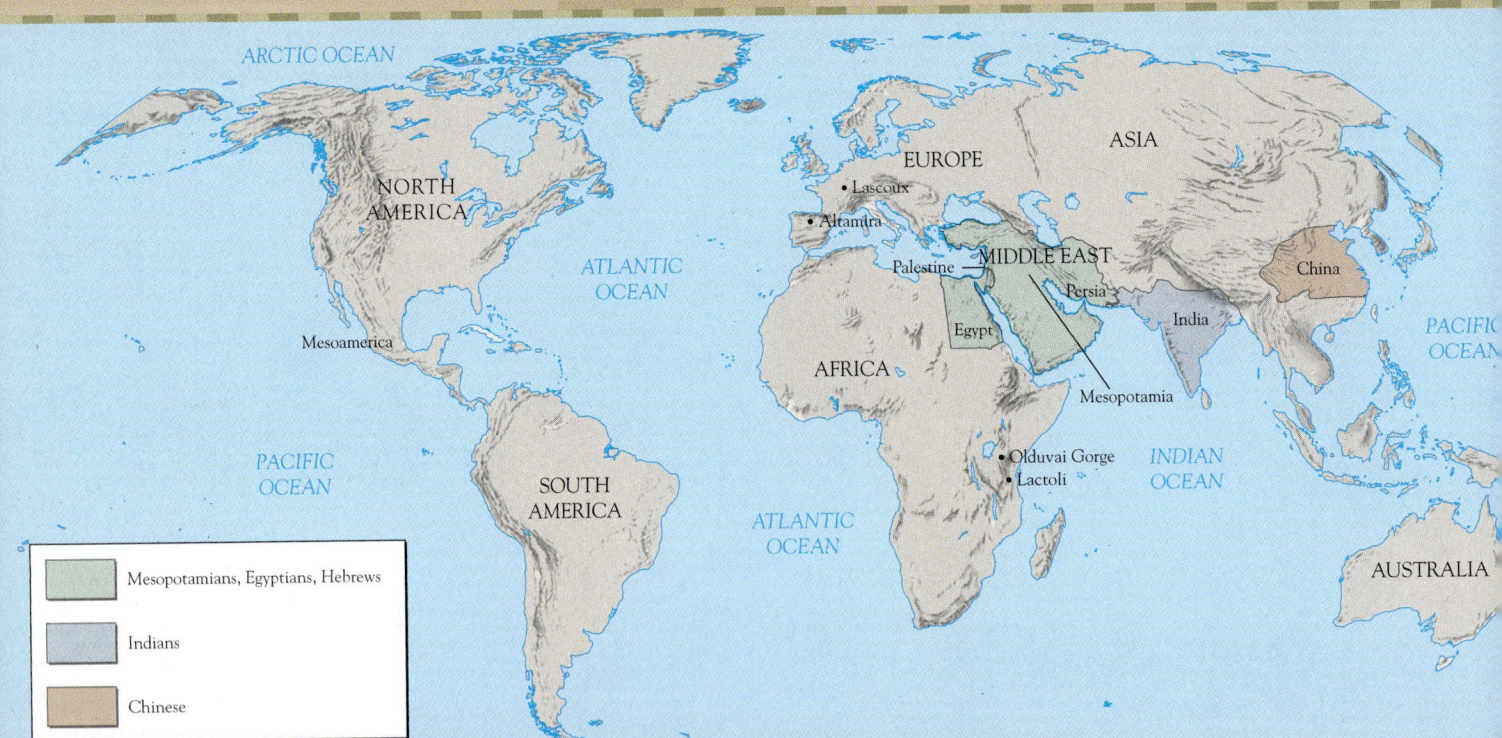

ARCTIC OCEAN

NORTH AMERICA

EUROPE

ASIA

• Lascoux

• Altamira

Palestine

MIDDLE EAST

Persia

China

Egypt

India

Mesoamerica

AFRICA

Mesopotamia

ATLANTIC OCEAN

PACIFIC OCEAN

PACIFIC OCEAN

SOUTH AMERICA

• Olduvai Gorge

• Lactoli

INDIAN OCEAN

ATLANTIC OCEAN

AUSTRALIA

	Mesopotamians, Egyptians, Hebrews
	Indians
	Chinese

ANCIENT CIVILIZATIONS, 3500–500 BCE

WHAT EXACTLY DO most people mean when they talk about "civilization" and "history"? This question is problematic because, for the most part, the particular civilization in which people live and how they record their history shape their general notions about what these terms mean. Since we live in a literate and technologically advanced civilization, for example, we naturally associate history with writing and civilization with relatively high levels of technology. But is it really fair to judge other civilizations only by one's own? More importantly, is it accurate? It is vital that we pose these questions at the outset. These are questions that you may best answer from the knowledge you will acquire from your studies of the world's civilizations and their places in history. Rather than providing facile answers, your authors hope that as you learn more about world civilizations—and there have been many that differed significantly from our own—you will return to these crucial questions again and again. However, we shall provide you with two clues: it is important that you approach this study with an open and inquiring mind, and that you be ready to assume a small measure of intellectual risk so that you benefit from your class discussions.

How and when did the first known civilizations begin? To answer that question, the first six chapters of this book examine the growth of organized ways of life in four quite different areas of the globe before 500 BCE and how each region developed civilizations that were at once distinctive yet similar. The first chapter deals with the period between the spread of *Homo sapiens* throughout much of the Earth, around 100,000 years ago, and 5000 BCE, by which time many societies had mastered the ability to produce food for themselves. We look at the general conditions of life and the achievements of human beings before some societies elaborated the first forms of writing and the capacity to record and maintain written records.

These early breakthroughs are truly impressive, and it is a mark of their fundamental importance that we so rarely think about them. For us who live in the modern world, it is hard to envision an existence in which they were unknown. From them sprang other triumphs of prehistoric humans' imagination and skill commonly associated with civilization, such as metalworking, art, settled habitation, and organized religions.

The commitment to growing—rather than chasing or gathering—food gradually took root among widely scattered groups in the late Neolithic Age (c. 10,000–5000 BCE). This Agricultural Revolution is one of the two epoch-making changes in human life to date, the other being the Industrial Revolution commencing in the late 18th century. Agriculture generated the material basis for further developments like urban living, government by officials, writing beyond mere record keeping (such as recorded law), military forces, and greater social complexity.

Chapters 2 through 6 examine the establishment and development of agriculture, urban life, and trading networks in western Asia, northeast Africa, India, and China. First in chronology was probably Mesopotamia, but it was quickly rivaled by development in the Nile valley of Egypt. Both of these cultures began to take definite form about 3500 BCE and reached their apex between about 1500 and 1200. Somewhat later, the plains of the Indus River in India's far west produced a highly organized, urban society that prospered until about the middle of the second millennium BCE, when it went into decline and was forgotten for many centuries. Simultaneous with the decline of the Indus valley civilization, the north-central region of China gave birth to a formal state ruled by the Shang dynasty. Like the others, this society was founded on a mastery of irrigated farming. Unlike the Mesopotamians and the Indus peoples, both the Egyptians and the Chinese maintained the major elements of their early civilizations down to modern days.

Part One also provides brief accounts of a few of the other major contributors to world civilizations before 500 BCE. Chapter 4 puts the warlike Assyrians and the first of the several Persian empires into perspective and examines the small but crucially important nation of the Jews and their religious convictions.

We open Part One and each of the other five parts in this book with a Worldview map that highlights the civilizations and cultures during the era covered by that part.

This map provides readers with a big-picture overview of the places and peoples discussed in the part, as a general frame of reference before they begin to study. At the end of each part, readers will find a Worldview chart, designed to provide a thumbnail comparison of the text's themes playing out across the various peoples of the part's epoch. The cultures in the Worldview maps are color-coded to match those in the end-of-part charts.

1 THE EARLIEST HUMAN SOCIETIES

Civilization is a movement and not a condition, a voyage and not a harbor.

—Arnold J. Toynbee

c. 200,000–100,000 BCE	*Homo Sapiens* appears
c. 75,000–15,000 BCE	Humans migrate out of Africa and populate the major continents
c. 10,000 BCE	Neolithic Age commences
c. 7000 BCE	Bronze Age begins
c. 3500 BCE	Agrarian civilizations in Mesopotamia, Egypt
c. 1500 BCE	Iron Age begins

A FEW DEFINITIONS OF TERMS

THE EVOLVING PAST

THE PALEOLITHIC AGE
Human Development During the Paleolithic

THE NEOLITHIC AGE: AGRICULTURE
Agrarian and Irrigation Civilizations

METAL AND ITS USES

HISTORY, IN THE STRICTEST sense, means a systematic study of evidence of the human past, in whatever form it exists—as written records or the spoken word, for example. But most people don't use "history" in the strict sense. They define the word *history* more simply as whatever has happened in the past to human beings, which, of course, is a much bigger proposition. Humans, however defined, have inhabited the Earth for a long time. Before the invention of writing, an extremely lengthy period of time elapsed during which human beings gradually mastered the various abilities of mind and body that together enabled their survival as a species on Earth. This period of human existence lasted for several million years. During this time, humans slowly and sporadically evolved from beings who were only slightly different from their genetic cousins among the great apes to creatures who have proven marvelously resourceful and adaptable. Tens of thousands of years before the beginning of the historical period, they populated the entire Earth (except Antarctica), developed religions, made tools, created art forms, mastered agriculture, and demonstrated many other talents and achievements.

By far the major portion of this long period of human development is and will remain unknown to us. From time to time, researchers are able to find some measurable remnants of ancient life amid the debris of the past, from which they might deduce informed guesses and even certainties regarding prehuman and very early human societies. Modern sciences, which do not depend on written evidence, are capable of occasionally penetrating the dark space of human development before recorded history. Bones and pottery shards help us understand the material conditions of life among our distant ancestors. But the bulk of the human evolutionary record will necessarily remain closed to us, insofar as it was nonmaterial and did not leave such artifacts.

TABLE 1.1 Evolution of the Genus *Homo*

Homo habilis (Toolmakers)	3.5–4 million years ago
Homo erectus (Bipedal walkers)	1.5–1.8 million years ago
Homo sapiens	200,000–100,000 years ago
Homo sapiens sapiens (Modern humans)	30,000 years ago

The development of human creatures from their earliest origins has become one of the most controversial of modern sciences. Every year, it seems, new evidence comes to light that purports to extend the age of the genus *Homo* farther back in time, and with a more tangled ancestry. Whereas until recently it was assumed that *Homo* evolved along a clear-cut and single-stemmed line, it is now generally accepted that human beings' family tree is more like a bush with many branches, of which almost all have died (see Table 1.1).

A humanlike creature, or **hominid,** was walking about in East Africa perhaps as early as 4.5 million years ago, by latest reckoning. In the usage of contemporary science, the fundamental differences between humans and apes are certain deviations in bone structures of the foot, the hip, and the hand, the size of the brain, and the use of language. Because language necessarily could leave no traces until the invention of writing, physical anthropology depends primarily on skeletal remains to establish the age and source of animal life, including humans. Bone fragments recovered at different sites in East Africa since the 1970s indicate that upright-walking (bipedal) animals possessing the essential anatomical attributes of modern humans were extant millions of years ago. A recent discovery shows bipedalism in a foot bone dating to more than 4.5 million years ago. This would put the creature it belonged to near the epoch when current anthropology places the genetic division between the genus *Homo* and its closest relations, the great apes.

Homo, we now know, subdivided into many species—a tree with many branches. Only one has survived to the present: the modern human being we see in our mirrors and all around us. Regardless of race or stature or any other physical characteristic, our fellow humans are all members of the species called ***Homo sapiens*** or, according to some authors, *Homo sapiens sapiens.* Both terms denote "thinking or skillful man," a type of being that has populated most of the Earth since roughly 45,000 years ago, at least, and that has outlasted its various predecessors among the hominids, such as *Australopithecus, Homo habilis, Homo erectus,* and others whom we know only from the fossil evidence they occasionally left behind. All of these eventually disappeared for reasons that we may only guess at. In any case, the evolutionary tree proved to have many limbs that died off. Only *Homo sapiens* and the great apes (that is, gorilla, orangutan, and chimpanzee) remain.

It is almost universally believed that *Homo sapiens* originated in Africa, probably in that continent's eastern regions, and migrated from there starting perhaps 100,000 years ago, first into the Middle East, then Europe, Asia, and finally the Western Hemisphere. By perhaps 15,000–10,000 years ago, the sole surviving representative of the genus *Homo* was found on every continent but Antarctica. Worldview Map 1.1 shows the spread of *Homo sapiens* across the globe.

Their origin seems to have been in East Africa. From there, they expanded into southwest Asia and Europe, and into East Asia by perhaps 75,000 years ago. The most recent Ice Age froze sufficient water in the Pacific Basin to enable crossing by land into North America by about 17,000 years ago. The rapid ensuing migration southward carried *Homo sapiens* into South America by no later than 13,000 years ago. The last great human passage, to the Pacific islands, happened between about 1200 BCE and 1250 CE.

A FEW DEFINITIONS OF TERMS

Let's start our exploration of the past with some definitions of certain key words and phrases:

History is the record of what people have done in the past. In this context, the past can mean 10,000 years ago or yesterday. History depends on evidence of the past. What has happened but been forgotten or for which no evidence exists—which is, of course, the vast majority of what has happened—is technically not history.

Historiography is the systematic study of history, as processed through an author's brain and bias, working on the raw materials he or she has found.

Archaeology is the study of past cultures and civilizations through examination of their artifacts (anything made by humans). The name means "the study of origins," and like almost every other scientific name in the English language, it is derived from Greek.

Anthropology refers to the science that studies humans as a species rather than studying a special aspect of their activity. Its name, too, is derived from Greek.

Archaeologists are crucial to the study of human societies that existed before recorded history. In that transitional period when the remembered and recorded past are just beginning to develop, *paleoanthropologists* (students of human evolution from a multidisciplinary point of view), *paleoenvironmentalists* (students of ancient natural environments), and *paleographers* (students of old writing) are also essential to the historian.

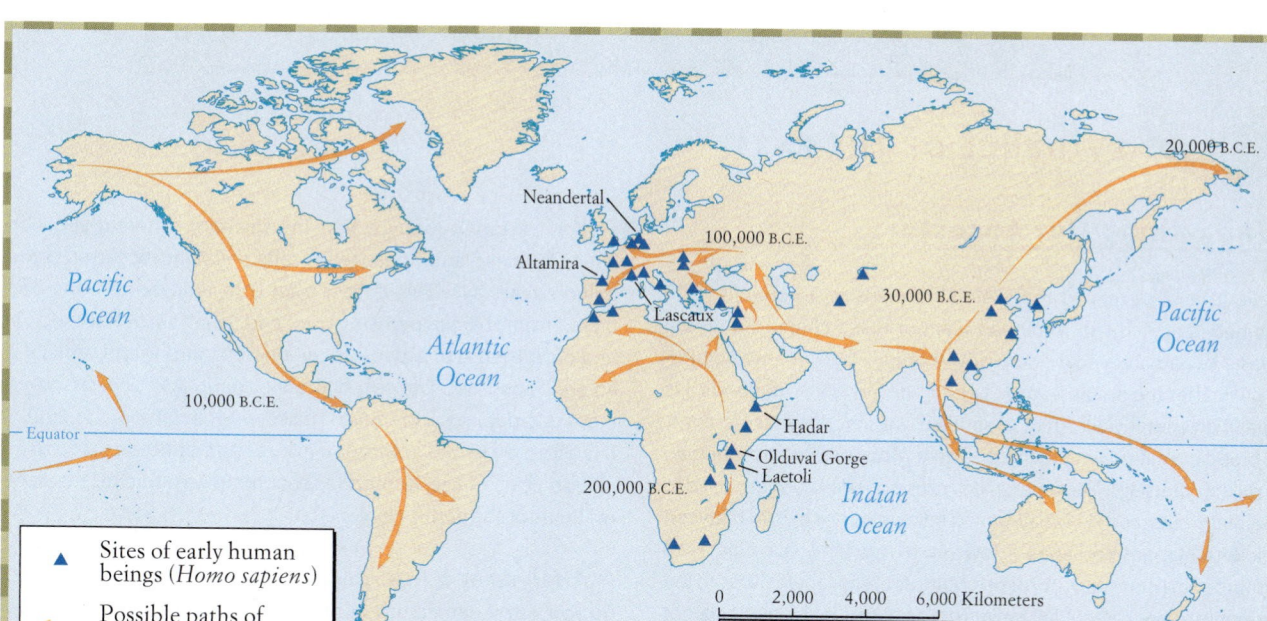

WORLDVIEW MAP 1.1   The Spread of Homo Sapiens

Anthropologists disagree on the detail but agree that human beings entirely similar to us probably existed in every continent but Antarctica by 10,000 BCE. Their origin seems to have been in East Africa. From there they expanded into Southwest Asia and Europe, and into East Asia by perhaps 75,000 BCE. The most recent Ice Age froze sufficient water in the Pacific Basin to enable crossing by land into North America by about 15,000 BCE. The rapid ensuing migration southward carried *Homo sapiens* into South America by no later than 10,000 BCE.

 View an interactive version of this or a related map at http://worldrc.wadsworth.com/

THE EVOLVING PAST

Probably no other science, not even nuclear or genetic biology, has evolved so swiftly in the last forty or fifty years as archaeology and its associated *paleoanthropology.* Each season brings its new discoveries about the age, the nature, and the locales of early humans, both before and after the emergence of *Homo sapiens,* as illustrated in the Evidence of the Past box. Throughout this book, in Evidence of the Past boxes, we will broaden the usual definition of *primary sources* (original documents of the time) to include objects, artifacts, and nonwritten sources such as the spoken word, human genetic history, and the study of past languages (called *linguistic history*).

Tool-making ability is a primary indicator of the development of the hominids and human beings. Recently, the archaeological evidence we are discussing has been brought forward from southern Africa's Blombos cave complex to show that refined tools of both bone and stone were being made much earlier than previously thought, dating back well into the Paleolithic, some 70,000 years ago. Some of the stone materials bear regular markings that had no discernible functional purpose and must therefore have been made for decoration or the aesthetic pleasure of the maker. In other words, they were rudimentary art forms, and as such, they predate by many thousands of years the earliest previously dated art, found in the caves of Paleolithic France and Spain.

THE PALEOLITHIC AGE

The lengthy period extending from about the appearance of the first tool-making hominids to about 10,000 BCE is known as the Paleolithic Age, or Old Stone Age, so called because tools were made of stone and other natural materials and were still quite crude (*paleo* = old; *lithos* = stone). By the end of the Paleolithic, humans inhabited all the continents except Antarctica. Late Paleolithic peoples were hunters and foragers, but life was not easy, and famine was always near at hand.

Paleolithic hunting and gathering was done in groups, and success depended more on organization and cooperation than

Musée National du Bardo, Tunis, Tunisia/ ©Werner Forman/Art Resource, NY

EVIDENCE OF THE PAST

Unearthing Our Ancestors

The 1974 discovery of the skeletal remains of a hominid nick-named "Lucy" by an American team of researchers in Ethiopia was a key advance in modern anthropology. Lucy (named whimsically after the Beatles' song "Lucy in the Sky with Diamonds") is the first generally accepted example of *Australopithecus afarensis*, a bipedal creature who roamed eastern Africa's savanna more than 3 million years ago. The immediate ancestor of *Homo*, as opposed to hominid, Lucy and her small-boned fellows were a hybrid between modern humans and apes. A few years later, the Leakey family of anthropologists found the fossil footprints of similar creatures in the volcanic ash of Laetoli, Tanzania. These footprints showed a pair of individuals walking upright for several yards and were dated at about 3.5 million years ago. Since then, further discoveries around the globe have pushed the frontier between human and hominid even farther back in time.

It is currently thought that the decisive differentiation between humans and apes, genetically speaking, occurred 6 to 8 million years ago. This is based on DNA analysis of bone fragments from the skeletons of Lucy and other australopithecines and on evidence of bipedal locomotion (standing and walking in an erect position). The oldest known exemplar of bipedal movement is *Ardepithecus ramidus*, discovered in Ethiopia in 2001. If it is accepted by the anthropologists as authentically dated at 5.5 million years of age, *Ardepithecus ramidus* approaches the earliest limits of the genus *Homo*.

▶ *Analyze and Interpret*

Do you find it demeaning or humiliating that you (and all of your friends and family) are closely related as a species to the great apes? Does the extent of body hair or posture have any essential connection with the moral or cultural refinement of a given creature?

Kenneth Garrett/National Geographic Image Collection/Getty Images

FOOTPRINTS FROM 3.5 MILLION BCE. The Leakeys in Laetoli found these fossilized prints in present-day Tanzania in East Africa. The stride and distribution of weight on the foot indicate that these creatures were walking upright and were thus some of the earliest of the hominids.

on individual bravery or strength. The family was the basic social unit, but it was normally an extended family, or clan, that included uncles, aunts, in-laws, and other relatives rather than the nuclear family (mother, father, children) that is common today. A unit larger than the nuclear family was necessary for protection. But the total number able to live and hunt together was probably quite small—no more than forty or so. More people than that would have been difficult to sustain when hunting was poor or wild fruits and seeds were not plentiful. Close family relations and interchange with other, similar groups among the Paleolithic hunters were critical to their survival, a fact that we will see reflected in many other locales in later history. The Society and Economy boxes throughout the book refer to this theme.

Although conflicts frequently arose over hunting grounds, water, theft, or other problems, the Paleolithic era probably saw less warfare than any time in later history. So much open space capable of sustaining life was available that the weaker units probably just moved on when they were confronted with force or threats. Violence tempered and controlled by consensual authority was a constant factor in determining historical and prehistoric life. The Law and Government boxes throughout the book will help us follow this theme.

Human Development During the Paleolithic

During the Paleolithic, both the physical appearance of humans and their vital capacity to reason, plan, and organize changed considerably. Because of the extensive work of anthropologists since World War II, we know that at least seventeen varieties of hominid evolved during this time. Much evidence uncovered in East Africa and the Near East as well as in Europe indicates that all of these species of *Homo* came to an evolutionary dead end except for *Homo sapiens*. Some time between 30,000 and 10,000 years ago, *Homo sapiens* seems to have become the sole species of *Homo* to survive anywhere.

Why this occurred is problematic. Some believe bloody warfare erupted between competing species of hominids; others posit a peaceable, gradual absorption by the more advanced species. A good example of these failed species is the famous **Neanderthal Man,** who flourished in many parts of Europe until 30,000 years ago and then disappeared at about the same time that *Homo sapiens* appeared in Europe.

What happened to Neanderthal Man? Climatic changes probably affected and perhaps even caused this and other evolutionary developments. We know that the end of the last of several Ice Ages—15,000–12,000 years ago—coincided with the appearance of *Homo sapiens* throughout the Northern Hemisphere. It is certain that the pre–*Homo sapiens* inhabitants of Europe, such as *Homo erectus* and Neanderthal Man, failed to adapt to the changed climate and dwindling plants and game animals, in the same way that some zoologists believe that the dinosaurs failed to adapt much earlier.

During the Paleolithic, hominids became more upright, and their skulls enlarged and became more rounded to encompass a gradually enlarging brain. Their bodies grew less hairy and their arms shorter. Hip structure changed to allow a more erect gait and became enlarged among females to permit delivery of infants with larger heads (as well as brains). Eyesight grew sharper and the sense of smell less so. Gradually, too, the shape of the lower jaw altered, and the larynx shifted into its present location to allow for speech. All of these modifications and many others were adaptations that reflected humans' changed physical environment, their increasing manipulation of that environment, and sophisticated forms of communication and social organization.

The changed physical environment was reflected in the substitution of semipermanent shelter for the nomadism of an earlier day. By the late Paleolithic (c. 100,000–10,000 years ago), groups were living in caves, lean-tos, and other shelters for long periods of time, perhaps several months. Whereas earlier a group rarely remained more than a few weeks at a given locale, now it could stay in one place several months to await the ripening of edible grasses and roots or the migration of the animals. Even more important, humans' ability to master their physical environment was constantly increasing as they learned to make clothing for cold seasons, to kindle fire where and when it was needed, and to devise new tools for new tasks. The earliest human artwork came in the late Paleolithic. Certain caves of southern France (Lascaux) and Spain (Altamira) are world famous for their lifelike portraits of deer and other animals (see Evidence of the Past). Other human explorations of the aesthetic, whether in art, architecture, sculpture, music, or literature, are the subjects of Arts and Culture boxes throughout the text.

In such ways, humans began to bend the physical world to their will. As they developed human speech 80,000–100,000 years ago, they acquired the ability to plan and to remember what had been successful in the past, so they could repeat it. Humans in the late Paleolithic were making rapid strides toward the remembered past, or "history." Soon after, they would reach the state of advanced mastery of tool making and innovative problem solving that we call the *Neolithic Age.*

THE NEOLITHIC AGE: AGRICULTURE

Although the Paleolithic saw notable developments, it was in the Neolithic, or New Stone Age, that humans made the breakthrough to more complex forms of civilization. As we saw, Paleolithic groups were essentially nomadic. Before about 800,000 years ago, they were scavengers. In the later Paleolithic, they depended more on hunting and gathering wild plants and animals for food. These hunter-gatherers had a mobile life. They moved with the seasons and the migration of the animals they hunted; therefore, they had no reason to attempt to settle down and every reason not to. In the Neolithic, this situation changed. The gradual adoption of agriculture demanded more *sedentary,* or settled, ways of life.

The beginnings of humans' ability to grow or breed their food used to be called the **Agricultural Revolution.** Now, we know that if this was a revolution, it was a very slow one. Most peoples took about five to ten generations (200 to 400 years) to complete it. Gradually, gathering and hunting as the primary ways to acquire food gave way to livestock breeding and herding, sowing and harvesting. Usually, such domesticated ways of obtaining food continued to go hand in hand with hunting for a long, long time. Some members of the group would hunt while others raised some form of grain from wild grasses, the usual form of agriculture, or raised livestock. When plant and animal husbandry became the primary ways

EVIDENCE OF THE PAST

Paleolithic Art

Paleolithic art in its most striking forms has been found in southern France and northern Spain, in caves that bear many marks of ancient human occupancy. The painting of horses here was found on one side of a large room in the recently discovered Chauvet Pont-d'arc cave in the southwest of France. This painting pushes back the time frame of European art by more than 15,000 years, to approximately 31,000 BCE. It is a section of a large mural depicting many different animals.

The reasons why these paintings came into existence are much guessed at by modern researchers. Many believe that the prehistoric hunter was attempting to capture the spirit of the animal prey he sought in the coming hunts. Some believe that the animals pictured were the totemic protectors of the inhabitants of the caves, like the "medicine" of the Native Americans. And others think that, apart from any religious or magical qualities, the pictures display early humankind's strong aesthetic urge, much as men and women have done ever since by capturing life-like representations of the living things around them.

▶ *Analyze and Interpret*
What do you believe might be the most persuasive argument for early artists' motivations?

French Ministry of Culture and Communication, Regional Direction for Cultural Affairs, Rhône-Alps region, Regional Department of Archaeology

HORSES. The Paleolithic artist demonstrates a mastery of his or her material that is the envy of any observer. These horses are a detail of a much larger fresco of animal sketches covering most of one side of a large room at the recently discovered Chauvet Pont-d'Arc cave in southern France. This painting pushes back the framework of European art by more than 15,000 years, to approximately 31,000 BCE.

Joy Tessman/National Geographic/Getty Images

MODERN HUNTER-GATHERER. This hunter-gatherer in Namibia, Southern Africa, takes aim at his quarry. His Khoisan kin are some of the last of the world's hunting-gathering folk. They range the Kalahari Desert much as their ancient forebears did.

of getting something to eat, the Agricultural Revolution was complete for that group. Throughout this book, we shall be watching traditional beliefs and lifestyles giving way, however grudgingly, to the challenges brought forth by changes in the natural or the manmade environments. The Agricultural Revolution was one of the vastest of such changes. The Science and Technology boxes will provide a perspective on others.

With such a slow transition, is *revolution* an appropriate word to describe the adoption of food producing? Archaeologists now know that humans were managing their environments in ways that included limited stock-breeding and plant growing long before the appearance of the settled ways of life commonly associated with the Agricultural Revolution. Therefore, what actually was "revolutionary" was not the transition to growing and breeding their food sources, but rather *the dramatic series of changes in human societies* that resulted from this change-over. First, it often—but not always, in cases where people had to rely principally on herding livestock—meant that people settled down in permanent locations. To be near the area used for cultivation, people settled in villages and then in towns, where they lived and worked in many new, specialized occupations that were unknown to pre-Neolithic society. These settlements could not depend on the luck of hunting or fishing or on sporadic harvests of wild seeds and berries to supply their daily needs. Only regularized habits of farming and herding could support the specialists who populated the towns, and only intensive methods could produce the dependable surplus of food that were necessary to allow the population to grow. Of course, occasional years of famine still occurred. But the lean years were far less frequent than when people depended on hunting-gathering for sustenance. Thus one major result of the food-producing revolution was a steadily *expanding population* that thrived primarily in *permanent settlements.*

Second, food production was the force behind creating the concept of "mine versus thine"—that is, *privately owned property* in land or livestock. Until farming and livestock breeding became common, there was no concept of private property; land, water, game, and fish belonged to all who needed them. But once a group had labored hard to establish a productive farm and grazing rights to land, they wanted permanent possession. After all, they had to clear the land, supply water at the right time, and organize labor for preparing the soil, planting, weeding, and harvesting or for tending their livestock. Who would do that if they had no assurance that next year and the next the land would still be theirs?

Third, food production necessitated the development of *systematized regulation* to enforce the rights of one party over those of another when disputes arose over access and use of resources, including land and water. Codes of law, enforced by organized authority (or government officials), were important results of the introduction of agriculture and animal husbandry. The function of law is to govern relations between individuals and groups so that security is established and the welfare of all is promoted. Law and the exercise of lawful authority is one of the recurrent themes in this book, and we will look at it in the Law and Government boxes.

A fourth change was the increasing *specialization of labor.* It made no sense for a Neolithic farmer to try to be a soldier or carpenter as well as a food grower. Efforts were more productive for the entire community if people specialized; the same principle applied to the carpenter and the soldier, who were not expected to grow or breed the food supply.

Agriculture also led to an *enlarged public role for women* in Neolithic societies based on farming, apparently a direct result of the fact that the first farmers were probably women. There is even some evidence of **matriarchy** (female social and political dominance) in Neolithic China, the Near East, and West Africa, as well as among many Native American societies. The association of women with fertility, personified in a whole series of Earth Mother goddesses in various cultures, certainly was related to this development. As those who brought forth life, women were seen as the key to assuring that the Earth Mother would respond to the villagers' prayers for food from her womb. In many areas where agriculture became important, *female-centered religious rituals,* female priestesses, and graphic reenactments of human reproduction were crucial components of cults intended to promote human, animal, and plant fertility. Changes in religious belief and practice carry the widest-ranging consequences for any society, ancient or modern. Often they have been manifested in the concepts of good and bad that dictated public and private behavior patterns, or morality. We will observe many such changes as we progress through this world history, and the Patterns of Belief boxes will reinforce the theme.

Alterations in lifestyle came about gradually, of course, as a group learned to depend on domesticated crops and animals for its main sources of food. When that change took place varied sharply from one continent or region to the next. In a few places, it has still not occurred. A few nomadic hunter-gatherer groups can still be found in regions that are useless for crop growing or animal grazing, although they are fast disappearing under the intrusions of modern communications and technology.

Where were the first food-producing societies? For many years, researchers believed that agriculture must have emerged first in a region of the Near East called the *Levantine Corridor* and spread gradually from there into Asia and Africa. According to this **diffusion theory** of cultural accomplishment, knowledge of new techniques spreads through human contacts, as water might spread on blotting paper. But now it is known that by 7000 BCE, agriculture had developed in at least seven separate

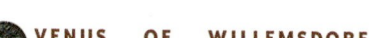

VENUS OF WILLEMSDORF. Unearthed near the small Austrian village of Willemsdorf one hundred years ago, this is one of the better-known "Earth Mothers" found in excavations throughout central and eastern Europe. Its age is approximately 28,000 years. The emphasis on fertility aspects and the deemphasis of individual features tells us something of the value of women in Neolithic societies.

Naturhistorisches Museum, Vienna, Austria/Ali Meyer/Bridgeman Art Library areas independent of outside influences: the Near East, Central America, South America, northern China, southern China and southeast Asia, northeast Africa, and West Africa. About the same time or slightly later, the first domesticated animals were being raised. The raising of pigs, sheep, cattle, goats, guinea fowl, dogs, and turkeys for food goes back at least as far as 4000 BCE. (The horse and donkey come considerably later, as we shall see.) Worldview Map 1.2 shows where some common plant and animal species were first cultivated or domesticated.

Agrarian and Irrigation Civilizations

Wherever ancient gathering and hunting peoples discovered how to grow and breed their food populations swelled dramatically; surplus wealth supported more complex societies; craft production and trade appeared; new farming technologies appeared, such as the use of draft animals and irrigation; urban life developed; ruling elites emerged; and the need to maintain records necessitated the invention of writing. In short, the most ancient civilizations known to us arose. As we shall see, each of these civilizations acquired

and elaborated its own unique characteristics and "style" of life. Yet, as distinctive as each of these earliest civilizations was, to a varying extent they shared eight attributes. Together, these features comprise a type of civilization called **agrarian civilization**. As we study a few of the earliest world civilizations, see how many of these features you can find in each one. These eight features were:

◆ *They were primarily rural societies.* Most people lived in country villages and had rural outlooks and ways of life. This does not mean that these civilizations had no cities. Since they were socially complex (stratified), cities were the locales where members of the ruling classes, as well as priests, craftspeople, merchants, and nobles, lived. Relationships between rural villages and cities were complex, but generally the city dwellers directed the productive activities of rural folk through their control of religious beliefs and rituals thought to be essential to fertility and through the enforcement of laws, customs, and traditions.

◆ *They were based primarily on peasant agriculture or livestock breeding.* The overwhelming majority in such civilizations relied on farming and herding to

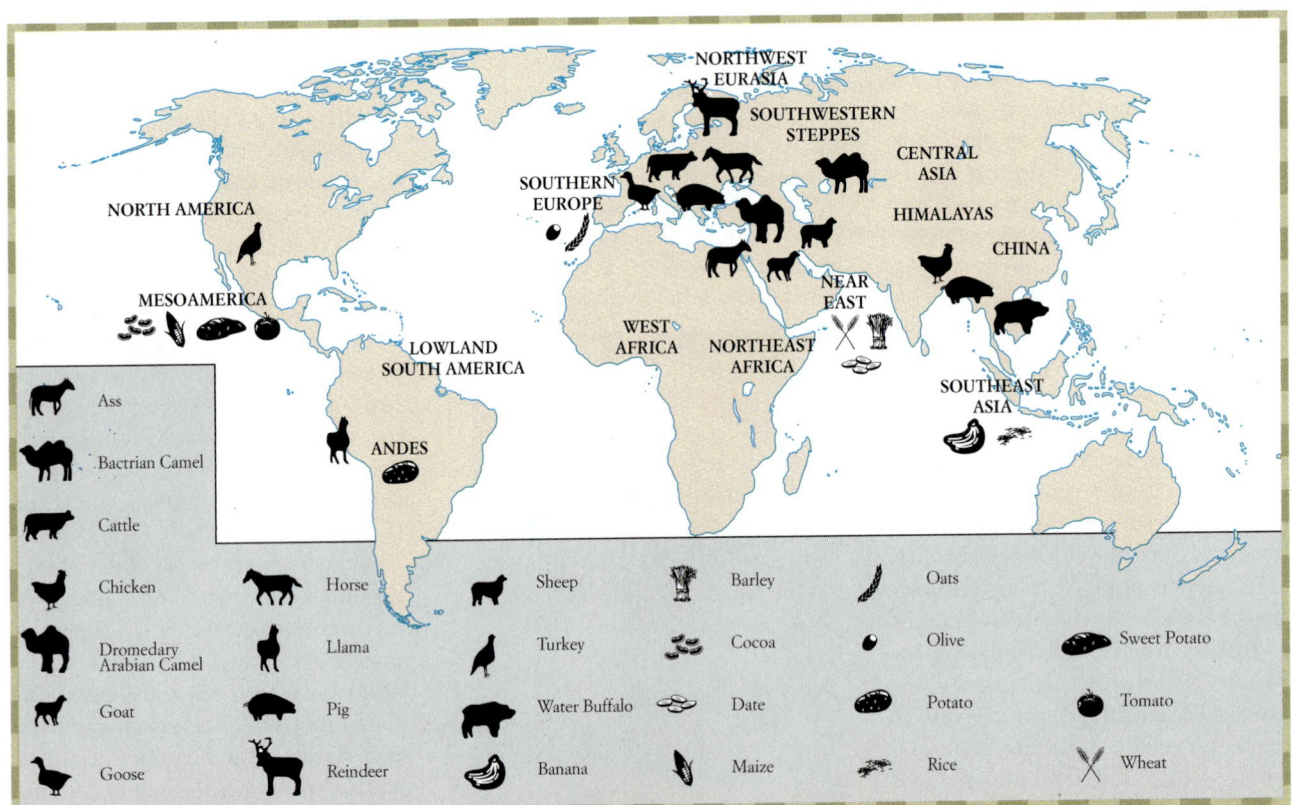

WORLDVIEW MAP 1.2 Origin of Crops and Domestic Animals

This map shows where particular plant and animal species were first cultivated or domesticated. Did these practices arise independently in different areas, or did they appear by diffusion? In the case of some species (for example, the pig), there seems to have been independent development in different areas. In most cases, however, the contact between neighboring cultures facilitated the rapid rise of plant and animal cultivation around the globe.

sustain themselves and their families, as well as to support nonfood-producing members of society, such as craftsmen, merchants, and ruling elites. They employed relatively simple technologies to perform their labors. They crafted their tools out of materials at hand—mud, clay, grasses, leather, wood, wattle, and stone. Wind, water, human strength, or animals powered what simple machinery they fashioned, such as irrigation devices and ploughs. The rulers often skimmed off what surpluses they produced as taxes, keeping the people poor.

◆ *Most people maintained life in balance with their natural environment.* In civilizations that relied on simple technology, people's survival and ability to produce food hinged on their understanding of their natural world. It was this ability, acquired from many generations of observation and experiment, that enabled them to work with what these surroundings provided them.

◆ *Their religion was based heavily on gods and spirits that controlled their natural environment.* Since the earliest civilizations relied so much on agriculture, the ability of humans to control natural phenomena was crucial to life. One way this was achieved was through an intimate understanding of the natural environment. But because total understanding and predictability were impossible, people came to believe that capricious gods and spirits controlled natural forces. Frequently, people believed these spirits could assume human and animal forms.

◆ *Their religion emphasized ritual and sacrifice as ways to control the deities.* Since the gods and spirits could control nature, another way people thought they could control nature was through control of the spirits. Communal religion centered on complex rituals and sacrifices to the gods to win their cooperation in controlling rainfall, river floods, soil and animal fertility, births, and even death.

◆ *They relied on religious specialists to communicate with the gods.* The rituals and sacrifices on which so many people relied were complicated and had to be carried out with great precision to be effective. Only trained specialists—priests, priestesses, spirit mediums, and medicine men and women—could perform them flawlessly.

◆ *They believed time to be cyclic.* Farmers and animal pastoralists lived their lives according to the rhythms of nature. Consequently, they perceived the workings of time and the universe as occurring in endlessly repeating rounds of birth and death, death and renewal.

◆ *Their social values emphasized kinship and the clan.* Another strategy employed as a hedge against natural disaster was to create wide social contacts among kin, fellow clans people, clients, and allies. These extensive groupings constituted networks of mutual rights and responsibilities as a form of "social insurance" that helped guarantee the survival of individual members. A corollary to this was a veneration of elders and the spirits of dead ancestors.

Several of these civilizations developed in the plains bordering on major rivers or in the valleys the rivers created. They depended on intensive, productive agriculture, and the development of agriculture depended in turn on the excellent soil and regular supply of water provided by the river. In ancient Mesopotamia, the dual drainage of the Tigris and Euphrates rivers made the first urban civilization possible. In Egypt, the Nile—the world's longest river at more than 4,000 miles—was the life-giving source of everything the people needed and cherished. At a slightly later date in West Africa, the Niger River nurtured the early development of agriculture and city life there. The earliest available evidence of the beginnings of Indian civilization are traced to the extensive fields on both sides of the Indus River, which flows more than 2,000 miles from the slopes of the Himalayas to the ocean. In northern China, the valleys of the Yellow River, which is about 2,700 miles long, and the Yangtze River were the cradles of the oldest continuous civilization in world history. Worldview Map 1.3 shows four of these earliest. Recent studies in the western valleys of the Andes in Peru also show an advanced, ceramic-making civilization that previously was unsuspected.

What else did the rivers provide besides good crops and essential water? They also offered a sure and generally easy form of transport and communication, allowing intervillage trade and encouraging central, usually city-based authorities to extend their powers over a much greater area than would have been possible if they had had only overland contacts. The interchange of goods and services between individuals or groups is a constant motivating force in human history as a strategy to avoid the catastrophic effects of crop failure through the creation of supplementary forms of wealth. We shall look at this theme in differing contexts in later chapters. Moreover, it was trade as well as migrations that provided the usual means by which early societies established and maintained connections with each other. Trade and other forms of human contact, such as migration and conquest, will be common themes throughout this text.

The rivers had very different natures. The Tigris and the Yellow were as destructive in their unpredictable flooding as the Nile, the Niger, and the Indus were peaceful and predictable. The Yellow River was so ruinous at times that its ancient name was the "sorrow of China." But without its water, early farming in northern China would have been impossible.

Climate, too, created differences among the earliest civilizations. Egypt and most of the Indus valley, for example, have temperate climates that change little over the course of the year and are suitable for crops all year long. It is not at all unusual for an Egyptian family farm to grow three crops annually. Northern China and Mesopotamia, on the other hand, experience much more severe changes of weather, not only from season to season but from day to day.

In deserts and steppe lands where soils or drier conditions made farming harder, people were forced to rely more (or exclusively) on stockbreeding for food and clothing.

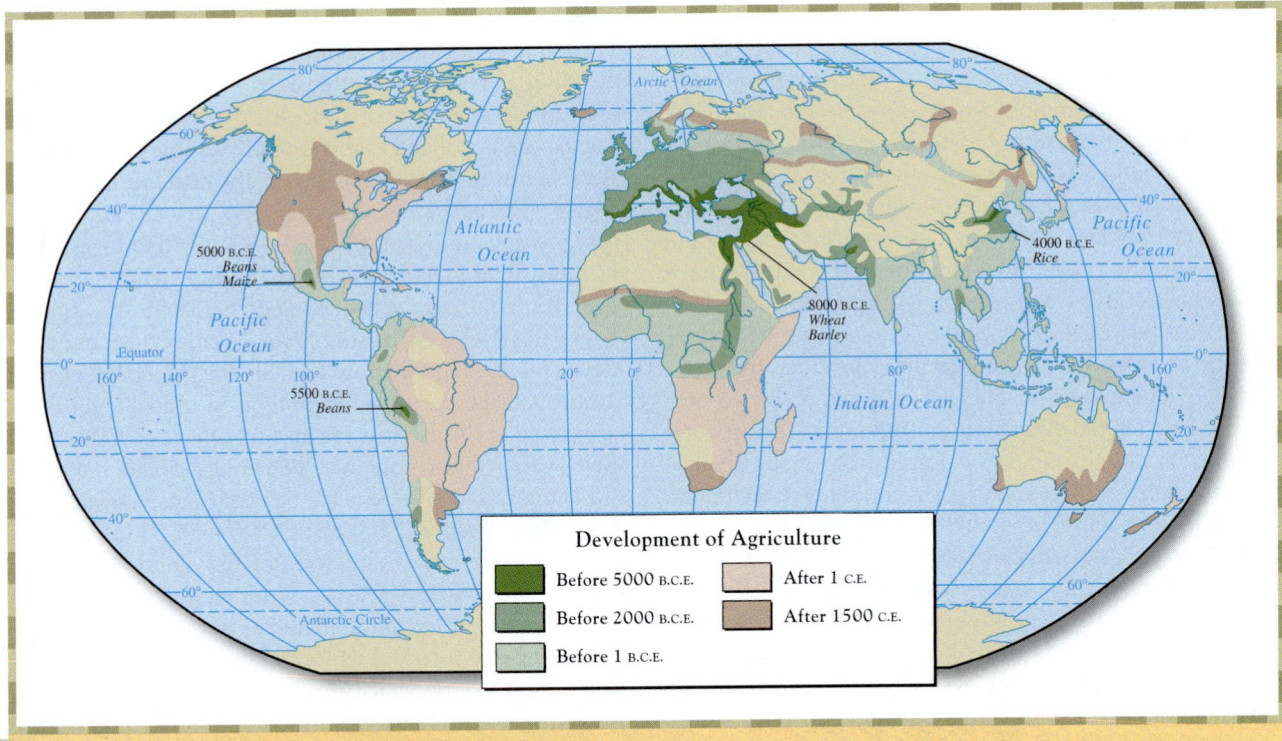

 WORLDVIEW MAP 1.3 Early Agriculture

Several of the earliest civilizations were centered around rivers, which provided good soil and water for agriculture. Ancient Mesopotamia grew up around the Tigris and Euphrates rivers. Egyptian civilization flourished along the Nile. Indian civilization began in fields along the Indus. The Yellow River supported early Chinese agrarian civilization.

MAP QUESTIONS
What do you suppose the new science of paleobotany might involve as its study, and how does it assist in dating early agriculture?

View an interactive version of this or a related map at http://worldrc.wadsworth.com/civilizations.

Conditions usually made settled life impossible, so they continually had to be on the move in search of water and pasturelands for their livestock. Their homes in the desert and grasslands usually bordered on terrain where farming was the principal mode of production and where farmers and their food stores were valuable as trading partners or, alternatively, as targets of raids. As a rule, the pastoralists' way of life made them heartier people, and their methods of mounted warfare made them formidable opponents whose movements and raiding could be held in check only by powerful, highly centralized states. As we shall see in the following chapters, the tension and frequent warfare between pastoralist tribesmen, such as Semitic-speaking nomads, Indo-European Iranians, and Turco-Mongolian peoples, and neighboring, agrarian civilizations formed one of the important constants in world history.

METAL AND ITS USES

The first metal used by humans seems to have been soft copper. When combined with lead and tin ores, copper becomes the more useful bronze. Bronze has some advantages over copper: it is harder (and therefore more suitable for weaponry) and more resistant to weathering. But it has several disadvantages when compared with other metals: it is relatively difficult to make, its weight is excessive for many uses, and it cannot keep a fine edge for tools and cutting weapons. Above all, bronze was difficult to obtain in the ancient world and expensive. The period when bronze art objects and bronze weapons predominated in a given part of the world is called its *Bronze Age.* In western Asia, where the earliest known civilizations appeared, the Bronze Age extended from about 7000 BCE to about 1500 BCE, when a major innovation in human technology made its first appearance: the smelting of iron.

The discovery of how to smelt and temper iron tools and weapons was a major turning point in the development of every people, ushering in an *Iron Age.* Iron has been the key metal of history. Wherever it has come into common use, certain advances have occurred. Iron plowshares open areas to cultivation that previously could not be tilled. Iron weapons and body armor gave warfare a new look. Iron tools enabled new technical progress and

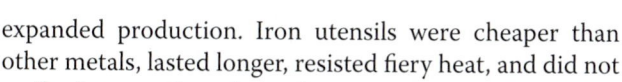

expanded production. Iron utensils were cheaper than other metals, lasted longer, resisted fiery heat, and did not easily shatter or lose their edge.

Iron ore is one of the more common metallic ores, and it is often found on or near the Earth's surface (unlike copper and lead). It is easily segregated from the surrounding soils or rock. The crucial breakthrough was learning how to temper the ore—that is, how to purify it so that the iron could be formed and used without shattering. The Indo-European people known as Hittites, who lived in modern-day Turkey, apparently were the first to smelt and temper iron. By 1200 BCE, this knowledge was spreading rapidly among Middle Eastern and Egyptian peoples.

SUMMARY

THE PREHISTORY OF the human race is immeasurably longer than the short period (5,000 years or so) of which we have historical knowledge. During the last 50,000 years of the prehistoric period, men and women became physically and mentally indistinguishable from ourselves and spread across the Earth. Developing agriculture to supplement hunting and gathering, humans slowly attained more advanced stages of development in the later part of the Neolithic Age, around 3000 BCE. Urban life was now possible, a system of government and record keeping evolved, and advanced weapons and tools of metal were invented.

In the next chapters, we examine four of the earliest known centers of civilization one by one and look at the reasons why each became a center. The similarities and contrasts among these civilizations gave each a particular character that would last for thousands of years and in some cases until the present day.

▶ Identification Terms

Test your knowledge of this chapter's key concepts by defining the following terms. If you can't recall the meaning of certain terms, refresh your memory by looking up the boldfaced term in the chapter, turning to the Glossary at the end of the book, or working with the flashcards that are available on the *World Civilizations* Companion Website: **academic.cengage.com/adler**

Agricultural Revolution	archaeology	history	matriarchy
agrarian civilization	diffusion theory	hominid	Neanderthal Man
anthropology	historiography	Homo sapiens	

▶ Test Your Knowledge

Test your knowledge of this chapter by answering the following questions. Complete answers appear at the end of the book. You may find even more quiz questions in CengageNOW and on the *World Civilizations* Companion Website: **academic.cengage.com/adler**

1. One term that is used to denote "thinking or skillful man" is
   a. Cro-Magnon.
   b. *Homo sapiens.*
   c. Paleolithic.
   d. Neanderthal.
   e. *Australopithecus.*
2. Human beings seem to have acquired speech about _____ years ago.
   a. 4.5 million
   b. 1 million–4.5 million
   c. 500,000 to 1 million
   d. 100,000–250,000
   e. 80,000–100,000
3. Which of the following statements most aptly describes Paleolithic society?
   a. The hunt was the only way to obtain food regularly.
   b. There was constant fighting among families and clans.
   c. The individual was more important than the group.
   d. Cooperation was necessary for survival.
   e. Extended family units usually numbered about sixty.
4. The Agricultural Revolution occurred first during the
   a. Neolithic.
   b. Bronze Age.
   c. Paleolithic.
   d. Mesozoic.
   e. Iron Age.

5. Among the major changes that occur as a result of the adoption of agriculture by any group is
   a. the abandonment of traditional village life.
   b. a decrease in trading.
   c. an increase in population.
   d. a reduction in animal raising.
   e. an increase in the percentage of people living in rural areas.

6. The first farmers were probably
   a. Andean.
   b. nomads.
   c. women.
   d. Indian.
   e. hunter-gatherers.

7. Which of these factors was of decisive importance to Neolithic agriculture?
   a. Use of beasts of burden for plowing
   b. Mastery of irrigation techniques
   c. Development of natural insecticides
   d. Existence of large cities as marketplaces
   e. Development of heavy iron plows for cultivation

8. The increase in the number of humans during the Neolithic Age was primarily caused by
   a. the disappearance of epidemic disease.
   b. a surplus of food.
   c. decreased intergroup violence.
   d. a greater respect for the aged.
   e. increasing understanding of the use of herbs for medicinal purposes.

9. The site of the oldest known continuous civilization in world history was in
   a. southern Africa.
   b. western Africa.
   c. the Nile River valley.
   d. Mesopotamia.
   e. northern China.

10. The use of bronze as the primary metal for tools and weapons
   a. came after iron.
   b. was dictated by its ease of making.
   c. started about 7000 BCE in western Asia.
   d. came after urban civilizations were established in the Near East.
   e. predated the use of copper

Enter *CengageNOW* using the access card that is available with this text. *CengageNOW* will assist you in understanding the content in this chapter with lesson plans generated for your needs and will provide you with a connection to the *Wadsworth World History Resource Center* (see description at right for details).

 ▶ **World History Resource Center**

Enter the Resource Center using either your *CengageNOW* access card or your standalone access card for the *Wadsworth World History Resource Center*. Organized by topic, this website includes quizzes; images; over 350 primary source documents; interactive simulations, maps, and timelines; movie explorations; and a wealth of other resources.

*They see the cedar-mountain, the
abode of the gods, . . .
On the mountain the cedars uplift
   their abundance.
Their shadow is beautiful, is all
   delight.
Thistles hide thereunder, and the
   dark prick-thorn,
Sweet-smelling flowers hide
   under the cedars.*
   —Epic of Gilgamesh

2 MESOPOTAMIA

c. 15,000–10,000 BCE	End of the last Ice Age
c. 10,000 BCE	First evidence of agriculture in the Levantine Corridor
c. 5000 BCE	Sumerians arrive in Mesopotamia
c. 3500 BCE	Cuneiform writing
c. 3000 BCE	Sumerian city-states develop
c. 2300 BCE	Sargon of Akkad
1700s BCE	Hammurabi/Oldest surviving law code
c. 1500 BCE	Hittites conquer Mesopotamia
c. 900 BCE	Rise of Assyria
539 BCE	Conquest by Persia

NEOLITHIC SOUTHWEST ASIA

SUMERIAN CIVILIZATION
Earning a Living ◆ Religion and the Afterlife ◆ Mathematics and Chronology ◆ The Evolution of Writing ◆ Law ◆ Government and Social Structure ◆ The Status of Women

TRADE AND AN EXPANSION OF SCALE

SUCCESSORS TO SUMERIA

THE DECLINE OF MESOPOTAMIA IN WORLD HISTORY

THE POPULATION INCREASE due to the Agricultural Revolution was first exemplified by the creation of farming villages, where previously nomadic food gatherers settled to plant and tend their crops. Grains were the usual basis of early agriculture, and those areas with fertile soil, sufficient rain, and a temperate climate to support wild grains were the pioneers of village development. From the farming village slowly evolved the much more socially differentiated town, with its various economic divisions and occupational specialties. And in some places from the town grew the larger centers of governmental power, religious ritual, and cultural sophistication termed *cities*. A combination of agrarianism, city life, social complexity, government, trade networks, and writing produced the earliest, known civilizations in world history.

NEOLITHIC SOUTHWEST ASIA

Around 15,000 BCE, the world's climate began warming after centuries of Ice Age conditions, melting glaciers in the northern hemispheres, raising sea levels, and covering the planet's landmasses with vast inland lakes, streams, and forests. In southwestern Asia, giant stands of oak and pistachio forests and the bounteous herds of game replaced Ice Age grasslands. Hunter-gatherers of the Near and Middle East, called *Natufians* (nah-TOO-fee-ans), stalked antelope and Persian gazelle and harvested wild nuts and grasses using flint-bladed sickles, enabling them to expand their populations dramatically. However, around 11,000 BCE, a catastrophe occurred. Known as the Younger Dryas Event, glacial melt water that had accumulated in a colossal, freshwater lake in northern Canada suddenly burst into the Atlantic Gulf Stream, triggering a thousand-year-long regression in Europe and southwestern Asia to the cooler and drier conditions of the late Ice Age.

The abundant sources of water and plant foods previously available to humans and animals alike disappeared, forcing Natufians to congregate in small, semi-permanent villages near surviving streams and rivers. Coming after a time when populations had grown dramatically, these catastrophic events forced small groups of western Asians to adopt more intensive ways of managing their food resources: basically, this encouraged them to switch from gathering and hunting to planting and domesticating cereals like barley and wheat, which grew in wild forms in their natural environment. Thus, the world's first farming settlements appeared in a section of the Near East called the **Levantine Corridor,** an arc of land that was endowed with especially high water tables and included much of present day Israel, Syria, and the Euphrates River Valley. Here, by 8000 BCE, cereal agriculture had become widespread and people had added to their food stocks by domesticating and breeding goats and sheep. Later still, cattle were introduced, possibly from Africa.

The switch to agriculture provided an abundance that allowed people to grow their populations and to congregate in towns and cities for the first time in history, and wherever this transformation occurred, the world's earliest recorded civilizations appeared. The first of these was in a part of the Levantine Corridor that included the valleys of the Tigris and Euphrates rivers, a land that the ancient Greeks called **Mesopotamia** ("land between the rivers")—now the southeastern portion of Iraq.

SUMERIAN CIVILIZATION

Along with agriculture and herding, some of the earliest towns and cities archaeologists have discovered appeared in southwestern Asia. The rivers, the Euphrates and the Tigris, originate in present-day Turkey and flow parallel to each other for about 400 miles before joining together to flow into the head of the Persian Gulf (see Map 2.1). In the lower courses of the rivers in the third millennium BCE, the first urban civilization of the world developed. This agrarian civilization was supported by extensive irrigation farming, pioneered by a people called **Sumerians** (soo-MAYR-ee-ans), who came into lower Mesopotamia from somewhere to the east about 5000 BCE. Gradually, the Sumerians created a series of small, competing kingdoms, or city-states. Here they developed a series of ideas and techniques that would provide the foundation of a distinct and highly influential civilization.

The Sumerians were the first people to do a number of highly significant things—all of them characteristics of what we call "civilization."

◆ They created the first large *cities*, as distinct from towns and small cities like Jericho. The largest of these cities may have contained upward of 100,000 people (about the size of present-day Charleston, South Carolina; Kansas City, Kansas; or Reno, Nevada). All early civilizations had an advanced center such as this, one that drew its necessities from a surrounding countryside subject to it. Each such city was encircled for miles by villages of farmers who built the canals and provided the agricultural surplus on which the city elite depended. Most of these centers originated as a place of ritual prayer and sacrificial offerings that honored one or more of the gods whose goodwill was purchased so agriculture could flourish. Gradually, the ceremonial aspects of the shrine and its attendant priesthood were joined by commercial and governmental pursuits, so it became a place in which a growing population of labor-specialized people was supported by sophisticated irrigation agriculture.

JERICHO. Located on the West Bank of modern Jordan, the ruins of Jericho date to about 8000 BCE, making it one of the oldest Neolithic cities in the world. This is a view of the round tower of the city, which the Biblical prophet, Joshua, is said to have blown down. Archaeologists believe that an earthquake in the second millennium BCE actually destroyed the fortifications.

©Israel/Ancient Art and Architecture Collection Ltd./ The Bridgeman Art Library

- They developed the first sophisticated system of *writing*.
- They built the first monumental buildings, using as the basic principle of support the post-and-lintel system (beams held up by columns, used today in structures as varied as monkey bars and bridges).
- They probably invented the wheel as a load-bearing transportation device and were the first to use bricks made from sun-baked clay.
- They were the first to design and build an irrigation system powered by the force of gravity.
- They were the first to use the plow and among the first to make bronze metal utensils and weaponry.

What we know of the Sumerians is extremely impressive. We know a good deal not only because they left extensive records and physical evidence of their own but also because they had enormous influence on their neighbors and rivals, such as the Akkadians and Egyptians, as well as their several conquering successors in Mesopotamia.

The early history of Mesopotamia under the Sumerians is a tale of great technological and cultural advances, marred by strife, disunion, and unceasing warfare. Trade wars and disputes over water assured that no centralized governing power was possible. Whenever one city managed to seize control of substantial supplies of water and trade, the others upstream or downstream would band together against it or its subjects would rebel. Conflicts seem to have been the order of the day, with city-state vying against city-state in a constant struggle for mastery over the precious irrigated lands.

Not until about 2300 BCE was the land between the rivers brought under one effective rule, and that was imposed by a Semitic invader known as Sargon the Great, who conquered the entire plain. Sargon established his capital in the new town of Akkad, near modern-day Baghdad, capital of Iraq. Although the Akkadian Empire lasted less than a century, its influence was great, for it spread Sumerian culture and methods far and wide in the Near and Middle East, through that wide belt of land reaching from Mesopotamia to Egypt that is called the **Fertile Crescent** (see Map 2.1).

Although the separate Sumerian city-states never united until outsiders overwhelmed them, their cultural and religious achievements and beliefs would be picked up by their conquerors and essentially retained by all their successors in Mesopotamia.

Earning a Living

Most Mesopotamians at this time drew their livelihood from the land either directly, as farmers and herders, or indirectly, as carters, wine pressers, millers, or any of the dozens of other occupations that transformed agrarian products into food and drink and delivered them to the consumer. For every person who lived in an urban setting and did not have to grow his or her own food, there

were ten or twenty who lived in the agrarian villages that surrounded the cities and who spent most of their labor in the fields or the pasture. As we know from both historical and archaeological evidence of many kinds and from many places, commerce was also primarily concerned with trade in foodstuffs, grain above all, although other commodities essential to living also had to be imported. It is easy for us to forget just how much of the time and energy of early civilizations went into the pursuit of sufficient caloric intake! Three square meals a day were often the exception, and the ordinary person rarely took them for granted.

Not all occupations involved farming or foodstuffs, however. A few required education and a degree of formal training: scribes, bookkeepers, and the priesthood, for example. Although each civilization had some learned occupations, they varied in prestige and in the number of persons who practiced them. Mesopotamian city dwellers seem to have been literate to an unusual degree and took writing for granted as a normal part of daily life. Many other occupations did not require literacy, but they did demand a lengthy period of apprenticeship. Most of these occupations were found in the towns. They included metalworking, leatherwork, jewelry making, all types of ceramics, fine and rough carpentry, masonry, and other building trades. Besides these skilled jobs, there were shopkeepers, their clerks and errand boys, casual laborers available for any type of manual task, and a large number of trades connected with the production of clothing and textiles. Many people were also involved in the preparation, distribution, and sale of food, whether in shops or eating places such as taverns and street booths. One crucial task, which we in the present-day United States rarely think about, was obtaining a regular supply of water. This was one of the most important tasks of women and children, and took great amounts of time and labor.

Some civilized centers employed more of one type of labor than others, but overall there was a rough parity. Most jobs were in very small-scale enterprises. These were usually family-owned and staffed, with perhaps two or three paid or slave laborers. Slavery was less common in some places than others, but in all ancient societies except early Egypt and China, slaves made up a sizable portion of the working population. They sometimes performed much of the particularly unpleasant or dangerous work (mining and handling the dead, for example).

Religion and the Afterlife

Our knowledge of the Sumerians' religion is sketchy and unsure. As in most agrarian civilizations, they believed in a host of nature gods (**polytheism**, Greek for "many gods") of various ranks. There were many male and female deities, each with specific competencies in natural and human affairs. Among the most important were *Innana*,

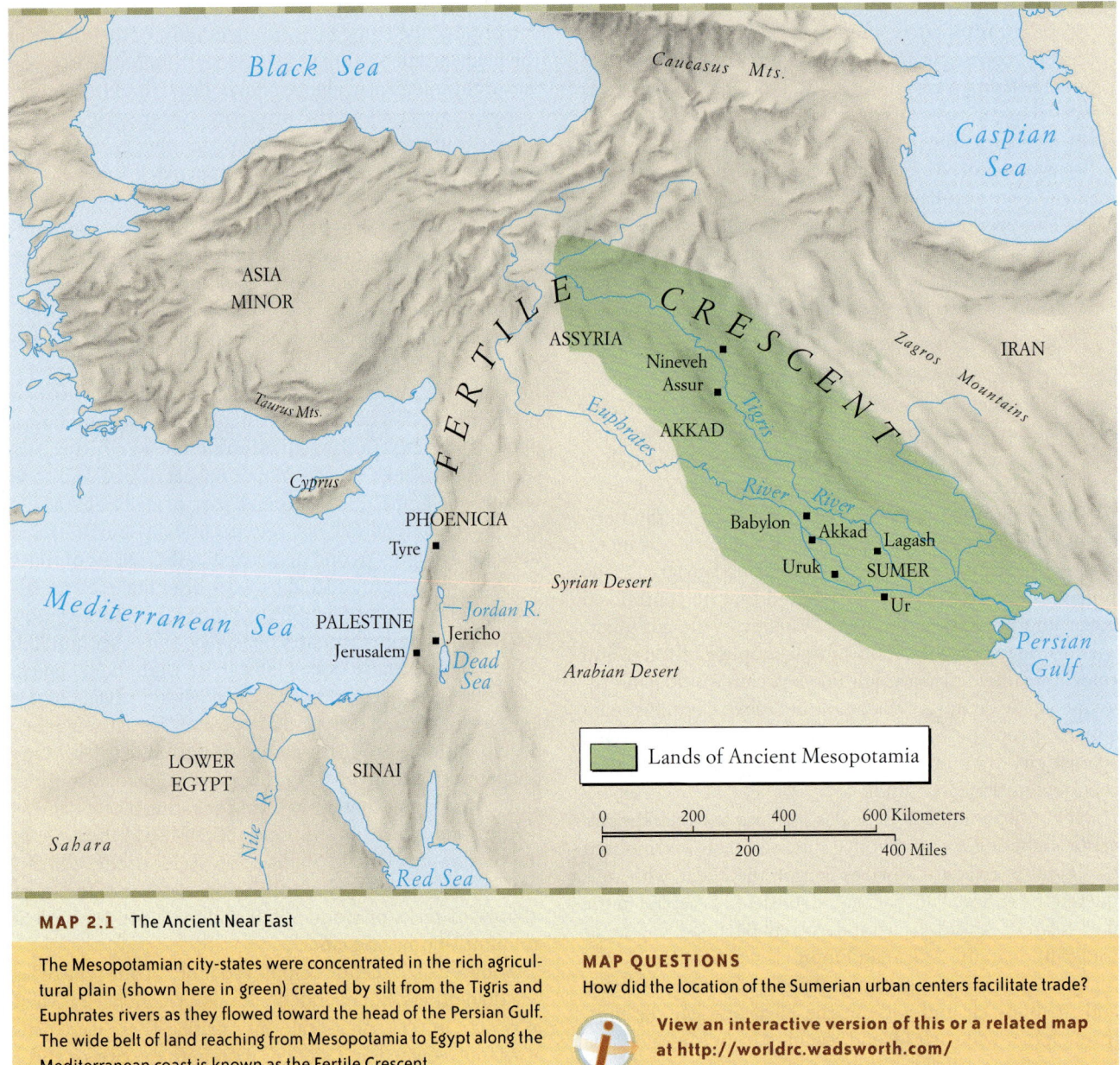

MAP 2.1   The Ancient Near East

The Mesopotamian city-states were concentrated in the rich agricultural plain (shown here in green) created by silt from the Tigris and Euphrates rivers as they flowed toward the head of the Persian Gulf. The wide belt of land reaching from Mesopotamia to Egypt along the Mediterranean coast is known as the Fertile Crescent.

MAP QUESTIONS
How did the location of the Sumerian urban centers facilitate trade?

View an interactive version of this or a related map at http://worldrc.wadsworth.com/

the goddess of love and fertility and the water-god, *Enki* (ENG-kee). These gods were much like superhumans, with all the faults and weaknesses of men and women. Some were immensely powerful: Their will affected all the Sumerian settlements, and they were believed to rule over all of nature and humanity. In addition, each city-kingdom had its local gods and spirits of the land and sky who were crucial to the prosperity of its citizens and who had to be carefully placated by professionally trained priests. The gods were thought to reside at times in the great temple complexes crowned and protected by the **ziggurats** (ZIHG-goo-rahts), or stepped pyramids, where hundreds of priests and their dependents ritually prayed and made offerings

to them on behalf of the city-state's welfare. The best-known ziggurat, erected by the powerful city of **Babylon** long after the Sumerian Epoch, was the Tower of Babel of biblical fame.

The two features of Mesopotamia's natural environment that stood out the most were the aridity of the climate and the unpredictability of the rivers' annual floods on which everyone relied for growing food. Like nature, which they controlled, the Mesopotamian gods frequently were cruel toward their human creatures and highly unpredictable. Men and women were the slaves of their god-creators, intended as the providers of the labors that the gods didn't wish to perform. Every religious function was performed on

Georg Gerster/Photo Researchers, Inc.

ZIGGURAT. The stepped pyramidal form for religious monuments has been used from one end of the Earth to the other. It combines an overpowering sense of mass and permanency with a mystical projection of divine superiority over earthbound humans. Pyramids like this Mesopotamian ziggurat can also be found in Egypt, Central America, and, in modified form, Southeast Asia. The Mesopotamian variety was constructed of earthen bricks, which demanded frequent renovation lest they dissolve into ruins through time's erosive force or an enemy's vandalism.

behalf of the community; hence, there is little evidence of a personal, loving relationship between deities and men. Nor is there any trace of ethics in Mesopotamian religion. The demands of the gods had no intrinsic connection with doing good or avoiding evil on Earth beyond what offerings and ritual acts could win from them to assure the regularity of the natural cycles on which a farm-based economy depended. The gods often punished humans, but not for "moral" failings, or what we would call *sin*. Being nature gods, the punishments often took the form of natural catastrophes, such as droughts or floods that harmed the entire community. To avert punishment, the gods had to be appeased with frequent, costly rituals and ceremonies, which were the responsibility of a hereditary priesthood and, to a lesser extent, the rulers.

The priests used their power as interpreters of the will of the gods to create large and wealthy temple communities supported by the offerings of the citizens. In some Sumerian cities, the priests seem to have been the true rulers for a time. This practice ended with the conquest by Sargon the Great, who made the royal throne, supported by a powerful army, the undisputed center of authority.

WARKA VASE. Sumerian priests from Uruk (3500–3000 BCE) used vases like this one to make offerings to the gods. The vase depicts water, wheat or barley growing from the water, and naked priests gratefully presenting the "first fruits" of a successful crop to Innana, the goddess of fertility.

©Gianni Dagli Orti/Corbis

The religion was certainly not an optimistic one, and it seems to have had no clear ideas on the nature of the afterlife or who, if anyone, could enjoy immortality. The best approach seemed to be to honor and obey the gods as well as you could, to appease them by making offerings through their powerful priests, and to hope to prosper in this life and the afterlife, if there was one. Much of what is known about Mesopotamian religious belief derives from their literature, in which several major myths of Western civilization, including the Flood and the Garden of Eden, find their first expression. Particularly important is the creation myth embraced in the ***Epic of Gilgamesh*** (GIL-gah-mesh)**,** the first epic poem in world literature. Gilgamesh is a man, a king of one of the city-states, who desires the secret of immortal life, but the gods, jealous of his power, defeat him. The excerpts in the Patterns of Belief box show the similarity between the flood stories in *Gilgamesh* and the Book of Genesis of the Judeo-Christian Scripture.

Monastery, Goettweig, Austria/ ©Erich Lessing/Art Resource, NY

PATTERNS OF BELIEF

The Epic of Gilgamesh

The collection of stories that is termed the *Epic of Gilgamesh* is one of the earliest approaches to analyzing the relations of gods and humans. It portrays a society in search of a religious basis for human action. Stories of the Flood occur in many ancient cultural traditions, such as the Noah story in the Old Testament of the Hebrews, the creation myths of the Hindus, and some of the North American Indian creation stories. In each case, the story tells of a disastrous flood that engulfed the entire Earth and nearly annihilated humanity.

In the Middle Eastern tradition, the narrative of the Flood is first found in the *Epic of Gilgamesh*. In this version, the main focus of the story is on the inevitability of death and the defeat of the hero as he attempts to achieve immortality. The Mesopotamian counterpart of the biblical Noah is Utnapishtim. Here his description of the flood is contrasted with the version recounted in Genesis:

Gilgamesh

The gods of the abyss rose up; Nergal pulled out the dams of the netherworld, Ninurta the war-lord threw down the dikes . . . a stupor of despair went up to heaven when the god of storms turned daylight into darkness, when he smashed the earth like a teacup. One whole day the tempest raged, gathering fury as it went, and it poured over the people like the tide of battle; a man could not see his brother nor could the people be seen from heaven. Even the gods were terrified at the flood, they fled to the highest heaven . . . they crouched against the walls, cowering . . . the gods of heaven and hell wept . . . for six days and six nights the winds blew, tempest and flood raged together like warring hosts. . . . I looked at the face of the earth, and all was silence, all mankind was turned into clay. . . . I bowed low, and I wept. . . .

Genesis

All the fountains of the great deep burst forth and the floodgates of the heavens were opened. And rain fell on the earth for forty days and forty nights. . . . The waters increased and bore up the ark, and it rose above the earth.

The waters rose higher and higher, and increased greatly on the earth . . . the waters rose higher and higher, so that all the highest mountains everywhere under the heavens were covered. All flesh that moved on the earth died: birds, cattle, wild animals, all creatures that crawl upon the earth, and all men. Only Noah and those with him in the ark were saved.

Gilgamesh is a grim tale that speaks of death and the afterlife in pessimistic and fearful tones. Indicative is this description by Gilgamesh's companion Enkidu of a vivid dream he had had, foreshadowing his approaching death:

I stood alone before an awful Being; his face was somber like the blackbird of the storm. He fell upon me with the talons of an eagle, and he held me fast, pinioned by his claws until I smothered; then he transformed me so that my arms became wings covered with feathers . . . and he led me away, to the house from which those who enter never return . . . whose people sit in darkness, dust their food and clay their meat. They are clothed like birds with wings for coverings, they see no light, they sit in darkness.

The epic ends with the failure of Gilgamesh's quest for the secret of immortal life. The somber funeral chant seems to underline the poet's sense of resignation and futility:

The king has laid himself down, and will not rise again. The Lord of Kullab [that is, Gilgamesh] will not rise again, He overcame evil, but he will not rise again, Though he was strong of arm, he will not rise again, Possessing wisdom and a comely face, he will not rise again.

▶ Analyze and Interpret

What does the emphasis on defeat and death in the *Gilgamesh* story signify in terms of the beliefs of the peoples who created these myths? Read the full accounts of the flood in *Gilgamesh* and Genesis. What do you make of the differences?

Source: Reprinted with permission from Penguin Classics, 1960, 2d rev. ed., 1972. Copyright N. K. Sanders, 1960, 1964, 1972.

You can read the entire *Epic of Gilgamesh* at the Wadsworth World History Resource Center.

Mathematics and Chronology

Like almost all agrarian civilizations, Mesopotamians' sense of time was shaped by the cyclic nature of seasonal change. The year was based on the passage of seasons and their way of reckoning this was by observing and recording the positions of heavenly bodies as well as the recurring changes in their surroundings. Their calendar was subdivided into lunar months, corresponding to the period between one full moon and the next. In calculating the year's length, the Sumerians arrived at a figure close to our own, although not quite as close as the Egyptians, by employing their solar calendar. All in all, Sumerian math, including its further development by the Babylonians and Persians, has held up very well and has been influential in all later Western science, including that of the Greeks.

After the invention of writing, perhaps the most dramatic advances made by these early inhabitants of Mesopotamia were in mathematics and chronology. Sumerian math was based on units of 60 and its divisors, and this, of course, is the reason that we still measure time in intervals of 60 seconds and 60 minutes. Much of our basic geometry and trigonometry, such as the 360 degrees of a circle, also stems from the Sumerians.

The Evolution of Writing

Spoken language was one of the key achievements of early human beings, enabling an intensity and variety of communication that was previously unknown. We have no certain idea when modern forms of speech occurred, but linguists theorize that this was around 80,000 years ago. Not until some time in the fourth millennium (4000–3000 BCE), however, was oral language joined to a written form, and so remained permanently accessible.

Perhaps the most important and lasting of all the Sumerian accomplishments was the gradual invention of a system of writing, which evolved from their need to have good records for keeping their calendar and predicting seasonal changes, as well as for commercial and religious taxation, marital and inheritance contracts, and some other activities in which it was important to have a clear, mutually agreed-upon version of past events. Some type of marks on some type of medium (clay, paper, wood, stone) had been in use long, long before 3500 BCE. What did the Sumerians of that epoch do to justify the claim of having invented writing? Significantly, they moved beyond pictorial writing, or symbols derived from pictures, into a further phase of conveying meaning through abstract marks.

All writing derives originally from a simplified picture. This is called *pictography*, and it has been used from one end of the Earth to the other. Pictography had several obvious disadvantages, though. For one thing, it could not convey the meaning of abstractions (things that have no material, tangible existence). Nor could it communicate the tense of a verb, the degree of an adjective or adverb, or many other things that language has to handle well.

The way that the Sumerians (and later peoples) got around these difficulties was to expand their pictorial writing gradually to a much more sophisticated level so that it included special signs for abstractions, tenses, and so on—signs that had nothing to do with tangible objects. These are called *conventional signs* and may be invented for any meaning desired by their users. For example, if both of us agree that the signs "cc" stand for "the boy in the blue suit," then that is what they mean when we see them on a piece of paper, or a rock surface, or wherever. If we further agree that by adding the vertical stroke "!"

©Iraq Museum, Baghdad/Photo ©Held Collection/Bridgeman Art Library

CUNEIFORM WRITING. This example of cuneiform writing is an astrological tablet from Uruk in Sumer. Probably recorded by a priest, it serves as a reminder of the linkage that existed between religious ritual and time keeping in ancient agrarian societies.

we make a verb into a future tense, then it is future tense so far as we're concerned. Very slowly, the Sumerians expanded their pictographic vocabulary in this way, while simultaneously simplifying and standardizing their pictures so that they could be written more rapidly and recognized more easily by strangers.

A big breakthrough came some time in the third millennium, when a series of clever scribes began to use written signs to indicate the sounds of the spoken language. This was the beginning of the *phonetic written language*, in which the signs had a direct connection with the oral language. Although the Sumerians did not progress as far as an alphabet, they started down the path that would culminate in one about 2,000 years later.

The basic format of the written language after about 3500 BCE was a script written in wedge-shaped characters, the **cuneiform** (KYOO-neh-form), on clay tablets about the size of your hand. Tens of thousands of these tablets covered by cuneiform writings have been dug up in modern times. Most of them pertain to contracts between private parties or between a private party and officials. But other tablets contain prayers of all sorts, proclamations by officials, law codes and judgments, and some letters and poetry. Sumerian cuneiform remained the basic script of most Near and Middle Eastern languages until about 1000 BCE, when its use began to fade out.

Law

One of the earliest known complete codes of laws originated in post-Sumerian Mesopotamia in the 1700s BCE during the reign of the emperor Hammurabi (ham-moo-RAH-bee). He is the first of the historic lawgivers whose work has survived into our times. (His accomplishments are described in the Law and Government box.) His code certainly had predecessors that have been lost, because its legal concepts and vocabulary are much too sophisticated for it to have been a first effort. The code is based on two distinctive principles: punishment depended on the social rank of the violator, and offenders were subjected to the same damages or injury that they caused to others. These ideas would be incorporated into many later codes over the next 2,000 years, although rejected by modern democratic theory. A commoner would get a different, more severe punishment than would a noble or official for the same offense. And a slave (of whom there were many) would be treated more harshly still. If in the same social class as

the victim, the offender would have to give "an eye for an eye, a tooth for a tooth." Another basic principle of Mesopotamian law was that the government should act as an impartial referee among its subject citizens, seeing to it that the wronged party got satisfaction from the wrongdoer. The victim had the right to demand personal compensation from the person who had caused him grief—a legal concept that is being reintroduced into American criminal law.

People were not equal before the law: husbands had a great deal of power over wives, fathers over children, rich over poor, free citizens over slaves. Nevertheless, a definite attempt was made to protect the defenseless and to see that all received justice.

Much of Hammurabi's code dealt with social and family problems, such as the support of widows and orphans, illegitimacy, adultery, and rape. Clearly, the position of women was inferior to that of men, but they did have certain legal rights and were not just the property of their male relatives. A wife could divorce her husband, and if the husband was found to be at fault, the wife was entitled to the property she had brought into the marriage. Women could also enter into contracts and have custody over minor children under certain conditions—two rights that many later civilizations denied them.

Government and Social Structure

Government in Mesopotamia can be divided into two types: the **theocracy** (rule by gods or their priests) of the early city-states of the Sumerians, and the kingdom-empires of their successors, starting with Sargon the Great of Akkad. A king, assisted by noble officials and priests, ruled the cities. In Sumerian times, the kings were no more than figureheads for the priests, but later they exercised decisive power.

The city, ruled by an elite headed by a king-emperor, was quite different in its social subdivisions from the village. In the village, social equality was rarely challenged, and a leveling interdependency in everyday life was taken for granted. In the urban areas, on the contrary, distinctions among people were essential and expected to be displayed in many fashions and activities. Above all, the lower classes supported the far less numerous upper classes through both labor and taxes.

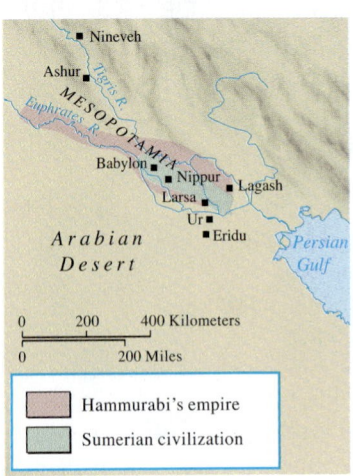

HAMMURABI'S EMPIRE

Nineveh
Ashur
Tigris R.
Euphrates R.
MESOPOTAMIA
Babylon
Nippur
Larsa
Lagash
Ur
Eridu
Arabian Desert
Persian Gulf

0   200   400 Kilometers
0   200 Miles

Hammurabi's empire
Sumerian civilization

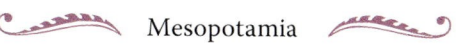

Kunsthistorisches Museum, Vienna, Austria/
©Erich Lessing/Art Resource, NY

LAW AND GOVERNMENT

Hammurabi

The emperor Hammurabi, who ruled Mesopotamia from about 1792 BCE to about 1750 BCE, is best known for the code of laws that bears his name, one of the earliest law codes yet discovered. Hammurabi's empire stretched from the desolate mountains of Zagros in western Iran to the edge of the Arabian Desert. It was centered on the great city of Babylon in central Mesopotamia. Although nature has not been generous with this region, its ruler was successful in bringing prosperity and peace to most of his subjects.

Like all Middle Eastern kingdoms, the Amorite Hammurabi's empire was originally created by conquest. He formed coalitions with his Semite neighbors and won the loyalty of the smaller Amorite city-states that surrounded his own. Babylon emerged as a center of both manufacturing and trade, and its influence reached from the head of the Persian Gulf to the eastern shore of the Mediterranean.

The emperor's main concern, however, was to maintain order in this large region through authority, which answered what he perceived to be the needs of his people. To that effect, he gave his subjects a complex law code. Its 282 decrees, collectively termed the Code of Hammurabi, were inscribed on stone *stelae*, or columns, and erected in many public places. The one shown here was discovered in Persian Susa in the nineteenth century and is now in the Louvre in Paris.

The code dealt primarily with civil affairs such as marriage and inheritance, family relations, property rights, and business practices. Criminal offenses were punished with varying degrees of severity, depending on the social status of the offender and the victim. Clear

STELA OF HAMMURABI. The stela is about five feet high, showing the king receiving the code from Shamash, god of justice, at the top and the actual text of the 282 laws below.

Louvre, Paris, France/Bridgeman Art Library

distinctions were made between the rights of the upper classes and those of commoners. Payments were generally allowed as restitution for damage done to commoners by nobles. A commoner who caused damage to a noble, however, might have to pay with his head. Trial by ordeal, retribution by retaliatory action, and capital punishment were common practices. But judges distinguished between intentional and unintentional injuries, and monetary fines were normally used as punishment where no malicious intent was shown. The "eye for an eye" morality often associated with Hammurabi's code was relatively restricted in application and applied only to crimes committed against social equals.

The code made theft a serious crime and devoted great attention to crimes against property in general. Workers had to do an adequate job or be punished for negligence. Official fee tables were ordained for medical care, and woe to the doctor who was found guilty of malpractice! Although the code did not concern itself with religious belief or practice, it did accord considerable powers to the administering judges, who were often priests. In general, it established strict standards of justice and public morality.

▶ Analyze and Interpret

How does the Code of Hammurabi show that property rights were superior to human rights? Is it unusual to show class distinctions in the application of laws?

You can read the entire Code of Hammurabi at the *Wadsworth World History Resource Center*.

The Mesopotamian civilization apparently had but three classes of people, the first of which were the small groups of priests and noble landlords (often two branches of a single group) who were great landlords and had a monopoly on the higher offices of the city. Behind the priesthood stood the immense power of the high gods of the Sumerians and their successors: the deities of earth, sky, fire, fresh water, salt water, and storm. The second group, the freemen, was the most numerous class. They did the bulk of the city's work and trading, and owned and worked most of the outlying farmlands. The relatively protected position of freemen is attested to by Hammurabi's code (see Law and Government box) and by the thousands of other documents recovered in the nineteenth and twentieth centuries from the ruins of Sumerian cities. Both priests and nobles depended on their skills and their labor, which was presumably given on a more or less voluntary basis.

Finally, the slaves who at times were very numerous often possessed considerable skills and were given some responsible positions. Freemen had some political rights, but slaves had none. As we will repeatedly see, slaves were common in most ancient societies, and enslavement was by no means the morally contemptible and personally humiliating condition it would frequently become later. Slavery had nothing much to do with race or ethnicity and everything to do with bad luck, such as being on the losing side of a war or falling into debt. Most slaves in Mesopotamia—and elsewhere—had run up debts that they could not otherwise repay. It was not at all uncommon to become someone's slave for a few years and then resume your freedom when you had paid off what you owed. Hereditary slavery was rare. Many owners routinely freed their slaves in their wills as a mark of piety and benevolence.

Maltreatment of slaves did occur, but mostly to field workers, miners, or criminals who had been enslaved as punishment and had had no personal contacts with their owner. On the other side, in all ancient societies many slaves engaged in business, many had advanced skills in the crafts, and some managed to accumulate enough money working on their own accounts that they could buy their freedom. The conditions of slaves in the ancient world varied so enormously that we cannot generalize about them with any accuracy except to say that slaves were politically and legally inferior to free citizens.

The Status of Women

Historians generally agree on some categorical statements about the women of ancient Mesopotamia and Egypt:

- ◆ In the earliest stage of civilization, women shared more or less equally with men in social prestige and power.
- ◆ This egalitarianism was undermined and overturned by the coming of militarized society (armies), the heavy plow in agriculture, and the establishment of large-scale trade over long distances.

- ◆ The trend toward **patriarchy** (PAY-tree-ahr-kee)—a society in which males have social and political dominance—proceeded at varying speeds in different societies but was impossible to reverse once it started.

Ancient law codes from Mesopotamia show a definite break between about 2000 BCE and 1000 BCE, with Hammurabi's code being a transition. In the earliest contracts and rulings (and to a lesser degree in Hammurabi's code), the female enjoys extensive rights; by about 1200 BCE, she is an object ruled by men.

In Mesopotamia, most of the household and artisan occupations were open to women as well as to men. Women could engage in small-scale business in their own name (but normally under a male relative's supervision). A woman only rarely operated in affairs completely independently.

Adultery was always considered the worst of all possible offenses between husband and wife because it put the children's parentage under a cloud of doubt and thus undermined the family's continuity. Punishment for wifely adultery could be death, not only for her but also for her lover if he were caught. Note that in Hammurabi's code adultery as a legal concept was limited to the wife's acts. The husband's sexual activity with slave girls or freeborn concubines, as he might see fit, was taken for granted. The double standard has existed since the beginnings of history.

Divorce and lawsuits arising from it were frequent in Mesopotamia, as the tablets attest. Husbands, who were disappointed by childless wives or were sexually attracted to another woman and did not wish to or could not support the first wife as well, initiated most divorces. The lawsuits resulted when the wife or her father protested the lack of provision made for her support or the husband's attempt to retain her dowry. Then as now, lawyers must have relied on divorce proceedings for a substantial part of their income.

Sexual and marital life. Because children and the continuity of the family were the real reasons for marriage, the marital bed was an honorable and even sacred place, and what took place there was in no way shameful. But the male and female had desires that went beyond the creation of children, and these were also nothing to be ashamed of, for these desires were implanted in humans by the all-wise gods. Everywhere in the Near East, starting apparently with the Sumerians and long continuing, the rites of the Sacred Marriage between a god and his high priestess, celebrating the fertility of the earth and of all creatures on it, were central to religious practice. The result was a fundamentally different attitude toward sex than we commonly find in civilized society today. Whether sexual pleasure outside marriage was permissible, however, depended on the status of the individuals concerned.

Marriage was always arranged by the two families—something so important could never be left to chance attraction. A great many of the clay tablets dug up in Mesopotamian ruins deal with marital contracts. Some

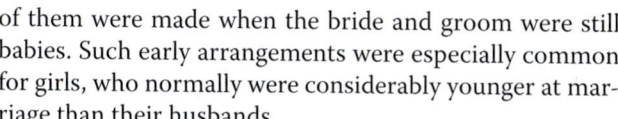

of them were made when the bride and groom were still babies. Such early arrangements were especially common for girls, who normally were considerably younger at marriage than their husbands.

Marriage usually involved the exchange of bride money and a dowry. Bride money was a payment by the groom's family to the bride's family as specified in the marital contract. The dowry was also specified in the contract and was paid by the bride's family to the groom when the couple began to live together. The dowry remained in the husband's control as long as the marriage lasted. When the wife died, the dowry was distributed among her children, if she had any.

Every ancient culture insisted that brides should be virgins. This was one of the reasons for the early marriage of women. Although many literary works and folktales describe the social condemnation that awaited a woman who lost her virginity before marriage, it is still quite clear that lovemaking between young unmarried persons was by no means unheard of and did not always result in shame. Loss of virginity was regarded as damage to the family's property rather than a moral offense. As such, it could be made good by the payment of a fine. Punishment for seducing a virgin was less severe than for adultery or rape. Some authorities believe that the early stages of civilization in all areas were more tolerant of nonvirginal marriage for women than were later ones. If premarital relations were followed by marriage, very little fuss was made.

TRADE AND AN EXPANSION OF SCALE

The Sumerians were not the only settlers of the broad plain on either side of the two rivers. In fact, they were not even the first people in those regions. Unlike most of their neighboring tribes, the Sumerians were not members of the **Semitic** (seh-MIH-tic) language family. (*Note*: A language group or family is related by its grammar and sometimes by its vocabulary and alphabet. The Semitic family is one of the major language families in the world and includes Hebrew and Arabic as well as many others.)

By 3000 BCE, the Sumerians had extended their domain upriver into Semite-inhabited regions, as far as the future city of Babylon. Trade grew rapidly, not only between food-growing villages and the towns but also with Semitic-speaking communities scattered for hundreds of miles along the banks of the rivers. Out of these large towns grew, with neighborhoods of craftspeople, merchants, and laborers. Sumerian civilization took root and matured among these so-called *barbarians* (a Greek word meaning simply people who speak a different language and are supposedly inferior). In the period of Sumerian greatness (to about 2000 BCE), political development never exceeded that of warring city-states. So, ironically,

it was their Semitic-speaking stepchildren, the Akkadians, the Babylonians, and the Assyrians who unified Mesopotamia and expanded the reach of Mesopotamian civilization over a considerably wider region than anything the Sumerians had ever imagined.

In the earliest days of Mesopotamian trade, Sumerian cities depended on importing basic materials like obsidian, wood, and later copper and more exotic goods from regions both east and west of the Tigris-Euphrates Valleys. Mesopotamian trade eventually extended across a broad expanse that stretched from the Indus Valley in modern-day Pakistan, to the Nile Valley and the lands bordering the eastern Mediterranean. Scholars think that this region comprised the earliest known global trade network in world history. Eventually, in many places where Sumerian commercial tentacles reached, Sumerian culture followed. Many centuries after the passing of Sumeria's greatness, its cuneiform system of writing and its literature continued to be the foundation of Mesopotamian culture. Epics like *Gilgamesh* remained popular, and the Creation account in the Hebrew Book of Genesis originated in Mesopotamia, quite likely from as far back as Sumerian times.

SUCCESSORS TO SUMERIA

After the conquest of Sumeria by Sargon of Akkad, nomadic peoples eager to enjoy the fruits of civilized life subjected Mesopotamia to a long series of foreign invasions and conquests. These barbaric nomads generally adopted the beliefs and values of those they had conquered. After the Akkadians, the most important of them were as follows, in sequence:

1. The *Amorites,* or *Old Babylonians,* a Semitic people who conquered the plains under their great emperor Hammurabi in the 1700s BCE.

2. The **Hittites,** an Indo-European group of tribes who came out of southern Russia into modern-day Turkey and constructed an empire there that reached as far into the east and south as the Zagros Mountains and Palestine. The first people to smelt iron, the Hittites were a remarkable group who took over the river plain about 1500 BCE. They were skilled administrators and established the first multiethnic state, which worked fairly well.

3. After the Hittites fell to unknown invaders about 1200 BCE, the *Assyrians* gradually rose to power around 900 BCE, operating from their northern Mesopotamian center at Nineveh. We will deal with the imperial Assyrian Period from about 800–600 BCE.

4. Finally, after a brief period under the *New Babylonians* (or *Chaldees,* as the Old Testament calls them), the plains fell to the mighty *Persian Empire* in the 500s BCE and stayed under Persian (Iranian) rule for most of the next thousand years (see Chapter 4).

THE DECLINE OF MESOPOTAMIA IN WORLD HISTORY

The valley of the Tigris and Euphrates rivers ceased to be of central importance in the ancient world after the Persian conquest. The Persians did not choose to make their capital there, nor did they adopt the ideas and the cultural models of their new province, as all previous conquerors had. The Persians were already far advanced beyond barbarism when they conquered Mesopotamia and perhaps were not so easily impressed.

Various problems contributed to the decline of Mesopotamia, but it is certain that it proceeded in part from one of the first known examples of long-term environmental degradation. Significantly, the cities' food supply declined as the irrigated farms of the lower plains no longer produced abundant harvests. Thanks to several thousand years of salt deposits from the evaporated waters of the canals and ditches, the fields—unrenewed by fertilizers and exposed to a gradually harshening climate of sandstorms and great heat—were simply not capable of producing as much as the population needed. The once-thriving city-states and rich fields were gradually abandoned, and the center of power and culture moved elsewhere.

Mesopotamia slowly receded into the background of civilized activities from the Persian conquest until the ninth century CE, when for a time it became the political and spiritual center of the far-flung world of Islam. But it was not until the mid-twentieth century, with the rise of Muslim fundamentalism and the coming of the Oil Age, that the area again became a vital world center.

SUMMARY

THE EARLIEST OF the mutually dependent agglomerations of agriculturalists and skilled trades that we call towns and cities were founded in fourth millennium BCE Mesopotamia, when an Asian people, the Sumerians, created them. Headed originally by a theocratic priesthood and later by warrior-kings, the Sumerian city-states left their various successors a rich variety of new techniques and viewpoints, including the load-bearing wheel, the first sophisticated writing system, an accurate chronology and mathematics, and impressive architectural skills. Their religion seems harsh and pessimistic to us now, but it apparently reflected their perceptions of the dangerous world around them, in which natural and manmade disasters were common and the gods cared little for their human slaves.

▶ Identification Terms

Test your knowledge of this chapter's key concepts by defining the following terms. If you can't recall the meaning of certain terms, refresh your memory by looking up the boldfaced term in the chapter, turning to the Glossary at the end of the book, or working with the flashcards that are available on the *World Civilizations* Companion Website: **academic.cengage.com/adler**

Babylon	Hittites	patriarchy	Sumerians
cuneiform	Levantine Corridor	polytheism	theocracy
Epic of Gilgamesh	Mesopotamia	Semitic	ziggurats
Fertile Crescent			

▶ Test Your Knowledge

Test your knowledge of this chapter by answering the following questions. Complete answers appear at the end of the book. You may find even more quiz questions in CengageNOW and on the *World Civilizations* Companion Website: **academic.cengage.com/adler**

1. The founders of ancient Mesopotamian civilization were the
   a. Sumerians.
   b. Amorites.
   c. Semites.
   d. Babylonians.
   e. Hittites.

2. The Tigris and Euphrates rivers were important to Mesopotamians primarily because
   a. they kept out potential raiders.
   b. they made irrigation possible.
   c. they drained off the water from the frequent storms.
   d. they brought the people together.
   e. they provided transportation to the sea.

3. The Mesopotamian ziggurat was a
   a. military fort.
   b. temple of worship.
   c. household shrine.
   d. royal palace.
   e. burial tomb.

4. Pictographs are a form of writing that
   a. uses pictures and words.
   b. uses agreed-upon signs to make pictures.
   c. puts abstract ideas into pictorial form.
   d. uses pictures of material objects to form meanings.
   e. uses conventional signs to designate parts of speech.

5. Mesopotamians considered their gods to be
   a. about equal in power.
   b. the creators of people and the universe.
   c. responsive to human needs and wants.
   d. disembodied spirits.
   e. always concerned with the well-being of human beings.

6. The *Epic of Gilgamesh* deals with the
   a. struggle between good and evil.
   b. details of death and the afterlife.
   c. proof of the existence of gods.
   d. conflict between men and women.
   e. conflict between humans and the gods.

7. The law code of King Hammurabi
   a. ensured equal treatment for all offenders.
   b. was the first law code ever written.
   c. used fines and financial punishments exclusively.
   d. ordered punishments in accord with the social rank of the offender.
   e. dealt mainly with matters of business.

8. In Sumerian and later government in Mesopotamia,
   a. theocracy succeeded the rule of kings.
   b. a warrior aristocracy was the rule from the beginning.
   c. a monarchy succeeded the rule of priests.
   d. the common people always had the last word.
   e. kings and priests usually worked together to create laws.

9. Becoming enslaved in Mesopotamia was most often the result of which of the following causes?
   a. Commission of crime or personal violence
   b. Being a prisoner of war or in debt
   c. Blasphemy
   d. Rebellion
   e. Defiance of the gods

10. A major reason for the decline of Mesopotamia in importance after the Persian conquests seems to have been
    a. an environmental change.
    b. unceasing warfare among the Persians.
    c. the conquest of the area by barbarians.
    d. the technological lag from which the area had always suffered.
    e. an alteration in trade routes which drew people elsewhere.

Enter *CengageNOW* using the access card that is available with this text. *CengageNOW* will assist you in understanding the content in this chapter with lesson plans generated for your needs and provide you with a connection to the *Wadsworth World History Resource Center* (see description at right for details).

 **World History Resource Center**

Enter the Resource Center using either your *CengageNOW* access card or your standalone access card for the *Wadsworth World History Resource Center*. Organized by topic, this website includes quizzes; images; over 350 primary source documents; interactive simulations, maps, and timelines; movie explorations; and a wealth of other resources. You can read the following documents, and many more, at the *Wadsworth World History Resource Center*:

Epic of Gilgamesh   Code of Hammurabi

> They [Egyptian priests] have
> told me that 341 generations
> separate the first King of Egypt
> from the last. Reckoning three
> generations as a century . . .
> a total of 11,340 years.
> —Herodotus, *Histories,*
> Book II

3 EGYPT

c. 3100–2200 BCE	Old Kingdom
c. 2600–2100 BCE	Pyramid-building age
c. 2200–2100 BCE	First Intermediate Period
c. 2100–1650 BCE	Middle Kingdom
c. 1650–1570 BCE	Second Intermediate Period
1500s BCE	Hyksos invasion
c. 1550–770 BCE	New Kingdom
c. 1550–1250 BCE	The Empire
1300s BCE	Akhnaton's monotheist experiment Tutankhamen
525 BCE	Persian conquest

THE NATURAL ENVIRONMENT AND PEOPLE OF EGYPT

THE PHARAOH: EGYPT'S GOD-KING
Government Under the Pharaoh ◆ The Old Kingdom, Middle Kingdom, and New Kingdom

CULTURAL ACHIEVEMENTS
Philosophy, Religion, and Eternal Life ◆ Egypt and Mesopotamia: Contrasts ◆ Trade and Egypt's Influence

I T WOULD BE HARD to find two other ancient civilizations that present as sharp a contrast in some respects as Mesopotamia on one end of the Fertile Crescent and Egypt on the other. The mainstay of Mesopotamian civilization was the Tigris and Euphrates Rivers, both of which were subject to frequent and unpredictable flooding. Because it had no natural barriers to protect it, Mesopotamia also lay open to destructive assault from several directions and was repeatedly conquered by alien forces. Egypt saw no such threats for millennia, and the Nile River was extremely dependable. Although we know that Mesopotamia exercised considerable influence on Egypt's cultural development though trade and although both civilizations rested on agrarian underpinnings, the two societies evolved patterns of beliefs and values that differed in significant ways. Quite unlike Mesopotamia, Egypt became an island in time and space that enjoyed more than one thousand years of peaceful existence with little disturbance from the outside world. When that disturbance did come at last, Egypt's reaction proved too inflexible to allow it to survive in its uniqueness.

THE NATURAL ENVIRONMENT AND PEOPLE OF EGYPT

Like Mesopotamia, Egypt depended on the waters of a great river system. Egypt is, and has always been, the valley of the Nile—a green strip averaging about thirty miles wide, with forbidding desert hills on either side. The 4,000-mile-long river—the world's longest—originates far to the south in the lakes of central Africa and flows north until it empties into the Mediterranean Sea at Alexandria.

Unlike the unpredictably flooding Tigris and Euphrates, the Nile is a benevolent river, and without it life in Egypt would have been unthinkable. In contrast to the Tigris, the Nile annually would swell gently in late summer until it

overflowed its low banks and spread out over the valley floor, carrying with it a load of extremely fertile silt. Two or three weeks later, the flood would subside, depositing the silt to renew the valley with a fresh layer of good top-soil. The Egyptians trapped receding waters in a series of small reservoirs connected to an intricate system of gated ditches that would later convey the water into the surrounding fields for irrigation.

PATTERNS OF BELIEF

Hymn to the Nile

Often called "The Gift of the Nile," more than anything else Egypt owed all life, all existence to the Nile River. As the bringer of life, little wonder that Egyptians not only made a god of the river itself, but even attributed gods and goddesses to the river in its several aspects, as seen in this ancient Hymn. For example, **Anuket** was the goddess of the river itself; **Khnum** was the god of the source of the river and Anuket's husband; while **Satis** was the goddess of the flood. Other gods mentioned in the poem include **Ra,** the universal god who subsumed and incorporated all others. **Seb,** the god of earth; **Ptah,** god of the primordial mound from which all life came, represented birth, life, and the renewal of life, like **Nepera. Maat** did not represent a specific thing, but rather the concepts of order, regularity, rectitude, and justice. (See Philosophy and Religion, below.)

©Erich Lessing/Art Resource, NY

EGYPTIAN IRRIGATION. Life in rural Egypt preserves many of the habits and simple, peasant technologies of its ancient past. Channel irrigation, maintained by farmers making use of the simplest hand implements like this, goes back at least 4000 years.

Hail to thee, O Nile! Who manifests thyself over this land, and comes to give life to Egypt! Mysterious is thy issuing forth from the darkness, on this day whereon it is celebrated! Watering the orchards created by [Ra], to cause all the cattle to live, you give the earth to drink, inexhaustible one! Path that descends from the sky, loving the bread of Seb and the first-fruits of Nepera, You cause the workshops of Ptah to prosper!

Lord of the fish, during the inundation, no bird alights on the crops. You create the grain, you bring forth the barley, assuring perpetuity to the temples. If you cease your toil and your work, then all that exists is in anguish. If the gods suffer in heaven, then the faces of men waste away.

. . . .

He shines when He issues forth from the darkness, to cause his flocks to prosper. It is his force that gives existence to all things; nothing remains hidden for him. Let men clothe themselves to fill his gardens. He watches over his works, producing the inundation during the night. The associate of Ptah . . . He causes all his servants to exist, all writings and divine words, and that which He needs in the North.

It is with the words that He penetrates into his dwelling; He issues forth at his pleasure through the magic spells. Your unkindness brings destruction to the fish; it is then that prayer is made for the (annual) water of the season; Southern Egypt is seen in the same state as the North. Each one is with his instruments of labor. None remains behind his companions. None clothes himself with garments, The children of the noble put aside their ornaments.

He night remains silent, but all is changed by the inundation; it is a healing-balm for all mankind. Establisher of justice [Maat]! Mankind desires you, supplicating you to answer their prayers; You answer them by the inundation! Men offer the first-fruits of corn; all the gods adore you! The birds descend not on the soil. It is believed that with your hand of gold you make bricks of silver! But we are not nourished on lapis-lazuli; wheat alone gives vigor.

▶ Analyze and Interpret

The Nile is personified in the poem in several ways and with several names, all in conjunction with each other. How do you interpret this? What does the author have to say about ritual and sacrifice? What does she infer about the connection between the River and order and justice (Maat)?

Source: Oliver J. Thatcher, ed., *The Library of Original Sources* (Milwaukee: University Research Extension Co., 1907), Vol. I: The Ancient World, pp. 79–83. From the Internet Ancient History Sourcebook.

But not only in agriculture was Egypt blessed by its environment, it was secure in its geographic isolation. The country was protected against invasion by the deserts on the east and west of the valley and by the so-called cataracts (rapids) of the northerly flowing Nile, which prevented easy passage into Egypt from the region south of the first cataract, where enemies, called the Nubians (NOO-bee-ans) dwelled. On the north, the sea gave the Nile delta some protection from unwanted intruders, while still allowing the Egyptians to develop maritime operations. Only on the northeast, where the narrow Sinai peninsula links Egypt to Asia (see Map 3.1), was a land-based invasion possible, and most of Egypt's eventual invaders and conquerors arrived from this direction.

The Egyptian population was composed overwhelmingly of peasants, who lived in the villages that crowded along the Nile. Most were free tenant farmers who worked on the estate of a large landholder or government official who had been granted the land as payment for services to the crown. Each village followed a similar pattern: The huts were set close together within, and the fields lay outside. Farm life was possible only on the Nile's floodplain, so fields and villages alike were seldom located more than a few hundred yards from the riverbanks. Each day the peasants would go out to work in the fields, care for the irrigation works, or tend the animals. The implements they used were simple, typically fashioned by the peasants themselves or village craftsmen from materials available to them in their natural surroundings. There was little mechanization, so all farm work was labor intensive: the sweat of humans or animals was the only energy source available to perform essential chores like digging or repairing channels, turning the soil, planting, weeding, and harvesting.

EGYPTIAN PEASANTS. Agriculture was the foundation of Egypt's great wealth. The overwhelming majority were peasant farmers who made the land productive and built the system of channel irrigation with simple hand tools like those in this picture. Here they can be seen winnowing grain.

©Erich Lessing/Art Resource, NY

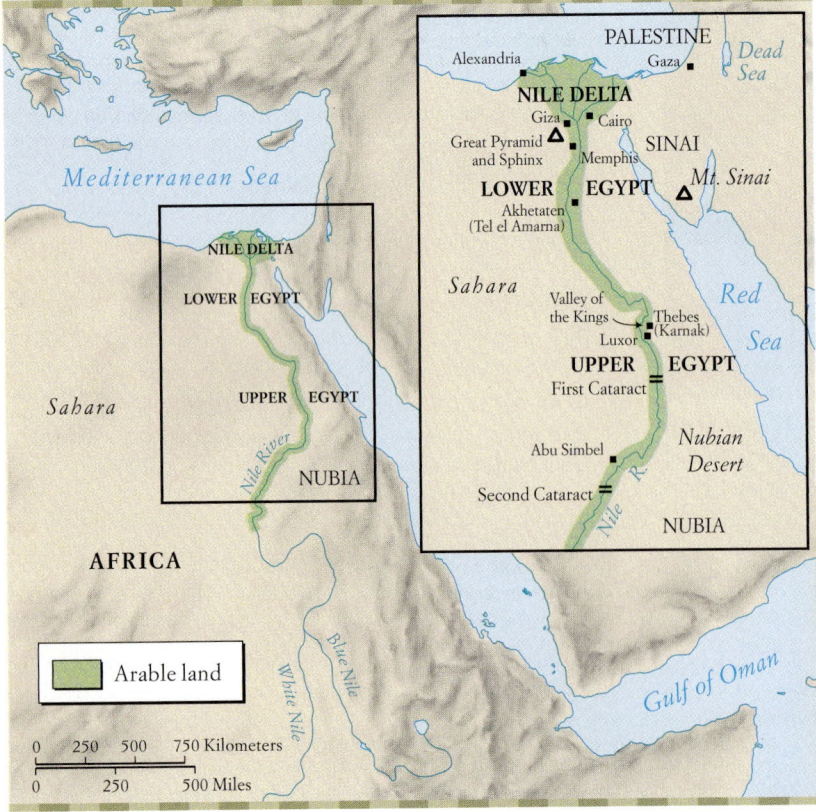

MAP 3.1 Ancient Egypt and the Nile

The first tourist to leave an account of Egypt was the Greek Herodotus in the fifth century BCE. He called Egypt "the gift of the Nile," a phrase that still describes the relation of the river and the people.

MAP QUESTIONS
Where did most of the village populations live?

As in Mesopotamia and other agrarian civilizations, Egypt's peasants had an intimate relationship with their natural environment that had grown from centuries of experience working it, making it productive, and passing on their accumulated understanding to their descendants. Soils, plants, insects, and animal life were known and exploited for all the life-giving secrets they held. Equally crucial to their success was the protection strong governments afforded them and the regularity of the seasonal cycles they could count on that made farming dependable and predictable. Above all, it was this regularity and predictability of all that man and nature could provide that was the secret of Egyptian civilization. It was such an important principle that Egyptians personified it as a goddess named **Maat.** (MAHT; See "Philosophy, Religion, and Eternal Life" below.)

As the centuries passed, daily life changed remarkably little in Egypt. Slavery was originally rare but increased during the Empire, when professional soldiers became necessary and prisoners of war became common. As in Mesopotamia, slavery was most often the result of owing debts to a landlord or committing a serious crime. A kind of serfdom—lifelong restrictions on one's physical and social mobility—also came into existence in later Egypt. Free tenant families were gradually turned into serfs, probably because of debt, and then had to work the land in a system of sharecropping that ensured that they remained in their village.

Besides farmers, many small merchants and craftspeople lived in the villages. But Egypt had no real cities as did Mesopotamia, places where neighborhoods were filled with specialized wholesale and retail markets, and where dozens of crafts were practiced in hundreds of workshops. Throughout most of its history, large-scale trade and commerce remained government monopolies. So, rather than being commercial centers, Egypt's capitals, Memphis, Tel el-Amarna, and Thebes, existed for purposes that were functionally more important to its civilization than craft production and trade. They contained the royal palaces and pleasure grounds for the wealthy, and from these capitals the kings and their officials exercised strong administrative control to assure the stability on which everything depended. Equally vital to this stability were the temples where the pharaohs and priests enacted the ritual prayers and sacrifices necessary to assure the favor of the gods who reigned over nature, the universe, and the afterlife.

THE PHARAOH: EGYPT'S GOD-KING

As is true of almost all early civilizations, the Egyptians' religious beliefs reflected their environment to a considerable degree, and the fully developed religion had an enormous impact on the nature of their government.

Much like Mesopotamia, Egypt was unified gradually. By 5000 BCE, the first hamlets and villages appeared along the Nile's banks, and initially the first settlers lived by a combination of gathering wild cereals and river fishing. Two thousand years later, near the end of the fourth millennium BCE, their descendants had cleared the Nile flood plain, and several late Neolithic states competed for control over a region that stretched from the delta in the north (called Lower Egypt) southwards to the first cataract (Upper Egypt). Around 3100 BCE, these tiny Nilotic states came under the control of one king, a **pharaoh** (FAYR-oh, meaning "from the great house"). Egyptian traditions claimed that this first pharaoh was named Narmer. Many scholars believe that he was merely a legend or that he represented, in oral tradition, a conflation of several kings of who came from Upper Egypt.

The period from 3100 to about 2500 BCE was Egypt's foundation period and the time of its greatest triumphs and cultural achievements. During these centuries, the land was ruled by an unbroken line of god-kings who apparently faced no serious threats either inside or outside their domain.

It is important to recognize that the pharaoh was not *like* a god. Instead, he *was* a god, a god who chose to live on Earth among his favored people for a time. From the moment that his days-long coronation ceremony was completed, he was no longer a mortal man. He had become immortal, a reincarnation of the god of order, **Horus.** His was not an easy life: he was surrounded by constant protocol and ceremony to protect him from profane eyes and spiritual pollution. The pharaoh's will was law, and his wisdom made him all knowing. What he desired was by definition correct and just. What he did was the will of the almighty gods, speaking through him as one of them. His regulations must be carried out without question. Otherwise, the gods might cease to smile on Egypt. His wife and family, especially his son who would succeed him, shared to some degree in this celestial glory, but only the reigning pharaoh was divine.

Government Under the Pharaoh

The pharaoh governed through a group of officials composed mainly of noble landowners and temple priests who were responsible to him, but who were granted great local powers. In his human and divine aspects, the pharaoh was *directly* responsible for the welfare of Egypt. This meant that, as king, he had to provide effective administration to protect his subjects, maintain order, and even direct their productive efforts—for example, by seeing to it that the irrigation system was built and maintained and by informing the farmers of impending seasonal changes. As a divinity, he was the mystical embodiment of the land and the people. His good relations with the gods assured prosperity and prevented natural catastrophes like droughts, insect infestations, and epidemics. When a weak pharaoh came to the throne, the prestige of the central authority could and occasionally did break down, and everyone suffered.

There were two short intervals in Egypt's long history when the pharaoh's powers were seriously diminished, in the so-called Intermediate Periods of 2200–2100 BCE and 1650–1570 BCE. The causes of the first breakdown remain unclear, but it was due partly to the pharaohs' loss of control over the governors of the southernmost provinces (called *nomes:* NOH-mays). The second of these periods is known to have been triggered by the invasion of the mysterious **Hyksos** (HICK-sohs) people, who crossed the Sinai peninsula and conquered the Nile delta. In both cases, a new, native Egyptian dynasty appeared within a century and reestablished effective central government. The monarchy's grip on the loyalties of the people was sufficient that it could reform the government in the same style, with the same values and officials as before.

What enabled the pharaoh to retain such near-magical power over his subjects for so long? For almost 2,000 years, the belief in the divinity of the king (or queen—there were at least three female pharaohs) persisted, as did the conviction that Egypt was specially favored and protected by the gods whose favor, Egyptians thought, was assured by the pharaoh and his priests. However, this was equally the result of the happy situation that Egypt enjoyed through climate and geography. Nature provided, as nowhere else, a perpetual agricultural abundance, making Egypt the only place in the known world at that time to be able to export grain surpluses. Furthermore, for 3,000 years of civilized life, until about 1000 BCE, Egypt was only rarely touched by war and foreign invasion. Until the Empire Period, no regular army—that great eater of taxes—was necessary.

The Old Kingdom, Middle Kingdom, and New Kingdom

It has long been customary to divide Egypt's ancient history into *dynasties* (periods of monarchic rule by one family). In all there were thirty-one dynasties, beginning with the legendary Narmer and ending with the dynasty that fell to the Persian invaders in 525 BCE. The greatest were those of the pyramid-building epoch and those of the Empire, about 1500–1300 BCE. The dynasties are traditionally grouped under three kingdoms: Old, Middle, and New.

Old Kingdom The **Old Kingdom** (3100–2200 BCE), which extended from Narmer to the *First Intermediate Period,* was ancient Egypt's most fertile and successful era. During these 900 years, both form and content were perfected in most of those achievements that made Egypt remarkable: art and architecture, divine monarchy, religion, social and economic stability, and prosperity. The pharaohs of this epoch governed from Memphis and seem to have been unchallenged leaders who enjoyed the willing loyalty and labor of their people. This was the period that saw the construction of Egypt's greatest monuments to the pharaohs, the pyramids of Giza. Later cultural and intellectual developments were almost always only a slight variation or a deterioration of the pattern established during the Old Kingdom.

Middle Kingdom The **Middle Kingdom** (2100–1650 BCE) followed the First Intermediate Period with 500 years of political stability and the continued refinement of the arts and crafts. The country under pharaoh's rule was extended further up the Nile to the south. Trade with neighbors, including Mesopotamia, Phoenicia (Lebanon), Crete, and Nubia (see Map 3.1) became more extensive. The condition of the laboring poor in the hundreds of Nile-side villages seems to have gradually worsened, however. Religion became more democratic in its view of who could enter the afterlife, and a small middle class of officials and merchants began to make itself apparent.

New Kingdom The **New Kingdom** (1550–700 BCE) is also called the *Empire,* although the name really belongs only to its first three centuries (1550–1250). The New Kingdom began after the defeat of the Hyksos invaders in the 1500s (the *Second Intermediate Period*). It lasted through the years of imperial wars against the Hittites and others for control of Mesopotamia, which ended with Egyptian withdrawal. Then came long centuries of sporadic weakness and resurgence that ended with Egypt's permanent conquest by foreigners.

The Empire was an ambitious experiment in which the Egyptians attempted to convert their eastern neighbors to their lifestyle and government theory. However, no one else was able to understand the Egyptian view of life or wanted it to be imposed on them. The Empire did not last because of both military reversals starting around the time of Pharaoh Akhnaton (1300s BCE) and internal discontent. By 1100, the pharaoh again ruled only the Nile valley.

During their last 300 years of independent existence, the Egyptians were frequently subjected to foreign invasion, both over the Sinai Desert and from the south by way of the great river. Before the Persians arrived in 525, others such as the Kushites (KUHSH-ites) and the Nubians had invaded repeatedly. But even after the Persian conquest, which marked the real end of ancient Egypt's existence as an independent state, the life of ordinary people in the fields and orchards saw no marked change. Only the person to whom taxes and rents were paid was different. The cultural forms and beliefs of the inhabitants were by now so deeply rooted that no foreign overlord could alter them.

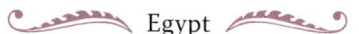
EVIDENCE OF THE PAST

The Egyptian Priesthood

With their belief in cyclic time, one of the most important duties of priests in ancient civilizations was devising and maintaining a calendar. Ancient peoples needed it to know when to anticipate crucial events like seasonal changes; the yearly rains or floods; dry seasons; changes in wildlife behavior; and, of course, the unfolding of the annual "liturgical" year when they had to honor certain gods associated with seasonal cycles. They based their calendars on astronomical phenomena and associated specific deities with heavenly events. They combined both astronomy with astrology, and believed that the constellations not only foretold earthly changes, but *caused* them.

A PRIEST PRAYING TO AN EGYPTIAN GOD. New Kingdom period.

©Erich Lessing/Art Resource, NY

EGYPTIAN CONSTELLATION FIGURES. These figures were painted on the ceiling in the sarcophagus chamber of the powerful New Kingdom pharaoh, Seti I. They show the stars and constellations of the northern sky.

©Werner Forman/Art Resource, NY

▶ *Analyze and Interpret*

What would have made the priests who mummified and interred Seti I in his tomb paint images of constellations of the Northern Sky? Could the painting have represented a map of some kind for Seti's soul? The four cardinal directions frequently had symbolic meaning in many ancient cultures. What particular significance could the north have had for a soul?

CULTURAL ACHIEVEMENTS

The wealth of the pharaoh and the willingness and skill of his people allowed the erection of the most stupendous monuments put up by any people or government anywhere: the pyramids and temples of the Old Kingdom. Visitors have marveled at these stone wonders ever since. The Great Pyramid of Khufu (KOO-foo), located a few

©Giza (El Gizeh), Cairo, Egypt/Bildarchiv Steffens/The Bridgeman Art Library

THE GREAT PYRAMIDS. These three massive stone monuments lie just outside the modern city limits of Cairo. The center one is the pyramid of Khufu, or Cheops, the largest masonry construct of all time. Aside from serving as the pharaohs' tombs, the pyramids apparently held great religious significance for the Egyptians, who believed it to be an honor to contribute their labor and skill to their construction. The pyramids were replaced by underground tombs beginning in the Middle Kingdom, probably because of both the expense and the difficulty of keeping them safe from tomb robbers, who were little deterred by religious principles.

miles outside present-day Cairo, is easily the largest and grandest commemorative edifice ever built. The pyramids (built between 2600 and 2100 BCE) were designed as tombs for the living pharaoh and were built while he was still alive. Much is still unknown about the pyramids' true purposes, but the perfection of their construction and the art of the burial chambers show Egyptian civilization at its most impressive.

The pyramids were not the only stone monuments erected along the Nile. In the period around 1300, several warrior-pharaohs celebrated the fame of their empire by erecting enormous statues of themselves and their favored gods, and even larger temples in which to put them. At the Nile sites of *Karnak* and *Tel el Amarna,* some of these still stand. Most losses of artistic and architectural wonders in Egypt have been caused not by time or erosion but by vandalism and organized tomb and treasure robbers over many centuries. All of the pharaohs' tombs discovered to date, except one, have long since been robbed of the burial treasure interred with the mummy of the dead god-king. The exception is that of the famous King Tutankhamen—King Tut—whose underground burial chamber was discovered in the early 1920s. **Tutankhamen** (Too-TAHNK-ah-men; ruled 1347–1339 BCE) died at the age of eighteen without having done anything of consequence during his short reign. The world probably would never have noted him had not the British archaeologist Howard Carter stumbled on his grave 3,000 years later. (See Evidence of the Past.)

Egyptian monarchic statuary is distinguished by the peculiar combination of graceful and natural lines in association with great dignity and awesomeness. This awe is reinforced by the art and architecture that surround the great statues, which are designed to impress all onlookers with the permanence and power of the Egyptian monarchy. The Egyptians' mastery of stone is rivaled in Western civilization only by the artistry of the classical Greeks and Romans. And artists and architects who did not know the principle of the wheel and had only primitive tools and what we would consider very clumsy math and physics apparently created most of this art!

Egyptian writing developed differently from that of Mesopotamia. **Hieroglyphics** (high-roh-GLIH-fiks; literally,

British Museum, London, UK/Bridgeman Art Library

EGYPTIAN HIEROGLYPHICS. The Rosetta Stone was discovered by French scientists accompanying Napoleon's army during its occupation of Egypt in the 1790s. It contains three versions of the same priestly decree for the second century BCE: hieroglyphic Egyptian, demotic (cursive) Egyptian, and Greek. By comparing the three, the brilliant linguist Jean François Champollion was able in 1822 to finally break the code of hieroglyphic symbols and commence the modern study of the Egyptian language.

"sacred carvings") were pictographs that could convey either an idea, such as "man," or a phonetic sound, by picturing an object that begins with a strong consonant sound. The word for *owl*, for example, began with the consonant "m" sound in spoken Egyptian, so a picture of an owl could be used to indicate that sound. This beginning of an alphabet was not fully developed, however. The use of hieroglyphics, which began as far back as 3000 BCE, was confined to a small group of educated people and gradually faded out after Egypt lost its independence in the sixth century BCE. The complete repertory of 604 hieroglyphic symbols is now deciphered, enabling the reading of many thousands of ancient inscriptions.

Philosophy, Religion, and Eternal Life

Egypt's religion was almost infinitely polytheistic. At least 3,000 separate names of gods have been identified in Egyptian writings, many of them the same deities but with different names over the centuries. Chief among them were the gods of the sun, *Amun* (Ah-mun) and *Ra* (Rah), who were originally separate but later combined into one being, **Amun-Ra**, and came to represent the embodiment of all the gods. Other important deities included *Anuket*, goddess of the Nile and of fertility; *Osiris* (Oh-sigh-ris), ruler of the afterlife; and *Anubis*, his consort, goddess of the underworld who weighed the souls (*ka*) of the dead; their son, *Horus*, made visible as the ruling pharaoh; and **Ptah**, who came from the primordial mound under the earth from which all living things emerged. As time passed, Ptah came to represent the rebirth and renewal of all life.

The Egyptians believed firmly in the afterlife. Originally, it seems to have been viewed as a possibility only for the upper class, but gradually the afterlife was democratized. By about 1000 BCE, most Egyptians apparently believed in a scheme of eternal reward or punishment for their *ka*, which had to submit to the moral Last Judgment by Osiris.

Ka (kah) referred to the life-essence that could return to life, given the correct preparation, even after the death of the original physical body.

Once again, it was nature that weighed most heavily not only on how ancient peoples understood earthly phenomena but also on what they imagined the structure of the cosmos to be and the kind of gods that governed it. For this reason, the gods of the Mesopotamians were capricious and angry (Chapter 2). But in the land that was "the Gift of the Nile," where the *Ra*, the Sun God, shined year in and out and where *Satis*, the goddess of the flood, was represented by the *ankh*, the symbol of fertility and life, Egyptians believed order and stability to be a fundamental, governing attribute of the cosmos. They incarnated this feature in the goddess, *Maat*. The impact of natural, time, with its circularity, implied that no event, no life was unique and all were consigned to endless repetition in a cosmic order that had no beginning or end. While Egyptians did not believe in reincarnation, as Hindus did (Chapter 5), they did believe in an afterlife where mortals went to dwell forever after leaving their earthly existence. There, judgment was passed on each soul when it was weighed against the feather of Maat. This was not a judgment that included any notion of morality as modern people would understand it (particularly by those who believe in a monotheistic God), but rather how it weighed against universal order and "rightness."

Mostly, it seems, Egyptians expected reward. They thought of eternity as a sort of endless procession by the deceased's *ka* through the heavens and the gods' abodes there. In the company of friends and family, watched over by the protective and benevolent gods, the individual would proceed in a stately circle around the sun forever. There was no need to work and no suffering. Such was heaven.

EVIDENCE OF THE PAST

"Wonderful Things!"

After several years of searching the Valley of the Kings, Howard Carter had found the buried tomb of the pharaoh Tutankhamen. He describes the experience in his own words:

The following day, November 26, was the day of days, the most wonderful I have ever lived through and certainly one whose like I can never hope to see again. . . . Slowly, desperately slowly, it seemed to us, the remains of the passage debris was removed, until at last we had the whole door before us. The decisive moment had arrived. With trembling hands I made a tiny breach in the upper left-hand corner. . . . Candle tests were applied as a precaution against foul gases and then, widening the hole a little, I inserted the candle and peered in. At first I could see nothing, the hot air escaping from the chamber causing the candle flame to flicker but presently, as my eyes grew accustomed to the light details of the room within emerged slowly from the mist; strange animals, statues and gold—everywhere the glint of gold. For the moment I was struck dumb with amazement, and when Lord Carnarvon [Carter's sponsor] unable to stand the suspense any longer, inquired anxiously, "Can you see anything?" it was all I could do to get out the words, "Yes, wonderful things!"

▶ Analyze and Interpret

Where are the various treasures Carter found in Tutankhamen's tomb displayed now? Who owns them? Why do you think the Egyptians made these burial objects out of gold? From where did it come? Why was it important to the pharaohs? How do contemporary archaeological digs in Egypt differ from those of eighty years ago in terms of leadership and ownership of what might be found?

Source: Christine Hobson, *The World of the Pharaohs* (New York: Thames & Hudson, 1987), p. 110.

©Egyptian National Museum, Cairo, Egypt/Giraudon/Bridgeman Art Library

THE GOLDEN DEATH MASK OF KING TUT. The burial site of young King Tutankhamen became one of the most spectacular archaeological finds of the twentieth century. For eight years, British archaeologist Howard Carter salvaged its magnificent treasure, after his discovery of it in 1922, classifying and restoring more than 5,000 objects, including a beautiful golden death mask, a gilded throne, statues, vases, and hundreds of artifacts made of wood covered in gold leaf and decorated with gems. A magnificent stone sarcophagus held the luxurious coffin, richly wrought in pure gold. The treasure offered scholars and the public a glimpse of the wealth of the ancient Egyptians and their Nile kingdom.

The notion of hell as a place where the evil paid for their sins came along in Egypt only during the New Kingdom, when things had begun to go sour.

The priests played an important role in Egyptian culture, although they were not as prominent as in several other civilizations. At times, they seem to have been the power behind the throne, especially when the king had made himself unpopular or was unusually weak in character.

In the reign of the young and inexperienced **Akhnaton** (Akh-NAH-tun; 1367–1350 BCE), the priests vehemently opposed a unique experiment: the pharaoh's attempt to change the basic polytheistic nature of Egyptian religion. Why the young Akhnaton (aided by his beautiful wife Nefertiti) chose to attempt to introduce a monotheistic ("one-god") cult of the sun god, newly renamed Aton, we can only guess. This attempt at **monotheism** was a great

©Réunion des Musées Nationaux/Art Resource, NY

THE FEATHER OF MAAT. Maat was the embodiment of many things: among them was truth and justice. A feather represented her, and when artists painted her she always had a feather in her hair. Egyptians believed that, when a person died, her soul passed into the underworld, where Anubis weighed it against truth, *maat*, to determine its fate. In this painting, the *ka*, shown as a heart, is being weighed in the scales against the feather of *maat*.

novelty in ancient civilization, and it was not to be heard of again until the emergence of Judaism five or six centuries later. The pharaoh announced that Aton was his heavenly father and that Aton alone was to be worshiped as the single and universal god of all creation. The priests naturally opposed this revolutionary change, and as soon as Akhnaton was dead (possibly by poison), they denounced his ideas and went back to the old ways under the boy-pharaoh Tutankhamen.

Egypt and Mesopotamia: Contrasts

The two outstanding early centers of Near Eastern civilized life—Egypt and Mesopotamia—were situated fairly close to each other and experienced considerable cross-cultural stimuli at times. But their differences were notable and permanent. Egypt enjoyed enormous stability, punctuated by occasional, decades-long interludes of low floods. Life was highly predictable: tomorrow was today and yesterday, under unchanged or only slightly changed circumstances. Mesopotamia, on the contrary, was frequently subject to violent change. Not only were invasions or war commonplace, but nature itself was as much a source of instability as of stability. Besides the unpredictability of the rivers, silting raised water levels, forcing farmers and townspeople to build earthen platforms on which to build their homes and elaborate irrigation systems to channel the river waters. Rising floods also brought salination to the soils and eventually made farming impossible. Little wonder their gods were so baleful!

Egypt was protected from outsiders for a very long time by natural barriers and could pick and choose among the cultural influences it wanted to adopt. Mesopotamia was a crossroads between the settled, farm-based civilizations of the rivers valleys and the migratory pastoralists who brought both war and opportunities for trade. Invasion, trade, and simple curiosity introduced new ideas, new techniques, new beliefs, and wider contacts throughout the region.

Great wealth and other blessings their gods brought Egypt bred complacency, so Egyptians viewed the world as consisting of the Egyptian people and the rest, whom they regarded as inferiors who had little to teach Egypt. Mesopotamia, on the other hand, was a melting pot. Repeatedly, large groups of outsiders would arrive with sufficient military or economic power to establish their ideas and beliefs among the conquered people, at least for as long as they needed to strike roots and change some elements of the previous civilization. Stagnation behind a wall of security could not occur—challenge was on the daily menu. In Egypt, the sense of superiority seems to have eventually become a sort of "defense mechanism" that prevented the rulers from seeing the truth and choked off badly needed reform. They viewed change as subversive and successfully resisted it for a long time—so long as to make successful adjustment almost impossible.

Of these two early civilizations, however, Mesopotamia proved to be a major cradle of later Western traditions and beliefs. Egypt remained something of an island in space and time, with the route of its cultural influences directed southwards into Nubia and beyond. In the next chapter, we will look at some of those neighbors in the Near East, including two peoples who eventually conquered Egypt—the Assyrians and the Persians.

Trade and Egypt's Influence

As a wealthy land, Egypt needed few imports. But there were some items Egyptians did need to import, and trade provided rare items whose monopoly was an important pillar of the monarchy. Wood was hard to find in a land where every acre of arable land was needed for agriculture, so large-scale projects like palaces, pyramids, and temples required the importation of timber. As early as the Old Kingdom, the pharaohs spent a great deal of time building trade, especially with timber-rich Byblos in Phoenicia, which provided valuable cedar. To the south, successive pharaohs sent expeditions into Nubia to obtain ivory and gold. Known to the Egyptians as the "Land of the Bowmen," Nubia also provided slaves whom Egypt's generals employed in special auxiliary units of archers in the pharaohs' powerful armies.

The pharaohs of the Middle and New Kingdoms embarked on ever-more ambitious campaigns to expand

Egypt's trade throughout southwestern Asia and south of the first cataract deep into the chiefdoms of Nubia. When bronze technology caught on, pharaohs of the Middle Kingdom extended conquests into the Sinai Peninsula where copper and gold were mined, and when the eastern Mediterranean emerged as an important commercial region (see Chapter 7), Egypt competed fiercely with other kingdoms of southwest Asia to maintain control of its lucrative trade routes. Yet, it was trade to the south of Egypt that remained the most valuable to Egypt. The pharaohs organized naval expeditions to the Land of **Punt,** where there was trade in luxuries like spices, frankincense, myrrh, and gold from India, southern Arabia, and eastern Africa. The New Kingdom pharaohs pushed their conquests down to the third cataract of the Nile, into the Nubian land of Kush. At Thebes a high court official, the "King's Son of Kush," administered it as an Egyptian province until 1070 BCE, when it achieved independence. With the might of Egypt weighing on it for so many centuries, it was in Nubia where Egypt's cultural influence was the most substantial. The population gradually became Egyptianized; its kings ruled in a style redolent of Egypt's pharaohs; its religion incorporated Egyptian gods; and its royalty were even interred in small pyramids (see Chapter 12).

SUMMARY

THE NILE VALLEY produced a civilized society as early as any in the world, thanks to an unusual combination of favorable climate and geography. Even before the emergence of central government under a god-king called pharaoh, the farmers along the river had devised an intricate system of irrigated fields that gave Egypt an enviable surplus of food. The unification of the villages was accomplished about 3100 BCE, giving rise to the highly centralized civilization of the Old Kingdom and its awesome monuments celebrating the linkage of Egypt and the protective gods. Aside from the abnormal collapse of central government in the brief Intermediate Periods,

the rulers of Egypt were uniquely successful, maintaining two thousand years of prosperity and isolation from contacts with others, except on their own terms. This success allowed the reigning group to assume a superiority that, although originally justified, gradually became a clinging to tradition for its own sake. When the misguided attempt at empire failed, Egypt faced the challenge of repeated foreign invasions after about 1000 BCE. The divine kings lost their stature, and the static civilization of the Nile fell under the sway of once disdained aliens from the east and south. The Persian conquest in 525 BCE completed the decline of the pharaohs' state into dependency.

▶ Identification Terms

Test your knowledge of this chapter's key concepts by defining the following terms. If you can't recall the meaning of certain terms, refresh your memory by looking up the boldfaced term in the chapter, turning to the Glossary at the end of the book, or working with the flashcards that are available on the *World Civilizations* Companion Website: **academic.cengage.com/adler**

Akhnaton	Hyksos	monotheism	Ptah
Amun-Ra	*ka*	New Kingdom	Punt
hieroglyphics	Maat	Old Kingdom	Tutankhamen
Horus	Middle Kingdom	pharaoh	

▶ Test Your Knowledge

Test your knowledge of this chapter by answering the following questions. Complete answers appear at the end of the book. You may find even more quiz questions in CengageNOW and on the *World Civilizations* Companion Website: **academic.cengage.com/adler**

1. Which of these adjectives would you *not* associate with ancient Egypt?
   a. Stable
   b. Predictable
   c. Poor
   d. Isolated
   e. Unique

2. The geographic status of Egypt destined the country to be
    a. vulnerable to repeated invasions.
    b. a crossroads of travelers through the ages.
    c. almost self-contained.
    d. divided into many different natural regions.
    e. left out of maritime expeditions.

3. The key element of Egypt's government was
    a. the pharaoh's efficient police.
    b. the code of royal law.
    c. popular respect for the god-king.
    d. a powerful military establishment.
    e. a nobility that was completely self-regulatory.

4. The Middle Kingdom was ended in Egypt by
    a. the coming of the Hyksos invaders.
    b. revolt against the pharaoh Akhnaton.
    c. invasion by the Nubians.
    d. the Persian conquest.
    e. a thirty-year drought.

5. Which of the following was *true* of Egypt's cultural achievements?
    a. The use of hieroglyphics eventually gave the Egyptians a complete alphabet.
    b. Most of early Egypt's architectural wonders have been destroyed by erosion.
    c. The use of the wheel aided the Egyptians' use of stone as art.
    d. The pyramids were constructed during the Middle Kingdom.
    e. Egypt's great statues were designed to illustrate the power and endurance of the pharaohs.

6. The key to understanding ancient Egyptian hieroglyphics was the
    a. conquest of Egypt by the Persians and their translations.
    b. discovery of the similarities between them and ancient Sumerian writing.
    c. translation of the Rosetta Stone.
    d. ability of modern linguists using computers to compare them with other languages.
    e. discovery and translation of a wall of writings in the tomb of King Tutankhamen.

7. Slavery in Egypt
    a. became rarer as the New Kingdom expanded Egypt's borders.
    b. was the result mainly of debt and crime.
    c. was quite different from that of Mesopotamia in nature and causes.
    d. was almost unknown.
    e. was most prevalent during the First Intermediate Period.

8. The pharaoh Akhnaton fostered a
    a. belief in a single god.
    b. return to traditional religious belief.
    c. major reform in landholding and agriculture.
    d. major change in government's nature.
    e. reverence for Egyptian ancestors.

9. Which of the following was least likely to have occurred in Egypt from 3000 to about 1000 BCE?
    a. Social rebellion against the government
    b. Drastic change in the prestige of various Egyptian deities
    c. Invasion from outside Egypt
    d. Attempt to extend rule over non-Egyptians
    e. Extensive trade with outside peoples

10. A chief difference between Egypt and Mesopotamia lay in
    a. their relative dependence on irrigation farming.
    b. Egypt's more democratic government.
    c. Mesopotamia's superior artistic creativity.
    d. Egypt's acceptance of monotheism.
    e. the relative importance of city life and commerce.

Enter *CengageNOW* using the access card that is available with this text. *CengageNOW* will assist you in understanding the content in this chapter with lesson plans generated for your needs and provide you with a connection to the *Wadsworth World History Resource Center* (see description at right for details).

 ▶ **World History Resource Center**

Enter the Resource Center using either your *CengageNOW* access card or your standalone access card for the *Wadsworth World History Resource Center*. Organized by topic, this website includes quizzes; images; over 350 primary source documents; interactive simulations, maps, and timelines; movie explorations; and a wealth of other resources. You can read the following documents, and many more, at the *Wadsworth World History Resource Center*:

Herodotus, *The Histories*

> *The Lord our God made a covenant, not only with our fathers, but with all of us living today. . . . The Lord said, "I am the Lord your God . . . Worship no God but me."*
>
> —The Bible

4 WARRIORS AND DEITIES IN THE NEAR EAST

1900s BCE	Hebrews leave Mesopotamia
c. 1250 BCE	Hebrew Exodus from Egypt
c. 1000 BCE	Hebrew Kingdom established; Phoenicians develop early alphabet
c. 800 BCE	Assyrian Empire expands; Carthage founded by Phoenicians
722 BCE	Assyrians conquer Samaria
612 BCE	Fall of Nineveh/end of Assyrian Empire
500s BCE	Establishment and expansion of Persian Empire
586–539 BCE	Babylonian Captivity of Jews

THE NEAR EAST, that area between the Nile valley and the western borders of Iran, was from earliest times a region of cultural overlap and interchange. First one people and then another would take command of a portion of the region for a century or more, only to fall under the sway of the next onslaught of newcomers. Petty states and kingdoms arose whose very names are sometimes forgotten but whose contributions to the ascent of civilization in this region were collectively impressive. In this chapter, we look at three of the most important of these—briefly at the transitory glory of Assyria and Phoenicia, and in more detail at the much larger and longer-lived monarchy of Persia. Then we review the history of the Hebrews, a people whose historic achievement lay in their gradual working out of a unique vision of the nature of the Divinity and the relation of God and humans, a vision that passed on into the very heart of Western civilization.

THE ASSYRIAN EMPIRE

The Assyrians were a Semitic tribal group who emerged from nomadism in what is now northern Iraq in the twelfth century BCE, following the decline of the Hittite monarchy based in Turkey. They entered history about 900 BCE as challengers to other Semites in the Tigris valley. Their chief town, **Nineveh** (NIH-neh-vay), lay in the upper valley of the Tigris, and their chief god was the fierce **Assur** (AH-sher), from whom the people derived their name. By 800 BCE, through their own ferocity and cunning in war, the Assyrian kings had conquered much of the Tigris-Euphrates region and were fighting the

Babylonians for the southern portion (see Map 4.1). The Assyrians displayed great talent in military affairs. Their army was large and seemingly invincible, using new tactics to negate the traditional advantage of charioteers over foot soldiers.

By this epoch, the horse and the chariot were the chief force in warfare. (It is believed that the chariot was introduced to Near Eastern warfare by the Hyksos invaders of Egypt in the 1500s BCE.) For centuries, leather-clad warriors armed with short swords had fought from chariots drawn by two or three horses. The chariots would split the loose ranks of the enemy foot soldiers, and the momentum of the horses combined with the raised platform gave the swordsmen an almost irresistible advantage over opposing infantry. The early Assyrian kings took away this advantage, however, by fielding tight-knit infantry formations with long spears and swords, protected on the flanks by bands of horsemen who engaged the enemy charioteers while they were still far off. The infantry were heavily armored and so disciplined that they would stand up to a chariot charge without breaking. The Assyrians were also

experts in siege warfare, and no enemy walled town or fort could hold for long against their artillery of stone-throwing catapults and rams.

Anyone who resisted the Assyrians and lost suffered a terrible fate: wholesale slavery, execution, pillage, and rape. Once conquered, the enemy was closely supervised, and any effort to spring free was immediately suppressed. The chronicles left by the Assyrians delight in telling of the huge piles of dead left by the triumphant armies of such kings as Tiglath-Pileser (TIHG-lath Pih-LEH-ser), who reigned in the seventh century BCE:

> Like the Thunder, I crushed corpses of their warriors in the battle. I made their blood flow over into all the ravines and over the high places. I cut off their heads and piled them at the walls of their cities like heaps of grain. I carried off their booty, their goods, and their property beyond all reckoning. Six thousand, the remainder of their troops who had fled before my weapons and thrown themselves at my feet, I took away as prisoners and added to the peoples of my

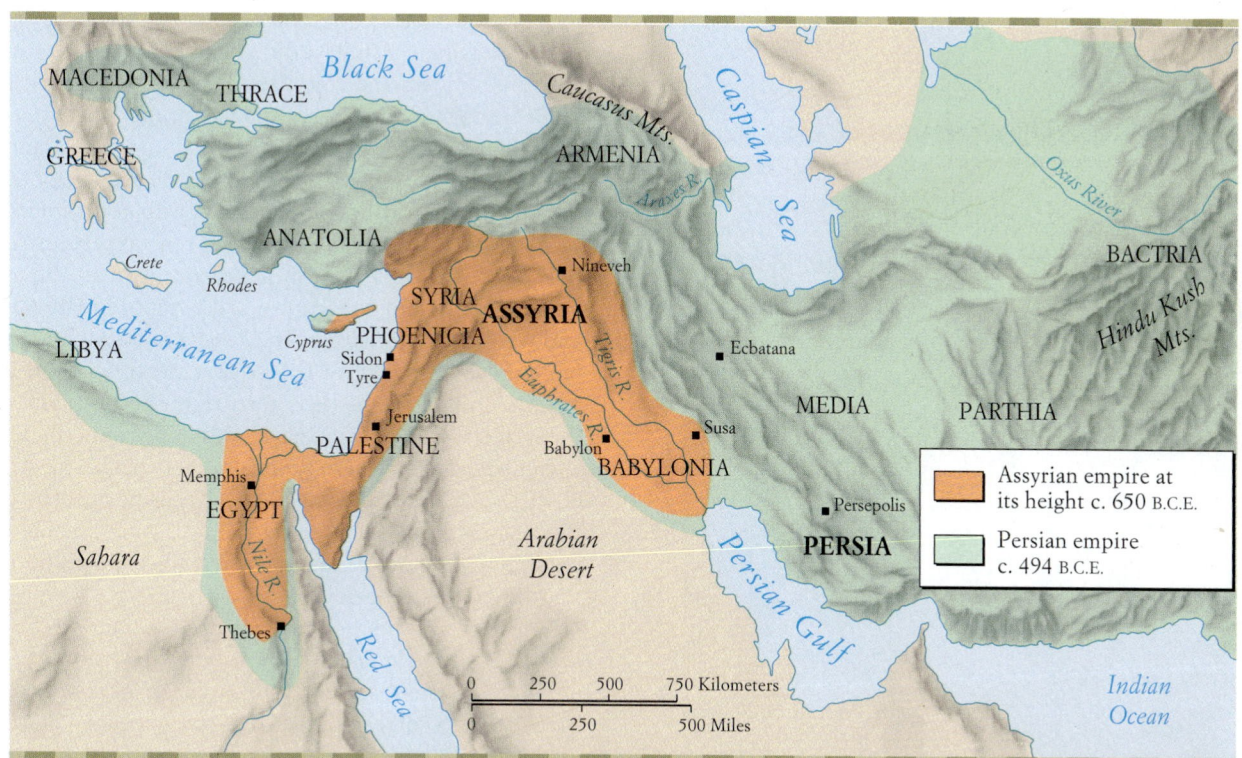

MAP 4.1 The Assyrian (*c.* 650 BCE) and Persian (*c.* 494 BCE) Empires

Although the Assyrians subdued most of the Near East and Egypt for a brief time, the later Persian Empire was much more extensive, reaching from Egypt to the borders of the Indus valley. The "King of Kings" held most of this huge area through a network of Persian-ruled satrapies, or tributary kingdoms whose rulers regularly acknowledged overlordship.

MAP QUESTIONS

Were the principal Assyrian cities in Mesopotamia or Iran?

 View an interactive version of this or a related map at http://worldrc.wadsworth.com/

country [that is, slaves]. (From J. B. Pritchard, ed., *Ancient Near Eastern Texts,* 3d ed. Princeton, NJ: Princeton University Press, 1969.)

The Assyrians were perhaps the most hated conquerors in ancient history. Only their expertly calculated plans to "divide and conquer" and their mass deportations of subject peoples enabled them to remain in power as long as they did. At one point their empire reached from the upper Tigris to central Egypt. It was governed from Nineveh by a network of military commanders who had no mercy for rebels and held large numbers of hostages for the good behavior of the rest of their people.

But less than a century after its high point of power, Nineveh was in total ruins ("not a stone upon a stone," asserts the Old Testament), and the Assyrians were swept from the pages of history as though they had never existed. Their many enemies and rebellious subjects, led by the Chaldees of New Babylon, finally united against their oppressor and took full revenge for Assyrian atrocities. When they captured Nineveh in 612 BCE, the victors even salted the fertile irrigated lands that ringed the city, to prevent the site from ever being inhabited again. It was indeed

forgotten until the middle of the nineteenth century, when Nineveh's ruins were unearthed by some of the earliest archaeological expeditions to the East.

With such determined erasure of their history, how can we know anything about the Assyrians' past? Remarkably, they combined their delight in slaughter with a sophisticated appreciation for all forms of pictorial and architectural art. Much of our knowledge about the Assyrians comes from their extensive portrayals of court life in bas-relief sculpture, as well as from archaeological discoveries from their ruined cities. One of the last kings of the Assyrians, Assurbanipal (ah-sher-BAH-nih-pahl), established the largest library known to the Near East in ancient times. More than 20,000 "books" of clay tablets have been recovered from the site in Nineveh since the nineteenth century.

THE PHOENICIANS

Another small but significant Semitic people were the unwarlike Phoenicians, who originally inhabited a strip along the coast of what is now Lebanon. From their ports of Tyre (tire) and Sidon (SIGH-don), they became the greatest maritime traders and colonizers of the ancient Near East. Their trade in luxury wares such as copper and dyes took them through the Mediterranean and into the Atlantic as far as the coast of Britain (Cornwall). Here they obtained the precious tin that could be mixed with copper and lead to form bronze, the main metallic resource before 1000 BCE. The Phoenicians also apparently spread the art of iron making from the Hittite settlements to the Greeks and westward into Africa. They established a whole series of colonies in the western Mediterranean. Some of these became important in their own right, and one of them, the rich city-state of Carthage, founded around 800 BCE, became the great rival to Rome until its final defeat around 200 BCE. The Phoenicians themselves were absorbed into the Assyrian and succeeding empires but remained the paramount Mediterranean traders and seafarers until the rise of Greece in the 600s BCE.

The Phoenicians' most notable contribution came in the linguistic field. They were the first to use a *phonetic alphabet,* a system of twenty-two written marks ("letters"), each of which corresponded to a specific consonant sound of the oral language. The Phoenicians' alphabet, which emerged about 1000 BCE, was a definite advance in simplicity and accessibility of written communication over both the cuneiforms of the Sumerians and the hieroglyphs of the Egyptians. The Greeks later improved the Phoenician alphabet; added signs for the vowels, which the Phoenicians did not employ; and thereby created essentially the same alphabet (although in a different letter form) that we use in Western scripts today.

©British Museum, London, UK/Photo ©Boltin Picture Library/ The Bridgeman Art Library

ASSURBANIPAL AT A LION HUNT. This Assyrian bas relief shows King Assurbanipal charging the lion in his war chariot, accompanied by picked spearmen who thrust away the fierce prey as the monarch loads his bow. The Assyrian genius for portrayal of violent motion comes through strongly in these reliefs, which date from the 600s BCE.

THE PERSIANS

Until the twentieth century, present-day Iran was called *Persia.* Its ruling group was for a millennium, 500 BCE to 500 CE, the most powerful of the many peoples in western Asia. Iran is mostly a high, arid plateau, surrounded on the north, west, and east by high mountains and on the south by the Indian Ocean (see Map 4.1). For a long time, the country has been a natural divide-point for travel from the eastern Mediterranean to China and India, and vice versa. Later, it became the great exchange point between the Arabic-Muslim and the Indic-Hindu worlds. Thanks to this strategic position, Iran and the Iranians have long been able to play a considerable role in world affairs.

The case of the Persians, and their cousins the *Aryans* who settled in India (Chap. 5), provides one of the earliest examples of wandering, pastoralists who conquered, then eventually settled regions that supported agriculture. They were an Indo-European speaking people who had migrated slowly south from the central Asian steppes into Iran. Actually, several related groups, collectively termed *Iranians,* moved south starting between 1500 and 1000 BCE. At this epoch they were still nomadic and knew nothing of agriculture or other civilized crafts and techniques. They

LION KILLING A BULL. This vivid depiction of a lion bringing down a wild onager is taken from the palace ruins at Persepolis. This complex was started in the sixth century and was added to by various Iranian rulers until its destruction by the triumphant Alexander the Great in 330. The Persian court shared the Assyrian pleasure in hunting scenes.

©Persepolis, Iran/Bridgeman Art Library

did, however, possess large numbers of horses, and their skill at cavalry tactics enabled them to gradually overcome their rivals for territorial mastery. Eventually, through both war and trading contacts with their Mesopotamian neighbors to the west, they learned the basics of agriculture and a sedentary, civilized life.

HALL OF A HUNDRED COLUMNS. This is the great assembly and banquet hall erected by Darius I in Persepolis and burned to the ground by the triumphant conqueror Alexander. Its vast size was symbolic of the great powers exercised by the Persian emperor.

©Persepolis, Iran/Bridgeman Art Library

PATTERNS OF BELIEF

Zarathustra's Vision

We usually think of the connection between religious belief and morality as intrinsic and logical: moral actions are the concrete manifestations of a belief in good and evil, ultimately determined by a supernatural code or by conscience. Yet in ancient times, people did not usually regard the supernatural gods as arbiters of human moral conduct. Rather, gods were seen as personifications of natural forces that made men their helpless playthings unless appeased by worship and sacrifice. This attitude was as prevalent among Iranians in the sixth century BCE as any other people, but it would change radically when a prophet arose among them called Zarathustra, or Zoroaster.

About Zarathustra's life we know nothing except that he was a Persian and lived probably in the 500s BCE. His teaching, however, was written down long after his death, possibly as late as the third century CE. This Zoroastrian scripture, known as the *Avesta* (Ah-ves-tah), tells in fragmentary fashion the beliefs of a man who founded a new type of religion, a faith that linked the gods and humans in a new fashion.

Zarathustra preached that two principles are in eternal conflict: good and evil, truth and lies. Good is incarnated in the impersonal deity Ahuramazda (ah-hoo-rah-MAHZ-dah) and evil by its twin Ahriman (AH-rih-mahn), a close approximation of the Christian Lucifer. The two would struggle for the souls of men, and eventually Ahuramazda would triumph. Humans, as the possessors of free will, could and must choose between the two gods, serving one and defying the other. In an afterlife, individuals would be made responsible for their choice. They would stand before a divine tribunal and have to answer for their lives on Earth. If the balance was found positive, they would enjoy heaven in eternity; if negative, hell awaited them.

The role of priests was very important, for they interpreted what was right and wrong conduct. The fire worship that had prevailed among Iranians before Zarathustra continued to play a significant role, and a sacred fire was at the heart of the worship of Ahuramazda. For a time, the teachings of the Zoroastrians became the state cult of imperial Persia, and both Darius I and his son Xerxes (ZERK-sees) were known to be sympathizers.

The similarities between Zarathustra's doctrines and Judaism and Christianity are not coincidental. The Last Judgment that all souls must undergo, the responsibility of the exercise of free will, the eternal bliss of heaven, and the torments of hell entered first Jewish and then Christian belief. Through Zoroastrian preaching and converts in the eastern Mediterranean, the image of an all-powerful God who allowed humans the supreme freedom of the choice between good and evil entered the mainsprings of Western religious culture. Zarathustra's teaching that Ahriman was closely bound up with the flesh, while Ahuramazda was a non-corporeal entity, a spirit, would come to haunt Christianity for ages, and it appeared again and again in various sects. The most famous of these was medieval Manicheism, which derived its beliefs from the Middle East and spread throughout Mediterranean Europe. It taught that the flesh is essentially evil, the province of the devil. Many people think that the puritanical element in Christianity is largely the product of this belated offshoot of the Zoroastrian creed.

What has become of the religion of Zarathustra? In Persia, it gradually declined into superstition and was almost extinguished in the wake of the Muslim conquest of Persia in the 600s CE. The Parsees of the region around Bombay, India, are the center of the cult in modern times. Their scripture, the *Avesta*, remains one of the first attempts to unite *religion*, worship of the immortal gods, with *ethics*, a code of proper conduct for mortal men.

▶ *Analyze and Interpret*
How do Christianity and Zoroastrian beliefs converge, and how do they contrast in their treatment of the nature of sin? Why is the concept of free will a necessary precondition for a code of ethics and an ethical religion?

The Persian Empire

In the mid–sixth century BCE, the Persians united under a brilliant warrior king, Cyrus the Great, and quickly overcame their Iranian cousins and neighbors, the Medes. In a remarkable series of campaigns between 559 and 530 BCE, Cyrus then extended his domains from the borders of India to the Mediterranean coast. By 525, his son and immediate successor, Cambyses, had broadened the empire to include part of Arabia and the lower Nile valley. The main Persian cities were at Susa (SOO-zah), Persepolis (per-SEH-poh-lihs), and Ecbatana (Ek-bah-TAH-nah) in Iran, not in Mesopotamia. The gradual decline of Mesopotamia's importance can be dated to this time.

Cyrus had a concept of imperial rule that was quite different from that of the Assyrians. He realized that many of his new subjects—peoples as radically different as the Hebrews from the Egyptians—were more advanced in many ways than his own Persians and that he could learn from them. Accordingly, his government was a sort of umbrella, sheltering many different peoples and beliefs under the supervision of the "King of Kings" at Persepolis.

The Persian subjects were generally allowed to retain their own customs and laws. Their appointed Persian supervisors (*satraps*; SA-traps) only interfered when the central government's policies were threatened or disobeyed. In the provinces **(satrapies),** the local authorities were kept in power after conquest by Persia, so long as they swore obedience to the monarch, paid their (relatively light) taxes, provided soldiers, and gave aid and comfort to the Persians when called upon to do so. Religion was totally free, and all sorts of beliefs flourished under Persian rule, from the freed-from-Babylon Hebrews to the fire worshipers of the Indian borderlands. Most remarkably, the initial move toward an ethical religion seems to have come with the teaching of **Zarathustra** (zah-rah-THOO-strah), as outlined in the Patterns of Belief box, "Zarathustra's Vision."

Darius I (522–486) was the third great Persian ruler, following Cyrus and Cambyses. During his reign, the empire reached its maximal extent (see Map 4.1). A stable coinage in gold and silver and a calendar that was commonly used throughout the Near East were introduced.

Darius's law code was also an advanced and refined distillation of earlier codes from Mesopotamia and Egypt. For the next century, the peoples of the empire flourished under enlightened Persian leadership.

THE HEBREWS

What we know of the ancient Twelve Tribes of the Hebrews is derived in large part from the poetic history of the Old Testament. In recent years, the Old Testament's stories have been partially borne out by modern archaeological evidence. It is clear that many events and stories previously regarded as mythological have a strong basis in fact.

The Hebraic tradition of a certain Abraham leading his people out of the wilderness and into the land of Canaan refers to what is now generally accepted as historical fact: nomadic, primitive Semitic tribes departed from someplace in northern Mesopotamia in the twentieth century BCE and wandered for a lengthy time through what is now Saudi Arabia. By the 1500s BCE, they were established in Canaan, the southern part of Palestine (see Map 4.2). Here they came under imperial Egyptian rule, and a good portion of the Twelve Tribes went off—perhaps voluntarily, perhaps as coerced slaves—to live in the Nile delta.

We know that, in the thirteenth century BCE, many semi-civilized peoples were moving about the eastern Mediterranean region. The Hebrews' **Exodus** from Egypt under their legendary leader Moses occurred during that century. The exact reasons for the Exodus are not clear, but it is entirely possible that the Hebrew Bible's (Old Testament) story of brutal treatment by the pharaoh is true. In any case, under Moses, the Hebrews resolved to

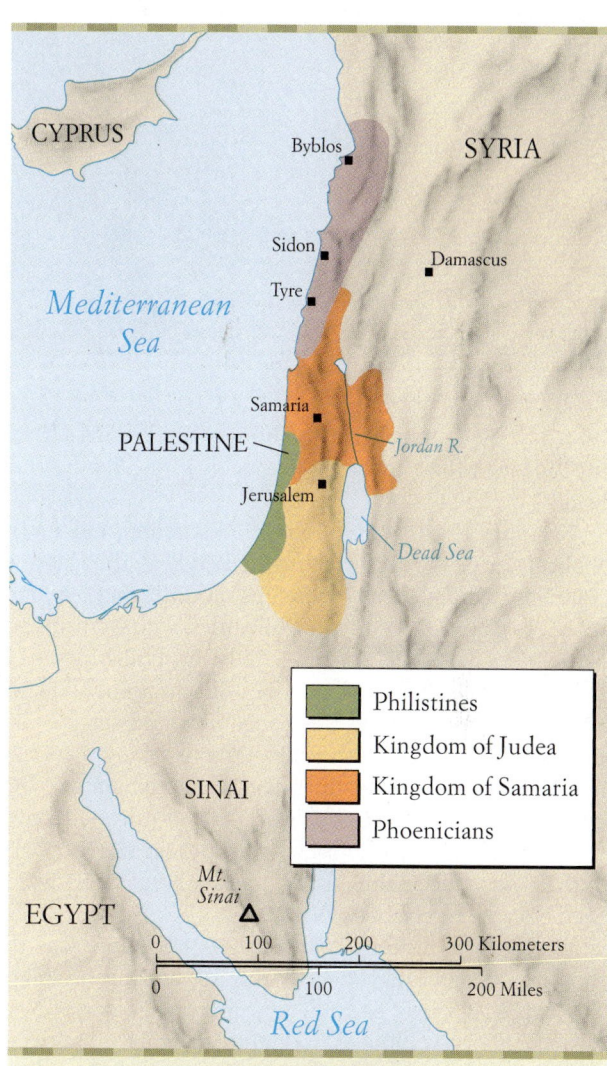

MAP 4.2 Ancient Palestine and the Jewish Kingdoms

The kingdoms of Judea and Samaria (Judah and Israel) divided the region once occupied by the Philistines and Canaanites before the Jews' return to the Promised Land. After the split, the Samaritans swiftly fell to the temptations of false gods such as the Golden Calf.

MAP QUESTIONS
Locate Canaan, the Jewish "land of milk and honey."

 View an interactive version of this or a related map at http://worldrc.wadsworth.com/

©Israel Images/Alamy

THE LANDSCAPE: A PROMISED LAND?
The harshness of the present-day Israeli landscape stands in sharp contrast to the biblical "land flowing with milk and honey" that the early Hebrews pined for in their Egyptian exile. There is much evidence that climatic change has indeed made desert from what once was a reasonably fertile and well-watered soil.

return to the "land of milk and honey," the Promised Land of Canaan, whose memory had been kept alive by their leaders in Egypt.

Escaping the pharaoh's wrathful pursuit (told in the Biblical story of Moses' parting the Red Sea), the Hebrews wandered across the Sinai peninsula until they encountered the Canaanites and the Philistines, who were already settled in coastal Palestine. At first the Philistines were able to hold the newcomers at bay. But by about 1000, the Hebrews had overcome the Canaanites and set up their own small kingdom, with Saul as the first king. Saul carried the war to the Philistines, and his lieutenant and successor, David, carried on his work. David (the victor over the giant Goliath in the Bible) was a great warrior hero, and he was successful in conquering Jerusalem, which then became the Hebrews' capital.

David's son, **Solomon** (ruled 970–935 BCE), was the most renowned king of the Hebrews. During his reign, the Hebrews briefly became an important factor in Near Eastern affairs, serving as trading intermediaries between Egypt and the Mesopotamians. The famous Temple of Jerusalem—which a triumphant Solomon constructed of stone and cedarwood, and decorated inside and out with gold—became a wonder of the ancient world. But many of his subjects hated Solomon because of his heavy taxes and luxurious living, as noted in Law and Government, "King Solomon." When he died, a revolt against his successor split the Hebrew Kingdom in two: Judea and Samaria, or, as they are sometimes called, Judah and Israel.

Although ethnically very close, the two kingdoms were hostile to each other. As time passed, Samaritans and Judeans (or Jews, as they came to be called) came to look on one another as different peoples. Their differences arose primarily because of differing religious beliefs but also because Judea came under the shadow of a briefly revived Egyptian empire, while Samaria fell to the successive conquerors of Mesopotamia.

The kingdom of Samaria/Israel was ended in 722 by a failed rebellion against the Assyrian overlords, resulting in the scattering of the populace far and wide (the first **Diaspora,** or "scattering") and the eventual loss of them (the ten Lost Tribes of Jewish tradition) to Judaic belief. Judea, however, survived under the Assyrians until the defeat of the latter in 612. It then fell under Babylonian (Chaldean; CAL-dee-an) overlordship. The ill-fated attempt to throw off this yoke led to the crushing defeat by King Nebuchadnezzar (neh-buh-kehd-NEH-zer) in 586 and the ensuing Babylonian Captivity (586–539 BCE), when thousands of Jews were taken off to Babylon as hostages for the good behavior of the rest. The great temple of Solomon was demolished. Becoming one of the provinces of the Persian Empire after 539 BCE, the Judeans continued under Persian rule until Alexander the Great toppled the King of Kings in the 330s (see Chapter 7). They then lived under the successors of Alexander until the gradual extension of Roman power reached Palestine.

JEWISH RELIGIOUS BELIEF AND ITS EVOLUTION

From the time of the kingdom of Saul, a great god known as *Yahweh* (Jehovah) was established as the Hebrews' chief deity, but by no means the only one. In Samaria, Yahweh

LAW AND GOVERNMENT

King Solomon

The story of King Solomon is an illuminating example of how tradition can be consciously or unconsciously adapted to fit the needs of a people. The Old Testament tells us that Solomon ruled the united tribes of the Jews with wisdom and justice and that his people looked up to him as an exemplary ruler. In fact, Solomon's wisdom and justice often seemed conspicuous by their absence, and his kingdom did not long outlast his own life.

The son of King David and his fourth wife, Bathsheba, Solomon succeeded his father, despite the existence of an older surviving son. His mother, with the help of the prophet Nathan, persuaded the old king to recognize Solomon as his heir shortly before his death. Several years later, Solomon secured the throne by eliminating his rival on charges of plotting against him.

Ignoring Hebrew traditions that emphasized the collective nature of leadership and the collaboration of king and priest, the young ruler established an absolute monarchy. He adopted a style of living and governing that was foreign to previous Jewish kings and subordinated all else to enriching his court and its prestige. The Canaanites, defeated by David but long allowed to go their own way, were now reduced to slavery and forced to work for Solomon's projects. Under Solomon's hand, the city of Jerusalem grew in commercial importance in the Near East. He was able to extend his influence into Mesopotamia and northern Egypt by marrying foreign brides, including the daughter of the pharaoh.

In place of the simple quarters that had sufficed for David, Solomon constructed a large royal home that rivaled those of the Persians in size and fittings. The famous Temple of Jerusalem became a wonder of the ancient world. Visitors from many countries came to marvel and to ask Solomon for solutions to their problems, for the king was reputed to have great wisdom. The Twelve Tribes of Israelites, so long isolated and ignored, became commercially versatile and sophisticated. But the king's extravagances were much resented, and they exacerbated the split that was already developing between Judea and Samaria-Israel.

During Solomon's reign, Judea received commercial advantages and paid less taxes. The northern ten tribes became indignant, threatening to sever their relations with Jerusalem and Judea even before Solomon's death. When the king died in 935, the Hebrew tribes split and formed the two separate, rival kingdoms of Judea and Israel, lessening their ability to rule their satellite peoples and exposing themselves to foreign threats. The vassal kingdoms that David had painfully conquered were lost, and the trading empire that Solomon had labored for forty years to create was destroyed forever. "Vanity of vanities, all is vanity."

©Private Collection/Christie's Images/Bridgeman Art Library

THE WAILING WALL, IN JERUSALEM. In the center of old Jerusalem stands the last remnant of Solomon's temple, shown here in a late nineteenth-century watercolor, where devout Jews today pray to the god of their forebears. In the years following the Temple's destruction by the Babylonians, the Romans prohibited Jews from entering Jerusalem at all, so the customary place for mourning the Temple's loss was instead the Mount of Olives, to the east of and overlooking the Temple Mount.

▶ *Analyze and Interpret*

What might explain the Old Testament's admiring view of Solomon? Can you give a modern example of how national or regional tradition has been bent to fit the current need or desire of a people? What does "the wisdom of Solomon" mean in modern times?

(YAH-way) was eventually relegated to an inferior position. But in Judea, Yahweh's cult gradually triumphed over all rivals, and this god became the only deity of the Jews of Jerusalem.

This condition of having a single god was a distinct oddity among ancient peoples. *Monotheism* was so rare that we know of only one pre-Jewish experiment with it—that of Akhnaton in Egypt (see Chapter 3). Some of the Hebrews were living in Egypt during Akhnaton's reign, and it is possible that the pharaoh's doctrines penetrated into Jewish consciousness. Zarathustra's doctrine of dualism between two almost-equal deities who wrestled over the souls of men undoubtedly had much to do with the later forms of Hebrew belief, but just how they are related is a subject for argument.

By the 600s, the Judean Jews, under the influence of a whole series of great prophets, including Amos, Hosea, Ezekiel, and Isaiah, came to believe themselves bound to Yahweh by a sacred contract, the Covenant (Promise), given to Moses during the Exodus. The contract was understood to mean that, if the Jews remained constant in their worship of Yahweh and kept the faith he instilled in them, they would eventually triumph over all of their enemies and be a respected and lordly people on Earth. The faith that Yahweh desired was supported by a set of rigid rules given to Moses by Yahweh on Mount Sinai, from which eventually evolved a whole law code that governed every aspect of Hebrew daily life. Known to later Jews and Christians as the Ten Commandments, these moral regulations have been adapted to much different social circumstances.

The Jewish faith was one of the earliest attempts to formalize an ethical system and to link it with the worship of supernatural deities. *Ethics* is the study of good and evil and determining what is right and wrong in human life and conduct. Yahweh's followers gradually came to regard him as an enforcer of correct ethical actions. Those who did evil on Earth would be made to suffer, if not in this world, then in the one to come. This belief was not unusual, for other religions had made at least some moves toward punishment of evildoers. The laws of Yahweh, however, also assured that the good would be rewarded—again, if not in this life, then in the eternal one to come.

How did people know whether they were doing good or evil? One way was by following the laws of Yahweh. Increasingly, though, they could also rely on the knowledge of what is right and what is wrong that Yahweh imprinted in every heart: conscience. The Ten Commandments were particularly the Jews' property, given to them as a mark of favor by their lord and protector Yahweh. But all men and women everywhere were believed to have been given conscience, and insofar as they followed conscience, they were doing the Lord's work and possibly gaining eternal salvation.

ECONOMIC CHANGE AND SOCIAL CUSTOMS

Although their religious beliefs would have immense influence on Western civilization, the Jews were mostly minor players on the Near Eastern stage in economic affairs and politics. They had never been numerous, and the split between Israelites and Judeans weakened both groups. With the rise of Assyria, both Israel and Judea had to engage in numerous expensive wars and suffered economically. Both became relatively insignificant backwaters under the direct or indirect rule of powerful neighbors.

When the kingdom was founded under Saul, most Hebrews were still rural herders and peasants, living as Abraham had lived. Over the next half millennium, however, many Hebrews made the transition from rural to town life. As many people shifted from subsistence farming to wage earning, social tensions dividing rich and poor began to appear. The strong solidarity that had marked the Hebrews earlier broke down. The prophets of the eighth through fifth centuries called repeatedly for social justice and remind us that exploitation of widows and orphans and abuse of the weak by the strong were by no means limited to the despised Gentiles (Jen-tiles: all non-Jews).

More than most, the Jews divided all humanity into they and we. This was undoubtedly the result of their religious tradition, whereby they had been selected as the Chosen. Jews looked upon non-Jews as distinctly lesser breeds, whose main function in the divine plan was to act as tempters and obstacles that the pious must overcome. In their preoccupation with the finer points of the Law laid down by Moses and his successors, the Hebrews deliberately segregated themselves from other peoples. Intermarriage with nonbelievers was tantamount to treason and was punished by immediate expulsion from the community. Ancient Judaism was almost never open to converts.

The Judaic Yahweh was definitely a male lawgiver, speaking to other males in a society in which women counted only as the relatives and dependents of men. The nomadic background of the Twelve Tribes is evident here, exhibiting the universal tendency of nomadic people to subordinate females and consider them as the possessions of their men. In the Old Testament, even when a Jewish woman acts in self-assertive fashion, the point is to secure some advantage or distinction for a male, not on her own behalf. Judith slays Holofernes not to avenge herself for her sexual exploitation, but to secure the safety of her people. Marriage and divorce reflected the patriarchal values. The married state was strongly preferred, and in fact, bachelors were looked on as failures and shirkers of duty. Young men were supposed to marry by no later than age twenty-four and preferably by twenty. Girls were thought ready for marriage at puberty, roughly about age thirteen. A man could have several legal wives and an unlimited number of concubines, but as in other societies, only the wealthy could afford this practice. The wife married into the husband's family and moved into his house. The property she brought into the marriage remained hers, however, and could be removed again if her husband divorced her for any reason but unfaithfulness. Divorce was easy enough for the husband but very unusual for a wife to initiate. Women caught in adultery could be killed, but typically they were divorced and sent back to their father's home. Infidelity by the husband was a crime only if committed with a married woman.

As with almost all early peoples, children were the whole point of marriage. The continuation of the family was the primary duty of both husband and wife. The oldest male child received the lion's share of the inheritance, but the other boys were not shut out. The girls, on the other hand, received nothing beyond their dowries, because through marriage they would be joined to another family, which would care for them. The education of all children was carried on within the family circle and was religious in nature. Literacy was uncommon among the country folk but not so among the urbanites.

Jewish arts and sciences were relatively undeveloped compared with those of their more sophisticated and richer neighbors. Excepting the Old Testament's poetry, the Jews produced little of note in any of the art forms. The representation of living things was thought to be sacrilegious and was banned. There is no record of any important Jewish contributions to the sciences.

A CHANGING THEOLOGY

In the centuries after the fall of the monarchies of Samaria and Judea, the Jews' conception of Yahweh changed in several significant ways, linked to their political relations with others. After losing their independence, the Jewish people went through a long spiritual crisis. Their hope for a triumph over their enemies was not realized. Indeed, quite the contrary happened: the *Babylonian Captivity* (586–539 BCE) was a particular low point. Many Jews never returned, having been seduced by the "Great Whore" Babylon into the worship of Mesopotamian deities, as had their erstwhile co-believers in Samaria. After the Persian king Cyrus released them, those who returned were the "tried and true" who had been tested and, strong in their faith, had survived. They rebuilt the destroyed Temple and restructured their theology. Aided by new interpretations of the Covenant (the *Talmud;* TAHL-muhd), the Jews reappraised and made precise the nature of God and their relation to him.

During this post-Captivity period, the image of Yahweh took on clearer lines. Not only was Yahweh the only god;

he was the *universal* god of all. Whether or not the Gentiles worshiped him, he was their all-powerful judge and would reward or punish them (mostly the latter) as they conformed or not to the demands of conscience.

God was a *just* god, who would reward and punish according to ethical principles, but he was also a *merciful* god who would not turn a deaf ear to the earnest penitent. His ways were mysterious to men such as the sorely tried Job in the Old Testament, but they would someday be seen for what they were: righteous and just.

God was an *omnipotent* and *omniscient* (all powerful and all-knowing) master, who could do whatever he desired, always and everywhere. The Creator of nature, he stood outside his creation, transcending it. There were no other opposing forces (gods) that could frustrate his will, but in his wisdom, Yahweh had granted his creature Man free will and allowed the principle of evil to arise in the form of the fallen angel, Lucifer or Satan. Humankind could ignore conscience and the Law and choose evil, much as Zarathustra had taught. If they did, they would face a Last Judgment that would condemn them to eternal punishment and deprive them of the fate that Yahweh desired and offered: salvation in blessedness.

Finally, Yahweh gradually came to be a *personal* deity, in a way in which no other ancient god had been. He could be prayed to directly; he was observant of all that affected a man's or a woman's life. His actions were not impulsive or unpredictable. He wanted his people not as slaves but as friends. The relationship between God and Man is meant to be one of mutual love. In a sense, God needed Man to complete the work of creation.

The promise to preserve the Jews as a people that Yahweh had given Moses was what held the Judean Jews together after the Assyrian and Babylonian conquests. But inevitably some of them, including many of the learned men (*rabbis*), came to think of this promise as one aimed not at simple preservation but at a counter-conquest by the Jews of their enemies. Instead of being a contemptible minority in the empires of the mighty ones, these Hebrews believed they would become the mighty and would bend others to their will.

In this way grew the hopes for a **messiah** (meh-SIGH-yuh), a redeemer who would take the Jews out of their humiliations and make them a people to be feared and respected (see Evidence of the Past). In this manner, the message of the Lord speaking through the great prophets was distorted into a promise of earthly grandeur rather than a promise of immortal salvation for those who believed. When a man named Jesus appeared, claiming to be the messiah and speaking of his kingdom "which was not of this earth," there was disappointment and disbelief among many of those who heard him.

By the time of the Roman conquest of the Near East, in the first century before Christ, some of the Jewish

EVIDENCE OF THE PAST

The Dead Sea Scrolls

Arab shepherd boys on watch over their family sheep in the rocky hills over the Dead Sea made a dramatic discovery in 1947, when they brought the so-called Dead Sea Scrolls to light. After two thousand or more years resting at the bottom of a shaft-like cave, these copper, leather, and papyrus manuscripts—more than 600 all told—would substantially increase our knowledge of the Jewish people and their beliefs at the era of Christ's birth and earlier.

The scrolls are the assorted documents deemed most worthy of preservation by a religious brotherhood that chose to withdraw from participation in public life in Judea, in favor of a type of monastic community. Convinced of the impending end of the world and the coming of a Last Judgment, these individuals studied and fasted while awaiting the coming of a messiah. In the last forty years, extensive archaeological work shows that the brotherhood (there seem to have been no females) lived in hermit-like isolation in a barren country that now forms part of the Israel–Jordan border, near a place called Qumran. There they devoted their lives to a spiritual odyssey that they hoped would place them among the saved.

Authorities have now dated the writing to between the third century BCE and the year 68 CE. They make no mention anywhere of the life of Jesus of Nazareth, but in several other fashions confirm previous scholarly presumptions about the events of those years in Roman Palestine. The final entries in the scrolls coincide with the brutal campaign of the Roman general Vespasian against the Zealots, the Jewish rebels against Rome's rule who ignited the Jewish War and the second destruction of the Temple of Solomon. It is thought that the scrolls were hidden away to preserve them from Roman destruction.

▶ *Analyze and Interpret*

How does the omission of any mention of Jesus in the scrolls affect the credibility of the New Testament? Would you expect that the life and message of Jesus would be well known to the Qumran brotherhood who wrote the scrolls? Would they necessarily accept him as the true Messiah?

THE DEAD SEA SCROLLS. These historic documents were found in a cave above the Dead Sea in 1947. The scrolls have been largely deciphered in recent years and have proven a rich source of knowledge of Jewish society and customs around the first century CE.

©Israel Museum, Jerusalem, Israel/ Ancient Art and Architecture Collection Ltd./Bridgeman Art Library

leaders had become fanatical, believing in the protection of mighty Yahweh against all odds. These **Zealots** (ZEH-luts) were unwilling to bend before any nonbeliever, however powerful he might be. This would cause the tension between the Jewish nation and the Roman overlords that eventually resulted in war and the second Diaspora, the forced emigration of much of this small people from their ancestral home to all corners of the great Roman Empire.

Wherever the Jews went, they took their national badge of distinction with them: the unerring belief in their identity as the Chosen and their particular vision of the nature of God and his operations in the minds and hearts of humans. This was a vision of the relationship between the deity and his creations that no other people had: mutually dependent, ethical, and just, but also merciful on the Lord's side; submissive but not slavish on Man's side. It was the relationship between a stern but loving father and an independent, sinful, but dutiful child. The mold for the evolution of Christianity had been formed. All that was needed was the appearance of the long-rumored messiah who would fulfill the promise that the Chosen would enter glory, someday.

SUMMARY

AFTER THE DECLINE of Mesopotamia and Egypt in the first millennium BCE, several smaller peoples contributed their diverse talents to the spread of civilized life. The Assyrian Empire, founded on an efficient army, lasted only a brief time. After it was toppled in the seventh century BCE by a coalition of enemies, most traces of it were wiped away in its Mesopotamian homeland. One of the Assyrians' conquests was Phoenicia, whose people are remembered for their maritime explorations and colonization, and for taking the first major steps toward a phonetic alphabet.

For more than 200 years after the conquests of Cyrus the Great, the Persian Empire brought relative peace and progress to much of the Near East. Learning from their more advanced subjects, the imperial governors allowed substantial freedom of worship, language, and custom, while upholding superior justice and efficient administration. Trade and crafts flourished throughout the immense empire. From the preachings of Zarathustra emerged a new, highly sophisticated ethics that was elevated to a state religion.

The contribution of the Jews to later history was of a different nature. The Twelve Tribes of the Hebrews wandered out of Mesopotamia and entered Palestine some time in the middle of the second millennium BCE. After a long duel with powerful neighbors, the Jews set up a monarchy that broke into two parts in the 900s. The larger segment, Samaria or Israel, gradually fell away from Judaism and was dispersed by Assyrian conquest. The smaller part, Judea with its capital Jerusalem, stayed true to Yahweh and survived as a province of other empires into Roman times.

What distinguished the Jews was their monotheistic religion and their linkage of a universal God with ethical standards in this life and immortal salvation in the next. Their gradually evolving vision of an omnipotent, just, and merciful Lord who would one day send a messiah to lead the Hebrews to glory would be the cement that held this small people together. It was a vision unique to them, and its power carried the Jews through a history of subjugation and torment.

▶ Identification Terms

Test your knowledge of this chapter's key concepts by defining the following terms. If you can't recall the meaning of certain terms, refresh your memory by looking up the boldfaced term in the chapter, turning to the Glossary at the end of the book, or working with the flashcards that are available on the *World Civilizations* Companion Website: **academic.cengage.com/adler**

Assur	messiah	satrapies	Zarathustra (Zoroaster)
Diaspora	Nineveh	Solomon	Zealots
Exodus			

▶ Test Your Knowledge

Test your knowledge of this chapter by answering the following questions. Complete answers appear at the end of the book. You may find even more quiz questions in CengageNOW and on the *World Civilizations* Companion Website: **academic.cengage.com/adler**

1. The people who conquered the Semites of the Tigris valley in the eighth century BCE were
   a. Babylonians.
   b. Assyrians.
   c. Phoenicians.
   d. Egyptians.
   e. Hittites.

2. The key to Assyrian success in empire building was
   a. cultural superiority.
   b. respectful treatment of conquered peoples.
   c. the bravery of the individual soldier.
   d. effective military organization.
   e. wholesale execution of their enemies.

3. The overthrow of the Assyrians was accomplished by
   a. an internal palace plot.
   b. a coalition of their enemies led by the Babylonians.
   c. the Egyptian and Hittite armies.
   d. a general rebellion of the slaves.
   e. the invasion of the Hyksos peoples.

4. The outstanding contribution of the Phoenicians to world history was the
   a. marine compass.
   b. phonetic alphabet.
   c. invention of coinage.
   d. gyroscope.
   e. chariot.
5. The creator of the Persian empire was
   a. Zoroaster.
   b. Xerxes.
   c. Cyrus.
   d. Ahura-mazda.
   e. Cambyses.
6. Which of the following is the correct chronological sequence of empires?
   a. Assyrian, Persian, Hittite, Sumerian
   b. Persian, Hittite, Sumerian, Assyrian
   c. Sumerian, Hittite, Assyrian, Persian
   d. Hittite, Assyrian, Sumerian, Persian
   e. Hittite, Persian, Sumerian, Assyrian
7. The first king of the Hebrew Kingdom founded after the Exodus was
   a. David.
   b. Saul.
   c. Solomon.
   d. Isaiah.
   e. Judah.
8. The Covenant of the Hebrews with their god Yahweh
   a. was given to Moses during the Exodus from Egypt.
   b. had nothing to do with individual conduct, only with group survival.
   c. was a contract that was allowed to lapse.
   d. guaranteed each believing Hebrew immortality.
   e. provided the basis for early Persian law.
9. Belief in the messiah among Jews of the first century BCE was focused on
   a. hope for a statesman who would lead the Jews to a new homeland.
   b. expectation of a military leader who would help the Jews repel the Romans.
   c. finding a political leader who would assert Jewish supremacy.
   d. a hermit who rejected society, such as John the Baptist.
   e. having the Son of God come to Earth to bring eternal salvation.
10. The critical new factor in the Jews' vision of God that had developed by the first century CE was the
    a. link between the merciful deity and humans' ethical conduct on Earth.
    b. belief that God was all-powerful and that He controlled all human affairs.
    c. belief that God was supreme over all other deities.
    d. promise of an eternal life given by God to those whom He deemed worthy.
    e. belief in a messiah who would remove his people from their troubled lives on Earth.

Enter *CengageNOW* using the access card that is available with this text. *CengageNOW* will assist you in understanding the content in this chapter with lesson plans generated for your needs and provide you with a connection to the *Wadsworth World History Resource Center* (see description at right for details).

 **World History Resource Center**

Enter the Resource Center using either your *CengageNOW* access card or your standalone access card for the *Wadsworth World History Resource Center*. Organized by topic, this website includes quizzes; images; over 350 primary source documents; interactive simulations, maps, and timelines; movie explorations; and a wealth of other resources. You can read the following documents, and many more, at the *Wadsworth World History Resource Center*:

2 Kings 17:1–16
Psalm 137

*He who worships God must stand
distinct from Him,
So only shall he know the joyful
love of God. For if he say that
God and he are one,
That joy, that love, shall vanish
instantly away.*
    —"Song of Tukaram"

5 INDIA'S BEGINNINGS

c. 2500–1900 BCE	Mohenjo-Daro and Harappa flourish
c. 1500 BCE	Invasion of Aryans
c. 1500–500 BCE	The Vedic Epoch
563–483 BCE	Life of the Buddha
326 BCE	Invasion by Alexander the Great
320–232 BCE	Mauryan Dynasty

INDUS VALLEY CIVILIZATION AND EARLY TRADE
Mohenjo-Daro and Harappa

THE VEDIC EPOCH
The Beginnings of the Caste System

HINDUISM

BUDDHISM

DAILY LIFE AND THE POSITION OF WOMEN

THE MAURYAN DYNASTY

TRADE AND THE SPREAD OF BUDDHISM

HOW OLD ARE THE MOST ancient civilizations? Is it possible that the oldest of all are yet to be discovered? Until fairly recently it was believed that the civilization of India had been founded only some 2,000 years ago, far later than China, Egypt, or Mesopotamia. But in the early twentieth century, archaeologists found that a highly advanced, urbanized civilization had existed since the middle of the third millennium BCE in the valley of the Indus River in what is now Pakistan. The discovery of this chapter in world history is a dramatic story, and much of the detail is still being pieced together. Enough is known, however, to whet our appetite to know much more, especially about the possible contributions of this civilization to two of the world's leading religious beliefs, Hinduism and Buddhism.

INDUS VALLEY CIVILIZATION AND EARLY TRADE

As in Mesopotamia and Egypt, the earliest Indian civilization was located in the plain bordering two great streams, the Indus and the Saraswati Rivers. Both flow south and west from the foothills of the Himalayan range, the world's loftiest and most forbidding mountains. The Himalayas are the highest of several ranges that separate India and Pakistan from Tajikistan and China (see Map 5.1).

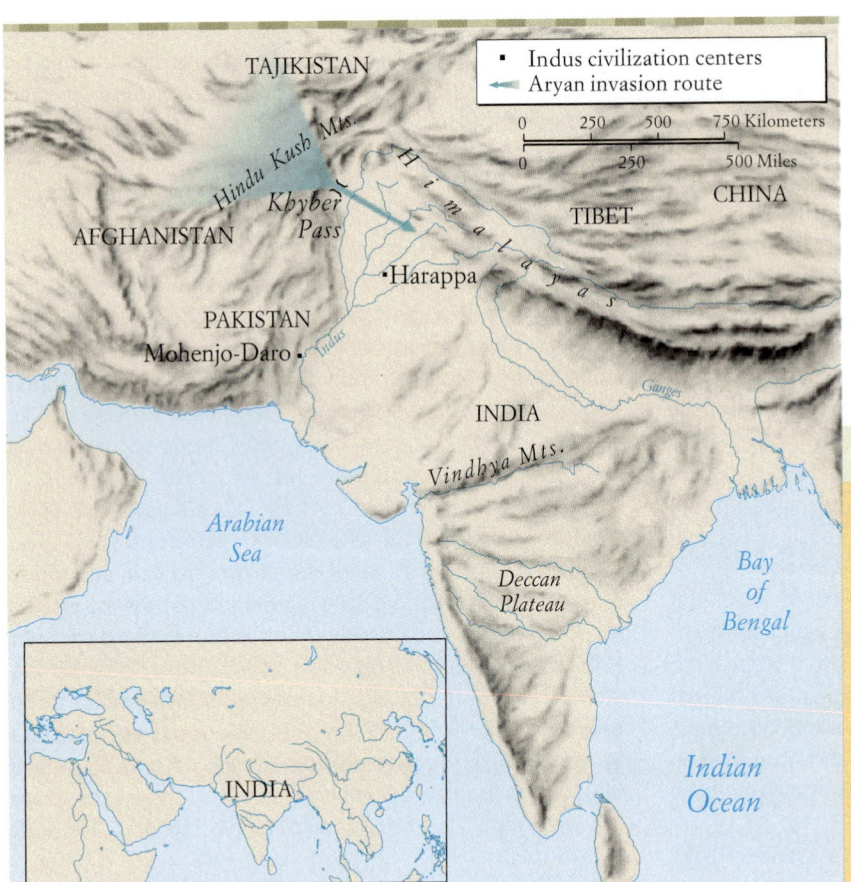

MAP 5.1   The Indian Subcontinent

India is a very large and diverse geographic entity, ringed by the Himalayas and other high mountains to the north and northeast. The usual routes of contact with other peoples have been from the northwest and by sea from both eastern and western directions. Mohenjo-Daro and Harappa were part of a highly advanced, urbanized ancient civilization that flourished in the valley of the Indus River before the Aryan invasions.

MAP QUESTIONS
Examine the map and explain why India is classified as a subcontinent.

Archaeologists are still unsure about the precise origins of this **Indus Valley civilization,** but because it was linked with the north and west by trade even before agriculture appeared, Mesopotamian civilization might have influenced its emergence. Farming on the flood plains of the Indus Valley began around 6000 BCE, and by 4000 BCE the region had a dense population and numerous fortified farming villages. Soil erosion and frequent, violent flooding constantly plagued settled life along these riverbanks, so preplanning was essential. Evidence of flood control systems and grid-like street layouts show up in the very deepest (earliest) layers in excavations that archaeologists have carried out in early Indus Valley farming sites.

The third millennium BCE saw explosive growth in the region and the enlargement of towns into cities. As in other early civilizations like Mesopotamia and Egypt, Indus Valley civilization rested firmly on the agrarian base of cereals cultivation, dry land crops like wheat, barley, and cotton. But even more than in other civilizations, it seems, the central role of trade was striking, considering its importance and its endurance. Finds of items manufactured from cotton, metals, and ivory from the Indus Valley show that southwest Asia had an extensive trade with northwest India already by 2600 BCE, and by 2350 BCE there

even existed Indian settlements in southern Mesopotamia. Professional merchants gave this trade a high degree of organization, and it is likely that it had a major impact on the growth and wealth of Indus urban life. In its earliest stages, this trafficking relied chiefly on land routes, although there was some waterborne trade within the Gulf and along coastal regions of southern Asia. Gradually, sea routes opened into the Indian Ocean, the Red Sea, and the Persian Gulf, allowing for the expansion of this early trade. This development placed India at the center of a huge trade network that linked it with the eastern Mediterranean, East Africa, Arabia, and other parts of Asia.

Mohenjo-Daro and Harappa

At two locations on the Indus River called *Mohenjo-Daro* (mo-HEN-jo-DAH-ro) and *Harappa* (hah-RAP-pah), archaeologists have found the remnants of large, carefully constructed walls and the cities they enclosed. Each was more than three miles across and probably housed more than 100,000 people at some time in the distant past. Many smaller towns and villages have also been found under the dust of centuries, scattered along the Indus and its several tributaries in western India.

INDUS VALLEY JEWELRY. The fine workmanship and imagination exhibited here allow us to draw some conclusions about the state of Indus civilization at this epoch, about 2000 to 1800 BCE. Some of the precious stones in this jewelry had to have been brought from as far away as China. Discoveries of such manufactures as well as others made from metals and ivory throughout the western Indian Ocean suggest the impact trade had on Indian civilization as early as the third millennium BCE.

National Museum of India, New Delhi, India/Bridgeman Art Library

RUINS OF MOHENJO-DARO. Systematic excavation commenced in the ruins of Mohenjo-Daro in the late nineteenth century, under the auspices of the British colonial government. It continues today, directed by the Pakistani government. Shown here is the Great Bath, a pool and surrounding cells that clearly existed for ritual bathing. Some have suggested that the emphasis on purification by water in present-day Hinduism may go back to these origins.

Robert Harding Picture Library

The cities and villages were built of fired brick and carefully planned. The streets ran at precise right angles, and they were of two widths. The main thoroughfares were thirty-four feet wide, large enough to allow two large carts to pass safely and still leave room for several pedestrians. The smaller avenues were nine feet wide. Many of the buildings had two or even three stories, which was unusual for residences in the ancient world. They were built of bricks that are almost always of two sizes, but only those two. The interior dimensions of the houses were almost identical. A sewage canal ran from each house to a larger canal in the street that carried off household wastes. Small statues of gods and goddesses, almost always of the same size and posture, are frequently found in the house foundations.

All this regularity suggests a government that was very powerful in the eyes of its subjects and probably gained its authority from religious belief. Some experts on Indus civilization believe that it was a *theocracy* (thee-AH-crah-see), in which the priests ruled as representatives of the gods. In no other way, they think, could the government's power have been strong enough to command residential uniformity over a period of centuries, as happened in Mohenjo-Daro and Harappa.

Both cities also contain monumental buildings, probably a communal granary and the temples of the local gods, situated on a citadel. Harappa differs from Mohenjo-Daro in building style and other details, but the similarities are strong enough that the two cities and the surrounding villages are believed to constitute one civilization, sometimes termed *Dravidian*.

For their food, the cities depended on the irrigated farms of the surrounding plain. Like the people of Egypt, the ordinary people apparently enjoyed a high standard of living for many generations. Although a good many works of art and figurines have been found, the occasional writing has not yet been deciphered. This, as well as the long period when this civilization was forgotten, has hindered scholars' efforts to obtain a detailed knowledge of these people. We still know next to nothing about their religion, their government, the social divisions of the people, and their scientific and intellectual accomplishments. One thing now seems clear, however: the cities and villages were prosperous, expanding settlements from at least 2500 to about 1900 BCE. Around 1900, for reasons still only guessed at, they began a long decline, which ended with the abandonment of Mohenjo-Daro about 1200 BCE and Harappa somewhat later. Some evidence indicates that landslides changed the course of the lower Indus and prevented the continuation of the intensive irrigation that had supported the cities. Some people think that the population may have fallen victim to malaria, as the blocked river created mosquito-ridden swamps nearby. Others think that the irrigated land gradually became alkaline and non-productive, as happened in lower Mesopotamia. Whatever the role of natural disasters, it is certain that the decline of the Indus Valley was accelerated when the same Indo-European nomads who created the Persian empire began a series of migrations out of their homelands, somewhere north of the Caspian Sea, into Iran and Afghanistan after 1500 BCE. However, for many of these Proto-Iranians, this was not the end of their pastoralist wanderings. Some continued their movement south from Afghanistan, through the Khyber Pass, and into the Indus Valley. The name by which these people called themselves was closely related to that of their Iranian cousins to the north, namely the **Aryans** (AYR-yanz).

THE VEDIC EPOCH

These Aryans and their Indo-European-speaking relatives were among the earliest nomadic, horse-breeding people of ancient Asia, and their aggressive ways were the terror of other civilizations besides that of the Indus Valley. Many scholars believe that they overwhelmed the agrarian Indian civilizations and set themselves up as a sort of master group, using the Indians as labor to do the farming and trading that the Aryan warriors despised as inferior. As we noted, their conquest of the more advanced peoples may have been aided by natural disasters that had severely weakened the economy.

Our knowledge of the Aryans comes largely from their **Vedas** (VAY-dahs), ancient oral epics that were written down only long after the Aryan invasion. So the pictures the Vedas present may be deceptive. We know that the Aryans worshiped gods of the sky and storm, and made impressive use of bronze weaponry and horse-drawn chariots in battle. (Apparently, the Indus Valley people knew the horse only as a beast of burden and were at a disadvantage against the Aryan chariots.) The **Rigveda** (rig-VAY-dah), the oldest and most important Veda, paints a picture of a war-loving, violent folk, led by their *raja* (RAH-jah), or chieftain, and their magic-working priests.

The Aryans moved on from the agriculturally played-out Indus Valley, preferring instead better-watered regions to the east and south. In time, the Aryans extended their rule across all of northern India, but centered it on the Ganges River and its tributaries. Gradually, they abandoned their nomadic ways and settled down as agriculturists and town dwellers, just as they had elsewhere. Two factors probably contributed to this: the new iron technology the Aryans introduced, which gave them better tools, and the introduction of rice cultivation from the east, supplemented by pepper and spices, which provided more and better foods

for their diet. They never conquered the southern half of India, and as a result, the southern culture and religion still differ from those of the north in some respects.

The Beginnings of the Caste System

The Vedas describe the beliefs of a warlike people who saw themselves as the natural masters of the inferior Indians and who underlined their difference by dividing society into four groups or classes. The two highest classes of priests and warriors were reserved for the Aryans and their pureblooded descendants. The priests were called **Brahmins** (BRAH-mihns) and originally were superior in status to the warriors, who were called *kshatrija* (shah-TREE-yah) and evolved over time from warriors to the governing class. The third class, the *vaishya* (VIE-shyah), was probably the most numerous and included freemen, farmers, and traders. In the fourth and lowest group within the system were the unfree: the serfs or *shudra* (SHOO-drah).

Over the long course of the Vedic Epoch (over a thousand years, from 1500 to about 500 BCE), these four classes evolved into something more complex by far: multiple social groups defined by birth, or **caste** (cast). A caste is a social unit into which individuals are born and that dictates most aspects of daily life. It confers a status that cannot be changed. Each caste except the very lowest has special duties and privileges, some of which are economic in nature, whereas others are manifested by dietary and marital restrictions. A high-caste Indian normally has very little contact with lower castes and none at all with the outcastes, or *pariahs* (pah-REYE-yahs). Perhaps a seventh of Indian society still falls into this last category—the untouchables—whose members until recently were treated worse than animals.

The stratification of Indian society begun by the Aryan conquest persists to the present day. The Aryans were gradually absorbed into the indigenous Indian peoples through intermarriage with high-status individuals, but the caste system took ever-stronger root. By the eighteenth century CE there were more than 3,000 separate subcastes, or *jati* (JAH-tee). Although the number has probably declined since then, the belief that one is born into a group that is fixed by age-old traditions and allows no change is still strong among rural Indians.

Throughout Indian history, caste has had the effect of inhibiting any type of change, particularly social change. Why? Combined with the beliefs of Hinduism (see the next section), caste made it next to impossible for someone born into a low state to climb the ranks of social prestige and privilege. It also limited political power to the uppermost ranks. Caste discouraged or prohibited cultural innovation by those in the lower ranks. Meanwhile, those on top were very content to have things go on forever as they were. Under the Aryan-founded caste system, India became a highly stratified and immobile society.

HINDUISM

The religion of the overwhelming majority of Indians is Hinduism, the fourth largest in the world with about one billion adherents. Hinduism is both more and less than a *religion* as the West understands that term: it is a way of life, a philosophical system, an inspiration for art, and the basis of all Indian political theory in the past. But it is not a rigid set of theological doctrines that must be believed to find truth or to be saved in eternity. And it possesses almost innumerable localized variations in manner and content.

The Hindu faith is a product of the slow mixing of the Aryan beliefs with those of the native agrarian cultures. Many of Hinduism's basic principles reflect the patriarchal and class-conscious society that the Aryan conquerors founded and that was strengthened in its stratification by the conquerors' beliefs. A revealing glimpse at early Hinduism is given by the Laws of Manu, as excerpted in the Society and Economy box. One's birth family determines his caste, as is the relation of men to women and husbands to wives.

National Maritime Museum, Haifa, Israel/ ©Erich Lessing/Art Resource, NY

SOCIETY AND ECONOMY

The Laws of Manu

The Laws of Manu are an ancient compilation of teachings from Hindu India. Manu was a being simultaneously human and divine, from whom devout Hindus could learn what was needed for perfection and the attainment of *moksha*. Manu's laws were the cornerstone of Hindu traditional opinion on the rights and duties of the sexes and of family members, as well as castes. These opinions and prejudices did not change substantially until recent times. The attitude of the Laws of Manu toward women and the lower castes are especially revealing. (*Note:* The *shudra* (SHOO-drah) are the lowest of the original four castes of India established during the Aryan epoch.)

> That place where the shudra are very numerous . . . soon entirely perishes, afflicted by disease and famine.
>
> A Brahmin may confidently take the goods of his shudra, because the slave cannot have any possessions and the master may take his property.
>
> A Brahmin who takes a shudra to wife and to his bed will after death sink into Hell; if he begets a child with her, he will lose the rank of Brahmin. The son whom a Brahmin begets through lust upon a shudra female is, although alive, a corpse and hence called a living corpse. A shudra who has intercourse with a woman of a twice-born caste [that is, a Brahmin] shall be punished so: if she was unguarded he loses the offending part [his genitals] and all his property; if she was guarded, everything including his life.
>
> Women . . . give themselves to the handsome and the ugly. Through their passion for men, through their unstable temper, through their natural heartlessness they become disloyal toward their husbands, however carefully they may be guarded. Knowing their disposition, which the lord of creation laid upon them, to be so, every man should most strenuously exert himself to guard them. When creating them, Manu allotted to women a love of their bed, of their seat and of ornament, impure desire, wrath, dishonesty, malice, and bad conduct. . . .
>
> It is the nature of women to seduce men in this world; for that reason the wise are never unguarded in the company of females. For women are able to lead astray in this world not only the fool, but even a learned man, and make of him a slave of desire and wrath.

But the exhortations of Manu are not completely one-sided:

> Reprehensible is the father who gives not his daughter in marriage at the proper time [namely, puberty]; reprehensible is the husband who approaches not his wife in due season, and reprehensible is the son who does not protect his mother after her husband has died.
>
> Drinking spirituous liquors, associating with wicked ones, separation from the husband, rambling abroad, sleeping at unseasonable hours, and dwelling in houses of other men are the six causes of ruin in women.

▶ Analyze and Interpret

How do these laws differ, if at all, from the attitudes toward women reflected in the code of Hammurabi? Where did women find better protection and justice, by modern standards?

Source: D. Johnson, ed., *Sources of World Civilization*, Vol. 1. ©1994, Simon & Schuster.

You can read more of the Laws of Manu at the *Wadsworth World History Resource Center*.

But Hinduism is different from the religions of the West in its insistence on the illusory nature of the tangible world and the acceptance of the individual's fate in earthly life. Its most basic principles and beliefs are as follows:

1. The nonmaterial, unseen world is the real and permanent one.
2. The universe works as a Great Wheel, with epochs, events, and lives repeating themselves never endingly. The individual dies, but her soul is immaterial and undying; so it reincarnates (*samsara*), being born, living, and dying again and again and again as the Great Wheel turns and its karma determines the next caste into which it will pass.
3. Conceptually, **Karma** (KAR-mah) resembles the ancient Egyptian *maat* (Chapter 3), the notion of order and "rightness" that is built into the structure of the universe. Like *maat*, too, it has a moral dimension: as a soul goes from one life to the next and good and bad deeds committed by an individual in a given life are tallied up. "Justice" is rendered as good karma, which results in birth into a higher caste in the next life; bad karma, into a lower one.
4. One must strive for good karma through following the code of morals prescribed for one's caste, called **dharma** (DAR-mah), as closely as one can. One meaning of dharma is "duty;" one has a "duty" to obey the rules of caste.

The gods *Brahman* (BRAH-mahn: the impersonal life force), *Shiva* (SHEE-vah: the creator and destroyer), and *Vishnu* (VISH-noo: the preserver) dominate an almost endless array of supernatural beings. Most Hindus are devotees of either Shiva or Vishnu as the foremost deity, but they worship them in a huge variety of rituals.

When a person has lived a life in perfect accord with his or her dharma, death will lead to final release from reincarnation and the great Wheel of Life. This release is **Moksha** (MOHK-shah), and it is the end for which all good Hindus live. Moksha is the end of individuality, and the individual soul is submerged into the world-soul represented by Brahman. A classic analogy is a raindrop, which, after many transformations, finds its way back to the ocean that originated it and is dissolved therein.

Vedic (VAY-dik) Hinduism was highly ritualistic and exclusive in nature. The priestly caste—Brahmins—had power by virtue of their mastery of complex ceremonies and their semi-magical knowledge of the gods. Gradually, the more educated people became alienated from this ritual formalism and sought other explanations for the mystery of human fate that allowed them to experience the divine in ways that met their personal, spiritual yearnings in more satisfying ways. Following the fifth century BCE, three new modes of thought gradually became established in India: *Jainism* (JEYE-nism), *Buddhism* (BOO-dism), and *Bhakti* (BAHK-tee) Hinduism. Jainism is limited in its

©Government Museum and National Art Gallery, Madras, India/Lauros-Giraudon/Bridgeman Art Library

SHIVA IN THE DANCE OF LIFE. One of the great trinity of Hindu deities, Shiva is sometimes portrayed as a male, sometimes as a female. Shiva is the god who presides over becoming and destroying, representing the Great Wheel of the universe.

historical appeal. It is less a supernatural religion than a philosophy that emphasizes the sacredness of all life. In modern India, the Jains are a small number of high-caste people representing perhaps 2 percent of the total Indian population.

In contrast, Buddhism is and has long been one of the great religions of the world. It has adherents in all South and East Asian nations, and includes several sects. Buddhism today has the third largest membership of all faiths after Christianity and Islam. Historically, its appeal has lain always in its highly "democratic" nature: anyone who seeks the divine can experience it in the Buddhist nirvana.

Hinduism retained its caste-based, ritual formalism, but gradually a new version, called *Bhakti*, surfaced. Those who resisted conversion to Buddhism and who remained faithful to the old tradition began apprehending the old Hindu gods in different ways. Rather than remaining as mere abstractions or as capricious super beings demanding worship and sacrifice, these gods steadily assumed more personal attributes that made them more approachable. This change allowed individual to seek spiritual fulfillment by devoting (*Bhakti*) themselves to individual gods.

BUDDHISM

Buddhism began in India as an intellectual and emotional revolt against the emptiness of Vedic ritualism. Originally an earthly philosophy that rejected the idea of immortal life and the gods, it was turned into a supernatural belief system soon after the death of its founder, the Buddha.

Siddhartha Gautama (sih-DAR-thah GAW-tah-mah; 563–483 BCE), an Indian aristocrat, was the Buddha, or Enlightened One, and his life is fairly well documented (see the Patterns of Belief box). As a young man, he wandered for several years through the north of India seeking more satisfying answers to the riddle of life. Only after intensive meditation was he finally able to come to terms with himself and human existence. He then became the teacher of a large and growing band of disciples who spread his word gradually throughout the subcontinent and then into East Asia. Buddhism eventually came to be much more important in China and Japan than in India, where it was practically extinct by 1000 CE.

PATTERNS OF BELIEF

The Buddha

Siddhartha Gautama (*c.* 563–483 BCE) was the pampered son of a princely Indian family in the northern borderlands, near present-day Nepal. A member of the *kshatrija* caste of warrior-governors, the young man had every prospect of a conventionally happy and rewarding life as master of a handful of villages. Married young to a local aristocrat like himself, he dedicated himself to hunting, feasting, and revelry—the usual pursuits of his class and time.

But in his late twenties, a notable change occurred. According to a cherished Buddhist legend, on successive excursions he encountered an aged man, then a sick man, and finally a corpse by the roadside. These reminders of the common fate set the young man thinking about the nature of all human life in a (for him) novel way. Finally, he abandoned home, wife, and family, and set out to find his own answers. In the already traditional Indian fashion, he became a wandering ascetic, begging a handful of rice to stay alive while seeking truth in meditation.

Years went by as Siddhartha sought to answer his questions. But for long he found no convincing answers, neither in the extreme self-denial practiced by some nor in the mystical contemplation recommended by others. At last, as he sat under the bodhi tree (the tree of wisdom) through an agonizingly long night of intensive meditation, enlightenment reached him. He arose, confident in his new perceptions, and began to gather around him the beginnings of the community known as Buddhists ("the enlightened ones").

From that point on, the Buddha developed a philosophy that was a revision of the ruling Vedic Hindu faith of India and, in some important ways, a denial of it. By the Buddha's death, the new faith was firmly established, and some version of his teaching would gradually grow to be the majority viewpoint before being extinguished in the land of its birth.

In the original Buddhism, little attention was given to the role of the supernatural powers in human life or to reincarnation. The gods were thought to exist but to have minimal influence on an individual's karma, or fate. Gods could not assist a person to find

RECLINING BUDDHA. A so-called reclining Buddha, one of the frequent colossal representations of the Buddha on the island of Sri Lanka, the center of the Theravada school of the religion.

©Polonnaruwa, Sri Lanka/Bridgeman Art Library

what Hindus call *moksha* and Buddhists *nirvana*, or the state of release from earthly life and its inherent suffering. But in time, this changed among the majority, or Mahayana Buddhists, who came to look on the Buddha and other *bodhisattvas* as divine immortals who could be called on for spiritual assistance.

How would the Buddha have received this development during his own lifetime? The answer is not hard to guess because his rejection of supernatural deities was well known. But it remains true that the very breadth of Buddhist doctrines and practices, which range from simple repetitive chants to the most refined intellectual exercise, has allowed a sizable proportion of humankind to identify with this creed in one or another of its forms.

▶ *Analyze and Interpret*

Contrast the Buddhist emphasis on human beings' capability of finding their own way to serenity with the Zoroastrian convictions you read about in Chapter 4. Which seems more persuasive? Why?

The **Eightfold Path** to spiritual bliss, or **nirvana** (ner-VAH-nah), demands right (or righteous, we would say) ideas, right thought, right speech, right action, right living, right effort, right consciousness, and right meditation. The person who consistently follows these steps is assured of conquering desire and will be, therefore, released from suffering. The heart of the Buddha's message is that suffering and loss in this life are caused by the desire for an illusory power and happiness. Once the individual understands that power is not desirable and that such happiness is self-deception, the temptation to pursue them will gradually disappear. The individual will then find the serenity of soul and the harmony with nature and fellow human beings that constitute true fulfillment.

Buddhism quickly spread among Indians of all backgrounds and regions, carried forth by the Buddha's disciples during his lifetime. What made it so appealing?

Much of the popularity of Buddhism stemmed from its *democracy of spirit*. Everyone, male and female, high and low, was able to discover the Four Truths and follow the Eightfold Path. No one was excluded because of caste restrictions or poverty.

Soon after the Buddha's death, his followers made him into a god with eternal life—a thought foreign to his own teaching. His movement also gradually split into two major branches: *Theravada* and *Mahayana* Buddhism.

Theravada (thayr-rah-VAH-dah, or Hinayana), which means "the narrower vehicle," is the stricter version of the faith. Theravada Buddhism emphasizes the monastic life for both men and women, and takes a rather rigorous approach to what a good person who seeks nirvana must believe. It claims to be the pure form of the Buddha's teachings and rejects the idea of the reincarnation of the Master or other enlightened ones (*bodhisattva;* boh-dih-SAHT-vah) appearing on Earth. It is particularly strong in Sri Lanka and Cambodia.

Mahayana (mah-hah-YAH-nah) Buddhism is much more liberal in its beliefs, viewing the doctrines of the Buddha as a sort of initial step rather than as the ultimate word. The word *Mahayana* means "the larger vehicle," reflecting the belief that there are many ways to salvation. Its faithful believe that there are many buddhas, not just Siddhartha Gautama, and that many more will appear. Monastic life is a good thing for those who can assume it, but most Mahayana Buddhists will never do so and do not feel themselves disadvantaged thereby. Mahayana adherents far outnumber the others and are found in Vietnam, China, Japan, and Korea.

DAILY LIFE AND THE POSITION OF WOMEN

The almost entirely self-governing Indian villagers led lives controlled by the seasons, caste, and local tradition, punctuated by the feast days of the deities. It was not, so far as we can see, a bitterly impoverished existence.

The abject rural misery often experienced in India's modern history is a relatively recent phenomenon—usually the product of a shortage of agricultural land—and until the last two or three centuries, shortages were almost unknown or limited to small areas. Although the material conditions of village life could not have been high by today's standards, the natives and the Aryan invaders had extensive areas of both irrigable and undeveloped land suitable to agriculture in various forms, and they brought these lands into production steadily for a millennium. When a shortage did threaten the food supply of large numbers or was seen as a menace, emigration to another, less crowded area was the usual, effective solution. As in the Near East, Indian tradition regarding the relative status of women shows an initial period of near equality or possibly matriarchy. But with the arrival of the Aryan nomads, female prestige began a descent that continued in the Vedic Hindu era. **Manu,** the legendary lawgiver, established the proper relation between the sexes once and for all (see box). Gradually, the ritual of widows' suicide (*sati:* SAH-tee) and isolation

©Government Museum and National Art Gallery, Madras, India/Lauros/Giraudon-Bridgeman Art Library

KALI. The Indian goddess of destruction was frequently portrayed in a sexual context, but in this stone representation (15th century CE) from south India, she takes a Buddha-like position while extending her four arms with traditional household implements.

from all nonfamily males (*purdah*; PURR-dah) became established. The female's fundamental dharma in all castes was to obey and serve her husband and her sons.

Interestingly, in conjunction with this subordination went an emphasis on female sexuality. The female was often seen as being more sexually potent than the male.

It is now sometimes argued that this attitude arose from men's fears about "the devouring woman," represented by the ferocious goddess of destruction, Kali (KAH-lee). Some equivalent of the woman who is sexually insatiable and physically overpowering is found in several ancient religions. It is notably absent from those that arose during a period of female predominance (matriarchy) or when the sexes were more or less equal in public life.

THE MAURYAN DYNASTY

For a century and a half after the Buddha's death, the philosophy he founded gained adherents steadily but remained a distinctly minority view in a land of Hindu believers. In the 330s BCE, however, the invasion of India by Alexander the Great (see Chapter 7) not only brought the first direct contact with Western ideas and art forms but also enabled a brief period of political unity under the Mauryan (MOH-ree-yan) Dynasty, which moved into the vacuum left by Alexander's retreat. The founder of this first historical dynasty in India was Chandragupta Maurya (chan-drah-GUP-tah MOH-ree-yah), who succeeded in seizing supreme powers in northwestern India upon the withdrawal of the Greeks. The rule of the dynasty was brief but important for India's future. The third and greatest of the Mauryan rulers, **Ashoka** (ah-SHOH-kah; 269–232 BCE), was the outstanding Indian emperor of pre-modern times, admired by all Indians as the founding spirit of Indian unity and nationhood.

Ashoka's significance stems in large part from his role in spreading the Buddhist faith in India, thereby initiating the tradition of mutual tolerance between religions that is (or used to be) one of the subcontinent's cultural boasts. After a series of successful wars 'against the Mauryans' neighbors and rivals, Ashoka was shocked by the bloodshed at the battle of Kalinga at the midpoint of his reign. Influenced by Buddhist monks, the king became a devout Buddhist and pacifist. The last twenty years of his reign were marked by unprecedented internal prosperity and external peace, thanks mostly to the support he and his Buddhist advisors gave to trade. The inscriptions enunciating his decrees were placed on stone pillars scattered far and wide over his realm, and some of them survive today as the first examples of Indian written language. They, and the accounts of a few foreign travelers, are the means by which we know anything of Indian government in this early epoch.

After Ashoka's death, his weak successors soon gave up what he had gained, both in defense against invasion and in internal stability. New waves of nomadic horsemen entered India through the gateway to Central Asia, the Khyber Pass (see Map 5.1). Most of them soon enough became sedentary in habit, adopted Indian civilization, and embraced the Buddhist faith. But the political unity established by the Mauryan rulers disintegrated. Four centuries passed before the Gupta Dynasty could reestablish it in the 300s CE.

TRADE AND THE SPREAD OF BUDDHISM

Most of India's land connections with the outer world have been northwestward, across the same routes through the passes of Afghanistan and the Hindu Kush mountains that invaders followed again and again. From the northwest came the Aryans, then the Greco-Macedonians under Alexander, then the Persians in the early centuries CE, and eventually the Turks and Afghani Muslims. Most of these intruders, even the course horsemen from the Asian steppe, soon adopted settled habits and enriched India's Hindu-Buddhist culture in one way or another.

In contrast, early India had remarkably little cultural interchange with China, its sophisticated and powerful neighbor to the northeast. The main reason for this lack of contact was that the mountains ringing India to the north provided no easy passages to the east. There were, however, some exceptions to this mutual lack of contact. By far the most significant one was the export of the Buddhist faith from India to China. In the first century CE, Buddhist merchants, drawn by the lucrative trade that passed along the Silk Road linking Han China and the Roman Empire, braved the difficult passages through the northern mountain ranges that took them to Central Asia. There, in its Mahayana form, the new doctrine won converts among

©Borromeo/Art Resource, NY

THE LIONS OF SARNATH. Sarnath was the site where Siddhartha Gautama first preached. The Lions of Sarnath were created by King Ashoka to symbolize the proclamation of Buddhism to the world. The modern republic of India has adopted the lions as the official symbol of state.

the tribespeople who controlled the east-west corridors. From the caravan centers, the new religion was conveyed eastward and took root in China, where it entered deeply into Chinese cultural life, blending the new ideas with traditional Confucian practice and ethics (see Chapter 16).

India's commercial and cultural preponderance in regions that made up the (appropriately named) Indian Ocean domain was even weightier than in central and eastern Asia. Again, it was Ashoka's conversion that helped India position itself in the very center of this arena of continents. The reason lay in the fact that, while Hindu priests frowned on dealings with foreigners, Buddhists taught that trade contributed to everyone's welfare. Ashoka and his Buddhist advisors encouraged the extension of trade along sea-lanes to Southeast Asia, a development aided by two other major advances. The first was the Mauryan conquest of the Ganges River port of Tamluk, which faced the Bay of Bengal. The other, more crucial, development

was the discovery of the prevailing directions of the Indian Ocean's monsoon winds.

From June to September, the winds blew from the southwest to the northeast; then from November to March they shifted to the opposite direction. This realization enabled Indian merchants to complete roundtrip voyages either to eastern or western destinations in a year or less, and allowed traders to develop routing strategies that turned the Indian Ocean into the center of a vast mercantile world that, when combined later with the Silk Road, placed the Indian Ocean at the southern end of an Asian commercial nexus that was the largest in the world prior to the advent of the modern era. Besides trade goods, along the strands of this web of interconnectedness passed people and ideas that helped shape whole civilizations. Thus Indian merchants introduced Southeast Asia to Buddhism, and once there it became as integral to its civilization as in China (see Chapter 17).

SUMMARY

SETTLED LIFE IS now known to have emerged in India much earlier than previously believed. By 2500 BCE, people of the Indus River valley had developed irrigated fields and good-sized towns that traded widely with both the surrounding villagers and distant neighbors to the west. These towns seem to have been governed by a priesthood, but information on their history is still sparse. The civilization was already in decline, possibly from natural causes, when it fell to Aryan nomads, who instituted the beginnings of the caste system.

In the thousand years after the Aryan conquest—the Vedic Epoch (1500–500 BCE)—the Hindu religion was gradually constructed from a combination of Aryan beliefs and the Indus Valley faith. When this ritualistic Hinduism

was challenged by other, more ethically conscious doctrines such as Buddhism and Jainism, it gave way.

Buddhism, in particular, became an international religion and philosophy, as several variants took root throughout East and Southeast Asia through India's growing trade networks.

Although arts and sciences flourished, the cultural and political unity of India was only sporadically enforced by a strong central government. Many invasions from the northwest kept India in a frequent state of political fragmentation. Religious belief, rather than government, was the cement that held its people together and gave the basis for their consciousness of being a nation.

▶ *Identification Terms*

Test your knowledge of this chapter's key concepts by defining the following terms. If you can't recall the meaning of certain terms, refresh your memory by looking up the boldfaced term in the chapter, turning to the Glossary at

the end of the book, or working with the flashcards that are available on the *World Civilizations* Companion Website: **academic.cengage.com/adler**

Aryans	dharma	Mahayana	Rigveda
Ashoka	Eightfold Path	Manu	Siddhartha Gautama
Brahmin	Indus Valley civilization	moksha	Theravada
caste	karma	nirvana	Vedas

▶ *Test Your Knowledge*

Test your knowledge of this chapter by answering the following questions. Complete answers appear at the end of the book. You may find even more quiz questions in CengageNOW and on the *World Civilizations* Companion Website: **academic.cengage.com/adler**

1. The excavation of Mohenjo-Daro indicates that India's earliest civilization
   a. had a strong central government.
   b. was governed by merchants.
   c. had little if any commercial contacts with other civilized lands.
   d. had no dependence on irrigation agriculture.
   e. flourished despite the absence of any large building projects.

2. The evolution of Indian castes came about because of
   a. economic necessities.
   b. the application of Vedic beliefs to Indian realities.
   c. the teachings of the Buddhist monks.
   d. climate and geography.
   e. the need for major social reforms.

3. In Indian society after the Aryan conquest, the highest social group was that of the
   a. priests.
   b. warriors.
   c. tillers of the soil.
   d. educated.
   e. vaishya.

4. The Laws of Manu show a society in which
   a. there were no essential differences between male and female.
   b. there was a strong sense of social justice.
   c. children were not valued.
   d. women were considered a source of temptation.
   e. slaves were afforded some measure of protection.

5. *Karma* is a Sanskrit word meaning
   a. the soul.
   b. release from earthly cycles.
   c. the uppermost caste in Hindu society.
   d. the tally of good and bad acts in a person's life.
   e. the code of morals for one's caste.

6. Which of the following religions of India emphasizes above all the sacred nature of all life?
   a. Jainism
   b. Buddhism
   c. Hinduism
   d. Mithraism
   e. Zoroastrianism

7. The Buddha taught all but which one of the following?
   a. All persons are destined for immortal happiness in an afterlife.
   b. Sorrow is generated by desire.
   c. Every individual is capable of attaining nirvana.
   d. Gods are of little or no significance in attaining true happiness.
   e. Nirvana is achieved by successfully following the Noble Eightfold Path.

8. The first true dynasty in India was founded by
   a. Ashoka.
   b. Manu.
   c. Chandragupta Maurya.
   d. Kautilya.
   e. Siddhartha Gautama.

9. Women's status in India could best be described as
   a. improving during the Vedic Period.
   b. developing a true matriarchy as time passed.
   c. offering more choices to women of higher caste.
   d. supporting the role of mother, but rejecting the sexual side of marriage.
   e. entering into a period of decline after the Aryan invasion.

10. The most significant contribution of India to world history is probably
    a. the model of good government given by Ashoka.
    b. the development of higher mathematics.
    c. the passing of Buddhism to China.
    d. the spiritual precepts of the Vedas.
    e. its model of respect for women.

Enter *CengageNOW* using the access card that is available with this text. *CengageNOW* will assist you in understanding the content in this chapter with lesson plans generated for your needs and provide you with a connection to the *Wadsworth World History Resource Center* (see description at right for details).

 **World History Resource Center**

Enter the Resource Center using either your *CengageNOW* access card or your standalone access card for the *Wadsworth World History Resource Center*. Organized by topic, this website includes quizzes; images; over 350 primary source documents; interactive simulations, maps, and timelines; movie explorations; and a wealth of other resources. You can read the following documents, and many more, at the *Wadsworth World History Resource Center:*

Laws of Manu

*The people of our race were created by Heaven
Having from the beginning distinctions and rules
Our people cling to customs
And what they admire is seemly behavior.*
—The Zhou Book of Songs

6 ANCIENT CHINA TO 500 BCE

EARLIEST CHINA: THE SHANG DYNASTY
Writing ◆ Art and Architecture

THE ZHOU DYNASTY
Culture and Daily Life Under the Zhou ◆ Metals, Salt, and Silk

CONFUCIUS AND THE CONFUCIAN PHILOSOPHY

RIVALS TO CONFUCIUS
Daoism ◆ Legalism

THE MOST STABLE AND in many ways the most successful civilization that history has known began in China in the second millennium BCE. It continued in its essentials through many changes in political leadership, meanwhile subjecting an enormous area and many different peoples to "the Chinese way." The Chinese educated classes, who considered themselves the hub of the universe, formed the most cohesive ruling group the world has ever seen. They combined scholarship and artistic sensitivity with great administrative abilities. Much of China's permanent culture was already firmly established by about 500 BCE, and it would change only very slowly.

EARLIEST CHINA: THE SHANG DYNASTY

Of all the ancient civilizations, China was the most isolated from outside influences, even more so than Egypt. Both agriculture and metalworking apparently originated independently in China. No connections with either Indian or Mesopotamian arts and sciences are known until much later, after the civilization along the Yellow and Yangtze Rivers had developed its own characteristics and technology. The exact time and place in which agriculture first appeared in the Far East is disputable. Yet once in place, Chinese civilization had features that were typical of other early civilizations we have encountered: It rested on an agrarian foundation (Chapter 1); it produced a long series of dynastic monarchies; and, bordered by deserts and steppe lands, it endured episodic warfare and invasion from nomadic, Turco-Mongolian tribespeople who roamed the west and northwest.

The Chinese heartland was divided between the dry northern flatlands and the better-watered southern valleys. Late Paleolithic Chinese roamed the grasslands of the great Northern Plain, gathering wild varieties of millet; around

7000–6000 BCE, they began settling in villages along the Yellow River, elevating their villages above the flood plain on rammed earth platforms and surrounding them with earthen walls. They developed terracing and irrigation techniques to grow millet, barley, soy, and hemp in the yellow, wind-blown soils called *loess* (LOW-us). It was this region that became the cradle of Chinese civilization. However, another river would play almost as important a role in China's later history: the Yangtze (YAHNG-tzuh). This great stream is much tamer than the Yellow and runs far to the south through a warmer and wetter landscape. Agriculture actually might have appeared south of the Yangtze first, where non-Chinese peoples hunted pigs and gathered wild varieties of rice that grew in swamplands along the river. Between 10,000 and 7000 BCE, settled farm life appeared, and it became the center of China's wet rice culture. Both regions gave rise to a number of competing Neolithic civilizations. But eventually, the northern Chinese conquered the south, and the rice of the Yangtze became even more important to the their food supply than the millet of the Yellow River drainage.

Unlike the floods of the Nile, the Yellow River's floods were tremendously damaging and had to be controlled by extensive levees, painfully erected and maintained. Perhaps, as in other early civilizations, it was this need to control the floods and to coordinate the labor of thousands in vast construction projects that contributed most toward political unification. The worship of clan ancestors and nature spirits seems to have been an early feature of Chinese religion. And it was this, particularly the need for the ritual appeasement of the ancestors of landowning senior lineages, that assured that unification and dynastic rule went hand in hand in Neolithic and Bronze Age China.

Slightly before the Aryan invaders arrived in the Indus Valley, around 1600 BCE, several of the Neolithic cultures along the central course of the Yellow River were drawn into an organized state for the first time (see Map 6.1 inset). This state was the product of military conquest by a Bronze Age people who were ruled by a dynastic monarchy called *the Shang*. The **Shang Dynasty** replaced the villagers' earlier political overseers, and its rise appears to have been associated with two important innovations: bronze casting and writing. Another dynasty, the Hsia (shah), which is mentioned in the ancient histories as the first of the Chinese ruling groups, may have preceded the Shang Dynasty. Like the Shang, the existence of the Hsia has recently been confirmed by archaeological evidence, but our knowledge of the Hsia is still in a beginning stage.

Most of what we know of ancient China comes from archaeology rather than from history, because Shang writings were limited. Since the 1920s, Chinese and foreign archaeologists have been excavating many rich grave sites. From the elaborate order followed by the tomb remains and their contents, we can infer that Shang society was strictly hierarchical. At the top was a powerful king with his warrior court. War was commonplace, and warriors were favored in every way, much as in feudal Europe.

On a level below the warriors were many skilled artisans and a growing class of small traders in the towns. In the countryside lived the great majority, the peasants in their villages. Scholars are not sure to what degree the early Chinese shared a common religion in which all participated or whether belief in the afterlife was commonplace.

Being agrarian, the early Chinese believed in deities and ancestor spirits who controlled natural forces. Scholars know precious little about the actual gods in whom the peasant classes believed and about their religious activities, but there was a public cult of the royal ancestors. One of the king's most important functions was divining their will and controlling them to the benefit of all. To accomplish this, they used *oracle bones*, which provide us with some of the earliest examples of Chinese writing. Questions were written on tortoise shells or the shoulder bones of sheep, and then a heated rod was applied to produce cracks. Priests interpreted their patterns as answers.

Several fundamental aspects of Chinese life were already visible in the Shang Epoch:

◆ *The supreme importance of the family.* More than any other culture, the Chinese rely on the family to serve as a model for public life and the source of all private virtue.
◆ *The reverence shown to ancestors and the aged by the young.* The Chinese believe that experience is far more important than theory and that the young must learn from the aged if harmony is to be preserved and progress achieved.
◆ *The emphasis on this world.* No other civilization of early times was so *secular* in orientation. Although the emperor was titled Son of Heaven, China never had a priestly caste, and the government usually subordinated religious affairs to earthly, practical tasks.
◆ *The importance of education, particularly literacy.* No other culture has made the ability to read and write so critical for success. The ancient Chinese written language was extremely complex (it has since been simplified). Years of hard study were required to master it, but once acquired, it opened the doors to both wealth and power.

In the eleventh century BCE, the Shang rulers seem to have faced internal conflicts that weakened the dynasty. Somewhat later they fell to the **Zhou** (Choh) **Dynasty,** a related but alien group from farther west. The Zhou would be the most enduring of all the Chinese ruling dynasties.

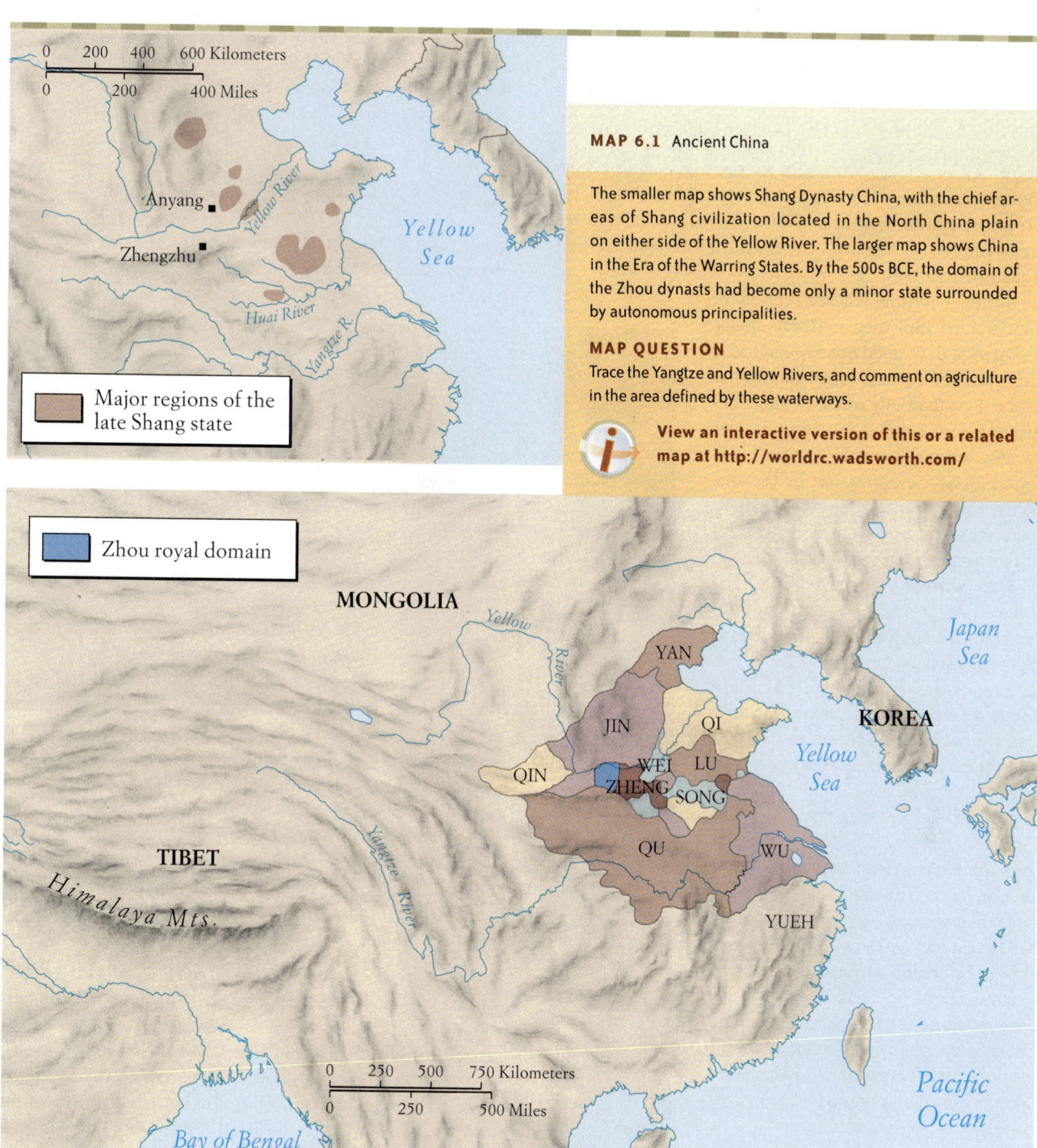

MAP 6.1 Ancient China

The smaller map shows Shang Dynasty China, with the chief areas of Shang civilization located in the North China plain on either side of the Yellow River. The larger map shows China in the Era of the Warring States. By the 500s BCE, the domain of the Zhou dynasts had become only a minor state surrounded by autonomous principalities.

MAP QUESTION
Trace the Yangtze and Yellow Rivers, and comment on agriculture in the area defined by these waterways.

View an interactive version of this or a related map at http://worldrc.wadsworth.com/

Writing

The written language was critically important in China. Its beginnings date to about 1500 BCE, and it is still in essentially the same format today. How did it differ from other written languages, and how did it develop (apparently without input from non-Chinese sources)?

Like most languages, written Chinese was originally pictographic, but it soon developed a huge vocabulary of signs that had no picture equivalents and were not at all related to the spoken word (that is, they were not alphabetic). These characters are called *logographs*, or "words in signs." Chinese spoken language is monosyllabic (each word has but one syllable), and a single logograph can take the place of as many as several words in other languages, conveying whole descriptions or actions in one sign. Some logographs were derived from certain common pictorial roots, but others were not connected in any way, which made learning them difficult. All in all, students had to memorize about 5,000 logographs to be considered literate. Understandably, literacy was rare, and those who knew how to read and write entered a kind of elite club that carried tremendous prestige.

Although writing emerged considerably later in China than in Mesopotamia or Egypt, it developed quickly and had a richer vocabulary and more conceptual refinement than any other written language before the first century CE. The earliest writing beyond pictography is found on oracle bones, but by the end of the Shang Period, about 1100 BCE, histories and stories were being written, and some have been preserved.

The written language was immensely important in unifying the groups and subgroups who came to call themselves Chinese. China has dozens of spoken dialects, which are mutually unintelligible, but it has only one way of writing, which can be understood by all who can read.

Art and Architecture

The greatest artistic achievement of the ancient Chinese was undoubtedly their bronze work. Craftsmen in the late Shang and early Zhou periods turned out drinking cups, vases, wine vessels, brooches, and medallions, whose technical excellence and artistic grace were stunning. Metal technology in general was advanced in early China. Besides bronze, cast iron and copper were widely used for both tools and weaponry.

The Shang buildings that have been partially unearthed by modern archaeologists are impressive in both size and design. The upper class built large palaces and strong forts around towns such as Anyang and Zhengzhou (chung-choh) in the middle reaches of the Yellow River plain. The distinctive Chinese architectural style, with pagoda-type

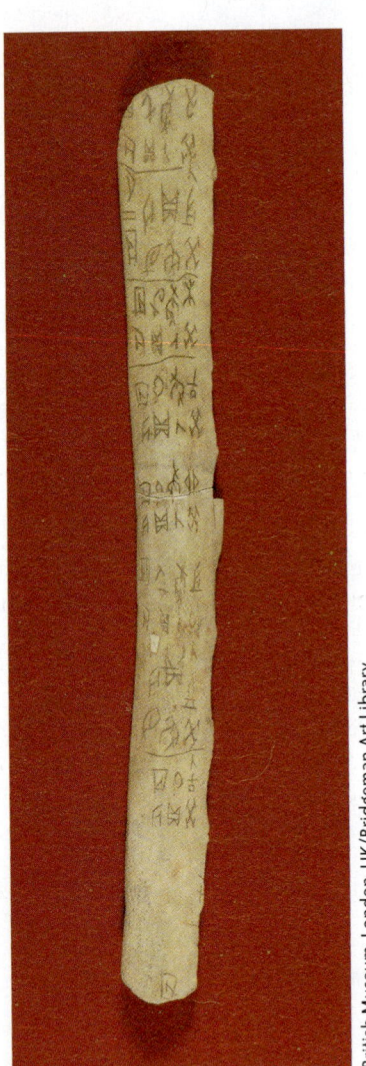

British Museum, London, UK/Bridgeman Art Library

ORACLE BONE. On the flat surface of bones such as this, Shang sages incised the earliest surviving examples of Chinese ideographs. The messages are questions addressed to the gods, and the sages read the answers by examining the patterns of cracks in the bones after hot irons had been pressed against them.

roof lines and diminishing upper stories, was developed at this time, although it was carried out much more elaborately later. Most of the art forms of modern China had their roots in very early times.

THE ZHOU DYNASTY

From time to time, pastoralist groups from the north or west succeeded in conquering China's ruling warlords and seating their own tribal leaders in power. The Zhou were the first of a series of ruling dynasties of nomadic origins that came from China's borderlands to the west.

During the 700 years that they ruled, at least in name, the Zhou greatly extended China's borders. Where the Shang had been content to rule a relatively restricted segment of north-central China on either side of the Yellow River, the Zhou reached out almost to the sea in the east and well into Inner Mongolia in the west. We know much more about the Zhou Era than the Shang because an extensive literature survives. Much history was written, and records of all types from tax rolls to lists of imports and exports have been found. The dynasty falls into two distinct phases: the unified empire, from about 1100 to about 750 BCE, and the Later Zhou, from about 750 to about 400 BCE. The earlier period was the more important. The Later Zhou Dynasty experienced a series of constant provincial revolts until, finally, the central government broke down altogether (see Map 6.1).

One of the novelties of the Zhou Period was the idea of the **mandate of heaven.** As did most tribespeople who originated in the west, the Zhou worshipped sky gods, principally one named *Tian.* So, to justify their forcible overthrow of the Shang, the first Zhou rulers developed the idea that "heaven"—that is, the supernatural deities who oversaw all life—gave the chosen earthly ruler a mandate, or vote of confidence. As long as he ruled well and justly, he retained the mandate, but it would be taken from him if he betrayed the deities' trust. A ruler who failed to protect his people from invaders or failed to contain internal revolt had betrayed this trust. Thus, if a Chinese ruler fell to superior force or a successful conspiracy, it was a sign that he had "lost the mandate" and should be replaced. This marvelously self-serving theory (it was used to justify innumerable conspiracies and rebellions) was to be highly influential in Chinese history.

The first Zhou kings were powerful rulers who depended mainly on their swords. The royal court employed hundreds of skilled administrators, and we see the faint beginning of a professional bureaucracy in the Zhou Era. China led the world in this development, as in so many others. As the centuries passed, however, power slipped from the monarch's hand and a feudal society developed, as the kings delegated more and more of their military and administrative duties to local aristocrats. These men stood to gain from the acquisition of new territory, and they did so at every chance. As a result, China expanded, but at the same time the control of the royal government weakened.

By the 500s, the local aristocrats were in command of much of the empire, and by 400, the central power had broken down completely—one of the few times that has happened in China.

Culture and Daily Life Under the Zhou

Although the Zhou rulers eventually failed to keep the nation together, their era saw great advances in every area of arts and crafts. Silkworm cultivation and the weaving of silk have been demonstrated to be an important part of Shang and Zhou culture and trade with foreign states. The famous Silk Road, the caravan route to the Near East and the Black Sea, did not yet exist, but regional trade did and goods flowed between China and its western neighbors. Along China's borders, there was great demand for products like metal and jade wares, salt, and above all, silk that issued from the shops of China's artisans. In exchange for these, the Chinese aristocracy prized the sturdy horses supplied by nomads who wandered the Central Asian steppes.

With China's incessant need to defend itself against the nomads on its borders, the importation of the war chariot from Western Asia led to a technical breakthrough of the first rank: a harness or collar that allowed the horse to pull with the full strength of its shoulders and body without choking. This type of harness transformed the value of horses, not only in warfare but also as beasts of burden. Only much later did other civilizations recognize and copy this fundamental change.

As for living standards in Zhou China, the evidence we have suggests that peasants were moderately prosperous and rarely enslaved at this time. Although their life was undoubtedly difficult, it was not miserable. Zhou peasants were in more or less the same economic situation as Egyptian peasants: they were sharecropping tenants on

©China Newsphoto/Reuters/Corbis

BATTLE CHARIOT. Chariots were invented in western Asia, but came into use in China during the Shang period, greatly revolutionizing warfare. Chinese archaeologists recently excavated burials at Anyang that included both chariots and horses.

the aristocracy's land, with some rights, and at least in the early Zhou years were usually protected from the worst excesses of grasping landlords by a powerful and respected government.

In the literary arts, many of the classics that have been taught to Chinese children through the centuries originated in the Zhou era. The earliest surviving books stem from the 800s BCE, much earlier than any from other civilized centers. They were written either on strips of specially prepared bamboo, strung together with silken cord, or on silk scrolls. Professional historians, employed by the court, wrote chronicles of the rulers and their achievements. Poetry made its first appearance in Chinese letters during the early Zhou, beginning a tradition of sensitive, perceptive nature poetry that continues to the present day. The revered collection called *The Book of Songs* was produced by one or several hands at this period, remaining a mainstay of Chinese education ever since. Calligraphy also began at this time, and officials were expected to master this art form as a qualification for office.

Metals, Salt, and Silk

Agriculture was the foundation of royal authority in China, but as elsewhere, manufacturing and trade played important supporting roles. There was no long-distance overland or oceanic trade during the Bronze Age and later—those materialized during the Qin and Han periods (Chapter 16)—but the governments of the Shang and Zhou kings tightly regulated or monopolized the manufacture of certain high-demand rare goods. Trade in these items took place, throughout the territories over which their rule

©Giraudon/Art Resource, NY

BRONZE ELEPHANT. The form of bronze casting known as *cir perdue* (lost wax) was widely used by the Zhou Dynasty artists. But using clay molds that locked tightly together before the liquid metal was poured into them produced the finest work. This enabled them to achieve a particularly fine detailing of the surface, as seen here.

©Eastern Asian Collection, Brandenburg, Berlin, Germany/Bridgeman Art Library

BRONZE WARE. Bronze was rare and treated virtually as a precious metal during Shang and early Zhou times. However, the kings employed skilled craftspeople at their courts who could provide a wide range of implements, such as this exquisite tripod cooking vessel.

extended and even beyond to the lands and peoples of the north and northwest.

Although bronze making had existed for at least 3,500 years before 700 BCE, until then bronze was still rare enough that for most practical applications China remained a Neolithic society. Early dynasties like the Shang, the Zhou, and the Qin (Chin) held sway because they monopolized warfare and public religion. They reached this position by strictly controlling access to the accoutrements of warfare and public ritual, namely weapons, particularly bronze weapons, and ritual objects (see the battle chariot and bronze artifacts). Royal workshops turned out all manner of weaponry, vessels, and statues, and reached an apex of perfection in Shang times. Much of it was produced using the lost wax method of casting into molds, a method that allowed greater production and more delicacy of form and design than in the West, where hammering and forging methods were employed.

Starting in the sixth century BCE, iron came into common use for tools and utensils, as well as weapons. Iron making produced stronger materials than bronze, but more importantly, once perfected, iron could be produced in far greater quantities than bronze and could be used to for tools as well as sacred objects and weapons. The iron plowshare opened up huge areas of northern and central China to agriculture, enabling unprecedented growth, perhaps 400 percent, of both the economy and the population during the Zhou Era.

Salt is so basic to modern diets that it is hard to think of it as a valued commodity—which it was in the ancient world. The high demand for salt made it an obvious target for government control and an important source of revenue for the emperors, who needed the income to support their large armies; there have been estimates that 50–80 percent of the emperors' purses derived from the salt monopoly. Through China's long run of dynastic rulers, there were periods when the monopoly on salt and metals was relaxed, but so fundamental were these goods to royal authority that these rare exceptions proved the rule.

Yet, as central as was the place occupied by salt and iron in its political economy, it is silk that comes to mind when thinking of imperial China. Woodcarvings of silkworms and weaving apparatus have turned up in excavations of Chinese Neolithic sites, suggesting that the craft had

©SEF/Art Resource, NY

SILK: A WOMAN'S BUSINESS. Throughout history, certain crafts have tended to be gender-related. Weaving was one of these, and as one of China's most important crafts, silk weaving was women's work, as shown in this Ming period vase.

production and population, plus the introduction of patterned weaving—no doubt contributed to expanded trade. Demand for silk also increased noticeably when new uses were found for silk during late Zhou times. For the first time, scribes and artists found it to be a useful medium for writing and painting, while the government officials discovered it was useful as currency to purchase war horses from nomadic tribespeople and to pay them bribes when demanded. Kings collected taxes in the form of silk textiles and paid their officials with it. There was little state control over silk production before 221 BCE, but in many respects the steadily rising levels of useful applications, demand, and trade in silk that occurred after 1000 BCE created opportunities later emperors like Shi Huangdi or Wudi were quick to use to their advantage.

CONFUCIUS AND THE CONFUCIAN PHILOSOPHY

China's greatest single cultural force, the historical figure Kung Fu-tzu (551–479 BCE), or **Confucius** (con-FYOO-shus), appeared toward the end of the Zhou Era. For twenty centuries, Confucius was the most respected name in China, the molder of Chinese patterns of education, and the authority on what a true Chinese should and should not do. (See his biography in the Law and Government box.)

Confucius's interests were practical, centered on the hierarchy of ethical and political relations between individuals, and especially between the citizenry and the governor. The great model for Confucius's politics was the Chinese family.

Among the Chinese, the *yin-yang principles* identified the female as the passive element and the male as the active, creative one. Although all civilizations we have thus far studied gave pride of place to the father, none applied this principle so systematically as the Chinese. In ancient China, children and grandchildren accorded the father absolute obedience, whereas the mother supposedly never raised her voice in contradiction to her husband. A widow owed the same obedience to her father and sons. This arrangement remained the ideal in modern China before the communist takeover, although one can question whether it was a reality. (There is no scarcity of reports of independent Chinese wives within the four walls of the home in modern times.) But without a doubt, the principle of male superiority and female inferiority was adhered to and implemented systematically throughout Chinese history. For Confucius, whose teachings formed the basis of Chinese education for 2,300 years, women scarcely existed. He

prehistoric beginnings. From its inception, it was a craft specifically associated with women: most silk deities were female, for example, and China's queens had the responsibility for successfully enacting state procedures in honor of the goddess of silk weaving. The critical importance of silk weaving is indicated by the fact that its ritual honors were carried out on the state level. Furthermore, silk itself played a critical role in all public rituals. In conjunction with bronze and jade objects, it was a ubiquitous, key element of royal ancestral offerings.

More commonly, of course, silk was prized for its usefulness and beauty. It was an enormously strong, tough fabric that was superior to all others in its ability to hold dyes, so it far outshone all fabrics in popularity wherever it came to the attention of local elites. No Silk Road existed until imperial times (beginning with the First Emperor, Shi Huangdi; see Chap. 16), but already by 1000 BCE some trade existed with peoples to the west. By 500 BCE Central Asian elites were importing silk from China. Developments during the Eastern Zhou period—iron making, dramatically increased agricultural

LAW AND GOVERNMENT

Confucius (551–479 BCE)

The most revered of all Chinese statesmen and philosophers was Master Kung, or Kung Fu-tzu, known in the West as Confucius. As a lasting influence on a nation, he has no equal in world history. During his long lifetime, he acquired a devoted group of followers who gave educated Chinese their moral and ethical landmarks for 2,000 years. Confucianism has, of course, evolved considerably over the centuries, and no one now knows precisely what the Master's original thoughts may have been. But by reading what his disciples said about him and about their own understanding of his message, we can appreciate his greatness and his importance in the life of the Chinese people. He established a tradition of cultural values that has changed, not in its essentials, but in its degree of acceptance.

Confucius was born into an impoverished but aristocratic family in the state of Lu at the time when the Zhou Empire was falling apart and the Era of the Warring States was beginning. Given a good education, the young man set out to find a suitable place for himself in the world. His ambition was to acquire a post in the government of his home state, which would allow him to exert a real influence for good and to assist the princely ruler in providing wise and benevolent rule.

Frustrated by the intrigues of his rivals in Lu, where he briefly obtained a post in the ministry of justice, Confucius was forced to seek a position elsewhere. But in the neighboring states, too, he was disappointed in his quest, never securing more than minor and temporary positions before running afoul of backbiting competitors or speaking his mind when that was a dangerous thing to do. He had to return to Lu to earn his living as a teacher, and for the rest of his life he subsisted modestly on the tuition fees of his wealthier students.

Confucius accepted this fate with difficulty. For many years he continued to hope for appointment as an adviser to the prince and thus to translate his beliefs into government policy. Only gradually did he realize that by his teaching he could have more influence on the fate of his people than he might ever attain as a minister to a trivial and corrupt ruler. By the end of his life, his fame had already reached much of China's small educated class, and his students were going out to found schools of their own, reflecting the principles the Master had taught them.

Confucius taught that all human affairs, public and private, were structured by the Five Relationships: father and son,

PORTRAIT OF CONFUCIUS. This undated illustration, much like other depictions of Confucius after his death, was based on a relief from the stela in the Pei Lin de Sigan-fou.

©FPG/Getty Images

husband and wife, elder and younger brother, ruler and official, and friend and friend. The fact that three of these relationships are within the family circle shows the Confucian emphasis on the family. He believed it to be the model and building block of all other social or political arrangements. This emphasis continues in Chinese life to this day.

Confucius was not so much an original thinker as a great summarizer and reformulator of truths already embraced by his people. He did not attempt a complete philosophical system and was not at all interested in theology or what is now called *metaphysics*. Rather, his focus was always on the relation of human being to human being, and especially on the relation of governor to governed. He was an eminently secular thinker, and this tradition, too, has continued among educated Chinese to the present.

Two of the sayings attributed to him in the collection of his sayings called the *Analects* give the flavor of his teaching:

Tsi-guang [a disciple] asked about government.

Confucius said: "Sufficient food, sufficient armament, and sufficient confidence of the people are the necessities." "Forced to give up one, which would you abandon first?" "I would abandon armament." "Forced to give up one of the remaining two, which would you abandon?" "I would abandon food. There has always been death from famine, but no state can exist without the confidence of its people."

The Master always emphasized the necessity of the ruler setting a good example:

Replying to Chi Gang-tsi who had asked him about the nature of good government, Confucius said, "To govern is to rectify. If you lead the people by virtue of rectifying yourself, who will dare not be rectified by you?"

▶ Analyze and Interpret

After a generation of contemptuous treatment and proscription, the Chinese communist government has recently allowed the reintroduction of Confucian teaching and commentary in the schools. Why do you think this has happened? Do you think Confucius has anything to say to modern people?

You can read more from the Analects at the *Wadsworth World History Resource Center*.

mentions them rarely and only in the context of male activity. As late as the seventeenth century, Chinese philosophers debated whether the female was fully human.

In Confucius's view, the state should be like a harmonious family: the father was the undisputed head, each person had his or her special rights and duties, and the wisdom of the aged guided the young. The oldest male was responsible for protecting and guiding the others, who owed him absolute obedience even when he appeared to be wrong.

Confucius insisted on *gentility*—that is, courtesy, justice, and moderation—as the chief virtue of the public man. He taught that the rich and the strong should feel a sense of obligation toward the poor and the weak. A gentleman was made, not born. An aristocrat might not be a gentleman, whereas a lowborn person could learn to be one. The proper calling of a gentleman was government. He should advise the ruler and see to it that government policies were fair and promoted the general welfare. A ruler who followed the advice of his gentlemanly counselors would surely retain the mandate of heaven.

This philosophy of public service by scholarly, virtuous officials was to have enormous influence on China. Rulers came to be judged according to whether they used the Confucian prescriptions for good government. A corps of officials educated on Confucian principles, subscribing to his values, and believing him to be the Great Teacher came into existence. These *shi*, or **mandarins** (MAN-dah-rihns), as the West later called them, were the actual governing class of China for 2,000 years.

An unfortunate result of this system was the tendency of most rulers to interpret Confucian moderation and distrust of violence as resistance to needed change. The rulers naturally tended to see, in Confucius's admonition that the state should resemble a well-run family, a condemnation of revolt for any reason. In time, many of the Confucian-trained bureaucrats not only agreed but also came to believe that the status quo was the only natural and proper way of doing things. The insistence that harmony was the chief goal of politics and social policy sometimes was twisted into an excuse for stagnation. Also, like many Chinese, Confucius had a low opinion of people who lived by trade, so the Confucian notion of the ideal society placed merchants at the bottom of the social ladder. Both of these led to contempt for the new, a fear of change, however necessary, and a distrust of foreigners. From time to time in China's long history, these tendencies led to acute problems.

RIVALS TO CONFUCIUS

In the later Zhou Period, two especially persistent rival philosophies arose to challenge the Confucian view. Neither was as successful in capturing the permanent allegiance of the educated classes, but both were repeatedly seized upon as an alternative or a necessary addition to the Great Teacher.

Daoism

Daoism (Taoism) is a philosophy centered on nature and following the "Way" (*Dao*; dauw). It was supposedly the product of a teacher-sage called **Lao Zi (Lao-tzu; LAUW-tzuh)**, who purportedly was a near contemporary of Confucius but may be entirely legendary. The book attributed to him, the famous ***The Way of the Dao (Dao de Jing)***, was probably written by his followers much later.

Unlike Confucius, Daoism (dauw-ism) sees the best government as the least government, a minimum of correction and guidance for those who are *inherently unable and unwilling to govern themselves.* In so doing, the rulers should follow the Way of Nature, as it is perceived through meditation and observation. The intelligent man seeks a lifestyle that is in tune with the natural world, a harmony of parts in a serene whole. The excerpt from the *Dao de Jing* in the Patterns of Belief box shows this harmony through paradoxical examples drawn from everyday life. All extremes should be avoided, even those meant to be benevolent. The truly good ruler does little except *be*; excessive action is as bad as no corrective action at all.

Daoism has taken so many forms through the centuries that it is almost impossible to provide a single description of it. Originally, it was a philosophy of the educated classes, but it eventually degenerated into a superstition of the peasants. Yet for many centuries, it was a serious rival of Confucius's ideas and was often adopted by Chinese seeking harmony with the natural world and escape from earthly conflicts. This dichotomy was summed up in the saying that the educated classes were "Confucian by day, Daoist by night." In their rational, public lives, they abided by practical Confucian principles of conduct, but in the quiet of their beds, they sought immersion in mysterious, suprarational nature.

Legalism

Legalism was more a philosophy of government than a philosophy of private life. It was popularized in the **Era of the Warring States** (c. 400–c. 225 BCE) between the collapse of central Zhou dynastic authority (around 400 BCE) and the rise of the Qin emperor in the 220s (see Chapter 16). The general breakdown of authority that characterized this period provided the motivation for Legalist ideas.

PATTERNS OF BELIEF

Dao de Jing of Lao Zi

Confucian philosophy was by no means universally accepted in ancient China. It had to overcome several rival points of view among the educated class and was only partly successful in doing so. Among the ordinary people, Daoism was always stronger because it lent itself more readily to personal interpretation and to the rampant superstitions of the illiterate. It drew many of its principles from close observation of nature, emphasizing the necessity of bringing one's life into harmony with nature. Rather than the illusions of well-bred Confucians or the brutality of the Legalists, the followers of the Way sought serenity through acceptance of what is.

The *Dao de Jing*, or *The Way of the Dao*, is a collection of sayings attributed to Lao Zi (Lao-tzu), who supposedly lived in the sixth century BCE. Like much Chinese philosophy, the essence of the *Dao de Jing* is the search for balance between opposites, between the *yin* and *yang* principles. Unlike Confucianism, Daoism puts little faith in reason and foresight as the way to happiness. Instead, it urges its followers to accept the mystery of life and stop striving for a false mastery. It delights in putting its truths as paradoxes.

Chapter II

It is because every one under Heaven recognizes beauty as beauty, that the idea of ugliness exists.

And equally, if every one recognized virtue as virtue, this would create fresh conceptions of wickedness.

For truly Being and Non-Being grow out of one another; Difficult and Easy complete one another; Long and Short test one another; High and Low determine one another.

The sounds of instruments and voice give harmony to one another.

Front and Back give sequence to one another.

Therefore the Sage relies on actionless activity, Carries on wordless teaching. . . .

Chapter IV

The Way is like an empty vessel That yet may be drawn from Without ever needing to be filled.

It is bottomless; the very progenitor of all things in the world.

In it is all sharpness blunted, All tangles untied, All glare tempered, All dust smoothed.

It is like a deep pool that never dries.

Was it, too, the child of something else? We cannot tell.

Chapter IX

Stretch a bow to the very full And you will wish you had stopped in time; Temper a sword edge to its very sharpest, And you will find that it soon grows dull.

When bronze and jade fill your halls It can no longer be guarded.

Wealth and position breed insolence That brings ruin in its train.

When your work is done, then withdraw!

Such is Heaven's Way.

Chapter XI

We put thirty spokes together and call it a wheel; But it is on the space where there is nothing that the utility of the wheel depends.

We turn clay to make a vessel; But it is on the space where there is nothing that the utility of the vessel depends.

We pierce doors and windows to make a house; But it is on these spaces where there is nothing that the utility of the house depends.

Therefore, just as we take advantage of what is, we should recognize the utility of what is not.

▶ **Analyze and Interpret**

What application of Daoist thought can you find in your own experiences? Does the paradox of saying that doors and windows can be appreciated only if one keeps in mind the house walls strike you as truthful? as memorable?

Source: *The Way and Its Power: A Study of the Dao de Qing*, ed. and trans. A. Waley. ©1934.

You can read more from the *Dao de Jing* at the *Wadsworth World History Resource Center*.

The Legalists were convinced that a government that allowed freedom to its subjects was asking for trouble. Legalism was a rationalized form of governmental manipulation. It was not so much a philosophy as a justification for applying force when persuasion had failed. Its basis was the conviction that most people were inclined to evil selfishness, and it was the task of government to restrain them and simultaneously to guide them into doing "good"—that is to say, whatever the governors wanted. This task is to be accomplished by controlling people even before their evil nature has manifested itself in their acts. In other words, the Legalists advocated strict censorship, prescribed education (differing by social rank), and immediate crushing of any signs of independent thought or action that could upset the status quo.

In a later chapter, we shall investigate how the Chinese government and state were definitively formed in the second and first centuries BCE. But Chinese political culture, as distinct from the state, was already shaped by 500 BCE and would not change much until the modern era. The emphasis on the family, the respect due to elders, the subordination of women to men, the focus on this life on Earth rather than on a life to come, and the lofty position of the educated were already deeply rooted in Chinese society long before the Romans had established their empire.

SUMMARY

THE CIVILIZATION OF China originated in the Neolithic villages of the northern plains near the Yellow River in the second millennium BCE. Under the first historical dynasties of the Shang and the Zhou, this agrarian civilization displayed certain characteristics that were to mark China for many centuries to come: reverence for ancestors, the tremendous importance of the family, and the prestige of the educated and of the written word. Fine arts and literature were cultivated in forms that persisted: bronze ware, ceramics, silk, historical literature, and nature poetry.

The Shang dynasts were a warrior aristocracy who took over the village folk as their subjects in the eighteenth century BCE. What we know of them is almost entirely through a smattering of oracular fragments and archaeology performed in recent times. They were succeeded after several centuries by another warrior group called *the Zhou*, which established perhaps the most influential of all Chinese dynasties in the realm of culture. The arts flourished, and the limits of the state expanded greatly. Gradually, however, power to hold this vast realm together escaped from the dynastic ruler's hands and flowed into those of the provincial aristocrats.

The breakdown of central government that ended the long Zhou Dynasty and introduced the Era of the Warring States demanded further definition of basic values.

In response, three great schools of practical philosophy arose between 500 and 250 BCE: Confucianism, Daoism, and Legalism. Of these, the most significant for later Chinese history was the secularist, rationalist, and pragmatic thought of Confucius, the Sage of China for the next 2,000 years.

▶Identification Terms

Test your knowledge of this chapter's key concepts by defining the following terms. If you can't recall the meaning of certain terms, refresh your memory by looking up the boldfaced term in the chapter, turning to the Glossary at the end of the book, or working with the flashcards that are available on the *World Civilizations* Companion Website: **academic.cengage.com/adler**

Confucius
The Way of the Dao (Dao de Jing)

Era of the Warring States
Lao Zi
Legalism

mandarins
mandate of heaven

Shang Dynasty
Zhou Dynasty

▶ Test Your Knowledge

Test your knowledge of this chapter by answering the following questions. Complete answers appear at the end of the book. You may find even more quiz questions in CengageNOW and on the *World Civilizations* Companion Website: **academic.cengage.com/adler**

1. China's geography
   a. isolated it from other civilizations.
   b. was semitropical.
   c. is much like that of Mesopotamia.
   d. made it a natural marketplace and exchange point.
   e. made the development of agriculture difficult.

2. The Shang Dynasty was established in northern China at roughly the same time as the
   a. rise of the Assyrians.
   b. Aryan conquest of northern India.
   c. beginnings of Sumerian civilization.
   d. first dynasty in Egypt.
   e. founding of the first civilization in the Yangtze River region.

3. Early Chinese religious thought is noteworthy for its
   a. insistence on the existence of only two gods.
   b. emphasis on devotion to the spirits of the ancestors.
   c. superstition about heaven and hell.
   d. clear and detailed theology.
   e. development of a priestly class.

4. A significant long-term advantage of the Chinese style of writing is its
   a. easiness to learn.
   b. independence of regional dialects.
   c. effective use of an alphabet.
   d. small vocabulary.
   e. use of simple pictographs.

5. After seizing power from the Shang, the Zhou rulers adopted a
   a. theory of government that justified their actions.
   b. militarized dictatorship.
   c. theocracy in which the priests had final powers.
   d. democracy.
   e. comprehensive bureaucracy.

6. Which one of the following products was undeveloped in ancient China?
   a. Iron weaponry
   b. Silken cloth
   c. Fine bronze ware
   d. Iron plowshares
   e. Porcelain tableware

7. Which one of the following statements is *contrary* to Confucian teaching?
   a. The family is the proper model for good government.
   b. The young should be constantly seeking new and more effective modes of action.
   c. The gentleman is made and not born.
   d. The interactions of social groups should be controlled by formalities and courtesy.
   e. Virtuous scholarly gentlemen should involve themselves in public service.

8. In many aspects of philosophy, Chinese thought generally aimed at
   a. attaining union with the immortal gods.
   b. inspiring loyalty and fear in the common people.
   c. teaching myths and magical formulas.
   D. attaining harmony and avoiding disorder on Earth.
   e. developing innovations in government and finance.

9. Daoist political views emphasized that people
   a. get the government they deserve.
   b. are naturally evil and government must restrain them.
   c. should be enslaved to ensure peace.
   d. should be left to their own devices as much as possible.
   e. should defer to their rulers, who are naturally much wiser.

10. Legalism could best be described as
    a. a form of government that recognized the worth of individuals.
    b. a justification for forcing people to do what their government said they should.
    c. supportive of societal freedom.
    d. an ethical system that supported the independent actions of the people.
    e. a way of encouraging people to develop constraints on their own behavior.

Enter *CengageNOW* using the access card that is available with this text. *CengageNOW* will assist you in understanding the content in this chapter with lesson plans generated for your needs and provide you with a connection to the *Wadsworth World History Resource Center* (see description at right for details).

 **World History Resource Center**

Enter the Resource Center using either your *CengageNOW* access card or your standalone access card for the *Wadsworth World History Resource Center*. Organized by topic, this website includes quizzes; images; over 350 primary source documents; interactive simulations, maps, and timelines; movie explorations; and a wealth of other resources. You can read the following documents, and many more, at the *Wadsworth World History Resource Center*:

Confucius, *Analects*
Lao Zi, *Dao de Jing*

Worldview One

LAW AND GOVERNMENT

SOCIETY AND ECONOMY

MESOPOTAMIANS, EGYPTIANS, HEBREWS

Mesopotamia: Early law based on different treatment for differing classes. Property better protected than people, but some care is shown for all. Government originally theocratic; becomes monarchic after c. 2000 BCE, when city-states conquered by external invader and centralized.

Egypt: Law the divine wisdom and justice of the pharaoh, administered by officials. Government displays stability under god-king until c. 1000 BCE, when foreign invasions multiply.

Israel: Law based on Moses' Covenant provides divinely ordained ethical foundation for Hebraic custom. Twelve tribes long for messiah to lead them to earthly dominion but repeatedly disappointed after collapse of Solomon's kingdom and division into the hostile successor states Israel and Samaria.

Mesopotamia active in commerce originating in large towns and cities, themselves dependent on intensive irrigation farming. Extensive trade with other regions attested by archaeology.

Egypt is most fertile part of the world; exports grain, copper to neighbors, while remaining almost self-sufficient. No large urban areas developed and relatively little contact made with others.

Hebrews sporadically play intermediary role in trade between Nile and eastern Mediterranean, but their economy basically agrarian and pastoral.

As elsewhere, patriarchy the rule for Mesopotamians, Egyptians, Hebrews. Most routine occupations open to women as well as men in all ancient societies, but women normally under male supervision.

INDIANS

Government presumed to be theocracy in Indus valley civilization. Law remains customary and unwritten long after Aryan invasion (c. 1500 BCE). Brahmins retain lawmaking position as Aryan-Indian amalgam produces Vedic Hinduism. Important concepts memorized by succeeding generations, dominated by self-interest of uppermost castes.

Indian and other South Asian cultures agrarian into modern times. Large towns exist from earliest times, but large majority live in villages, with little contact outside their region.

Position of women in earliest Indian civilizations unclear. According to tradition, woman intended to serve and obey males.

CHINESE

China develops writing early and keeps records from c. 1000 BCE. Chinese law looks to protection of property and maintenance of the clan/family as determining factors for justice. Government monarchic and warrior-oriented, with Shang models for succeeding Zhou.

Most Chinese live in villages. A few large towns exist but play only minor role in economy. Trade with others negligible in this era.Rice culture has not yet begun, as south remains unconquered.

Evidence suggests period of matriarchy in Neolithic China, but father gets absolute obedience.

CROSS-CULTURAL CONNECTIONS

Migrations

Indo-Europeans: Pastoralists migrate from Caspian-Black Sea to Europe, C. Asia, Indus and Ganges Valleys.

Chinese: Millet cultivators of northern plain conquer Yangtze, southern China, adopt rice farming.

Austronesians: Cultivators master boat building and stellar navigation. Migrate to Melanesia.

Africans: Neolithic peoples adopt cattle breeding and cereal cultivation, migrate out of Sahara and settle major river valleys of Northeast and West. Bantu speakers of northwest rainforest migrate through equatorial rainforest, inhabit sub-equatorial Africa.

Northeast Asians: Late Paleolithic peoples cross Beringia in late Ice Age and settle Americas.

Trade and Exchange Networks

W. and S. Asia Network: Indian trade with Mesopotamia and Persia; later, maritime trade with eastern E., W. shores of Indian Ocean and with early SE Asian states.

NE Africa-Red Sea Network: Egypt, Nubia, Yemen, S. Arabia trade slaves, gold, aromatics, animals, hides.

Eastern Mediterranean Network: Egyptians, Greeks, Phoenicians trade in metals, obsidian, precious oils, aromatics, precious stones.

Eastern Asia Network: China and C. Asian pastoralists exchange horses and silk.

Central American Network: Kingdoms of Caribbean coast, plateau, rainforest, and N. America trade in cacao, precious stones, metals, birds, feathers, shells.

ANCIENT CIVILIZATIONS, 3500–500 BCE

PATTERNS OF BELIEF

ARTS AND CULTURE

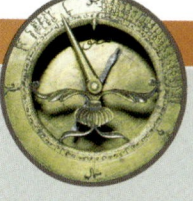

SCIENCE AND TECHNOLOGY

Religious belief dictates type of government in the earliest period, but gradually separates king from priest. Mesopotamia adopts pessimistic view of the human-god relationship and afterlife, elevating priests.

Egypt had optimistic view of afterlife and role of the protecting gods, which lasted until collapse of its empire.

Hebrews draw on Zoroastrian traditions to pioneer monotheism and elevate Yahweh into universal lawgiver to all humanity, with special relationship with his chosen people, based mutual love and justice in life to come.

Mesopotamians produce first monumental architecture, first urban society, first writing system. Arts flourish but little has survived.

Egypt's pyramids most impressive ancient construction; massive sculpture, interior fresco painting, and ceramics other Egyptian strengths in art.

At the end of period, Hebrews produce Bible as literature and history of their people.

Mesopotamians play huge role in early science: chronology, calendar, math, physics, astronomy all highly developed by 2500 BCE. Technology (e.g., mud brick construction, city sanitation, hydraulics) also has major place in daily life of city-states.

Egypt develops considerable science but not so innovative. Medicine and pharmacy are strengths, as are skill in construction and stonework. Solar calendar developed.

Hebrews lag in science and technology, remaining dependent on others.

Religion mixture of Indus belief and Aryan gods. Vedas brought by Aryans become sacred scripture by 1000 BCE. Brahmins co-rulers with warriors who conquer North India and impose Aryan rule. South India not conquered, but strongly influenced by Vedic beliefs. At end of period, Buddhism gains ground rapidly and has enormous impact on philosophy and theology.

Art reflects religious mythology. Some sculpture and minor arts survive ruins of Indus valley towns. Stone temples and carvings survive in limited numbers; sacred literature entirely oral into first centuries CE, when Vedas, Upanishads, and other Hindu and Buddhist epics are first written.

Indians master metalworking early, progressing rapidly through Bronze Age to Iron Age by 1000 BCE. Mathematics especially important, navigation arts well developed, engineering skills enable them to erect massive temples and fortresses.

Religion is conditioned by ancestral continuity; honor of lineage important, with gods playing minor roles. No state theology, but emperor enjoys the "mandate of heaven" serves as high priest of royal ancestral cult. At end of period, Confucian ethical and philosophical system beginning. Peasant majority goes on with Dao.

Arts in several formats take on lasting features during Zhou Dynasty: bronzes, landscape painting, nature poetry, ceramics, silk, pagoda architecture. Language arts highly developed. Reverence for education and for the aged already apparent. Supreme importance of the family continually emphasized.

Metal technology well advanced in China: Bronze Age commences 3000 BCE, and iron introduced, probably from Western Asia, by the 600s. Shang bronzes the finest ever cast, while Zhou Dynasty sees improvements in agricultural productivity and weaponry. Copper coins circulate; lacquer ware and silk processing major home industries.

Spread of Ideas and Technologies

Western Asia: Early bronze, then later iron making invented in Western Asia and spread to Europe, Northwest India, the Mediterranean coast, North Africa, and Northeast Africa. Sumerian cuneiform became the basis of writing and literature for all subsequent Western Asian civilizations.

India: Spread of farming and iron making from northwest to Ganges River and south. Indo-European-speaking Aryans spread early, priestly version of Hinduism. Aryan version of Indo-European speech became the root of most later Indian languages; Sanskrit is the basis of the Vedic tradition.

China: Some aspects of Chinese iron making (casting instead of smelting and forging) probably invented independently of Western Asian influences. Spread with extension of northern dynastic rule.

North and Northeast Africa: Probable routes of the spread of iron technology from Nile Valley southwards into East, Central, and Southern Africa, and from North Africa into West Africa. Egyptian deities and symbols of divine kingship spread up (south) the Nile Valley and influenced many aspects of religion and royal authority in Kerma and Meroe phases of Nubian civilizations.

Africa: Spread of pastoralism and dry cereals (millets and sorghums) agriculture from north to south in grassland savannahs and highlands of Atlas and Ethiopian mountains; spread of yams throughout equatorial rainforest zone from north to south and southeast; Southeast Asian yam and cocoanut cultivation spread from east to west; iron-making spread south from North and Northeast Africa.

Central and South America: Spread and sharing of many religious elements, including ritual ball games, blood (human and animal) sacrifice, and deities. Sharing of symbols and ritual duties of kingship, such as royal bloodletting and royal record keeping using a similar writing system.

Part TWO

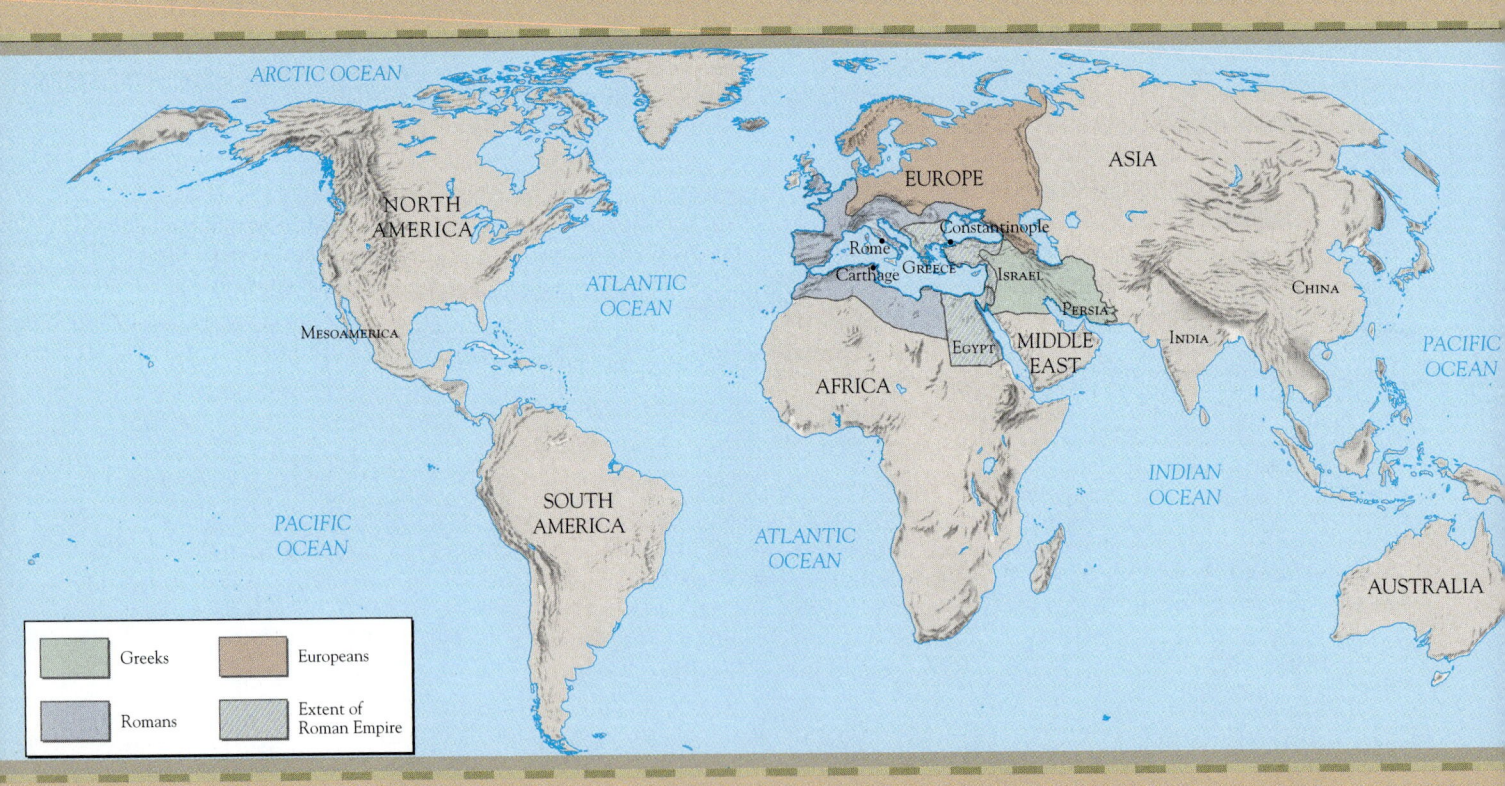

ARCTIC OCEAN

NORTH AMERICA

ATLANTIC OCEAN

Mesoamerica

PACIFIC OCEAN

SOUTH AMERICA

ATLANTIC OCEAN

EUROPE

Rome
Carthage
GREECE
Constantinople
ISRAEL
EGYPT
MIDDLE EAST
PERSIA

ASIA

INDIA

CHINA

AFRICA

INDIAN OCEAN

PACIFIC OCEAN

AUSTRALIA

| Greeks | Europeans |
| Romans | Extent of Roman Empire |

CLASSICAL MEDITERRANEAN CIVILIZATIONS, 500 BCE–800 CE

WHY DO WE use the word *classical* to identify the thousand-year epoch from 500 BCE to roughly 800 CE? In the eastern Mediterranean and the East and South Asian river valley civilizations, this period saw an impressive cultural expansion and development, especially in philosophy, the arts, and language. The monuments and methodologies created then served as benchmarks for many centuries for the Mediterranean, Indian, and Chinese peoples. Some have even endured to the present day. For example, the use of the architrave and exterior columns to lend both dignity and accessibility to the facade of public buildings (such as the Parthenon shown in Chapter 8) has persisted through 2,500 years in Western architecture.

The two other early centers of civilization—Mesopotamia and the Nile Valley—did not undergo similar expansion. In Egypt, invaders from both Asia and Africa eroded the heritage of 2,000 years of cultural and political sovereignty. After about 500 BCE, Egypt was under foreign masters and would endure governments led by foreign-born strangers for the next 2,500 years. Somewhat similar was the fate of Mesopotamia, where ecological damage intensified the negative effects of the Persians' decision to locate their chief cities elsewhere. The once-blooming fields surrounding cities such as Uruk and Lagash have long since been reduced to stark desert.

A hallmark of this period was the larger territorial size of the new civilizations of the world and their more pronounced cultural attractions for the nomadic pastoralists on their fringes. Urban centers were both more numerous and more important. Economic sophistication was evident in the expanded long-distance trade for the more numerous upper classes and in the more refined instruments of payment and credit employed by the merchants. For example, the beginning of the letter of credit was introduced in China to facilitate merchants' exchanges. Social strata were more differentiated and more complex than in the ancient age, and social tensions more evident. Wars were fought on a much larger scale and provided the impetus for much development of government.

Knowledge of the natural world (that is, science) made great strides in certain fields, such as physics, but was paltry in many others, such as geology. Technology, on the other hand, remained primitive in an age of easy access to slave labor. Supernatural and salvationist religions, especially Christianity, came to play an ever-increasing part in daily life after about 300 CE in the Mediterranean basin.

In this part of our book, we look at the classical civilization of the Mediterranean and western Europe, established first by the Greeks and then expanded and modified by the Romans. (We will turn to the classical age in South and East Asia in Part Three.) Chapters 7 and 8 outline the history of the Greeks. Although we note the Greeks' debts to their Mesopotamian and Egyptian predecessors, our emphasis is on the remarkable two centuries between 500 and 300 BCE. Chapters 9 and 10 follow the story of the rise and accomplishments of the Roman Empire between about 500 BCE and 200 CE, as well as its decline and transformation, and the beginnings of medieval Europe, between about 200 and 800 CE.

The function of the ruler is to use his best endeavors to make his subjects happier.
—Socrates

7 THE GREEK ADVENTURE

GEOGRAPHY AND POLITICAL DEVELOPMENT

THE MINOAN AND MYCENAEAN CIVILIZATIONS

EARLY HELLENIC CIVILIZATION

ATHENS AND SPARTA
Early Athens ◆ Athenian Democracy ◆ Spartan Militarism

THE PERSIAN WARS

THE PELOPONNESIAN WAR

THE FINAL ACT IN CLASSICAL GREECE

ALEXANDER AND THE CREATION OF A WORLD EMPIRE
A Mixed Culture ◆ Greeks and Easterners in the Hellenistic Kingdoms

THE ISLANDS OF THE Aegean Sea and the small, rocky peninsula in the eastern Mediterranean Sea that is now called Greece proved to be the single most important sources of later civilization in the Western world. In this sea and unpromising landscape emerged a vigorous, imaginative people who gave later human beings a tradition of thought and values that is still very much alive.

The history of the ancient Greeks can be divided into three epochs:

1. The *Minoan-Mycenaean Age* lasted from about 2000 BCE to the conquest of the Greek peninsula by invaders in the 1100s.

2. The *Hellenic Period* extended from the time of Homer to the conquest of the Greek city-states by the Macedonians in the mid-300s. It includes the Classical Age, when Greek philosophical and artistic achievements were most impressive.

3. The *Hellenistic Age* was the final blossoming of Greek cultural innovation, lasting from about 300 BCE to the first century CE. During this age, emigrant Greeks interacted politically and intellectually with other peoples to produce a hybrid culture that was extraordinarily influential on the arts and science of both Western and Asian civilizations.

We will look now at the political and social aspects of the Hellenic and early Hellenistic periods, and then we will focus on intellectual and artistic developments in Chapter 8.

GEOGRAPHY AND POLITICAL DEVELOPMENT

More than most societies, Greece was shaped by its geography. In ancient times it consisted of the numerous, small islands of the Aegean, the western end of Asia Minor, and the mountainous southern tip of the European mainland. Most of this area had little land that was suitable for large-scale farming, no broad river valleys, and no expansive level plains. No place within it was located more than eighty miles from the sea. Dozens of protected harbors and bays were found all along the coast. From the beginnings of their civilization on the island of Crete, the Greeks were expert sailors, so ships and shipping were a major part of their livelihood since its establishment. The mountains of the peninsula made overland travel there difficult, so it had almost always been easier to travel and trade by sea than by land.

This geography also encouraged political fragmentation. The people in each island, valley, and river basin developed their own separate sense of community and identity, much as the people of the valleys of our own Appalachians did. Greeks grew up thinking of themselves first as residents of a given place or town and only secondarily as sharing a common culture and language with the other inhabitants of the peninsula. This would be a critical weakness in the development of a united Greek nation.

THE MINOAN AND MYCENAEAN CIVILIZATIONS

Traditionally, scholars have traced the origins of Greek civilization not to the rocky mainland, but to the island of Crete. This large island supported an urbanized civilization of its own, dating back to at least 2000 BCE. Historians and archaeologists call the Cretan culture **Minoan** (MIHN-oh-ahn) after Minos (MY-nohs), the mythical king of Crete. The Minoan towns, led by *Knossos* (NAW-sus) on the northern coast (see Map 7.1 inset), were masters of a wide-ranging maritime empire, including coastal Greece, by about 1600 BCE. Nobody knows whether or not the Minoans actually were Greeks—their written records have never been deciphered—but they played a part in the formation of Greek civilization.

Like the ancient Indians, these islanders established a seaborne commercial network that spanned most of the eastern Mediterranean, becoming wealthy through their mastery of the sea as a highway of commercial transport. This wealth produced a socially complex society that was organized into tiny states centered on powerful, palace-dwelling kings. Some of these palaces were architectural and artistic masterpieces, as archaeologist Arthur Evans discovered more than a century ago when he excavated the most spectacular of these, the Great Palace at Knossos. Evans unearthed a palace complex that consisted of hundreds of rooms built on three levels and arranged loosely around a series of courtyards. The original structure was constructed around 2000 BCE. Through the centuries, earthquakes destroyed it several times, but the Minoans rebuilt it every time, usually on an even grander scale. Around 1450, however, an Indo-European speaking people from the mainland, the **Mycenaeans** (my-suh-NEE-uns), invaded Crete and destroyed many of the island settlements, aided by either volcanic explosions or earthquakes. Subsequently, they settled on Crete themselves, took over most of its trading network, and rebuilt the palace at Knossos.

©Ashmolean Museum, University of Oxford, UK/Bridgeman Art Library

RECONSTRUCTED THRONE ROOM AT KNOSSOS. Its excavator, the English archaeologist Arthur Evans spent a fortune rebuilding portions of the Great Palace at Knossos. This artist's depiction is a faithful rendering of what its throne would have looked like c. 1600–1400 BCE.

The ancestors of the Mycenaeans entered the mainland peninsula about 2000 BCE as stock-raising nomads from the eastern European plains. By about 1600, they had become sedentary, and some of them lived in fair-sized towns, notably *Mycenae* and *Tiryns* on the eastern side of the Peloponnesus (see Map 7.1 inset). Like the Minoans, the Mycenaean kings ruled from palaces. However, by the time they invaded Crete, the kings had strongly fortified these palaces, suggesting that theirs was a more warlike society than that of the Minoans. Walls described by some as "Cyclopean," after Homer's gargantuan Cyclops, surrounded royal graveyards and stone-built palaces that included a

megaron, a central hearth and "mead hall," where kings and their warriors retreated to drink and feast.

Our knowledge of this period comes largely from archaeological excavations and from the **Iliad** and the **Odyssey,** two epics of ancient Greece written by the magnificent poet **Homer** in the eighth century BCE. The *Iliad* deals with the Mycenaeans' war against the powerful city-state of Troy, and the *Odyssey* tells of the adventures of the hero Odysseus (Ulysses) after the war (see Arts and Culture). For a long time, historians believed that the Trojan War was simply a fiction created by a great poet about his ancestors. But thanks to archaeology, we know

MAP 7.1 Early Greece

At the height of Greek power, there were more than 200 independent poleis, many of them quite small and located on the numerous islands of the Aegean Sea and the Ionian coast. A few were entirely urban, but most combined a town with surrounding rural agricultural areas. The inset shows Mycenaean Greece, the earliest period in the history of the peninsula.

MAP QUESTION

What are two ways in which its distinctive geography shaped Greek culture?

 View an interactive version of this or a related map at http://worldrc. wadsworth.com/

that there actually was a Troy and that it was destroyed about the time that Homer indicates—about 1300 BCE. Whether it was destroyed by the Greeks or not, we do not know, but there is no reason not to believe so. Ancient Troy, now a great pile of rubble, was situated on a hill commanding the entrance into the straits called *the Hellespont*. Much evidence indicates that the Greek towns, led by Mycenae, were engaged in commercial rivalry with Troy throughout this period and may well have made war on their nearby enemy.

The Mycenaeans themselves seem to have engaged in extensive internal warfare among the competing towns. These wars weakened them sufficiently that they fell to a new wave of nomads from the north, the *Dorians.* From about 1100 BCE to about 800, the culture of the Greek peninsula declined, so much so that this period is called the *Dark Age.* Not only did arts and crafts decline, but even the ability to write seems to have been largely lost during these centuries. Were the Dorians to blame, or did the Mycenaeans simply fight one another to mutual exhaustion and destruction, as many experts think?

EARLY HELLENIC CIVILIZATION

Starting about 800 BCE, the Greek mainland slowly recovered the levels of civilization created during the Mycenaean Period and then went on to far greater heights.

During and after the Dark Age, the institution of the **polis** (POH-lis; plural, *poleis*) gradually developed. In Greek, *polis* means the community of adult free persons who make up a town or any inhabited place. In modern political vocabulary, the word is usually translated as "city-state." A polis could be almost any size. It is thought that Classical Athens, the largest and most powerful, had almost 300,000 inhabitants at its peak (about the size of our present-day Buffalo, New York), whereas the smallest were scarcely more than villages. At one time the Greek mainland and inhabitable islands (all told, about the size of Maryland) were the home to more than 200 poleis. Each thought of itself as a political and cultural unit, independent of every other. Yet each polis also thought of itself as part of that distinct and superior family of peoples calling themselves *Greek.*

The polis was much more than a political-territorial unit. It was the frame of reference for the entire public life of its citizens and for much private life as well. The mutual interdependence of the citizenry was exhibited in different ways. A sense of common life and shared destiny was promoted by governmental policies and techniques. The inherent superiority of the local format of governing for the public welfare was taken for granted, even when these ways might differ sharply from one polis to its nearest neighbor. Citizenship was greatly prized, and by no means

was everyone who lived in a polis a full citizen. Women were entirely excluded from political life. There were many resident aliens, who were excluded from citizenship, as were the numerous slaves.

Normally, only free males of twenty years of age or more possessed full civil rights. That meant that as much as 80 percent of the population might be excluded from political life because of their gender, age, or social status.

Each large polis had more or less the same economic and demographic design: a town of varying size, surrounded by farmland, pasture, and woods that supplied the town with food and other necessities. In the town lived artisans of all kinds, small traders and import–export merchants, intellectuals, philosophers, artists, and all the rest who make up a civilized society. Life was simpler in the countryside. Like all other peoples, most Greeks were peasants, woodcutters, ditch diggers, and all of those others of whom formal history knows little except that they existed.

ATHENS AND SPARTA

The two poleis that dominated Greek life and politics in the Classical Age were Athens and Sparta. They were poles apart in their conceptions of the good life for their citizens. Athens was the center of Greek educational, artistic, and scientific activity as well as the birthplace of political democracy. Sparta was a militaristic, authoritarian society that held the arts and intellectual life in contempt and dreaded the extension of freedom to the individual or the community. Eventually, the two opposites came into conflict. Interestingly, it was the artistic, philosophical, and democratic Athenian polis that provoked the unnecessary war that ultimately ruined it.

In general, the Greeks knew four types of government:

1. A **monarchy** is rule by a single person, a king or equivalent (either sex), who has the final word in law by right. Most of the poleis were monarchies at one time or another, and many of them apparently began and ended as such.

2. An **aristocracy** is rule by those who are born to the leading families and thereby are qualified to rule, whether or not they are particularly qualified in other ways. Aristocrats are born to the nobility, but not all nobles are born aristocrats.

3. An **oligarchy** (OH-lih-gar-kee) is rule by a few, and almost always the few are the wealthiest members of society. Many poleis were ruled by an oligarchy of landlords whose land was worked by tenant farmers.

4. A **democracy** is rule by the people, almost always by means of majority vote on disputed issues. Voting rights in executive and legislative acts are limited to citizens, and in the Greek poleis, this meant freeborn adult males.

Musée d'Art et d'Histoire du Judaisme/
©Reunion des Musées Nationaux/
Art Resource, NY

ARTS AND CULTURE

Odysseus and the Cyclops

The Homeric hero Odysseus (Ulysses) served as one of the chief role models for the ancient Greeks. He embodied in an epic work of literature, the *Odyssey*, the qualities of craftiness and effective action that the Greeks considered most commendable in a man.

One of Odysseus's most formidable challenges came when he and his shipboard companions found themselves at the mercy of the dreadful one-eyed giant, the Cyclops. The Cyclops invited the sailors to land on his island and then entertained himself by dismembering and devouring the Greeks two at a time. Then the sly Odysseus devised his counterblow:

I, holding in my hands an ivy bowl full of the dark wine stood close up to the Cyclops and spoke out: "Here, Cyclops, have a drink of wine, now you have fed on human flesh, and see what kind of drink our ship carried. . . ." Three times I brought it to him, and gave it him, three times he recklessly drained it, but when the wine had got into the brain of the Cyclops, then I spoke to him, and my words were full of beguilement.

[The Cyclops falls asleep.]

I shoved the sharp pointed beam underneath a bed of cinders, waiting for it to heat. . . . [W]hen the beam of olivewood, green as it was, was nearly at the point of catching fire and glowed, terribly incandescent, then I brought it close up from the fire and my friends about me stood fast. . . .

They seized the beam of olive, sharp at the end, and leaned on it into the eye [of the now sleeping giant],

HOMERIC HEROES. Archaeologists have discovered Mycenae and Troy. Was there truly a Trojan War? This Mycenaean vase dates to 1300 BCE, soon after the time of Homer's Trojan war, and shows two warriors of the period. Could King Agamemnon, Achilles, Odysseus, Helen, and the rest actually have lived? Are these their images?

© Nimatallah/Art Resource, NY

while I from above, leaning my weight on it twirled it . . . and the blood boiled around the hot point, so that the blast and scorch of the burning ball singed all his eyebrows and eyelids, and the fire made the roots of his eye crackle. . . .

He gave a giant, horrid cry and the rocks rattled from the sound. . . .

[The now-blinded Cyclops attempts to capture the Greeks by feeling for them, but they escape his wrath by suspending themselves beneath sheep that walk past him to the waiting boat.]

When I was as far from the land as a voice shouting carries, I called aloud to the Cyclops, taunting him:

"Cyclops, in the end it was no weak man's companions you were to eat by violence and force in your hollow cave, and your evil deeds were to catch up with you, and be too strong for you, ugly creature, who dared to eat your own guests in your own house, so that Zeus and the rest of the gods have punished you."

▶ *Analyze and Interpret*

What qualities of character does this anecdote reveal as admired by the Greeks?

Source: Excerpts from pages 146, 147, 149, from *The Odyssey of Homer* by Richard Lattimore. Copyright© 1965, 1967 by Richard Lattimore. Copyright renewed. Reprinted by permission of HarperCollins Publishers, Inc.

You can read more from the *Odyssey* at the Wadsworth World History Resource Center.

Additionally, the Greek word *tyranny* originally meant rule by a dictator who had illegally seized power. That person might be a good or bad ruler, a man or a woman.

Early Athens

Athens went through all of these forms of government in the period after 750 BCE, when we begin to know something

definite about its history. The original monarchy was gradually forced aside by the aristocrats, who ruled the polis in the seventh and early sixth centuries. The aristocrats gave way in the 500s to oligarchs, some of whom were nobly born and some of whom were rich commoners. The most important oligarch was Solon (SO-lun), who ruled in the early sixth century. When the polis faced a social and economic crisis generated by lack of agrarian land, the other oligarchs gave him supreme power to quell the discontent. Solon responded by establishing a constitution that struck an uneasy balance between the desires of the wealthy few and the demands of the impoverished and indebted masses. Neither group was satisfied, however, and the contest soon resumed.

Eventually, an aristocratic tyrant named Pisistratus succeeded in making himself the sole ruler and made certain important concessions to the common people to gain their support for his plan to start a new monarchic dynasty with his sons as his successors. But the sons were not nearly as clever as their father and were swept from power by rebellion in 510 BCE. The winner of the ensuing free-for-all was **Cleisthenes** (KLEYES-theh-nees), an aristocrat and the true founder of the Athenian democracy. Cleisthenes believed that the people should have the last word in their own government, both because it was just and because he believed it was the best way to keep civil peace.

Athenian Democracy

Cleisthenes (ruled 508–494 BCE) in effect gave away his tyrannical powers to a series of political bodies that were unprecedentedly democratic in character: the *ekklesia, boule,* and *deme.* The *ekklesia* (ek-KLAY-zee-ah) was the general "town meeting" of all free male Athenians, called on an ad hoc basis to make critical decisions affecting the future of the polis. All could speak freely in an attempt to win over the others; all could be elected to any office; all could vote at the meetings of the ekklesia in the center plaza of Athens below the Acropolis hill.

The *boule* (BOO-lay) was a council of 500 citizens who were chosen by lot for one-year terms. It served as a day-to-day legislature and executive, making and implementing policy under the general supervision of the ekklesia. The boule and its officers supervised the civil and military affairs of the polis and carried out many of the functions of a modern city council. All male citizens could expect to serve at least one term on it.

The *deme* (deem) was the basic political subdivision of the polis. It was a territorial unit, something like a modern precinct or ward, but smaller in population. Each deme was entitled to select a certain number of boule members and was represented more or less equally in the officers of the polis.

To enforce the will of the majority without resort to bloodshed and possible civil war, Cleisthenes introduced the idea of *ostracism,* or the "pushing out" of a citizen who would not conform to the will of his neighbors. An ostracized person must go into exile and lost all rights of citizenship for a certain length of time, normally ten years. So attached were the Greeks to their poleis that some preferred to kill themselves rather than submit to ostracism.

Of all the Athenian political institutions, democracy has attracted the most attention from later history. Americans tend to think of political democracy as a natural and normal way to govern a state, but in actuality, until the twentieth century, democracy was a very abnormal system of government. It was talked about a good deal but was not put into practice outside the West and in only a limited way within it. A great many modern countries still give only lip service to the idea of democracy, and sometimes not even that. The idea that the ordinary man or woman was capable of governing wisely and efficiently was quite daring when first introduced. After the initial democracy failed in Athens, as it did after about a century, it was so discredited that after the fourth century BCE it was not resurrected as a legitimate and practical system of government until the eighteenth century CE— 2,200 years later!

How many other poleis became democracies at some time? The answer is not clear, but under the strong pressure of powerful Athens, probably quite a few adopted similar governments between 500 and 400 BCE. But even within Athens (as well as everywhere else), there was strong resistance to the idea that did not cease until democracy had been abandoned and condemned as "the rule of the mob." Ironically, it was the democratic leadership in Athens that created the conditions that allowed their opponents to win out.

Spartan Militarism

By about 500 BCE, Sparta differed from Athens in almost every possible way, although the two were originally similar. The Spartan polis, located in the southern Peloponnesus about eighty miles from Athens, was a small city surrounded by pastoral villages. As the population grew in the 700s, the Spartans engaged in a bloody territorial war, the **Messenian** (mehs-seh-NEE-an) **Wars,** with their nearest Greek neighbor, Messenia, and finally won. The defeated people were reduced to a state of near slavery *(helotry)* to the Spartans, who from this point on became culturally different from most other Greeks. The most striking example of their divergence was their voluntary abdication of individual freedoms. During the 600s, the Messenians rebelled again and again, and as a result the Spartans made themselves into a nation of soldiers and

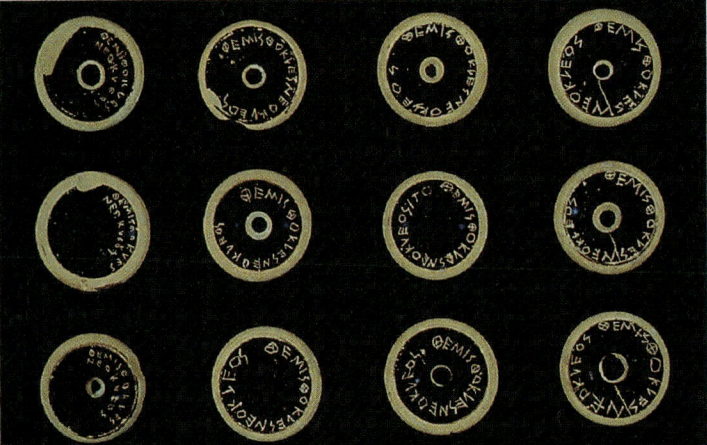

OSTRAKA SHARDS. Each year the citizenry of Athens was allowed to vote to ostracize any of their colleagues. The ballot was a ceramic token inscribed in advance with a name (top) or a piece of broken pottery (above). If someone received a predetermined number of votes, that person was expelled from the polis. How did this relate to the creation of a political democracy?

©American School of Classical Studies at Athens: Agora Excavations

helpers of soldiers so that they could maintain their endangered privileges.

The captive helots largely met Sparta's economic needs. They worked the fields and conducted the necessary crafts and commerce under close supervision. The Spartans themselves devoted their energies to the military arts. Male children entered a barracks at the age of seven and were allowed only sufficient free time thereafter to ensure that another generation of Spartan warriors would be born of Spartan mothers.

Unlike other Greeks, the Spartans held the arts in contempt and rejected individualism as being unworthy of them. Public life was expressed in total obedience to the state, which was headed by a group of elected officers called *ephors* (EE-fors), under the symbolic leadership of a dual monarchy. This strange combination seems to have worked satisfactorily into the 300s.

What did the other Greeks think of Sparta? One might think they would detest such a regime, but on the contrary, most Greeks admired the Spartan way of life, especially its undoubted self-discipline, courage, rigid obedience, and physical vigor. Even many Athenians thought the Spartan way was superior to their own and envied the single-minded patriotism displayed by the Spartans in all their public affairs.

Despite its military nature, Sparta was a conservative and nonaggressive state. The Spartan army was so large and so feared that after about 600, Sparta rarely had to use it in war. Sparta actually became a peaceable polis and directed all of its attention to keeping the political status quo within its own borders and, so far as possible, outside them.

THE PERSIAN WARS

Throughout the early fifth century BCE, the foreign policy interests of Athens and Sparta more or less coincided. Both were primarily concerned with maintaining their independence in the face of foreign threats. These threats originated from imperial Persia, which had expanded rapidly in the 500s, as we described in Chapter 4. They took the form of two Greco-Persian wars.

The First Persian War ended with an Athenian victory. The Persian emperor Darius I was faced with spreading rebellion among some of his subjects, Greeks on the Turkish coast (Ionia). When he attempted to subdue them, Athens went to their aid. Determined to punish the Athenians for their boldness and wishing in any case to expand his domains still further, Darius sent an army across the Aegean Sea to the Greek mainland. Aided by brilliant generalship, the Athenians were waiting and defeated the Persian expedition at the battle of Marathon in 490.

The Second Persian War (480–478 BCE) was fought on both land and sea and resulted in an even more decisive Greek victory. Ten years passed before Darius's successor, Xerxes (ZERK-sees), could find time to take up the challenge. This time, not only Athens but several other Greek poleis assisted the defensive effort. Spartan troops lived up to their fame at the battle of Thermopylae in 480 and again at the decisive defeat of the Persian force at Platea in 479. The Athenian navy completely routed the larger Persian fleet at Salamis and established Athens as the premier naval force in the eastern Mediterranean.

By the end of these **Persian Wars,** the Greeks had decisively turned back the attempts of the Asian empire to establish a universal monarchy over the Mediterranean basin. It was in retrospect a crucial turning point for Western civilization. The idea that, at least in the long run, the common man was capable of perceiving the common good and of ruling wisely and effectively toward that end—the belief in democracy—would have been submerged, perhaps indefinitely, beneath the acquiescence to the rule of the privileged, for the privileged.

THE PELOPONNESIAN WAR

The Greeks' victory in the Persian Wars did not lead to harmony among the Greek poleis, however. Athens used its new prestige and growing wealth to form a group of unwilling satellites (the Delian League) among the nearby poleis. The democrats, led by the great orator **Pericles** (PAYR-rih-clees), were now in command and were responsible for bringing Athens into conflict with Corinth, one of Sparta's Peloponnesian allies. Corinth asked Sparta for help, and when the Spartans warned the Athenians to back down, Pericles responded with war. Athens was embarked on an imperial adventure, with the goal of extending its authority over not only Greece but the surrounding coasts as well. It turned out to be a fatal error, although Pericles did not live to realize it. (See Law and Government.)

With its strong navy, Athens believed that it could hold off the land-based Spartans indefinitely while building up its alliances. These allied forces would then be able to challenge the Spartan army on Sparta's home territory.

For most of its duration, the **Peloponnesian War** (pehl-luh-puh-NEE-zhan; 431–404 BCE) was an intermittently fought deadlock. Neither side was able to deal the other an effective blow, and long truces allowed the combatants to regain their strength. After Pericles died in 429, the Athenian democrats argued among themselves while the antidemocratic forces within the polis gained strength. An ambitious attempt to weaken Sparta by attacking its allies on Sicily went astray and turned into disaster. Finally, in 404 the Spartans obtained effective naval aid (from Persia!) and defeated the Athenians at sea. After that, it was a simple matter for their large army to lay siege to Athens and starve it into surrender.

The Peloponnesian War ended with a technical victory for Sparta, but actually it was a loss for all concerned. The Spartan leadership was not inclined or equipped to lead the squabbling Greeks into an effective central government. Defeated Athens was torn between the discredited democrats and the conservatives favored by Sparta.

©Erich Lessing/Art Resource, NY

GREEK VASE. This vase shows a fight between a Greek hoplite (infantryman) and his Persian cavalry enemy. A product of the late fifth century BCE, it was probably a commemoration of the great Greek triumph over Darius's troops.

THE FINAL ACT IN CLASSICAL GREECE

After the war, the Greeks fought intermittently among themselves for political supremacy for two generations. Whenever a strong contender emerged, such as the major polis of Thebes, the others would band together against it. Once they had succeeded in defeating their rival, they would begin to quarrel among themselves, and the fragile unity would break down once again. The Greek passion for independence and individuality had degenerated into endless quarrels and maneuvering for power with no clear vision of what that power should create.

To the north of Greece were a people—the Macedonians (ma-sih-DOH-nee-ans)—whom the Greeks regarded as savage and barbarian, although they were ethnically related. Philip of Macedonia, the ruler of this northern kingdom, had transformed it from a relatively backwards society into an effectively governed, aggressive state. One by one he began to absorb the northern Greek poleis, until by the 340s he had made himself the master of much of the mainland.

After much delay, the Athenians finally awoke to the danger and convinced Thebes to join with them against the menace from the north. In the battle of Chaeronea (kie-roh-NEE-ah) in 338 BCE, however, Philip's forces defeated the allies. The former city-states became provinces in a rapidly forming Macedonian Empire. Chaeronea was the effective end of the era of polis independence and of the Classical Age. From the latter part of the fourth century BCE onward, Greeks were to be almost always under the rule of foreigners to whom the daring ideas of polis democracy were unknown or inimical.

ALEXANDER AND THE CREATION OF A WORLD EMPIRE

After the battle at Chaeronea, which brought him mastery of the former poleis of Greece, King Philip of Macedonia was assassinated, and his young son, Alexander, succeeded to the throne. In his thirteen-year reign (336–323 BCE), Alexander conquered most of the world known to the

LAW AND GOVERNMENT

Pericles (c. 495–429 BCE)

One of the great figures of democratic politics, the Greek general and democratic statesman Pericles (c. 495–429 BCE) is also a prime example of the dangers of the imperial vision. Desiring originally to bring his fellow Greeks into a mutually supportive defensive alliance against Persia, by the end of his career he was viewed as the chief villain of an imperialist scheme to reduce all Greeks to Athenian subjects. The seduction of power granted by the democratic majority proved too much for him.

Pericles was born into an aristocratic Athenian family and received a traditional education in rhetoric under Anaxagoras, a leading philosopher. Committing himself to the emergent democratic party in the hurly-burly of polis politics, he rose quickly to prominence. At the age of thirty-two, he became chief magistrate (the equivalent of mayor). For the next thirty-three years, Pericles was the leading political figure in Athens, a feat that speaks volumes not only about his abilities but also about his sensitivity to popular opinion in a city where every free male saw himself as a co-maker of policy.

In power, Pericles showed himself sincerely committed to the extension of democracy, although he was not above using a bit of demagoguery to retain his grip on popular affection. By appealing to the emotions of the populace, he reformed the political and judicial systems to allow greater participation by the ordinary citizen. He instituted a system of paying jurors and established new courts to hear criminal cases, thus lessening the powers of the aristocratic judges. He raised the payment citizens received for attending the great debates in the agora in the town's center where questions of policy were decided. By paying for jury duty and attendance at the assemblies, Pericles ensured that ordinary men could take time off from work to participate.

Pericles was a master orator, and his speeches were deemed masterpieces of effective rhetoric. Only one has come down to us: the famous Funeral Oration given near the end of his life to commemorate the Athenians who had fallen in the Peloponnesian War. Here is a sample:

Our constitution is called democracy because power is in the hands not of a minority but of the whole people. . . . No one, so long as he has it in him to be of service to the state, is kept in political obscurity because of poverty. . . . [We] do not say that a man who takes no interest in politics is minding his own business; we say that he has no business here at all. . . .

Under Pericles, Athens became the center of the extraordinary intellectual and artistic life that is always associated with the term "Classical Age." But in relations with other Greek city-states, Pericles was not so fortunate. (It was he who transformed the Delian League from a defensive alliance against the Persians into an instrument of Athenian empire building.) It was he who spent the forced contributions of the other members of the Delian League on the beautification of Athens and the expansion of its navy, which was then used to blackmail the other Greeks into submission to the will of Athens. And, it was Pericles who refused to take the warnings of the Spartans seriously when they sought to protect their allies against Athenian aggression. This made war inevitable, and the Peloponnesian War wrecked all hopes of Greek unity. It ended in a decisive defeat for Athens and for the Periclean policy of expansion. The following epoch saw the beginning of the long decline of classical Greece, rendering the poleis into mere provinces of new and alien empires.

PERICLES. This idealized bust of Pericles—here a Roman copy—was created just after his death.

British Museum, London, UK/Bridgeman Art Library

▶ Analyze and Interpret

The Peloponnesian War was originally popular among the Athenians. Although he had severe reservations, Pericles felt himself duty bound as democratic leader to follow their will. What does this tell you of the nature of democracy? What limits, if any, would you put on the exercise of authority in government by the majority?

You can read all of Pericles' Funeral Oration at the *Wadsworth World History Resource Center.*

Greeks and proved himself one of the most remarkable individuals in world history. His boldness and vigor became the stuff of legend among the Greeks who fought under him. Both traits are attested to by the story Plutarch (PLOO-tark) tells in the anecdote in this chapter (see the Society and Economy box "Plutarch on Alexander"). Alexander's break with previous military tradition regarding the status of the conqueror is also memorable.

At the time of his death, Philip had been organizing a large combined Macedonian–Greek army with the announced purpose of invading the huge Persian Empire. After swiftly putting down a rebellion in Thebes, Alexander continued this plan and crossed the Dardanelles (dahr-dah-NELS) in 334 with an army of about 55,000 men (very large for the times). In three great battles fought in Asia Minor, the young general brought down the mightiest empire the

SOCIETY AND ECONOMY

Plutarch on Alexander: *Parallel Lives*

Alexander of Macedonia is known to us through several eyewitness accounts. A Greek citizen of the Roman Empire who lived several hundred years after Alexander, however, wrote the best biography of all. Plutarch wrote his *Parallel Lives* to provide the youth of Rome with examples of both Greek and Roman heroes for them to emulate. It has been a favorite ever since and includes this famous anecdote:

> Philonicus the Thessalian brought the horse Bucephalus to Philip, offering to sell him for thirteen talents of silver; but when they went into the field to try him they found him so very vicious and unmanageable that he reared up when they endeavored to mount him and would not suffer even the voices of Philip's attendants. Upon which, Alexander, who stood nearby, said, "What an excellent horse do they lose for want of boldness to manage him! . . . I could manage this horse better than the others do."

Philip, who was a harsh father, challenged his son to prove his boast:

> Alexander immediately ran to the horse and taking hold of his bridle turned him directly toward the sun, having, it seems, observed that he was disturbed by and afraid of the motion of his own shadow. . . . Then, stroking him gently when he found him beginning to grow eager and

ALEXANDER. This marble bust of the conqueror is a Roman copy of a Greek original. It emphasizes Alexander's youthful beauty but may have been close to the reality of his appearance.

Pinacoteca Capitolina, Palazzo Conservatori, Rome, Italy/Index/ Bridgeman Art Library

fiery, with one nimble step he securely mounted him, and when he was seated by little and little drew in the bridle and curbed him so, without either striking or spurring him. Presently, when he found him free from all rebelliousness and only impatient for the course, he let him go at full speed, inciting him now with a commanding voice and urging him also with his heel. Philip and his friends looked on at first in silence and anxiety, till seeing him turn at the end of the course and come back rejoicing and triumphing for what he had performed, they all burst out into acclamations of applause; and his father, shedding tears of joy, kissed Alexander as he came down from the horse and in his exultation said, "O my son, look thee out for a kingdom equal to and worthy of thyself, for Macedonia is too little for thee!"

▶ *Analyze and Interpret*

Why might Plutarch, writing in the second century CE, want to use Alexander as one of his *Parallel Lives* for the instruction and entertainment of Roman youth? Besides bravery and intelligence, what other characteristics of Alexander are hinted at here that would appeal to a patriotic Roman?

You can read Plutarch's "Life of Alexander" at the *Wadsworth World History Resource Center*.

world had yet seen, the empire of Darius III of Persia, who was slain by his own troops after the third and decisive loss at Gaugamela in present-day Iraq (see Map 7.2).

Conquering an unresisting Egypt, Alexander then invaded the Persian heartland and proceeded eastward into the unknown borderlands of India. After spending five years defeating the numerous tribal kingdoms of the Indus basin and the wild highlands to its north (present-day Pakistan and Afghanistan), his remaining troops finally mutinied and refused to go farther. In 324, Alexander led his exhausted men back to Persia. A year later, he died in Babylon at the age of thirty-three. The few years of his reign and his much-disputed view of the desirable form of imperial government would have a lasting effect on much of the world's history.

A Mixed Culture

Alexander the Great (as he was soon called) had founded the largest empire yet seen in history, but it began to disintegrate almost on the day of his death. He left an infant son by his last and favorite wife, Roxana, but the child became a mere pawn as Alexander's generals struggled to succeed him as sole ruler. (The son was eventually put to death at age sixteen by one of the contestants.) Finally, the exhausted combatants tired of the civil war and split up the vast territories conquered by Alexander into a series of kingdoms, each originally ruled by one of Alexander's generals. Collectively, these successor states in southwestern Asia and the eastern Mediterranean are called the **Hellenistic kingdoms.**

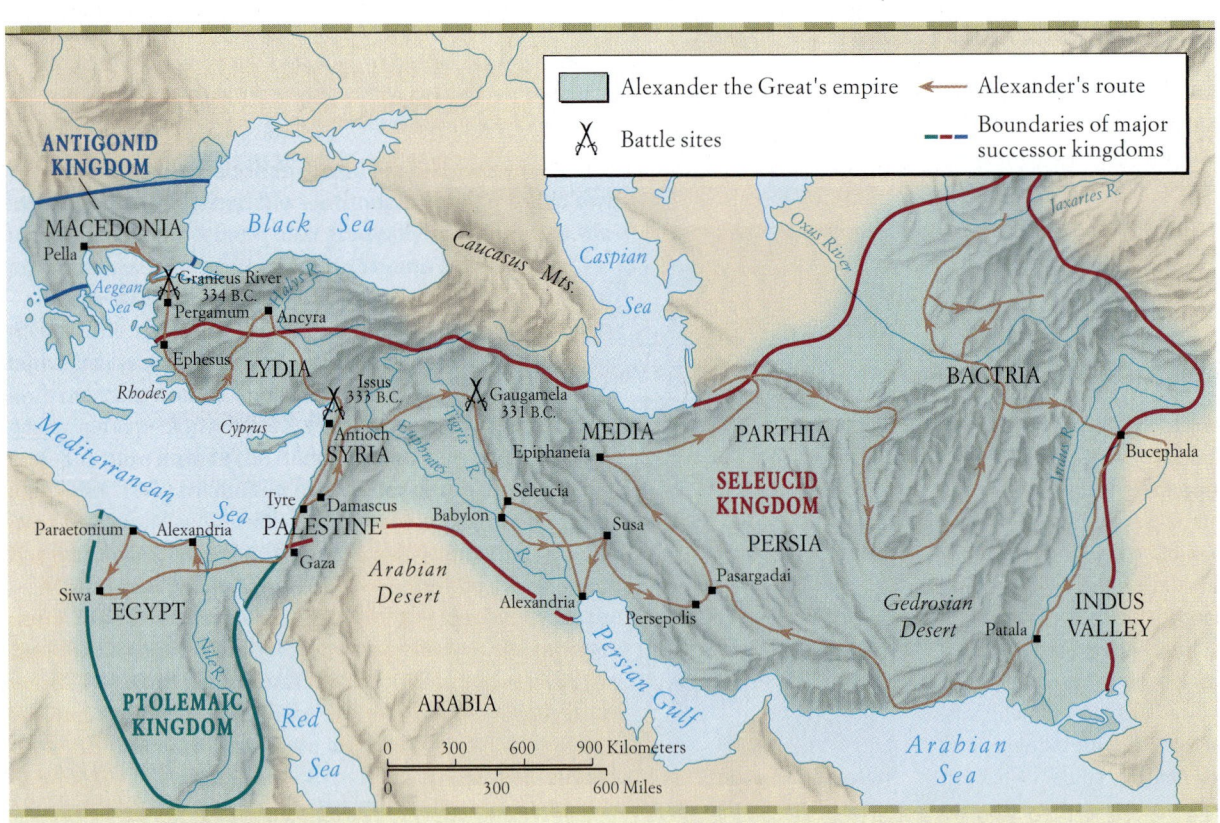

MAP 7.2 Alexander's Empire and the Successor Kingdoms

The huge area conquered by Alexander between 334 and 324 BCE was too large to control from a single center. It quickly broke down after the conqueror's death into regional kingdoms under several of his generals.

MAP QUESTIONS
Using the map scale, measure the east-to-west distance of Alexander's Empire. Locate and name the three successor kingdoms.

 View an interactive version of this or a related map at http://worldrc.wadsworth.com/

Everywhere Alexander led his armies, he founded new cities or towns, several of which bore his name. He then recruited Greeks from the homeland to come and establish themselves as a ruling group in the new cities. He encouraged them to follow his own example and intermarry with the locals. Tens of thousands of Greeks took up the invitation, leaving overcrowded, resource-poor Greece to make their names and fortunes in the countries now under Greco-Macedonian control. Inevitably, they brought with them the values they had cherished in their native land. As the conquerors, the Greeks could and did impose their ideas on the Asiatics and Egyptians with whom they had contact or intermarried.

The result was a mixed culture that blended Greek and Asiatic attitudes. A major example of this is the fate of the Greek civic community. The conquering Greeks first tried to reconstruct the polis mode of shared government and interdependent community in their new homes but quickly found that this was impossible. The Easterners had no experience of the polis form of government and did not understand it. They had never governed themselves but had always had an all-powerful king who ruled through his appointed or hereditary officials and generals. Soon the ruling Greeks themselves adopted the monarchical form of government. Thus, instead of the small, tight-knit community of equal citizens that was typical of the polis of the Classical Age, a Hellenistic state was typically a large kingdom in which a bureaucracy governed at the king's command. The inhabitants, whether Greek or native, were no longer citizens but subjects.

Although Alexander never conquered India's heartland, the Greek invasion of the Indus plains also had lasting effects. It introduced the Indian Hindu/Buddhist world to the Western world, and from this time onward, there were direct trade contacts between India and the eastern end of the Mediterranean. The invasion also disrupted the existing political balance in northern India, opening a vacuum that paved the way for the conquering Mauryan dynasty, including the great Ashoka (see Chapter 5).

Greeks and Easterners in the Hellenistic Kingdoms

The civil wars after Alexander's death resulted in the formation of three major successor kingdoms, each ruled by a former Greek general who had fought his way into that position (see Map 7.2):

1. The **Ptolemaic** (tah-leh-MAY-ihk) **Kingdom of Egypt.** A general named Ptolemy (TAH-leh-mee) succeeded in capturing Egypt, the richest of all the provinces of Alexander's empire. There he ruled as a divine king, just as the pharaohs once had. By the 100s BCE, the many immigrant Greeks and the Egyptian upper class had intermixed sufficiently to make Egypt a hybrid society. Many Greeks adopted the Egyptian way of life, which they found pleasant. Meanwhile, ordinary Egyptians remained exploited peasants or slaves.

2. The **Seleucid** (seh-LOO-sihd) **Kingdom of Persia.** The Seleucid kingdom, which was the successor to most of the once-mighty empire of Darius III, reached from India's borders to the shores of the Mediterranean. It was founded by a former general named Seleucus (seh-LOO-kus), and, like Ptolemaic Egypt, it lasted until the Roman assault in the first century BCE. Many tens of thousands of Greek immigrants came here as officials, soldiers, or craftsmen, and the contact between the locals and Greeks was extensive in the western parts of the kingdom, especially Syria and Turkey. The kingdom was too large to govern effectively, however, and it began to lose pieces to rebels and petty kings on its borders as early as the 200s. By the time the Romans were invading the western areas, most of the east was already lost.

3. The **Antigonid** (an-TIH-guh-nihd) **Kingdom.** This kingdom was also founded by a general, who claimed the old Macedonian homeland and ruled part of what had been Greece as well. The rest of Greece was divided among several leagues of city-states, which vied with each other for political and economic supremacy, until both they and the Macedonians fell to the Romans in the middle 100s BCE.

SUMMARY

THE GREEKS WERE an Indo-European nomadic group who entered the Greek peninsula around 2000 BCE and were gradually civilized, in part through the agency of the Minoans on Crete. By 1200, the Greeks had developed to the point that they were able to conquer their former overlords and mount an expedition against Troy. Following the coming of the Dorian invaders, however, Greece entered a Dark Age of cultural regression. This period ended around

800, and the Greeks began their ascent to becoming one of history's most remarkable civilizations, a rise that culminated in the Classical Age from 500 to 325 BCE.

In the Classical Age, the democratically led polis of Athens became the most important of the more than 200 city-states. Athens evolved through the various types of Greek government to achieve a limited but real democracy in the early fifth century. Through its commercial and maritime supremacy, it became the richest and most culturally significant of the poleis.

Victory over the Persians in the two Persian Wars encouraged democratic and imperialist Athens to attempt dominion over many other city-states. Its main opponent was militaristic and conservative Sparta, and the two came to blows in the lengthy Peloponnesian War, which ended with a Spartan victory in 404. Seventy years later, the real winner, however, proved to be the Macedonians, whose king Philip took advantage of the continuing intra-Hellenic disharmony and warfare to impose his rule over all of Greece at the battle of Chaeronea.

Alexander extended his father's ambitions by conquering the entire eastern world as it had been known to the Greeks at that time, creating an empire that incorporated all the old eastern civilizations that had preceded Alexander's, save that of China. Alexander died just ten years after having set forth on his own path to fame, and his empire failed to survive him. Had he lived long longer, perhaps Alexander might have derived satisfaction from witnessing the diverse peoples of the eastern Mediterranean and western Asia learning the language of their conquerors and colonizers and imbibing deeply from the wellsprings of their civilization, as indeed they did. Greek became the common language of discourse; it and Greek urban civilization were the twin foundations of most nations throughout this vast expanse, as we shall see in the next chapter. In the end, though, it would be the Romans who reaped the greatest rewards of Greece's and Alexander's triumphs (Chapters 9 and 10).

▶ Identification Terms

Test your knowledge of this chapter's key concepts by defining the following terms. If you can't recall the meaning of certain terms, refresh your memory by looking up the boldfaced term in the chapter, turning to the Glossary at the end of the book, or working with the flashcards that are available on the *World Civilizations* Companion Website: **academic.cengage.com/adler**

Alexander the Great	Hellenistic kingdoms	monarchy	Pericles
Antigonid Kingdom	Homer	Mycenaeans	Persian Wars
aristocracy	*Iliad*	*Odyssey*	*polis*
Cleisthenes	Messenian Wars	oligarchy	Ptolemaic Kingdom of Egypt
democracy	Minoans	Peloponnesian War	Seleucid Kingdom of Persia

▶ Test Your Knowledge

Test your knowledge of this chapter by answering the following questions. Complete answers appear at the end of the book. You may find even more quiz questions in CengageNOW and on the *World Civilizations* Companion Website: **academic.cengage.com/adler**

1. The Mycenaean period of Greek history
   a. preceded the Dark Age.
   b. followed the Dark Age.
   c. was the high point of Greek political culture.
   d. saw the Greeks ruling several other peoples.
   e. contributed a great deal to Dorian culture.
2. In Homer's poem, Odysseus (Ulysses) conquered the Cyclops by
   a. killing him in a duel.
   b. blinding him.
   c. tricking him to jump into the sea.
   d. tying him down while he was sleeping.
   e. convincing him to drink a poisonous concoction.

3. The polis was a
   a. warrior-king.
   b. community of citizens.
   c. commercial league of merchants.
   d. temple complex.
   e. barracks for military youth in Sparta.
4. Athenian women were
   a. secluded within the home after marriage.
   b. considered the collective sexual property of all free Greek males.
   c. excluded from any political role.
   d. viewed as the more talented of the two sexes.
   e. considered vital to the production of strong warrior offspring.
5. Which of the following was *not* a form of classical Greek government?
   a. Monarchy
   b. Hierarchy
   c. Oligarchy

d. Democracy
e. Aristocracy

6. The founder of the Athenian democracy was
a. Solon.
b. Cleisthenes.
c. Pisistratus.
d. Plato.
e. Homer.

7. The critical factor in transforming Sparta from an ordinary polis into a special one was
a. the war against the neighboring Messenians.
b. the invasions by the Persians.
c. the war against Athens.
d. its commercial rivalry with Athens.
e. its use of slavery to advance its standing as a polis.

8. The battle of Marathon was fought during the
a. Peloponnesian War.
b. Second Persian War.
c. Siege of Sparta.
d. Athenian navy's rout of its enemy at Salamis.
e. First Persian War.

9. The Peloponnesian War is best described as
a. a struggle between Athens and the rest of Greece.
b. the start of an era of Spartan dictatorship in Greece.
c. the discrediting of the Athenian democracy as leader of Greece.
d. the establishment of Persian influence in Greece.
e. simply one more in a line of victories for Athens.

10. According to Plutarch, Alexander most impressed his father by
a. slaying the giant Hercules.
b. riding a wild horse.
c. leading the Macedonian army.
d. constructing a bridge over the Hellespont.
e. invading the Persian Empire.

Enter *CengageNOW* using the access card that is available with this text. *CengageNOW* will assist you in understanding the content in this chapter with lesson plans generated for your needs, and provide you with a connection to the *Wadsworth World History Resource Center* (see description at right for details).

 **World History Resource Center**

Enter the Resource Center using either your *CengageNOW* access card or your standalone access card for the *Wadsworth World History Resource Center*. Organized by topic, this website includes quizzes; images; over 350 primary source documents; interactive simulations, maps, and timelines; movie explorations; and a wealth of other resources. You can read the following documents, and many more, at the *Wadsworth World History Resource Center*:

Pericles, Funeral Oration
Homer, the *Odyssey*

For we are lovers of the beautiful, yet simple in our tastes; we cultivate the mind without loss of manliness.

—The Funeral Oration
of Pericles

8 GREEK HUMANISM, 800–100 BCE

PHILOSOPHY: THE LOVE OF WISDOM
Pre-Socratic Philosophy ◆ The Classic Age: Socrates, Plato, and Aristotle ◆ Three Hellenistic Varieties

SCIENCE

GREEK RELIGION

THE ARTS AND LITERATURE

SOCIETY AND ECONOMY
Slavery ◆ Gender Relations

THE GREEK LEGACY

THE GREEK CONTRIBUTION to the creation of Western civilization equals that of the Jews and the Christians. In addition to the concept of democratic government, the Greek achievement was exemplified most strikingly in the fine arts and in the search for wisdom, which the Greeks called *philosophy*. In both areas, the Greeks developed models and modes of thought that have remained appealing for twenty-five centuries and are still valid and inspiring today. The overall achievement of the Greeks during their great age is summed up in the term *Hellenic culture*. After the Greeks fell to the Macedonian barbarians in 338 BCE, Hellenism in a diluted and corrupted form was spread into the East and Egypt by the conquerors and their Greek associates. This altered form of Hellenism is known as *Hellenistic* culture or civilization. It retained some of the values and attitudes of the classical Greek polis, but it also gradually dropped many in favor of the very different values and attitudes of the Eastern kingdoms and empires.

PHILOSOPHY: THE LOVE OF WISDOM

The Greek word *philosophy* means "love of wisdom." The Greeks used it to mean examination of the entire spectrum of human knowledge and not just the narrower fields of inquiry, such as the rules of logic, to which it is conventionally limited today. The ancient Greeks can legitimately be called the originators of philosophy. Of course, other peoples before them had attempted to work out the nature and meaning of human existence, but none pursued their studies so systematically or with as much boldness and imagination as the Greeks.

Greek philosophy can be divided into three periods: the Pre-Socratic period, the Classical Age, and the Hellenistic era. The first period extends from the earliest surviving philosophical writings around 600 BCE to the life of Socrates (470–399 BCE). The second period extends from Socrates through about 300 BCE. The third was from 300 to about 50 BCE.

Pre-Socratic Philosophy

The greatest contribution of the Pre-Socratics was the concept of law in the universe. Unlike any previous thinkers, these Greeks believed that what happened in the physical cosmos was the result of laws of causation and thus understandable and predictable on a purely natural level. They did not deny the gods or the powers of the gods, but they did not look to the gods as the normal and usual causes of phenomena. Instead, they conceived of what we now call *natural law*—a set of phenomena in nature that, when properly understood, explain why certain things occur.

Two of the greatest of the Pre-Socratics were Anaximander and Hippocrates. Anaximander was the father of the theory of natural evolution of species—long before Darwin ever dreamed of it. He also thought the physical universe had no limits. He conceived of it as boundless and constantly expanding, much as modern astronomers do. Hippocrates is best known as a founder of scientific medicine, but curing people was really only incidental to his intellectual interests. First and foremost, he wished to teach people to observe the life around them. He was the first great **empiricist** (ehm-PEER-ih-sist) in the natural sciences, arriving at his general theories only after careful and prolonged observation of those aspects of the world that could be weighed and measured.

The Classical Age: Socrates, Plato, and Aristotle

Socrates (470–399 BCE) was the first philosopher to focus on the ethical and epistemological (truth-establishing) questions that have haunted the thoughtful since the dawn of creation. Like most of the Classical Age figures, he concentrated on human rationality rather than on physical nature. He was more interested in "How do I know?" than in "What is to be known?" Systematic questioning is the essence of the *Socratic method,* which teachers have used ever since. He would systematically question his young disciples, allowing them to take nothing for granted. He challenged them to examine fearlessly and justify everything before taking it for truth.

Our knowledge of Socrates comes not from him directly but from the numerous works of his pupil and admirer, **Plato** (427–347 BCE). The conservative elders of the polis,

(rotated text at right of image) Museo Archeologico Nazionale, Naples/Alinari/Bridgeman Art Library

SOCRATES. Plato tells us that his master Socrates was considered extraordinarily ugly, but his mastery of logic and beauty of expression made all those who heard him forget everything else about him.

Plato tells us, accused Socrates, of poisoning the minds of the youth of Athens. Brought to trial, he was found guilty and forced to drink poisonous hemlock. Plato defended his teacher from the unjust accusation, but he was a different thinker from his predecessor. Plato tried above all to solve the problem of how the mind can experience and recognize Truth and ultimate reality (see the description of his *metaphor of the cave* in the Patterns of Belief box). He also ventured into an analysis of politics as it should be (in the *Republic*) and as it existed (in the *Laws*). During his lifetime, Greece was in constant turmoil, which probably predisposed him towards views which were notably anti-democratic.

PATTERNS OF BELIEF

Plato's Metaphor of the Cave

The classical Greeks were the ancient world's great pioneers into the question of how the mind works. Seeing Man as a part of the natural world, they wished to know as much as possible about him. Of the great trinity of Greek classical philosophers, Plato distinguished himself by wrestling with the eternal question: How does the human brain penetrate appearances to attain Reality? Our impressions of the outer world originally are entirely dependent on sensory data: what can be touched, or smelled, or seen and heard. How, then, can we formulate ideas that go beyond the specific detail of particular objects that the senses perceive? Or is there any idea, beyond the specific object? Could there be an abstract Idea of, say, a chair? Or only of *this* chair, with rounded legs and a straight back made of walnut wood? Most particularly, are there ideals of Truth, Beauty, and Goodness that lie behind the weak and unstable versions of those virtues that human experience can conceive of?

Plato thought that such abstractions existed and were far more perfect in their nature than any specific version of them that the senses might perceive. But he also believed that most people were unable to apprehend such Ideals in anything like their pure forms. Few men and women possessed the mental powers and the desire to allow them to penetrate beyond mere appearances into Truth and Reality.

Seeking to convey his meaning, Plato came to write the metaphor of the cave, which has remained one of the best-known philosophical anecdotes in history. Most people, he said, were like prisoners condemned to existence in a dark cave. They peered constantly through the dim light trying to make out what was happening around them:

Imagine the condition of men living in a cavern underground, with an entrance open to the daylight and a long passage entering the cave. Here they have been since childhood, chained by the leg and by the neck, so that they cannot move and can see only what is directly in front of them. At some higher place in the cave, a fire burns, and between the prisoners and the fire is a track with a parapet built in front of it, like a screen at a puppet show which hides the performers while they show their puppets. . . .

Now behind this parapet, imagine persons carrying along various artificial objects, including figures of men and of animals in wood or stone or other material which

project above the parapet. . . . The prisoners, then, would recognize as reality nothing but the shadows of those artificial objects.

Our sense impressions, unenlightened by wisdom, deliver us into a prison of ignorance, where men mistake blurred shadows for reality.

Plato further says that if a prisoner were released and allowed to go out into the unaccustomed sunlight, he would, of course, be blinded by the light and utterly confused.

But this would change as he became accustomed to his new condition; his ability to see this huge new world would gradually increase:

He would need, then, to grow accustomed before he could see things in the upper world. At first, it would be easiest to make out shadows, and then the images of men and things reflected in water, and later on the things themselves. After that, it would be easier to watch the heavenly bodies and the skies by night, looking at the light of the moon and stars rather than the sun and the light of the sun in daytime.

Plato drew his conservative political and social conclusions from these beliefs about the nature of Reality and human ability to perceive it. He thought that relatively few people would ever be released from the cave of ignorance and shadow-play. Those who did attain to the upper world of Truth and slowly and with difficulty worked through the ever-higher, more accurate stages of Reality should be given the leadership positions.

They deserved to be leaders not only because they merited power and prestige, but also because they—and not the masses who remained in the cave—were able to make proper choices for the welfare of the whole society. Plato, who lived through the Peloponnesian War, remained a convinced antidemocrat all his life.

▶ *Analyze and Interpret*

Does the metaphor employed by Plato explain to you his point about the difference between Reality and appearances?

In what way does this story link with Plato's contempt for democratic politics?

Source: F. M. Cornford translation, *The Republic of Plato* (Oxford: Oxford University Press, 1941). By permission of Oxford University Press.

You can read more of *Plato's Republic* at the Wadsworth World History Resource Center.

Aristotle (AYR-rih-stah-tuhl; 384–322 BCE) was a pupil of Plato, but he, too, differed sharply from his teacher. Aristotle is the nearest equivalent to a universal genius that Greece produced. His interests included practically every field of science yet known, as well as the formal analysis of thought and actions that we now know as philosophy. His best-known works are the *Politics, Physics,* and *Metaphysics,* but he was also a first-rate mathematician, an astronomer, the founder of botany, and a student of medicine. So great was his renown in the medieval world that both European Christians and Arab Muslims referred to him simply as "the Master." Christian scholars thought of him as a sort of pagan saint, while learned Muslims thought of him as the greatest natural philosopher and man of science the world had yet produced.

Greek philosophy was marked at all times by the strong sense that humans were quite capable of understanding the cosmos and all that lived within it by use of reason and careful observation. They were not overawed by the gods, but created the gods in their own image and never resorted to supernatural powers to explain what natural law could explain. The knowledge the Greeks sought in their "love of wisdom" was that which was reachable by the unaided human intellect.

Three Hellenistic Varieties

During the Hellenistic era, the lower classes were attracted by the new mystery religions (below), but three new philosophies appealed to the more educated. The first was **Cynicism,** which emerged as an organized school in the middle 300s. Its major figure was the famous Diogenes, who called for a return to absolute simplicity and a rejection of artificial divisions, whether political or economic. Relatively few people could adapt to the rigid poverty and absence of egotism that the Cynics demanded, but the philosophy nevertheless had a great impact on Hellenistic urban life.

The second philosophy was **Epicureanism,** named after its founder, Epicurus, who taught in Athens during the third century BCE. Epicurus taught that the principal good of life was pleasure, which he defined as the avoidance of pain. He was not talking about physical sensation so much as mental or spiritual pleasure and pain. He believed that inner peace was to be obtained only by consciously rejecting the values and prejudices of others and turning inward to discover what is important to you. Like Daoism and Buddhism, Epicureanism taught that it was better to focus on finding your own serenity and to ignore the affairs of the world.

The third philosophy, **Stoicism,** captured the largest following among the Hellenistic population. It was the product of a freed slave, a Phoenician named Zeno, who emphasized the unity of all humanity and disdained the social conventions that falsely separated the human race. He taught that good people were obliged to participate in public life to help the less fortunate as best they could. Whether or not they were successful was not so important as the fact that they had tried: virtue was its own reward.

The Stoics popularized the concept of an overarching natural law that governed all human affairs. This concept was to gain a following among the Romans and became the normal belief of their ruling class. It was a philosophy of noble acts, which strongly emphasized the necessity of service to one's fellows and the recognition that all are essentially equal under the skin.

SCIENCE

The pursuit of scientific knowledge did not really come into its own until the Hellenistic Period. The most important areas of inquiry were biology, astronomy, geography, physics, and math. The biggest center of science was the great city of Alexandria, Egypt, where the Ptolemaic kings established and supported many research centers and the ancient world's largest library and museum. Both were destroyed much later by fire and earthquake (see the Science and Technology box).

Why did science flourish in the Hellenistic period? For one, the Greek habit of rational and logical thought was especially useful in the sciences. Aristotle, who had tutored young Alexander, insisted on the necessity of careful observation of phenomena before attempting to explain their causes. His successors at the *Lyceum,* the famous school he founded in Athens, proceeded along those lines and obtained worthwhile results in several fields.

Another of the chief stimuli to scientific work was the new exposure of the Greeks to the Babylonian mathematicians and astronomers/astrologers, thanks to the conquests of Alexander. Now in the Hellenistic Age, the Greek world was brought for the first time into extensive contact with the cumulative knowledge of the Middle East. Scientists profited from the work done by Egyptian, Mesopotamian, and especially Babylonian scholars during the previous three millenia.

The work in astronomy done at this time would stand without serious challenge until the sixteenth century CE. Among the outstanding astronomers were Aristarchus of Samos (310–230 BCE) and Hipparchus of Nicaea (260–190 BCE). Aristarchus proposed a *heliocentric* model of the universe in which the Earth revolved around the sun. Hipparchus and others attacked it, however, and in the second century CE, a later astronomer named Ptolemy picked up the theory of a *geocentric* universe (that is, centered on the Earth). The geocentric model became the standard wisdom of astronomy for the next 1,500 years, until

Museum fuer Islamische Kunst, Staatliche Museum zu Berlin, Berlin, Germany/©Bildarchiv Preussischer Kulturbesitz/Art Resource, NY

SCIENCE AND TECHNOLOGY

Hellenistic Scientists

Egyptian Alexandria under the dynasty of the Ptolemaic kings was the largest city of the Hellenistic world. Founded and named by the world conqueror in the late fourth century BCE, it grew steadily, fattened by the increasing trade of the Nile valley with the remainder of the Greco-Roman world. At some point in the third century BCE, a museum and library were established there, which quickly became the intellectual and scientific center of the Mediterranean region. A recent British historian of science tells us about the type of research carried on there, the nature of the museum, and three of the Hellenistic researchers. Quoting the Roman author Cicero, he says:

> Strato the physicist was of the opinion that all divine power resides in nature, which is a power without shape or capacity to feel, containing within itself all the causes of coming-to-be, of growth, and of decay. Final causes, such as Aristotle posited, are out; nor is there any place in Strato's world for divine providence. Further . . . it seems clear that Strato endeavored to solve his problems by means of experimentation [a much debated question in the history of science].
>
> [T]he second of our Hellenistic scientists, Philo of Byzantium, worked in Alexandria around 200 B.C. Philo's work was concerned with artillery, comprising mechanical arrow-firing catapults and stone-throwing ballistas. . . . The most important fact revealed by recent research is the indication of *repeated experiment* as a means of establishing a method and a formula to be incorporated in the specification for the construction of different types of missile launchers.
>
> While Philo's name is associated with a variety of writings on scientific subjects, that of Ktesibios is linked with an equally wide range of inventions, most of which are based on the application of the principles of hydraulics. . . . His inventions included, in addition to the twin-cylinder

water pump, a water-clock, a pipe organ powered by an ingenious combination of water and compressed air, and an improved catapult which operated by bronze springs instead of twisted animal sinews. He is also credited with a considerable number of inventions designed for entertainment, the so-called automata. . . .

It is an easy step from the most famous inventor of his day [that is, Philo] to the Museum with which he was associated. The House of the Muses [the Museum] was evidently a research organization, supported, like the Library, by a royal endowment. Traditional accounts . . . assume that the Library, which rapidly acquired a worldwide reputation, was separate from the Museum; but it is more likely that both were parts of what might be called a research institute, which provided facilities for workers in a wide variety of disciplines belonging to what we would now call the humanities and the sciences.

Contrary to the commonly held opinion that under Rome the Museum and the Library suffered a rapid decline into total obscurity, we have evidence that both were still operating many centuries later, even if not as vigorously as in their heyday. . . . Medicine was in the most flourishing condition of all the sciences there, enjoying such a high reputation that the only qualification an intending practitioner needed to produce was a statement that he had received his training at Alexandria. The most important scientific advances seem to have been made in pure mathematics, mechanics, physics, geography, and medicine.

▶ Analyze and Interpret

Why do you think it was important whether scientists of this age employed experiments to determine factual knowledge?

What might be a modern equivalent to the Alexandria institute?

Source: K. D. White, in *Hellenistic History and Culture*, ed. P. Green (Berkeley: University of California Press, 1991), p. 216f. Used by permission.

Copernicus questioned it. The most important figures in geography were the Greek Eratosthenes (air-ah-TOS-thenees; c. 276–c. 194 BCE) and Strabo (c. 64 BCE–c. 23 CE). Eratosthenes calculated the circumference of the Earth accurately. His data provided the first reliable maps of the globe (see Worldview Map 8.1).

In physics, the outstanding researcher was Archimedes (ark-ih-MEE-dees; c. 287–212 BCE), who was equally

important in mathematics. In the third century BCE, Euclid (YOO-clid), an Egyptian Greek, produced the most influential math treatise ever written, the *Elements of Geometry.*

The Greeks in general were not interested in the practical aspects of science, which we now call technology. Most discoveries and experimental results were forgotten because no one saw any need to transform these theo-

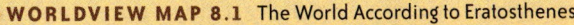

Parallel of Thule · *Thule* · **EUROPE** · *Northern Ocean* · **BRITAIN** · *Hyrcanian Forest* · *Don R.* · *Maeotic Lake* · Ostimii · *Dnieper R.* · *Caucasus Mts.* · *Jaxartes R.* · **SCYTHIA** · Pyrenees Mts. · *Rhône R.* · *Danube R.* · Byzantium · *Euxine* · Dionysia · *Caspian Sea* · *Oxus R.* · **SOGDIANA** · Corsica · *Adriatic Sea* · *Aegean Sea* · Athens · *Phaselis R.* · *Cyrus R.* · **OCHUS** · **BACTRIA** · *Ganges R.* · Parallel of Rhodes · Sardinia · Issus · *Taurus* · Mts. · Parallel of Alexandria · *Strait of the Columns* · Carthage · Sicily · *Syrtis* · Crete · Rhodes · Cyprus · Gaugamela · **A S I A** · Palibothra · Cyrene · *Euphrates R.* · **PERSIS** · **ARACHOSIA** · **INDIA** · Alexandria · **LIBYA** · **ARABIA** · *Tigris R.* · **SUSIS** · **CARMANIA** · **ARIANA** · Thebes · **MINACI** · Syene · *Arabian Gulf* · *Persian Gulf* · **GEDROSIA** · Tropic · **NUBIANS** · **SABAEI** · **FISHEATERS** · **CONIACI** · Parallel of Meroe · Ptolemais · **CHATRAMOTITAE** · Meroe · Sembrivae · Southern Limit of Known World · *Atlantic Ocean* · **CINNAMON LAND** · *Meridian of Alexandria* · *Erythraean Sea (Red Sea)* · *Taprobane (Ceylon)* · Equator · Stadia · 2,000 3,000 · 8,000 · 13,500 · 6,300 · 10,000 · 14,000 · 16,000 · 3,000 2,000

WORLDVIEW MAP 8.1   The World According to Eratosthenes

This is the first world map that bears substantial relation to the globe as modern people know it. It was drawn by the Greek geographer Eratosthenes in the third century BCE, relying on his own observations and on reports by mariners and other travelers.

MAP QUESTIONS
Compare Eratosthenes's map with a modern world map. What areas were unknown to the Greeks?

retical breakthroughs into practical applications for daily life. Laborsaving devices were not much in demand in the Hellenistic Period because an abundance of labor was available for all tasks: slaves were much more numerous then than they had been earlier, and their situation could be affected only marginally by technology.

By about 200 BCE, Hellenistic science had begun a slow decline. Astronomy was being replaced by astrology, and the initial advances in physics and math were not followed up. Only in medicine were some significant advances made, notably by the so-called **Empiricists,** doctors who were convinced that the answer to the ills of the body was to be found in the careful analysis of diseases and their physical causes. Building on the work of the great Hippocrates, these men identified much of the body's physiology, including the circulation of the blood and the functions of the nerves, the liver, and other vital organs. Medical knowledge would not reach so high a level again in the West until the end of the Middle Ages.

GREEK RELIGION

Not all Greeks were able to find the truth they needed in philosophy. Probably the large majority of people were not exposed to the complex reasoning of the philosophers, so they turned instead to religion. Like most of the other peoples we have discussed, the Greeks were polytheistic, but theirs were *anthropomorphic gods,* that is to say, they were creatures molded in the human image, with the foibles and strengths of men and women. Among them were Zeus (zoos), the father figure; Hera, the wife of Zeus; Poseidon (poe-SIE-dun), god of the seas; Athena, goddess of wisdom and also of war; Apollo, god of the sun; and Demeter, goddess of fertility.

Greek religion was different from the religions of most agrarian civilizations in other important ways. First, Greek civilization of the Hellenic era was **humanistic:** Greeks were convinced that human beings occupied a position in the cosmos that was second only to that of the gods themselves. They believed that the human race and the race of the gods were related, in fact, since both were descended from the Earth Goddess. They had enormous confidence in human qualities and the ability of humans to solve any problem, believing that "Man is the measure of all things," and deserved serious study. This attitude was reflected in their art, their philosophy, and their religion. From early times, the Greeks' anthropomorphic gods were less threatening and less powerful than other peoples' gods. Second, the Greeks never created a priestly class or caste, but used their priests only as informal leaders of loosely organized services. After about 500 BCE especially, the priests and priestesses receded more and more into the background, and many of the gods themselves became mere symbolic figures.

As with the Chinese Confucians, it was *human existence in this world* that engaged the educated Greeks and provided the frame of reference for defining good and evil. Normally, the educated people did not speculate about the afterlife and saw no reason to fear it. By the opening of the Classical Era, most of them apparently no longer believed in immortality, if they ever had. For them, philosophy, as an exercise in humanism and reason, increasingly took the place once occupied by supernatural religion, with its emphasis on the gods and myth. The acts of the gods came to be viewed as myths, simply allegories that served a useful moral purpose in educating the people to their duties and responsibilities as good citizens of the polis. Behind and above the gods was an impersonal and unavoidable Fate, a force that could not be successfully defied by either humans or gods.

In Classical philosophy, the ideal of the **golden mean,** the middle ground between all extremes of thought and action, was a particular attraction. The Greeks distrusted radical measures and tried to find that which embraced the good without claiming to be the best. They believed that the person who claimed to have the perfect solution to a problem was being misled by **hubris** (HYOO-brihs)**,** a false overconfidence. The gods were "setting him up," as we might put it, and disaster was sure to follow. The wise person always kept this in mind and acted accordingly.

Adherence to the golden mean should by no means be seen as a sign of humility. The Greeks were not humble by nature but were quite willing to take chances and to stretch their intellectual powers to the utmost. They believed passionately in the human potential, but they did not defy Fate or the gods without expecting to be punished.

The great tragedies written by Sophocles (SOFF-oh-cleez; c. 497–406 BCE) are perhaps the most dramatically effective expressions of this expectation, particularly his trilogy about the doomed **Oedipus** (EH-dih-puhs) **Rex** and his vain struggle to avoid the fate that lay in wait for him.

The Hellenistic religions that evolved after the conquests of Alexander were different from both the Greek religion of the Classical Age and the earlier religions of China and India. Worship of the traditional Greek gods such as Zeus and Athena died out completely in the East, and the Greek immigrants turned more and more to the native cults. Because they offered eternal life or earthly prosperity, they provided some concrete emotional support and responded to human longing for security. Three of the most important cults were those of Isis, goddess of the Nile and renewal; Mithra, god of eternal life; and Serapis, the Egyptian god of the underworld and the judge of souls.

All three shared certain characteristics, which allow them to be grouped as **mystery religions,** that is, they demanded faith rather than reason as the ultimate justification for their teachings. To believers who followed the instructions of the powerful priests, they promised eternal life. Life would overcome death, and the afterworld would be an infinitely more pleasant place than this one. These deities were universal gods who had final jurisdiction over all people everywhere, whether individuals recognized the god or not. The stage was thus being set for the triumph of the greatest of the mystery religions: Christianity.

THE ARTS AND LITERATURE

The classical Greeks gave at least three major art forms to Western civilization: (1) drama, a Greek invention that arose in the 600s, presumably in Athens, as a sort of pageant depicting scenes from the myths about the gods and their interventions in human affairs; (2) lyric poetry, originating in the pre-Classical Era and represented best by surviving fragments from the work of Sappho, a woman who lived on the island of Lesbos in the 600s; and (3) "classical" architecture, most notably the temples scattered about the shores of the Mediterranean by Greek colonists, as well as on the Acropolis in Athens and in many other poleis. Besides these forms, which they originated, the Greeks excelled in epic poetry (represented by the *Iliad* and *Odyssey*); magnificent sculpture of the human form and face at a level of skill not previously approached; dance, which was a particular passion for both men and women; fine ceramic wares of every sort; and painting, mainly on ceramic vessels and plaques.

The particular strengths of Greek pictorial and architectural art were the harmony and symmetry of the parts with the whole; the ability to depict the ideal beauty of the human form, while still maintaining recognizable realism in their portrayals; and the combination of grace and strength balanced in vital tension. The models established during the Classical Age have remained supremely important to artists of the West ever since.

Greek literature took several distinct forms. Poetry of all types was very highly developed from the time of

Acropolis, Athens, Greece/Alinari/Bridgeman Art Library

THE PARTHENON. Atop the hill in central Athens called the Acropolis, the Parthenon was designed to be the center of Athenian spiritual life and its most sacred temple. Constructed in the fifth century BCE, the now-empty interior once featured a massive statue of the patroness of the city, the goddess of both war and wisdom, Athena. An explosion of gunpowder then seriously damaged it during a seventeenth-century war between Turks and Italians. The style of its building has been praised and imitated throughout the world.

Homer (eighth century) onward. The outstanding names besides Sappho are Hesiod, Euripides, Aeschylus, Sophocles, Aristophanes, and Pindar. Most of these were dramatists as well as poets. Drama was one of the Greeks' most popular arts, and the plays that have survived represent possibly one-hundredth of what was written in the fifth and fourth centuries. The great trio of Euripides, Aeschylus, and Sophocles created the tragic form, while Aristophanes is the first noted comic playwright.

The ancient Greeks prized craftsmanship. They evidently learned much of their skill in ceramics and metalwork from the Egyptians and the Minoans, but they improved on their models. Greek ceramics were in great demand throughout the Mediterranean world, and Greek ships frequently set sail loaded with wine jugs, olive oil vessels, and other household utensils made from clay, as well as fine work. Much of the Athenian population evidently worked for the export trade, making objects of clay, metal, leather, and wood.

Generally speaking, art and literature in the Hellenistic age declined noticeably from the high standards of the preceding age. The fine arts were generally modeled on the art of the Hellenic Age but tended to be more realistic. They also lacked some of the creative vigor and imagination that had so marked Greek art in the earlier period, and they sometimes tended toward a love of display for its own sake—a sort of boastfulness and pretentiousness.

Much more literature has survived from the Hellenistic Age than from the Classical Age. Unfortunately, both artistic inspiration and execution seem to have declined. There were many imitators but few original thinkers. The main centers of literature were in Alexandria, Rhodes, Pergamum, and other eastern areas rather than in Athens or Greece itself.

The same was true of the plastic arts. Great sculpture and buildings were more likely to be created in the East than in Greece, in large part because the richest cities of the Hellenistic Age were found there, along with the wealthiest

Scala/Art Resource, NY

DISCOBOLUS. This Roman copy of a fifth-century Greek original by the great sculptor Myron is deservedly famous for its combination of manly strength and graceful control. The athlete prepares his body for an extreme effort at tossing the heavy stone disc, one of the feats at the original Olympic Games. Competition in the nude was the norm for both Greeks and Romans.

Casa di Lucrezio Frontone, Pompeii, Italy/Roger-Viollet, Paris/ Bridgeman Art Library

VENUS AND MARS. Frescoes humanizing the divinities were a favorite mode of art in the Hellenistic Age. This one shows the wedding of Venus and Mars, as the Romans called their epitomes of feminine beauty and virile manhood. It was painted on an interior wall in Pompeii, Italy.

inhabitants. In imagination and execution, much Hellenistic sculpture and architecture was extremely impressive. Indeed, it was much superior to the literary works of the time. The absolute mastery of stone that was already established by the artists of the Classical Age continued and developed even further. Such great sculptures as *Laocoön, The Dying Gaul,* and *The Old Shepherdess* show an ability to "make the stone speak" that has been the envy of other ages. But even in sculpture, there was a great deal of copying of earlier forms and an abundance of second-class work.

SOCIETY AND ECONOMY

Most Greeks farmed, yet the polis was the heart of Greek life. It usually was a small place (Athens was the exception), and its inhabitants were generally racially and culturally homogeneous. At its center was a town of moderate size, with a population of 10,000 to 20,000 as a rough average. It supported all of the usual urban trades and crafts. Most—including many who farmed and lived outside its

walls—debated about and participated in civic culture and politics, which were matters of wide concern.

The general level of education among the Greeks of the Classical Age was remarkably high and was not approximated again in the Western world until much later. The citizen-based, participatory nature of community life in the Classical polis necessitated high levels of education, and some scholars believe that Athens might have been the first literate society in history. Neither the Romans nor the medieval Europeans came close.

During the Hellenistic Age, a true urban civilization, in which the towns and cities were far more important than the more numerous rural areas, came into existence for the first time since the decline of the Mesopotamian cities. Large cities—such as Alexandria in Egypt, Antioch in Syria, and Susa in Persia—dominated the life of the Hellenistic kingdoms. Like modern cities, Hellenistic towns were centers of commerce and learning with great museums, libraries, and amusement halls. One or two of them possibly had more than 500,000 inhabitants, drawn from a vast variety of ethnic backgrounds. Even the free majority felt little sense of community, largely because they came from so many different social and ethnic groups.

Originally, the Greeks were the governing class of the cities, but gradually they intermarried and were absorbed by the larger group that surrounded them. The Greek language remained the tongue of the cultured, but in most other respects, the Eastern way of life and thought became predominant.

Slavery

It has frequently been remarked that Athenian democracy was built on and supported by a large population of slaves. This statement is true, but it may not be as damning as it seems at first, since there were ameliorating circumstances. Both Greeks and foreigners could be enslaved, usually as the result of debt, and for many slavery was neither lifelong nor hereditary. Masters normally did not abuse slaves, and many slaves were prized workers and craftsmen who worked for pay but were not free to go off at will to other employment. Many of these men and women were employed directly by the state, and most of the rest were used in a variety of domestic ways, rather than as chattel, farm labor. Only in the polis-owned silver mines near Athens were slaves abused as a matter of course, and these slaves were normally criminals, not debtors.

During the Hellenistic Era, most people were free, but there was a dramatic rise in the numbers of slaves. Also, for the first time, large groups of people were pulled into a slave status that lasted for their lifetimes; worse still, slavery became hereditary and was passed by parents on to their children.

Gender Relations

The degree of freedom accorded to women in classical Greek society has been a topic of intense debate in recent years. Historians agree that women were generally excluded from any effective exercise of political and economic powers, and that the Greeks were the Western originators of *misogyny*, the distrust and dislike of women by men. Any women who took political action did so only under certain closely defined conditions, and unless they did so at least ostensibly on behalf of a male relative, they and those around them came "to a bad end." The great tragic heroines such as Electra, Antigone, and Medea and the mythological heroines such as Cassandra and Artemis are examples of women who met such a fate.

One modern scholar notes that the antifemale prejudice exhibited in later Greek literature is not present in the Homeric period. The women of Sparta were free and equal with their men folk. Spartan women allegedly shared the sexual favors of their men, regardless of marriage. The men were so frequently away in the field or in barracks that both they and the government saw this practice as essential to Sparta's survival. Because our knowledge of Sparta comes exclusively from non-Spartan literary sources, it is impossible to know whether this very unusual attitude was actual fact, however.

In contrast, we have a good deal of definite information about Athens. Respectable Athenian women were limited to the home. Their work was closely prescribed for them: management of the household and supervision of children and servants. Within the four walls of the home, one or two rooms were reserved for their use. In multistoried houses, these rooms were normally upstairs, but in any house, they would be in the back, away from the street. This segregation served one purpose: keeping women, as the valuable possession of men, away from the prying eyes of non-family members and all sexual temptations. Poor urban women undoubtedly had more freedom to leave the home and enter the workplace unescorted, as did rural women, who had a great many essential tasks to perform daily, some of them outdoors. A freeborn, native Athenian woman was recognized as having some civic rights, but her citizenship was limited and very different from that enjoyed by males. Its main advantage was that Athenian citizenship could be passed on to (male) children through her.

Homosexuality seems to have been relatively common, at least among the educated, and to have been looked on as a tolerable, although somewhat disreputable, practice. It was viewed as particularly disreputable for the older man, because he was sometimes led to ignore his family responsibilities by a younger lover. From the glancing attention paid to the subject in the surviving literature, it is impossible to know how common such relations were, what the non-homosexual majority thought of them, or indeed much else regarding the sexual practices of the time.

Mainly on the basis of literary sources, historians generally agree that women's overall status gradually rose in the Hellenistic and Roman imperial eras. Of course, this statement applies more to the upper classes than to the lower ones. In the Hellenistic cities, upper-class women played an active role in business affairs, and the older prohibitions about leaving the family home seem to have faded. They were no longer regarded as the property of husbands and fathers, but as independent legal personages.

Women also had more opportunities for education in this age. The founder of the Epicurean philosophy, for example, admitted females to his school on the same criteria as males. Even physical exercise, always a justification for segregating males and females in classical Greece, was now opened to some females as well.

THE GREEK LEGACY

The dimensions and lasting importance of the Greeks' bequest to Western civilization cannot be overemphasized. When the poleis fell to the Macedonians, this bequest was retained, although in diluted forms. When the Greco-Macedonian world was then itself overtaken by the all-conquering Romans a couple of hundred years later, the new masters adopted much of the Greek heritage with great enthusiasm and made it their own. In this way, the Greek style and the content of their art, philosophy, science, and government gradually infiltrated much of Europe. In the process, though, parts were lost permanently, and much of it was radically altered by other views and conditions of life.

SUMMARY

HELLENIC CULTURE REPRESENTS a high point in the history of the Western world. The two or three centuries embraced by the Classical Age produced a series of remarkable achievements in the fine arts and in the systematic inquiry into humans and nature that we call philosophy. In some of these affairs, the Greeks built on foundations laid by others, including the Egyptians and the Phoenicians. In other fields, such as drama and lyric poetry, they were pioneers. In philosophy, the mighty trio of Socrates, Plato, and Aristotle defined most of the questions that the world would ask of the universe ever since. In drama, Aeschylus, Sophocles, and Euripides played the same pathbreaking role. Poets such as Sappho and Pindar, sculptors such as Phidias, and the mostly unknown architects of the Classical Age created monuments that remain models of excellence. They believed, as they said, that "Man is the measure of all things" and that what could not be analyzed by the educated mind was probably best left alone as being unworthy of their efforts.

The Hellenistic Age is a convenient although deceptively simple label for a widely varying mix of peoples and ideas. For about three centuries, from the death of Alexander to the Romans' coming into the East, the world affected by Greek ideas increased dramatically in physical extent, encompassing Mediterranean and western Asian cultures.

The philosophies and religious thought of the Hellenistic world eventually became the basic lenses through which the entire European continent (and its North American offspring) would perceive the world of the spirit. Our cultural debts to these Greco-Eastern forebears are beyond easy measure. In the next two chapters, we will see how the unimportant and provincial city of Rome became the inheritor of the Hellenistic East. We will also look at the way the Romans altered Hellenistic culture until it became a specifically Roman civilization.

▶ Identification Terms

Test your knowledge of this chapter's key concepts by defining the following terms. If you can't recall the meaning of certain terms, refresh your memory by looking up the boldfaced term in the chapter, turning to the Glossary at the end of the book, or working with the flashcards that are available on the *World Civilizations* Companion Website: **academic.cengage.com/adler**

Aristotle	Epicureanism	hubris	Plato
Cynicism	golden mean	mystery religions	Socrates
Empiricists	humanistic	*Oedipus Rex*	Stoicism

▶ Test Your Knowledge

Test your knowledge of this chapter by answering the following questions. Complete answers appear at the end of the book. You may find even more quiz questions in CengageNOW and on the *World Civilizations* Companion Website: **academic.cengage.com/adler**

1. The pre-Socratic philosophers sought most of all to explain the
   a. human capacity to reason.
   b. motion of the stars.
   c. composition and laws of the natural world.
   d. reasons for the existence of good and evil.
   e. creation of the world.

2. The cave metaphor in Plato's writings refers to
   a. the need of humans to have a place of refuge from their enemies.
   b. the ability of humans to form a community.
   c. the difference between reality and falsely understood images.
   d. the importance of a stable physical environment.
   e. the desire of humans to create a stable home environment.

3. Greek religion was
   a. controlled by a powerful priesthood.
   b. the same from one end of the country to the other.
   c. filled with gods created in man's image.

d. dominated by fear of the afterlife.

e. centered around an ethical system of high moral conduct.

4. Sophocles and Euripides are best known as Greek
   a. dramatists.
   b. poets.
   c. sculptors.
   d. painters.
   e. architects.

5. In the Greek polis, the majority of urban adults
   a. spent some time each year working in the surrounding fields.
   b. owned between five and ten slaves.
   c. allowed women more freedom than they achieved in rural areas.
   d. rented slaves occasionally from the very wealthy.
   e. participated in civic affairs as a matter of course.

6. Which adjective is *least* appropriate for the classical Greeks?
   a. Intimidated
   b. Rational
   c. Proud
   d. Curious
   e. Creative

7. *Hellenistic* refers to a
   a. blend of Greek and Eastern ideas and forms.
   b. blend of Greek and Roman ideas and forms.
   c. purely Greek style later transferred to Rome.
   d. mixed style limited in extent to Europe.
   e. blend of Greek, Roman, and Eastern style.

8. Stoicists believed in
   a. the brotherhood of all men.
   b. the natural superiority of Greeks over all others.
   c. the quest for personal pleasure being the only meaning in life.
   d. the impossibility of finding an honest man or woman.
   e. the acceptance of one's lot in life.

9. The scientific interests of the Hellenistic Period
   a. were limited to math.
   b. led to an industrial revolution.
   c. were limited to agriculture.
   d. had little connection with technology.
   e. tended toward the practical application of knowledge.

10. In the Hellenistic Period, the sociopolitical unit replacing the classical polis was the
    a. village.
    b. city.
    c. city-state.
    d. family.
    e. kingdom.

Enter *CengageNOW* using the access card that is available with this text. *CengageNOW* will assist you in understanding the content in this chapter with lesson plans generated for your needs, as well as provide you with a connection to the *Wadsworth World History Resource Center* (see description at right for details).

 World History Resource Center

Enter the Resource Center using either your *CengageNOW* access card or your standalone access card for the *Wadsworth World History Resource Center*. Organized by topic, this website includes quizzes; images; over 350 primary source documents; interactive simulations, maps, and timelines; movie explorations; and a wealth of other resources. You can read the following documents, and many more, at the *Wadsworth World History Resource Center*:

Plato, the *Republic*
Sophocles, *Oedipus Rex*

9 ROME: CITY-STATE TO EMPIRE

It is the nature of a Roman to do, and to suffer bravely.

—Livy

c. 750–509 BCE	Etruscans rule Rome
c. 509–31 BCE	Roman republic
300s–200s BCE	Conquest of Italy
264–202 BCE	The First and Second Punic Wars
50s–30s BCE	The two triumvirates
27 BCE–14 CE	Reign of Augustus
31 BCE–180 CE	Pax Romana
14 CE–69 CE	Julio-Claudian emperors
69 CE–96 CE	Flavian emperors
161 CE–180 CE	Marcus Aurelius

ROMAN FOUNDATIONS

REPUBLICAN GOVERNMENT
Rome's Conquest of Italy ◆ The Punic Wars ◆ The Conquest of the East ◆ The Late Republic's Crisis ◆ The Triumvirates

THE AUGUSTAN AGE
Augustus's Reforms ◆ Imperial Government Policies ◆ Peace and Prosperity ◆ The Succession Problem

IMPERIAL UNIFICATION

ROMAN CULTURE
Law ◆ The Arts ◆ Patterns of Belief

SOCIETY AND ECONOMY
Slave and Free ◆ Gender Relations ◆ Children and Education

THE SUCCESSOR TO THE Greek and Persian civilizations in the Mediterranean basin and the Near East was Rome, the Italian city-state that grew to be an empire and the dominant power in East and West alike. Although Rome is considered the successor to Hellenistic Greece, they actually overlapped in time, and Rome itself is in many ways a Hellenistic entity. In this chapter we will look at several centuries of Rome's growth from an insignificant Italian town dominated by a traditional upper class to an unusual combination of aristocracy and merit, subscribing to pseudo-democratic principles: the Roman *res publica*, or republic. Eventually, the disparity of civic means and ends generated by territorial expansion became too much, and from the ruins of this Roman republic then arose a vision of empire that has served the Western world as a model ever since. For two and a half centuries, Rome maintained peace and relative prosperity throughout most of Europe and the Mediterranean basin. Striking an uneasy but sustainable balance between the powers of a policy-making group in Rome and provincial officers drawn from many peoples, the system proved successful in a variety of circumstances, meeting needs both local and imperial.

ROMAN FOUNDATIONS

Rome is situated about halfway down the western coast of the Italian peninsula, where one of the country's few sizable rivers, the Tiber, flows through fertile plains before emptying into the sea (Map 9.1).

Very early Italy and the Italians are even more of a mystery than Greece and the Greeks. We do know that Indo-European peoples settled central and southern Italy at least as early as 1500 BCE. They developed farming villages but lagged seriously behind the peoples of the eastern Mediterranean and the Near East.

About 800 BCE, three peoples from the East began to enter Italy first as colonists and then as rulers of various segments of the peninsula: the Etruscans, the Greeks, and the Phoenicians. Each of these civilized groups contributed substantially to Italian development, and the first two had a decisive effect on Roman civilization's early forms.

The **Etruscans,** already highly civilized, came into Italy about 800, probably by following a route along the northern Adriatic Sea. They established a series of small city-states in the northern and central areas of the peninsula, ruling over the native Italic people by virtue of their superior weaponry and organization. They left a small amount of writing, but it has never been deciphered, so we have

MAP 9.1 Ancient Italy

The Italian peninsula was invaded innumerable times in history. The native Italic peoples of the north and center were taken over by the more civilized Etruscans in the tenth to eighth centuries BCE. Rome was probably founded by the uniting of several villages under a single government in the eighth century, as Roman legend states.

MAP QUESTIONS

How did being a peninsula affect Italy's ancient history?

no historical record in the strict sense. We do know that a federation headed by Etruscan kings ruled over early Rome from about 750 to about 509 BCE. The pictorial record left by the Etruscans, mainly in recently rediscovered underground tombs, makes it clear that the early Romans derived much of their religious beliefs, art forms, and architecture from these peoples.

According to Roman sources that may be unreliable, the Romans eventually rebelled against the idea of monarchy and were able to defeat the Etruscans because the pleasure-loving Etruscans could not stand up to the rigors of war as long as their rivals. After the Roman victory, the Etruscans gradually fade from history, absorbed by their former subjects.

In the long run, the Greeks had even more influence on Roman attitudes and manners than did the Etruscans. Whereas the Romans viewed the latter as rivals and defeated enemies, they regarded the Greeks as the one alien group that was superior to them in some ways. The early Romans were impressed by the advanced culture of the Greek migrants who had settled in southern Italy during the 700s. Overcrowding at home had caused these Greek colonists to leave their homes in Corinth, Thebes, and other Greek cities and settle in foreign places. They soon transformed southern Italy into a prosperous and commercially advanced civilization but found they had to fight both the Etruscans and the Phoenicians to hold onto it. True to Greek tradition, they made the job much harder by fighting among themselves.

Phoenician influence on Italian events came through **Carthage.** This great trading city had become independent of its homeland, Phoenicia, by 700. During this epoch, Carthage was the most powerful force in the western Mediterranean, sending ships as far away as Britain and the North Sea, as well as up the Nile, and founding colonies of its own all over the coasts of Spain and France. The Carthaginians fought the Greek cities of southern Italy and Sicily to a draw until the Romans were able to take advantage of their mutual exhaustion to conquer both groups.

REPUBLICAN GOVERNMENT

According to ancient Roman tradition, Rome was founded by the twin brothers Romulus and Remus, legendary descendants of the survivors who fled burning Troy after the Trojan War. Modern historians agree with tradition that the city-state of Rome was founded by the voluntary unification of seven agrarian villages at approximately 753 BCE. According to Roman history written much later, the town was under Etruscan rule until 509 BCE. In that year, a rebellion ousted the last king, and the city became

Museo Etrusco, Lazio, Rome, Italy/Bernard Cox/Bridgeman Art Library

ETRUSCAN WINGED HORSES. The vivid quality of Etruscan statuary is one of our few sources of knowledge about these people, who were the forerunners of and cultural models for the Romans in central Italy. The superb mastery of anatomy displayed here was a particular strength of Roman sculpture at a later date.

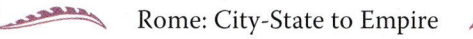
a *res publica*—a state without a monarch, ruled by a combination of the Senate and the citizens—in the original Latin, the *Senatus et populus.*

How did the new republic govern itself? The Senate was composed of the upper class, the **patricians** (from the Latin *patres,* "fathers"), who made up perhaps 5 to 10 percent of the total population and had considerable power even under the Etruscan king. The **plebeians** (pleh-BEE-ans), or commoners (from Latin, "the mass"), composed the other 90 percent and were represented in political affairs by delegates to the elective General Assembly. The executive was a small staff of officials who were elected by the Senate and Assembly for short terms. The chief executive power resided in two **consuls,** elected from among the members of the Senate for one-year terms that could not be repeated. Each consul had veto power over the other. When one consul was in the field as leader of the republic's forces, the other was the head of the civil government at home. Below the consuls in authority were the **censors,** always drawn from the ranks of the senators. The censors (from *census*) were originally tax assessors, but later they came to have the power to supervise the conduct and morals of their fellow senators. The tiny Roman bureaucracy also included a few other offices, which were dominated by the patricians until a series of plebeian revolts or threats to revolt gradually opened them up to the commoners.

Originally, the General Assembly was intended to be as powerful as—perhaps more so than—the Senate, which had only advisory powers. But soon after the foundation of the republic, the Senate had obtained decisive power while the Assembly became a seldom-summoned rubber stamp. For two centuries, the plebeians made considerable progress in their struggle to attain equality.

By about 250, the Roman political structure offered to all appearances a nice balance between the aristocrats and the common people. The chief officers of the plebeians were the **tribunes.** There were about ten tribunes, and they had great power to speak and act in the name of the common Romans. At first, the tribunes were chosen from the common people and were their true representatives. Later, however, after about 200, the tribunes were offered membership in the Senate, and as they sought to become censors and consuls, they came to identify increasingly with the interests of the patricians and less with those of the plebeians. This development was to be fateful for the republic.

After the passage of the Hortensian Law (named after the consul of the day) in 287, plebeians and patricians had equal voting rights and supposedly equal access to office. But in practice, this nod toward democratic principles was not authentic. A combination of wealth and aristocratic birth retained control of the Senate. Democracy eventually would fail in Rome, just as it had in Athens.

Rome's Conquest of Italy

Under this mixed government of aristocrats and commoners, the Roman city-state gradually and painfully became the master of the Italian peninsula. Down to about 340, the almost constant conflicts focused on a strip of land along the west coast. The Romans led a federation of tribes living in this plain of Latium, first against the Etruscans and then against other Italians (see Map 9.1).

Although Rome suffered a devastating invasion by Celtic tribes called Gauls in 390, the Romans and their Latin allies ruled most of central Italy by 340 or so. When the Latins then attempted to revolt against Roman overlordship, the Romans crushed them. Next they turned their attention to the Samnites, a group of Italic tribes in the south and east of the peninsula.

The war against the Samnites was lengthy and difficult. During this conflict the Romans perfected their military organization and created the myth of Roman invincibility. The surrender of the Samnites in 282 BCE brought the Romans a new neighbor and rival: the Greek city-states of southern Italy, which were supported by Pyrrhus, a powerful Greco-Macedonian general. After a couple of costly victories, Pyrrhus was defeated. Rome thus inserted itself into the ongoing struggle between the Greeks and the Carthaginians in Sicily. It would be only a matter of time before the two burgeoning powers of the western Mediterranean engaged in a contest for supremacy.

During these almost continuous conflicts, the Romans learned how to assure that yesterday's enemies became today's friends and allies. A pragmatic and flexible people, the Roman governing groups very soon realized that their original practice of humiliating and enslaving the conquered was counterproductive. Instead, they began to encourage the subject populations to become integrated with Rome—to become "good Romans" regardless of their ethnic or historical affiliations. The Romans gave partial citizenship rights to the conquered Italians as long as they did not rebel and agreed to supply troops when Rome called. This arrangement was advantageous to the conquered because it eased their tax burden, assured them of Roman assistance against their own enemies, and gave them wide-ranging powers of self-government.

Some of the conquered were eventually allowed to become full citizens, which meant they could run for office and vote in Roman elections, serve in the Roman army and bureaucracy, and have protection for property and other preferential legal rights that were not available to noncitizens.

The upper classes of the conquered Italians and Greeks were soon eager to latinize themselves and thus to qualify as full citizens. They achieved this status by intermarrying with Romans, adopting the Latin language, and accepting the basic elements of Roman custom and law.

The Punic Wars

Although the Romans were nearly constantly at war between 500 and 275 BCE, these conflicts generally dealt with peoples who were similar to themselves and whose conquered lands were adjacent to Roman possessions. Not until the First **Punic War** (264–241 BCE) did Rome more or less openly embark on imperial expansion. With that war, Rome started down the road to an *imperium* (empire), although it retained the laws and politics of a quasi-democratic city-state. This created internal tensions that ultimately could not be resolved.

The First Punic War broke out over the question of dominance in Sicily and ended twenty years later with the surrender of the important colonies of Sicily and Sardinia to Rome. Carthage, however, was far from completely subdued, and during the ensuing truce, it built up its forces and then invaded Italy. The brilliant Carthaginian general Hannibal won battle after battle against the desperate Romans but lost the war. Finally, after ravaging Italy for fifteen years in the Second Punic War (218–202), he was finally forced to return to Carthage to defend the city against a Roman counterinvasion. The decisive **battle of Zama** in 202 was a clear Roman victory, and Carthage was forced to give up most of its extensive holdings in Africa and Spain. These were made into new provinces of what by now was a rapidly growing empire (see Map 9.2). The Punic Wars determined that Roman, and not Carthaginian, culture and civilization would control the Mediterranean basin for the foreseeable future.

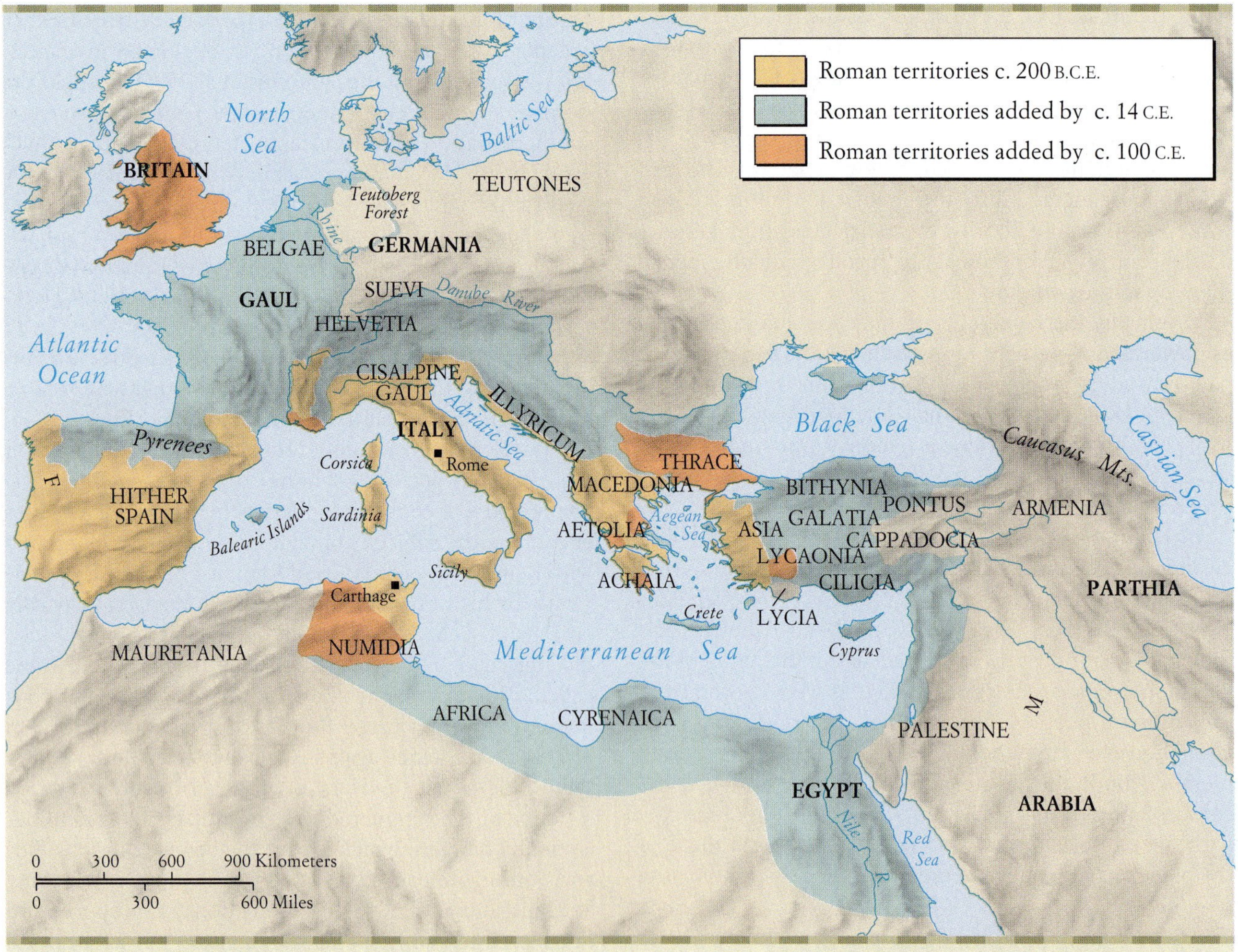

MAP 9.2 Expansion of Roman Territories to 100 CE

Rome's empire was created not by plan but by a series of wars that had little or no relation to one another. Roman influences were permanently barred from central Europe after the massive defeat in the Teutoburg Forest in 9 CE and the establishment of the Rhine and Danube borders thereafter. In Asia, the Romans created a series of client kingdoms that relieved them of having to station large numbers of troops there.

MAP QUESTIONS

Which of these areas were conquered from Carthage?

 View an interactive version of this or a related map at http://worldrc.wadsworth.com/

The Conquest of the East

Victorious against Carthage, the Romans at once turned their eyes eastward. Until now they had tried to stay out of the continuous quarreling of the Hellenistic kingdoms. But in the 190s, immediately after the Punic Wars, ambitious consuls saw an opportunity to profit from the internal Greek struggle. Within a very short time, the Greco-Macedonian kingdom was under Rome's control.

Roman armies soon defeated the other Hellenistic kingdoms around the eastern edge of the Mediterranean. These petty kingdoms could have been at once made into Roman provinces. But some senators expressed strong opposition to this move, believing that the expansive, materialistic society being created by military conquests was far from what Roman traditions of thrifty living and modest ambition honored. A seesaw struggle between conservatives, who wished Rome to remain an ethnically homogeneous Italian city-state, and imperialists, who wanted expansion (and wealth!), went on for about a century (150–50 BCE). The conservatives were fighting for a lost cause, however. By the latter date, the question had become which of the pro-imperialist groups would eventually seize supreme power.

The conquest of the East was executed by an outstanding military machine. It was composed mainly of infantry, which was recruited from all male citizens. In the early republic, only property holders were allowed citizenship, and only citizens could bear arms. The commanders were all patricians, whereas the plebeians served in the ranks. Service was for an indefinite term, and as the wars multiplied in the fourth and third centuries BCE, many citizens were away from their homes for lengthy periods. The effects were ruinous for many simple peasant-soldiers, who could not tend their fields adequately and had no other

source of income (because army service was considered an honor, soldiers were not paid).

As early as the mid-300s, military needs were urgent enough that a group of permanent commanders/governors called **proconsuls** was created. The custom of electing commanders annually fell into disuse, as it was clear that men of talent would be needed for more than a year. In this way, a group of men emerged who were both politically potent through their connections in the Senate and militarily potent through their command responsibilities. So long as they continued to regard the Senate and the consuls whom the Senate elected as their rightful superiors, all went well.

But it was inevitable that an ambitious commander would come along who would look first to personal advancement and only later or never to the welfare of the state. Such men began to appear regularly after the First Punic War, which created myriad opportunities to get rich in the new territories won from Carthage. These opportunities redoubled after the Second Punic War. By then, Rome was rapidly developing a volunteer, professional army that would look to its field commanders and not to a distant Senate as its legitimate director.

The Late Republic's Crisis

All through this imperial expansion, Rome's government had remained technically that of an ethnically homogeneous city-state, with traditional powers allocated between the senatorial upper class and the masses. By the end of the second century, the real Rome had deviated far from this ideal, and the strains were beginning to show, as the Society and Economy box reveals.

Many poverty-stricken former farmers flocked into the city, seeking any kind of work and ready to listen to anyone promising them a better existence.

ROMAN INFANTRYMAN. This picture shows a bronze figure of a Roman legionary in full dress at the time of the empire in the second century CE. The soldier's vest is constructed of overlapping metal bands that, although heavy and awkward, protected him effectively from enemy thrusts.

British Museum, photo © Michael Holford, London

Many of them had served in the army for years and were then discharged only to find that their lands had been seized for debt or confiscated through the maneuvers of wealthy speculators. The new landowners created great estates that were worked by the vast numbers of slaves that the Roman overseas conquests were bringing into Italy.

The members of this new urban **proletariat** (proh-leh-TAY-ree-uht)—people without sources of income except the daily sale of their labor—were citizens with votes, and they were ready to sell those votes to the highest bidder. They were also ready to follow any general who promised them a decent living in his army of long-serving veterans. Men would serve out their time and then be given a good mustering-out pension or a bit of land to support themselves in old age. That land could easily enough be taken from the victims of new Roman-incited wars around the Mediterranean and in what is now western Europe. But in Italy itself, this "land problem"—the forcing of the peasant-soldiers off their ancestral land—proved insoluble.

Starting about 150 BCE, Roman public life thus became a complex struggle between those upper-class individuals who saw the growing need for social and political reform and those who rejected reform under the banner of sacred tradition. Among the former was a certain Marius. This former consul saw his chance for fame in a war against African rebels and had himself reelected consul for six terms—a first that was to become commonplace within a couple more decades. Marius also abolished the property qualification for his soldiers, thereby opening the way for an army composed of men who had nothing to lose by enlisting and would follow any leaders who made sure they got plunder and pensions. More and more, the Roman military was becoming a force for instability and the essential base for all who had political ambitions.

In 83 BCE the harsh soldier-consul Sulla made himself dictator and packed the Senate with new men who would obey him. Sulla instituted several beneficial political reforms as well, but they were abolished as soon as he died in 78, and the government reverted immediately to open or covert warfare of wealthy senatorial groups against each other.

The Triumvirates

The final collapse of the pseudo-democracy and the republican system was brought on by the patrician general and politician Julius Caesar (died 44 BCE), who saw that it had become corrupt and was unsuited for governance of a far-flung empire. He conspired with others who were also discontented with the Senate leadership to form an alliance known as the *First Triumvirate* (rule of three). The other members were the wealthy speculator Crassus and the brilliant general Pompey.

During the 50s BCE, Caesar made his reputation by conquering the semicivilized Gauls in what is now France, which he turned into a Roman province of great potential. His ambitions fully awakened, he now wished to become consul and use that powerful office to make basic changes in the structure of government. He was opposed by his former ally Pompey and the large majority of the Senate, who viewed him as a dangerous radical. Emerging the victor after a difficult struggle, Caesar made himself dictator and fully intended to start a royal dynasty. He subordinated the Senate entirely to himself and initiated several major reforms of the existing system, including even the Roman calendar. But, in March 44, conservative senators assassinated him. His only surviving male relative was his adoptive son Octavian Caesar, whom he had made his political heir. But Octavian was only eighteen when Caesar died. He had little political experience and lacked military prowess, so it appeared unlikely that he would ever fill the office of his adoptive father.

When the senatorial assassins of Julius Caesar could not agree on what should be done to restore the republic, Octavian, the financier Lepidus, and the general Mark Antony formed an alliance known as the *Second Triumvirate*. The three allies crushed the assassins and then divided the empire: Antony took the East and Egypt; Octavian, Italy and the West; and Lepidus, Africa. Octavian soon showed himself a gifted politician, but he stood in the shadow of Mark Antony. (Lepidus had no independent political hopes and could be ignored.) Antony made himself unpopular in Rome by apparently succumbing to the charms of the queen of Egypt, Cleopatra, and maltreating his noble Roman wife and her influential family. Octavian cleverly built his political strength in Italy and acquired much experience in handling men. When the test came, he was ready. In 32 BCE, Octavian maneuvered Antony into declaring war against him. The victory of Octavian's forces at the decisive **Battle of Actium** in 31 BCE marked the effective beginning of the Roman Empire.

The Augustan Age

Octavian's victory had made him master of the Roman world. The question was, how would he respond to this opportunity? Like his predecessor Julius Caesar, Octavian knew that basic reforms were necessary if the Roman state was to survive. But he also knew how resistant the Roman people were to innovations that challenged ancient custom.

Augustus's Reforms

Octavian's response was to *retain the form, while changing the substance.* Mindful of the Romans' respect for tradition, Octavian pretended to be simply another elected consul, another *pontifex maximus* (high priest of the state

SOCIETY AND ECONOMY

"Rape of the Sabine Women"

From earliest times, the Roman ruling class saw itself as ordained to be the proud culmination of civilization and the executors of the will of their gods.

A favorite story was told by the first-century writer Livy, the official historian of the city in the time when Rome was transforming itself into an empire. It deals with the manner in which the first settlers, led by the mythical Romulus, procured wives for themselves: the "Rape of the Sabine Women." The tale shows not only the Romans' admiration for the warrior but also their vision of the proper relations between male and female.

Having lured the neighboring Sabine people to come to join in watching an athletic contest, Romulus and his fellow Romans sprang their trap:

> The day for the spectacle arrived and while [the Sabines'] eyes and minds were intent on it, a prearranged free-for-all began, with the Roman men scattering at an agreed upon signal to seize the unmarried girls. . . . As the games broke up in confusion and fear, the grieving parents of the maidens ran off, accusing the Romans of violating their sacred obligations as hosts and invoking the god to whose festival and games they had been deceitfully invited contrary to religion and good faith. The abducted maidens had no better hopes than their parents, nor was their indignation less. But Romulus repeatedly went about in person to visit them, arguing that what had happened was due to the arrogance of their parents, who had refused intermarriage with their neighbors. Despite this, he promised that they would enjoy the full rights of a proper marriage, becoming partners in all the fortunes the couple might share, in Rome's citizenship, and in the begetting of children, the object dearest to every person's heart. So let them now abate their anger, let them give their hearts to those whom chance had given their bodies. . . .

To Romulus's entreaties the husbands added their own honeyed words, claiming that they had acted out of desire and love,

an avowal calculated to appeal most to a woman's nature. While the Sabine women were thus soon soothed, their fathers and brothers were definitely not, and a fierce war between them and Rome quickly ensued. A great deal of slaughter seemed inevitable, but Livy goes on:

> [A]t this moment the Sabine women boldly interposed themselves amid the flying spears. Their misfortunes overcame womanish fear: with hair streaming and garments torn they made a mad rush from the sidelines, parting the battling armies and checking their angry strife. Appealing to fathers on one side and husbands on the other, they declared their kin by marriage should not defile themselves by impious carnage, nor leave the stain of blood upon their descendants, grandfathers upon grandsons, fathers upon children. "If you cannot abide the ties between you that our marriage has created, turn your anger against us. We are the cause of this war, we the cause of husbands and fathers lying wounded and slain. Only one side can win this battle. As for us, it is better to die than to live, for we must do so as widows and orphans."

Their appeal moved both leaders and rank and file: silence and a sudden hush fell upon the field. The commanders then came forward to strike a treaty by which they not only made peace but united the two peoples in a single community.

▶ *Analyze and Interpret*

What does the story tell you of Roman notions of fair play? Can you defend this view, or does armed might never make moral right in human relationships?

Source: Livy, *The Histories*, trans. F. J. Luce (Oxford: Oxford University Press, 1998), p. 14f.

You can read more of Livy's *Histories* at the Wadsworth World History Resource Center.

religion), and another general of the Roman legions. In reality, he became consul for life, his priestly duties were crowned with semidivine status, and his military resources overshadowed all possible rivals. He enlarged the Senate, packing it with loyal supporters. He made a great show of working with the Senate, while giving it enough busy-

work to keep it out of mischief. Meanwhile, he made all real policy decisions. He cut the army's size by half, while retaining all key military posts under his direct control.

Early in his reign, Octavian accepted the title *Augustus* ("revered one") from a grateful Senate, and it is as "Augustus Caesar" that he is best known. He preferred to be called **princeps** ("first citizen"), and his rule is often called the Principate. It lasted from 27 BCE, when he was elected consul for life, until his natural death in 14 CE. In those forty years, Augustus placed his mark on every aspect of public affairs. He was so successful overall that his system lasted for the next two and a half centuries without fundamental change. Augustus created a type of constitutional monarchy that was suited to contemporary Roman realities. To many people, it long remained the model of what effective and just imperial government should be.

Imperial Government Policies

In government and constitutional matters, Augustus kept the republican institutions intact. Supposedly, the *Senatus et populus* together were still the sovereign power, with the consul simply their agent. In practice, however, Augustus had the final word in everything important through his control of the military and the Senate. His steadily increasing prestige with the commoners also helped him. Ordinary Romans were appalled by the rebellions, civil wars, and political assassinations that had become commonplace in the last decades of the republic. After 31 BCE, however, Augustus was strong enough to intimidate any would-be troublemakers. He became immensely popular among the common people as a result.

In social policy, Augustus recognized the problems presented by the numbers of propertyless, impoverished citizens, especially in the cities. He therefore provided the urban poor with basic food rations from the state treasury, supplemented by "gifts" from the consul, from his own resources. This annual dole of grain and oil became an important means of controlling public opinion for Augustus and his successors. He also instituted huge public works programs, both to provide employment and to glorify his government. Projects were carried out all over the empire, but especially in Rome. Many of the surviving Roman bridges, aqueducts, roads (the famous, enduring Roman roads), forts, and temples were constructed during his reign or were started by him and completed later.

Augustus also attempted to institute moral reform and end the love of luxury that had become characteristic of the aristocratic class during the late republic. In his own life with his wife Livia, he set an example of modest living. He also tried to discourage the influx of slaves because he believed that the vast number of slaves being imported into Italy represented luxury and, as such, threatened the traditional lifestyle. But none of these moral reform attempts proved successful over the long run. His imperial successors soon gave up the struggle.

Segovia, Spain/Ken Welsh/Bridgeman Art Library

ROMAN AQUEDUCT IN SPAIN. This modern photo shows the enduring nature of Roman civic architecture all around the Mediterranean basin. This aqueduct might still be employed by the citizens of Segovia, Spain, to bring fresh water to them. Similar structures stand in southern France and in Turkey.

Augustus also tried to revive the faith in the old gods and the state cult by conscientiously serving as high priest. Here, too, he was unsuccessful in the long run. The educated classes emulated the Greeks by turning from supernatural religion toward philosophy, and the masses sought something more satisfying emotionally than the barren ceremonies of the state cult. This they found in the mystery religions, with their promise of salvation.

In foreign policy, the northern frontiers in Germany and the Low Countries had long been a problem that Augustus was determined to solve by conquering the fierce tribes who lived there. This foray ended in spectacular failure: in 9 CE, Germanic tribes ambushed and exterminated a Roman army that had pushed eastward into the Teutoburg forests. The entire Germania province was thereby lost, and the borders between Roman and non-Roman Europe were henceforth the Rhine and Danube rivers (see Map 9.2). After Augustus, Rome's only significant territorial acquisitions were in the British Isles and in present-day Romania.

To govern this vast empire of about 60 million, Augustus reformed its protection and administration. The outermost provinces, including Spain, Mesopotamia, and Egypt, were either put directly under his own control as "imperial" provinces or turned over to local rulers who were faithful satellites. Most of the army was stationed in the imperial provinces, enabling Augustus to keep the military under his surveillance and control.

Augustus initiated other reforms in military matters as well. The standing army had become increasingly large

and unwieldy, as well as politically dangerous, so he reduced its size by more than half, to about 250,000 men. The army was made thoroughly professional and used extensively as an engineering force to build roads and public works all over the provinces. Twenty-eight legions, each with about 6,000 highly trained and disciplined infantry, were supported by cavalry and by a large number of auxiliaries, taken from the non-Roman populations of the provinces. The volunteers who made up the legions served for twenty years and were given a mustering-out bonus sufficient to set them up as small landowners or businessmen.

The legionaries were highly mobile, and a common soldier often served in five or six different provinces before retirement. The auxiliaries served for twenty-five years and were normally given citizenship on retirement. In and around Rome, Augustus maintained his personal bodyguard and imperial garrison, the **Praetorian Guard.** Containing about 10,000 men, it was the only armed force allowed in Italy. Whoever controlled its loyalty had a potent lever for political power in his hand.

Augustus also reorganized the Roman navy and used it effectively to rid the major rivers and the Mediterranean of pirates, who had been disrupting shipping. For the next 200 years, the navy protected the provinces and Italy from waterborne threats. Not until recent times were the seas around Europe as safe as in the first and second centuries.

Peace and Prosperity

The **Pax Romana,** the Roman peace from 31 BCE until 180 CE, was the greatest of Augustus's achievements. For nearly two and a half centuries, the Western world from Syria to Spain and from Bristol to Belgrade was unified and generally peaceful under a single central authority enjoined by common law. This record has not been approached since. With Augustus's reign, Rome entered six generations of peace and prosperity. Literature and the arts flourished, supported by generous subsidies from the state treasury and commissions from a new class of wealthy men who wished to celebrate their achievements. Augustus set the tone by encouraging the arts in public spaces and buildings of all sorts and providing personal financial support for many of the outstanding literary figures of his time.

How did the Pax Romana benefit people throughout the far-flung Roman Empire? It allowed, for example, Syrian merchants to move their textile goods safely from Damascus to Alexandria. From there, Egyptians would transport the goods through a peaceable sea to Gibraltar, and from there, the goods would go on to Cornwall in Britain, where they would be exchanged for tin ore, which would then be brought back to a bronze foundry in Damascus. Under the Pax Romana, people throughout the empire lived under a common concept of peaceful order, expressed and upheld through laws that were as valid in London as in Vienna or Barcelona (all cities founded by the Romans). Governors (proconsuls) appointed in Rome supervised the provinces, but they were allowed considerable freedom of action in local affairs while being protected by Roman garrisons.

The Succession Problem

One important problem that Augustus was unable to solve was that of succession to his office and powers. Having only a daughter (the scandalous Julia), he adopted her husband, Tiberius, as his son and co-ruler. He thus set an example that would be followed by most of his successors: a combination of *heredity*, meaning succession by blood, and co-option, meaning succession by designation of the ruler. But this method often resulted in chaos and was at times disregarded in favor of heredity alone.

Tiberius was an effective ruler, although by no means the equal of Augustus in popularity or ability to manipulate the Senate. Whereas a grateful Senate had deified (declared to be a god) Augustus almost immediately after his death, Tiberius was much resented. He was followed by other members of the family of Augustus (the Julio-Claudians) until 68 CE, when the succession system experienced its first crisis. The last of the Julio-Claudians, the unpopular Nero, committed suicide in 69, and after some bloodstained maneuvering was replaced by the Flavian emperors from 69 to 96. They based their right to rule simply on having imposing military force behind them. Even though these generals were effective and wise rulers, they set an ominous precedent of coerced selection that would come back to haunt Rome in the third century.

IMPERIAL UNIFICATION

The successors of Augustus continued his work of bringing together the very diverse peoples over whom they ruled. Gradually, the Latin language became the common denominator of higher culture in the western half of the empire, while Greek continued to serve that function in the East. The government used both languages equally in its dealings with its subjects.

The imperial government became increasingly centralized. Roman directives curtailed the freedoms of the cities of the ancient East and governors were sent out from Italy or selected from the Romanized locals. In the western half of the empire, the Roman authorities founded many ***municipia.*** These were towns with their surrounding countryside that formed governmental units similar in size and function to our own counties. The municipal authorities were partly appointed by Rome and partly elected from and by leading local families. The provincial governor (usually an Italian given the job as political patronage) was responsible for their good behavior. He was backed by a garrison commander, who had wide-ranging authority in matters both military and civil.

Everywhere, the government became open to non-Italians, as soon as they had Romanized themselves sufficiently to become citizens. (Citizenship was eventually granted to all freemen by a popularity-seeking emperor in 212.) From the time of the emperor Hadrian (the 120s CE), half of the members of the Senate were of provincial origin. Men of talent could rise swiftly to the highest offices regardless of their ethnic background. Religious differences were ignored, so long as one was willing to make the undemanding ceremonial tributes to the official Roman gods (Jupiter, Neptune, and the like). Most individuals had no difficulty combining this state cult with the more intimate religions of their preference.

ROMAN CULTURE

In general, the Romans borrowed heavily and willingly from the Greek heritage in philosophy, the sciences, and the arts, but that does not mean that they developed no native culture. Their own genius and inclinations lay more in the fields of law and administration than in the realm of imagination or the fine arts. In the practical aspects of public life, such as engineering, sanitation, finance, and a system of justice, the Romans had few equals. They were always willing to experiment until they found a winning combination or at least one that was acceptable to the majority of citizens. At the same time, they never failed to make elaborate bows to a sometimes fictional tradition and to insist that they were following in the footsteps of the hallowed past when, in fact, they were making changes demanded by new circumstances.

Law

An indisputably great Roman achievement was the development of a system of law with the flexibility to meet the needs of subject peoples as diverse as the Britons and the Syrians. This law system and a government that combined effective central controls with wide local autonomy are perhaps the most valued Roman gifts to later civilized society. Many types of law originally existed within the borders of the empire, but these gradually gave way to the system that the Romans had hammered out by trial and error during the republic and that continued to be developed in the empire. The basic principles of this legal system were (1) the notion of *precedent* as coequal to the letter of the law, (2) the belief that *equity* (fairness) was the goal of all

law, and (3) the importance of *interpretation* in applying the law to individual cases.

The Romans had various codes of law. One originally applied only to citizens, and another applied only to aliens and travelers on Roman territory. During the early empire, the law code that governed relations between citizens and non-Romans, known as the **jus gentium** (yoos GEHN-tee-uhm; "law of peoples"), gradually came to be accepted as basic. The rights of citizens and noncitizens, of natives and aliens, came to be seen as worthy of protection by the Roman authorities. These rights were not equal, but they were recognized as existing. This concept paved the way for what we call "international law," and it gradually took Roman justice far beyond the usual concepts of "us against you" that other ancient peoples normally employed with foreigners.

Later, in the third and fourth centuries, the Romans evolved *natural law,* the idea that all humans, by virtue of their humanity, possess certain rights and duties that all courts must recognize. As the Romans adopted Christianity, this natural law came to be viewed as the product of a God-ordained order that had been put into the world with the creation of Adam.

The Arts

Roman art forms varied sharply in development and imagination. The Latin language evolved rapidly as the republic expanded its contacts with others. Roman literature began in the third century BCE, when poetry of some excellence, historiography of a rather inferior sort, and drama modeled on that of the Greeks began to appear. During the republic's last century, Cicero, Julius Caesar, Terence, Polybius, Cato, and Lucretius were major contributors. The best days of Roman literature, however, were still ahead, in the early imperial epoch, when a brilliant constellation around the emperors Augustus and Tiberius created a memorable body of poetry and prose. Virgil's *Aeneid* (ah-NEE-id) became the official version of the founding of Rome by refugees from the burning Troy; Ovid, Horace, and Catullus established Latin poetry equal to yet different from its Greek models. In the hands of prose masters such as the historian Tacitus, the satirist Juvenal, and the storytellers Pliny, Petronius, and Suetonius, the Latin language became an extraordinary instrument capable of extreme directness and concision.

In the pictorial and plastic (three-dimensional) arts, the early Roman sculptors and architects worked from both Etruscan and Greek models without much elaboration of their own. With few exceptions, the "Greek" statues in the world's fine arts museums are Roman copies of originals that have long since disappeared. By the end of the republican era this was changing, and a specifically native style was emerging. One of its greatest strengths was portrait

Louvre, Paris, France/Lauros-Giraudon/Bridgeman Art Library

**A ROMAN EMPEROR.** The Roman preference for realism in their ictorial arts is shown by this bust of a man assumed to be Emperor Macrin. Although their techniques were generally dependent on classical Greek models, the Romans soon progressed beyond the desire merely to imitate.

sculpture, especially the busts that were produced in large numbers. These are amazingly realistic and seem modern in a way that other ancient art generally does not.

The architectural style favored in the republic was strongly reminiscent of the Greek temple, but it also incorporated Hellenistic arches and circles, as in the frequent cupola roofs and semicircular altars, to a much greater degree. Roman skill in masonry work and affinity to the grand style combined to give magnificent expression to public works and buildings throughout the empire. The Forum and the Coliseum still stand in modern Rome, witnesses to the exceptional quality of Roman stone work.

Patterns of Belief

"How best to live?" was a question that preoccupied imperial Romans. Perhaps the greatest of all the emperors after Augustus was Marcus Aurelius (ruled 161–180 CE),

the last of the Five Good Emperors who ruled in the second century CE. He left a small book of aphorisms called *Meditations,* which has been a best-seller ever since (see the Patterns of Belief box). Marcus settled on a pessimistic Stoicism as the most fitting cloak for a good man in a bad world, especially a man who had to exercise power. This was a common feeling among upper-class Romans, and it became ever more popular in the third and fourth centuries as civic difficulties multiplied. Like Marcus Aurelius, Roman Stoics often opposed Christianity because they rejected external prescriptions for morality. Instead, they insisted that each person is responsible for searching and following his own conscience. Seneca, another Stoic and the most persuasive of the Roman moralists, had a somewhat different way of looking at things. He introduced a new note of humane compassion, a belief that all shared in the divine spark and should be valued as fellow creatures.

The Roman character, insofar as one can sum up a heterogeneous people's character, leaned toward the pragmatic and the here and now. Romans admired the doer more than the thinker, the soldier more than the philosopher, and the artisan more than the artist. The educated class could and did appreciate "the finer things." They admired and cultivated art in many media and many forms and spent lavishly to obtain it for their own prestige and pleasure. But they did not, generally speaking, provide that sort of intense, sustained interest that led to superior aesthetic standards and to the inspiration of superior and original works of art, such as the Greeks possessed in abundance. The early empire's successes in several fields were magnificent and long lasting, but they were not rooted in an original view of earthly life or a new conception of humans' duties and aspirations.

The religious convictions of the Romans centered on duty to the state and the family hearth. Toward the state, the Roman patricians felt a personalized attachment, a sense of duty, and a proud obedience to tradition handed down from generation to generation. Toward the patriarchal family and its symbol, the hearth, the Romans felt the same attachment as most ancient peoples, with the honor of the lineage being of the usual great importance to them.

Roman religion was a matter of mutual promises: on the gods' side, protection for the community and survival for the individual; on the human side, ceremonial worship and due respect. Priests and priestesses existed in Rome but had relatively little power and prestige among the people. It was a religion of state, rather than of individuals, and it was common for Romans to worship other gods besides those of the official cult. In the imperial period, many emperors were deified, and most of the mystery religions of the Hellenistic world eventually were taken up by Rome.

Chief among the many Roman gods was Jupiter, a father figure modeled on the Greek Zeus. Also important

PATTERNS OF BELIEF

The *Meditations* of Marcus Aurelius

Marcus Aurelius (121–180 CE) was perhaps the greatest of all the Roman rulers, in the sense of moral grandeur. As the last of the Five Good Emperors who ruled in the second century CE, he inherited an empire that was still intact and at peace internally.

But on its eastern borders, the first of the lethal challenges from the Germanic tribes materialized during his reign (161–180), and he had to spend much of his time organizing and leading the empire's defenses.

Even during his campaigns, his mind was attuned to the Stoic philosophy, which the Roman upper classes had acquired from the Greeks. In *Meditations*, he wrote a personal journal of the adventure of a life consciously lived. His book, which was never meant for publication, has lived on into our day because of its nobility of thought and expression. Some excerpts follow:

> Begin each day by reminding yourself: today I shall meet with meddlers, ingrates, insolence, disloyalty, ill-will and selfishness—all of them due to the offenders' ignorance of what is good and what evil. But I have long perceived the nature of good and its nobility, the nature of evil and its meanness, and also the nature of the culprit himself, who is my brother . . . therefore, none of those things can injure me, for no one can implicate me in what is degrading. . . .
>
> Never value the advantages derived from anything involving breach of faith, loss of self-respect, hatred, suspicion, or execration of others, insincerity, or the desire for something which has to be veiled or curtained. One whose chief regard is for his own mind, and for the divinity within

him and the service of its goodness, will strike no poses, utter no complaints, and crave neither for solitude nor yet for the crowd. . . .

> Hour by hour resolve firmly, like a Roman and a man, to do what comes to hand with correct and natural dignity, and with humanity, independence, and justice. Allow your mind freedom from all other considerations. This you can do if you will approach each action as though it were your last, dismissing the wayward thought, the emotional recoil from the commands of reason, the desire to create an impression, the admiration of self, the discontent with your lot. See how little a man needs to master, for his days to flow on in quietness and piety; he has to observe but these few counsels, and the gods will ask nothing more.

▶ *Analyze and Interpret*

Of the various world religions encountered thus far in this book, which seems closest in its ethical principles to Marcus's *Meditations*? Can you see why the *Meditations* was a particular favorite with Christians after Constantine's time?

Source: Excerpt from Marcus Aurelius, *Meditations*, trans. Maxwell Staniforth, © 1964, Penguin Classics. Reprinted by permission of Penguin, Ltd.

You can read more from Marcus Aurelius's *Meditations* at the *Wadsworth World History Resource Center.*

---

were Apollo, Neptune (Poseidon), Venus (Aphrodite [af-roh-DIE-tee]), Minerva (Athena), and Mars (Ares). Like the rituals of the Greeks, the worship given to these deities was more like a present-day patriotic ceremony than a modern church service. Even less than among the Greeks did the Romans look to the civic gods for ethical guidance or to secure personal immortality by passing a last judgment. The Roman notion of an afterlife changed from person to person and from age to age during Rome's long history. In broad terms it resembled that of the educated Greeks: the existence of an afterlife was an open question, but if it did exist, one could know nothing about it or secure admission to it through the gods.

Ideally, and in their own musings about the good life, educated Romans generally affirmed Stoicism, believing that service to the state and the human community was the highest duty. They thought that the only way to ensure against the disappointments of earthly life was to renounce the pursuit of wealth and power and live a life of modest seclusion. But few Romans who had a choice did that! As a governing class, they were very much attuned to the delights of wealth and power and very much willing to make great efforts to get them. A people who made much of military virtue and unquestioning obedience, they also insisted on the autonomy of the individual's conscience. A people who were notably conscious of the concept of

justice and the rule of law, they also had many moments of collective blind rage when they exerted sadistic power over others. Nobility of thought was sometimes marred by base actions and even baser motives.

SOCIETY AND ECONOMY

In general, the Romans were successful in creating a single, unified vision of what life was about—and how it should best be lived—that was accepted from Britain to Egypt and from Spain to Romania. We have a great deal of information about the economic and cultural life in the first and second centuries CE, when the empire was prospering.

Trade and manufacturing enjoyed a considerable boom. Trade was conducted mainly within the borders of the empire but also extended beyond them to India, Africa, and even China during the Han Dynasty, which closely paralleled the rise and fall of the Roman hegemony in Europe. Trade with China was focused on luxuries and was not direct but conducted through Asian intermediaries.

Increasingly, the balance of trade within the empire shifted to favor the East (meaning the area from the Adriatic to Mesopotamia and Egypt). Italy became more and more dependent on imports from other parts of the empire, mainly from the East, where the levels of skills far exceeded those of the West. In the East lived the bulk of the population and the majority of the urbanites. Here, too, were the sophisticated, civilized traditions of the Hellenistic world. Even the skilled slave labor in Italy came almost exclusively from Eastern sources.

During Rome's imperial age, the methods by which the ordinary man made a living changed little from earlier days. Farming or herding animals remained the paramount occupation. At the same time, the urban population grew considerably, especially in the West. (See the Society and Economy box for details of what these people ate.) In the towns, the number of people—both men and women— engaged in skilled or semiskilled labor increased steadily. But the real growth of urban population came from the influx of country people who had lost their land and their livelihood. They came to town hoping for a better life, but many ended up as beggars.

SOCIETY AND ECONOMY

The Roman Cuisine

The differences between the items on the Roman table and those we are accustomed to on our own were perhaps not so great as generally imagined, but there were indeed some:

> [T]he Romans had no coffee, tea, sugar, liquors, truffles, potatoes or beans; tomatoes were unknown, dried herbs rare and imported. Sweets were made with honey, and sometimes with honey and cheese. The only intoxicating drink was wine; even in bars (thermopolia), which, to judge from Pompeii, were as common then as now, hot wine was drunk....
>
> The use of bread seems to have become general only at the beginning of the second century BCE. Besides special types of bread, like barley and spelt bread, there were three main grades: 1) black bread, of coarsely ground flour, 2) whiter, but still coarse, and 3) the best quality.
>
> The commonest vegetables were lentils and chickpeas, and among green vegetables lettuce, cabbage and leeks.... The Romans were great devotees of mushrooms, as is shown by many references, particularly in Martial. The olive, which we regard simply as a hors d'oeuvre, was much more highly esteemed....

> The commonest fruits were those we still have: apples, pears, cherries, plums, grapes (fresh, dried or preserved), walnuts, almonds, and chestnuts.... The apricot was introduced from Armenia, and used in the preparation of certain dishes, for example chopped ham. Dates (imported from warmer countries) seem to have been very common.
>
> The animal world contributed to the Roman table a little more widely than it does to ours. Besides beef and pork the Romans ate venison, the flesh of wild asses (onager), and dormice, to the raising of which tremendous care was paid.
>
> ... Animals which have disappeared from our table but were much prized by the Romans were the flamingo, of which the tongue was particularly esteemed, the stork, the crane and even the psittacus, a small talking bird of the parrot family.
>
> The peacock was an object of great gastronomic enthusiasm among the Romans.

▶ *Analyze and Interpret*
From your reading of this selection, why can you believe that obesity was not a common Roman health problem?

Source: Ugo Paoli, *Rome: Its People, Life, and Customs* (New York: Greenwood, 1963).

Most Roman subjects, as always, worked the land. But much of this land was now owned either by the imperial government or by wealthy absentee landlords. Small free farmers were a declining species by the second century. They were replaced not so much by slaves as by sharecropper-tenants, who were still free in most of the empire but would not long remain so.

In the Italian and western European countryside, the land controlled by the *villa,* or country estate of the wealthy, was steadily gaining at the expense of the impoverished small farmers. More and more people were tempted or coerced into giving up their independence to obtain regular income and protection against rapacious tax collectors. Another ominous trend in the empire was the increasing social stratification, particularly in the towns of Italy. The rich were more numerous than ever before, and the poor were both more numerous and more miserable. Wealth seems to have become the main qualification for public office.

Slave and Free

The number of slaves climbed sharply in the first century BCE. Roman legions took over one province after another and made off with the human booty. The alien slaves were often more educated and better skilled than the native Italians, and slaves from Greece, in particular, brought high prices in the market. Augustus tried to protect the free citizens by banning the importation of additional slaves into Italy, but his measures were evaded and later revoked.

Roman slavery was harsher than had been the case earlier. The large merchant fleet and the navy depended on galley slaves. The extensive Roman mining industry also depended on slave labor, because this job was so dangerous that few freemen could be lured into it. Slave families were broken up and sold to the highest bidders.

Slaves supposedly could own no property of their own, nor could they inherit or bequeath property. The children from a marriage of slaves were automatically the property of the parents' owners. Rape of another's slave was considered an injury to the slave owner, not to the slave, and was paid for accordingly. The rape of a slave by his or her owner was not an offense at all.

Despite such treatment, by the third and fourth centuries CE, free persons were increasingly selling themselves into voluntary slavery, which promised them a better material life than freedom could. Sometimes, too, the self-sale was a dodge to avoid the tax, which a free person had to pay but a slave did not. It is not possible to know which motive predominated.

Gender Relations

The earmark of female status was the far-reaching authority of the father over his daughter and, indeed, over all his *familia,* defined as wife, children, grandchildren, and

© Scala/Art Resource, NY

A ROMAN APARTMENT HOUSE. This model has been reconstructed from archaeological evidence found at Ostia, Rome's port. The building on the right is the home of a wealthy family, possibly the owners of the multistory tenement to the left. Although some tenements were solidly built, many were thrown up to maximize the income for the landlord and allowed to become filthy nests.

household slaves. This ***patria potestas*** (PAH-tree-ah poh-TESS-tahs), literally, the "power of the father") extended even to life and death, although the exercise of the death penalty was rare.

All Roman law was concerned primarily with the protection of property, and the laws concerning women clearly show that they were considered the property of the male head of the familia. It is worth noting that the father's powers exceeded those of the husband. For example, if a wife died without leaving a will, the property she left reverted not to her husband but to her father. A woman who passed from her father's control and was not under that of a husband was termed ***sui juris*** (SOO-ee YOO-riss; "of his or her own law"). This status was quite unusual. Women who were neither married nor possessing sui juris had to be under tutelage—that is, a male relative was legally responsible for her.

Roman girls married young by our standards, and betrothal was often much earlier still. Marriage at age thirteen was not unusual. The girl's consent was not necessary. Unlike many other civilizations, the Roman widow was expected to remarry if she could, and she was normally then sui juris, legally equal to her new husband in terms of control over property.

Divorce of wives by husbands was common among the upper classes. Augustus, scandalized by the habits of some of his colleagues, decreed that a man catching his wife in adultery must divorce her or be considered her procurer and be punished himself. Divorce was much harder for a woman to obtain, and sexual impotence was one of the few grounds accepted. Because marriage was considered a consensual union rather than a legal obligation of the spouses, the lack of continued consent was itself grounds for its dissolution. This is the source of the modern divorce by "irreconcilable differences." Abortion was legal until the first century CE, and when it was then declared a crime, it was because the act affected the property of the father of the fetus—a typical Roman viewpoint. Infanticide by exposure also continued, but no one knows how common it may have been or whether it favored the male over the female child, as is frequently assumed. A large proportion of slaves and prostitutes originated as girl babies picked up "from the trash heap," as the Roman saying went.

Women worked in all trades not requiring the heaviest labor. Textile trades were still the most common occupation for women of all classes, slave and free. Midwives, many physicians, scribes, and secretaries were female. Personal servants, hairdressers, nannies, and masseuses (a Roman passion) were always women. Entertainers of all sorts—acrobats, clowns, actresses, musicians, dancers— were in high demand. They were often female and frequently combined their stage talents with a bit of prostitution on the side. The tradition that female artistes are

sexually available continues in Mediterranean folklore to the present day.

Like most peoples, Romans attempted to legislate morality. Rape and female adultery were two of the most serious offenses. Both were punishable by death, although actual prosecutions seem to have been few. Homosexuality does not appear to have been as widespread in Rome as it had been in Greece, although it was certainly not unusual among the upper classes. Prostitution was not itself illegal, but it carried with it *infamia,* meaning disrepute and shame for the practitioners. Prostitutes were expected to register with the local authorities, and they paid heavy taxes on their earnings. Nevertheless, they were not criminals but were simply engaged in business and were so treated. Brothel keeping in Roman times, as earlier and later, was one of the more dependable sources of wealth for the (generally female) proprietors.

Children and Education

The male child of patrician birth was important as the continuer of the familia, and much attention was devoted to his education, sometimes at a school, but more often by a live-in tutor. Strict demands for achievement were placed on him from the earliest years. Learning was acquired for a communal purpose: to advance the welfare of the state. Therefore, the most important subjects to master were law and the principles of government. All men of affairs were

GIRL READING. This tender rendition of a young girl daydreaming over her studies is marked by a sentiment not often encountered in Roman painting.

Museo e Gallerie Nazionali di Capodimonte, Naples, Italy/Lauros-Giraudon/ Bridgeman Art Library

also taught rhetoric and philosophy. Science and the fine arts were of secondary importance and were viewed as personal matters, possibly important to the individual but only incidental to the community.

The segregation of the sexes that was so marked in classical Greece was largely overcome in Roman theory and, to some extent, in practice. Roman females gradually received increased freedom to enter the "great world" of male concerns. They could do this through advanced studies and larger political responsibilities. Hence, by the second century CE, it was no longer absurd for a middle class Roman girl to study mathematics or philosophy or to become an instructor in one of the arts—all careers that had been closed even to upper-class Greek females.

SUMMARY

THE PECULIAR BALANCE of political power between aristocrats and commoners that the Roman republic established lasted as long as Rome remained a socially and ethnically homogeneous state and extended its rule only to Italy. This situation ended with Rome's hard-fought success in the Punic Wars of the third century BCE, when the city-state became in fact, but not yet in name, an empire.

The failure of the republic's pseudo-democratic political structure to adapt to the changed circumstances led to civil war and constant upheaval during the last century of its existence. Reformers attempted in vain to find a solution during these unstable years. Julius Caesar tried to establish a monarchy but was cut down by his conservative enemies. His adoptive son Octavian had better success, as the first emperor, Augustus Caesar. For more than 200 years, the Augustan reforms, continued by a series of able successors, enabled Rome to prosper in peace while creating a Mediterranean and west European hegemony.

Roman republican culture and art forms were originally based on Greek and Etruscan models, with the Greeks of the Hellenistic Age being particularly important.

In form and content, philosophy and religious belief resembled the Greek originals from which they were largely derived. More innovation was shown during the late republican and imperial epoch, but the creative artistic imagination was generally not the Romans' strong point. In law and government and in the practical application of scientific knowledge to everyday problems of society, however, few surpassed them.

▶ Identification Terms

Test your knowledge of this chapter's key concepts by defining the following terms. If you can't recall the meaning of certain terms, refresh your memory by looking up the boldfaced term in the chapter, turning to the Glossary at the end of the book, or working with the flashcards that are available on the *World Civilizations* Companion Website: **academic.cengage.com/adler**

Actium, battle of	*jus gentium*	plebeians	Punic War
Carthage	*municipia*	Praetorian Guard	*sui juris*
censors	*patria potestas*	*princeps*	tribunes
consuls	patricians	proconsuls	Zama, battle of
Etruscans	Pax Romana	proletariat	

▶ Test Your Knowledge

Test your knowledge of this chapter by answering the following questions. Complete answers appear at the end of the book. You may find even more quiz questions in CengageNOW and on the *World Civilizations* Companion Website: **academic.cengage.com/adler**

1. The peoples who exerted the greatest influence on early Rome were the
   a. Etruscans and Hittites.
   b. Greeks and Egyptians.
   c. Greeks and Etruscans.
   d. Egyptians and Etruscans.
   e. Etruscans and Phoenicians.

2. Chief executive authority in the Roman republic was exercised by
   a. a king.
   b. two consuls.
   c. four praetors.
   d. ten tribunes.
   e. three censors.

3. The first decisive change in the political nature of Rome from a homogeneous city-state to an empire came after the
   a. conquest of Greece.
   b. triumph of Octavian Caesar over his partners in the Second Triumvirate.
   c. attainment of supreme power by Julius Caesar.
   d. winning of the wars against Carthage.
   e. death of Julius Caesar.

4. The first province outside the Italian "boot" to be added to the Romans' sphere of government was
   a. Gaul.
   b. Greece.
   c. Sicily.
   d. Egypt.
   e. Carthage.

5. The group of Roman officials who came to govern the new provinces was
   a. the proconsuls.
   b. the censors.
   c. the triumvirates.
   d. the tribunes.
   e. the senators.

6. Roman law is notable for its
   a. egoism and arrogance.
   b. brutality and vengeance.
   c. gentleness and mercy.
   d. practicality and flexibility.
   e. rigidity and stagnation.

7. A chief strength of Roman arts was their
   a. portrait painting.
   b. dramatic tragedy.
   c. miniature goldwork.
   d. sculpted busts.
   e. well-developed historiography.

8. The Roman state religion consisted mainly of
   a. ritual and ceremony.
   b. prayer for personal salvation.
   c. theological discussions.
   d. emotion-charged public devotions.
   e. rejection of Greek polytheism.

9. Slavery after about 100 BCE was usually
   a. harsher and more common than had been the case earlier.
   b. a temporary condition that was easily overcome.
   c. granted only for cases of homosexuality in the husband.
   d. possible only when no children could be conceived.
   e. difficult but obtainable on a few grounds.

10. For Roman women, divorce was
    a. as easily obtained as for men.
    b. an absolute impossibility because of patria potestas.
    c. a punishment reserved for serious crimes against the state.
    d. reserved for non-Italians.
    e. much more difficult than it was for men.

Enter *CengageNOW* using the access card that is available with this text. *CengageNOW* will assist you in understanding the content in this chapter with lesson plans generated for your needs and provide you with a connection to the *Wadsworth World History Resource Center* (see description at right for details).

 World History Resource Center

Enter the Resource Center using either your *CengageNOW* access card or your standalone access card for the *Wadsworth World History Resource Center.* Organized by topic, this website includes quizzes; images; over 350 primary source documents; interactive simulations, maps, and timelines; movie explorations; and a wealth of other resources. You can read the following documents, and many more, at the *Wadsworth World History Resource Center:*

Livy, *Histories*

10 IMPERIAL DECLINE AND THE BIRTH OF CHRISTIAN EUROPE

> *They have no fixed abode, no home or law or settled manner of life, but wander.*
> —Ammianus Marcellinus (Roman historian, speaking of the German tribes)

c. 6 BCE–29 CE	Life of Jesus of Nazareth
284–305 CE	Diocletian/Empire divided East and West
313–337 CE	Constantine/Christianity tolerated
381 CE	Theodosius makes Christianity official religion
late 300s–400s CE	Germanic invaders enter western empire
527–565 CE	Justinian I/Corpus Juris
c. 500–800	"Dark Age"/Germanic kingdoms
768–814	Charlemagne/Carolingian renaissance
800s–900s	Rise of feudalism

INTERNAL UPHEAVAL AND INVADING BARBARIANS

RESTRUCTURING OF THE EMPIRE

CHRISTIANITY
The Appeal of Christianity ◆ Christianity's Spread and Official Adoption ◆ Early Church Organization and Doctrine

GERMANIC INVADERS

GERMAN CUSTOMS AND SOCIETY
Conversion to Christianity ◆ Germanic Law ◆ Female Status ◆ Beginnings of Feudalism ◆ The Dark Age

CHARLEMAGNE AND THE HOLY ROMAN EMPIRE
Carolingian Renaissance ◆ Disintegration of the Carolingian Empire ◆ Renewed Invasions ◆ Development of Feudalism

THE BYZANTINE EMPIRE

AFTER MARCUS AURELIUS'S REIGN (161–180 CE), Rome's power and its convictions of a mandate to rule began to decline. Germanic tribes in the mid-200s invaded several of the outer provinces briefly, and the whole empire was wracked by internal strife that threatened to bring its traditional authority down entirely. At the beginning of the fourth century came an effort at renewal and realignment based in part on the official embrace of the formerly condemned Christianity and in part on absolute monarchy as the new style of rule. But this effort was doomed in the longer run. Germans increasingly forced their way into the empire's heartlands and imposed their own partially digested forms of Roman law and governmental technique on the populace at large. Only after the slow process of conversion to Christian belief had effected some softening of the Germanic warrior culture did the general regression in the art and craft of civilization become less apparent and this so-called Dark Age begin to lift. Charlemagne's interlude as reviver of Roman authority and belief, however bravely undertaken, proved to be a transitory moment.

Internal Upheaval and Invading Barbarians

After the unfortunate reign (180–193) of the corrupt and incompetent Commodus, son of Marcus Aurelius, the central government fell into the hands of military usurpers for almost a century. Agriculture, which had always provided the livelihood of most Roman subjects, was increasingly dominated by large estates employing unfree labor. Cities declined in size and importance as civil wars among the generals reduced one urban center after another to ashes or strangled its commerce. Some of the provinces were relatively untouched by these conflicts, particularly in the East. This fact reinforced the ever-clearer political and economic dominance of the eastern half of the empire over the western.

In the half-century between 235 and 284, Rome had twenty emperors, eighteen of whom died by violence. This was the infamous age of the Barracks Emperors. An ambitious commander who had the momentary support of a legion or two might attempt to seize power in Rome or in one or another of the provinces. Those who had the allegiance of the Italian garrison, the Praetorian Guard, were the most powerful at any given moment, and the guard was easily bought with promises of booty.

Ordinary citizens were not involved in these struggles, of course, but they suffered the effects in many ways. Respect for imperial authority disappeared, the courts of law were overruled by force, and bribery and corruption of officials became commonplace. The long-distance trade that had sustained much of Roman prosperity was badly disrupted.

It was Rome's bad luck that the Barracks Emperors coincided with the first really serious challenges from the barbarian tribes beyond its borders. In the later third century, the "Wandering of the Peoples," the long-sustained nomadic migrations begun much earlier from Asia and eastern Europe, reached the outer provinces from the Low Countries all the way to the Balkans. When these tribal peoples reached the river frontiers (the Rhine and the Danube), they found large gaps in the defenses, caused by the army's dissolution into a series of quasi-private forces. Sometimes peaceably and sometimes by force, the newcomers crossed into the civilized areas in groups both small and large.

Almost miraculously, the last few general-emperors in the 270s were able to beat off the barbarian attacks and manipulate the various tribes and nations into fighting one another more than the Romans. Rome gained breathing space that was utilized by the last of the Barracks Emperors, Diocletian, to reorganize the badly wounded government.

Restructuring of the Empire

Under Diocletian (ruled 284–305), a capable general who had fought his way to supreme power, the fiction created by Augustus Caesar that he was merely first among equals was finally buried. From now on, the emperor was clearly the absolute ruler of a subservient *Senatus et populus.* His bureaucrats were his instrument to affect his will, rather than agents of the Roman people. Diocletian brooked no opposition, not because he was a tyrant, but because he saw that if the empire was to survive, something new must be tried immediately.

To make the huge empire more governable, Diocletian divided it into western and eastern halves and underlined the dominance of the East by taking that half for his personal domain (see Map 10.1). The other he gave to a trusted associate to rule from Rome as his deputy. Each of the two co-emperors appointed an assistant, who was to follow him in office. This system, called the **Tetrarchy** (TEHT-rahr-kee: rule of four), was supposed to end the civil wars. It failed as soon as Diocletian retired (305 CE), but the reorganization of the empire into two halves remained.

Diocletian also attempted to revive the economy by lowering inflation, which had been rampant since the early Barracks Emperors. He issued the first governmental "price ceilings" on consumer goods in Western history (which failed, of course). He attempted to restore the badly damaged faith in the value of Roman coinage, whose gold and silver content had been steadily and surreptitiously reduced. He also increased the tax burden and insisted that the tax collectors were personally responsible for making up any arrearages in their districts. The net result was to make taxes more hated than ever and the tax collectors' posts almost unfillable.

Constantine the Great (ruled 313–337), Diocletian's successor to supreme power after an eight-year civil war, generally continued these policies and increased the restrictions on personal freedoms that the central government was steadily imposing. The measures were aimed especially at the free peasants, who were being forced into debt by the big landlords and who often ran away or sold themselves into slavery or were otherwise lost to the tax collector.

In the 330s, Constantine took the long-expected step of formally transferring the government to the East. Perched on the shore of the strait between Europe and Asia in a highly strategic location, the new capital city of Byzantium was well defensible from both land and sea. In time, the city of Constantine (Constantinople in Greek) became the largest city in the Christian world. Greek was the dominant language in the new capital, and Greeks were the dominant cultural force from the beginning.

What happened to the old Rome in the West? Although the deputy emperor maintained his government there for another century and a half, that city and surrounding Italy were in steady decline. Rome was ravaged by two Vandal raids (in 410 and 455), which left parts of it in permanent ruin. Finally, in 476, a German chieftain pushed aside the insignificant and powerless deputy of Constantinople and crowned himself king of Italy, an event conventionally taken as the end of the Roman Empire in the West.

MAP 10.1 The Later Roman Empire

Note the outlines of the four subdivisions of the empire after Diocletian, whose reign ended in 305 CE. Although the West had more area, the East had much greater population. The total at this era has been estimated at about 60 million, actually a decline from the second century's total of about 65 million and attributable to the ravages of a plague that hit the West in the late second century.

MAP QUESTIONS

Locate the capital cities of the Western and Eastern Empires. Which capital was more vulnerable to attack? Why?

CHRISTIANITY

While the Roman Empire weakened and crumbled, a new force—Christianity—developed within it. *Jesus of Nazareth* (*c.* 6 BCE–29 CE), whom about one-third of the world's population assert to be the Son of God and Redeemer of Mankind, was born during the reign of Augustus Caesar, about a generation after Pompey had incorporated Judaea into the growing Roman Empire. We summarize his life and influence in the Patterns of Belief box.

During the last century BCE, the Hellenistic mystery religions had become widely popular. Egyptian, Persian, Greek, and Italian cults promising power and immortality appealed to the lower ranks of a population that was steadily being divided into economic haves and have-nots. The Jews were not immune to this appeal and subdivided into several factions that held different views of the deliverer—the messiah promised to them long ago (see Chapter 4). None of these factions were receptive to the pacifist and provocative message of love and forgiveness that Jesus preached between 26 and

Bridgeman Art Library

THE WALLS OF CONSTANTINOPLE. After the move from Rome, the government devoted much money and energy to making the new capital impregnable from both sea and land. On the land side, a series of gigantic walls were erected, which protected Constantinople from all attacks until 1453, when the Ottoman Turks succeeded in capturing it by breaking down the walls with newly discovered gunpowder.

29 CE. To the Sadducees and Pharisees, Jesus's admonition to stop confusing the letter of the law with its spirit was an attempt to seduce the Jews, who had survived and remained a distinct nation only because of their unbending adherence to their Mosaic laws. Zealots wished to fight the Romans and had no empathy with a prophet who asked them to "render unto Caesar the things that are Caesar's"—that is, to accept the legitimate demands of their Roman overlords.

Meanwhile, the Roman administrators must have regarded Jesus as a special irritant among an already-difficult, religiously obsessed people. The Jews' religious doctrines were of no concern to the Romans, but Jesus's challenges to the traditionalist rabbis did create difficulties in governing. In the most literal sense, Jesus was "stirring things up." As a result, when the Jewish leaders demanded that the Roman procurator, Pontius Pilate, allow them to punish this disturber of the peace, he reluctantly agreed, and Jesus was crucified on Golgotha near Jerusalem.

For a couple of decades thereafter, the Christian cult spread slowly in Judaea and was nearly unknown outside it. This situation changed as a result of two developments. First, the educated Jew Saul of Tarsus (*c.* 6–67 CE), a Roman citizen and sophisticate, was miraculously converted to Christianity on the road to Damascus. As the apostle Paul, he insisted on preaching to the Gentiles (non-Jews). Second, the fanatical element among the Jews rebelled against the Roman overlords in the **Jewish War** (67–71 CE). After the Romans crushed it, they decided to punish this troublesome people by dispersing them in what came to be known as the *Diaspora* (actually, the second Diaspora: see Chapter 4). One result of this forced eviction

from Judaea was the establishment of Jewish exile colonies that became breeding grounds for Christianity throughout the eastern Mediterranean basin and soon in Italy itself. Spurred by the strenuous efforts of the apostle Paul and his band of missionaries, the Christian doctrine was spreading steadily, if not spectacularly, among both ex-Jews and Gentiles by the end of the first century.

The Appeal of Christianity

What was the appeal of the new religion? First, it distinguished itself from all of the other mystery religions by its *universality*. All persons were eligible: men and women, Jew and Gentile, rich and poor, Roman and non-Roman. Second, Christianity offered a message of *hope and optimism* in a Hellenistic cultural world that appeared increasingly grim for the aspirations of ordinary people. Not only were believers promised a blessed life to come, but the prospects for a better life on this Earth also appeared to be good. The Second Coming of the Lord and its accompanying Last Judgment, when the just would be rewarded and the evil punished according to their desserts, were thought to be not far off. Third, Christians were far ahead of their rivals in the *spirit of mutuality* that marked the early converts. To be a Christian was to accept an active obligation to assist your fellows in any way you might. It also meant you could count on their help and prayers when needed. Finally, Christianity featured an *appeal to idealism* that was much more powerful than anything its rivals offered. It emphasized charity and unselfish devotion in a way that had strong appeal to people weary of a world that seemed to be dominated by the drive for wealth and power.

The Gospels ("good news") of the four evangelists, Mark, Luke, Matthew, and John, were the original doctrinal foundations of the faith. They were written and collected in the late first century CE, along with the letters of St. Paul to the communities of Christians he had founded in the eastern Mediterranean. By the second century, a written New Testament had appeared that was accepted by all Christians and largely superseded the Old Testament of the Jews in their eyes.

Christianity's Spread and Official Adoption

Slowly, Christian cells sprang up in the major towns all over the Mediterranean basin (see Map 10.2). The story of Peter the Apostle coming to Rome and dying a martyr's death shortly after the death of Christ may well be factual. Certainly several disciples, spurred on by Paul, left the strictly Jewish environment in which the religion had begun and "went out into the world" of Roman pagan culture. Paul himself is thought to have died a martyr in Rome under the persecution ordered by the emperor Nero.

By the early fourth century, it has been estimated that about 10 percent of the population of the East had become Christian and perhaps 5 percent of the West. In

PATTERNS OF BELIEF

Jesus of Nazareth (c. 6 BCE–c. 29 CE)

The life and works of Jesus have affected more people more directly than those of any other individual in world history. With more than 2 billion formal adherents, Christianity is the world's most widespread faith. As with other important world religions, its founder's life is known only in sketchy outline.

In the centuries of Hellenistic civilization, several religions arose in the eastern Mediterranean that shared certain fundamental features. They insisted that there was a better life to come after the earthly existence and that some individuals had the potential to share in that life. They also maintained that it was necessary to follow the teaching of a mythic hero-prophet in order to realize that potential. These were the "mystery" religions, whose members depended on an act of faith by the believer, rather than mere attendance at a priestly ceremony.

Christianity was by far the most important of the mystery religions. Its founder was not a mythic hero, such as the Egyptian Osiris or the Greek Cybele, but a real historical person, Jesus of Nazareth, later called by his followers the *Christos*, or Messiah. Jesus was born in the newly Romanized province of Judaea, the former kingdom of Judah and home of the two tribes of Israel that had stayed true to the Mosaic Law.

Of Jesus's early life until he embarked on his preaching career at about age thirty, we know next to nothing. The Christian disciples who wrote the books of the New Testament did not think it relevant to Jesus's work to tell us of his youth or the intellectual context in which he grew up.

It is reasonably sure that Jesus was born to a couple—Mary and Joseph—who were quite ordinary, practicing Jews. Their status was undistinguished before the miraculous selection of the young Virgin Mary as the mother of the Messiah. For many years thereafter, the family (Jesus may have had at least one half-brother, the apostle James) led an obscure life in the region of Galilee, probably in the town of Nazareth.

Around 26 CE, Jesus was introduced to the teachings of John the Baptist, one of the numerous wandering sages of the day. In that same year, Pontius Pilate was appointed governor of Judaea. He was an average official, concerned mainly with making money out of his position and keeping the subject population sufficiently quiet so as not to create difficulties for his reputation back in Rome.

During the next few years, a group of lower-class Jews attached themselves to Jesus, seeing in him truly the Son of God and the long-awaited Messiah, as he claimed to be. Most of the time, Jesus followed the precepts of Jewish law and tradition quite closely, and he repeatedly said that he did not intend to found a new religion. But his bold insistence on the spirit, rather than the letter, of the law and his flat statement that, although he was the Messiah, his kingdom was not of this world, cast him in a dubious light among the tradition-bound rabbis. Before long, his message of faith in God, hope in his mercy to secure salvation, and love of one's fellow man was being seen by the high-placed as potentially revolutionary. They carried their complaints to Pontius Pilate and induced him to let them crucify Christ as an enemy of Roman rule as well as of the Mosaic Law.

The Sermon on the Mount gives us the most coherent and concise overview of Jesus's message. It is a message of tolerance, justice, and humility, of turning the other cheek and keeping the peace. Jesus thus differentiated himself and his doctrines from all other mystery religions, in which the prospect of eventually triumphing over enemies and reveling in the "good things" of the world was a major motivation for keeping the faith. Already by the Resurrection three days after his crucifixion, the small cadre of believers in Christ the Messiah felt they were the possessors of a sacred truth. Led by the apostles, they prepared to carry out their heavy responsibility to "make smooth the path of the Lord" on Earth.

▶ Analyze and Interpret

Why do you think the Bible has nothing to say of the early years of Jesus? What does the spirit rather than the letter of the law being crucial mean? How does the Sermon on the Mount exemplify the spirit of early Christianity?

You can read about Jesus's life in the Gospel according to Mark and about the work of the apostles at the *Wadsworth World History Resource Center*.

San Apollinare Nuovo, Ravenna/Dagli Orti/ The Art Archive

CHRIST AND THE FISHERS OF SOULS. This Ravenna, Italy, mosaic dating from the sixth century shows Christ calling to his disciples Peter and Andrew and telling them that henceforth they would be "fishers of souls." Fishing was a common mode of making a living in the Near East, in both fresh and salt waters. The mosaic was done, like many others, while Ravenna was the capital of the Byzantine government's attempt to regain Italy for the emperor.

MAP 10.2 The Spread of Christianity, 300–800 CE

After the emperor Theodosius made Christianity the official imperial religion, Christianity spread dramatically throughout the Roman Empire.

View an interactive version of this or a related map at http://worldrc.wadsworth.com/

MAP QUESTIONS

How was Christianity disseminated so widely from the small pockets that existed in 300 CE?

this situation, the emperor Constantine (whose mother Helena was a Christian) decided to end the persecution of Christians that had been going on at intervals since Nero's time. In 313 he issued the *Edict of Milan*, which announced the official toleration of Christianity and signaled that the new religion was favored at the imperial court. Constantine seemingly became a Christian only on his deathbed in 337, but from this time on, all emperors in East and West, with the exception of Julian (361–363), were Christians. In 381, the emperor Theodosius took the final step of making Christianity the official religion of the empire.

Why did the suspicious and warlike Constantine decide to stake his own fate, and possibly the fate of the empire,

on a new religion that had distinguished itself by its pacifism and its rejection of the traditional Roman state cult? As the story has it, Constantine became convinced that the Christian God had aided him in a crucial battle during the civil war, but historians suspect that something more was behind such a momentous decision. Probably, he expected this move would assist him in shoring up a wounded political system by gradually creating a new unity between governors and governed. Certainly, too, he recognized the growing support that Christianity was attracting among those who counted in Roman society.

Constantine's recognition would both aid and hinder the new religion. Giving Christianity a favored status and

CHRIST IN BETHANIA. This masterpiece of late Byzantine art shows Christ with his disciples at Bethany. It is a fresco in the Ascension church at Decani, in southern Serbia, painted in the mid-fourteenth century by an anonymous group of Greek and Serbian artists who had been trained in Byzantine technique. Note the use of curvature to focus the viewer's attention on the prostrate figure at the bottom.

putting the resources of the secular government behind it spurred its growth. Soon Christians were a majority in the cities. (The countryside appears to have been much slower to adopt the new creed.) At the same time, Constantine's decision ensured that the Christian church would be linked with the state and the wishes of the state's governors. Church councils would soon find that civil questions would sometimes override purely religious considerations.

Early Church Organization and Doctrine

Under Constantine, Christians came out into the open and organized their church on Roman civil models. In each community of any size, bishops were elected as heads of a diocese. They in turn appointed priests on the recommendation of the local faithful. The early Christian emperors made the fateful decision to allow the bishops to create their own courts and laws (*canon law*) for judging the clergy and administering church property—a decision that later led to great friction between revenue-seeking kings and wealthy bishops.

Several bishops of important eastern dioceses, such as Jerusalem, Antioch, and Alexandria, claimed direct office-holding descent from the twelve apostles of Jesus and therefore possessed special prestige and the title of *patriarch*. But the bishop of Rome claimed to be first among equals through the doctrine of *Petrine Succession*. According to this concept, the bishop of Rome was the direct successor of Peter, the first bishop of Rome, whom Christ had pronounced the "rock [*petros*] upon which I build my church." He therefore succeeded Peter as the preeminent leader of the church. The patriarchs and other bishops stubbornly resisted this claim until a pope was able to get it acknowledged by a church council in the sixth century.

The early church experienced many serious disputes in theology as well. The efforts to settle such disputes led to two long-term developments: (1) the council of bishops became the supreme arbiter in matters of faith, and (2) the civil and religious authorities established a close and permanent relationship.

The first council was the **Council of Nicaea** [neye-SEE-ah], in Turkey, which was held in 325 during the reign of Constantine. More than 300 bishops attended and defined many important questions of theology and church administration. The secular government, thus bringing the second new principle into play, implemented some of the decisions of the council. From this time onward, the Roman emperors in the East and West saw themselves as possessing executive powers within the Christian community—a development that led to conflict when the emperor and bishops had differing opinions on the civic implications of theological issues.

Even after Emperor Theodosius, many educated Romans still could not bring themselves to adopt the new faith, which they regarded as a mixture of base superstition and a sort of cannibalism (the host, or Eucharist). The challenges that paganism presented to Christianity contributed to the rise of a school of Christian explainers of sacred doctrine, or *apologists*, in the 300s and 400s. The most important of these *Fathers of the Church*, as they are called, were Augustine and Ambrose, the bishops of Hippo (North Africa) and Milan, respectively. Their writings are the secondary foundation of the Christian faith, as the Gospels are the primary one. St. Augustine has been especially influential in molding belief. His *Confessions* and *The City of God* have been the most important repositories of Christian teaching after the Gospels.

By the early fifth century, the Christian faith was giving the tottering Roman Empire a new system of morality and ethics that challenged the old beliefs in myriad ways. After Theodosius's reign (378–395), the imperial government was a Christian entity, so Christians could actively support it and perhaps even defend it against its external enemies. But if this worldly empire fell, it was no tragedy. It was only the otherworldly kingdom of the Lord that should count in man's eyes. By thus shifting the focus to the next world, Christian doctrine made it easier to accept the sometimes painful ending of the western Roman Empire that was occurring at the hands of Germanic warriors.

AKG, London

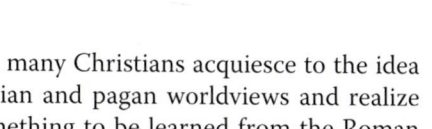
Only slowly did many Christians acquiesce to the idea of blending Christian and pagan worldviews and realize that there was something to be learned from the Roman secular environment while they awaited the Last Judgment. By the time they had arrived at this realization, however, much of that secular world had already been hammered to pieces.

GERMANIC INVADERS

After the capital was moved to Constantinople, the western provinces were gradually sacrificed to the Germans, who by this time were being pushed from behind by various Asiatic peoples. The invasion of the Huns, Asian nomads who suddenly appeared in the 440s and pillaged their way through Italy, confirmed the Romans' decision to more or less abandon the West (see Map 10.3). The Huns dispersed after the death of their warrior leader, Attila,

but the vulnerability of the West had been demonstrated, and the Germans would take full advantage of that fact.

What we know of the early Germanic people derives entirely from Roman sources, for they left no writings of their own and, in fact, had no written language until they learned Latin from the Romans. They spent much time fighting one another, and the Romans encouraged this behavior to keep the Germans weak. But once they learned to band together, the outer defenses of the Roman Empire came under frequent attack from a fierce and determined foe.

In the fourth and fifth centuries, the Germanic tribes roamed through the western provinces more or less at will. Replacing the demoralized Roman officials with their own men, the tribal war chiefs began to create rough-and-ready kingdoms:

1. The *Franks* established the core of the French kingdom in the fifth century.
2. The *Saxons* set up a kingdom in northern Germany from present-day Holland eastward.

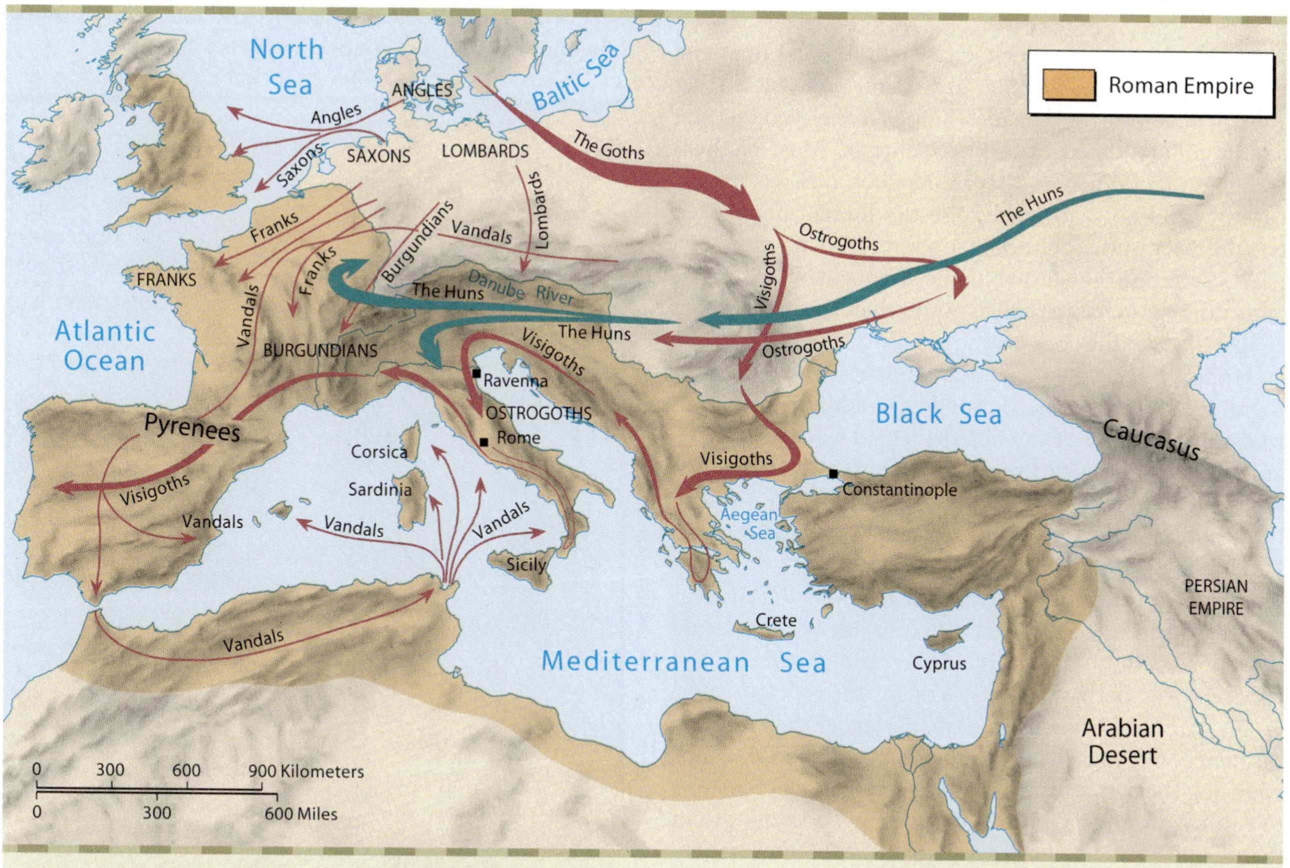

MAP 10.3 Barbarian Migrations in the Fourth and Fifth Centuries CE

This map shows the movements of the major Germanic and Asiatic invaders of Rome's empire. Originating in southern Scandinavia, the Germans spread rapidly south and west. The Huns were the first of several nomadic Asian peoples to follow "the grass highway" through southern Russia into Europe.

MAP QUESTIONS
Why was the Roman Empire vulnerable to invasion at this time?

 View an interactive version of this or a related map at http://worldrc.wadsworth.com/

3. The *Angles* and *Saxons* invaded and conquered England in the fifth century.

4. The *Vandals* invaded Roman North Africa, established a kingdom there, and from it made the raid on Rome (455), which gave their name to history.

5. The *West Goths (Visigoths)* took over Spain.

6. The *East Goths (Ostrogoths)* took over most of Italy after the Huns' raid.

By the 500s, the western half of the empire was an administrative and sometimes also a physical ruin. Germanic nobles had generally supplanted Italian or Romanized officials as the authorities. Small-scale wars, piracy, and general insecurity were the rule. Under such conditions, Roman government and traditions and the Roman lifestyle gradually disappeared except in a handful of cities and larger towns. Even there, trade and manufacturing dwindled, as the population supporting them shrank.

GERMAN CUSTOMS AND SOCIETY

It would take centuries for the two cultures—Roman and Germanic—to blend together to form the new culture that we call medieval European. The Germans were at first starkly differentiated from their subjects. Most of them wanted to be Roman, as they understood that term. They certainly did not hate or despise the Roman population or think themselves culturally superior. Intermarriage was practiced from the start. But they brought with them a large number of habits, beliefs, and values that were not at all like those of the conquered.

From the comments of the Romans who observed them, we know that the Germans had a highly personalized concept of government. An elected leader exercised authority. He received the sworn loyalty of his warriors, but the leader's final authority applied only in time of war. In peacetime, the Germans remained essentially large families led by the oldest male, each of whom was a little king in his own right. If the war leader was defeated or the warriors were dissatisfied with his leadership, he could be deposed. There was no hierarchy below the chief and apparently no permanent offices of any sort.

For many years, the new Germanic leaders had no fixed residences but traveled continuously about their domains "showing the flag" of authority and acting as chief justices to resolve disputes. Gradually, this changed to the extent that the king had a favorite castle or a walled town named for him, where he might stay for part of each year.

Very slowly also, the idea made headway that the subject paid tribute and gave loyalty to the *office* of king, rather than to the individual holder of the crown. This last development resulted from Roman influence, and its contribution to peaceable transfer of power and stable government was so clear that all of the tribal leaders adopted it sooner or later. The Christian church authorities helped in this by preaching that the crown itself was a sacred object and that its holder was a sacred person, ordained by an all-wise God to exercise civil powers over others.

Conversion to Christianity

The Germans had strong supernatural beliefs when they entered the Roman Empire, but we do not know much about their religion because it was thoroughly rooted out during the Christian Era. Originally, the Germans were *animists,* who saw spiritual powers in certain natural objects, such as trees. As with many other peoples around the globe (consider the Aryans in India or the Egyptians), their chief gods were sky deities, such as Wotan and Thor, who had no connection with either an afterlife or ethical conduct, but served as enforcers of the tribe's will. The Germans had no priests, no temples, and little, if any, theology.

The various tribes within the old Roman Empire converted to Christianity between about 450 and 700. Those beyond the empire's borders converted somewhat later. Last of all were the Scandinavians and Lithuanians, some of whom remained non-converts as late as 1100.

Bibliothèque Municipale, Laon, France/Bridgeman Art Library

POPE GREGORY I, "THE GREAT" (R. 590–604). As Pope, Gregory took in hand the conversion of the Anglo-Saxon tribes of Britain. His first deputation of Benedictine monks, led by Augustine the Missionary, succeeded in converting King Ethelbert of Kent, establishing a toehold for the later conversion of England and western Europe. Here he is depicted dictating the Book of Job to a copyist.

The method of conversion was similar in all cases. A small group of priests, perhaps headed by a bishop, secured an invitation to go to the king and explain to him the Christian gospel. If they were fortunate (rarely!), conversion of the king, his queen, or important nobles was achieved on the first try. After baptism (the outward sign of joining the Christian world), the new Christian would exert pressure on family and cronies to join also, and they, in turn, would exhort their vassals and dependents. When much of the upper class was converted, at least in name, and some native priests were in place, the tribe or nation was considered Christian, a part of the growing family of ex-pagans who had adopted the new religion.

Why did the German authorities accept Christianity? Their reasons were almost always a combination of internal politics, desire for trade, and recognition of the advantages that Christian law could give the ruler in his efforts to create a stable dynasty. It generally took decades for the faith to filter down to the common people, even in a rudimentary sense. Centuries might pass before the villagers could be said to have much knowledge of church doctrine and before they would give up their most cherished pagan customs. Medieval Christianity was in fact a hodgepodge of pagan and Christian images and beliefs. Most priests were satisfied if their faithful achieved a limited understanding of sin, heaven and hell, and the coming Last Judgment. More could not be expected.

Germanic Law

Germanic law was very different from Roman law and much more primitive. It derived from custom, which was unwritten and allowed for no fine points of interpretation. Law was the collective memory of the tribe or clan as to what had been done before in similar circumstances. It did not inquire into motivation but looked simply at the result.

The ultimate object of Germanic law was preventing or diminishing personal violence, which endangered the whole tribe's welfare. The guilty party, as determined by the assembly, was punished by the imposition of a money fine, or **wergeld** (VAYR-gehld), which was paid to the victim as compensation. In this way, the blood feuds that would have eventually wrecked the tribe's ability to survive were avoided and the honor of the victim maintained.

The Germans used trial by fire and by water to determine guilt in criminal cases in which the evidence was not clear-cut. In some capital cases in which the two parties were of equal rank, they sometimes reverted to the extreme measure of trial by combat to get a verdict. As in ancient Mesopotamia, the object of a trial was to ascertain whether illicit damage had been done to an individual and, if so, how much compensation the victim was owed by the perpetrator. As in Hammurabi's code, the court, which was the general meeting of the elders of the clan or village, acted as a detached referee between the opposing parties. Also reminiscent of the older code, but not so overtly, justice was to a large extent modified by social status.

Female Status

The status of women in pre-Christian Germanic society is a subject of much debate. According to some Roman sources, women who were married had considerable freedom and rights, more so than Roman matrons did. Although it was a warrior society, an extraordinary amount of attention seems to have been paid to the rights of mothers and wives, in both the legal and the social senses. In some cases, the widows of prominent men succeeded to their husband's position, a phenomenon the Romans found remarkable. After the Germans became Christian, there are many instances of queens and princesses exercising governmental power. The exercise of managerial powers by noble women was routine in their husband's death or absence.

The legal value (*wergeld*) of women of childbearing age was much higher than that of women who were too young or too old to have children. This reflects the view we have found in other ancient societies that women's chief asset was their ability to perpetuate the male family's name and honor. The Romans admired the Germans' sexual morality (although admittedly not to the point of adopting it themselves). Rape was a capital crime when committed against equals, as was adultery by a woman. Both concubinage and prostitution seem to have been unknown.

Beginnings of Feudalism

In the countryside, a process that had begun during the Barracks Emperors' rule accelerated dramatically. This was the establishment of large estates or **manors,** which were almost entirely self-sufficient and self-governing. The manor normally began as a villa, the country hideaway of a wealthy Roman official in quieter days. As order broke down and the province could ignore the central government, some of these officials became the equivalent of Chinese warlords, maintaining private armies to secure the peace in their own localities. Frequently extorting services and free labor from the villagers nearby, they evaded the central government's controls and taxes. These men grew ever more wealthy and powerful and began to acquire the peasants' lands through bribery, intimidation, and trade for the protection they offered.

When the invasions began, these strongmen simply took over the basic elements of government altogether. In return for physical protection and some assurance of order in their lives, the peasants would often offer part of their land and labor to the "lord" for some period, perhaps life. In this way were born both the later European nobility (or a large part of it) and the feudal system of agricultural estates worked by bound laborers. The serfs of later days were the descendants of these free men and women who were desperately seeking protection in a world of chaos and danger.

As the cities and towns declined, more and more of the population found itself in manorial villages, dependent on and loosely controlled by the Roman or German lord and his small band of armed henchmen. Economic life became much simpler, but it was more a daily struggle for survival than a civilized existence. The skills and contacts of Roman days fell into disuse, for there was little demand for them in this rough and sometimes brutal world. Trade in all but the barest necessities over the shortest distances became rare. Neither the roads nor the waters of western Europe were safe from marauders and pirates, and the Roman transport network fell to pieces.

The Dark Age

So backward did much of society become that it was once usual to refer to the centuries between 500 and 800 as the Dark Age in Europe. Similarly to its namesake in ancient Greece, this term refers as much to the lack of documentation as to the ignorance of people living then. Not only have many documents perished through vandalism and neglect, but relatively few records were kept in the first place. Only the clergy had much need of writing, and many of the priests and monks in the seventh and eighth centuries did well to read or write more than their names. They were almost always illiterate in the official Latin language of the church and knew their church history and doctrines only by hearsay. Many a bishop could not write his sermon.

The venal and immoral conduct of some clergy gave rise to scandal. In many places church offices were bought and sold like so many pounds of butter. Rome was far away and could be easily ignored in church affairs, as it was in civil ones. Besides, the pope in this era was always an Italian nobleman who rarely gave much attention to things spiritual. This was particularly the case after 700.

In some countries, notably the German lands east of the Rhine, the bishops were more or less forced by the king to take on secular and even military duties as the king's lieutenants. The churchman was often the only

Musée Condé, Chantilly, France/Giraudon/Bridgeman Art Library

THE FARMER'S TASKS. Pastoral life in medieval Europe required the work of men, women, and children. This painting shows some details of the manor and its peasants at work shearing sheep and harvesting a summer wheat crop.

educated person in the area and the only one who had some concept of administration and record keeping. The combination of civil and religious duties was, however, injurious to the religious. The bishop or abbot (the head of a monastery) often devoted more time and energy to his secular affairs than to his spiritual ones. All too frequently, important clergymen bribed their way into their position with the intention of using it as a means of obtaining wealth or influence in political matters. Their ecclesiastical duties played little or no role in these considerations. In the circumstances, it is more remarkable that some clergy *were* good and gentle men who tried to follow the rules than that many were not.

Having said all that, it is still true that the Christian church was the only imperial Roman institution that survived the Germanic onslaught more or less intact. The church was changed, usually for the worse, by German custom and concepts, but it did survive as recognizably the same institution that had won the religious allegiance of most Roman citizens in the fourth century. The church, which also operated whatever charitable and medical institutions that existed, supplied all of the education that was available in early medieval Europe. When the higher concepts of Roman law were recovered in Europe, the church adopted them first in its canon law and spread them to secular life by its teaching.

The *Age of Faith* had opened, and the church's teachings and preachings about the nature of humans and their relations with God were to have tremendous influence on every facet of human affairs, an influence that did not diminish noticeably for about a thousand years.

CHARLEMAGNE AND THE HOLY ROMAN EMPIRE

The greatest of the Germanic kings by far was *Charlemagne* (SHAR-luh-mane; Charles the Great), king of the Franks (768–800) and the first Holy Roman Emperor (800–814). The kingdom of the Franks had been in a favored position since its founder, Clovis, had been the first important German ruler to accept Roman Christianity, in or about 500. Charlemagne became king through the aggressive action of his father, a high official who seized royal power. An alliance with the pope in Rome did much to cement the new king's shaky legal position. Charlemagne earned the papacy's lasting gratitude by crushing the Lombards,

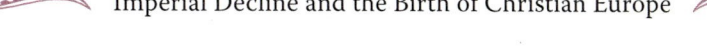

a Germanic people who had settled in northern Italy and were pushing south, threatening Rome.

For more than thirty years (772–804), Charlemagne was at war with one or another non-Christian German neighbor. His persistence was rewarded by the establishment of by far the largest territory under one ruler since Roman times and by the granting of the title *emperor* by Pope Leo III. (See Society and Economy box and Map 10.4.) Charles's new empire was an attempt to revive the Roman order in Europe, in close cooperation with the Christian church. According to medieval theory, the civil government and the ecclesiastical establishment were two arms of a single body, directed by one head: Christ. Charlemagne's coronation by Leo in the papal city on Christmas Day 800 was looked on as the culmination of that dream of proper governance and as the greatest event since the birth of Christ.

The emperor in Constantinople was not pleased, to put it mildly.

Carolingian Renaissance

Charlemagne's claims to fame stem more from his brave attempts to restore learning and stable government to Europe than from his coronation as the first emperor. He revived the Roman office of *comes*, or count, as the representative of the king in the provinces. He started the **missi dominici**, special officers who checked up on the counts and others and reported directly to the king. Knowing that most people were touched more directly by religion than by government, Charlemagne also concerned himself with the state of the church. Many of his most trusted officials were picked from the clergy, a practice that would lead to problems in later days.

Charles admired learning, although he had little himself (supposedly, he, too, could not sign his name!). From all parts of his domains and from England, he brought men to his court who could teach and train others. Notable among them was *Alcuin*, an Anglo-Saxon monk of great ability, who directed the palace school for clergy and officials set up by the king. For the first time since the 400s, something like higher education was available to a select few. Not overly pious himself, Charlemagne still respected and encouraged piety in others. At his orders, many new parishes were founded or given large new endowments, and the establishment of many more monasteries reinforced these.

But all Charlemagne's efforts were insufficient to turn the tide of disorder and violence. His "renaissance" was short lived, and his schools and governmental innovations were soon in ruins. The times were not ripe for them. In the first crises, they collapsed, and the darkness descended again.

Disintegration of the Carolingian Empire

Charlemagne eventually bequeathed his empire to his only surviving son, Louis the Pious, a man who was unfit for the heavy responsibility. By Louis's will, the empire was divided among his three sons: Charles, Lothar, and Louis. Charles received France; Lothar, the midlands between France and Germany reaching down into Italy; and Louis, Germany. Fraternal war for supremacy immediately ensued. The *Treaty of Verdun* in 843, which established the peace, is one of the most important treaties in world history, for the general linguistic and cultural borders it established still exist today, 1,160 years later (see inset, Map 10.4). When Lothar died a few years later, the midlands were divided between the survivors, Charles and Louis. After a brief period, the title of Holy Roman Emperor was settled on the king of Germany, the successors of Louis, who retained it until the nineteenth century.

Renewed Invasions

In the late ninth century, the center and western parts of Europe were attacked from three directions: The Vikings swept down from the north, the Magyars advanced from the east, and the Muslims attacked from the Mediterranean. In the ensuing chaos, all that Charlemagne had been able to do was extinguished, and government reverted back to a primitive military contract between individuals for mutual defense.

The Vikings or Norsemen were the most serious threat and had the most extensive impact. Superbly gifted warriors, these Scandinavians came in swift boats to ravage the coastal communities and then flee before effective countermeasures could be taken. From their headquarters in Denmark and southern Sweden, every year after about 790 they sailed forth and soon discovered that the Franks, Angles, and Saxons were no match for them. In 834, a large band of Vikings sailed up the Seine and sacked Paris. Seventy years later, they advanced into the Mediterranean and sacked the great city of Seville in the heart of the Spanish caliphate.

By the late 800s, the Vikings were no longer content to raid. They came to conquer. Much of eastern England, Brittany and Normandy in France, Holland, and Iceland fell to them. In their new lands, they quickly learned to govern by intimidation rather than to plunder and burn, and taxes took the place of armed bands. They learned the advantages of literacy and eventually adopted Christianity in place of their northern gods. By about 1000, the Vikings had footholds ranging from the coast of the North Sea to the eastern Mediterranean. They had become one of the most capable of all the European peoples in government and administration, as well as the military arts.

The Magyars were a different proposition. They were the next-to-last version of the Asiatic invasions of western Europe, which had begun as far back as the Huns. This resemblance earned their descendants the name *Hungarians* in modern nomenclature. The Magyars arrived in Europe at the end of the ninth century and for fifty years

SOCIETY AND ECONOMY

Charlemagne

The monk Einhard was a German. In the 790s, he went to join the school founded by Charlemagne and administered by Alcuin in the Carolingian capital at Aachen. After Charles's death, Einhard found time to write the most famous biography of the Christian Middle Age. He was particularly concerned with giving his readers a view of Charles as a human being. Very brief and easily read, the *Life of Charlemagne* is our chief source of information about the character of the first Holy Roman Emperor.

Chapters 18 and 19: Private Life

At his mother's request he married a daughter of the Lombard king Desiderius but repudiated her for unknown reasons after one year. Then he married Hildegard, who came from a noble Swabian family. With her he had three sons, Charles, Pepin, and Louis, and as many daughters.... [H]e had three more daughters with his third wife Fastrada.... When Fastrada died he took Liutgard to wife.... After her death he had four concubines....

For the education of his children, Charles made the following provisions.... [A]s soon as the boys were old enough they had to learn how to ride, hunt, and handle weapons in Frankish style. The girls had to get used to carding wool and to the distaff and spindle. (To prevent their getting bored and lazy he gave orders for them to be taught to engage in these and in all other virtuous activities).... When his sons and daughter died, Charles reacted to their deaths with much less equanimity than might have been expected of so strong-minded a man. Because of his deep devotion to them he broke down in tears.... For Charles was by nature a man who had a great gift for friendship, who made friends easily and never wavered in his loyalty to them. Those whom he loved could rely on him absolutely.

He supervised the upbringing of his sons and daughters very carefully.... Although the girls were very beautiful and he loved them dearly it is odd that he did not permit any of them to get married, neither to a man of his own nation nor to a foreigner. Rather, he kept all of them with him until his death, saying he could not live without their company. And on account of this, he had to suffer a number of unpleasant experiences, however lucky he was in other respects. But he never let on that he had heard of any suspicions about their chastity or any rumors about them.

Chapter 25: Studies

Charles was a gifted speaker. He spoke fluently and expressed what he had to say with great clarity. Not only was he proficient in his mother tongue (Frankish) but he also took trouble to learn foreign languages. He spoke Latin as well as his own language, but Greek he understood better than he could speak it—He also tried his hand at writing, and to this end kept writing tablets and notebooks under his pillow in bed—But since he had only started late in life, he never became very accomplished in the art.

Louvre, Paris/Peter Willi/Bridgeman Art Library

CHARLEMAGNE (R. 742–814). The first Holy Roman Emperor briefly succeeded in unifying Western Europe. Within two generations after his death, however, his empire was divided into three parts. This casting was made within a few years of his death and is probably a close likeness.

▶ *Analyze and Interpret*

How does Charles's possessiveness toward his daughters make him more believable as a human being? What do you make of Einhard's statement that Charles "had to suffer a number of unpleasant experiences"? What do you think about the fact that this pillar of the church took at least four wives and four concubines?

You can read more selections from Einhard's *Life of Charlemagne* at the *Wadsworth World History Resource Center*.

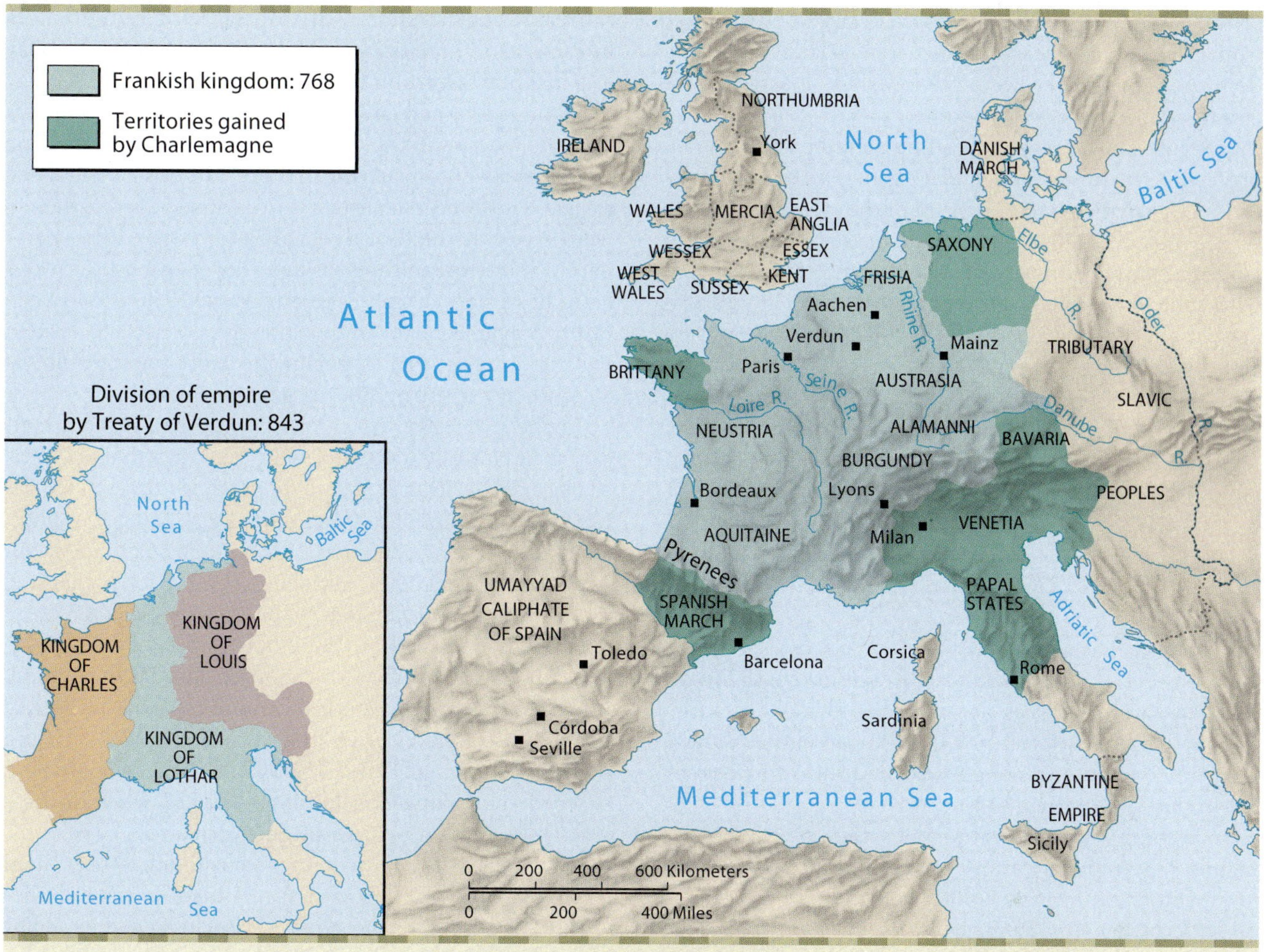

MAP 10.4 Charlemagne's Empire

Charlemagne intended for the territories of the first Holy Roman Empire to be divided among his three sons. However, two died before their father, so the entire realm passed to Louis. Louis then repeated his father's plan and divided the empire among his three sons: Louis, Lothar, and Charles.

MAP QUESTIONS

Why was Charlemagne's Empire known as the Holy Roman Empire?

 View an interactive version of this or a related map at http://worldrc.wadsworth.com/

fought the Christianized Germans for mastery. Finally, in a great battle in 955, the Magyars were defeated and retired to the Hungarian plains, where they gradually settled down. In 1000, their king and patron saint, Stephen, accepted Roman Christianity, and the Magyars joined the family of European nations.

The Muslims of the Mediterranean were descendants of North African peoples who had been harassing southern Europe as pirates and raiders ever since the 700s. In the late 800s, they wrested Sicily and part of southern Italy from the Italians and thereby posed a direct threat to Rome. But the Muslims were checked and soon settled down to join the heterogeneous group of immigrants who had been coming to southern Italy for a long time. The Muslims' highly civilized rule was finally disrupted by the attacks of the newly Christian Vikings, who began battling them for mastery in the eleventh century and eventually reconquered Sicily and the southern tip of the peninsula from them.

Development of Feudalism

The invasions fragmented governmental authority, as the royal courts in France and Germany were unable to defend their territories successfully, particularly against the Viking attacks. It fell to local strongmen to defend their own areas as best they could. Men on horseback had great advantages in battle, and the demand for them rose steadily. Thus, the original **knights** were mercenaries, professional warriors-at-horse who sold their services to the highest bidder. What was bid normally was land and the labor of those who worked it. In this way, large tracts passed from the king, technically the owner of all land in his kingdom, to warriors who were the lords and masters of the commoners living on these estates.

The invasions thus greatly stimulated the arrival of the professional army and the feudal military system in northern Europe, which bore the brunt of the attacks.

Any headway Charlemagne had made in restoring the idea of a central authority was soon eradicated. The noble, with control over one or more estates on which manorial agriculture was practiced with serf labor, now became a combined military and civil ruler for a whole locality. The king remained the object of special respect, and all acknowledged the sacred powers of the royal crown. But the feudal nobles and their hired men-at-arms carried out all day-to-day administration, military defense, and justice.

THE BYZANTINE EMPIRE

The eastern half of the early Christian world is usually known as the **Byzantine Empire** (BIZ-an-teen: from *Byzantium*, the original Greek name for the town Constantine renamed for himself). It proved to be an extraordinarily resilient competitor among the several rivals for supremacy in the eastern Mediterranean.

In keeping with Eastern traditions, the nature of the imperial throne became even more autocratic than in Rome. The emperor became a semi-divine figure, ruling through a large and efficient bureaucracy. Despite occasional religiously inspired revolts (notably the *Iconoclastic* uprising against the imperial decree forbidding worship of images), the government and the population were strongly bonded by Christianity and a belief in the emperor as Christ's deputy on Earth. In fact, this spiritual bond enabled the long life of the empire in the face of many trials, until its ultimate death at the hand of the Ottoman Turks in the fifteenth century.

Unlike the West, the East accepted the emperor as the dominant partner in affairs of church and state. He appointed his patriarchs, and he had the power to remove them. This **Caesaro-Papism** (the monarch as both head of state and head of church) was to sharply distinguish the Byzantine from the Latin world of faith. The founder of this tradition was the powerful emperor *Justinian* (ruled 527–565), who also put his stamp on the appearance of the capital through a huge program of public works. The most spectacular was

San Vitale, Ravenna/Giraudon/Bridgeman Art Library

FRESCO DEPICTING JUSTINIAN (R. 527–565). Justinian, the Emperor of the eastern Roman Empire, tried to re-conquer the western Empire after the various barbarian tribes had occupied it. His armies were successful in retaking most of Italy and parts of North Africa, but most of this territory reverted to Germanic control within a few years. He is remembered more as the builder of the Hagia Sophia and for his *Corpus Juris*.

the great central church of Constantinople, the **Hagia Sophia,** or Church of Holy Wisdom, which remains today as a magnificent reminder of past glories.

As already noted, after the transfer of imperial government to Constantinople, the western provinces became expendable. The heartlands, those areas that had been assigned to the eastern half as organized by Diocletian, were given the bulk of the army and received the major part of state expenditures (as it produced by far the greater amount of state taxes). Even after large regions had been lost to Slavic, Persian, and Asiatic invasions, the Christian Eastern Empire would remain the most potent political and military entity in the Mediterranean basin.

In the mid-500s, the ambitious Justinian made a concerted and initially successful effort to recover the lost Western provinces. The dream of re-creating the empire was ultimately a failure, however. Within just two generations, almost all of the reconquered areas (in Italy, Spain, and north Africa) had fallen to new invaders. The effort had exhausted the Byzantines and would never be attempted again.

From the early 600s, the empire was under more or less constant attack for two centuries. During this period, it lost not only the western reconquests but also most of its own eastern territories, first to Avars and Persians and then to Arabs and Slavs. The besieging Muslims nearly succeeded in taking Constantinople in 717, when the desperate defenders used "Greek fire," a combustible liquid, to beat them off at sea. While the imperial defenders were occupied, their tributary Slavic subjects in the Balkans (Bulgars, Serbs) established independent states that soon became powerful enough to threaten the Greeks from the north. Yet again and again the Constantinople authorities would somehow find the energy and skill to foil their opponents or set them against one another.

In the long term, perhaps the most outstanding achievement of the Byzantine rulers was the Christianization of eastern Europe. By the 700s, priests of the Western church, supported by the bishop of Rome, had made many converts among the Germanic tribes and kingdoms. But they had not yet ventured into eastern Europe, which had never been under Roman rule. Here, the field was open to the Byzantine missionaries.

The mission to the Slavic peoples was pursued with energy and

devotion. Beginning in the 800s, Greek monks moved into the nearby Balkans and then to the coast of the Black Sea and into Russia. Their eventual success in bringing Christianity to these regions meant that the inhabitants of the present-day states of Russia, Romania, Serbia, Bulgaria, and, of course, Greece would look for centuries to Constantinople rather than Rome. Constantinople molded their religious and cultural values, their laws and their literature, their styles of art and architecture, and, thanks to their ethnically organized churches, their very sense of nationhood.

The conversion of the Slavs to Greek-rite Christianity proved to be a crucial and permanent turning point in European history. The split that originated in the rivalry between the bishops of Rome and Constantinople gradually deepened. It was reflected in the cultural and religious differences between Greek and Latin. After many years of alternating friction and patched-up amity, the rift culminated in the division of Christianity between West and East. In 1054, a headstrong pope encountered a stubborn patriarch who refused to yield to the pope's demands for complete subordination in a matter of doctrine. The two leaders then excommunicated each other in a fit of theological egotism. Despite several efforts—most recently, Pope John Paul's visit to Orthodox Ukraine in 2001—their successors have not been able to overcome their differences.

One other enormously influential result of Byzantine initiative was the huge collection called the ***Corpus Juris*** (COHR-puhs YOO-rihs). This sixth-century distillation of Roman law and practice was undertaken (once again!) at the emperor Justinian's command and passed on to posterity. It is the foundation for most Western medieval and early modern law codes, and its basic precepts are operative in many Roman Catholic countries of Europe and Latin America to the present day.

SUMMARY

THE GERMANIC INVASIONS of the third and fourth centuries found a Roman society that was already sorely tried under the burdens of heavy taxes, declining productivity, population loss, and instability at the top. The demoralization was slowed but could not be stopped by the authoritarian reforms of Diocletian and Constantine. In the meantime, the new mystery religion named after Jesus Christ gathered strength within the Roman realm. Christianity spread rapidly after winning the favor of Constantine and his successors, but it could not halt the constellation of forces laying waste to the western provinces.

The Germanic tribes took note of Rome's weakness and acted accordingly. A regressive Dark Age of violence and ignorance ensued, from which relatively little documentation has survived. In time, the efforts of missionaries and the examples of civic organization demonstrated by the Romanized subject populace showed results, as the Germanic warriors set up royal or princely governments of a rough-and-ready sort. By the 700s in the former Roman provinces, these attempts had become stabilized and Christianized, at least in the governing classes.

The most important of the early medieval rulers was Charlemagne, the first Holy Roman Emperor as well as king of the Franks. His attempts to restore the ancient empire went astray almost as soon as he was dead, and the renaissance that he promoted also proved ephemeral. New invasions by Vikings, Magyars, and Muslims, and the chaotic conditions they created in Europe, were too much for the personal system of government that Charlemagne had established. It collapsed and was replaced by a highly decentralized administration based on agrarian manors and local military power in the hands of a self-appointed elite, the nobility.

In the eastern half of the old empire, a form of semi-divine monarchy possessing great power continued for a thousand years after the collapse in the West. After the failed attempt of Justinian to recover the western provinces, attacks came from all sides. The most persistent and successful attackers were the Arab Muslims, who by the 700s had taken most of the former imperial lands of the eastern Mediterranean. The conversion of the Slavs and some other peoples to Greek-rite Christianity was an outstanding achievement, but the split with the Roman church that came in the eleventh century was to be fateful.

▶ *Identification Terms*

Test your knowledge of this chapter's key concepts by defining the following terms. If you can't recall the meaning of certain terms, refresh your memory by looking up the boldfaced term in the chapter, turning to the Glossary at the end of the book, or working with the flashcards that are available on the *World Civilizations* Companion Website: **academic.cengage.com/adler**

Byzantine Empire	Council of Nicaea	knights	Tetrarchy
Caesaro-Papism	Hagia Sophia	manor	*wergeld*
Corpus Juris	Jewish War	*missi dominici*	

▶ *Test Your Knowledge*

Test your knowledge of this chapter by answering the following questions. Complete answers appear at the end of the book. You may find even more quiz questions in CengageNOW and on the *World Civilizations* Companion Website: **academic.cengage.com/adler**

1. The reforming emperor who created the Tetrarchy was
   a. Commodus.
   b. Constantine.
   c. Diocletian.
   d. Augustus.
   e. Justinian.
2. Which of the following does *not* help explain the appeal of early Christianity?
   a. Encouragement of military valor
   b. Sense of supernatural mission
   c. Receptivity to all potential converts
   d. Promotion of a sense of community among its adherents
   e. Emphasis on moral behavior and concern for others
3. Christianity became a universal faith rather than a Jewish sect in large part due to the efforts of
   a. the Roman officials in Judaea.
   b. the apostle Paul.
   c. the apostle Peter.
   d. the Zealots.
   e. the emperor Constantine.
4. The emperor Theodosius is important to Christian history for
   a. his final persecution of Christians.
   b. making Christianity the official religion of the empire.
   c. beginning the practice of intervening in internal church affairs.
   d. moving the church headquarters to Constantinople.
   e. issuing the Edict of Milan, which was the first official acceptance of Christianity.
5. The first attempt to clarify matters of church administration was the
   a. Treaty of Verdun (843).
   b. Edict of Milan.
   c. Corpus Juris.
   d. Carolingian revival.
   e. Council of Nicaea.
6. The first Holy Roman Emperor was
   a. Pippin I.
   b. Richard the Lion-hearted.
   c. Charlemagne.
   d. Leo III.
   e. Diocletian.
7. The biographer of Charlemagne tells us that the king
   a. cared greatly about the manners of his courtiers.
   b. enjoyed the company of his daughters.
   c. despised physical exercise.
   d. read and wrote a great deal.
   e. encouraged his children to marry and bear him grandchildren.
8. The decisive advantage held by the Vikings in their raids on Europe was their
   a. overwhelming numbers.
   b. superior weapons.
   c. great courage under attack.
   d. use of naval tactics to strike swiftly.
   e. willingness to adopt the ways of those they conquered.
9. The Treaty of Verdun in 843
   a. divided Europe between Muslims and Christians.
   b. created the kingdom of the Franks.
   c. was a compromise between Eastern and Western Christianity.
   d. divided Charlemagne's empire into three states.
   e. provided for religious toleration within the Holy Roman Empire.
10. Which of the following was *not* accomplished by Justinian?
    a. Temporary reconquest of part of the western empire
    b. Construction of the Hagia Sophia
    c. Defeat of the Arab invaders
    d. Composition of a new code of law
    e. Establishment of the concept of the monarch serving as head of the church

Enter *CengageNOW* using the access card that is available with this text. *CengageNOW* will assist you in understanding the content in this chapter with lesson plans generated for your needs and provide you with a connection to the *Wadsworth World History Resource Center* (see description at right for details).

 ▶ **World History Resource Center**

Enter the Resource Center using either your *CengageNOW* access card or your standalone access card for the *Wadsworth World History Resource Center*. Organized by topic, this website includes quizzes; images; over 350 primary source documents; interactive simulations, maps, and timelines; movie explorations; and a wealth of other resources. You can read the following documents, and many more, at the *Wadsworth World History Resource Center*:

Gospel According to Mark
Einhard, *Life of Charlemagne*
Marcus Aurelius, *Meditations*

Worldview Two

LAW AND GOVERNMENT

SOCIETY AND ECONOMY

GREEKS

After eclipse of original Mycenaean civilization and ensuing Dark Age, evolution of written law and developed monarchy begins with reforms of Draco and Solon in the sixth century BCE. There is a noticeable shift toward the latter in lawgiving. Strong differences continue between slaves and freemen and between aliens and citizens. Mass political activity within framework of polis stimulated by democratic reforms of the fifth century in Athens. Sparta emerges as opposite pole to Athens. Ensuing Peloponnesian War leads to Macedonian takeover. Polis ideals die out under Hellenistic monarchies, then under conquering Romans.

Small farms, home crafts, and maritime trade backbone of the Classical Age economy. Overpopulation becomes major problem by the 600s but solved by emigration and establishment of colonies around Mediterranean. Trade becomes critical to maintenance of home country prosperity; city-states become market centers. Coinage introduced. In Hellenistic period (after 300 BCE), large numbers of Greeks emigrate to East as favored citizens. Massive urban development in Hellenistic monarchies creates stratified society. Use of Greek coinage greatly facilitates commercial development. Slavery becomes commonplace, as does large-scale manufacturing and estate agriculture. Under Roman rule, Greek homeland diminishes in economic importance, becomes impoverished.

ROMANS

Evolution of Roman law and government particularly marked over this millennium. Roman republic produces written codes by the fifth century BCE and eventual balance of patrician–plebian powers. Punic Wars and resultant imperial outreach corrupt this balance, and bring about social problems that cannot be solved peacefully. Augustus's administrative reforms answer most pressing needs for civic peace and stability for next two centuries, while law continues evolution on basis of equity and precedent. Central government's authority sharply weakened in West by transfer to Constantinople, then destroyed by Germanic invaders after 370s CE. Eastern provinces remain secure.

Small peasants the bulk of original Roman citizenry but, after Punic Wars, are overshadowed by hordes of slaves and immigrants from Africa and eastern Mediterranean. Italy becomes dependent on food imports. Plantations and estates replace farms, while urban proletariat multiplies. Importation of luxury goods from Asia via the Silk Road during the period of the Empire. After 200 CE, western provinces lose ground to richer, more populous East, a process hastened by the Germanic invasions. Reforms of Diocletian and Constantine (295–335 CE) do not stop declining productivity of western provinces and resultant vulnerability to invaders.

EUROPEANS

Roman institutions transformed by Germanic admixtures; government evolves slowly from imperial model through feudal decentralization to monarchies of the late Medieval Age.

Economic activity increasingly mixed between agrarian and nonagrarian fields, but peasant farmers and pastors still make up majority.

CROSS-CULTURAL CONNECTIONS

Migrations

Southern Europeans: Greeks colonize northern Mediterranean perimeter and islands and Black Sea region; under Alexander, they conquer and occupy parts of western Asia. In Hellenistic period, large numbers of Greeks emigrate to East as favored citizens.

Western Asia: Phoenicians colonize southern periphery of Mediterranean. Later, Arab Islamic conquests occupy most of eastern and southern Mediterranean perimeter.

Central Asians: Huns and Central Asian Turkish tribes migrate westward, driving Germanic and Slavic tribes before their advance.

Northern Europeans: Germanic peoples migrate from northern Europe eastwards, then driven westwards by Central Asians; eventually overrun Western Europe and North Africa.

Trade and Exchange Networks

Northeast Africa-Red Sea Network: Greco-Roman trade with Egypt, Kush, Axum, Southern Arabia, and India.

Greco-Roman Mediterranean Network: Thriving network between Europe, Near East, and North Africa; later largely in hands of Muslim and Italian merchants.

European Network: Overland and river trade routes extended into Europe from Mediterranean during centuries of Roman Empire.

CLASSICAL MEDITERRANEAN CIVILIZATION 500 BCE–800 CE

PATTERNS OF BELIEF

ARTS AND CULTURE

SCIENCE AND TECHNOLOGY

Greeks of the Classical Age founders of philosophy as rational exercise. Explore most of the questions that have occupied Western philosophy in metaphysics, ethics, and epistemology. Religion conceived of as civic duty more than as a path to immortality. Gods seen as humans writ large, with faults and virtues the same. Theology and ethics sharply separated; educated class turns to philosophy as guide to ethical action: "Man the measure." After second century BCE, the religion–philosophy divergence stronger as masses turn to mystery religions from East.

Classical Age brings brilliant flowering of literary and plastic arts, giving models for later Western civilization. Mastery of sculpture, architecture, poetry, drama, and history achieved. In Hellenistic period, Roman overlords adopt Greek models for their own literature and sculpture, spreading them through out Europe. Greeks patriarchal in public and private culture. Large cities dominate culture of Hellenistic kingdoms and contribute to continuing differentiation between rich and poor.

In Classical Age, physical science subordinated to philosophy in broad sense. In Hellenistic period, physical sciences selectively advanced, especially mathematics, physics, and medicine. Little or no interest in technology apparent. Scientific knowledge pursued for its own sake rather than for applications.

Romans adopt notions of supernatural and immortality from Etruscans and Greeks, modifying them to fit their own civic religion. Roman adaptations of Greek Stoicism and Epicureanism become most common beliefs of educated. Government of Constantine adopts Christianity in fourth century to sustain faltering empire, and it becomes equal or senior partner of civil regime in the West. Roman papacy assumes governmental powers for Italy when empire's attempt to recover under Justinian fails.

Art of high technical quality but lacks creative imagination. Artists generally content to follow models from abroad in plastic and literary forms. Exceptions are some minor literary genres, mosaic work, and architecture. Public life not so patriarchal as that of Greece but is more affected by class divisions. Romans give respect to tradition while demonstrating considerable flexibility in governance and social organization. Urban life increasingly the dominant matrix of Roman culture as empire matures, but gives way in western half as invasions begin.

Roman science depends on Hellenistic predecessors, which entered Italy from the East. As with Greeks, abundance of slaves and other cheap labor argues against search for labor-saving techniques. Only interest shown in technology is in construction and engineering fields. Novel use of brick and cement, construction of bridges, forts, aqueducts, hydrology systems, and road building extensive and sophisticated throughout Italy and provinces.

Roman Christianity gradually superimposed on western and central Europe through missionary activity in the 500s to 800s. Western Europe becomes single religious community, though remaining divided into political realms.

Greco-Roman models lost to northern and central Europe after the Roman collapse.

Natural sciences stagnate or worse until late medieval period.

Spread of Ideas and Technologies

Western Asia: *Mesopotamian and Egyptian skills in mathematics and the physical sciences passed to Greeks. Some deities borrowed from Egypt.*

North and Northeast Africa: *Spread of Greek and Roman humanism during early centuries; later Christianity and Islam.*

Europeans: *Roman urbanization and spread of Greek and Roman political ideals. Conversion of Germans and Scandinavians to Roman Catholic Christianity.*

Part THREE

EQUILIBRIUM AMONG POLYCENTRIC CIVILIZATIONS, 500–1500 CE

BEFORE ABOUT 500 CE, contacts among the major civilizations were limited and tenuous. Usually, they were made through intermediate, less developed societies. Rome, for example, had only the most sparing contacts with China, and they were all indirect. Its contacts with Hindu India were more direct but still very limited. For that matter, India and China had very little contact with one another despite their geographic proximity. Thanks to the mountain walls and the deserts that separated them, few Chinese and still fewer Indians dared make that journey. After 500, however, entirely new civilizations emerged, quite detached from the original West Asian and Mediterranean locales.

In still-isolated America, throughout this period a series of ever more skilled and more populous Indian societies arose in the middle latitudes of the continent and along its western fringe. They were mysteriously (to us) dispersed or overcome by later comers, until the most advanced and skilled of all fell prey to the Spanish conquistadors.

In sub-Saharan Africa, urban life and organized territorial states were emerging by about 300 CE. About the same epoch, the Mesoamerican Indians and the Muslims of Asia and northern Africa had achieved a high degree of city-based civilization, the former developing independently of all other models and the latter building on the ancient base in western Asia.

As one example, commercial relations between Mediterranean Christians and the Hindu/Buddhist regions became closer and more extensive. Both overland and by sea, the Muslims of the eastern fringe of the Mediterranean were the essential mediators between these distant centers and profited from the middleman role as they extended their influence over the Indian Ocean and Central Asian trade network. At the end of the period, a reinvigorated Islam extended its conquests in both southern Europe and Africa. Indeed, with the great advantages enjoyed by the civilizations of Asia over the relatively backward West, an observer in the fifteenth century hardly could have guessed that it would be Europe that would emerge as the dominant force in the world in the coming centuries.

In Asia, this millennium was an era of tremendous vitality and productivity—the South and East Asian Classical Age—which was only briefly interrupted by the Mongol conquests of the thirteenth century. But the Mongols were soon assimilated or expelled by their Chinese/Turkic/Persian subjects.

In the West, the entire thousand-year epoch from 500 to 1500 CE carries the title Middle Age. But this term has no relevance to the rest of the world, of course, and should be avoided when speaking of any culture other than the Christian Europeans. In Europe, the Middle Age began with the gradual collapse of the Roman West under the assaults of the Germanic tribes and ended with the triumph of the new secularism of the Renaissance.

Chapter 11 surveys the chief actors in the pageant of pre-Columbian America. Sub-Saharan Africa's immense variety is examined in Chapter 12, as parts of the continent emerge into historical light. Chapters 13 and 14 deal with the rise of Islam and its culture. The next several chapters look at the stable and technically advanced South and East Asian societies. The first of this series (Chapter 15) surveys India's flourishing Hindu and Buddhist cultures. The second (Chapter 16) looks at China in the great age of Confucian order and prosperity. Then comes Japan (Chapter 17) as it evolved from an adjunct of China and Korea into cultural and political sovereignty, along with the early histories of the islands and mainland of southeastern Asia.

The focus returns to the West in Chapter 18, as we look at the European revival that occurred during its Middle Ages. Chapter 19 deals with the Mongol eruption and its impact on the major civilizations of Asia and Eastern Europe. In the end, however, their conquests enabled the unification of lands and peoples on an unprecedented scale and brought both peace and prosperity to a large part of the Old World. Returning to Europe, Chapter 20 describes the trials it faced during its "disastrous" fourteenth century. However, these setbacks were only temporary. With a return to the conditions that had produced the revival of the Middle Ages (Chapter 18) and benefiting from the flow of ideas and trade from the East that reached Europe from the Mongol unification (Chapter 19), in Chapter 21 we see how Europe began its modern era with the period of its "rebirth" during the Renaissance.

And the man took an ear of corn and roasted it, and found it good.

—Frank Russell, *Myths of the Jicarilla Apaches*, 1898

c. 20,000–10,000 BCE	Arrival of Ancestral Native Americans
c. 9500–8900 BCE	Clovis and Folsom hunting cultures
c. 8000–2000 BCE	Archaic gathering cultures
c. 5500–2000 BCE	Agriculture begins
c. 1500–300 BCE	Olmec culture
c. 900–200 BCE	Chavín culture
c. 600 BCE–1300 CE	Mississippian civilizations/Cahokia
c. 400 BCE–800 CE	Classical Mayan civilization/Teotihuacan
c. 400–800 CE	First Puebloan pit house communities
c. 800–1150 CE	Chaco Canyon
c. 1100–1532	Inca Empire
c. 1300s–1521	Aztec Confederation

PALEOINDIAN AMERICA

THE ARCHAIC PERIOD

THE AGRICULTURAL REVOLUTION IN THE AMERICAS

EARLY MESOAMERICAN CIVILIZATIONS
The Olmecs ◆ The Maya ◆ Teotihuacan

THE MILITARISTIC AZTECS

SOUTH AMERICAN CIVILIZATIONS
The Chavín ◆ Ancient Andean Lifeways ◆ The Inca

NORTH AMERICANS
The Ancestral Puebloan Civilization ◆ The Mississippian and Cahokia Civilizations

LIKE AFRICA, THE AMERICAS exhibit a tremendous range of cultures and physical environments, from the Inuit Eskimos of northern Canada to the sophisticated city builders of Central America, from the deserts of the American Southwest to the jungles of the Amazon basin. The first Native Americans arrived in the New World much later than humans *(Homo sapiens sapiens)* had evolved and spread elsewhere in the world. Reliable linguistic, genetic, and dental studies suggest that they came in three distinct waves, probably between 20,000 and 10,000 BCE. The **Amerindians** were the first migrants to come, probably from northeast Asia. They were the ancestors of the numerous Native American peoples found throughout the Western Hemisphere today, from southern Canada to Tierra del Fuego at the southern tip of South America. Following them came a second group, from Central Asia, most of whose descendants today are located in western Canada, with the exception of the Navajo and Apache peoples, who migrated to the American Southwest between 1300 and 1500 CE. The last group to arrive again came from northeastern Asia. Their modern descendants are the Inuit Eskimo peoples of northern Canada and Alaska.

Just how these varied peoples came to the New World is fiercely debated. The most widely accepted theory is that they arrived near the end of the last Ice Age by means of a "land bridge" that, because of lower sea levels, connected Northeast Asia and Alaska. Archaeologists have named this land bridge **Beringia** [beh-RIHN-jee-ah] because it covered what is now the Bering

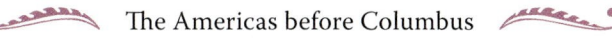

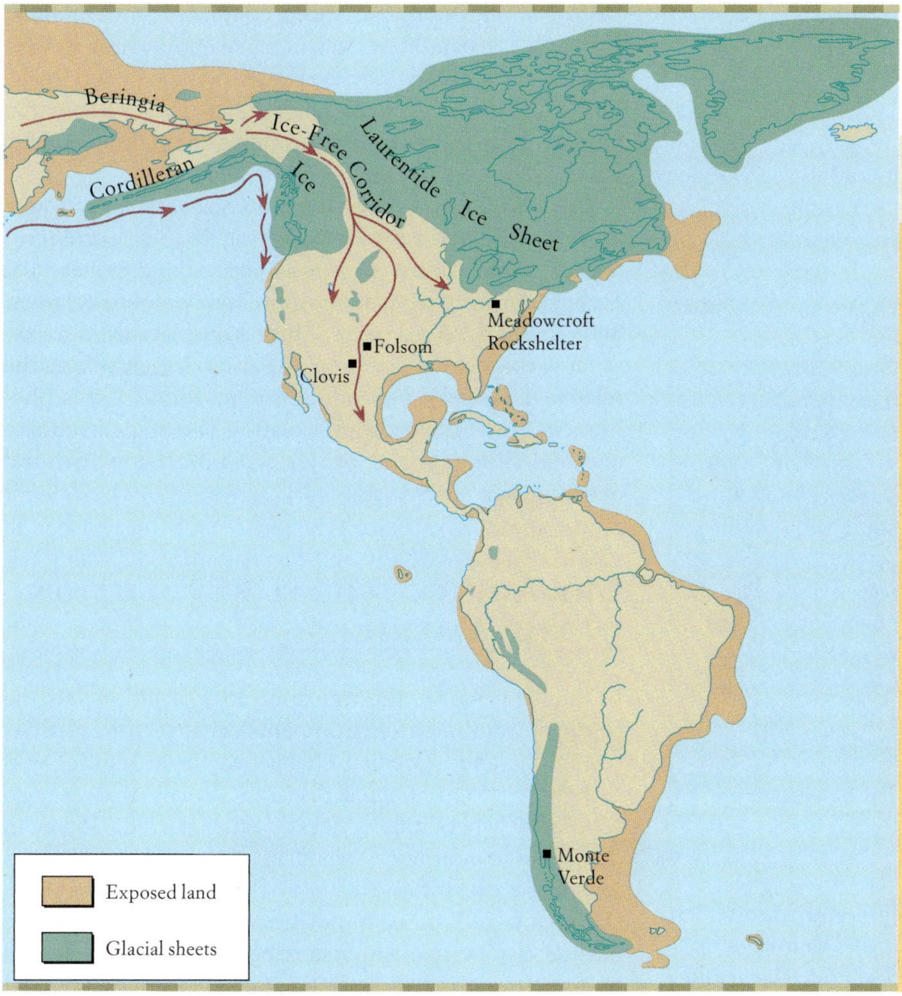

MAP 11.1 Migrations of Ancestral Native Americans

In the Late Pleistocene era, glaciers covered most of Canada and the northern parts of the United States. With so much water taken up in ice, the ocean levels were lower and a land bridge, called Beringia, made it possible for Ancestral Native Americans to migrate into the Western Hemisphere. Some made it through an ice corridor into regions south of the ice cap.

Source: Reprinted with permission of The Free Press, a Division of Simon & Schuster Adult Publishing Group, from *In the Hands of the Great Spirit: The 20,000 Year History of American Indians* by Jake Page. Copyright© 2003 by Jake Page. All rights reserved.

MAP QUESTIONS
From what area did the ancestral Native Americans migrate?

View an interactive version of this or a related map at http:// worldrc.wadsworth.com/

Strait (see Map 11.1). Although massive glaciers covered Canada at that time, these early immigrants made their way southward on foot through an opening in the glacial sheets and by small boats along the Pacific coast into what is now North and Central America. Eventually they populated the entire hemisphere. Where conditions were favorable, some eventually settled down to become farmers. For many centuries before this, however, from about 11,000 to 8900 BCE, they lived as late Paleolithic hunters and gatherers during what is usually called the **Paleoindian Period.**

PALEOINDIAN AMERICA

Once south of the glaciers, the earliest ancestral Native Americans arrived in a North America whose climate was considerably cooler and moister than it is today. Here they found a world with abundant plant and wild animal life, which included many forms of megafauna; that is, giant, now extinct beasts such as the woolly mammoth, the giant

sloth, and the giant bison. Not surprisingly, therefore, the earliest Native American cultures that archaeologists have uncovered were hunters of both large and small game. The **Clovis** (CLOH-vihs) **culture** was the earliest-known hunting culture, dating between about 9500 and 8900 BCE. Associated with this archaeological culture in particular were large and deeply notched, leaf-shaped spearheads called "Clovis points," which early Native Americans of North America used to kill their megafauna prey. In addition to the spearheads, archaeologists have discovered varieties of smaller stone implements which Paleoindians appear to have employed for preparing smaller game for their cooking as well as for skinning and tanning hides used for clothing.

Later, the climate gradually became drier, and the megafauna gradually died out. As this occurred, hunters turned increasingly to bison, elk, and deer as their prey, and smaller, fluted **Folsom points** (FOHL-suhm) replaced the larger Clovis spearheads. Wherever archaeologists have discovered Folsom sites, associated with these missile (spear, dart, and arrow) heads have been such items

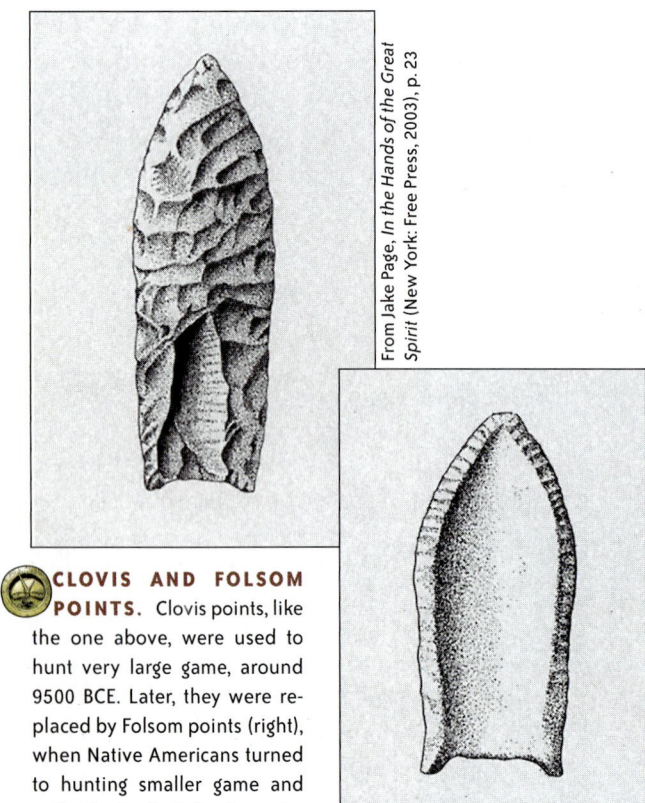

From Jake Page, *In the Hands of the Great Spirit* (New York: Free Press, 2003), p. 23

CLOVIS AND FOLSOM POINTS. Clovis points, like the one above, were used to hunt very large game, around 9500 BCE. Later, they were replaced by Folsom points (right), when Native Americans turned to hunting smaller game and gathering for their food supply.

as hammer stones, used for breaking bones from which marrow was extracted; stone end scrapers that were used for scraping hides; and cutting tools and bone eye needles for preparing hides as clothing and containers. As these missile heads grew smaller, they were placed at the head of spear throwers called *atlatls* (ah-tuh-LAH-tuhls). (Bows and arrows remained unknown among many Native Americans until about 400 CE.)

THE ARCHAIC PERIOD

As had happened with the Clovis culture, the Folsom complex disappeared as the climate continued changing. Conditions everywhere became warmer and drier, and in the American Southwest and in northern Mexico, where Native Americans first turned to agriculture, desert conditions eventually replaced what once had been grasslands. Therefore, during what archaeologists call the **Archaic Period,** people were forced to rely more on gathering wild plants as their primary sources of food. In contrast to the specialized hunting implements of the Paleolithic period, Archaic tool kits were less specialized and included more equipment for processing plant foods, such as rice grass, goosefoot, and dropseed, as well as prickly pear cactus.

Deer, elk, and mountain sheep continued to be hunted, although discoveries of snares, small traps, and smaller cutting tools among the bones of rabbits, desert mice, rats, squirrels, birds, snakes, and other reptiles imply that humans were forced to rely on much more humble daily fare.

Precious little is known about the social organization of these early Americans. However, the small size and temporary nature of most Archaic campsites suggest that most groups consisted of relatively few, highly mobile families. Such mobility seems to have been considerably more restricted than in the Paleoindian Period, largely due to the relative scarcity of groundwater. One result of this phenomenon was the growing isolation of groups from one another. Gradually out of this separation grew cultural and language differences.

THE AGRICULTURAL REVOLUTION IN THE AMERICAS

In the New World, the transition to agriculture was the result of continued environmental change toward drier conditions and a gradual changeover from hunting and gathering. Archaeological research reveals that Mexico was likely where this process first occurred. There, in desertlike conditions, Canadian archaeologist Richard MacNeish excavated a cave in the state of Tamaulipas (tah-maow-LEE-puhs) in northeastern Mexico, which indicated that Native Americans began growing chile and pumpkin for food as early as 5500 BCE to supplement their meager diet of small desert creatures. By about 2500, they had added beans. Maize (corn), however, eventually became the foundation of the Native American diet. At Tehuacán (tey-wah-CAHN), just south of modern Mexico City, MacNeish uncovered evidence that suggests maize was gradually grown and domesticated between about 4000 and 2500 BCE.

Farming seems to have become general throughout Mexico, Central America, and the coastal plain of Peru in South America by 1500 BCE. By then, farmers were living in small villages, usually in structures called "pit houses." Although these varied somewhat in form, pit houses typically consisted of a framework of wood poles thatched with tree branches and leaves, built over a pit dug into the ground. Their technology remained Neolithic, but Mexican farmers were, archaeologists estimate, able to grow enough corn, beans, squash, and chile peppers in just eight to ten weeks to support a small family for up to an entire year. This level of productivity made it possible for the great civilizations of Mexico, Central America, and the Andean Mountain nations of South America to develop.

EARLY MESOAMERICAN CIVILIZATIONS

Mesoamerica (Middle America) extends from central Mexico to encompass all of modern Central America. The Sierra Madre Mountains are a prominent geographical feature of Mesoamerica. The Central Valley of Mexico is located on a high plateau near the convergence of the Eastern, Western, and Southern Sierra Madres. Beyond the mountain ranges, a vast rainforest covers southern Mexico and Guatemala. The earliest Mesoamerican civilizations did not locate in river valleys but on the elevated plateaus of the Central Valley or the tropic lowlands inland from the Caribbean Sea. Generally speaking, these early civilizations were polytheistic theocracies ruled by astronomer-priests of semi-divine status who used extremely accurate calendars to regulate the cycles of agriculture and religion. Their cities were religious centers with great stone pyramids, temples, palaces, and ritual ball courts. The laboring masses periodically gathered to witness awe-inspiring, sometimes bloody, ceremonies in which the priests exerted their control by invoking ancient gods of rain and fertility. The jaguar—a species of great cat indigenous to the Americas—was particularly revered. The elites created writing and numerical systems to keep the records of their increasingly complex societies. Extensive trade networks disseminated goods and functioned as catalysts for cultural exchange. Goods were transported by water or by human porters, since there were no draft animals or wheeled conveyances.

The Olmecs

The earliest civilization we know about—between 1500 and about 300 BCE—bears the name **Olmec** (OHL-mehk),

Werner Forman/Art Resource, NY

THE MERCHANT. This deerskin manuscript shows the patron god of merchants (upper left), Lord Nose, carrying the crossroad symbol of traders, with footprints that indicate travel. The merchant on the right holds the characteristic fan and staff, and a load of quetzal birds on his back.

or "People of the Land of Rubber," because of the solid rubber balls they made for the sacred Mesoamerican ballgame. The Olmec arose in what is now southern Mexico, where they developed the first culture with regional influence. Surviving art (sculpture) indicates that a small, elite group centering on the priests of the official religion had great powers and the ruler was probably a hereditary king/high priest. The Olmecs established vast trade networks in Central America. Olmec pottery and decorative ceramics have been found throughout Mexico and Guatemala, and as far south as Costa Rica (see Map 11.2). Their main sites thus far discovered, east of Mexico City and near the Caribbean port of Veracruz, consist of central fortified complexes of governmental halls, religious shrines, and ball courts.

A pervasive religious faith centering on the worship of ancient feline gods was the inspiration for much of their art and architecture. The enormous heads of basalt that they left behind most remarkably express the Olmecs' skill in stonework. Standing up to nine feet high and weighing up to twelve tons, these mysterious heads may represent prominent individuals in the guise of were-jaguars. (There is no evidence to support speculation that the unique features of the Olmec heads may indicate African or Asian influence). Olmec masonry skills also enabled them to build ceremonial stone pyramids, one of which reached 110 feet high. This Great Pyramid speaks of a high degree of organization and a ready supply of labor, suggesting that Olmec agriculture must have been sufficiently advanced to support a large population. The Olmec had a primitive form of writing and a number system, neither of which is understood but which enabled them to survey and build a large number of massive edifices. More than this is not known.

The Maya

Before or around 300 CE, the Olmecs declined in importance, supplanted by their Maya neighbors. The **Maya** (MAH-yah) became the most advanced of all the pre-Columbian Amerindians by building on ancient cultural traditions. For example, the Mayan written language and complex calendar were derived from Olmec prototypes. The Mayan understanding of mathematics included the concept of zero and was far more advanced than European mathematics in the twelfth century. The recent decipherment of over half of the Mayan written language has enabled scholars to more accurately reconstruct the events portrayed in the rich pictorial images of Mayan stonework, although much remains obscure. All in all, more is known about the life of the Mayan people than about any of the other Mesoamericans. They are the models for the classical image of Amerindian civilization.

MAP 11.2 Mesoamerican Civilizations

The Aztec empire was at its height when the Spanish arrived. The Mayan cities of Palenque and Tikal were abandoned in the tenth century for unknown reasons, possibly failure of the food supply.

MAP QUESTIONS
Which geographical areas of Mesoamerica saw the rise of pre-Columbian urban centers?

The historical outline is by now fairly clear. From about 400 BCE, there emerged a hierarchy of Mayan cities ruled by hereditary kings. The earliest great Maya ceremonial centers arose in the rainforest that straddles present-day Mexico and Guatemala. Recent discoveries in Guatemala reveal that the first flourishing of Mayan cities occurred in the second century BCE, much earlier than previously thought. After the decline and fall of these cities, the same rainforest saw a rebirth of Maya grandeur, known as the classical era (400–800 CE). Some cities contained several tens of thousands of people (see Map 11.2), but most of the population were peasant villagers who lived in satellite settlements on the cities' periphery. The whole population of the Mayan Empire or federation may have reached 14 million—far and away the largest state under one government outside Asia at that time.

Public buildings of truly amazing dimensions were the heart of the cities. Temples, palaces, and ballcourts, many of them employing the blunt-tipped pyramid form, are so arranged as to construct a massive arena or assembly ground. To these sacred precincts at designated times would stream tens of thousands, to experience the priest-led worship ceremonies or the installation of a new monarch.

The cities seem to have been more religious and administrative centers than commercial and manufacturing centers. None of them approached the size of the Mesopotamian towns of a much earlier epoch. The Maya further developed and expanded the previous trade networks, sending traveling merchants to trade salt and cacao beans for jade, obsidian, and tropical bird feathers, among other goods. The political and social power rested, as with the Olmec, in the hands of a hereditary elite. To judge from their costumes in surviving artwork, they were very wealthy. The common folk appear to have been divided into freemen, serfs, and slaves, as in much of the ancient

Werner Forman/Art Resource, NY

MAYAN CALENDAR STONE AND BALL PLAYER. Agrarian Native Americans believed in natural time. Their calendars were circular and carefully represented and recorded key astronomical phenomena, usually solar and lunar cycles, on which they based their time cycles. To keep the sky in motion and thus to assure the regularity of the seasons, many Mesoamerican civilizations played a ritual ballgame whose purpose was to keep the ball—the sun—in constant motion. The connection between time and the game is represented here.

world. Stone carvings show that Maya noblewomen held important positions in religion and politics, and enjoyed certain rights. Women of the lower classes tended the family garden and domestic animals, did the weaving, and probably led the home religious rites.

Religious belief was paramount in ordering the round of daily life. The ruling class included priests, who had magical powers given to them by the gods. The pyramids were sacred mountains with cave-like inner chambers where priests mediated with the supernatural sphere. In the Mayan cosmology, there existed thirteen heavens and nine hells. The Mayan underworld seems to have been as fearsome as that of Mesopotamia. No hint of ethical religion exists, however. The gods, like those of Sumeria, played multiple roles in human affairs, and in their persons they combined beastly and human traits. Human sacrifices apparently were common and provided the rulers with companions on their journey to the next world.

Again, prosperity inevitably brought decline, as overpopulation and ecological collapse forced the people to abandon the great centers. A final revival occurred in the Yucatán between about 1000 and 1300 CE, this time with artistic influence from the Valley of Mexico. By the time the Spanish under Cortés arrived in the Valley of Mexico

two hundred years later, the Mayan achievements had been forgotten.

Their memory has been revived by the nineteenth- and twentieth-century discoveries of great stone pyramids and temples in the remote Mexican rainforest and in the Yucatán peninsula. These sites have now become major tourist attractions, especially **Chichén Itzá (chee-CHEN ee-TSAH),** where a vast complex of Mayan buildings has been excavated. The Mayan ruins are an American version of Egypt's Tel Amarna or Karnak; indeed, some anthropologists postulate that a human link existed between ancient Egypt and Mexico. However, most scientists think that ancient peoples around the globe independently devised the concept of pyramidal structures as a tribute to the gods and to the priestly elites.

The most notable accomplishment of the Maya in science was their astoundingly accurate astronomy, based on an equally refined mathematics. The Mayan calendar had two distinct numeration systems, allowing them to construct a chronology that could date events for a space of more than two thousand years. In literature, little survived the Spanish colonial censorship, but the Maya were the only pre-Columbian people who completed the transition to full literacy. The handful of codices (ancient documents) is supplemented by the extensive sculpted glyphs decorating the exterior and interior of the monuments the Maya left behind. Unfortunately, these materials tell us little to nothing of the political or social life of the era because they are mostly concerned with the events in the reign of one or another monarch.

Teotihuacan

During the same era when the classical Mayan surge was reaching its peak, another high culture was appearing in the Valley of Mexico, some hundreds of miles west of Yucatán. The metropolis of **Teotihuacan** (TAY-oh-tee-WAH-kahn) rose in the rich farmlands in the northern part of the valley around 200 BCE. Later arrivals in the Valley named the city Teotihuacan, which means "Place of the Gods." It was an unfortified city, a theocracy devoted more to agriculture, crafts, and commerce than to war. Like the cities of the Olmecs and the Maya, Teotihuacan's great pyramids and temples were centers of religious rituals and offerings to the gods of nature who were so crucial to settled agriculture. Two of the pyramids at Teotihuacan, the so-called Pyramids of the Sun and the Moon, are among the largest masonry structures ever built. The Pyramid of the Sun is actually larger in total volume than the Great Pyramid of Egypt.

Teotihuacan, perhaps the first true city of the Western Hemisphere, was unusual in that its inhabitants included more than just the priests and nobles. Although the houses of the elites filled its center, it was laid out in *barrios,* or quarters, for the ordinary people who farmed the fields surrounding the city. It grew to become the largest and most

Sean Sprague/Mexicolore/Bridgeman Art Library

AVENUE OF THE DEAD AT TEOTIHUACAN. The ceremonial heart of the city, the Avenue of the Dead was lined with dozens of temples and pyramids, like the gigantic Pyramid of the Sun, shown at the upper left. Here, feather-clad priests carried out elaborate daily rituals and sacrifices to gods like Quetzalcoatl, who regulated such matters as fertility, rainfall, childbirth, and even the arts.

impressive of all the ancient pre-Columbian centers, with a population as high as 200,000—far greater than that of any contemporary European city. Teotihuacan was a hub of commerce; its trade networks reached from northern Mexico to Central America. Recent discoveries show that Teotihuacan was allied with Classical Maya kings who proudly traced their lineage back to an invading ruler of Teotihuacan.

In the final years of its dominance, Teotihuacan seems to have become more militaristic, perhaps to enforce tribute demands to support its burgeoning population. Invading warriors destroyed Teotihuacan in about 650 CE, ushering in two centuries of chaos and conflict among rival groups in the Valley. Over the next two centuries, the cultural heritage of Teotihuacan would endure, and subsequent regimes would revive and expand its trade networks. The identity of Teotihuacan's builders was lost, but they would be revered by later arrivals in the Valley as creator gods whose ruined city became a sacred site.

THE MILITARISTIC AZTECS

After the fall of Teotihuacan, several waves of warlike nomads from the north migrated into the Central Valley.

Modern Mexico derives its name from the last of these groups, the **Mexica** (meh-SHEE-kah) known later as the **Aztecs** (AZ-teks). Beginning in the 1300s, in the space of two hundred years, the Mexica-Aztec people converted themselves from despised nomads into the elite of a huge militaristic state embracing many millions of Amerindians. By 1500, after alliances and aggressive territorial expansions, the Aztec Confederation dominated the center of present-day Mexico from coast to coast and reached down into Mayan lands in present-day Guatemala (see Map 11.3). Their capital, the splendid city of **Tenochtitlán** (teh-NOHSH-teet-LAHN), was the largest in the New World in the 1400s, and one of the largest anywhere. These achievements were based on the foundation provided by earlier Amerindian civilizations, but the Aztecs contributed some new characteristics.

The lives of the ruling elites revolved around conquest and continual warfare; they carried militarism and human sacrifice to unprecedented extremes. War shaped the state religion and imposed a social structure that was unique in America. The chief war god was also god of the sun at noon, provider of warmth for the growing crops. The Aztecs believed that this god survived on human blood, preferably the warm hearts of brave captive warriors, which were ripped out on altars in the

MAP 11.3 The Aztec, Incan, and Mayan Civilizations

The relative size of the three best-known pre-Columbian states at their maximum extents is shown here.

MAP QUESTIONS
Only the Incan Empire relied on a vast network of roads. What purposes did these roads serve?

middle of their great city. At the height of Aztec dominance, priests vastly increased the numbers of victims for each major ceremony, and ritual cannibalism also increased.

The most widely accepted practical explanation for this scale of mass slaughter is that the Aztec elite tried to prevent rebellions by terrorizing the population into submission. The Aztecs were thus a sort of super-Assyrians, ruling their unfortunate neighbors by fear and random raids. These vengeful subjects readily allied themselves with the Spanish conquerors to topple the hated Aztecs in the early 1500s.

How was the Aztecs' militaristic society organized? We know a good deal about the Aztec state, thanks to its pictographic records, or *codices*. The Spanish preserved some of these records so they could learn more about their new subjects and control them more efficiently. The emperor, who acquired semi-divine status, was elected by

the male members of the ruling family. At the top of the social hierarchy were the emperor's officials, ex-warriors of distinction who governed like feudal lords in the provinces conquered by the Aztec armies. The Aztecs also had a large and powerful group of priests, the highest of whom served as advisers to the emperor in his palace.

Next came a class of warriors, who were continuously recruited from the ordinary freemen. After taking at least four prisoners for sacrifice, a warrior was allowed to share in the booty of the Aztecs' constant warfare. Interestingly, any woman who died in the childbirth "battle" received the honors afforded all fallen warriors. A specialized class of merchants (seen previously among the Maya) traveled throughout the realm, enriching themselves through trade and serving as spies for the emperor and as vanguards for future conquests. The great majority of the Aztecs fell into

SOCIETY AND ECONOMY

Aztec Family Role Models

In the mid-sixteenth century, some thirty years after the Spanish conquest, a learned and industrious monk named Bernardino de Sahagun undertook a remarkable mission: to create an ethnographic portrait of the Aztecs as they lived before the European invasion. Sahagun held many interviews with Indians of all social classes and ages, to hear their own versions of their culture and beliefs. Included are several thumbnail summaries of what was expected of men and women, of family members, of the upper and lower strata of Aztec society, and even of some professions. A few examples follow:

> The Father: the father is the founder of lineage. He is diligent, compassionate, sympathetic, a careful administrator of his household. He is the educator, the model-giver, the teacher. He saves up for himself and for his dependents. He cares for his goods, and for the goods of others. . . . He is thrifty and cares for the future. He regulates and establishes good order. . . .
>
> The bad father is not compassionate, he is neglectful and not reliable. He is a poor worker and lazy. . . .
>
> The Mother: the mother has children and cares for them. She nurses them at her breast. She is sincere, agile, and a willing worker, diligent in her duties and watchful over others. She teaches, and is mindful of her dependents. She caresses and serves others, she is mindful of their needs. She is careful and thrifty, ever vigilant of others, and always at work.
>
> The bad mother is dull, stupid and lazy. She is a spendthrift and a thief, a deceiver and a cheat. She loses things through her neglect. She is frequently angry, and not heedful of others. She encourages disobedience in her children. . . .
>
> The Nobleman: the man who has noble lineage is exemplary in his life. He follows the good example of others. . . . He speaks eloquently, he is mild in speech, and virtuous . . . noble of heart and worthy of gratitude. He is discreet, gentle, well reared in manner. He is moderate, energetic, inquiring. . . . He provides nourishment for others, comfort. He sustains others. . . . He magnifies others and diminishes himself from modesty. He is a mourner for the dead, a doer of penances. . . .
>
> The bad nobleman is ungrateful, a debaser and disparager of others' property, he is contemptuous and arrogant. He creates disorder. . . .
>
> The Physician: the physician is knowledgeable of herbs and medicines from roots and plants; she is fully experienced in these things. She is a conductor of examinations, a woman of much experience, a counselor for the ill. The good physician is a restorer, a provider of health, one who makes the ill feel well. She cures people, she provides them with health again. She bleeds the sick . . . with an obsidian lancet she bleeds them and restores them.

▶ Analyze and Interpret

Do these descriptions of good and bad persons differ in substantial ways from modern ones? How do the expectations of men and of women differ in Aztec society, from these examples?

Source: Bernardino de Sahagún, *The General History of the Things of New Spain* (Santa Fe, NM: School of American Research, 1950)

---

the next category: ordinary free people who did the usual work of any society. Organized in age-old kinship groups called **calpulli** (kahl-POO-lee), they tilled the fields, carried burdens, built the buildings and roads, and so on. They might also be called for military duty in a pinch and thus shared in the essential purpose of the state.

At the bottom were the serfs, whose rights and duties were similar to those of medieval European serfs, and the slaves, who had been captured from other Indians or were victims of debt. If the priests did not destine them for human sacrifice, Aztec slaves were usually able to gain their freedom.

Upper-class Aztec women seem to have had some private rights and freedoms that many sixteenth-century European women might have envied. Common women could be market vendors and midwives, and perhaps could own property. However, the destruction of the Aztec written sources and the absence of others make it impossible to know for sure. Certainly, the Spanish witnesses in Mexico and Peru gave no indication of female governors or high officials.

SOUTH AMERICAN CIVILIZATIONS

Another major Amerindian civilization existed far to the south of Mexico, almost certainly remaining in ignorance of the Aztec realm and its accomplishments. In the Andes Mountains of modern Peru, an extraordinarily talented people—the **Inca** (INK-ah)—had recently constructed a militaristic empire, as the Aztecs had done in Mexico. The Inca achieved the first unification of the entire Andean area. The Inca Empire was the culmination of many centuries' developments in agriculture, commerce, religion, architecture, and government.

Pre-Columbian Peru was a complex mosaic of ethnic and linguistic groups, living in a region where the climate changes drastically according to altitude rather than latitude. Moving east from the arid Pacific coastal plains, the terrain rises steadily to the river valleys, then the Andes foothills, finally reaching the frigid peaks and plateaus of the Andes. Continuing east, the downward slopes of the mountains are covered with dense tropical forests leading to the Amazonian jungle basin. The success of Andean civilizations depended upon expansion and refinement of interregional exchange networks. The collective food basket provided more nourishment than in Mesoamerica. For example, the coastal fisheries provided needed protein to inland peoples in exchange for tubers from the highlands and fruit from the tropical forests. However, the Andean peoples had to contend with formidable natural disasters: The unpredictable but frequent *El Niño* (ehl NEE-nyoh) phenomena brought warm currents that devastated the fisheries. Floods and earthquakes periodically disrupted the delicately balanced irrigation systems.

The earliest farmers settled (in what is modern Peru) on the coastal plains near the abundant Pacific Ocean fisheries. The fairly dependable supply of protein-rich seafood allowed the inhabitants to thrive. Some groups then settled farther east, along the many mountain-fed rivers that drain to the Pacific Ocean. Over the centuries, the inhabitants of the coastal plains and the inland river valleys developed enterprises that are still important today: the fishing industry, irrigation systems for their fields, and exquisite textiles woven from their native cotton. Vast trading networks promoted the exchange of goods among the inhabitants of diverse terrains both east and west of the Andes range. Trade with Mesoamerica brought maize to South America, while metallurgy spread to Mesoamerica from the Andes area. The usage of metal was considerably more common in Peru than in Mexico.

The Chavín

In South America at the same epoch as the Mesoamerican Olmec flourished, the **Chavín** (cha-VEEN) culture showed a comparable development (900 to 200 BCE). The capital city, Chavín de Huántar (day WAN-tahr), was well located on the trade routes connecting the coast with the mountains. During the Chavín era, use of the llama, a small camel-like pack animal, fomented trade and led to the construction of roads. Most scholars agree that the Chavín hegemony came about through trade and cultural exchange, rather than through political power or military might. Furthermore, the elaborate Chavín jaguar cult, a synthesis of elements from previous coastal and highland beliefs, spread quickly and lasted for centuries. Chavín de Huántar's blunt-tipped pyramids, platform mounds, and artificial water works provided the stage for priests to demonstrate their god-given powers over nature. The Chavín priests organized the irrigation projects and supervised the labor force throughout the area. The triumph of the Chavín lay above all in the provision of adequate food for a dense population in such topographically difficult areas. This achievement has barely been replicated in modern Peru even with late-twentieth century technology. Eventually, the Chavín culture collapsed, possibly due to overpopulation, increased social stratification, and rising militarism in the region. The Chavín never became a true political state. However, their heritage is evident in the succeeding theocratic kingdoms of north and central Peru.

Ancient Andean Lifeways

The formation of ancient Peru's first states (200 BCE–600 CE) corresponded roughly in time with the rise in Mesoamerica of Teotihuacan and the classical Maya. During this time, the fundamental features of Andean civilization reached maturity. The basic unit of both society and government was the **ayllu** (ah-YOO), or clan. A village would normally possess two to four clans, headed by a male in the prime of life to whom all members of the clan owed absolute loyalty. He handled the clan's business dealings with outsiders. Improved irrigation and terracing techniques, as well as the introduction of fertilizer and metal tools, produced the agricultural surpluses to feed growing populations. The food surpluses supported elites that devoted themselves to government and religious duties. Tuber crops, especially the potato in a freeze-dried form, spread from the highlands, becoming a staple food. Maize became an additional staple, and was used to make a fermented drink. The priests devised accurate calendars for regulating the planting and harvesting of crops. Furthermore, the priests marshaled the ayllus to provide the labor for agriculture and building projects. More cities and ceremonial centers were built, with residential sections for different groups of artisans (as in Teotihuacan).

Andean religion included the worship of spirits that dwelled in rivers, caves, and mountains. (Even today, miners in the Andes follow the ancient practice of giving coca leaves and other offerings to the mountain spirits in exchange for extracting the silver and copper.) Among some groups, the sacrifice of captives provided blood offerings to the deities, although not to the extent reached among the Aztecs. The cloth-wrapped mummies of ancestors were also revered. The rulers were demigods, and their elaborate mummy bundles contain exquisite gold and silver ornaments. The most valuable commodity was cotton and (alpaca) woolen cloth of intricate design.

Textiles and fibers held great importance in the Andean culture. Artisans fashioned fishing nets, wove roofs for houses, and braided cords for rope bridges over Andean chasms. Knotted, abacus-like cords called *kipus* (KEE-pooz) were the only means of calculating and recording numerical data. Women and girls of all social classes labored at spinning and weaving; even aristocratic women who had servants for other chores had to make textiles. Textiles, the most exquisite of Andean art, were highly prized as status symbols and as gifts. No known writing system existed in ancient Peru, so we know much less about the pre-Inca peoples than about the pre-Aztec civilizations.

Catastrophic natural upheavals (*c.* 600–1100 CE) periodically interrupted development of a series of wealthy coastal kingdoms in northern and central Peru. Earthquakes, two major El Niño events, and a prolonged drought brought famine and the downfall of these states. Meanwhile, the southern and central mountain civilizations had begun widening their spheres of influence by alliances, colonizing, and warfare. The Incas, who adopted the same strategies and traced their origins to Lake Titicaca, then subjugated these expansionist regimes.

The Inca

The Inca began as one of many competing groups in the southern Andes near Lake Titicaca. Like the Aztecs, the Inca rose from humble beginnings to conquer the entire Andean region. (The title "Inca" really refers to the ruler of this empire, but it is also commonly used to refer to the tribal group that ruled the surrounding peoples and to the empire they created.) Centered on the town of **Cuzco** (COOS-koh) in one of the high valleys that penetrate the massive wall of the Andes, the Inca started bringing their immediate neighbors under their rule in the 1200s. By the mid-1400s, they had created a state that rested on the obligatory labor of the conquered peoples, who are thought to have numbered as many as 8 million. (If this number is accurate, the Inca, like the Aztecs, ruled over more people than any European state at the time.) The Inca practice of labor allotment, perhaps adopted from one of the conquered groups, provided room and board for the workers in exchange for their mandatory labor tribute.

The critical breakthrough to empire, rather than merely regional dominance, came with the rule of Pachacuti Inca in the 1450s. He adopted the practice of split inheritance, meaning that each deceased Supreme Inca (in mummified form) kept all his lands. Henceforth each new emperor had to conquer new territories in order to validate his own authority. Pachacuti Inca created an elaborate new cult to an ancient sun deity, elevating him above other nature gods. The Inca rulers claimed direct descent from the Sun, a convincing way to maintain control. Eighty years before the Spaniards came, the original petty kingdom had expanded to boundaries that reached into present-day Argentina in the south and what is today central Ecuador to the north.

Like the Aztecs, their success in conquests kept the Inca under the constant pressure of keeping a large group of subjects under strict control. The Incas excelled at organization and administration. Taxes were collected by an efficient administrative system. After conquering a new area, the Inca often deported the inhabitants, moving them from their native region to an alien place, where they would be entirely dependent on Cuzco's protection from resentful neighbors—a practice that is reminiscent of Assyrian and early Roman techniques of rule. Another strategy was to break up the old ayllus and replace them with new ones based on place of residence, rather than common kinship. The head of the new ayllu was appointed by the emperor because of good service or demonstrated loyalty. He served the central government in about the same fashion as a feudal baron served the king of France. The ordinary people, organized in these new artificial clans, were his to do with as he liked, so long as they discharged their labor duty and paid any other tax demanded of them by the Cuzco government. The Inca also established colonies among their subjects. The colonists helped encourage the conquered people to transfer their loyalty to their new masters and also ensured that a military force would be available if needed to suppress a rebellion.

Regimentation and enforced conformity were prominent features of Incan government, but it also displayed a concern for social welfare that was unusual for early governments. In times of poor harvest, grain was distributed to the people from the government's enforced-collection granaries, as in China. Natural disasters, such as flooding mountain rivers, were common, and a system of central "relief funds" provided assistance for the areas affected. The central authorities also enforced a sort of pension system that provided for the destitute and the old. These features of the Incan regime have attracted much attention from modern historians, who see in them a tentative approach to the welfare state of the twentieth century.

The Incas' cultural impact on their subjects is evident from the linguistic changes that occurred. Along the west coast, the Incas' **Quechua** (KETCH-wah), now the official language of most Peruvians (along with Spanish), supplanted the variety of unwritten languages that had previously existed among the South American Indians. Unlike the Mesoamericans, however, the Inca did not

develop a written language. They continued to rely on different types of kipus for keeping numerical records and as a means of controlling their empire. The Inca probably also used certain kipus as memory devices for reciting oral traditions.

The Inca built on previous feats of engineering to become superb road builders and architects. The greatest road network in the hemisphere unified the empire from north to south both along the coast and in the mountains. As their predecessors had done, the Inca constructed irrigation systems, dams, and canals, and built terraces on the steep hillsides so crops could be planted on every square inch of soil. The stone buildings of royal Cuzco, cut and fitted perfectly without mortar, are among the finest erected in the Americas. One of the most magnificent achievements of Incan rule was **Machu Picchu** (MAH-choo PEET-choo), a city in the clouds of the high Andes, whose ruins were discovered only in 1911. The Inca accomplished the awe-inspiring feat of moving thousands of massive stone blocks to build the walls of this fortress-city on a mountaintop, in the absence of almost all technology (probably even without the wheel). No one knows why the city was built or why it was abandoned.

Like most other ancient and pre-modern societies, Incan society exhibited sharp class divisions. A small elite of nobles was at the top, under their divine king, the Inca, from whom all authority issued. A large army maintained obedience. Most rebellions against the Inca were, in fact, fraternal wars in which the rebel leader was a member of the imperial house. The Spaniards under Francisco Pizarro used one of these civil wars to great advantage when they arrived in 1533 to steal the gold of Cuzco.

NORTH AMERICANS

Agriculture came to Native Americans more slowly than it did to those people in Central and South America. Corn and squash made their way into the mountainous parts of southern New Mexico sometime around 1500 BCE and then quickly moved into other parts north of the Rio Grande River.

The Ancestral Puebloan Civilization

By the early centuries of the Common Era, **Ancestral Puebloans** (PWEH-bloh-ans) sometimes called the *Anasazi* (ah-nah-SAH-zee) were taking to more settled ways in the Four Corners area, where the states of Utah, Colorado, New Mexico, and Arizona meet today (see Map 11.4). Most continued their hunting and gathering ways, but their migratory routes had become noticeably more confined, and they appear to have spent longer periods in specific locations. They had begun growing corn and squash, and by 400 CE, bows and arrows had replaced the atlatl, making hunting more efficient. (See Patterns of Belief for Native American oral traditions about the origins of corn.) Beans also had been added to their diet, making them less dependent on meat for protein. People had begun living in pit house villages, often for an entire growing season. The fact that they made baskets for both storage and cooking (using heated cooking stones in waterproof baskets) has led archaeologists to call the phase to about 700 CE the *Basketmaker Period*.

Beginning around 700, they started erecting rectangular, adobe houses above ground, beginning the so-called

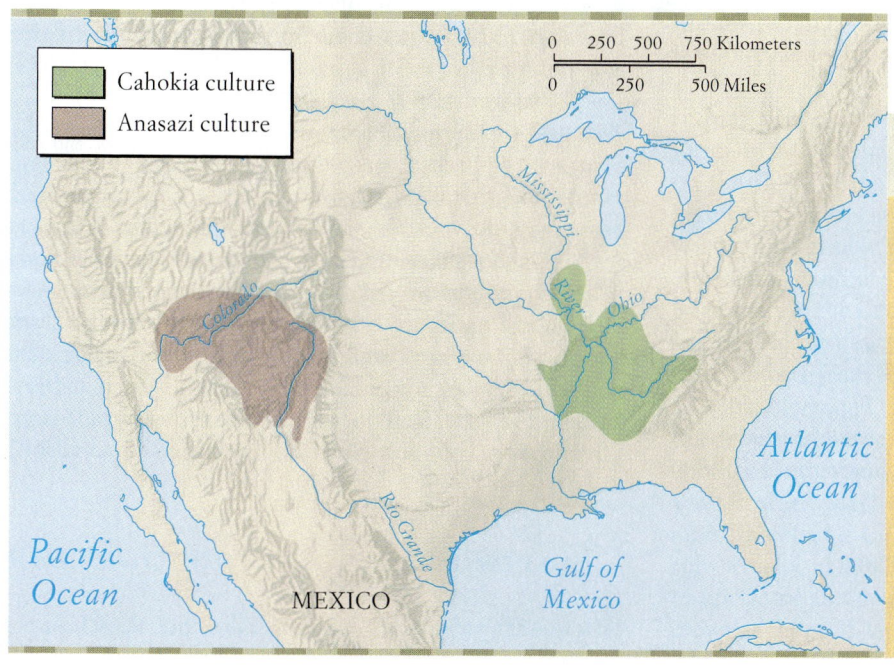

MAP 11.4 Anasazi and Cahokia Cultures of North America

Some time before 500 CE, the nomads of the southwestern quarter of the present-day United States began to farm the riverine wetlands, raising maize, beans, and squash, which had been developed earlier in Mexico. Their success allowed the maintenance of cliffside pueblos of more than 200 people. Later, the Cahokia Indians of the midwestern Mississippi valley erected large burial mounds near their extensive agricultural villages.

MAP QUESTIONS
What modern U.S. states correspond to the Cahokia and Anasazi culture areas?

Pueblo I period. The Pueblo II (*c.* 800–1150) saw a dramatic increase in population as a result of noticeably higher rainfall and groundwater levels. Pueblo villages were both larger and more numerous across the American Southwest. However, the most remarkable development of this period was what is sometimes called the **Chaco phenomenon** (CHAH-coh). This refers to the construction of fourteen "Great Houses" in Chaco Canyon, located in northwestern New Mexico.

The Great Houses were multistory stone-and-timber pueblos. The largest of these, Pueblo Bonito, numbered more than 600 rooms, contained more than 40 ritual enclosures, and possibly stood as high as five stories. Excavations have shown convincingly that it served a largely ceremonial function. Although few burials have been found in Pueblo Bonito and other Great Houses, archaeologists have unearthed large caches of rich ceremonial artifacts, such as turquoise-encrusted ceremonial beakers, feathers and skeletal remains of macaws from Mexico, and seashells. Furthermore, scholars have discovered that Pueblo Bonito and other Chacoan Great Houses were aligned with such exactitude that they comprised a gigantic, highly precise structural assemblage for predicting the annual solar and eighteen-year lunar cycles, which rivaled in sophistication those of the Mesoamerican civilizations.

Chaco Canyon appears to have been the center of an extensive network of roads and "outlier" Great Houses. Questions have arisen, quite naturally, over the reason for the system of roads, constructed in almost perfectly straight lines for many miles in all directions. Clearly, both ritual and trade were factors, because all of these roads converged on Chaco Canyon, giving it the appearance of a regional center where people came to pay tribute and participate in religious rituals performed in underground ceremonial chambers called **kivas** (KEE-vahs), that were found in the Great Houses. The discovery of items that Chacoans imported from as far away as Mexico (macaws, copper bells), the Gulf of Mexico and the Gulf of California (seashells), the upper Rio Grande region (turquoise), and the Chuska Mountains to the west (timber) supports the theory that Chaco functioned as a center of trade and ceremony that exercised vast authority throughout the Four Corners region.

The Pueblo II period, one of exceptionally clement weather for the Chacoans, came to a rudely abrupt end around 1150, when a thirty-year drought forced the abandonment of the Great Houses and the thousands of smaller pueblos that were part of the Chacoan system. Many fled north to the Four Corners area. There they settled in what scholars call the "Great Pueblos," some of which were built in the alcoves of cliffs. Today, Mesa Verde National Park is where the most famous of these cliff dwellings can be found. Yet another devastating drought, from 1280 to 1300, caused the Ancestral Puebloans to finally abandon the Four Corners area completely.

From about 1300 to 1500, the Puebloan clans migrated westward, southward, and eastward. Their descendants today live in the Hopi, Zuni, Acoma, Laguna, and Upper Rio Grande Pueblos of Arizona and New Mexico. About the time they abandoned the Four Corners area, the ancestors of the Navajo and Apache peoples moved from

Richard A. Cooke/Corbis

PUEBLO BONITO. Built in stages between 850 and 1150, Pueblo Bonito was the largest of the Chacoan Great Houses. It had more than 600 rooms, stood up to five stories tall, and contained more than forty ceremonial *kivas*. Despite their size, it is believed that the primary purpose of Great Houses like Pueblo Bonito was not habitation but ceremonial and, like Mesoamerican structures, astronomical.

 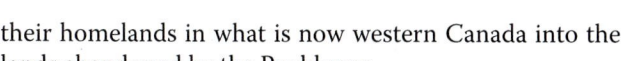

their homelands in what is now western Canada into the lands abandoned by the Puebloans.

The Mississippian and Cahokia Civilizations

When knowledge of agriculture gradually altered people's life ways in the American Southwest, it was having similarly revolutionary effects on areas to the east. Mysterious mound-building cultures, based on hunting the abundant resources of the Ohio and Mississippi river valleys, appeared around 600 BCE. Scholars call these the Adena and the Hopewell civilizations. By the early centuries CE, another mound-building civilization had evolved out of these earlier ones. This one was based on farming and was far more

PATTERNS OF BELIEF

North American Corn Myths

In many non-western societies, history and religious myth are not considered separate views of human existence. These two examples of Native American traditions provide explanations for the origins of corn (maize).

The first of these is a condensation of the *Popol Vuh*, a religious and philosophical tract that presents Mayan ideas about the structure of the universe and the world, as well as the nature of humanity. The *Popol Vuh* was a myth that would have been passed on orally from generation to generation, even acted out in ceremonies.

[Speaking to Creator gods, Heart of Sky and Plumed Serpent]

Fox: We bring you great news! We have found ears of yellow corn and white corn.

Coyote: This is the ingredient you have been looking for to create human flesh!

Parrot: The mountain we have just come from is thick with corn.

Crow: Hundreds of plants grow there, strong and straight and tall....

Plumed Serpent: Let us grind the corn nine times!

Narrator 2: And then the yellow corn was ground
      And then the white corn.

Heart of Sky: Let us add water!

Narrator 2: The food came
      With water to create strength,
   And it became man's grease
      And turned into his fat.

Heart of Sky: The story of our beginnings will be told!

Narrator 2: Only yellow corn
      And white corn were their bodies.
   Only food were the legs

      And arms of man.
   Those who were our first fathers
      Were the four original men
   Only food at the outset
      Were their bodies.

—Narine Polio

The following story is anthropologist Frank Waters's condensed version of the Hopi account of the relationships between the corn and the human race:

With the pristine wisdom granted [the Hopi], they understood that the earth was a living entity like themselves. She was their mother; they were made from her flesh; they suckled at her breast. For her milk was the grass upon which all animals grazed and the corn which had been created specially to supply food for mankind. But the corn plant was also a living entity with a body similar to man's in many respects, and the people built its flesh into their own. Hence, corn was also their mother. Thus, they knew their mother in two aspects which were often synonymous—as Mother Earth and the Corn Mother.

▶ *Analyze and Interpret*

What do these traditional accounts seem to be saying about the relationship between humans and their food? Why do you suppose Native Americans relied on such stories rather than on more scientific explanations? How do such stories compare, for example, with the Book of Genesis in the Bible?

Sources: From website http://www.yale.edu/ynhti/curriculum/units/1999/2/99.02.09.x.html. Copyright ©1978–2004 by the Yale–New Haven Teachers Institute, all rights reserved, and Frank Waters, *Book of the Hopi. The First Revelation of the Hopi's Historical and Religious Worldview of Life* (New York: Penguin Books, 1963), p. 7.

You can read the entire *Popol Vuh* at the Wadsworth World History Resource Center.

sophisticated. With locations throughout much of the United States east of the Mississippi River, scholars have called this the *Mississippian civilization.*

The largest and most important mound-builder settlement of this period was at **Cahokia** (cah-HOH-kee-ah), located near today's East St. Louis, Illinois. Although its exact relationship to other Mississippian locations is not yet archaeologically well-defined, it appears that the people who built Cahokia were Mississippians who had moved there from somewhere east of it around 600 CE. With a peasant base capable of producing large surpluses of squash, beans, and maize, the Cahokian civilization might have had a social hierarchy from its inception. Ordinary Cahokians built their dwellings from simple materials like wood slats and mud, but nobles built their houses on the terraces of a large, pyramid-like mound, which today is called Monks Mound. Covering about eighteen acres and

reaching nearly 100 feet at its highest point, Monks Mound was made entirely out of earth. It is the largest pyramid ever built in North America and the fourth largest in the entire world.

The entire Cahokia site included about eighty mounds of differing sizes and, apparently, purposes. Some, where excavators have found ceremonial objects, were meant simply as places for religious rituals. Others were evidently tombs, as they contained human remains. We know that human sacrifice was practiced, because in one instance, an especially important individual was buried amid copper sheets, baskets of mica, and 180 sacrificial victims from all ranks of Cahokian society. Cahokia ended somewhat mysteriously around 1300. Archaeologists have suggested several explanations, such as environmental degradation, overpopulation, or climatic change, but nobody knows for sure why the site was abandoned.

SUMMARY

THE ACHIEVEMENTS OF the Amerindian civilizations are imposing in some respects but paltry in others. When compared with the works of the Mesopotamian peoples, the Egyptians, or the Chinese, the relative absence of written documents and the small number of permanent monuments make it difficult to get a clear and comprehensive view of the Amerindians' abilities. Also, the physical isolation of the American continent from other centers of civilization assured that the Amerindians did not benefit from outside stimuli. What they produced came from their own mental and physical resources, so far as we can now tell. Yet the physical evidence that survives is certainly impressive. That the Inca could govern a huge empire without

benefit of writing or the wheel seems to us almost a miracle. And yet it was done. That the Mayan pyramids in southern Mexico could soar upward of 300 feet without benefit of metal tools or any of the technological innovations of the Mesopotamians, Egyptians, and Hindus seems equally incredible. Yet it, too, was done.

The Amerindian civilizations are perhaps the most forceful argument against the diffusion theory of human progress. Most likely, the Amerindians created their own world through their own, unaided, intellectual efforts. What would have been an admirable achievement under any circumstances becomes astounding if the Amerindians did these things alone.

▶ *Identification terms*

Test your knowledge of this chapter's key concepts by defining the following terms. If you can't recall the meaning of certain terms, refresh your memory by looking up the boldfaced term in the chapter, turning to the Glossary at

the end of the book, or working with the flashcards that are available on the *World Civilizations* Companion Website: **academic.cengage.com/adler**

Amerindians	Cahokia	Cuzco	Mexico
Ancestral Puebloans	*calpulli*	Folsom points	Olmec
Archaic Period	Chaco phenomenon	Inca	Paleoindian Period
ayllu	Chavín	*kivas*	Quechua
Aztec	Chichén Itzá	Machu Picchu	Tenochtitlán
Beringia	Clovis culture	Maya	Teotihuacan

▶ *Test Your Knowledge*

Test your knowledge of this chapter by answering the following questions. Complete answers appear at the end of the book. You may find even more quiz questions in CengageNOW and on the *World Civilizations* Companion Website: **academic.cengage.com/adler**

1. Most archaeologists today accept the theory that the first inhabitants of the New World
   a. settled down to farming by 9500 BCE.
   b. brought "Clovis points" with them from Asia.
   c. developed *atlatls* hundreds of years before their arrival in North America.
   d. arrived on primitive ships from West Africa.
   e. crossed a land bridge from Asia into Alaska.

2. The most important factor leading to the gradual abandonment of hunting and gathering in favor of farming among Native Americans was
   a. increasing technological sophistication.
   b. political pressure exerted by chiefs.
   c. climatic change.
   d. growing trade and the need for surpluses.
   e. enforced settlement into towns by clan leaders.

3. The most advanced system of writing among the Amerindian civilizations was that of the
   a. Maya.
   b. Inca.
   c. Toltecs.
   d. Aztecs.
   e. Olmecs.

4. The overridingly important principle of Aztec society and government was
   a. cannibalism.
   b. war and its requirements.
   c. trade and the creation of wealth.
   d. art and excellence in its production.
   e. the establishment of great cities.

5. Generally speaking, pre-Columbian cultures shared which of the following?
   a. Divine kings
   b. Worship of nature gods
   c. The importance of trade networks
   d. Use of pack animals
   e. a, b, and c above

6. Teotihuacan, called the city of the gods,
   a. was a planned city.
   b. has one of the world's largest pyramids.
   c. was fortified.
   d. had residences for artisans and peasants.
   e. a, b, and d above.

7. South America was home to which of these Amerindian civilizations?
   a. Aztecs
   b. Olmecs
   c. Maya
   d. Toltecs
   e. Inca

8. All of the following helped the Inca build and maintain their empire *except*
   a. the Quechua language.
   b. the reformed ayllu or clan organization.
   c. their excellent road system.
   d. wheeled transport.
   e. agricultural advances.

9. The Ancestral Puebloans (Anasazi) were
   a. rivals to the Incan rulers in Peru.
   b. inhabitants of Mexico City before the Aztecs.
   c. the builders of "Great Houses."
   d. part of the Cahokia culture.
   e. some of the earliest mound builders.

10. The Cahokia civilization was
    a. related to the Mississippian civilization.
    b. derived from the Ancestral Puebloan civilization.
    c. founded by the Toltecs.
    d. based primarily on hunting and gathering.
    e. centered in the Four Corners region.

CENGAGENOW™

Enter *CengageNOW* using the access card that is available with this text. *CengageNOW* will assist you in understanding the content in this chapter with lesson plans generated for your needs and provide you with a connection to the *Wadsworth World History Resource Center* (see description at right for details).

▶ *World History Resource Center*

Enter the Resource Center using either your *CengageNOW* access card or your standalone access card for the *Wadsworth World History Resource Center*. Organized by topic, this website includes quizzes; images; over 350 primary source documents; interactive simulations, maps, and timelines; movie explorations; and a wealth of other resources. You can read the following documents, and many more, at the *Wadsworth World History Resource Center:*

Popol Vuh

12 AFRICA FROM KUSH TO THE FIFTEENTH CENTURY

Not even God is wise enough.
—Yoruba Proverb

8000–3000 BCE	Food-producing revolution in Africa
2500–1000 BCE	Desiccation of the Sahara begins; first permanent settlements south of the Sahara
3100–1070 BCE	Egypt flourishes in the Nile Valley
c. 1500 BCE–350 CE	Kingdom of Kush
100s–700s CE	Kingdom of Axum
300–1100 CE	Kingdom of Ghana
641–710s CE	Arabs conquer Egypt and North Africa
800s–1200s CE	Many Swahili city-states founded
c. 500s CE	Origins of Sudanese kingdoms/trans-Saharan trade increases
c. 900s–c. 1400s CE	Great Zimbabwe flourishes
1250–1450 CE	Kingdom of Mali flourishes
1375–1591 CE	Songhay Kingdom flourishes

AFRICAN GEOGRAPHY AND CLIMATES

EARLY MOVEMENTS OF PEOPLE AND IDEAS
The Bantu Expansion into Subequatorial Africa

SOCIAL ORGANIZATION AND STATE FORMATION

THE KINGDOMS OF THE NILE
Kush ◆ Axum

TRANS-SAHARAN TRADE AND KINGDOMS OF THE SUDAN
Ghana ◆ Mali ◆ Songhay

THE SWAHILI CITY-STATES

GREAT ZIMBABWE

AFRICAN ARTS

EUROPEAN IMPRESSIONS

THE HISTORIOGRAPHY OF AFRICANS has made impressive advances in the past fifty years. The greater part of the continent's people had no written language until relatively recent days. Historical research in the usual literary sense was therefore difficult, but a combination of new methods of obtaining information about the past and new techniques for using that information has changed the situation radically. Now, archaeology, historical linguistics, art forms, and oral traditions have brought considerable illumination to Africa's past, and these sources are gradually revealing an extraordinary panorama of peoples and achievements.

Africa is a huge place—the second largest of the world's continents—and the chief characteristic of its history is its variety. Most of its several different climates and topographies have produced civilizations of various levels of sophistication. More even than elsewhere, Africa has repeatedly demonstrated that racial categorization has little meaning generally and even less so as a way of explaining the successes or failures of peoples all over the world in their struggles to achieve better lives and to create distinctive civilizations. Rather than race, the natural environment in which people live and their location on routes of trade and travel usually have proved to be the more decisive factors in their history.

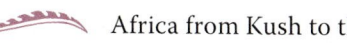 

AFRICAN GEOGRAPHY AND CLIMATES

Before the Europeans arrived during the fifteenth century CE, many parts of Africa were isolated by their geography from other centers of human activity. The great exception was its Mediterranean coast and the northeastern portion, where both Egypt and the Horn of Africa (present-day Ethiopia and Somalia) were in continuous contact with the Near and Middle Eastern civilizations from at least as early as 2000 BCE.

The continent rises from the surrounding waters like an inverted saucer, with its coastal lowlands quickly giving way to deserts (in the north, northwest, and southwest), inland plateaus, or to highlands and mountains (in the east and southeast) that dominate the vast interior (see Map 12.1). A coastal strip along the Mediterranean Sea quickly gives way to the Atlas, the enormous Sahara Desert divides the continent into its North African and sub-Saharan components. The coastal areas stretching from modern-day Liberia to Angola are marked by rainforest, which restricted travel to the rivers until recent times. Where the great rivers of the eastern interior flow from high grasslands of the interior to low-lying coasts, tremendous waterfalls and rapids block human travel and transport. The inland plateaus and rolling country until recently could be reached only after a dangerous and lengthy overland journey from the eastern coast. Long reaches of the continent's Atlantic coasts lack good harbors, and heavy surf makes the open beaches unusable by small craft almost everywhere except the Mediterranean. The coastal lands on the eastern side of the continent, those facing the Indian Ocean, however, have many excellent natural harbors that have served as places of trade and settlement for at least 2,000 years, as we shall see.

Although geography plays a major role, part of the reason for Africa's interior isolation is climatic. The continent is divided into five climatic and vegetative zones (see Map 12.1). One of these, the desert, has been unsuited to sedentary life for any concentrated number of people, and a third, the Sahel or Sudan, is frequently afflicted with extreme droughts. Perhaps 55 to 65 percent of the total area falls into one or another of these categories, in which sustenance for humans was (and is) difficult.

The five zones are as follows:

1. The *Mediterranean and extreme southern coasts* lie outside the tropical zones and enjoy temperate weather and good soil.
2. The *Sahel*, or the dry, mainly treeless steppes (semiarid grass-covered plains between the desert and the savanna) that cross Africa from the Atlantic to the Indian Oceans.
3. The *deserts*, of which the enormous and growing Sahara is the chief but not the only one, the others being the Namib and Kalahari deserts of the southwest.
4. The *rainforest*, which extends on either side of the equator in the west and center.
5. The *savanna*, the grassland regions of the interior plateaus, mainly south of the Sahara Desert and north of the rainforest in West Africa, and in most of East, Central, and South Africa.

The various peoples of Africa developed sharply different ways of life, which depended primarily on the zone where they lived. The Mediterranean coast was for most of its history closely linked to Europe and the Middle East. Egypt, as we have seen, was almost a land to itself in its isolated but benevolent Nile Valley. In much of the center and west of the continent, the rainforest's infestation by the *tsetse* fly, the cause of sleeping sickness, and the presence of a multitude of other diseases inhibited large-scale development almost to the present. In the desert regions, nomadic pastoralism and small-scale oasis agriculture were the only possible lifestyles in historical times, and vast areas were left uninhabited. The dry Sahel also could support only a pastoral economy. Beyond the coastal strip, only the savannas of the west and the eastern plateaus and the equatorial forests had enough precipitation and reasonably good soil to sustain crop agriculture and dense village populations.

EARLY MOVEMENTS OF PEOPLE AND IDEAS

Like its climate, geography, and lifestyles, Africa's people are also diverse. In the coastal strip along the Mediterranean, the Nile valley, and the northern Sahara dwelled Egyptians and **Berbers**, later joined by Arabs after the Muslim expansion in the seventh century CE. Along the northeastern coasts and upper Nile valley were Abyssinians (Ethiopians), Nubians, and Somalis. Various **Bantu** (BAN-too) speaking ethnic groups made up the large majority in the center and south by about 400 CE. In the huge bulge of West Africa below the Sahara lived, and still live today, an assortment of peoples and language groups most (but not all) of which are closely related to the Bantu languages.

In the far south and southwest, the original inhabitants were the Khoisan (koi-SAHN) speaking peoples who still survive in much reduced numbers in a hunting-gathering culture in the Kalahari Desert. To the north of them in the center of the African forest belt live the Pygmies, also traditionally a hunting-gathering people. Today, hunting and gathering continue to supply the largest part of the daily diet in those few remaining regions of Africa that are blessed with more protein-bearing game than any other part of the globe.

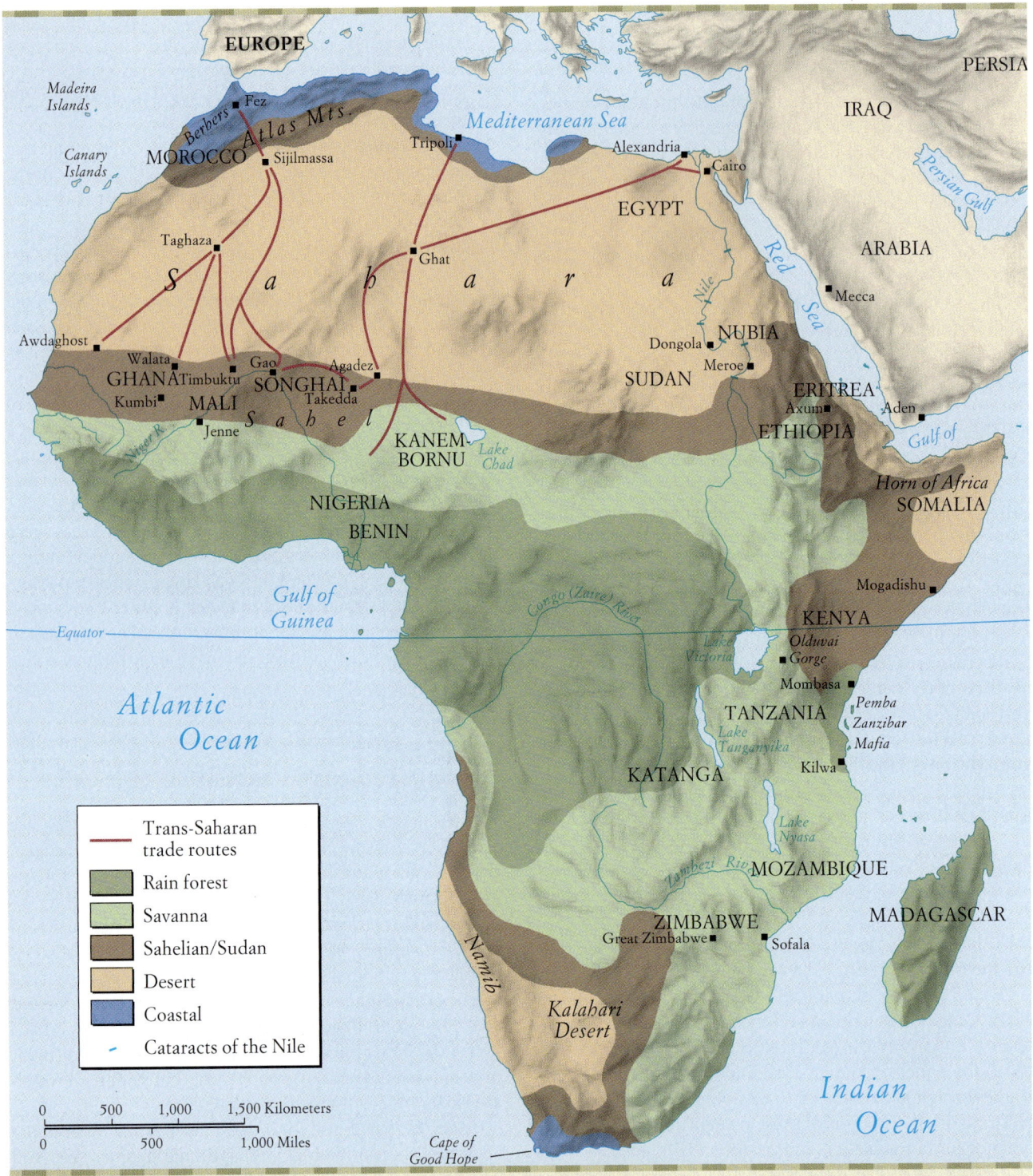

MAP 12.1 The Continent of Africa

Africa, the second-largest continent, has a highly diverse geography and climate. This map shows the five major subdivisions of climate and vegetation. The enormous Sahara Desert divides the continent into its North African and sub-Saharan components. Note Great Zimbabwe, the source of the East African gold trade.

MAP QUESTIONS

Where on the map were the major trade routes that linked Africa's interior with the Islamic world and Europe?

In the forests and grassland savannas, many villages depended on either pastoralism or farming for their food supply. Many combined both of these subsistence activities in what scholars call "mixed farming." Hunting was often a subsidiary resource, especially in the grasslands where big game abounded. Traditionally, women performed most of the daily drudgery associated with farming: sowing, weeding, hoeing, and preparing the food. In some regions, such as present-day Kenya and Tanzania, the pastoral lifestyle predominated, and agriculture was limited. The same was true of the Sahel and the Sahara, where there was too little rainfall for agriculture. But in the more densely settled areas, farming supplied Africans, as all other peoples, with the essentials of life and represented the usual work.

As we saw in Chapter 1, the key element in the development of settled existence normally is the availability of adequately watered farmland and metal tools. In Africa, these elements were closely associated, although tools such as hoes and even pottery continued to be made from stone during the early centuries of Africa's food-producing revolution. Most of the land suitable for intensive agriculture in pre-modern Africa was in the savanna south of the Sahara and in the Nile valley, with only bits and pieces elsewhere. The evidence provided by rock paintings and archaeology reveals that cattle pastoralism might have been practiced in the region of the Sahara during a wet phase that lasted from about 7500 to 2500 BCE. Once the Sahara began drying up, to become the desert it is today, these Saharan herding peoples migrated north and south of the desert, largely confining their settlements to the banks of rivers and surviving lakes.

Archaeologists have found evidence that demonstrates that between about 4000 and 2500 BCE the cultivation of native millet, sorghum, and rice began in the Nile River valley and the Niger (NEYE-jer) River valley of West Africa. When agriculture spread south into the rainforests, conditions did not favor cereals. In these regions, Africans learned to grow bananas and root crops such as yams, which could thrive in the humid climate and rain-drenched soils.

The Bantu Expansion into Subequatorial Africa

Although stone tools continued to be in use for several centuries, the growing use of iron greatly facilitated the spread of agriculture into the southern half of Africa. The Bantu speakers, a large group of distantly related peoples, profited from their mastery of yam agriculture to begin a steady expansion south and east from the general region of present-day Nigeria and Cameroon in West Africa through the rainforest some time well before 1000 BCE. To accomplish this, they appear to have used canoes to navigate the waters of the Congo River and its many tributaries, and polished, stone axes to clear the forest for farming. Around 1000 BCE, they emerged from the forest and reached the drier savanna to the west of Lake Victoria. They acquired iron technology and learned to breed livestock and grow the grain crops that did better than yams in the grasslands. These innovations helped them enlarge their numbers primarily through natural increase and the absorption of other peoples. By these means, they established a series of small kingdoms stretching across eastern, central, and southern Africa, and by 400 CE, they had reached the southern tip of the continent in present-day South Africa.

The bulk of the Bantu-speaking inhabitants of central, eastern, and southern Africa are thought to be the descendants of these migrants. As the Bantu had no written language and built few monuments that have survived, most of what we know about this process has been inferred from archaeological and linguistic research. Only when they arrived on the coast of the Indian Ocean and built the port cities of the Swahili coast (below) do we know much more than that they had created kingdoms dependent on agriculture and trade in the interior. Some of these states and kingdoms existed when the Portuguese arrived in the 1500s, and accounts of Portuguese travelers provide valuable additional information that supplements what archaeological and linguistic data provide.

SOCIAL ORGANIZATION AND STATE FORMATION

In sub-Saharan Africa, the basic unit of society was not the nuclear family but the clan, or **lineage** (LIN-ee-ehj), a much larger unit supposedly descended from a common ancestor. Within lineages, children took their names from and had specified status and rights through their lineage. Some societies seem to have followed **patrilineal descent** (descent and rights were determined by the father's lineage), but others followed **matrilineal descent** (names and rights were received from the mother's side). Clans lived together in compounds that grew in time to become villages or towns. People occasionally formed guild-like organizations to specialize in a certain craft, such as iron or copper smelting, pot making, basketry, salt-making, or even regional or long-distance trade. But most clans depended on either farming or herding activity to sustain them.

Several clans made up an ethnic group (sometimes called a "tribe"), and the local village was usually the keystone of all social organization and responsible for enforcing the rules of daily life—what many would call "government." Because age was highly venerated, it was customary for the clan elders to make most of the important decisions for the village, although everyone usually had rights to participate in deliberations, and matters were usually discussed until a consensus opinion was reached. Religion and the maintenance of social order were closely linked, but we know little about the exact practices that were followed in the remote past. Religious sacrifices were demanded before any important action was taken. Excepting the Christian northeast, animism in a multiplicity of forms was universal before the influence of Islam began to be felt in the ninth century.

Arab travelers' accounts tell of the "shocking" freedom (to Muslims, at least) of women in African society in the tenth through thirteenth centuries. There was no attempt to seclude women, except among some upper-class Muslims, or to restrict them from business dealings. As a rule, women were subordinate to men in public life, although they exercised their rights to be heard on public issues and there were instances when women occupied positions of power within African states, for example, as queen mothers or even occasionally as rulers. Women played a much stronger hand in the family and in the economies of their communities. They enjoyed rights equal to men's in the life of their clans, particularly where it came to rights of access and inheritance of clan resources like land and livestock. Since women performed most of the work on the family farms, they organized local markets for the sale of their produce. In this capacity, they played a crucial part in regional trade.

Male polygamy was the universal rule, and the number of wives a man had was taken as a sign of his wealth and social status. Taking additional wives as a man matured was considered a natural and desirable way of extending his kinship network. The offspring of these unions were considered the responsibility of the females, thus reinforcing the prevalent African custom of seeing the clan rather than the nuclear family as the primary unit of social life. When African people fell under the sway of Islam, women's personal and public lives were controlled more closely. Moreover, where matrilineal descent existed, it was usually replaced by patrilineal descent, and women's rights of inheritance were reduced to the general rule of Islamic law that restricted a woman's inheritance to only half that of a man.

Early European explorers/traders remarked on the existence of large numbers of people throughout sub-Saharan Africa who lived without any form of what they recognized as government. Perhaps as many as one-fourth of the African population, it has been estimated, lived in such apparently stateless societies at the advent of the Europeans. In making their judgment, the newcomers looked for the earmarks of government with which they were familiar in their European homelands: monarchs surrounded by subordinate officials, tax-collecting systems, defined frontiers,

permanent military establishments, and, most important, written laws. They also assumed that the larger the state, the more advanced must be its civilization. These assumptions led most Europeans to conclude erroneously that Africans must be severely retarded in their political development, as some or most of these elements of the state were lacking in the sub-Saharan civilizations, especially where they did not have written language.

What can we say today about the early Europeans' assessment? In fact, the social controls necessary for the peace and security of any large group were always present but went unrecognized by the Westerners who came to Africa during the colonial era. In the absence of written laws, controls typically would have included conflict and dispute resolution by medicine men or women having spiritual access to clan and village ancestors; social rules and norms that regulated rights and duties between kin groups or lineages when one or more of their members were involved in dispute; and certain duties and privileges accorded to an age group. In all or several of these fashions, the village elders usually performed the functions that early Europeans normally expected a state and its officials to perform.

Where states did emerge, they typically were organized around the principle of divine kingship. These had no bureaucracies but did include large numbers of court functionaries who individually did not have the king's power, but whose collective will could negate that of the king if they believed his actions had exceeded the bounds of custom or propriety. Typically, these included such figures as the queen mother, a prime minister, the royal historian and praise-singer, royal drummers, commanders of the army, diviners, keepers of court protocol, and medicine men and women. The king was a member of a royal lineage that enjoyed great prestige or was thought to be sacred. He acted as intermediary between the living and the dead, and he was thought to be able to discern the wishes of the royal ancestors through divination or even spirit possession. Maintaining the ritual purity and strength of the king was thought to be essential to the welfare of the land and people, and a weak, sick or aged king threatened the state. He then could be deposed. Usually, too, the divine king was surrounded by symbols of office, or regalia. These typically (but not always) would have included ivory horns that were blown on ceremonial occasions, royal drums, ceremonial swords, umbrellas or fans, and a palanquin on which he was transported.

THE KINGDOMS OF THE NILE

Trade runs like a golden thread throughout the history of Africa. Agriculture and livestock breeding were the cornerstones of daily existence for most Africans, but

wherever regional states and kingdoms overlaid village life, trade was one of the primary bases on which kingly or queenly authority relied. Africa exported few manufactures internationally, but local production and export of high-value commodities like gold, ivory, animal hides (processed and unprocessed), dyes, gums, and aromatics—as well as the traffic in human beings—created a lot of wealth. As in the case of Africa's earliest state, Egypt, when ambitious individuals were able to control and tax such wealth, they could wield enough power to extend their sway over large populations. Goods that Africans imported, likewise, often became symbols of prestige and power that kings could regulate and control to their political advantage if they were especially prized and not locally obtainable. Besides women and livestock, political power in Africa rested on control over imports like salt, dates, weapons, Chinese porcelain, textiles, and beads.

All this means that large portions of Africa maintained links to the larger world through international trade and commercial networks. As we shall see, the earliest trade was with the Nile Valley and the Mediterranean world; then, with the rise of the trading states of the western Sudan, the coastal Swahili, and Great Zimbabwe, these contacts extended to a wider Islamic commercial nexus that covered the eastern Mediterranean, the Indian Ocean community, and Asia.

Kush

Up the Nile (which actually is south) from the lush irrigated ribbon that is Egypt, the river flows across a series of cataracts (rapids) and makes a huge S turn through what is now one of the harshest deserts in the world. This area, which was never brought under the pharaoh's rule despite numerous attempts, is modern southern Egypt and northern Sudan. In ancient terminology it was called *Nubia* (see Chapter 3). East and south of Nubia, across the Horn of Africa and reaching to the Red Sea, are present-day Eritrea, Ethiopia, and Somalia. These modern states are the successors to the ancient kingdoms of Kush and Axum. And these kingdoms were, in their turn, the successors of pharaonic Egypt as centers of a flourishing civilization.

Kush (cush as in "cushion") was an African kingdom that emerged in the fifteenth century BCE and prospered until its overthrow in the fourth century CE. Its original capital was Kerma; then, after 900 BCE, the capital was moved further south to Napata (nah-PAH-tah) near the fourth cataract of the Nile. Archaeologists, who commenced work only about seventy years ago, have unearthed the extensive ruins of its cities, especially its last capital at Meroe. The Kushites had a written language. Archaeologists have uncovered Kushite script inscribed on many stone monuments, but it is still undeciphered. Remarkably, it is alphabetic and thus rivals the achievement of the ancient Phoenicians.

Darryl Plowes

PYRAMIDS AT MEROE. Standing from 50 to 100 feet high, this roofless shrine and its surrounding pyramids are thought to be part of a royal tomb complex in the ancient capital of the Kushites.

Kush was at once the partner and the rival of the pharaohs in keeping open the busy maritime trade routes that spanned the eastern Mediterranean, the Red Sea, and the western reaches of the Indian Ocean. These routes connected the Mediterranean basin with southern Asia. They became increasingly profitable as the Hellenistic and Roman rulers developed a taste for the gold, spices, and aromatics like frankincense and myrrh from East Africa, India, and China.

In its early history, when its capital was at Kerma, Kush was closely associated with Egypt and was strongly influenced by its culture and religion. However, when the Assyrians invaded Egypt in the eighth century BCE, the capital was moved a second time, farther up the Nile to Meroe (MEH-roh-way). Once at Meroe, the kingdom cut most of its ties with Egypt and became increasingly African in character. From the sixth century BCE, Meroe was a major industrial center whose principal product was iron. Archaeologists have discovered numerous iron-smelting furnaces and large mounds of slag, an industrial by-product of iron making. By the third century BCE, Meroe was at its height. Its strength derived from its grip on the trade coming downriver from the African interior and on the perhaps more important trade with southern Arabia across the Red Sea. The most valuable commodities were gold and slaves, followed by such exotic luxury wares as animal hides, ostrich feathers, spices, ebony, and ivory, all of which were destined for the Mediterranean region or Arabia.

Axum

By the first century CE, a rival power was rising on Kush's eastern flank. **Axum** (AX-uhm) in the Ethiopian highlands was the main city of a kingdom that had been established when local people and immigrants from southwestern Arabia arrived and intermarried during the last centuries

BCE. After establishing its own Red Sea port at Adulis, Axum became strong enough by the 300s to challenge Kush for control of the Red Sea trade and the upper Nile corridor. About 350 CE, Axum conquered Kush. The kingdom flourished until the eighth century, after which it gradually descended into oblivion and was abandoned. The city's sparse ruins were not rediscovered until the late eighteenth century by the earliest European explorers.

The rise of Axum coincided with its conversion to Christianity by Byzantine missionaries. Only a generation after Constantine accepted the faith, King Ezana of Axum made the same choice. Thus began the extraordinary history of Christianity in Ethiopia, the modern name for Axum and its surrounding lands. It is the oldest and most distinctive version of that religion in all of Africa. In later centuries, the rugged mountains and physical isolation of much of the country enabled the Ethiopians to hold off repeated Muslim attempts to conquer it, both from the Nile Valley and the Red Sea coasts. It also allowed the growth of a unique legend of royal descent, the Solomonic dynasty of Ethiopian Christian kings that commenced in biblical times and lasted until an army rebellion in 1970. Like its predecessor, Axum depended for its prosperity on its function as exchange depot for the Indian Ocean–Red Sea trade, as well as the Nile Valley route. In the sixth century, about the time the Muslim prophet Muhammad was born (Chapter 13), Axum had become strong enough to cross the Red Sea and conquer southwestern Arabia. However, the seventh-century Arab conquest of Egypt and South Arabia changed this situation dramatically, and within a century Christian Axum was driven from its Red Sea coast and under siege. From the eighth century, Arab Muslims dominated the seaborne trade. Nubian society, which gradually had matured into the three small states of Noba, Makuria, and Alowa, took Axum's place along the Nile. Little is known about them except that they had converted to Christianity through Egyptian influence in the seventh and eighth centuries and managed to hold out against Muslim pressure until as late as the 1200s in some areas. Throughout this lengthy period from Axum's fall to the coming of Muslim hegemony in the upper Nile, a diminished commercial traffic along the great river bound Egypt with its southern borderlands in Nubia and the Sudan. But the level of urban, sedentary life reached by the Kushite and Axumite kingdoms was not again approached in northeastern Africa.

TRANS-SAHARAN TRADE AND KINGDOMS OF THE SUDAN

The Sudanese kingdoms were a series of states that were formed starting about 400 CE in the bulge of West Africa below the great Sahara Desert. Here iron tools, good soils, and the transport afforded by the Niger River enabled agriculture to advance and provide for a rapidly growing population and some of the first cities south of the Sahara. In the early centuries CE, gold was discovered in the Senegal River region and early **trans-Saharan trade** routes developed that connected the western Sudan with North Africa. In the late seventh century, Islam established itself in North Africa and the western Sudan, and Muslim Berber and Arab merchants brought western Sudan into an international commercial system that eventually spanned southern Europe, Africa, and Asia (see Chapters 14 and 16). As in the Nile Valley, trade supported state formation. Three of these kingdoms are especially well known to modern historians: Ghana, Mali, and Songhay.

Ghana

Ghana (GAH-nah), the first of these kingdoms, endured for at least 500 years before it fell apart in the eleventh century as a result of a combination of events, including the onslaught of a Muslim *jihad.* Its exact origins are conjectural, but the Soninke people probably founded it some time in the first centuries CE, perhaps as early as 400. Its kings established a monopoly of trade in gold obtained from a mining region to the southwest of Ghana on the Senegal River, so the kingdom grew and became a regional power after it began dealings with the Muslims to the north in the eighth century. The *ghana* was the title given to its divine king who ruled through a network of regional officials in an area that at one point reached the size of Texas. Kumbi Saleh, the capital town, was sufficiently impressive that the sophisticated Muslim geographer al-Bakri spent some time describing it in a well-known travel and sightseeing guide of the eleventh century.

The Muslims, both Arabic and Berber, were influential in Ghana and, for that matter, in most of the Sudanese West African kingdoms that followed. The largely agrarian peoples of the Sudan believed in nature and ancestor spirits, but many experienced little difficulty converting to the monotheistic doctrines of Islam that Berber merchants and missionaries introduced. Like the earlier Christians of Rome, the missionaries concentrated their efforts on the upper class, usually in the towns where trade flourished. By adopting the new doctrine, their African merchant partners quickly gained advantages: literacy; access to new commerce and financial connections; a written law code (the *Sharia*) that helped facilitate commerce; and access to the Muslim trade network that extended across Africa and Asia. The Muslims introduced their concepts of law and administration, as well as religious belief. Kings who chose to continue following their traditional religions often relied on Muslim advisers for political and administrative advice.

Mali

Ghana's sources of gold dried up, which fatally weakened it when confronted by a Berber-led holy war in the eleventh century. Its regional segments warred with one another until one emerged under a semi-mythical king, Sundiata, who was powerful enough to subdue most of the western Sudan around 1250 (see Evidence of the Past). This was the kingdom of **Mali** (MAH-lee), which survived to about 1450. Mali was larger and better organized than Ghana, and the gold trade on which its kings depended, like those of the *ghanas* before them, seems to have come from a new region closer to the headwaters of the Niger River, which lay at the heart of the new kingdom (see Map 12.1). The original ruling clan, the Keitas (KEYE-tahs), were nominally Muslims, but they ruled primarily as divine kings who governed with the help of their court officials and regional representatives. The adoption of stricter forms of Islam early in the fourteenth century by a new ruling clan, the Mansas, encouraged good relations with the Berbers, whose trading activities were essential to the prosperity of the kingdom.

Like the earlier Kush and Axum, the Sudanese kingdoms were first and foremost the products of a strategic position in international trade. In this case, controlling movement along a lengthy stretch of the southern fringe of the Sahara allowed them to monitor the movements of trade goods from sub-Saharan to North Africa (and on to both Europe and the East). Both Ghana and Mali relied heavily on the taxes imposed on the Saharan traders in three vital commodities: gold, salt, and slaves. Although the king had other means of support, these taxes made it possible to support a hierarchy of governing officials and chiefs and a large army that included both infantry and cavalry units.

African gold was essential to Roman and medieval European commerce, as well as to the Muslim world. Gold ore was rare in Europe, but it was found in large quantities in parts of sub-Saharan Africa that were controlled by western Sudanese merchants and those of Swahili city-states like Kilwa in East Africa.

Salt was almost as prized as gold in the ancient world. Although it was a necessity, supplies were limited in most areas except near the sea, and it was difficult to transport without large loss. This made salt highly valuable, and saltpans in oases like Taghaza (tah-GAH-zah) and Tassili (tahs-SIH-lee) on the southern side of the Sahara were major sources.

Slaves were common in African markets long before the Europeans began the Atlantic slave trade. European, African, and Muslim cultures had no scruples about slave trading or possession in this epoch. As in every other part of the ancient world, slavery was an accepted consequence of war, debt, and crime. Being captured in raids by hostile neighbors was reason enough for enslavement. Large numbers of slaves passed northward through Ghana and Mali, bound for collection points on the Mediterranean coast. From there they were traded all over the known world.

The kingdom of Mali expanded by military conquests in the thirteenth century, until it came to dominate much of West Africa. Early Africa's most noted ruler, the far-traveled *Mansa Musa* (MAHN-sah MOO-sah), ruled from 1307 to 1332. He extended the kingdom as far north as the Berber towns in Morocco and eastward to include the great mid-Saharan trading post of Timbuktu. Perhaps 8 million people lived under his rule—at a time when the population of England was about 4 million.

Like his immediate predecessors, Mansa Musa was a Muslim, and in 1324 he made the pilgrimage to the holy places in Arabia. His huge entourage, laden with gold staffs

A SAHARAN SALT CARAVAN IN MALI. The foundation of the Sudanic empires was the Saharan trade. As in China, salt was an important commodity in the diet of most West Africans, so it was highly valued. It was mined from Saharan oases, then transported south to the Niger River "port" cities like Timbuktu. There it was traded for gold, ivory, and slaves.

Images&Stories/Alamy

and plates, entered Cairo like a victory procession and made an impression that became folklore. Thanks to Mansa Musa's support, Islam gained much ground in West Africa during his lifetime.

Thereafter, the religion gradually passed through the upper classes to the common people. Since then, the Muslim presence in sub-Saharan Africa has been growing slowly for many generations. It has had almost the same impact there as Christianity did in the Germanic kingdoms. Much African law, social organization, and literature, and many political institutions stem from it. Mansa Musa and his successor, Mansa Sulayman, especially encouraged scholarship, and Musa founded a *madrasa* (university) at the famous Sankore (san-KOH-ray) mosque in Timbuktu. The city gradually gained fame as a center of Islamic book production as well as trade.

Songhay

The Niger River city of Gao was already the focus of central Sudanic trade at the time of Ghana's greatness in the western Sudan. It remained in the shadow of its more powerful western Sudanic neighbors through the centuries of Mali's greatness, and in fact, realizing its importance, Mansa Musa subjugated Gao in 1325. Its dominance of

EVIDENCE OF THE PAST

Ibn Khaldun's Account of the Decline of Ghana and the Rise of Mali and Mansa Musa

Abu Zayd 'Abd ar-Rahman Ibn Khaldun is a well-known and highly regarded historian of the fourteenth century. He was born in Tunis in 1332 and died in 1406. The following selection is taken from the introduction of his great work of history and geography, *Kitab al-Ibar*, whose full title, loosely translated, is "The Book of Examples and the Register of the Origin and History of the Arabs, the Persians and the Berbers." Although he never traveled to the Sudan, as a secretary to various Moroccan rulers Khaldun would have had access to correspondence between Mali and Morocco, and he apparently used Malian oral historians (*griots*) as additional sources of information.

> When Ifriqiya and the Maghrib were conquered [by the Arabs] merchants penetrated the western part of the land of the Sudan and found among them no king greater than the king of Ghana. Ghana was bounded on the west by the Ocean. They were a very mighty people exercising vast authority. The seat of their authority was Ghana, a dual city on both banks of the [Niger River], one of the greatest and most populous cities in the world. . . .
>
> The neighbors of Ghana on the east, as chroniclers assert, were another people known as [Soso] . . . and beyond them another people known as Mali, and beyond them another known as . . . [Gao] . . . then beyond them another known as Takrur. . . . Later the authority of the people of Ghana waned and their prestige declined as that of the veiled people, their neighbors on the north next to the land of the Berbers, grew (as we have related). These extended their domination over the Sudan [black people], and pillaged, imposed tribute and poll tax, and converted many of them to Islam. Then the authority of the rulers of Ghana dwindled away and they were overcome by the [Soso], a neighboring people of the Sudan, who subjugated and absorbed them.
>
> Later the people of Mali outnumbered the peoples of the Sudan in their neighborhood and dominated the whole region. They vanquished the [Soso] and acquired all their possessions, both their ancient kingdom and that of Ghana as far as the Ocean on the west. They were Muslims. . . . Their greatest king, who overcame the [Soso], conquered their country, and seized the power from their hands, was named Mari Jata. Mari, in their language, means "ruler of the blood royal," and jata "lion". . . .
>
> Their rule reached from the Ocean and Ghana in the west to the land of Takrur in the east. Their authority became mighty and all the peoples of the Sudan stood in awe of them. Merchants from the Maghrib and Ifriqiya traveled to their country. Al-Hajj Yunus, the Takruri interpreter, said that the conqueror of [Gao] was Saghamanja, one of the generals of Mansa Musa. . . .
>
> Mansa Musa was an upright man and a great king, and his tales of justice are still told. He made the Pilgrimage [to Mecca] in 724/1324. . . .

▶ Analyze and Interpret

Why do you think the capital city of the king of Ghana is described as having been two cities? (*Hint:* It had to do with religion.) What role does religion seem to have played in the downfall of Ghana? At times the author uses the word *Sudan* to refer to a region and at other times to a people. What do you think *Sudan* means in Arabic?

Source: J. F. P. Hopkins (trans.) and N. Levtzion (ed. and ann.), *Corpus of Early Arabic Sources for West African History* (London: Cambridge University Press, 1981), pp. 332–334.

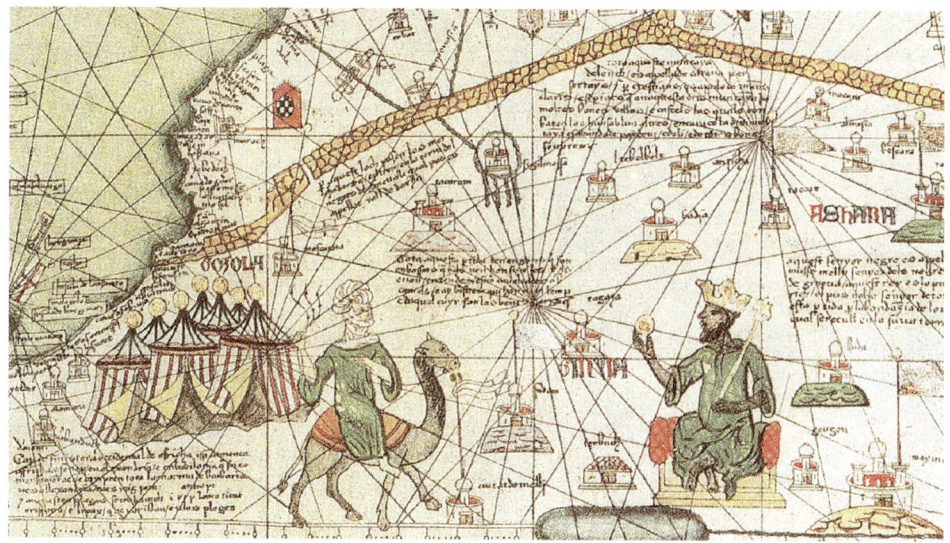

THE KING OF MALI IN THE EUROPEAN IMAGINATION. This fourteenth-century European map shows a rather fanciful rendering of a king of Mali, often presumed to be Mansa Musa, holding a large nugget and a large gold scepter.

the Niger River trade and most of the major trans-Saharan routes to the east of Timbuktu enabled it to exercise great commercial and military power. This power was realized when its first great king, Sonni Ali (1464–1492), employed a strategy that combined coordinate attacks of a robust cavalry of armored warriors with a sturdy navy of river canoes to extend his conquests to create the core of what became the kingdom of **Songhay** (song-GEYE). Under Sonni Ali and his successors, Songhay eventually became the mightiest of the great Sudanic states of West Africa.

Askia (ahs-KEE-yah) Muhammad (1493–1528) continued his predecessor, Ali's, expansionist ways. But, as important as his conquests were, Askia Muhammad's most lasting contribution to West African history lay in his support of Islam. Following the example of the great Malian emperors, Mansas Musa and Sulayman, Muhammad was an enthusiastic Muslim who gave Muslim scholars (*ulama*: oo-lah-MAH) important positions in his state apparatus; enforced orthodox practices among his subjects; built mosques; and subsidized book production and scholarship in the intellectual centers of Gao, Timbuktu, and Jenne.

Despite the works of Muhammad and his successors, simultaneous attacks by non-Muslim Mossi peoples from the south and Tuareg (TWAH-rehg) Berbers from the north gravely weakened the Songhay state during the 1500s. Its final overthrow came when Moroccan forces invaded it in 1591.

THE SWAHILI CITY-STATES

The East African city-states also had a large hand in the gradual commercial development of the continent. Well before the Common Era, Greek, Roman, and Egyptian ships that traveled down the Red Sea were trading with coastal ports of the Horn of Africa and "Azania," the name given to East Africa at that time. One account from the first century CE, the *Periplus of the Erythraean Sea*, described Arab and Greco-Roman trade for ivory and tortoise shell with an East African town called Rhapta, for example.

An enormous expansion of this trade came after the seventh century, when the entire Indian Ocean became virtually an Islamic lake. Thereafter, Persian, Arab, and Indian traders arrived with the annual trade winds to trade with the local Bantu-speaking people, whom the Arabs called "the Zanj." Imports that were especially popular with these Zanj, known to us as the **Swahili** (swah-HEE-lee), were dates, glassware, Persian ceramics, Chinese porcelains and silks, Indian cotton fabrics, and glass beads. In return, they traded locally manufactured iron, timber, ivory, and sundry animal by-products such as hides, ambergris, rhinoceros horn, and tortoise shell. By the time the Portuguese arrived in the region in the late fifteenth century, Swahili ships also seem to have been making the reverse journey, building and sailing fully seaworthy ships of their own to ports of southern Arabia and India. Thus, the vast ocean separating Africa and India was well known to both African and Muslim travelers long before the arrival of the first Portuguese explorers.

Foreign Muslims and local, Bantu-speaking, coastal people steadily intermarried, and the children of these unions were raised as Muslims. Many coastal Africans opted to convert to Islam for many of the same reasons that West Africans did; however, the mixture of African and non-African peoples typically found in the major commercial entrepôts of the coast, like Kilwa and Mombasa, was probably even greater than what one typically would have encountered in the western Sudan. The greatest period of conversion seems to have been 1000 to 1500 CE.

©The Granger Collection

Peter Garlake, *The Making of the Past: The Kingdoms of Africa*
(Elsevier/Phaidon, 1990), p. 101

THE PALACE OF HUSUNI KUBWA (hoo-SOO-nee KOO-bwah). Meaning "Great Palace" in Swahili, the Abu'l Mawahib sultans built this structure around the time Ibn Battuta visited Sultan Abu'l Mawahib Hasan al-Mahdali in 1331. The front part included rooms for the sultan's harem, as well as various audience courts and even an octagonal bathing pool. The large, open space at the rear appears to have been a warehouse area where trade goods were off-loaded from ships and stored. Archaeological excavation by H. N. Chittick in the early 1960s indicated that the palace was only lived in for a few decades and was abandoned by the late 14th century. Use of carved coral blocks and cupolas, as seen on the roof, were common features of medieval Swahili religious architecture.

EVIDENCE OF THE PAST

Ibn Battuta's Visit to East Africa

The following is taken from the account of the great fourteenth-century traveler from Morocco, Muhammad ibn Abdallah ibn Battuta, or Ibn Battuta (ihbn Bah-TOO-tah) for short. Little is known about him aside from his account of his travels. He was born in Tangier in 1304 and died in 1377. He was in East Africa around 1331–1332, includ ing the cities of Mogadishu, Mombasa, and Kilwa in his visit.

> Then I set off by sea from the town of Mogadishu for the land of the Swahili and the town of Kilwa, which is in the land of Zanj. We arrived at Mombasa, a large island. . . . The island is quite separate from the mainland. It grows bananas, lemons, and oranges. . . . The people [of the island] do not engage in agriculture, but import grain from the [people of the mainland, opposite the island]. The greater part of their diet is bananas and fish. They follow the Shafi'i [sect of Islam], and are devout, chaste, and virtuous. . . .
>
> We spent a night on the island and then set sail for Kilwa . . . the greater part of whose inhabitants are Zanj of very black complexion. . . .
>
> Kilwa is one of the most beautiful and well-constructed towns in the world. The whole of it is elegantly built. The roofs are built with mangrove pole. There is very much rain. The people are engaged in a holy war, for their country lies beside the pagan Zanj. Their chief qualities are devotion and piety: they follow the Shafi'i sect.

> When I arrived, the Sultan was Abu al-Muzaffar Hasan surnamed Abu al-Mawahib [loosely translated, "The Giver of Gifts"] . . . on account of his numerous charitable gifts. He frequently makes raids into the Zanj country [neighboring mainland], attacks them and carries off booty, of which he reserves a fifth, using it in the manner prescribed by the Koran [Qur'an]. That reserved for the kinsfolk of the Prophet [Muhammad] is kept separate in the Treasury, and when Sharifs [descendants of the Prophet] come to visit him, he gives it to them. They come to him from Iraq, the Hijaz, and other countries. I found several Sharifs from the Hijaz at his court. . . . This Sultan is very humble; he sits and eats with beggars, and venerates holy men and descendants of the Prophet.

▶ *Analyze and Interpret*

How credible do you think this source is? Do you know anything that suggests it might be accurate or inaccurate? What interesting things does the author say about the quality of Islamic practices in remote East Africa? Why do you think the Sultan of Kilwa and his descendants came to be called "The Giver of Gifts"?

Source: G. S. P. Freeman-Grenville, *The East African Coast, Select Documents* (London: Oxford University Press, 1962), pp. 31–32.

You can read more from Ibn Battuta's *Travels* at the *Wadsworth World History Resource Center.*

By the ninth century, a series of small city-states were established whose community life centered on manufacturing and trade. The earliest of these city-states, such as Mogadishu, Shanga, and Manda, were concentrated along the coasts of modern Somalia and Kenya. Once the gold from the coast of Mozambique, coming from Great Zimbabwe (see following section), began to dominate coastal trade, the great East African emporium of **Kilwa** became prominent. In most coastal centers, local Swahili controlled these sophisticated commercial states. In the late thirteenth century, however, the Mahdali (MAH-dah-lee) clan from southwestern Arabia established an Arab Sultanate in Kilwa. Calling themselves the Abu'l-Mawahibs (ah-BOOL mah-WAH-hibs; loosely translated as "The Givers of Gifts"), their position was based on Islamic piety, claims of descent from the Prophet Muhammad, and a monopoly of Kilwa's gold trade with Great Zimbabwe. The Moroccan traveler, Ibn Battuta, visited the court of the reigning Abu'l-Mawahib in 1331 and provided one of the best accounts available from that period (see Evidence of the Past).

early as the fourth century CE. Nevertheless, the spread of mixed farming into areas that previously had been purely pastoralist or even hunting-gathering seems to have been slow.

The chief center of early settled life in southern Africa was not near the coast but far inland: **Great Zimbabwe** (zihm-BAH-bway). Today the ruins of what was once a large capital city and fortress can be seen in the present-day nation of Zimbabwe inland from Mozambique. Great Zimbabwe was not discovered until 1871, and unfortunately, we know nothing of its history from written sources. Nevertheless, its massive walls and towers make it one of the most impressive monuments in Africa south of the pyramids. Apparently, the first stages of its construction were begun in the tenth and eleventh centuries by kings whose wealth and power rested, just as did that of the kings of Ghana and Mali, on the control of gold production. Trade in gold and ivory passed down to the Swahili ports on the coast, while exotic imports such as glass beads and pottery passed hand to hand in the opposite direction to Zimbabwe.

GREAT ZIMBABWE

Southern Africa has a moderate climate and good soil, which encouraged settlement by Bantu-speaking farming peoples who reached it around the fourth century CE. Later reports by shipwrecked Portuguese sailors indicate that, by the 1500s, Bantu-speaking mixed farmers and Khoisan-speaking hunter-gatherers and cattle pastoralists were living in agricultural villages, pastoralist communities, or hunter-gatherer camps all across the tip of the continent. Archaeology reveals that iron had come into use as

ZIMBABWE SOAPSTONE BIRD. The ruins at Great Zimbabwe include a large, enclosed area on the hills overlooking the Great Enclosure. It served as a center for the cult of the Rain God, presided over by the King. Carved soapstone images of fish eagles topped the walls. The fish eagle was a migratory bird that returned to the Zimbabwean plateau at the beginning of the rainy season; hence, the agrarian Zimbabweans associated the bird with the Rain God.

THE GREAT ENCLOSURE AT GREAT ZIMBABWE. These stone walls are the only remnants of the once-important center of the gold trade in the south-central African interior. Europeans discovered them only in the late nineteenth century, and typical of attitudes of the time, believed they were built by some "white" race and not by the local Shona people.

The region flourished as a political, religious, and trading center. Additional stone structures continued to be built at the Great Zimbabwe site, and other *zimbabwes* (courts and burial places for royal clan members) were constructed until the fifteenth century, when the state broke apart into several smaller, competing kingdoms. We also know from early Portuguese sources that the supply of Zimbabwe's gold had begun to peter out by the early 1500s. As happened with other great world civilizations, the population might also have grown to the point that it tipped the delicate balance with the natural environment. In a sense, they become victims of their own success. The most likely explanation, however, as is usually the case in history, is that all of these factors combined caused the decline and abandonment of the site of Great Zimbabwe.

African Arts

In the absence of written languages, African art was necessarily visual and plastic, and the sculpture and inlay work of all parts of sub-Saharan Africa have lately aroused much interest and study in the Western world. Perhaps the most famous are the Benin bronzes from the West African kingdom of Benin, one of the successors to Mali. The highly stylized busts and full-length figures in bronze, gold, and combinations of metal and ebony are striking in their design and execution. They are obviously the product of a long tradition of excellence. Benin's enemies vandalized many of these pieces during the constant warfare that marred West African history. Many others were carried off as booty by the early Europeans and have since disappeared. Enough remain in museums, however, to give us some appreciation of the skill and imagination of the makers.

The same is true of the wood sculptures of the Kanem and Bornu peoples of central Sudan, who assembled, between the twelfth and fifteenth centuries, a series of kingdoms in the vicinity of Lake Chad that lasted in one manifestation or another until the eighteenth century.

The ivory and gold work of the Swahili city-states is also remarkable and greatly appreciated, especially by Middle Eastern buyers. Some Muslims looked on this infidel artwork depicting human figures as a mockery of Allah and destroyed much of it, either in place in Africa or later, in the countries to which it was transported.

The earthenware heads of the Nok people of prehistoric Nigeria, on the other hand, have come to light only in this century. Dating from roughly the first five centuries before the Christian era, these terra cotta portrait heads are the oldest examples yet found of African art. Their probable religious significance is not known.

European Impressions

Unfortunately for the Africans' reputation, the fifteenth century Europeans arrived on the African coast at about the very time that the most powerful and most advanced of the sub-Saharan kingdoms collapsed or were in decline. In the absence of written sources, the causes of decline are not easily identified. They seem to have involved a lethal combination of internal quarrels among the nobility who served the king and conquest from outside, sometimes by Muslims from Morocco.

As a result, the European explorer-traders perceived the kingdoms of Africa as subservient and backward. This impression was reinforced by the Africans' relative lack of knowledge in military and technological matters, and later by the readiness of some of the African kings and chieftains to allow the sale of competing or neighboring people into slavery—a practice that had been commonplace in Europe for a thousand years but that Christian and Jewish teaching had by that time effectively forbidden.

The Europeans (largely the Portuguese in the first century of contacts) concluded that the Africans were backward in their sensitivity and degree of civilization and that it would not be wrong to take advantage of them. Africans were perceived as not quite human, so what would have been a despicable sin against God and humanity if it had been done back home in Lisbon was quite forgivable—perhaps not worth a second thought—here. This callousness was undoubtedly reinforced by the desperate nature of business enterprise in the first centuries of the colonial era, when it is estimated that Europeans who went to the African coast had a 25 percent mortality rate per year. It was not an affair that encouraged second thoughts on the morality of what one was doing.

Other Europeans who as slavers came into contact with the West Africans shared the Portuguese attitude. Early attempts to convert the Africans to Christianity were quickly subordinated to business interests by the Portuguese and never attempted at all by their English, Dutch, and French successors until the nineteenth century. The tendency to see Africans as a source of profit rather than as fellow human beings was soon rationalized by everything from biblical quotations to Arab and Berber Muslim statements reflecting their own prejudices. The basis of European (and later American) racism directed against the dark-skinned peoples is to be found in these earliest contacts and the circumstances in which they were made.

SUMMARY

AFRICA IS A continent of vast disparities in ethnic background, climate, and topography. Much of its interior remained shut off from the rest of the world until a century ago, and little was known of its history from either domestic or foreign sources. Only the Mediterranean coastal region and the Nile valley came to be included in the classical world, while the great Saharan desert long secluded the African heartland from northern penetration.

In a prehistoric migration, the Bantu-speaking inhabitants of the western forest regions gradually came to occupy most of the continent in the early Christian era, aided by their mastery of iron and of advanced agriculture. African state formation proceeded slowly and unevenly. The first were in the northeast, where ancient Egypt was

followed by Kush and Axum as masters of the Indian Ocean–Mediterranean trade routes. Their decline followed upon Arab Muslim expansion in the eighth century. In the tenth and succeeding centuries, several large kingdoms arose in the western savanna lands, largely dependent on an active trade in gold and slaves across the desert to the northern Muslim regions. Ghana was the first of these commercially oriented kingdoms, followed by the larger and more permanent Mali and Songhay empires. A Muslim elite formed the governing class. In the Swahili city-states along the eastern coast, an Islamicized African population known as the Swahili ruled. Islam, carried by proselytizing Arab merchants into the interior, was the prime force for political, legal, and administrative organization in much of pre-European Africa.

▶ Identification Terms

Test your knowledge of this chapter's key concepts by defining the following terms. If you can't recall the meaning of certain terms, refresh your memory by looking up the boldfaced term in the chapter, turning to the Glossary at

the end of the book, or working with the flashcards that are available on the *World Civilizations* Companion Website: **academic.cengage.com/adler**

Axum	Great Zimbabwe	Mali	Swahili
Bantu	Kilwa	matrilineal descent	trans-Saharan trade
Berbers	Kush	patrilineal descent	
Ghana	lineage	Songhay	

▶ Test Your Knowledge

Test your knowledge of this chapter by answering the following questions. Complete answers appear at the end of the book. You may find even more quiz questions in CengageNOW and on the *World Civilizations* Companion Website: **academic.cengage.com/adler**

1. Pastoralism seems to have first appeared in Africa in the
   a. Mediterranean region.
   b. Sahara region.
   c. grassland savanna.
   d. Sahel.
   e. western Horn.
2. An important population movement in Africa was the
   a. drift of Bantu speakers from West Africa to the south and east.
   b. movement of the Pygmies from central to northern Africa.

   c. settlement of North Africa by the Tuaregs.
   d. coming of the Portuguese to colonize the coast.
   e. settlement of the Sahel by Arab traders.
3. The kingdom of Axum
   a. succeeded the kingdom of Kush in northeast Africa.
   b. was crushed by the Egyptians during the New Kingdom of Egypt.
   c. was the original home of the Bantus.
   d. was converted early to Islam.
   e. was ruled by Mansa Musa and his descendants.
4. By about the fifth century CE, the population of the western Sudan had increased dramatically as a result of
   a. immigration from the eastern regions.
   b. changes in climate.

c. increased food production.
d. the practice of polygamy.
e. large populations of slaves captured in battle.

5. Which factor has contributed to the greatest misunderstandings of Africans and their history?
   a. Religion
   b. Race
   c. Government
   d. Social organization
   e. Trade practices

6. The outside people having the greatest cultural influence on the kingdom of Ghana were the
   a. European colonists.
   b. Muslim Berbers and Arabs.
   c. Ethiopians.
   d. Egyptian Christians.
   e. Sudanese merchants.

7. Trade in slaves in both East and West Africa before the fifteenth century was
   a. commonplace.
   b. limited to extraordinary circumstances.
   c. controlled by the Muslims.
   d. rarely encountered.
   e. completely unknown.

8. The Swahili city-states were essentially populated by
   a. Arabs
   b. Arabs, Persians, and Indians
   c. Bantu animists
   d. Bantu-speaking Muslims
   e. Refugees from Kush

9. Mansa Musa was
   a. the outstanding Muslim geographer who described early Africa.
   b. the wealthy African king who journeyed to Arabia on pilgrimage.
   c. the founder of the kingdom of Mali.
   d. the Arab missionary who converted the king of Mali.
   e. the Moroccan traveler who visited Great Zimbabwe.

10. Which of the following, according to the text, was *not* a likely reason for the decline of Great Zimbabwe?
    a. Invasion by outsiders
    b. Dynastic quarrels
    c. Overpopulation of the land
    d. A decline in gold production
    e. Environmental upsets

Enter *CengageNOW* using the access card that is available with this text. *CengageNOW* will assist you in understanding the content in this chapter with lesson plans generated for your needs and provide you with a connection to the *Wadsworth World History Resource Center* (see description at right for details).

 World History Resource Center

Enter the Resource Center using either your *CengageNOW* access card or your standalone access card for the *Wadsworth World History Resource Center.* Organized by topic, this website includes quizzes; images; over 350 primary source documents; interactive simulations, maps, and timelines; movie explorations; and a wealth of other resources. You can read the following documents, and many more, at the *Wadsworth World History Resource Center:*

Accounts of Meroe, Kush, and Axum, *c.* 430 BCE– 550 CE
Ibn Battuta, *Travels in Asia and Africa, 1325–1354*

There is no god save God, and Muhammad is His Messenger.
—Muslim profession of faith

c. 570–632	Life of Muhammad
640s	Conquest of Persian Empire and Egypt completed
661–750	Umayyad Dynasty at Damascus
711–733	Conquest of Spain/ Muslims defeated at Tours
750–1258	Abbasid Dynasty at Baghdad

THE LIFE OF MUHAMMAD THE PROPHET

PATTERNS OF BELIEF IN ISLAMIC DOCTRINE

ARABIA IN MUHAMMAD'S DAY

THE JIHAD

THE CALIPHATE
The First Period, 632–661 ◆ The Umayyad Dynasty, 661–750 ◆ The Abbasid Dynasty, 750–1258

CONVERSION TO ISLAM

EVERYDAY AFFAIRS

I N THE ARABIAN TOWN of Mecca, late in the sixth century, an individual was born who founded a religion that is now embraced by about one-fifth of the world's population. Muhammad created a faith that spread with incredible speed from his native land throughout the Near and Middle East. Carried on the strong swords of his followers, and later through conversions, Islam became a major rival to Christianity in the Mediterranean basin and to Hinduism and Buddhism in East and Southeast Asia. Like these faiths, Islam was far more than a supernatural religion; it also created a culture and a civilization.

THE LIFE OF MUHAMMAD THE PROPHET

The founder of Islam was born into a people about whom little documentary information exists prior to when he made them the spiritual and political center of a new civilization.

Arabia is a large and sparsely settled peninsula extending from the Fertile Crescent in the north to well down the coast of Africa (see Map 13.1). Mecca, Muhammad's birthplace, was an important interchange where southern Asian and African goods coming across the Indian Ocean and the narrow Red Sea were transferred to caravans for shipment farther east. Considerable traffic also moved up and down the Red Sea to the ancient cities of the Near East and the Nile delta. For these reasons, the Mecca of Muhammad's time was a cosmopolitan place, with Egyptians, Jews, Greeks, and Africans living there, alongside the local Arab population. Long accustomed to trading and living with foreigners, the Arabs of towns like Mecca were using a written language and had well-developed systems of tribal and municipal governments. In such ways, the Arabs of the cities near the coast were far more advanced than the Bedouins (nomads) of the vast desert interior.

Several tribes or clans inhabited Mecca. The most important was the Quraysh (KOO-resh), the clan into which Muhammad was born about 570. According to traditional Muslim accounts, the first forty years of his life were uneventful. He was orphaned by the time he was six years old; his paternal uncle reared him and gave him the traditional protection of his clan. He married Khadija, a rich widow, and set himself up as a caravan trader of moderate means. The marriage produced six children, only one of whom survived, a daughter named Fatima.

Around 610 CE, Muhammad began having mystical experiences that took the form of visits from a supernatural messenger. For days at a time he withdrew into the low mountains near Mecca, where long trances ensued in which the Archangel Gabriel began telling him of the One True God (**Allah**), and warning him of a coming Day of Judgment. For about three years he dared speak of these visions only to his immediate kin. (See Evidence of the Past.)

Finally, Muhammad began to preach about his visions in the street. Meccan authorities, however, supported a form of worship centered on nature deities and various cult objects, such as a Black Stone protected in a religious shrine called the ***Ka'ba*** (KAH-bah), which Muslims now believe God had once given to the Prophet Ibrahim (Abraham). Consequently, during his Meccan

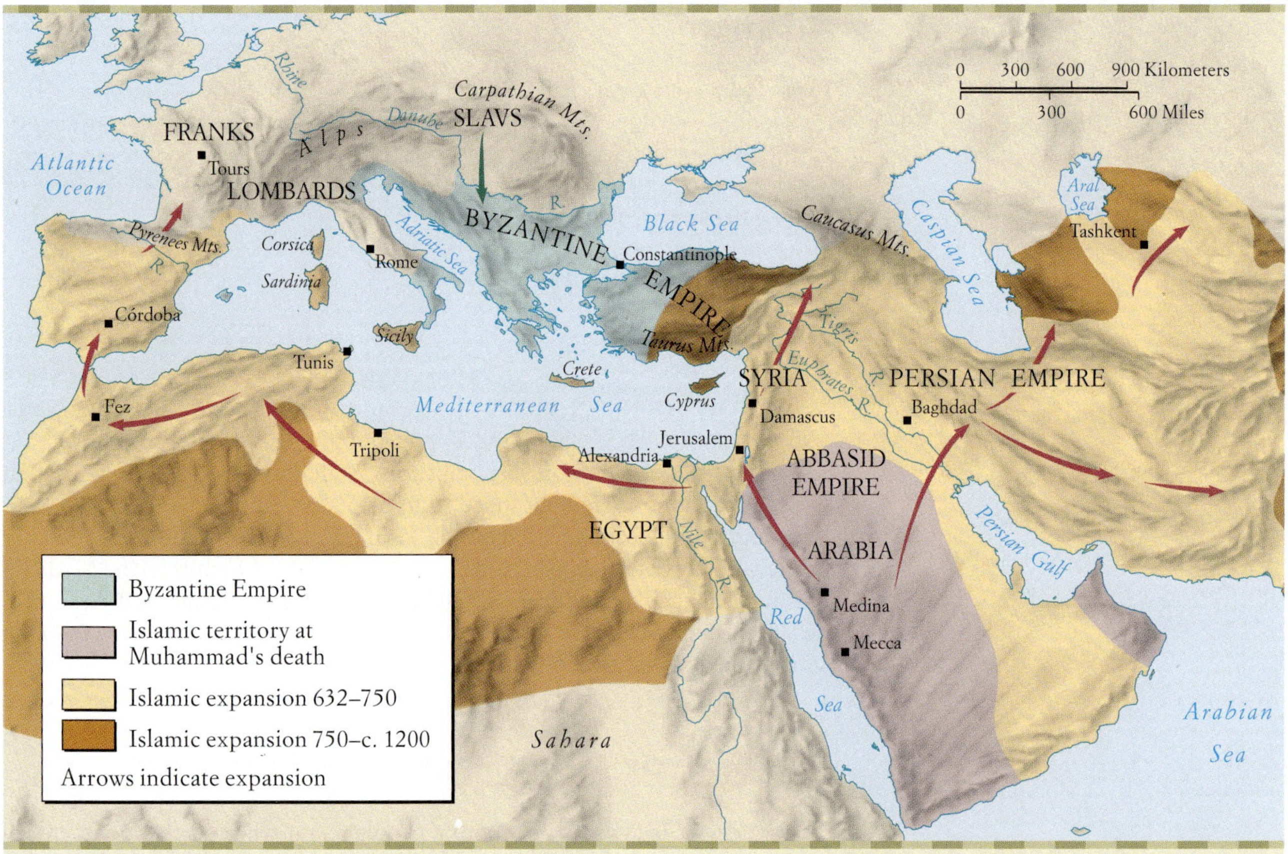

MAP 13.1   Spread of Islam

The lightning-like spread of the new faith throughout a belt on either side of the equator is evident in this map. About one-third of the world's populations known to the Christians converted to Islam in the space of a long lifetime, 630–720 CE.

 View an interactive version of this or a related map at http://worldrc.wadsworth.com/

MAP QUESTIONS
Considering the directions of Islam's expansion (arrows), what seemed to be the factors that prevented its further expansion? (Example: the expansion from Syria and from Spain?)

EVIDENCE OF THE PAST

Muhammad Receives His First Revelation

Muhammad Ibn Ishaq was the first person to write a biography of Muhammad, the Prophet of Islam. He lived a little more than a century (died, c. 768) after Muhammad and based his information on oral accounts he collected from the descendants of Muhammad's close associates. This is his account of the day, when Muhammad was about forty years old, of the Prophet's first visit by the Archangel Gabriel.

> "Relate to us, 'Ubayd, what the beginning of the Messenger of God's prophetic mission was like when Gabriel came to him." I was present as 'Ubayd related the following account to 'Abdallah b. al-Zubayr and those with him. He said, "The Messenger of God used to spend one month in every year in religious retreat on [Mount] Hira." . . . feeding the poor who came to him. When he had completed this month of retreat the first thing which he would do on leaving, even before going home, was to circumambulate the Ka'bah seven times, or however many times God willed; then he would go home.
>
> When the month came in which God willed to ennoble him, in the year in which God made him his Messenger, this being the month of Ramadan, the Messenger of God went out as usual to Hira accompanied by his family. When the night came on which God ennobled him by making him his Messenger . . . Gabriel brought him the command of God. The Messenger of God said, Gabriel came to me as I was sleeping with a brocade cloth in which he was writing. He said, "Recite!" and I said, "I cannot recite." He pressed me tight and almost stifled me, until I thought that I should die.
>
> Then he let me go and said, "Recite!" I said, "What shall I recite?" only saying that in order to free myself from him, fearing that he might repeat what he had done to me. He said: Recite in the name of your Lord who creates! He creates man from a clot of blood. Recite: And your Lord is the most Bountiful, he who teaches by the pen, teaches man what he knew not.
>
> I recited it, and then he desisted and departed. I woke up, and it was as though these words had been written on my heart.

▶ Analyze and Interpret

How accurate might this account be? What historical (not religious) reasons can you think of for believing or not believing this passage? How does this compare with the believability of similar passages about the prophets in the Old Testament and the accounts of Jesus in the New Testament of the Bible?

Source: From *The History of al-Tabari, Volume VI. Muhammad at Mecca.* Trans. W. Montgomery Watt and M. V. McDonald (Albany, NY: SUNY Press, 1988), pp. 70–71.

You can read a selection from Ibn Ishaq's Life of Muhammad at the *Wadsworth World History Resource Center*.

years, Muhammad's successful conversions were primarily (although not exclusively) among members of his own family, the Meccan poor, and some slaves. The deaths of his wife Khadija in 619 and of his uncle and protector in 620 produced a major crisis for Muhammad. Growing concerns for his and his followers' safety forced him to flee Mecca in 622, which came to be known as the year of the *Hijra* (HIJ-rah: "flight"). It became the first year of the Muslim calendar.

Muhammad fled to the rival city of Medina, where, despite the opposition of its three Jewish tribes to his claims of being God's prophet, he gradually gained the support he had vainly sought in Mecca. From 622 to 624, he gradually won over enough followers to begin a kind of trade war against the Meccan caravans and to force the city fathers there to negotiate with him on spiritual matters. He also won the support of nearby Bedouin tribes, and by 630 he was able to return to Mecca on pilgrimage (*hajj*) to the Ka'ba at the head of a victorious community of converts. By the time of his death two years later, most of western Arabia was under Islamic control. A *jihad* (jee-HAHD), a war of holy conquest in the name of Allah, was under way.

PATTERNS OF BELIEF IN ISLAMIC DOCTRINE

What message did Muhammad preach that found such ready acceptance? The doctrines of Islam (the word means "submission," in this case to God, or Allah) are the simplest and most readily understood of any of the world's major religions. They are laid out in written form in the **Qur'an** (koor-AHN), the most sacred scriptures of the Muslim world, which the third caliph, Uthman (see the "Umayyad Dynasty" section), ordered to be collected from oral traditions twenty-three years after the Prophet's death. The basic ideas are expressed in the **Five Pillars of Islam**, which are described in the Patterns of Belief box. Without doubt, the simplicity of these teachings and their ritual requirements were important factors in winning many converts to Islam as the Islamic Empire expanded—in the first instance, through the sword.

Muhammad and his followers were able to achieve what they did for various reasons. First, Muhammad preached a straightforward doctrine of salvation, ensured by a God who never failed and whose will was clearly delineated in comprehensible principles and commands. Second, those who believed and tried to follow Muhammad's words (as gathered a few years after his death in the Qur'an) were assured of reward in the life to come. On the other hand, God's Messenger warned unbelievers of a fiery end that awaited them in Hell.

Finally, Muhammad's preaching contained large measures of an elevated yet attainable moral and ethical code. It deeply appealed to a population that wanted more than the purely ritualistic animist doctrine could give them but were repelled by the internal conflicts of Christendom or unsympathetic to the complexities of Judaism. His insistence that he was not an innovator, but the finalizer of the

PATTERNS OF BELIEF

The Five Pillars of Islam

From the outset, Islam has rested on the Five Pillars taught by Muhammad. In more or less flexible forms, these beliefs are recognized and observed by all good Muslims, wherever and in whatever circumstances they may find themselves.

1. There is one God (whom Muslims call Allah), and Muhammad is His prophet. Islam is a thoroughly monotheistic faith. There are neither saints nor Trinity.

2. God demands prayer from His faithful five times daily: at daybreak, noon, in the mid-afternoon, twilight, and before retiring. Prayer is always done in the direction of Mecca. It is the outward sign of complete submission to the Lord.

3. Fasting and observance of dietary prohibitions are demanded of all who can. The month of Ramadan and some holy days are particularly important in this respect. Alcohol and all other mind-warping substances are forbidden, as insults to the handiwork of the perfect Creator.

4. Almsgiving toward the poor faithful is a command, enforced through the practice of tithing. Gifts and bequests to the deserving fellow Muslim are mandatory for those who would attain worldly distinction and the respect of their neighbor.

5. If possible, every Muslim must make the *hajj* ("pilgrimage") to the holy cities of Arabia at least once. In modern days this command has filled Mecca with upward of 2 million visitors at the height of the holy season.

Bibliothèque Nationale, Paris

THE ENTRY INTO MECCA BY THE FAITHFUL. In this thirteenth-century miniature from Baghdad, the *hajj*, or pilgrimage, is depicted in its glory. Supposedly devoted to pious purposes, the *hajj* was also an opportunity to display one's wealth.

▶ Analyze and Interpret

Considering this list of religious requirements, if you were a Muslim, and if your knowledge of your religion extended only to the performance of these duties, would Islam seem a spiritually satisfying religion to you? Why or why not? (*Hint:* Consult the next chapter's discussion of *Sufism* as a follow-up to this question.)

message of the Jewish and Christian prophets and gospel writers was also of great significance in the success of his religion among the Eastern peoples.

ARABIA IN MUHAMMAD'S DAY

The Jews and Christians with whom Muhammad had contact in Mecca undoubtedly influenced the strict monotheism of Islam. Many other aspects of the Muslim faith also derive in some degree from other religions, such as the regulations against eating pork and using stimulants that alter the God-given nature of man. But the Muslim creed is not just a collection of other, previous beliefs by any means. It includes many elements that reflect the peculiar circumstances of Arabs and Arabia in the seventh century CE.

At that time, much of the interior of the Arabian peninsula was barely inhabited except for scattered oases. The Bedouin tribes that passed from one oasis to the next with their herds were continually at war with one another for water and pasture. The virtues most respected in this society were those of the warrior: strict social and material equality, bravery, hardiness, loyalty, honor, and hospitality to strangers.

The Arabs' religion before Muhammad involved a series of animistic beliefs, such as the important one centering on the Ka'ba, a cubical stone shrine that contained the Black Stone. (Recall that *animism* means a conviction that objects such as rivers, trees, or stones possess spirits and spiritual qualities that have direct and potent impact on human lives.) In the coastal towns, these beliefs coexisted side by side with the monotheistic beliefs of Judaism, Christianity, and Zoroastrianism. There is evidence that belief in a principal, creator deity also existed in Arabia before Muhammad, although such evidence is vague and indirect. In towns such as Mecca, commerce had bloomed to such an extent that many Arabs were seduced away from their traditional social equality by this newfound wealth.

Traditions that underscored social and economic equality were being cast aside in favor of materialist values and social hierarchy. The cultural gap between town Arab and Bedouin had widened to such an extent that it threatened to become irrevocable. Worship at the Ka'ba shrine had become linked to trade for the merchants of Mecca, who profited greatly from the many thousands of Arabs from the interior who made annual processions there during the month of Ramadan (RAH-mah-dahn) to worship tribal and clan idols that were housed in the shrine.

From this standpoint, some scholars have interpreted Muhammad's religious message as the work of a reformer, a man who perceived many of the problems facing his people and responded to them. The verses of the Qur'an excerpted in the Patterns of Belief box contain many references to these problems and propose solutions. For example, the condition of women in pre-Muslim Arabia was

apparently poor. A man could have as many wives as he wished, regardless of whether he could support them all.

Women were practically powerless in legal matters, had no control over their dowries in marriage, and could not have custody over minor children after their husband's death, among other things. In his preaching, Muhammad took pains to change this situation and the attitude that lay behind it. In this way he was an innovator, reacting against a tradition that he believed to be ill founded. He imposed an absolute limit of four wives *per man,* although he made no restrictions on the number of a man's concubines. If additional wives could not be supported equally, they were not permitted. Although Muhammad denied that women were equal to men, he made it clear that women were not mere servants of men; that they had some inherent rights as persons, wives, and mothers; and that their honor and physical welfare needed protection by the men around them. The status of women in early Muslim teaching was relatively elevated. It might actually have been higher and more firmly recognized than the status accorded to women in the medieval West as well as in rural southern and eastern Asia.

THE JIHAD

One of the unique aspects of Islam is the jihad, the effort or war for the establishment of God's law on Earth. Allah enjoined Muslims to fight against unbelief, both internal and external. The word *jihad* derives from the Arabic term *jahada,* which means "to strive," to exert oneself to eradicate disbelief. Disbelief can arise within oneself in the form of doubt, as well as in others. God commands the believer always to strive against doubt or the outright rejection of Him, so taking part in a jihad is a way of fighting Satan. To take up the Sword of God (*Sayf Allah*) is the highest honor for a good Muslim. Dying in such an effort, whether through eradicating internal doubts or through external holy war, is a way of fulfilling one of God's commandments, so it assures one of a heavenly reward.

Aside from the salvation of one's soul, what was the earthly appeal of the jihad? It seems to have been based on several aspects of Arabic culture. The desert Bedouins were already a warlike people, accustomed to continual violence in the struggle for water and pasture. Much evidence also indicates that they faced an economic crisis at the time of Muhammad—namely, a severe overpopulation problem that overwhelmed the available sparse resources. Under such conditions, many people were willing to risk their lives for the possibility of a better future. It is likely that many of those who participated in the early conquests saw Muhammad as a successful war leader as much or as well as a religious prophet.

Once the jihad was under way, another factor favored its success: exhaustion and division among Islamic opponents.

PATTERNS OF BELIEF

The Qur'an

The Qur'an is not only the bible of the Muslims but also an elaborate and poetic code of daily conduct. It is a compilation, like the Christian and Jewish Bibles, formed in the memory of Muhammad's associates of his words and instructions after the Prophet's death. As the literal word of God, the holy book is held by all devout Muslims to be the unfailing source of wisdom, which, if adapted to the changing realities of daily life, can be as usable in the twenty-first century as it was in the seventh when it was written. Many of its verses have formed the basis of law in the Muslim countries. Now translated into every major language, the Qur'an was long available only in Arabic, one of the world's most poetic and subtle languages. This circumstance both helped and hindered the religion's eventual spread. Some excerpts follow:

The Jihad

Fight in the cause of God against those who fight against you, but do not begin hostilities. Surely, God loves not the aggressors. Once they start the fighting, kill them wherever you meet them, and drive them out from where they have driven you out; for aggression is more heinous than killing. But fight them until all aggression ceases and religion is professed for the pleasure of God alone. If they desist, then be mindful that no retaliation is permissible except against the aggressors.

Do not account those who are slain in the cause of God as dead. Indeed, they are living in the presence of their Lord and are provided for. They are jubilant . . . and rejoice for those who have not yet joined them. . . . They rejoice at the favor of God and His bounty, and at the realisation that God suffers not the reward of the faithful to be lost.

Piety and Charity

There is no piety in turning your faces toward the east or the west, but he is pious who believeth in God, and the last day, and the angels, and the scriptures, and the prophets; who for the love of God disburses his wealth to his kindred, and to the orphans, and the needy, and the wayfarer, and those who ask, and for ransoming. . . .

They who expend their wealth for the cause of God, and never follow what they have laid out with reproaches or harm, shall have their reward with the Lord; no fear shall come upon them, neither shall they be put to grief.

A kind speech and forgiveness is better than alms followed by injury. Give to the orphans their property; substitute not worthless things of your own for their valuable ones, and devour not their property after adding it to your own, for this is a great crime.

Society and Economy

Ye may divorce your wives twice. Keep them honorably, or put them away, with kindness. But it is not allowed you to appropriate to yourselves any of what you have once given them. . . . No blame shall attach to either of you for what the wife shall herself give for her redemption [from the marriage bond].

Men are superior to women on account of the qualities with which God hath gifted the one above the other, and on account of the outlay they make from their substance for them. Virtuous women are obedient, careful, during the husband's absence, because God hath of them been careful. But chide those for whose obstinacy you have cause to dread; remove them into beds apart, and whip them. But if they are obedient to you, then seek not occasion to abuse them.

Christians and Jews

Verily, they who believe and who follow the Jewish religion, and the Christians . . . whoever of these believeth in God and the Last Day, and does that which is right shall have their reward with the Lord. Fear shall not come upon them, neither shall they be grieved.

We believe in God and what has been sent down to us, and what was sent down to Abraham, Ishmael, Isaac, Jacob and their descendants, and what was given Moses, Jesus and the prophets by their Lord. We do not differentiate between them, and are committed to live at peace with Him.

▶ Analyze and Interpret

Does some of this excerpt remind you of the Laws of Manu? What similarities are most prominent? Note the fine line walked by the Qur'an between self-defense and aggressive war. What in the background of the Bedouin might have made this close distinction necessary and natural?

Source: From T. B. Irving, trans., *The Quran: Selections* (n.p.: Islamic Foundation, 1980).

You can read more of the Qur'an at the *Wadsworth World History Resource Center.*

THE KA'BA IN MECCA. In this huge mosque courtyard assemble hundreds of thousands of worshipers during the Muslim holy days each year. The Ka'ba is the cubicle of stone in the center. It contains a piece of black meteorite worshipped by the Arabs before their conversion to Islam. During Muhammad's lifetime, it became the symbol of God's relationship to humanity and a symbol of Islamic unity.

Mecca, Saudi Arabia/Bildarchiv Steffans/ The Bridgeman Art Library

Both of the major opponents, the Byzantine Greeks in Constantinople and the Persians, had been fighting each other fiercely for the previous generation and were mutually exhausted. As a result, by 641, only nine years after the death of the Prophet, all of the huge Persian Empire had fallen to Arab armies, and much of the Byzantine territory in Asia (present-day Syria, Lebanon, and Turkey) had been taken as well (see Map 13.1). In place after place, the defenders of the Byzantine provinces put up only halfhearted resistance or none at all, as in Damascus. The religious differences within Christianity had become so acute in these lands that several sects of Christians preferred surrender to the Muslims to continuing to live under what they regarded as a high-handed, wrong-thinking emperor and his bishops. This was true not only in Syrian Damascus but also in several Christian centers in North Africa and Egypt, which were in religious revolt against the church leaders in Constantinople and Rome.

THE CALIPHATE

The nature of Muslim leadership changed markedly from epoch to epoch in the 600 years between the founding of Islam in Arabia and 1258 CE, when it passed from Arabic to Turco-Mongolian hands. While he had remained alive, Muhammad had been seen as a direct link to God for his little community. The ***Umma*** (OO-mah), the Muslim community that he had founded, was unique in Arabia inasmuch as it was held together by belief and acted under the command of God, rather than being united by blood ties, as the clans and tribes had been. God took an interest in everything a Muslim did. There was no division between religious and secular affairs. Therefore, as God's mouthpiece and as the last of God's prophets, Muhammad was both a religious and a temporal ruler. His sudden death in 632 after a short illness, therefore, caused a crisis of leadership that has never been resolved to the satisfaction of all his followers to this day.

The First Period, 632–661

Muhammad's unexpected death necessitated choosing another leader if the Muslim community was going to avoid falling apart. His closest followers at Medina argued over this choice, some believing the leadership should fall to a close family member, in particular his cousin and son-in-law, Ali, others thinking that it should be the "best qualified," the person who was closest to the Prophet and who best represented his teachings. They decided on Abu Bakr (AH-boo BAH-ker), Muhammad's closest friend, his father-in-law, and one of his first converts. Unsure what Abu Bakr's exact status was, most addressed him simply as *Khalifat ar-Rasul Allah*, Deputy of God's Messenger. Although the title was humble in origin and meaning, the term stuck as **caliph** (kah-LEEF).

Abu Bakr was elected by a committee of his closest associates, as were the next three caliphs. Soon after fighting

Bridgeman Art Library

THE DOME OF THE ROCK. This great edifice, erected by Muslims in Jerusalem in the late seventh century, has been used by three religions as a sacred place of worship. Supposedly Muhammad ascended into heaven from this spot.

a brief war to reunite the Muslims, Abu Bakr (632–634) died and was succeeded by a general, Umar (634–644), who ruled over Islam for ten years. Umar was the real founder of the early Muslim Empire. His Arab armies pushed deep into North Africa, conquering Egypt by 642. At the same time, he invaded Persia and the Byzantine territory in the eastern Mediterranean. By the time of Umar's death in 644, mounted Arab raiders were penetrating as far as western India.

With such rapid expansion, administration of this vast and growing empire had to be done on an ad hoc basis. The system Umar devised was brilliant at first but proved troublesome in the longer term. As the Arab tribesmen poured into one conquered land after another, the caliph created a system of rule called an "Arab Islamic theocracy." It was an Islamic theocracy because, in theory at least, God's commands, as preserved through the Qur'an, provided the principles by which the Caliph and his lieutenants ruled. Ethnically, it was Arab because the caliph kept the conquering Arabs segregated from the vanquished in fortified encampments. To maintain this system, the Caliph pensioned the Arab tribes out of booty taken in battle and from a special poll tax (*jizya*) that was collected from non-Muslim subject peoples.

This stunningly rapid expansion came to a halt because of a civil war in 656 for mastery within the Muslim world, which brought Ali, husband of Fatima and Muhammad's son-in-law, to the fore. Ali was the last "orthodox" caliph for a long time. His assassination by a dissident in 661 marked the end of the first phase of Muslim expansion.

The Umayyad Dynasty, 661–750

The first four caliphs had been elected, but three of the four died by murder. At this point, because the elective system had clearly failed, the system of succession became dynastic, although the elective outer form was preserved. From 661, two dynasties of caliphs came to rule the Islamic world: the Umayyads from 661 to 750, and then the Abbasids from 750 to 1258.

Following the murder of Ali, the governor of Syria, Muawiya (moo-AH-wee-ah), initiated the **Umayyad** (oo-MAY-yad) **Dynasty.** This change from electing the caliph to dynastic succession proved fateful. Ali's supporters continued to believe that he possessed a special spiritual knowledge (*ilm*) that he had inherited from Muhammad's bloodline, and therefore that he had been the rightful caliph. These supporters of Ali came to be known as **Shi'ites** (SHEE-ites), and they formed a significant minority within Islam that continues to the present. They believed that only the lineal descendants of the Prophet through Ali and Muhammad's daughter, Fatima, were qualified to become caliphs, and they looked on the Umayyad dynasty as illegitimate usurpers. Another minority, called **Kharijites** (KAH-rih-jites), rejected the caliphs for another reason. They disallowed any form of dynastic succession, believing that only a Muslim free of all sin was fit to lead. Pointing to the increasingly secular lifestyles of the caliphs, as well as to their greater concerns for the secular aspects of ruling than for religious principles, this group frequently fought against the rule of the majority and of the caliphs.

The supporters of Muawiya and his successors were known as **Sunni** (SOO-nee), and they constituted the large majority (currently, almost 90 percent) of Muslims at all times. They largely acquiesced to the legitimacy of the caliphal dynasties. Primarily out of concern for maintaining the unity of Allah's community of believers, they rejected the politically divisive claims of the radical Kharijites and of the Shi'ites that the family of Muhammad possessed some special enlightenment in spiritual matters. In any case, exactly the opposite situation came about: continual rivalries and battles between Shi'ite, Kharijite, and Sunni were to have decisive effects on the political unity of the Muslim world. Most members of these minorities came to be concentrated in Persia and the Near East, but they had support in many other areas and were always a counterweight to the policies of the Sunni central government. From their ranks came many of the later sects of Islam.

Muawiya proved to be a skillful organizer and statesman. He moved the capital from Medina (where Muhammad had established it) to his native Damascus, where he could be more fully in charge. He made the office of caliph more powerful than it had been before and also laid the foundation for the splendid imperial style that would characterize later caliphs, in great contrast to the austerity and simplicity of the first days. Muawiya made clear the dynastic quality of his rule by forcing the reluctant tribal leaders to accept his son as his successor. From that time on, the caliphs were normally the son or brother of the previous ruler.

The Umayyads continued the advances to east and west, although not quite so brilliantly and rapidly as before. To the east, Arab armies penetrated as far as western China before being checked, and they pushed deep into central Asia (to Tashkent in Uzbekistan). Afghanistan became a Muslim outpost. In the west, the outstanding achievement was the conquest of North Africa between 665 and 742, and of Christian Spain between 711 and 721. At least part of Spain would remain in Muslim hands until the time of Christopher Columbus. The Arab horsemen actually penetrated far beyond the Pyrenees, but they were defeated in 732 at Tours in central France by Charlemagne's predecessor, the Frankish leader Charles Martel, in one of the key battles of European history. This expedition proved to be the high-water mark of Arab Muslim penetration into Europe, and soon afterward they retreated behind the Pyrenees to set up a Spanish caliphate based in the city of Córdoba.

Expansion and time, however, brought unanticipated changes that spelled trouble for the regime. Partly out of religious conviction and, no doubt, partly too as a way of avoiding the poll tax (*jizya*), many non-Muslims started converting to Islam. The administration handled this situation by joining converts to existing Arab tribes as "clients" (*mawali*; ma-WAH-lee). However, they consigned these non-Arab converts to the status of second-class Muslims by requiring that they continue paying the burdensome *jizya*. This was necessary to maintain the pension system, but it caused widespread resentment of the caliphs and the privileged Arabs.

Dispersal of the Muslims during the conquests over a wide empire also fostered religious problems. Trouble began with the third caliph, Uthman. Fearing that diverse versions of the Qur'an were beginning to appear, in 655 the caliph ordered that an official edition be issued. Many accused him of setting the power of the state over religion.

Later Umayyad caliphs also led notoriously secular lifestyles, so many accused them of being indifferent Muslims and failing to provide religious leadership.

In the 740s, rebel armies, consisting largely of *mawali* demanding social and religious equality with Arab Muslims, overthrew the Umayyad dynasty. After a brief period of uncertainty, the Abbasid clan was able to take over as a new dynasty of caliphs. One of their first moves was to transfer the seat of government from unfriendly Damascus to the entirely new city of **Baghdad** in Iraq, which was built for that purpose. Their 500-year reign from the fabled capital of Baghdad was the golden age of Islamic civilization.

The Abbasid Dynasty, 750–1258

The **Abbasid Dynasty** (ah-BAH-sid) of caliphs claimed descent from Abbas, the uncle of Muhammad, and for that reason they initially were more acceptable to the Shi'ite faction than the Umayyads had been. The Abbasids also differed from the Umayyads in another important way. Whereas the Umayyads had favored the Arabs in matters of taxation, social status, and religion, the Abbasids opened up the faith to all comers on an essentially equal basis. Such changes enabled Islam to develop into a true world religion during their long reign. Arab officials attempted to retain their monopoly on important posts in the central and provincial administration. But gradually, Persians, Greeks, Syrians, Berbers from North Africa and the Sahara, Spanish ex-Christians, and many others found their way into the inner circles of Muslim authority and prestige. In every area, experienced officials from the conquered peoples were retained in office, although supervised by Arabs.

Through these non-Arab officials, the Abbasid administration incorporated several foreign models of government. As time passed, and more conquered peoples chose to convert to Islam, other ethnic groups steadily diluted the Arab ruling group. These non-Arab converts to Islam transformed it into a highly cosmopolitan, multiethnic religion and civilization. Like the doctrines of Islam, the community of believers was soon marked by its eclecticism and heterogeneity.

Even with the cement of a common faith, the empire was simply too large and its peoples too diverse to hold together politically and administratively. Within little more than a century of the founding of the Abbasid caliphate, the powers of the central government underwent a gradual but cumulatively severe decline. Many segments of the Islamic world broke away from the political control of Baghdad. Spain became fully independent as the Caliphate of Córdoba. North Africa, Egypt, the eastern regions of Persia, and Afghanistan also freed themselves. But the Muslim faith was strong enough to bind this world together permanently in a religious and cultural sense. With the sole exception of Spain, where the Muslims were always a minority, those areas captured at one time or another by the Islamic forces after 629 remain mostly Muslim today. Those areas reach halfway around the globe, from Morocco to Indonesia.

Conversion to Islam

Contrary to widespread Christian notions, Islam normally did not force conversion. In fact, after the first few years of conquest, the Arab leaders came to realize the disadvantages of mass conversion of the conquered and discouraged it. By the time of the Umayyads, conversion was looked on as a special allowance to deserving non-Muslims, especially those who had something to offer the conquerors in the way of talents, wealth, or domestic and international prestige.

No effort was made to convert the peasants or the urban masses. Life in the villages went on as before, with the peasants paying their rents and taxes or giving their labor to the new lords just as they had to their old rulers. When and if they converted, it was because of the genuine appeal of Islam as a faith, as well as specific local circumstances, rather than from pressure from above. Centuries passed before the peasants of Persia and Turkey accepted Islam. In Syria, Lebanon, and Egypt, whole villages remained loyal to their Christian beliefs during ten centuries of Muslim rule.

Intermarriage between Muslim and practicing non-Muslim was strictly prohibited. This restriction was a result of Qur'anic injunctions that Muslims marry Muslims. Moreover, Muslims had restricted social contact with non-Muslims, although the two groups did mix together in business transactions, administrative work, and even, at times, intellectual and cultural interchange (especially in Spain).

The Muslims did not view all non-Muslims the same way. Instead, they were categorized according to what the Qur'an and Arab tradition taught about their possession of spiritual truth. The Jews and the Christians were considered meritorious because both shared the same basic beliefs in the one God and His prophets (such as Abraham and Jesus of Nazareth), as did Islam. The Zoroastrians were viewed in much the same way. All three were classed as **dhimmis** (THIH-mees), or "Peoples of the Book," and were thought to have risen above what Muslims regarded as the superstitions of their many other subject peoples.

The *dhimmis* were not taxed as severely as pagans were, and they had legal and business rights that were denied to others. Restrictions on the *dhimmis* were generally not severe, and in many places evidence shows that they prospered. They could worship as they pleased, provided they observed limitations placed on public displays of belief and avoided proselytization, and they elected their own community leaders. Their position was normally better than that of Jews or Muslims under contemporary Christian rule, although there were instances of persecution in later centuries.

Everyday Affairs

In the opening centuries of Muslim rule, the Muslims were a minority almost everywhere outside Arabia, so they had to accustom themselves to the habits and manners of their subjects, to some degree. Because the Bedouin pastoralists who formed the backbone of the early Islamic armies had little experience with administrative organization, manufacturing, or commerce and finance, they were willing to allow their more sophisticated subjects considerable leeway in such matters. Thus, Christian, Jewish, or pagan merchants and artisans were generally able to live and work, as they were accustomed to doing, without severe disturbance. They managed routine government and economic affairs not only for themselves but also for the ruling Arabs. This gradually changed as the Bedouins settled into urban life and as converts to Islam became numerous, but in the meantime, the habit of using the conquered "infidels" to perform many of the ordinary tasks of life had become ingrained and was continued.

Similar patterns could be found in finance and administration: the conquered subjects were kept on in the middle and lower levels. Only Muslims could hold important political and military positions, however. The Muslim "aristocracy" maintained an advantage over the neo-Muslim converts as late as the ninth century, but Greek, Syrian, Persian, and other converts found their way into high posts in the central government in Baghdad under the Abbasids. And in the provinces, it was common to encounter neo-Muslims at the highest levels. With the native peoples playing such a large role in public affairs, it is not surprising that economic and administrative institutions came to be an amalgam of Arab and Greek, Persian, or Spanish customs.

Society in the Muslim world formed a definite social pyramid. During the Umayyad period, descendants of the old Bedouin clans were on top, followed by *mawali* converts from other religions. Once the Abbasids took power, this distinction ceased to exist. Below the Muslims came the *dhimmis*, then other non-Muslim freemen, and the slaves at the bottom. All five classes of society had their own rights and duties, and even the slaves had considerable legal protections. Normally, little friction existed between Muslims and non-Muslims, but the non-Muslims were always clearly second-class citizens, below every Muslim in dignity. Different courts of law had jurisdiction over legal disputes, depending on whether Muslims or non-Muslims

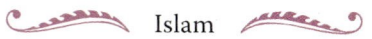

were involved. Non-Muslims were taxed heavily, although, as we have seen, the burden on the *dhimmis* was less than on other non-Muslims.

As this discussion suggests, religion was truly the decisive factor in Muslim society. Like Christians and Jews, but even more so, good Muslims believed that a person's most essential characteristic was whether he or she adhered to true faith—Islam. The fact that all three faiths—Christianity, Judaism, and Islam—believed in essentially the same patriarchal God was not enough to minimize the differences among them. Rather, in time those differences became magnified.

SUMMARY

THE SWORDS OF the jihad armies propelled the surge of Islam outward from its native Arabia in the seventh century. But the attraction of the last of the Western world's major religions rested finally on its openness to all creeds and colors, its ease of understanding, and its assurance of heaven to those who followed its simple doctrines. The Prophet Muhammad saw himself as completing the works of Abraham and Jesus, as the final messenger of the one omnipotent God. Divisions among the Christians of the Near East assisted his work, as did economic rewards to the Muslim conquerors and the momentary exhaustion of both Byzantium and Persia. Already by the mid-600s, the new faith had reached Egypt and the borders of Hindustan. By the early 700s, the fall of Spain had given Islam a foothold in Europe. Not only was this the fastest spread of a creed in world history, but Islam would also go on spreading for many years to come.

The caliphs held the political leadership of the faith, at first through the Umayyad dynasty at Damascus, then through the Abbasids at their new capital at Baghdad.

The unity of Islam was split as early as the first Umayyad caliph by the struggle between the Sunni majority and the Kharijite and Shi'ite minorities, the former of which insisted that a strict observance of religious principles mattered most in a caliph and the latter that a blood relationship with Muhammad was essential for the caliphate office.

The upshot of the Muslim explosion out of Arabia was the creation of a new civilization, which would span Iberia and a large part of the Afro-Asian world by the twelfth century and be carried deep into Christian eastern Europe in the fourteenth century. In the next chapter, we will look at the cultural aspects of this civilization in some detail.

▶ Identification Terms

Test your knowledge of this chapter's key concepts by defining the following terms. If you can't recall the meaning of certain terms, refresh your memory by looking up the boldfaced term in the chapter, turning to the Glossary at the end of the book, or working with the flashcards that are available on the *World Civilizations* Companion Website: **academic.cengage.com/adler**

Abbasid Dynasty	*dhimmis*	*jihad*	Shi'ite
Allah	Five Pillars of Islam	*Ka'ba*	Sunni
Baghdad	*hajj*	Kharijites	Umayyad Dynasty
caliph	*Hijra*	Qur'an	*Umma*

▶ Test Your Knowledge

Test your knowledge of this chapter by answering the following questions. Complete answers appear at the end of the book. You may find even more quiz questions in CengageNOW and on the *World Civilizations* Companion Website: **academic.cengage.com/adler**

1. Muhammad's religious awakening came
   a. as a result of a childhood experience.
   b. in his middle years, after a series of visions.
   c. in response to the Christian conquest of Mecca.
   d. after an encounter with a wandering holy man.
   e. after his rejection of the Jewish faith.

2. Muhammad began his mission to reform Arab beliefs because
   a. he was desperate for social prominence.
   b. he could not tolerate the evil behavior of his associates.
   c. the Archangel Gabriel convinced him he was chosen to do so.
   d. he was inspired by the example of the early Christians.
   e. he became angry over the interference of Meccan traders in religious matters.

3. Which of the following is *not* one of the Five Pillars of Islam?
   a. Frequent and regular prayer to Allah
   b. Fasting at prescribed times
   c. Almsgiving
   d. A pilgrimage to Mecca, if one is able
   e. Taking arms against the infidel

4. Which of the following statements about Islamic belief is *false*?
   a. A Last Judgment awaits all.
   b. The faithful will be guided by the Qur'an to salvation.
   c. Mortals must submit to the will of the one all-powerful Lord.
   d. The divinity of Jesus is beyond doubt.
   e. The Qur'an is the inspired word of Allah.

5. The farthest reach of Muslim expansion into western Europe was at
   a. Palermo.
   b. Tours.
   c. Córdoba.
   d. Gibraltar.
   e. the Pyrenees Mountains.

6. The conflicts between Sunni and Shi'ite Muslims centered on the
   a. divinity of Muhammad.
   b. authenticity of Muhammad's visions.

   c. location of the capital of the Islamic state.
   d. importance of blood kinship to Muhammad in choosing his successor.
   e. origin of the Qur'an.

7. The basis of all Muslim political theory is
   a. a person's religion.
   b. the wealth possessed by a given group of citizens.
   c. the social standing of an individual.
   d. the historical evolution of a given social group.
   e. the patriarchal family unit.

8. Which of the following areas had not fallen to Islam by the beginning of the Abbasid dynasty?
   a. Afghanistan
   b. Spain
   c. Iraq
   d. Syria
   e. Italy

9. Until 750, the social prestige and position of the Arab Bedouins
   a. varied according to their wealth.
   b. was sometimes below even that of slaves.
   c. was at the top of the pyramid.
   d. was above that of *dhimmis* but below that of converts.
   e. was lower than that of the *dhimmis.*

10. The *dhimmis* in early Muslim societies were
    a. Christians and Jews who had not converted to Islam.
    b. the merchants.
    c. the original Arabic believers in Islam.
    d. non-Arab converts to Islam.
    e. regarded by the Muslims as still mired in superstition.

Enter *CengageNOW* using the access card that is available with this text. *CengageNOW* will assist you in understanding the content in this chapter with lesson plans generated for your needs and provide you with a connection to the *Wadsworth World History Resource Center* (see description at right for details).

 World History Resource Center

Enter the Resource Center using either your *CengageNOW* access card or your standalone access card for the *Wadsworth World History Resource Center.* Organized by topic, this website includes quizzes; images; over 350 primary source documents; interactive simulations, maps, and timelines; movie explorations; and a wealth of other resources. You can read the following documents, and many more, at the *Wadsworth World History Resource Center:*

Ibn Ishaq, *Life of Muhammad*
The Qur'an

We believe in God and what has been sent down to us, and was sent down to Abraham, Ishmael, Isaac, Jacob, and their descendants, and what was given Moses, Jesus, and the prophets by their Lord.

—The Qur'an

14 MATURE ISLAMIC SOCIETY AND INSTITUTIONS

750	Abbasid caliphate founded in Baghdad
786–809	Harun al-Rashid
1055	Seljuk Turks take power
1258	Mongols plunder Baghdad

THE CALIPHATE

THE FURTHER DEVELOPMENT OF ISLAMIC RELIGIOUS THOUGHT

LITERATURE AND THE NATURAL SCIENCES

THE ARTS IN THE MUSLIM WORLD

MARRIAGE AND THE STATUS OF WOMEN

THE FIRST "WORLD" CIVILIZATION, 632–1500

THE DECLINE OF THE ABBASIDS AND THE COMING OF THE TURKS AND MONGOLS

THE CONSOLIDATION OF ISLAMIC civilization took place during the period from the founding of the Abbasid Dynasty in 750 through the degeneration of that dynasty in the tenth century. In these 200 years, Islam created for its varied adherents a matrix of cultural characteristics that enabled it to survive both political and religious fragmentation, while still expanding eastward into Asia and southward into Africa. In the arts and sciences, the Muslim world now occupied the place once held by the classical Greeks and Romans, whose own accomplishments were largely preserved to a later age through Muslim solicitude.

Challenges to the caliphs' supremacy, not least from the Christian crusades to the Holy Land, temporarily checked the faith's expansion after about 900. A nearly complete breakdown of the Baghdad caliphate ensued in the eleventh and twelfth centuries, before first the all-conquering Mongols from the Central Asian deserts and then the Ottoman Turks took over the leadership of Islam and infused it with new vigor (see Chapters 19 and 24).

Even after all semblance of central governance of the vast empire had been destroyed, a clear unity was still visible in Islamic culture and lifestyle, whether in the Middle East, India, or Spain. Conflicts with other civilizations and cultures (African, Chinese, Hindu, Christian) only sharpened the Muslims' sense of what was proper and necessary for a life that was pleasing to God and rewarding to humans. How well such a sense was converted into actuality varied, of course, from country to country and time to time. But at its height, Islamic civilization was the envy of its Christian neighbors, with achievements in the sciences and arts that could rival even those of the Chinese.

193

THE CALIPHATE

We have seen how the Abbasid clan seized power from the Umayyads and transferred the capital to the new city of Baghdad in the 760s (see Chapter 13). This city quickly became one of the major centers of culture, manufacturing, and trade in the world, as the Abbasids adorned it with every form of art and encouraged its educational establishments with money and personal participation. They also further developed the Umayyad institutions of government. The Abbasid caliphs had come to power on the promise to establish equality among all Muslims, regardless of their ethnicity. More important still, they had promised to provide more religious leadership. The Islamic community, as it had expanded into a vast empire and as Muslims had become widely scattered, started to show signs of sectarian division. Much of this centered on questions regarding the applicability of religion in people's everyday lives. With the sponsorship of the caliphs, religious scholars called the *ulama* (oo-lah-MAH) operated to gradually bring into existence the *Sharia* (shah-REE-yah), or sacred law, based on the words of the Qur'an and the example, or *Sunna* (SOO-nah), set by the Prophet Muhammad in Muslim living. The Sharia involved far more than religious or doctrinal matters, strictly speaking. In the Muslim view, religion entered into virtually all spheres of what we consider civil and private life, so that the decisions of the ulama and the applications of the Sharia affected almost all aspects of public and private affairs.

Unlike the Western world, the Muslims' sacred book and the Sunna of the Prophet remained the twin bases of all holy law and hence of all administration and government to a very late date. The Qur'an was still the fount of all legal knowledge into modern times, and for some Islamic fundamentalists, it still is (for notable examples, in Afghanistan under the Taliban; in Iran since the revolution of 1979–1980; and in Libya and Saudi Arabia).

In Baghdad, an elaborate, mainly Persian bureaucracy exercised governing powers. The major institutions of the central government were the *diwan,* or state council, and the *qadis* (KAH-dees), or judges who had jurisdiction in all disputes involving a Muslim. A **vizier** (vih-ZEER), a kind of prime minister for the caliphs who had enormous powers, headed this council. Many of the other officials were eunuchs (castrated male slaves), who were thought more likely to be devoted to the government because they could have no family interests of their own. In the provinces, the *emir,* or governor, was the key man. His tax-collecting responsibility was crucial to the well-being of the Baghdad government. Rebellions normally started in the provinces and were led by independent-minded emirs.

The Muslim army in the Abbasid era was international in composition. Many of the soldiers were slaves, taken from all the conquered peoples but especially from the Africans and Egyptians. They were well trained and equipped, and their commanders came to have increasing political power as the caliph became weaker. The Abbasid forces were undoubtedly the most impressive of the era and far overshadowed the Europeans' feudal levies and the Byzantines' professional soldiery. Abbasid raids into Afghanistan and western India established footholds that were gradually expanded by later Muslim regimes.

THE FURTHER DEVELOPMENT OF ISLAMIC RELIGIOUS THOUGHT

By the tenth century, the ulama had succeeded in systematizing the application of the Sharia to all spheres of Muslims' lives. This triumph was so complete that by then the ulama had succeeded in eclipsing even the caliphs as the primary source of authority on religious matters. While the caliphs remained the symbolic heads of the Islamic community, people turned to the ulama for religious guidance and education. Even more critical was the fact that the system and the sources of written law they had developed for seeking God's will in all things was considered to be complete, and therefore closed to further development. Known as the "Closing of the Gates," this closure discouraged all future independent thought and intellectual innovation after that time. From the tenth century on, the practice of religious law became thoroughly conservative, and the ulama exercised almost total control over defining acceptable, orthodox practices in God's eyes.

Equally noteworthy was the burgeoning success of the movements known collectively as Sufism. **Sufis** (SOO-fees) are, generally speaking, the equivalent of Christian and Buddhist mystics; they believe in a direct, personal path to the experience of God's presence. They rely as much on emotional connections to divine truth as on the workings of reason and the revealed word. Although they certainly revere the Qur'an, they do not necessarily see it as the sole path to God. They wish to bring the individual into the state of grace through his or her (Sufis were of both sexes) own commitment to the Divine. Sometimes this search for grace took the form of ecstatic dancing, which continued until the participants fell into a trance. One example was the Turkish Whirling Dervishes of the seventeenth and eighteenth century mentioned in accounts by Western travelers into the Muslim East. Many varieties of Sufism existed, among both Sunni and Shi'ite Muslims, and they were particularly active in mercantile circles. This practice assisted in the spread of the movement to all corners of Islam because of the Sufis' greater tolerance of local customs than most ulama were willing to allow.

Whether ecstatic dervish or reserved intellectual in his study, the relation between the Sufi and the ulama authorities was often strained to the point of mutual

Victoria & Albert Museum, London, UK/The Stapleton Collection/Bridgeman Art Library

WHIRLING DERVISHES. This Persian miniature shows a group of Sufis, or dervishes, the members of popular Muslim religious associations called *tariqas*, which began forming in the century after the death of the great Sufi teacher al-Ghazzali. In this particular tariqa, prolonged dancing was aimed at inducing a trance in which the faithful witnessed God's presence.

condemnation and even bloodshed. An Iranian Sufi, the great philosopher-theologian Abu Hamid Muhammad al-Ghazzali (al-gah-ZAH-lee; 1058–1111), managed to bring together the mystic enthusiasts and the conservative clerics into a fragile but lasting truce, with his profound synthesis of both points of view in the early twelfth century. Known as the "Renewer of Islam" because of his services, al-Ghazzali is one of the most important theologians of Islam. From Ghazzali's time, Sufism became very popular. Soon, other Sufi masters came forward and gathered circles of students and devotees around them. Some of these circles organized into religious associations, or **tariqas** (tah-REE-kahs), most of which were named after the Sufi master on whose teachings they were based. Such tariqas helped spread Islam into parts of Asia and Africa where it previously had only a weak hold at best. (See Evidence of the Past for an example of Sufi poetry.)

LITERATURE AND THE NATURAL SCIENCES

The Arabic language became an important source of unification in the Muslim world, spreading into its every part. Because the sacred book of the Qur'an could be written only in Arabic, every educated Muslim had to learn this language to some degree. The Arabs also came to possess a cheap and easily made writing medium—paper (picked up from the Chinese, as so much medieval technology would be). A paper factory was operating in Baghdad as early as 793, providing a great stimulus to making books and circulating ideas.

The university was also a Muslim creation. The world's oldest still-functioning higher educational institution is the Azhar Mosque University in Cairo, which was founded in the ninth century by Shi'ite ulama as a place of study in the religious sciences. Long before the names of Aristotle and Plato were known in the Christian West, the Muslims of the Middle East had recognized the value of classical Greek learning and acted to preserve and expand it. Harun al-Rashid, one of the greatest of the Baghdad caliphs in the early ninth century, and his successors created a special

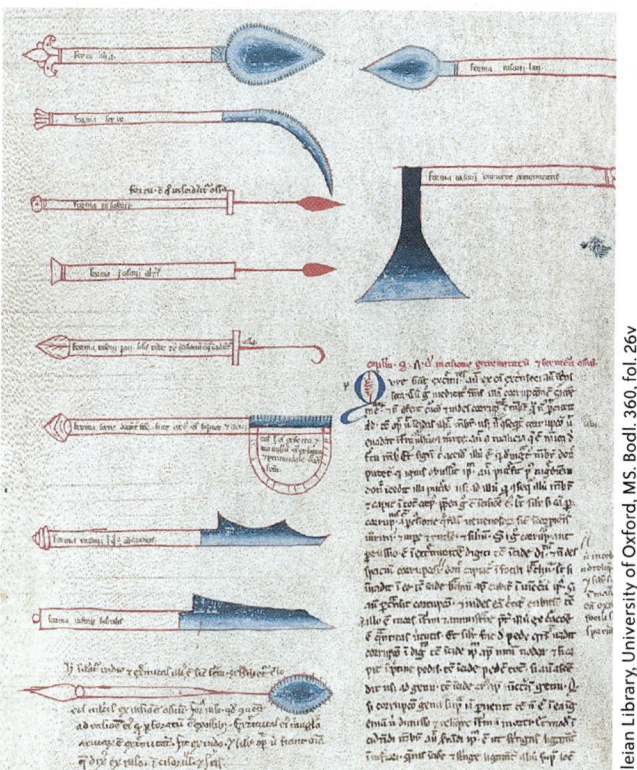

Bodleian Library, University of Oxford, MS. Bodl. 360, fol. 26v

SURGICAL INSTRUMENTS. Islamic medicine was so far ahead of medieval European practice that, despite the enmity between Christianity and Islam, Arab doctors were frequently invited to spend time teaching in Europe. The Muslim practitioners were particularly adept at eye surgery and amputations.

EVIDENCE OF THE PAST

The Sufi Verses of Al-Rumi

Following al-Ghazzali's death, Sufism spread rapidly throughout the Islamic world. Many Sufis organized into associations, called *tariqas*, which functioned much like clubs or secret societies. Each of these had its own unique "way" (tariqa) of achieving spiritual ecstasy as well as its own body of religious literature and lore, some of which took the form of music and spoken poetry. Here is an example of such Sufi poetry by the great thirteenth-century Persian mystic, Jalal al-Din al-Rumi:

> No joy have I found in the two worlds apart from thee, Beloved
> Many wonders have I seen: I have not seen a wonder like thee.
> They say that blazing fire is the infidel's portion:
> I have seen none, . . . excluded from thy fire.
> Often I have laid the spiritual ear at the window of the heart:
> Of a sudden didst thou lavish grace upon thy servant:
> I saw no cause for it save thy infinite kindness.
> O chosen Cup-bearer, O apple of mine eyes, the like of thee
> Ne'er appeared in Persia, nor in Arabia have I found it.
> Pour out wine till I become a wanderer from myself;
> For in selfhood and existence I have felt only fatigue.

> O thou who art milk and sugar, O thou who art sun and moon,
> O thou who art mother and father, I have known no kin but thee.
> O indestructible Love, O divine Minstrel,
> Thou art both stay and refuge: a name equal to thee I have not found.
> We are pieces of steel, and thy love is the magnet:
> Thou art the source of all aspiration, in myself I have seen none.
> Silence, O brother! Put learning and culture away:
> Till Thou namedst culture, I knew no culture but Thee.

▶ Analyze and Interpret

Rumi uses the language of a suitor or lover: Whom is he actually addressing? Why does he choose this kind of language? Is it appropriate? Throughout the poem, he disavows all sense of earthly pleasure and even of himself. Why do you suppose he does this? What does it suggest about the method used by the religious mystic to achieve an ecstatic experience of God?

Source: Taken from *Selected Poems from the Diwani Shamsi Tabriz* (by Rumi), trans. by R. A. Nicholson (London: Cambridge University Press, 1898). Quoted in William H. McNeill and Marilyn R. Waldman, *The Islamic World* (Chicago: University of Chicago Press, 1973), pp. 243–244.

---

bureau, called the "House of Wisdom," whose highest purpose was translating the great works of medicine, science, mathematics, astrology, alchemy, logic, and metaphysics from Greek and Sanskrit into Arabic. There, too, students of philosophy and the various sciences congregated and debated the writings of the Greek and Indian masters. The Muslims especially revered Aristotle, whom they regarded as the greatest teacher of all time. They passed on this esteem for Aristotle to their Christian subjects in Spain, who in turn transmitted it to the rest of Christian Europe in the twelfth and thirteenth centuries.

In the sciences, the Muslim contribution was selective but important. Unlike the Classical and Hellenistic civilizations, the contributions brought forth by Muslim scientists were often of substantial practical application. In the medical sciences, the four centuries between 800 and 1200 saw the world of Islam considerably ahead of any Western civilization. Pharmacology, physiology,

anatomy, and, above all, ophthalmology and optical science were special strong points. In geography, Arabic and Persian writers and travelers were responsible for much new information about the known and the hitherto unknown world. In astronomy and astrology, the Muslims built on and expanded the traditions of careful observation they had inherited in the Near East. In mathematics they developed and rationalized the ancient Hindu system of numbers to make the Arabic numbers that are still in universal use. They also introduced the concepts of algebra and the decimal system to the West. One of the most important figures in Muslim science was Ibn Sina (Avicenna), a physician and scientist of great importance to medieval Europe and author of the famous handbook on clinical practice *The Canon of Medicine.* Other important individuals include the philosophers al-Kindi and Ibn Rushd (Averroës), and al-Zahrawi, a surgeon and medical innovator.

THE ARTS IN THE MUSLIM WORLD

The Abbasid era was witness to an extraordinary flourishing of many of the arts—plastic, literary, and poetic. Some of them employed novel forms; others carried forth established tradition. Because the Qur'an prohibited the lifelike representation of the human figure as blasphemous to the creator, Allah, the Muslims had to turn to other motifs and developed an intricate, geometrically based format for the visual arts. The motifs of their painting, ceramics, mosaics, and inlay work—in all of which the Muslim world excelled—were based on garlands, plants, or geometric figures such as triangles, diamonds, and parallelograms. Because of the religious prohibition, the Muslims produced no sculpture beyond miniatures and, for a long time, no portrait painting.

In architecture, the Muslims, especially the Persians, developed a great deal of lastingly beautiful forms and executed them with great skill. The "most beautiful building in the world," the Taj Mahal in India, is a thoroughly Muslim creation (see the photo in Chapter 24). The use of reflecting pools and landscapes of great precision and intricate design was common in parks and public buildings. Great wealth and a love of luxury were earmarks of rulers throughout the world of Islam, and it was considered a mark of gentility and good manners for a ruler to spend lavishly on public and private adornments.

Calligraphy was a special strength of the Muslims, whose Arabic script is the product of aesthetic demands as much as the desire to communicate. As in ancient China, a beautiful script was considered to be as much a part of good breeding as beautiful clothing. Arabic lettering was incorporated into almost every form of art, generally as quotations from the Qur'an.

In literature, the Persian language replaced Arabic as the preferred instrument of expression. The epic *Shah-Nama*, a prodigious collection of tales and anecdotes from the great poet Firdawsi, attempts to sum up Persia's history from the origins. Written in the early eleventh century, it is far better known and revered in the Muslim East than the *Rubaiyat* of Umar Khayyam (see the Patterns of Belief box in Chapter 24). Arabs developed storytelling to a high art and are generally credited with the invention of fiction—that is, stories told solely to entertain. The most famous book of stories in the history of the world is **The 1001 Nights** (also called **The Arabian Nights**), which was supposedly created by a courtier at the court of Harun al-Rashid. Poetry was also a strongly cultivated and popular literary art form, especially among the Persian Muslims.

The Metropolitan Museum of Art, Rogers Fund, 1942 (42.63) Photograph, all rights reserved, The Metropolitan Museum of Art

DECORATIVE TILES. These magnificent tiled spires are part of the shrine to Fatima, the daughter of Muhammad, in Qom, Iran.

©Mark Shenley/Alamy

ARABIC CALLIGRAPHY. Only the Oriental scripts rival the beauty of written Arabic. Several different styles evolved in different places and times, quite as distinct as the various alphabets of the Western world. Here is an eleventh-century Persian script.

MARRIAGE AND THE STATUS OF WOMEN

How did women fit into the social scheme of the Muslim world? The Qur'an openly states that men are superior to women and grants men the right to rule over them. On the other hand, the Qur'an also accorded women many protections from male abuse—far more than in pre-Islamic Arab society. How many of these beliefs were actually put into practice is difficult to know. As a generalization, the relatively elevated status of women in the early Islamic period appears to have undergone some decline in later centuries, as a result of expansion and the process of absorption of other cultures into Islam. Veiling and the seclusion of women, for example, were Indian practices in origin. Slave women were allowed more freedom than were the freeborn, but only because of and as a sign of their inferior position. Many were concubines.

The Qur'an allows but does not encourage a man to marry up to four wives if he can maintain them properly. If additional wives cannot be supported properly, they are neither expected nor permitted. The marriages may be either serial or simultaneous. There is no limit on the number of concubines he can have. In practice, though, few Muslims had as many as four wives, and fewer still could afford concubines. The children of a concubine, if acknowledged by the father, were provided for in law and custom equally with those of a legal wife.

Many households kept at least one slave (sometimes the concubine). Slavery was common but usually not harsh.

TOWNSCAPE OF GRANADA. This striking view of one of the strongholds of the Moors (Muslims of Spain, from *moro*, "dark") shows the remnants of the medieval walls and the castle sitting on its hill below the high mountains of southern Spain.

Ken Welsh/Bridgeman Art Library

Most slaves worked in the household or shop, not in the fields or mines. It was common for slaves to be freed at any time for good behavior or because the owner wished to ensure Allah's blessing. Most people fell into slavery for the usual reasons: debts, wars, and bad luck. Muslims were not supposed to enslave other members of their faith, but this rule seems to have been frequently ignored or rationalized.

In theory at least, the household was ruled by the man, whose foremost duty toward it and himself was to maintain honor. Muslim society was dominated by honor

SOCIETY AND ECONOMY

Care of the Ill: Egypt in the Thirteenth Century

In the mid-thirteenth century, the Marmaluke governor of Egypt decided to ensure his soul's ascent to paradise by leaving a generous bequest to his subjects. In accord with imprecations frequently encountered in the pages of the Qur'an, the Emir Mansur ordained in his *waqf*, or testamentary gift, that a new hospital should be founded. It would contain not only a mosque but also a chapel for the Christian Copts; there would be separate buildings for male and female, as well as separate wards for several different diseases. There would be a library for the doctors and patients, and a pharmacy on premises.

The Mansur foundation would minister to as many as 8,000 people simultaneously, and the waqf stated that

> the hospital shall keep all patients, men and women, until they are completely recovered. All costs are to be borne by

the hospital, whether the people come from afar or near, whether they are residents or foreigners, strong or weak, low or high, rich or poor, employed or unemployed, blind or sighted, physically or mentally ill, learned or illiterate. There are no conditions or consideration of payment; none is objected to even indirectly, for non-payment. The entire service is through the magnificence of Allah, the generous one.

Mansur's plan was put into effect at his death, and the hospital's lineal descendant exists today in Cairo.

▶ Analyze and Interpret

Why do you suppose a person would make such a bequest? From what you know about the Qur'an, what seems to have been the attitude of Muhammad toward the destitute? How does this belief compare with the attitudes of Christians and Jews?

and shame, and such notions often were tied up in social perceptions of how the women of a particular household behaved. Consequently, in most upper-class households, women's status was restricted the most. Here, women of reproductive age and children were restricted to the harem, the private areas of the house where they were kept in hiding (called **purdah**) from the prying eyes of visitors and strangers. Visiting other women outside the home was permitted, although it was usually restricted to the evening and nighttime hours.

In practice, however, women's status was not always as limited as Islamic law and custom demanded. Although such rules of honor and behavior were common in well-to-do households in the Islamic heartlands, among the lower echelons of society, women often enjoyed considerably greater personal freedom. The same held true for Muslim women who lived in many parts of Asia and Africa. Sheer economic necessity, for example, usually made observing the rules of purdah impossible. Women often were occupied outside their households, fully participating in many breadwinning activities, as were male members of their homes and communities. Moreover, local traditions frequently overrode written law. Islamic "orthodoxy" made more allowance for local social traditions than called for by the written legal codes. Ample recent scholarship has shown that women in many Islamic societies exercised powers within the private sphere that sometimes exceeded those of male members. Houses, for example, sometimes actually belonged to the female members of a Muslim society, rather than to the males. Where divorces occurred, these women were left in possession of the house and the marriage goods, often ruling them as powerful matriarchs. Many such examples exist and deserve further exploration by interested students of history.

THE FIRST "WORLD" CIVILIZATION, 632–1500

Islamic civilization flourished most brilliantly between about 900 and about 1200. At its height, Islam was the most lavish and innovative civilization of the world, rivaled only by China, with which it had extensive commercial and some intellectual contacts. Innovations in thought and culture turned Islam into a world religion, but trade provided the opportunities for conversion and the expansion of the Muslim world in this era. The Qur'anic exhortation to "honor the honest merchant" meant that commerce and manufacturing held places of honor in the world of Islam that was rivaled only among (Mahayana) Buddhists and some Hindus castes. The Muslim faithful saw nothing wrong in getting rich. In contrast to Christians, they considered a wealthy man to be the recipient of God's blessings for a good life. The rich had an obligation to share their wealth with the poor, however. Most schools, dormitories, hospitals, orphanages, and the like in Muslim areas are to this day the result of private donations and foundations, the **waqf**, which are commonly included in Muslim wills. (See Society and Economy.)

The Islamic world at this time extended from Spain to China, and Muslim traders were found on every known continent and sea (see Map 14.1). Between them, Muslims and Hindus nearly reduced the trade of the Indian Ocean to a monopoly, and Muslims exercised almost equal control over the Asian land routes. Imperial China and the Islamic West were the greatest producers and consumers of wealth in the World, and the Indian Ocean and Silk Road routes were the links that tied these two great zones of prosperity together. Manufactured goods, principally silks, porcelains, carpets, textiles, gold coins, and metal wares, were transported in ships or by camels and mules. Southeast Asia and India added beads, textiles, and high-value goods like pepper and spices. Africa occupied an important, although somewhat subordinate rank in this network, provisioning the great markets of Asia with slaves, gold, leather goods, and raw materials like animal byproducts, cowry shells, timber, and foodstuffs. Of greater significance was the movement of people, technologies, and ideas throughout this vast commercial domain.

Islam provided a precise place for every person in its social scheme without severely limiting freedom of movement. Believers could move throughout this network without hindrance all around a huge belt of settlements on either side of the equator, from Spain to the Philippines. Travelers could journey to distant lands, secure in the knowledge that they would be welcomed by their co-religionists and would find the same laws and religious values, the same literary language, and the same conceptions of justice and truth that they had known at home. The Arabic language provided a common medium that facilitated the flow of trade, ideas, and customs. Wherever they were, all Muslims knew they were members of a great community, the Muslim Umma.

The cities of this world were splendid and varied. Córdoba and Granada were cities of perhaps a half million people in the tenth century; their ruling class was Muslim, from the North African Berber people, but their inhabitants included many Jews and Christians as well. Anything produced in the East or West could be purchased in the markets of Córdoba. The same was true of Baghdad, which had an even larger population and featured the most lavish imperial court of all under caliph Harun al-Rashid and his ninth-century successors. The annual pilgrimage to Mecca drew Muslims from every part of this Old World community, and again provided a locale where, despite differences in local culture, Muslims could rediscover the common heritage that bound them together over the vast distances that separated their homelands.

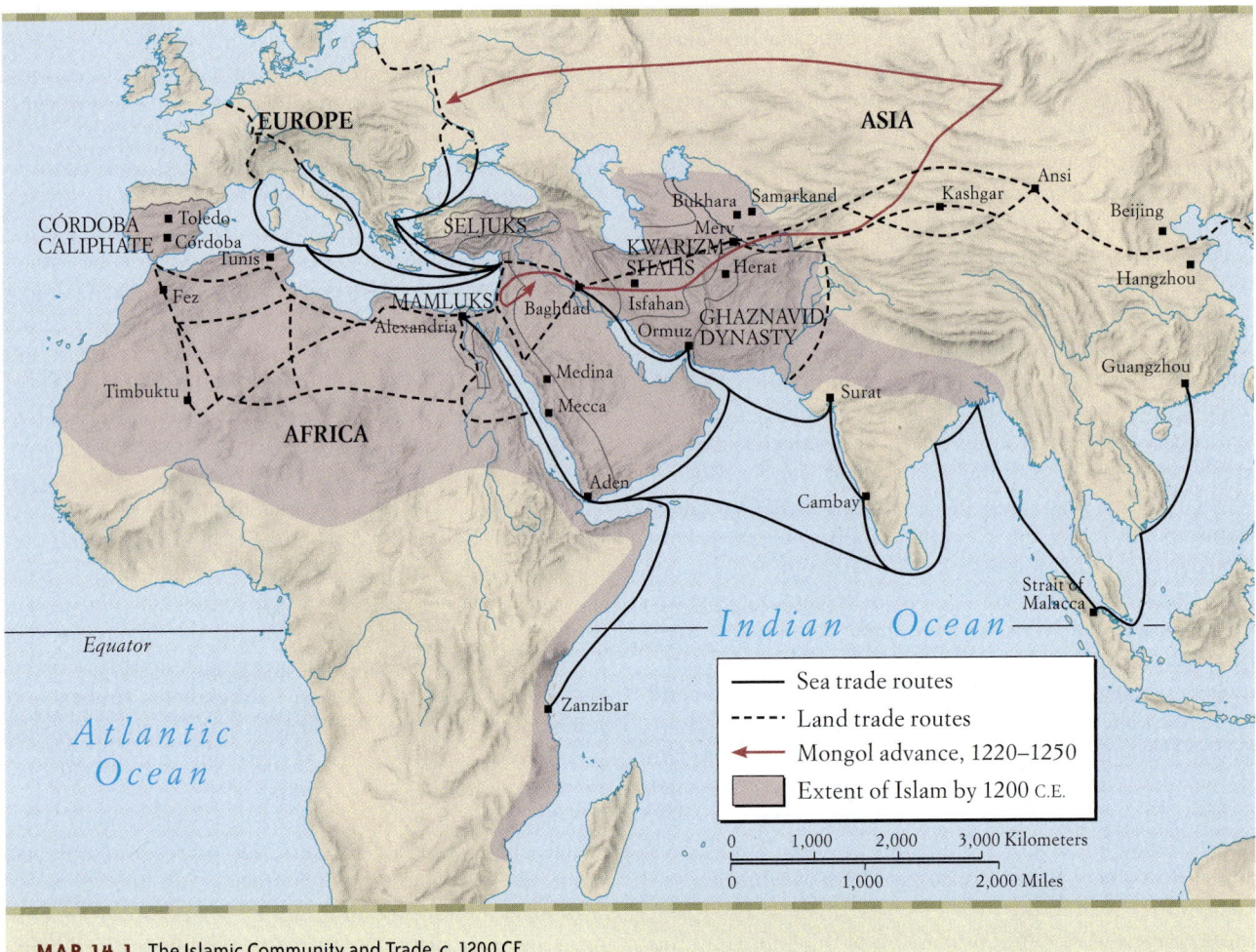

MAP 14.1 The Islamic Community and Trade, *c.* 1200 CE

In this period, the Islamic community extended from the Atlantic to Southeast Asia. By about 1200, the Baghdad caliph's hold on territories beyond Arabia and Iraq was minimal, if it existed at all. Persia and Egypt, as well as Spain and Afghanistan, were autonomous under their own shahs and caliphs. African Muslims had never had direct contact with Baghdad.

MAP QUESTION
What features of geography favored the spread of Islam over such a vast region?

THE DECLINE OF THE ABBASIDS AND THE COMING OF THE TURKS AND MONGOLS

Despite all of their efforts, the Abbasids were unable to restore the political unity of the empire they had taken over in 750. Even great caliphs such as Harun al-Rashid, who was well known in the West, could not force the Spaniards and the North African emirates to submit to their rule. Gradually, during the 800s, almost all of the African and Arabian possessions broke away and became at least semi-independent, leaving the Abbasids in control of only the Middle East. More and more, they came to depend on tough Turkish tribesmen, most of whom had converted to Islam, for their protection against rebellion.

It was inevitable that, as time passed and the caliphs became ever more dissolute, these tribesmen would turn on their weak masters and turn them into pawns.

In the mid-1000s, a new group of Turks, known as **Seljuks**, surged out of Afghanistan into Iran and Iraq. In 1055, they entered Baghdad as victors. Keeping the Abbasid ruler on as a figurehead, the Seljuks took over the government for about a century, until they, too, fell prey to internal rivalries. The central government ceased to exist, and the Middle East became a series of large and small Muslim principalities, fighting one another for commercial and territorial advantage.

Into this disintegrated empire exploded a totally new force out of the East: Chinghis Khan and the **Mongols**. Chinghis started out as a minor tribal leader of the primitive Mongols, who inhabited the semi-desert steppes of

northern Central Asia as nomadic horse and sheep breeders. In the late twelfth century, he was able to put together a series of victories over his rivals and set himself up as lord of his people. Leading an army of fearsome horsemen in a great campaign, he managed to conquer most of Central Asia and the Middle East before his death in the early 1200s.

Chinghis's immediate successor as Great Khan (the title means "lord") was victorious over the Russians and ravaged about half of Europe before retiring in the 1230s. But a few years later, the Mongols felt ready to settle accounts with the Seljuks and other claimants to the Baghdad throne. They took Baghdad in a violent assault followed by considerable slaughter and rape—most estimates say that some 80,000 people were killed. In this debacle, the Abbasid caliphate of Baghdad finally came to an end in 1258 and was replaced by the Mongol Khanate of Central Asia. The Mongols' story continues in Chapter 19.

SUMMARY

MUSLIM CIVILIZATION WAS an amalgam of the many civilizations that had preceded it and its own legal and cultural innovations. It was eclectic, taking from any forebear anything that seemed valuable or useful, then adapting it to satisfy the spiritual needs of Muslims. In the opening centuries, the Arabs who had founded it by military conquest dominated the civilization, but it gradually opened up to all who professed the true faith of the Prophet and worshiped the one god, Allah. Much of the territory the Arabs conquered already had seen previous great civilizations, with well-developed religions. During the first century and a half of conquest, the invading Arabs contented themselves with establishing a minority of rulers and traders and gradually intermarrying with the peoples they conquered. It would be a mistake to over-emphasize force and conquest as the principal causes for the spread of Islam; the record suggests that religious minorities were tolerated and that by the eleventh century most non-Arabs had converted to Islam of their own, free will. Based on the easy-to-understand principles of an all-embracing religious faith, Muslim civilization was a world into which many streams flowed to comprise a vast new sea in which many traditions were tolerated, helping it to become the first "world" civilization.

▶ Identification Terms

Test your knowledge of this chapter's key concepts by defining the following terms. If you can't recall the meaning of certain terms, refresh your memory by looking up the boldfaced term in the chapter, turning to the Glossary at the end of the book, or working with the flashcards that are available on the *World Civilizations* Companion Website: **academic.cengage.com/adler**

Arabian Nights, The	*purdah*	Sufis	*ulama*
(The 1001 Nights)	Seljuks	*Sunna*	vizier
Mongols	*Sharia*	*tariqas*	*waqf*

▶ Test Your Knowledge

Test your knowledge of this chapter by answering the following questions. Complete answers appear at the end of the book. You may find even more quiz questions in CengageNOW and on the *World Civilizations* Companion Website: **academic.cengage.com/adler**

1. Which of the following cities was *not* a center of Muslim culture in this era?
   a. Cairo
   b. Constantinople
   c. Córdoba
   d. Baghdad
   e. Granada

2. Sufism is the Islamic version of the intellectual phenomenon known in the West as
   a. communism.
   b. mysticism.
   c. individualism.
   d. feminism.
   e. agnosticism.

3. The common Muslim attitude toward trade and mercantile activity was
   a. that they were best left to the "infidel."
   b. reluctant acceptance of their necessity.
   c. that nothing was morally or ethically wrong with them.

d. condemnation as temptations to evildoing.

e. that only the upper class was to be involved.

4. Many Muslim scholars especially revered the work of

   a. Gautama Buddha.

   b. Aristotle.

   c. Confucius.

   d. Socrates.

   e. Harun al-Rashid.

5. Muslim knowledge significantly influenced the West in all of these areas except

   a. philosophy.

   b. law.

   c. medicine.

   d. mathematics.

   e. a written language.

6. The major area from which Muslim culture entered Christian Europe was

   a. Greece.

   b. Spain.

   c. Italy.

   d. Russia.

   e. Turkey.

7. *The Canon of Medicine* was the work of

   a. Aristotle.

   b. Harun al-Rashid.

   c. Avicenna.

   d. Averroës.

   e. al-Zahrawi.

8. The application and interpretation of Islamic law was largely in the hands of

   a. the caliphs.

   b. the Sharia.

   c. the ulama.

   d. Sufis.

   e. the viziers.

9. Before the time of al-Ghazzali, Sufism was

   a. organized into associations.

   b. highly unpopular.

   c. encouraged by the caliphs.

   d. discouraged by the ulama.

   e. popular only among slaves.

10. The concept of veiling and secluding women appears to have come from

   a. the Qur'an.

   b. Muhammad.

   c. Afghanistan.

   d. Avicenna.

   e. India.

Enter *CengageNOW* using the access card that is available with this text. *CengageNOW* will assist you in understanding the content in this chapter with lesson plans generated for your needs and provide you with a connection to the *Wadsworth World History Resource Center* (see description at right for details).

 World History Resource Center

Enter the Resource Center using either your *CengageNOW* access card or your standalone access card for the *Wadsworth World History Resource Center*. Organized by topic, this website includes quizzes; images; over 350 primary source documents; interactive simulations, maps, and timelines; movie explorations; and a wealth of other resources. You can read the following documents, and many more, at the *Wadsworth World History Resource Center*:

   Ibn Sina (Avicenna), *On Medicine*

   Harun al-Rashid, *The 1001 Nights*

INDIAN CIVILIZATION IN ITS GOLDEN AGE

The people are numerous and happy. . . . if they want to go, they go; if they want to stay on, they stay. . . . Throughout the whole country the people do not kill any living creature.

—Fa Xian

THE GUPTA DYNASTY
Economic and Cultural Progress

POLITICAL FRAGMENTATION: SOUTH AND NORTH
South: Hinduism and Buddhism ◆ North: Islam Comes to India

HINDU DOCTRINES IN THE CLASSICAL AGE

DEVELOPMENT OF THE CASTE SYSTEM

SOCIAL CUSTOMS
Sexuality

INDIA AND EAST ASIA

UNDER THE GUPTA DYNASTY of kings (320–480 CE), India experienced a great flourishing of Hindu culture. At about the time that the Roman Empire was weakening, Hindu civilization stabilized. The caste system assured everyone of a definite place in society, and political affairs were in the hands of strong, effective rulers for a century and a half. Vedic Hindu religious belief responded to the challenge of Buddhism and reformed so effectively that it began to supplant Buddhism in the country. Indian merchants and emigrants carried Hindu theology and Sanskrit literature to Southeast Asia, where they merged with native religions and cultures. Long after the political unity under the Guptas ended, India continued to produce scientific advances and technological developments that are still not fully recognized in the West. The invasions of Muslim Turks and others from the northwest redivided India into political fragments, but the essential unity of its Hindu civilization carried on.

THE GUPTA DYNASTY

After the fall of the Mauryan Dynasty in the 200s BCE (see Chapter 5), India reverted to a group of small principalities fighting one another for mastery. This was the usual political situation in India, where one invader after another succeeded in establishing only partial control, usually in the north, while Indian princes controlled the rest.

Not until 320 CE was another powerful native dynasty founded—that of the Gupta kings, who ruled from their base in the valley of the Ganges River on the east side of the subcontinent. They overcame their rivals to eventually create an empire over most of India, which lasted until about 500 when it was destroyed by a combination of internal dissension and external threats. The Gupta Dynasty was the last Indian-led unification of the country until the twentieth century. Long after the dynasty had disappeared, memories of its brilliance remained. As time wore on and India remained divided and subject to foreign invaders, the Guptas and their achievements became the standard by which other rulers were measured.

The Gupta Period is the first in Indian history for which more or less reliable firsthand accounts have survived. The most interesting is that of the Chinese Buddhist monk Fa Xian (fah SHAN), who visited India for a long period around 406 and left a diary of what he saw and did. According to his account, India was a stable society, well ruled by a king who was universally respected because he brought prosperity and order everywhere. Nevertheless, despite such sources, we know relatively little about Gupta India compared with what we know of other world civilizations of this date. Indians did not begin to keep historical records until very late, so, aside from works such as Fa Xian's, the main written materials we have are religious poetry and folklore. Even these sources are sparse, for the tradition of both Hinduism and Buddhism was not literary but oral. What was important was memorized, generation after generation, but inevitably with some changes. It was not written down until much later, and then only in a much-altered version. For this reason historians have few definite records to work with in India until perhaps as late as 1500 and must depend heavily on both archaeology and travelers' reports, such as Fa Xian's.

Economic and Cultural Progress

In this classical age, the overwhelming majority of Indians continued to gain their daily sustenance from farming and herding, perhaps even more so than in other parts of the world. The agrarian villages, not the handful of towns and cities, were the vital center of Indian life. These villages changed little in activity or appearance over the centuries.

In the Gupta Period and for some time thereafter, India remained free from the problems of insufficient land and overpopulation in its rich river basins. The average villager seems to have been a landowner or tenant who worked a small plot that he had inherited and that he would pass on to an oldest son or sons.

In most of the subcontinent, rice was the chief crop, as it had become in most of South Asia. The huge demands this crop imposed on labor determined many aspects of life in the village: the cycle of rice planting, transplanting, and harvesting was the fundamental calendar. Water was crucial for rice growing, and control and distribution of water were the source of constant controversy and in some

cases even wars between the numerous small principalities. In this respect and in its dependence on intensive, irrigation agriculture, India resembled both Mesopotamia and South China.

The arts flourished during the Gupta Period, and several models in architecture and sculpture were developed that remained the standards of beauty for a long time. The greatest of ancient India's playwrights, **Kalidasa** (kah-lee-DAH-sah), wrote a series of works that remain popular today. He was a major contributor to the upsurge of Sanskrit literature at this time. Sanskrit, the language of the Aryans, was now formally adopted as a sacred literary script, but literacy remained exceptional.

The Gupta Period also produced notable achievements in the sciences. Mathematicians worked out the concept of zero, which enabled them to handle large numbers much more easily; zero is closely associated with the decimal system, which was probably also an Indian invention. The "Arabic" numbers that are used universally today also originated in Gupta India, so far as historians can determine. Indian astronomers also made several breakthroughs in explaining eclipses of the moon and in calculating geographic distances.

The medical sciences developed significantly during and after the Gupta Period. Pharmacy, surgery, and diagnosis of internal ills were Indian specialties, and wealthy Muslims from the West often came to Indian doctors for treatment. In this way began the active interchange between the Muslim and Hindu medical men that so profited the Muslims in the period after 850 and was eventually passed on to the backward Europeans.

POLITICAL FRAGMENTATION: SOUTH AND NORTH

After the demise of the Gupta Dynasty, India divided into political-cultural regions: South and North (see Map 15.1). Each of these regions further subdivided into several units ruled by hereditary or aristocratic leaders, but each region shared some common features distinguishing each from the other.

South: Hinduism and Buddhism

Below the Deccan plateau, dark-skinned peoples whose languages came from the Dravidian and Pali families, quite different from those of the North, inhabited the South. The South's political history is almost unknown for several centuries, as it was never brought under direct Gupta rule, and few written records have survived. The invasions that perennially wracked the North had little effect on the South, whose contacts with foreigners were in the nature of peaceful commerce both east and west over the Indian Ocean. From the Gupta Period onward, little

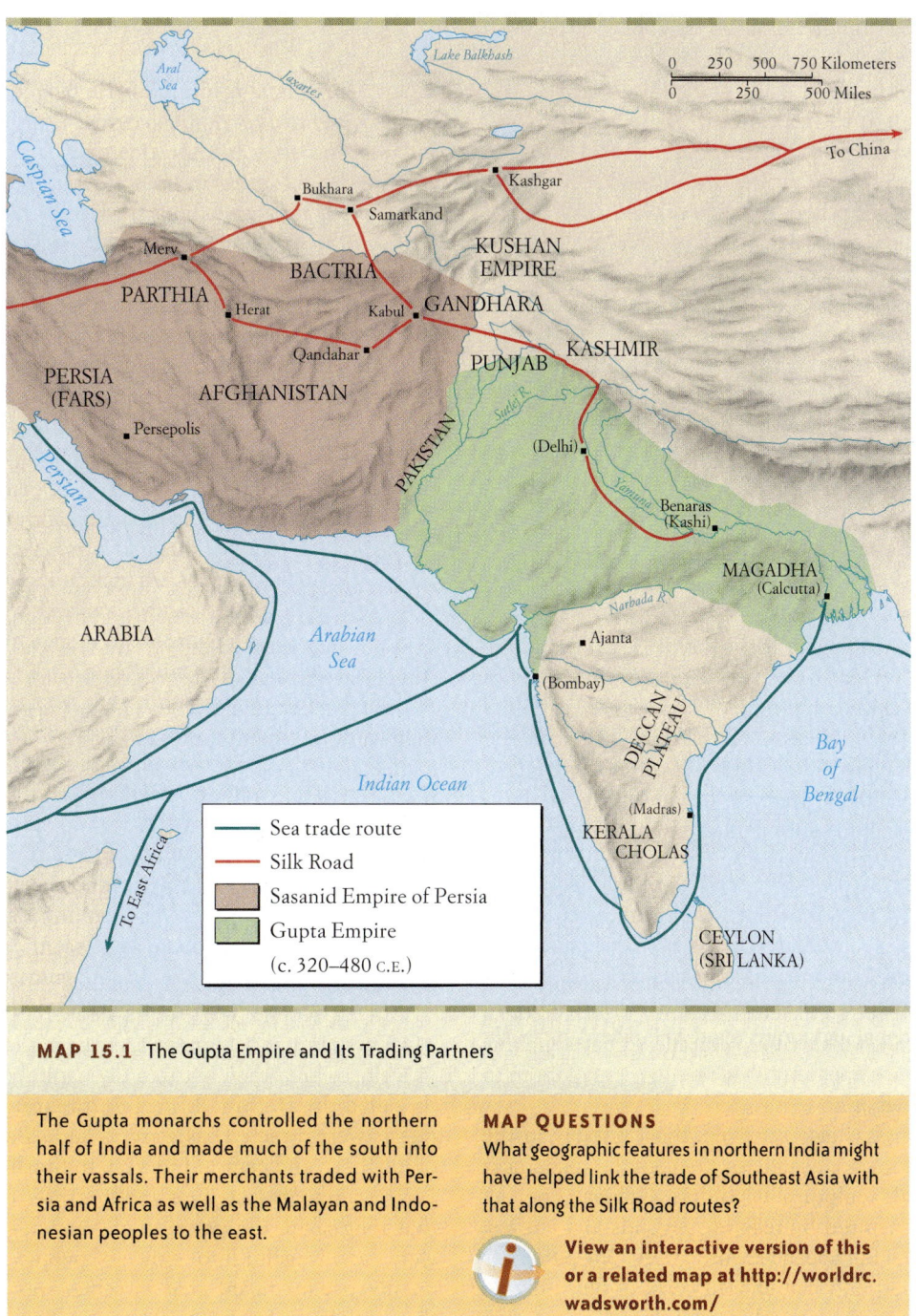

MAP 15.1 The Gupta Empire and Its Trading Partners

The Gupta monarchs controlled the northern half of India and made much of the south into their vassals. Their merchants traded with Persia and Africa as well as the Malayan and Indonesian peoples to the east.

MAP QUESTIONS
What geographic features in northern India might have helped link the trade of Southeast Asia with that along the Silk Road routes?

View an interactive version of this or a related map at http://worldrc. wadsworth.com/

common political bond existed between the two regions for many centuries.

The culture of the South was strongly influenced by varieties of Hinduism and particularly Buddhism, which differed from those of the North. The Theravada (Hinayana) form of Buddhism became dominant in the South, especially in Sri Lanka. Sri Lankan holy men and monasteries were instrumental in the conversion of much of Southeast Asia. The Theravada devotees tended to look down on the relatively flexible doctrines of the Mahayana adherents and rejected many as unworthy or inauthentic.

This attitude contributed to the differentiation of South and North, which was already apparent in linguistic and ethnic spheres. Only the near extinction of Buddhism and the revival of Hinduism throughout the subcontinent allowed Indians to begin the slow development of a modern, politically expressed sense of nationhood.

The South saw a great flourishing of both Buddhist and Hindu architecture and sculpture between 300 and 700 CE.

©John Elk/Stock Boston

STUPA RELIEFS. The candid emphasis on sexual attributes in Hindu sculpture was considered to be justified recognition of a source of human pleasure. Throughout history, most peasant-based civilizations placed great importance on fertility; hence, sexuality was celebrated.

conquerors of the Hindu and Buddhist areas had harassed northwestern India.

The first wave of conquests of the seventh century had carried Islam only as far as northwestern India, reaching the Indus Valley and Multan in 711, and no farther. For another three centuries, Hindu dynasties in central India had proved sufficiently vigorous to discourage further invasion. By the early eleventh century, the military balance of power had shifted dramatically, however. A strong regime had been established in Afghanistan. Its military power rested on highly trained and mobile, professional slave troops of Turkish origins for whom the riches of India beckoned like ripe fruit. Between 1001 and 1030, their warlord, Mahmud al-Ghazni (mah-MOOD al-GHAZ-nee), launched powerful raids into northwestern India for the purpose not of empire building but of seizing booty. In one raid alone against the Temple of Shiva in Gujarat, Mahmud reportedly carried off nearly 3,000 pounds of gold. Yet the effects of these first raids hardly outlived Mahmud's death in 1030, and for another 165 years, Islamic rule languished. By the late 1100s, effective Islamic control had shrunk only to the region of the Punjab.

After a second wave of invasions beginning in 1192, Muslim commanders made their headquarters in the city of Delhi, which then became the capital of what came to be called the **Delhi** (DEL-ee) **Sultanate.** Additional conquests were directed eastward as far as Bengal, until most of northern and central India fell to Muslim arms.

The sultanate lasted for another three centuries, and in that long span, the patterns of Muslim–Hindu relations were cast. Muslim intolerance of people they considered openly pagan meant that violence was the keynote of these relations from the beginning. Successful raids and victories frequently led to excessively high losses of life for Hindus and Buddhists defending their temples, monasteries, and homes. Mahmud's raid on the Temple of Shiva was followed by a slaughter of 50,000 Brahmins, or high-caste Hindus. Similar massacres occurred in Muslim attacks on the last remaining major Buddhist monastery.

Culturally speaking, the contacts between Islamic and Hindu/Buddhist civilizations were important. Beginning as early as the 800s, many Muslim merchants visited the west coast of India. Some of their travel accounts survive and are important sources of Indian history. So many

Both religions encouraged the construction of massive stone *stupas* (STOO-pahs), rounded temples that stood in the midst of extensive complexes for both worship and living quarters. In the interiors stood statues of the gods and goddesses and all types of holy shrines. Sculpture, mainly in stone but also in bronze, seems to have been the art form of choice among Hindus during most of their history. Some of their life-size and larger-than-life-size works have survived to demonstrate the artists' skills. Even more impressive are the many panels and figures that decorate the exteriors of the stupa temples and show us the vigor and life-affirming nature of Hindu art. Much of it was erotic and created a great deal of embarrassment among nineteenth-century British colonial observers. What would have been considered pornographic in a Western context apparently had no such connotations to Indians, either then or now.

Some painting has also survived, most notably in the **Ajanta Caves** (ah-JAHN-tah) in the South. Like most architecture and sculpture of India's Golden Age, all paintings were inspired by religious legends and stories, much as medieval European artworks were. The paintings portray gods good and bad and all sorts of quasi-divine demons taken from the rich religious folklore.

North: Islam Comes to India

We have a good deal more political and military data from the North of India during the 700 years between the fall of the Gupta Dynasty and the erection of the Muslim sultanate in Delhi. The major question facing all North Indian rulers was how to defend themselves against the repeated and ever-fiercer assaults coming from Muslim forces out of Afghanistan on the northwestern frontier. From the eighth century onward, bands of Muslim raiders and would-be

©The Bridgeman Art Library

FRESCOS AT AJANTA CAVES. The Ajanta Caves complex was begun some time in the second century BCE and completed in 478 CE. Originally a Hindu project, it became a Buddhist retreat, and the hundreds of frescos and sculptures that grace it are mainly representative of Buddhist belief. The picture shows a multitude of seated bodhisattvas.

resident Muslims lived in some of the coastal towns as to justify building mosques. In addition to carrying cottons, silks, and fine steel swords from India to the world of Islam, these merchants, traders, and other Muslim visitors took back the Indians' knowledge of algebra and astronomy and other cultural achievements. Indian visitors came to Harun al-Rashid's Baghdad to train Islamic scholars at the request of the caliph. When Harun fell seriously ill, an Indian physician, who was then rewarded with the post of royal physician, cured him.

Muslim conquest brought on the final stage of the long decline of Buddhism in India. Buddhism was a proselytizing religion, like Islam, and the two competitors did not get along well. Whereas the Muslims were able to ignore or come to terms with Hinduism, they attacked Buddhism and its institutions, especially the few remaining monasteries that were the heart of the faith. Already weakened by a revitalized Hinduism, the Buddhist faith was now, in the twelfth century, wiped out in the land where it had originated. Its strong roots on the island of Sri Lanka, as well as in China, Korea, Japan, and much of Southeast Asia, guaranteed its continued existence, however.

HINDU DOCTRINES IN THE CLASSICAL AGE

The doctrines of Hinduism stem from a great mass of unwritten tradition but also from three written sources: the Vedas, the Upanishads, and the *Mahabharata.* The *Vedas* (see Chapter 5) are four lengthy epic poems that were originally brought to India by the Aryans and were then "nativized" over many centuries. Dealing with the relations between the many gods and their human subjects,

they relate tales of the god-heroes who created the Earth and all that lies in it. The most significant is the *Rigveda,* which was written down in relatively modern times; it contains a great deal of information about the Aryan-Indian gods and their relations with humans. The chief deities are Indra and Varuna. Indra, the god of war and revelry, resembles the old Germanic god Thor in several ways. Varuna was the caretaker of proper order in the universe, the first hint of an ethical element in Indian religion. Vedic religion was one of ritual and sacrifice, with priests playing the leading role.

The **Upanishads** (oo-PAH-nih-shads) are a series of long and short philosophical speculations, apparently first produced in the eighth century BCE; gradually, they were expanded to number more than 100 by a body of poems that deal with the human dilemma of being alive on Earth as a partial, incomplete being. The Upanishads are a long step forward from the relatively unsophisticated rituals and anecdotes of the Vedas; with them begins the tradition of involved speculation that became a characteristic of later Hindu thought.

The supreme deities of all Hindus are Brahman, Vishnu, and Shiva. Although individuals may worship many gods, all Hindus believe in the paramount importance of these three. **Brahman** is the world-spirit, the source of all life and all objects in the universe—roughly equivalent to the Christian God the Father, but entirely impersonal. Hindus are generally subdivided into the devotees of either Vishnu or Shiva.

Vishnu is the Preserver, a sort of Christ figure without the ethical teachings. He (or sometimes, she; the Hindu deities are often bisexual) has appeared in nine incarnations thus far in world history, and there will be a tenth. The most popular of all Hindu gods, Vishnu is particularly beloved in the form of Krishna, the instructor and protector of all humans. The last of the Hindu trinity is **Shiva**, the Destroyer and also Creator. Shiva is best appreciated as the god of becoming, lord of both life and death. At times he or she is depicted as a beneficent bringer of joy; at other times he is the ruthless and irresistible destroyer, making way for new life to come.

Some of these beliefs, and particularly the position of the priests who interpreted them—the Brahmins—were challenged by the Buddhists and the Jains (see Chapter 5). By the first century CE, Buddhism and Jainism had attracted

Vedic religion into something different. The *Mahabharata* (mah-hahb-ah-RAH-tah) is the world's longest poem. It contains about 200,000 lines, relating the exploits of the gods and some of their favored heroes on Earth. The most popular part, known by all Hindus, is the *Bhagavad-Gita* (bah-gah-vahd-GEE-tah), a segment in which the god Krishna instructs a warrior, Arjuna, in what is entailed in being a human being who strives to do good and avoid evil to his fellows (see Patterns of Belief). This new Hinduism was capable of arousing strong adherence among ordinary souls by giving them a meaningful guide to moral and ethical belief.

Both Buddhism and especially Hinduism in time evolved into many subdivisions, or sects, which worshiped somewhat differently and had different gods and prophets. All of these sects are notable for their tolerance toward others; in contrast to the historical Western religions and Islam, they do not assert that there is but one true path to heaven.

HINDU GOD VISHNU. Vishnu, the god of preservation (right), is depicted with his consort Lakshmi, riding the huge bird demon Garuda as it circles the cosmos in search of prey.

the allegiance of a large part of the population. The old Vedic Hinduism proved unable to match the appeal of these religions to people seeking an emotionally and intellectually fulfilling experience.

As Buddhism gradually evolved into a supernatural religion after its founder's death, Hinduism responded to the Buddhist challenge by developing a less formal and more speculative approach to the mysteries of eternal life and the gods who ordained human fate. The Upanishads and the *Mahabharata* are the embodiment of this response, which changed the old

DEVELOPMENT OF THE CASTE SYSTEM

By the end of the Gupta Period, the caste system founded by the Aryan conquerors reigned supreme. It had grown ever more refined in its applications and more complex in its structure as time passed. Sub-castes had multiplied and were determined by geographic, ethnic, and kinship factors as well as the traditional social and economic categories. Along with the restructured Hindu belief, caste had

EVIDENCE OF THE PAST

A Father's Lesson

The complexities of Hindu religious and philosophical speculations as they developed in the first millennium CE are often baffling to the reader. But occasionally help is forthcoming through one or another of the frequent Indian folk sayings that have evolved in the oral tradition:

> A learned father wished to instruct his son in the mysteries of the spirit that informs all earthly creatures but can never be apprehended by the senses.
>
> Father: Now you ask for that instruction by which we hear what cannot be heard, by which we perceive what cannot be perceived, by which we know what cannot be known.
>
> Son: What is that instruction, sir?
>
> F: Fetch me a fruit of the Nyagrodha tree.

> S: Here is one, sir.
>
> F: Break it.
>
> S: It is broken.
>
> F: What do you see?
>
> S: These seeds, almost infinitesimal.
>
> F: Break one.
>
> S: It is broken.
>
> F: What do you see there?
>
> S: Not anything, sir.
>
> F: My son, that subtle essence which you do not perceive there, of that very essence this great Nyagrodha tree exists.

▶ *Analyze and Interpret*

What is the meaning of this lesson?

Source: *Sacred Books of the East*, ed. F. Max Mueller (Oxford: Oxford University Press, 1999).

PATTERNS OF BELIEF

An Excerpt from the *Bhagavad-Gita*

Of the myriad Hindu sagas and poems, the *Bhagavad-Gita* is the most popular and the best known among Westerners. Indian holy men and parents have also used it to teach moral behavior to succeeding generations. It is a part of the larger poem *Mahabharata*, a tale of the distant and mythical past, when two clans fought for supremacy in India. Just before the decisive struggle, one of the clan leaders, the warrior Arjuna, meditates on the meaning of life. His charioteer, who is the god Krishna in human disguise, answers his questions. Arjuna regrets having to kill his opponents whom he knows and respects, but Krishna tells him that his sorrow is misplaced because what Arjuna conceives of as the finality of death is not that:

> You grieve for those beyond grief,
> and you speak words of insight;
> but learned men do not grieve
> for the dead or for the living.
> Never have I not existed,
> nor you, nor these kings;
> and never in the future
> shall we cease to exist.
> Just as the embattled self enters
> childhood, youth, and old age,
> so does it enter another body;
> this does not confound a steadfast man . . .
> Our bodies are known to end,
> but the embodied Self is enduring,
> indestructible, and immeasurable;
> therefore, Arjuna, fight the battle!
> He who thinks this Self a killer
> and he who thinks it killed,
> both fail to understand;
> it does not kill, nor is it killed.

> It is not born,
> it does not die;
> having been,
> it will never not be;
> unborn, enduring,
> constant, and primordial,
> it is not killed when the body is killed.
> Arjuna, when a man knows the Self
> to be indestructible, enduring, unborn,
> unchanging, how does he kill
> or cause anyone to kill? . . .
> Weapons do not cut it [the Self],
> fire does not burn it,
> waters do not wet it,
> wind does not wither it.
> It cannot be cut or burned;
> it cannot be wet or withered,
> it is enduring, all pervasive,
> fixed, immobile, and timeless. . . .
> The Self embodied in the body
> of every being is indestructible;
> you have no cause to grieve
> for all these creatures, Arjuna!

▶ *Analyze and Interpret*

What does Krishna attempt to show Arjuna about the nature of his duty as a warrior? Is his counsel coldhearted or realistic, in your view? How could devout Hindus take comfort from this poem?

Source: From *Bhagavad Gita: Krishna's Counsel in Time of War,* trans. B. S. Miller, copyright 1986 by Barbara Stoler Miller. Used by permission of Bantam Books, a division of Random House, Inc.

You can read the *Bhagavad-Gita* at the Wadsworth World History Resource Center.

become one of the two defining factors in the lives of all Indians. At the bottom were the outcastes or untouchables, who were condemned to a marginal existence as beggars, buriers of the dead, and dealers in animal products that were thought to be polluting. Above them were hundreds of varieties of farmers, craftsmen, and merchants, as well as laborers, each of which constituted a more or less closed grouping with its own (unwritten) rules of religious belief and social conduct (dharma).

Although caste members tended to belong to a distinct occupation, caste membership could also differ according to its territory or doctrines. For example, members of the caste that specialized in credit and money lending in Calcutta were not members of the caste that dominated the same activity in Bombay or in Delhi. They could be seen as higher or lower in the intricate gradings of social prestige that caste imposed. Although it was possible to raise one's status by marriage with a higher-caste member, it was also possible

Ellora, Bombay, India/Bridgeman Art Library

ELLORA CAVE TEMPLES. The immensity of these constructions can be gathered in this photo of one of the several courtyards dug out of the solid rock. The work is believed to have started around 600 CE. Over the centuries, Hindu, Jain, and Buddhist artists and laborers contributed.

to debase oneself by marriage to a lower one. It seems that impoverished members of the high-prestige castes who sought material advantage from marriage with a lower, but wealthy, individual attempted the usual rationalizations. All in all, such mixed marriages with their attendant changes of caste were rare in India, and the stratification of society, which commenced in Aryan times, grew ever stronger.

By about the ninth or tenth century CE, the system had become so entrenched as to be a fundamental pillar of the revitalized Hindu culture. It was the cement holding the nation together, giving everyone a definite, easily comprehended place in society. Yet at the same time, the caste system created permanent barriers among individuals—separations that persist today. The modern Indian constitution, adopted after independence in 1947, outlaws caste privilege and guarantees all Indians equality before the law. Yet the old categories persist, especially in the villages, where about 75 percent of Indians still live.

SOCIAL CUSTOMS

How did the Hindu masses organize their day-to-day lives? For Indians as for most early peoples, blood ties were the basis of social life. The extended family was universal: in-laws, cousins, and second and third generations all lived together under the same roof or in the same compound. The oldest competent male always exercised authority. Polygamy (the practice of having several wives) was common, as was concubinage for those who could not afford another wife. Children, especially the oldest boy, had an honored place and were often pampered.

Females were clearly and unequivocally subservient to the male. Women were expected to be good wives and mothers and to let the husband decide everything that pertained to affairs outside of the house. Marriage was arranged early in life by the parents of the bride and groom. As in most

societies, marriage was primarily an economic and social affair, with the feelings of the individuals being distinctly secondary. Ideally, the girl was betrothed (formally engaged) immediately after coming into puberty, at about age thirteen or fourteen, and given into the care of her much older husband soon after. The reality usually differed, however, as many families began to betroth children as young as one to two years of age to ensure that they would have proper partners, always within their caste. The actual wedding did not take place until both parties were at least at the age of puberty, however. The wife was to be the faithful shadow of her husband and the bearer of children, preferably sons. A barren wife could expect that her husband would take additional wives to ensure the continuance of the family name, much as among the Chinese. Divorce was rare among the upper castes; we know little about the others.

Considerable evidence indicates that in early times, Hindu women, at least in the upper classes, had more freedoms than in other ancient societies. The Rigveda, for example, makes no mention of restricting women from public affairs, and women composed some of the numerous sacred texts, but later this freedom declined. In the *Mahabharata* epic, composed about 400 BCE, the female's status is generally inferior to that of any male. The veiling and strict social isolation of women among Hindus was reinforced with the Muslim conquests in the twelfth century. From that time onward, the Hindu population began a much stricter seclusion of respectable women and treated them as the property of fathers and husbands. The position of widows was especially pitiful. A widow was expected to be in permanent mourning and never to remarry. She was looked on with disdain, even by her relatives, and as the bringer of bad luck. It is no wonder that some women chose to follow their dead husbands into voluntary death through **sati** (sah-TEE), the ritual suicide of a wife after her husband's death, which was so shocking to Westerners. Actually, it seems, few widows, even in the priestly castes that were supposed to be a model to others, ever went so far in their devotion. But on occasion, a widow did fling herself into the flames of the cremation pyre, which was the usual way to dispose of bodies in India.

Sexuality

One of the attributes of Hindu culture that is noted by almost all foreigners is its readiness to accept all forms of pleasure that the day might bring. In sharp contrast to Jewish and Christian suspicion of the senses' delights, Hinduism taught that human beings had a positive duty to seize pleasure where they might, so long as dharma was not violated. This was particularly the case in terms of sexual matters, which were given prominence in the famous *Kama Sutra* (kah-mah SOO-trah), composed some time before the first century CE as a treatise on one of the four spheres of Hindu life.

Prostitutes were as common in Indian life as elsewhere. Many were attached to the temples, where their services

were offered to those who donated for the temples' support. Others were educated and artful women who served the upper class and held a position of general respect. Although the sacred texts denounced prostitution as being unworthy, the attitude of the ordinary man and woman was apparently more flexible. The Indian male's attitude toward women was marked by a strong duality: woman is both saint and strumpet, to be cherished and to be guarded against. The goddess Kali, who is sometimes pictured as a maternal guardian and sometimes as a demonic destroyer, is the classic example (see Chapter 5).

INDIA AND EAST ASIA

The culture and customs of Hinduism were rarely disseminated to other peoples. The Hindu faith was peculiarly interwoven with the historical experience and ancient beliefs of the peoples of the Indian subcontinent. Lacking a sacred book that defined a uniform dogma, Hindus normally showed little or no interest in converting others to the path of righteousness or initiating them into the mysteries of dharma. Most Hindus are, and have always been, residents of India.

There was, however, a major exception to this rule. In part of Southeast Asia, Indian colonies gradually were established during the sixth through the thirteenth centuries CE (see Chapter 17). Why this emigration started, why it continued, and who participated are questions that cannot be answered definitively, although it clearly was a byproduct of India's commercial expansion that started during the late Mauryan period (Chapter 5). These colonies must have been the result of invitation rather than conquest and were small in comparison with their host population. We know of but one example of Indian conquest in Southeast Asia over this lengthy period. Local rulers must have recognized the advanced civilization of the subcontinent as desirable in certain aspects for their own subjects. Precisely what the colonists offered is not certain and probably varied from place to place and situation to situation. It seems reasonable to assume that the Indian element functioned generally as teachers and administrators. Whether Brahmin priests, craftsmen, or artists of some type, the Asian hosts saw them as useful and non-threatening instructors or models, and they allowed them to settle in numerous places. Indians seem always to have remained a small minority, and the relationship between hosts and guests was both peaceable and productive.

The Southeast Asians were highly selective in what they chose to adopt, however. They rejected major aspects of Hindu culture, notably the caste system, which never spread into Asia beyond India. The adoption of Indian custom by the host nation was normally limited to linguistic, commercial, and some artistic spheres. Certain elements of

Hindu religious and philosophical belief were introduced into the native animisms. What eventually emerged was a mélange of the flexible Hindu theology and ceremonies with the native belief and practice. Southeast Asian religion remains to this day one of the outstanding examples of *syncretism* (SING-krah-tism; mixed-source belief).

Buddhism succeeded Hinduism in India's cultural exports to the east. As their religion declined in India proper, thousands of Buddhist monks were encouraged to emigrate and establish their monasteries and temples among the peoples of the Asian islands and mainland. Eventually, by about the eleventh century, Buddhist practice completely supplanted Hinduism in Myanmar, Thailand, Cambodia, Laos, and Vietnam. The Hindu worldview seems to have depended largely on the peculiar traditions and conditions of the Indian peninsula for its flourishing, particularly on caste.

This transplantation of Hinduism and Buddhism was linked to the development of the Indian Ocean trade, in which Indians played a central role. From the time of the Emperor Ashoka, merchants and mariners from southern India were carrying on a lively trade in luxury items with Southeast Asian and South Pacific ports. Cinnamon, pepper, cloves, nutmeg, mace, and Chinese silk were transshipped via South Indian ports across the western Indian Ocean and eventually to the Near East and the Mediterranean. After the seventh century, Arab and other Muslim entrepreneurs carried on most of this lucrative trade (Chap. 14) and Islam supplanted Buddhism in most of India and Southeast Asia. But the commercial colonies established in the islands remained ethnically Indian.

In the large **Khmer** (keh-MER) kingdom of Cambodia, both Hindu and Buddhist merchants, craftsmen, and artists found markets and patrons. The largest building in the world devoted to religion is the temple of **Anghor** (ANG-kor) in present-day northern Cambodia. It was built as a Hindu shrine under Indian inspiration, and possibly supervision, in the tenth century. Somewhat later it was converted into a Buddhist temple. After the conquest of the Khmers by the neighboring Thais in the twelfth century, the great temple was neglected and forgotten for 700 years. Only since World War II has it been reclaimed from the surrounding jungle and become a major tourist attraction.

If the Khmers were the most notable partners of Indian cultural exchange on the mainland, the maritime empire of Sri Vijaya (sree vee-JAH-yah) based on the island of Sumatra expanded Hinduism throughout the huge Indonesian archipelago. Originally a small city-state, Sri Vijaya had become a large state by the seventh century and remained so for 300 years. By about 1000 CE, its power had sufficiently declined as to allow a successful piratical conquest by one of the south Indian principalities, Chola (CHOH-lah). For the next two centuries, Sri Vijaya served as the partner of

ANGHOR WAT. The enormous Buddhist temple at Anghor in Cambodia was the spiritual and political center of the ancient empire of the Khmer people. After the empire's fall, it was buried under jungle foliage for many centuries.

©Robert Harding Picture Library Ltd/Alamy

Chola in organizing the commerce of the nearby islands and Malayan peninsula. The upper classes became Hindu and spread the religion widely. As in India, the absorp-tive Hindu belief took myriad forms in Southeast Asia, sometimes so merging with the local animisms or with Buddhism as to be almost unrecognizable to outsiders.

SUMMARY

INDIA, IN ITS golden or classical age (which was much longer than the classical age of the Greeks or most other peoples), saw the slow evolution of a civilization that was centered on the quest for understanding the relation between the earthly and the unearthly, between material reality and spiritual reality. Both Hindu and Buddhist beliefs evolved into forms quite different from their originals; in time, the revived Hinduism became again the faith of the vast majority. Written history is scarce until modern times because of the predominantly oral culture. We know that the Gupta Dynasty was a particular high point; after it collapsed in the fifth century CE, the subcontinent broke up into political fragments, often ruled over by non-Indians in the North.

Beginning with the Islamic invasions from Afghanistan in the eleventh century, North and South went their separate ways, though they remained linked by the Hindu faith. Priestly and commercial migrants from the South into Southeast Asia established colonies and a Hindu presence there among the upper classes. In the North, waves of Turkic peoples eventually were able to conquer the natives in the twelfth century and set up a Muslim sultanate at Delhi that ruled much of the subcontinent for the next several centuries.

Indian science, particularly mathematics, ranked near or on par with the world's most advanced types. In the temple ruins and the cave shrines that dot the peninsula, we can also obtain at least a minimal appreciation of the Indians' achievement in the arts.

▶ Identification Terms

Test your knowledge of this chapter's key concepts by defining the following terms. If you can't recall the meaning of certain terms, refresh your memory by looking up the boldfaced term in the chapter, turning to the Glossary at the end of the book, or working with the flashcards that are available on the *World Civilizations* Companion Website: **academic.cengage.com/adler**

Ajanta Caves
Anghor Wat
Bhagavad-Gita
Brahman

Delhi Sultanate
Kalidasa
Khmers
Mahabharata

Rigveda
sati
Shiva
Upanishads

Vedas
Vishnu

▶ *Test Your Knowledge*

Test your knowledge of this chapter by answering the following questions. Complete answers appear at the end of the book. You may find even more quiz questions in CengageNOW and on the *World Civilizations* Companion Website: **academic.cengage.com/adler**

1. Hindus believe that the Vedas
   a. are sacred texts that introduced a caste system for society.
   b. are a remnant of the Aryan days that are no longer relevant.
   c. must be studied in old age.
   d. are forgeries by Westerners.
   e. were brought to their country from Afghanistan.
2. The best-known and most beloved Hindu scripture is the
   a. Rigveda.
   b. Upanishads.
   c. *Bhagavad-Gita.*
   d. Sangha.
   e. book of Vedas.
3. A peculiar facet of Indian civilization was its
   a. lack of interest in mathematics.
   b. avoidance of the pictorial arts.
   c. slowness in producing a literary culture.
   d. strong tendency toward political centralization.
   e. refusal to portray religious subjects in its art.
4. The major source of foreign troubles for India has been its
   a. sea frontiers to the east.
   b. borders with China.
   c. resident colonies of foreign traders.
   d. frontier with Afghanistan.
   e. lack of strong military leadership.
5. Southeast Asians experienced Hindu culture
   a. as a result of Indian conquests.
   b. in a selective and adapted fashion.
   c. mainly among the lower classes.
   d. both b and c
   e. as one imposed on them arbitrarily.
6. The religion that suffered most severely from the Muslim Turks' invasion of India in the twelfth century was
   a. Christianity.
   b. Hinduism.
   c. Buddhism.
   d. Jainism.
   e. Sikhism.
7. The Jains are especially concerned to
   a. avoid killing any creature.
   b. avoid being shamed by others.
   c. spread their religion.
   d. be seen as superior to Hindus.
   e. reject animal sacrifices.
8. The last native dynasty to rule over the greater part of the Indian subcontinent was the
   a. Guptas.
   b. Afghans.
   c. Maurya.
   d. Delhi sultans.
   e. Ghaznivids.
9. Mahmud al-Ghazni and his troops were
   a. Persian.
   b. Arabs.
   c. Turks.
   d. Mongols.
   e. Afghans.
10. It is believed that the Arabic numerals used today originated in
    a. Saudi Arabia.
    b. western Afghanistan.
    c. Dravidian India.
    d. the Ajanta region.
    e. Gupta India.

CENGAGENOW™

Enter *CengageNOW* using the access card that is available with this text. *CengageNOW* will assist you in understanding the content in this chapter with lesson plans generated for your needs, as well as provide you with a connection to the *Wadsworth World History Resource Center* (see description at right for details).

▶  World History Resource Center

Enter the Resource Center using either your *CengageNOW* access card or your standalone access card for the *Wadsworth World History Resource Center.* Organized by topic, this website includes quizzes; images; over 350 primary source documents; interactive simulations, maps, and timelines; movie explorations; and a wealth of other resources. You can read the following documents, and many more, at the *Wadsworth World History Resource Center:*

The Jain Respect for Life
The *Bhagavad-Gita*

EMPIRE OF THE MIDDLE: CHINA TO THE MONGOL CONQUEST

Tzu-kung asked about the true gentleman. The Master said, "He does not preach what he practices until he has practiced what he preaches."
—The *Analects* of Confucius

THE QIN EMPEROR: FOUNDATION OF THE STATE

THE HAN DYNASTY, 202 BCE–220 CE
Arts and Sciences ◆ The Economy, Government, and Foreign Affairs ◆ The End of the Dynasty

THE TANG DYNASTY, 618–907 CE

THE SONG DYNASTY, 960–1279
Song Internal Policies ◆ Foreign Affairs

BUDDHISM AND CHINESE CULTURE

THE TREMENDOUS VITALITY AND flexibility of Chinese civilization in the 1,500 years we examine in this chapter have no match in world history, anywhere. The longest-lived continuous political organism in the world, China was in these years able to combine the stability of an Egypt with the adaptability of a Japan. The government centered on the person of an emperor who, although by no means divine, was able to inspire the loyalty of a great many talented and ambitious servants in his bureaucracy—the world's first to be based more on merit than on birth. When the regime was at peace and working as designed, the life of the common people was about as good and secure as ever seen in the ancient world. Prosperity was widespread, and cities thrived while the villages were secure. When the regime broke down, however, the country fell into anarchy with cruel results for all. But for most of these 1,500 years, anarchy was held at bay, the emperor was seen by all to be the authentic Son of Heaven, and the arts and sciences prospered.

THE QIN EMPEROR: FOUNDATION OF THE STATE

The last years of the Zhou Dynasty (see Chapter 6) were a sad tale of governmental collapse and warring feudal lords. By about 500 BCE, effective central government had become nonexistent, and a long period of intra-Chinese struggle known as the Era of the Warring States ensued until 220 BCE. It is significant that many of the outstanding philosophical contributions of Chinese thinkers—Confucian, Daoist, and Legalist—matured during this period. They aimed at either restoring proper order to a world gone astray or making it tolerable.

The relatively small northwestern state of Qin (chin) adopted the Legalist doctrines wholeheartedly in the mid-200s BCE (see Chapter 6). Guided by them, the Qin ruler managed to reunify the country by a combination of military force and administrative reorganization. The dynasty thus founded would have a short span, but the general principles that guided the Qin rule could still be traced in Chinese government until the twentieth century. Even the name of the country in Western languages comes from Qin. It was an awesome achievement.

The king of Qin (246–221 BCE) and later **First Emperor** (221–210 BCE), ruled all China only eleven years, but he made an imprint that was to last, as he boasted, "10,000 generations." Shih Huang-di (sheer wahng-dee), as he was called, was a man of tremendous administrative gifts and huge personality defects. His subjects felt both. His generalship overwhelmed the rival Chinese states. In only nine years (230–221 BCE), the six largest states fell to Qin armies or surrendered, and for the first time in its long history China became a unified empire. At once the process of centralization got under way along ruthless Legalist lines. Guided by the minister Li Si (lee shoo) the emperor set out to make his rule irresistible and to eliminate the entrenched feudal aristocracy. The country was divided into administrative units that persisted throughout later history. To create a unified administration based on Legalist principles, the emperor fixed weights and measures, made

the size of the roads uniform so that all carts would fit the ruts, and introduced the first standard units of money. The system of writing was standardized so effectively that it is almost the same in the twenty-first century as it was then.

As a defense against the constant series of nomadic invaders from Mongolia, disconnected barriers that had been erected by various princes in the north and northwest were unified into the first version of the Great Wall (see Map 16.1). A whole list of other massive public works was started, including the tremendous imperial palace at Sian and the emperor's tomb in which more than 7,000 life-sized clay soldiers were buried with him. (They were discovered in 1974 and are now being restored.) Under Shih Huang-di, China expanded to both north and south. The region around Guangzhou (Canton) came under his control; it was to be China's premier port for many centuries to come. First contacts were made with the Vietnamese and with several other Asian peoples to the west and south.

The First Emperor's reign also had its negative side. Convinced by his Legalist principles of the inherent evil of human nature, Shih Huang-di apparently became paranoid

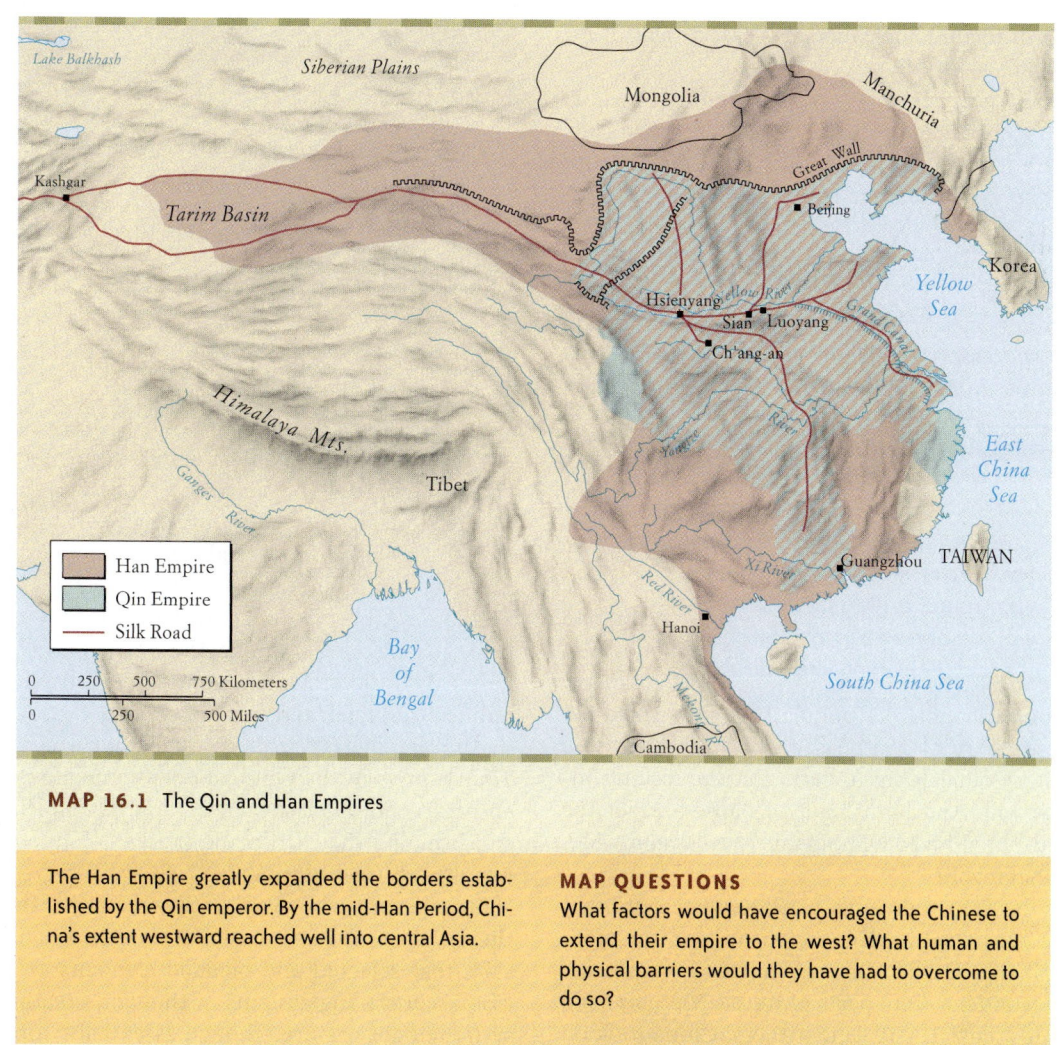

MAP 16.1 The Qin and Han Empires

The Han Empire greatly expanded the borders established by the Qin emperor. By the mid-Han Period, China's extent westward reached well into central Asia.

MAP QUESTIONS
What factors would have encouraged the Chinese to extend their empire to the west? What human and physical barriers would they have had to overcome to do so?

Bridgeman Art Library

THE GREAT WALL. The golden light of sunset illumines a stretch of "the only earthly object visible from an orbiting space vehicle." The wall extends more than 1,800 miles in the present time, but much of its mainly mud brick construction has been allowed to sink back into the surrounding terrain through lack of upkeep. Started on a more modest scale by the First Emperor in the 200s BCE, it was last renewed by the early Qing dynasts in the 1600s.

Ian McKinnell/Alamy

WARRIORS FROM THE FIRST EMPEROR'S TOMB. The accidental discovery of the tomb of Shih Huang-di, the First Emperor, at Sian in 1974 revealed the terra cotta statues of more than 7,000 warriors buried with him. Armed with spears, swords, and bows, and presumably meant as a bodyguard in the next world, each of the life-sized warrior statues has individual facial features taken from living models.

and engaged in torture and other harsh treatment of his subjects and officials.

He especially hated the doctrines of Confucius, which he regarded as a menace to his style of autocratic rule, and ordered a **burning of the books** in a vain attempt to eradicate the Confucian philosophy from Chinese consciousness, an episode deeply resented by later generations. Shih Huang-di died of natural causes in 210, but the cruelties and heavy taxation and labor levies he imposed on the peasants caused unrest and assured that his son and weaker successor would not last long as ruler. The son's overthrow in 206 BCE was followed by the establishment of one of the most successful of all the Chinese dynasties, the **Han Dynasty**, which lasted until 220 CE.

THE HAN DYNASTY, 202 BCE–220 CE

Han rule occurred almost simultaneously with the Roman heyday, and these two great empires of the East and West had other similarities as well. Both were basically urban in orientation, although the populations they ruled remained decidedly rural and peasant. Both depended on a nonhereditary officialdom to carry out the distant imperial court's will. And both finally collapsed under the combined impact of invading nomadic peoples and widespread regional revolts.

Why are the Han monarchs considered the primary shapers of China's national consciousness? Even more than Shih Huang-di, the Han rulers greatly expanded the Chinese frontiers—into parts of Korea, Vietnam, and westward into Central Asia. Under them, China took on

more or less the geographic boundaries that it has retained ever since (except for the much later conquest of Tibet). With the extension of their control westward, the eastern half of the Silk Road came into permanent existence, and Chinese trade began to reach as far as India and the Mediterranean world, although mainly through intermediaries. Chinese commercial contacts soon expanded into massive cultural influence on the Japanese, Koreans, and Vietnamese. Everywhere on the Asian mainland north of India and east of Cambodia, the "men of Han," as the Chinese called themselves, became the controlling factor in military, political, and commercial life.

The Han dynasts were not revolutionaries in any sense. They kept what the Qin had done to create the state and ensure its continued existence, while relaxing the strictness and brutality that had made the First Emperor hated. It was *Wu-di* (woo-dee; 141–87 BCE), the greatest of the Han emperors, who oversaw the creation of the **Han synthesis.** This was a new, imperial Confucian ideology of the state that selected and blended elements of all three of China's prevailing systems of thought, creating a unified system of governance. Though essentially Confucian, this

British Library/Bridgeman Art Library

CARAVAN. This detail from a fourteenth-century Spanish map depicts a caravan traveling on the Silk Road.

was a changed Confucianism, with a somewhat Legalist emphasis on the obedience owed by the people to the government. The person of the emperor was given a sacred aura by the renewed emphasis on the "mandate of Heaven," the theory that the gods approved and supported the emperor and all his actions until they showed otherwise. They showed otherwise by allowing the imperial armies to be defeated by the nomadic tribespeople, by allowing rebels to succeed, or by permitting the provincial administration to break down. In that way, the path was opened to a new ruler or new dynasty, as the mandate of Heaven was being transferred to more competent hands.

Arts and Sciences

Under the Han rulers, arts and letters experienced a great upsurge in quality and quantity. History came into its own as a peculiarly congenial mode of understanding the world for the Chinese, who are perhaps the globe's most historically conscious people. Records were scrupulously kept, some of which have survived in the scripts of the noted historian Sima Qian (soo-mah chen) and the Pan family of scholars dating from the first century CE. As a result, we know far more about ancient China than almost any other part of the ancient world insofar as official acts and personages are concerned. History for the Chinese, of course, was the record of what the uppermost 1 percent did and thought—the peasantry and other ordinary folk were beneath consideration as a historical force. (See the Law and Government box for anecdotes written by the great classical historian of China, Sima Qian.)

Mathematics, geography, and astronomy were points of strength in Han natural science, all of which led directly to technological innovations that were extremely useful to Chinese society. Some examples include the sternpost rudder and the magnetic compass, which together transformed the practice of navigation. The Han Period saw the invention of paper from wood pulp, truly one of the world's major inventions. By about the fifth century CE, paper had become sufficiently cheap as to enter common usage, paving the way for the advent of wood-block printing and the refinement of painting in later centuries.

Medicine was a particular interest of the Chinese, and Han doctors developed a pharmacology that was even more ambitious than the later Muslim one. Also, acupuncture first entered the historical record during the Han Period. Despite the persistence of superstition and folk medicine, a strong scientific tradition of healing through intensive knowledge of the parts of the body, the functions of internal organs, and the circulation of the blood was established during this period. This tradition has endured alongside the rather different approaches of the Western and Muslim medical practices and long ago made China one of the permanent centers of the healing arts.

In the fine arts, China continued to produce a variety of metallic and ceramic luxury items, which increasingly found their way into the Near East and even into Rome's eastern provinces. The production of silk was both an economic asset of the first rank and a fine art; for nearly 1,000 years, the Han and their successors in China maintained their monopoly, until the Byzantines were finally able to emulate them. Bronze work, jade figurines, and fine ceramics were particularly notable among the plastic arts, while poetry, landscape painting, and instrumental music figured prominently as part of the heritage of the Chinese educated class. The written language had become fully standardized by the end of the Han Period, and its adoption throughout the empire meant that educated citizens, regardless of their ethnic affiliation, could read and write the same way. This achievement was to be crucial for Chinese national unity.

The Economy, Government, and Foreign Affairs

The Han Period also saw major advances in economic affairs. Canals were built and the road system was extended to the south and west, improving communication and commerce between remote regions and the capital and contributing to a more unified economy. Large cities and numerous market towns came into existence. In the Chinese scale of values, merchants did not count for much; they were considered to be more or less parasites who lived off the work of the craftsmen and tillers of the land. They had none of the social prestige of the scholars or of the government officials and wealthy landowners. But they were still recognized as vital to the well-being of all and were seldom exploited as in some other civilizations. The urban markets were impressive; in both the variety of goods and the number of merchants, they seemed to have surpassed those of other contemporary civilizations, including Rome's.

Iron came into common use after about 500 BCE, greatly aiding the introduction of new and cheaper weapons, which led to the expansion of the armies under imperial command. As such a widely used metal, iron, along with salt and alcohol, became a government monopoly. Furthermore, the increased availability of iron led to the growing use of the plow, which allowed

LAW AND GOVERNMENT

The Virtuous Officials

The greatest of the classical historians of China, Sima Qian (c. 150–90 BCE), wrote during the rule of the ambitious emperor Wu, who had expanded China's borders at the price of imposing a cruel, Legalist-inspired internal regime.

Sima Qian regretted the emperor's style of governance, but he could not, as court historian, openly oppose it. Instead, he indirectly criticized Wu by writing about the virtue of emperors and officials in the distant past, when Confucian principles guided the government and proper attention was paid to the welfare of the people. These appeals to traditional virtues were well understood by Sima's audience. Some anecdotes from these histories follow; the first deals with the capable minister Sun Shu-ao, the second with the righteous Kung-i Hsiu, and the third with the relentlessly logical Li Li. All three men served kings of the Zhou Dynasty.

> The people of Ch'u liked to use very low-slung carriages, but the king did not think that such carriages were good for the horses and wanted to issue an order forcing the people to use higher ones. Sun Shu-ao said, "If orders are issued too frequently to the people they will not know which ones to obey. It will not do to issue an order.
>
> "If your Majesty wishes the people to use high carriages, then I suggest that I instruct the officials to have the thresholds of the community gates made higher. Anyone who rides in a carriage must be a man of some social status, and a gentleman cannot be getting down from his carriage every time he has to pass through the community gate."
>
> The king gave his approval, and after half a year all the people had of their own accord made their carriages higher so that they could drive over the thresholds without difficulty. In this way, without instructing the people Sun Shu-ao led them to change their ways.
>
> Kung-i Hsiu was an erudite of Lu. Because of his outstanding ability he was made prime minister. . . .
>
> Once one of his retainers sent him a fish, but he refused to accept the gift. "I always heard that you were fond of fish," said another of his retainers. "Now that someone has sent you a fish, why don't you accept it?" "It is precisely because I am so fond of fish that I don't accept it," replied Kung-i Hsiu. "Now that I am minister I can afford to buy all the fish I want. But if I should accept this gift and lose my position as a result, who would ever provide me with a fish again?"
>
> Li Li was director of prisons under Duke Wen. Once, discovering that an innocent man had been executed because of an error in the investigation conducted by his office, he had himself bound and announced that he deserved the death penalty. Duke Wen said to him, "There are high officials and low officials, and there are light punishments and severe ones. Just because one of the petty clerks in your office made a mistake there is no reason why you should take the blame."
>
> But Li Li replied, "I occupy the position of head of this office and I have made no move to hand the post over. . . . I receive a large salary and I have not shared the profits with those under me. Now because of an error in the trial an innocent has been executed. I have never heard of a man in my position trying to shift the responsibility for such a crime to his subordinates!" Thus he declined to accept Duke Wen's suggestion.
>
> "If you insist that as a superior officer you yourself are to blame," said Duke Wen, "then do you mean that I, too, am to blame?" "The director of prisons," said Li Li, "must abide by the laws which govern his post. If he mistakenly condemns a man to punishment, he himself must suffer the punishment; if he mistakenly sentences a man to death, he himself must suffer death. Your Grace appointed me to this post precisely because you believed that I would be able to listen to difficult cases and decide doubtful points of law. But now since I have made a mistake in hearing a case and have executed an innocent, I naturally deserve to die for my offense." So in the end he refused to listen to the duke's arguments, but fell on his sword and died.

▶ *Analyze and Interpret*

How effective do you think Sima's critiques of his emperor would be, given the Chinese reverence for traditional virtues in their governors? What effect would such an approach have, do you think, in present-day American politics?

Source: Excerpted from *Records of the Grand Historian*, trans. Burton Watson (New York: Columbia University Press, 1961), vol. 2, pp. 413–418. Reprinted with permission from the publisher.

newly conquered lands in the north and northwest to be cultivated. An improved horse harness was developed, enabling Chinese farmers to make much better use of the animal's strength. (This particular idea would not reach the West for another six centuries.) Animal fertilizer and crushed bones (phosphate) were applied to the land systematically. Through such methods, Chinese agriculture became the most productive in the premodern world.

Han government was more complex than anything seen earlier in China. The government functioned through the active recruitment of the educated elite into the bureaucracy. Its members were chosen by a written examination on the principles of correct action in given situations. The examinees were expected to be thoroughly familiar with the Confucian texts and commentaries on them, and by this time Confucius had become the mainstay of the Chinese educational system. To be eligible to take the final examination in the capital, candidates had to pass several preliminary tests and be recommended by their teachers at all levels. This **meritocracy** was designed to bring the best talent to the service of the central government, regardless of social origin. Despite many individual interventions to ensure preference for sons and grandsons, an exclusively hereditary nobility was not allowed to develop. The mandarins (scholar-officials) of China were to give generally good service to their countrymen for most of the next 2,000 years.

Traders and Buddhist monks made peaceful contacts with Western Asia and India; like the devout trader Fa Xian (see Chapter 15), the Buddhists wished to learn more about the religion in the land of its birth. In the first century CE, a Chinese trade mission was sent to make direct contact with the Romans in the Red Sea area. It reported back to the Han rulers that the Westerners' goods held little interest for China. The Chinese attitude that China had what the West wanted but the West had little to offer to the Middle Kingdom became steadily more rooted in the upper classes' mind as time wore on. Indeed, this belief was generally accurate, at least up to about 1500 CE, but when it was no longer true, it proved difficult or impossible to change. It then turned into the sort of unimaginative defensiveness and worship of the past that would also handicap the Muslim world in the face of the aggressive European challenge.

The ambitious visions entertained by the Han rulers in time generated familiar problems. The enormous building projects started by the emperors or continued from the Qin Period, such as the building of the Great Wall and the grand mausoleums for the emperors, imposed heavy burdens on the common people. The bane of all Chinese governments, an exploited and rebellious peasantry, began to make itself heard from in the first century CE. A reforming emperor, who in some ways resembled Rome's Augustus Caesar in his vision of the state, was killed before he could meet his goals. The result was an interval of chaos before order could be restored and the Later Han Dynasty established in 25 CE.

Corbis Collection/Alamy

 **TRADE AND BUDDHISM IN CHINA.** During the height of the Tang period, the Silk Road brought Buddhist merchants and missionaries to China. Many temples like these at Bezeklik in western China were carved out of cliffs and rocky overhangs.

The End of the Dynasty

China during the Later Han saw a continuation of its stable economy and population growth. It was also an era of transition that saw the social and political elite gradually changing character from one that had relied on military strength over the previous two millennia to one that based its power on land ownership and its status on its cultural sophistication.

In time, following the inexorable cycle of Chinese dynasties, the Later Han broke down into anarchy, with warlords and peasant rebels ignoring the weakened or corrupt bureaucracy. For a time the Era of the Warring States was replicated. This time, though, only three contestants participated, and the anarchy lasted only 135 years instead of 250. Out of the conflict came two major political divisions: the North, which was dominated by the kingdom of Wei, and the South, where various princely dynasties took turns fighting one another for supreme power. The dividing line was the Yangtze River, which flows across almost the entire width of China (see Map 16.2).

During this partial breakdown, an immensely significant agrarian advance came about: the cultivation of rice in paddies (wet rice farming) gradually became entrenched in the South. This development was to be highly important for all later Chinese history, because the grain allowed the Chinese population to expand greatly without putting intolerable strains on the economy. Ethnic minorities were forced off the land and sought refuge in the hills and mountains of the South. A Vietnamese import into South China, rice requires a great deal of hand labor but produces more caloric energy per acre than any other grain crop. Rice enabled the population to grow and provided the work to keep the new hands busy. The South now began to rival the North in civilized development.

THE TANG DYNASTY, 618–907 CE

The brief Sui Dynasty (580–618) was followed by the line of the **Tang Dynasty** of emperors (618–907), who

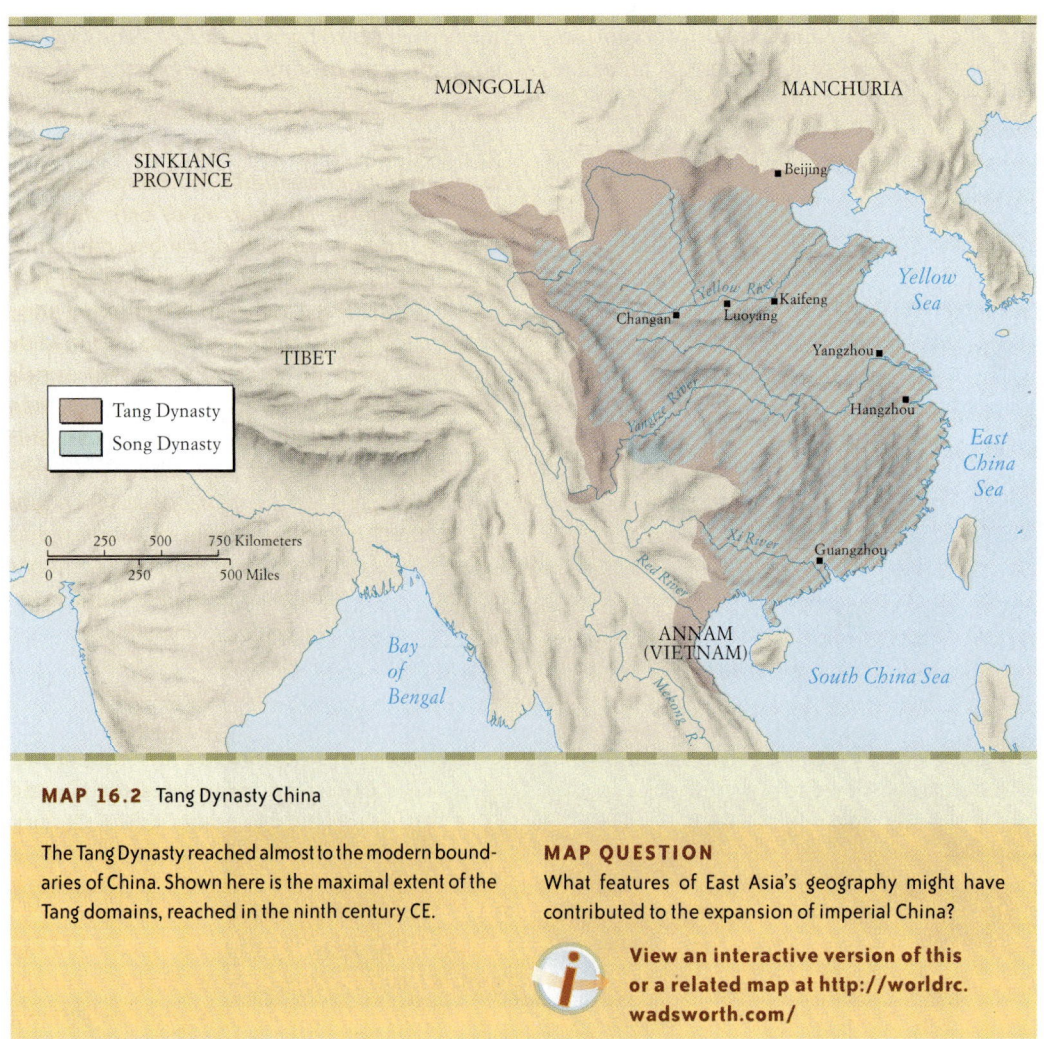

MAP 16.2 Tang Dynasty China

The Tang Dynasty reached almost to the modern boundaries of China. Shown here is the maximal extent of the Tang domains, reached in the ninth century CE.

MAP QUESTION

What features of East Asia's geography might have contributed to the expansion of imperial China?

View an interactive version of this or a related map at http://worldrc. wadsworth.com/

presided over one of the most brilliant epochs of China's long history. Like the Qin earlier, the two Sui rulers had reunified China and gone on to introduce unpopular but needed authoritarian reforms. The most notable was the reallocation of land every few years, known as the *well-field* reform, intended to give peasants more rights to land and to break the power of the landed elites. Failed military expeditions against the northern nomads brought the Sui down in the course of a widespread rebellion. But their Tang successors continued their reforms while avoiding their military misadventures, thus paving the way for an economic advance that supported a rich cultural epoch.

The early Tang rulers' primary concern was to improve the state of the peasant tenants, who had recently fallen into much misery because of the rapacity of their landlords. The landlords had taken full advantage of the collapse of the Han government by shifting the burden of taxation to their tenants while increasing the rents charged them. The early Tang rulers also adopted the *well-field* system from the Sui. Under the Tang, fertile farm land reverted to the state (that is, the imperial government) upon the death or old age of its peasant cultivator. It was then reassigned to another adult peasant in return for reasonable taxes and labor services. In this fashion, peasant needs and resources could be closely matched. For about a century there was a real improvement in the economic lives of the people.

The Tang re-created a generally efficient bureaucracy, which was firmly based, like the Han's, on Confucian ethics and the merit system. Although the wealthy and the families of officials often found ways of bypassing the exams or bribing their way into government service, the Tang open-examination system had so much to recommend it that it was still being employed in principle in modern times. Only the coming of democratic institutions in the early twentieth century ended its reign.

An imperial university originally created under the Han was now expanded to allow about 30,000 students to train annually for the demanding examinations. Only the very best candidates made it through this rigorous course to sit for the examinations that allocated posts at the central government level. Villagers would pool their resources to send a talented boy to a tutor and support him through the long years of preparation. They knew that if he were successful, he would bring back to the village far more than the cost to train him.

For about 150 years, the Tang dynasts were generally successful. From their capital Changan, they were active and aggressive in several directions. To the north and northwest, they managed either to purchase peace by paying tribute to their Turkish and Mongolian neighbors or by playing one tribe off against another. Conquests were extended farther to the west along the Silk Road. The economic and demographic growth of the Han era resumed

as the Silk Road and the opening of overseas trade with Southeast Asia brought ever more goods from foreign lands. The completion of the Grand Canal not only contributed to centralization as the south was linked with the capital at Changan but also permitted growing numbers of small entrepreneurs to benefit from the rapidly growing commercial economy. A byproduct of this was the rapid conversion of many to Buddhism (see below).

To the east, the initial era of Chinese–Japanese cultural contacts opened, and the Japanese proved to be enthusiastic admirers of Chinese culture at this time (see the next chapter). Contact with the Korean kingdoms was pricklier, but this less numerous people still fell under the powerful magnetism of the splendid civilization to their south. The same was true of the Tibetans in the far west, who were just being touched by Chinese expeditions for the first time. The Vietnamese in the far south, on the other hand, steadfastly resisted Chinese attempts to colonize them.

The emperor Xuanzong (shwan-tsung; reigned 712–765) presided over the Tang dynasty's greatest period of prosperity and cultural achievements. His reign coincided with the rapid expansion of the Islamic caliphate over western and central Asia; therefore, international trade brought unprecedented prosperity. Changan itself became one of the most cosmopolitan cities in the world, crowded with merchants and travelers from the lands of western Asia, the Indian Ocean world, and southeast Asia. His reign also coincided with one of the greatest eras in Chinese literary history, having produced three of China's greatest poets, Li Po, Du Fu, and Wang Wei (see Evidence of the Past).

In the mid-700s, the dynasty's successes ceased. An emperor fell under the sway of a beautiful and ambitious concubine and wholly neglected his duties; government was in effect turned over to her family. Unable to bear the humiliating situation longer, a general with a huge army rebelled, and the entire country was caught up in a devastating war from which the dynasty never recovered, although it did put down the rebels. Troubles on the northern borders mounted once again. Despite the brief intervals of strong rule in the early 800s, the Tang could not successfully quell the internal discontent that finally overwhelmed the dynasty with bloody anarchy in the later ninth century.

For a half-century China was again divided. Then, one of the northern provincial warlords made his bid for imperial power. Proving to be more adept as diplomat than as warrior, he was able to induce most of his rivals to join him voluntarily. The Chinese educated class always favored the idea of a single government center. Unlike Indians, medieval Europeans, and Middle Eastern peoples, educated Chinese regarded political fragmentation as an aberration, a throwback to the time before civilization. They saw it as something to be avoided at all costs, even if unity entailed submission to an illegitimate,

Werner Forman/Art Resource, NY

FLIGHT OF THE EMPEROR. The Tang style that first appeared in the tenth century became the mainstream of Chinese graphic art. Central to this style was a reevaluation of the place of human activity in the universe based on studies of patterns in nature. Finding "The Good" or "The Way" (*Dao*) centered more on finding harmony in nature. Human activity and structures were portrayed as being surrounded, and generally dwarfed, by natural phenomena, as can be seen in this painting of the flight of Emperor Ming Huan from rebels who threatened his court.

usurping ruler. When needed, the doctrine of the mandate of Heaven always provided a rationale for accepting new monarchs. Thus, they welcomed the coming of the **Song Dynasty**.

THE SONG DYNASTY, 960–1279

Armed with their newly discovered mandate, the successors to the Tang were able men. The Song (sung) rulers systematically promoted the many technical innovations that the Tang Period had produced and encouraged others. The most important of these was printing. At first printers used a separate carved wooden block for each page or column of ideographs, but by the eleventh century they had developed moveable wooden type, which sharply reduced the cost of printed material. Other labor-saving devices included the water pump and the spiral worm drive for transport of liquids. Together, they revolutionized the use of irrigation, made mining less difficult and more efficient, and allowed the construction and use of locks, which made canal boats a more widespread and useful form of transport. Avenues of internal trade opened along the network of canals that linked the South with the North. These have been used ever since to move most of China's bulk goods.

Manufactures were much advanced by the invention of the waterwheel and the forge bellows. The abacus and the water clock enabled accurate measurement of quantity and of time. Perhaps the best known of all the Tang/Song inventions was gunpowder, which the Chinese used only for pyrotechnic entertainments for a long while but then adapted to warfare to a minor degree. Strong oceangoing vessels were

armed with small rockets, for example, as defense against the frequent pirates. Gunpowder did not play a major role in Chinese military tactics until the 1200s, when it was used against the invading Mongols, who then carried it west to the Muslims and eventually the Europeans.

As in the Roman Empire and almost everywhere in the world, most people in Song China lived in villages, but the cities dictated the culture and defined the atmosphere of the empire. Along the canals in central and southern China sprang up several large cities, all with more than half a million in population. One of the largest was **Hangzhou**, whose delights and splendid vistas were described in wonder by the Venetian visitor Marco Polo (1254–1324) in the thirteenth century. Hangzhou was a port and grew in response to market forces and mercantile necessities rather than according to a government plan. Both Hangzhou and Kaifeng, the Song capital, are thought to have had more than a million inhabitants and contained all sorts of amusements and markets for rich and poor.

Song Internal Policies

For the most part, the Song continued the government style and policies of the Tang Period. In the South, the bureaucracy they commanded worked well for an unusually long period of almost 300 years. Most decisions had to be made at the top in the capital, many by the emperor himself. By some estimates, only 30,000 officials were needed to govern this large empire (the size of all of Europe, with a much larger population). The habits of obedience and self-discipline were already deeply ingrained in the people,

EVIDENCE OF THE PAST

Poets of China's Golden Age

Historians consider the long period covering the Tang and the Song dynasties, above all others, to have been China's golden age. It was an era above all that witnessed a flowering of thought and art in the ancient Daoist and Confucian traditions, while (Mahayana) Buddhism entered the Chinese cultural mainstream. Perhaps more than any other art form, poetry reflected these three traditions.

Some consider two poets of this era, Li Po (or Li Bo, 701–765) and Du Fu (712–770), to represent the Yin and the Yang, the passive and the active, the female and the male, or the Daoist and the Confucian aspects of traditional Chinese thought. Of these, Li Po clearly represented the former. He grew up in western China and became a devotee of Daoism. He spent long periods wandering, but in his middle years he served as a court poet under the Tang emperor Xuanzong. Above all, his poetry reflects the traditional Daoist *laissez-faire* approach to life: he enjoyed and wrote about the pleasures of drinking, friendship, nature, solitude, and the passage of time.

Sick Leave

> Propped on pillows, not attending to business;
> For two days I've lain behind locked doors.
> I begin to think that those who hold office
> Get no rest, except by falling ill!
> For restful thoughts one does not need space;
> The room where I lie is ten foot square.
> By the western eaves, above the bamboo-twigs,
> From my couch I see the White Mountain rise.
> But the clouds that hover on its far-distant peak
> Bring shame to a face that is buried in the World's dust.

Source: "The Poetry Store Archive, Li Po" (http://www.poetrystore.com/lipo.html)

In the Mountains: A Reply to the Vulgar

> They ask me where's the sense
>   on Jasper mountains?
> I laugh and don't reply
>   in heart's own quiet
> Peach petals float their streams
>   away in secret
> To other skies and earths
>   than those of mortals.

From Arthur Cooper, *Pi Po and Du Fu* (Bungay, Suffolk, 1973), p. 115.

Du Fu's work was very diverse, but above all his poems are highly autobiographical and much more concerned with real events in his life and those of others. He was raised as a Confucian, but he failed to pass the examinations on which government offices were awarded. Du Fu was an outspoken critic of the bloodshed and suffering that war visited on the common people.

Facing Snow

> After the battle, many new ghosts cry,
> The solitary old man murmurs in his grief.
> Ragged low cloud thins the light of dusk,
> Thick snow dances back and forth in the wind.
> The wine ladle's cast aside, the cup not green,
> The stove still looks as if a fiery red.
> To many places, communications are broken,
> I sit, but cannot read my books for grief.

Sources: "Humanistic Texts, Du Fu" (http://www.humanistictexts.org/dufu.htm); poem adapted from Henry H. Hart, *The Hundred Names: A Short Introduction to the Study of Chinese Poetry with Illustrative Translations* (Berkeley, 1933).

Poem on the Bend of a River (1)

> Each piece of flying blossom leaves spring the less,
> I grieve as myriad points float in the wind.
> I watch the last ones pass before my eyes,
> And cannot have enough wine pass my lips.
> Kingfishers nest by the little hall on the river,
> A unicorn lies at the tomb near the enclosure.
> One must go gladly at nature's gentle call,
> For what use is the trap of empty titles?

Source: "Chinese Poems, DuFu" (http://www.chinesepoems.com/du.html)

Wang Wei combined many talents. Besides being one of China's greatest poets, he had considerable talent as a painter and as a musician. His poems resemble those of Daoists inasmuch as they pay strong attention to nature and natural beauty, but they add a Buddhist's awareness of sensory illusion.

Replying to Sub-prefect Zhang

> Now in old age, I know the value of silence,
> The world's affairs no longer stir my heart.
> Turning to myself, I have no greater plan,
> All I can do is return to the forest of old.
> Wind from the pine trees blows my sash undone,
> The moon shines through the hills; I pluck the qin.
> You ask me why the world must rise and fall,
> Fishermen sing on the steep banks of the river.

Jinzhu Ridge

> Wingceltis and goldenrain shine at the empty bend,
> Fresh and green, rippling ever onward.
> A secret road leads up to Shangshan hill,
> Even the woodcutter does not know.

Source: "Chinese Poems, Wang Wei" (http://www.chinesepoems.com/wang.html)

▶ Analyze and Interpret

Try to pick out the Daoist, the Confucian, and the Buddhists themes in each of these poems.

who were educated along Confucian lines and living for the most part in self-governing villages.

The generals of the large army were kept under tight control and were not allowed those liberties in the outermost provinces that had often degenerated into warlordism in the past. The rest of society looked down on the military; a popular saying held that soldiers were the lowest types of humans and that good men should not be turned into soldiers any more than one would waste good iron to make nails. The military ranked even below the merchants, who gained somewhat in prestige during the Song Period but still occupied low rungs on the social ladder.

The Chinese economy reached an enviable state of smooth working and innovative production during this era. The final portion of the Grand Canal was completed in 611, an important link of the politically dominant North (the Yellow River plains) to the economically productive South (the Yangtze Valley). A population estimated at more than 100 million by the end of the Song Period was supported in decent conditions. The introduction of a new hybrid rice from Annam (Vietnam) helped feed this large population. It was now possible to grow two crops per year in South China, doubling the land's productivity with little additional expenditure of energy or resources. The volume of domestic and foreign trade increased markedly, aided by the development and use of paper money and sophisticated banking and credit operations.

Silk was now joined by porcelain as a major luxury export article. Despite the risk of breakage, it was exported to many lands, including such distant places as the Swahili cities in East Africa. Large ships that used the magnetic compass and the sternpost rudder—both Chinese inventions—were built for the active trade with Japan and Southeast Asia. The itinerant Chinese traders as well as colonies of Chinese peoples throughout Asia have their ancestors in this (Song) period of prosperity.

Foreign Affairs

Despite the triumphs and improvements in internal affairs under the Song Dynasty, China's control over its East Asian lands was drastically reduced from its high point during the Tang Dynasty. The emperors never succeeded in gaining firm control of the northern half of the country. Tibet and the far western province of Sinkiang were abandoned to the nomads who had continually contested the Han and Tang governments there. Fearful of the costs of reducing them to obedience, Vietnam and Korea were allowed to become autonomous regions, paying the Song a token tribute but effectively resisting any hints of Chinese sovereignty. The huge northeastern region of Manchuria, always a battleground between nomads and Chinese, broke away entirely.

These losses had a positive side, however. By giving up territories that were never firmly under China's hand, the Song were able to focus on the heartland, ruling the area between

the Yellow and Yangtze rivers from their capital at Kaifeng (Gaifung). For two centuries the Song rulers and their large armies were able to repel the increasing pressures from the northern and western tribes, but in the twelfth century they weakened. Toward the end of the 1100s, they lost any semblance of control over the far west to the Mongols. By the mid-1200s, the Song had been defeated by the descendants of Chinghis Khan and formally gave up the north and center of traditional China to them. The Song were able to hold on for a brief time in the South, but in 1279 there, too, dominion passed into the hands of the Mongols under Kubilai Khan—the first and only time China has been conquered in its entirety by outsiders. The Mongol **Yuan Dynasty** thus began its century-long reign (see Chapter 19).

BUDDHISM AND CHINESE CULTURE

The greatest single foreign cultural influence on China during the first millennium CE—and possibly ever—was the coming of Buddhism from its Indian birthplace. The Chinese proved responsive to the new faith, with all social and economic groups finding something in the doctrine that answered their needs. Buddhists believe in the essential equality of all. The enlightenment of the soul, which is the high point of a Buddhist life, is available to all who can find their way to it. Unlike Confucianism and Daoism, which are essentially philosophies of proper thought and conduct in this life and possess only incidental religious ideas, Buddhism, by the time it came to China, was a supernatural religion promising an afterlife of eternal bliss for the righteous. To the ordinary man and woman, this idea had far more appeal than any earthly philosophy. Another aspect of Buddhism's appeal was that the Mahayana version (see Chapter 5) adopted in China was very accommodating to existing beliefs—there was no conflict, for example, between traditional reverence toward the ancestors and the precepts of Buddhism in China.

The translation of Sanskrit texts into Chinese stimulated the literary qualities of the language, because the translators had to fashion ways of expressing difficult and complex ideas. Even more than prose, however, poetry benefited from the new religion and its ideals of serenity, self-mastery, and a peculiarly Chinese addition to classic Indian Buddhism—the appreciation of and joy in nature. Painting, sculpture, and architecture all show Buddhist influences, mostly traceable to India but some original to China in their conceptions. From about the fourth century onward, China's high-culture arts were strongly molded by Buddhist belief. They not only portrayed themes from the life of the Buddha but also showed in many ways the religion's interpretation of what proper human life should be.

So widespread was Buddhism's appeal that inevitably a reaction set in against it. In part, this reaction was a political power phenomenon. In the 800s, the Tang Dynasty exploited nativist sentiment against the "foreign" religion to curb the worrisome autonomy of the wealthy and tax-resistant Buddhist monasteries. Most of their property was expropriated. But the reaction was also philosophical and intellectual in the form of Neo-Confucianism and a general revival of the Confucian credo.

The Neo-Confucians were philosophers who sought to change the world through emphasis on aspects of the master's thought most fully developed by his later disciple, Mencius (370–290 BCE). In Neo-Confucianism, love and the responsibility of all to all were the great virtues. Unlike the Daoists and Buddhists, the Neo-Confucians insisted that all must partake of social life. Withdrawal and prolonged solitary meditation were impermissible. They also thought that formal education in morals and the arts and sciences was an absolute necessity for a decent life—it could not be left to the "enlightenment" of the individual seeker to discover what his fellow's welfare required.

The Confucians' efforts to hold their own against their Buddhist competitors were a major reason that the Song Period was so fertile in all philosophical and artistic fields.

Tang and Song era formal culture was supremely literary in nature. The accomplished official was also expected to be a good poet, a calligrapher, and a philosopher able to expound his views by quoting the "scriptures" of Confucian and other systems of thought. Skills in painting and music were also considered part of the normal equipment of an educated and powerful man. This was the ideal of the mandarin, the man who held public responsibilities and proved himself worthy of them by virtue of his rich and deep culture. This ideal was often a reality in Tang and later dynastic history.

SUMMARY

THE CHINESE IMPERIAL style was molded once and for all by the ruthless Legalist known as the First Emperor in the third century BCE. The Qin Dynasty he founded quickly disappeared, but for four centuries his Han successors built on the foundations he left them to rule a greatly expanded China. Softening the brutal Qin policies to an acceptable level, the Han dynasts made Confucianism into a quasi-official philosophy.

After the Han's dissolution and a period of anarchy, the 500 years of the Tang and Song dynasties comprised the Golden Age of Chinese culture. Despite intermittent internal dissension, the imperial government promulgated and was supported by a vision of proper conduct that was Confucian in essence and widely subscribed to by the educated classes.

Internally, both the Tang and the Song saw a tremendous development of the economy and its capacity to maintain a rapidly growing and urbanizing population. Thanks in large part to advances in agriculture and the expansion of international trade, few, if any, other civilizations could rival China's ability to supply all classes with the necessities of life. A series of technological inventions had immediate practical applications. It was also a period of extraordinary excellence in the fine arts and literature, which were supported by a large group of refined patrons and consumers in the persons of the landowning gentry and the mandarin officials. Buddhist influences were pervasive in both the popular and gentry cultures, rivaling but not overshadowing traditional Confucian thought.

In foreign affairs, the long seesaw struggle with the northern nomadic tribespeople was finally lost when the Mongols of Kubilai Khan defeated the last Song rulers and established the Yuan Dynasty. All of China thus fell under alien rule for the first and only time. Also during the Song, China took on more or less its modern territorial outlines, with its withdrawals from Vietnam, Korea, and Mongolia. Cultural and commercial contacts with Japan were expanded, and there was extensive commercial intercourse with the Muslims to the west and the Indians to the south.

▶ *Identification Terms*

Test your knowledge of this chapter's key concepts by defining the following terms. If you can't recall the meaning of certain terms, refresh your memory by looking up the boldfaced term in the chapter, turning to the Glossary at the end of the book, or working with the flashcards that are available on the *World Civilizations* Companion Website: **academic.cengage.com/adler**

burning of the books	Han Dynasty	meritocracy	Tang Dynasty
Era of the Warring States	Han synthesis	Song Dynasty	Yuan Dynasty
First Emperor	Hangzhou		

▶ Test Your Knowledge

Test your knowledge of this chapter by answering the following questions. Complete answers appear at the end of the book. You may find even more quiz questions in CengageNOW and on the *World Civilizations* Companion Website: **academic.cengage.com/adler**

1. The Qin First Emperor attained power by
   a. orchestrating a palace coup.
   b. playing on the superstitions of his people.
   c. assassinating the previous emperor.
   d. achieving triumph in battle.
   e. forging a political alliance with his strongest rival.
2. Which of the following was *not* a Chinese invention?
   a. The magnetic compass
   b. The waterwheel
   c. Paper from wood
   d. Decimals
   e. Gunpowder
3. Which of the following was not formally a requirement for joining the Chinese bureaucracy?
   a. Single-minded dedication
   b. Extensive formalized education
   c. Connections with the higher social classes
   d. Passing of written examinations
   e. A high degree of intellectual ability
4. The Tang Dynasty was extremely influential in Chinese history as the
   a. developer of the mandarin system of scholar officials.
   b. creator of the village democracy.
   c. reformer of the military.
   d. originator of the canal system.
   e. creator of an imperial university system.
5. The Song Dynasty was finally overturned by the
   a. Mongol conquerors.
   b. Korean invaders.
   c. Japanese pirates.
   d. Tang Dynasty.
   e. army of Shih Huang-di.
6. Marco Polo served as an official in the service of
   a. the Song emperor.
   b. the Mongol emperor.
   c. an Italian embassy to the Chinese government.
   d. Indian visitors to the Chinese court.
   e. an emperor of the Tang Dynasty.
7. Chinese Buddhism was different from the original conceptions of Siddhartha Gautama in
   a. the rigidity and uniformity of its doctrine.
   b. its insistence on the lifestyle of a hermit.
   c. its supernatural religious element.
   d. its appeal to only the upper classes.
   e. its emphasis on the study of religious works.
8. Buddhism found many sympathizers in China because it
   a. offered immortality to all social classes.
   b. was an import from Korea.
   c. came from a civilization that the Chinese regarded as superior to their own.
   d. demanded the rigorous intellectual effort that the Chinese so admired.
   e. echoed their long-held reverence for nature.
9. The burning of the books by the First Emperor was followed by the
   a. Song Dynasty.
   b. Sui Dynasty.
   c. Mongol Empire.
   d. Tang Dynasty.
   e. Han Dynasty.
10. The Grand Canal linked the Yellow River Plains to
    a. the South China Sea.
    b. the Korean peninsula.
    c. the Yangtze Valley.
    d. the Great Wall.
    e. northern India.

CENGAGENOW™

Enter *CengageNOW* using the access card that is available with this text. *CengageNOW* will assist you in understanding the content in this chapter with lesson plans generated for your needs and provide you with a connection to the *Wadsworth World History Resource Center* (see description at right for details).

▶  **World History Resource Center**

Enter the Resource Center using either your *CengageNOW* access card or your standalone access card for the *Wadsworth World History Resource Center*. Organized by topic, this website includes quizzes; images; over 350 primary source documents; interactive simulations, maps, and timelines; movie explorations; and a wealth of other resources. You can read the following documents, and many more, at the *Wadsworth World History Resource Center*:

Marco Polo, *Prologue to Travels*

17 JAPAN AND SOUTHEAST ASIA

> *In life there is nothing more than life; in death nothing more than death; we are being born and are dying at every moment.*
> —Dogen, Thirteenth-Century Zen Master

VERY EARLY JAPAN
Buddhism and Shinto ◆ Government and Administration

THE NARA AND HEIAN PERIODS, 710–1185

THE KAMAKURA PERIOD, 1185–1333

THE ARTS AND CULTURE IN MEDIEVAL JAPAN
Buddhist Evolution

THE ASHIKAGA SHOGUNATE, 1336–1573
Contacts with China ◆ Korea

THE EARLY SOUTHEAST ASIAN STATES
Funan and Champa ◆ Kampuchea ◆ Sri Vijaya ◆ Majapahit ◆ Burma and Thailand ◆ Vietnam

THE ISLAND NATION OF Japan emerges from the mists of pre-history in the early centuries CE, when Chinese travelers begin to report on their adventures there. Geography explains both Japan's receptivity to Chinese influence and its ability to reject that influence when it wished. Japan could adapt foreign ideas and values to its needs without having to suffer military or political domination from abroad. For the first thousand years of recorded Japanese history, until about 1500 CE, the Japanese state was successful in this adaptation, fitting imported governmental and cultural institutions to existing customs and the requirements of the native society.

VERY EARLY JAPAN

The Japanese islands (the four main ones are Hokkaido, Honshu, Kyushu, and Shikoku) are situated off the Korean peninsula and Siberia, separated from the mainland by 120 to several hundred miles of open water (see Map 17.1). Together, these mountainous volcanic islands are about the size of California. Only about one-fifth of the surface area is suitable for agriculture, and Japan's climate ranges from sub-arctic in the extreme north to temperate on the main island of Honshu (HAHN-shoo). The Japanese people are considered the most homogeneous in Asia, and this homogeneity has played a major role in the country's history right up to the present day. There has been no need to assimilate

MAP 17.1 Japan and Its Neighbors

The hundred-mile interval between Japan and Korea was not difficult to cross even in ancient times, and Chinese cultural influences came into Japan via Korean intermediaries until direct contacts were established in the seventh century.

MAP QUESTION

Considering the likelihood that the Japanese originally came from Korea, which Japanese island(s) might have continued to shelter Japan's original population?

numerous immigrants or to make conscious concessions to other cultures. Where the original settlers came from is uncertain, but the Koreans and Japanese are much closer ethnically than the Chinese and Japanese. The native oral language of Japan is entirely different from Chinese. The written language, which originally borrowed heavily from written Chinese, is still different in many ways.

According to ancient Japanese legends, the Japanese people are the descendants of the Sun Goddess (Jimmu Tenno), who continues to have a special relationship with the country through the person of the emperor. For many centuries, the Japanese thought of the emperor as divine, a status that was only finally and formally rejected by terms of the Japanese peace treaty after World War II. Archaeological data reveal that as early as the middle of the first millennium BCE, an early faming people known as the Jomon (joh-MAHN) people inhabited the southern island of Kyushu, burying their dead chieftains in elaborate mounds

with many pottery figures. The Jomon became masters of wet-rice culture, the nutritional basis of all later Japanese civilization. Their success in adopting rice growing laid the foundations for the Yayoi culture a few centuries later, when these people (who seem to have been the ancestors of the present day Japanese) moved northward from their original home on Kyushu (kee-OO-shoo) island. It was the Yayoi (YAH-yoi) who eventually organized the first regional governments and produced the first Japanese state. The first written records do not appear until as late as the eighth century CE, however; before that we must rely on archaeology and the occasional surviving travel reports of Chinese visitors.

Buddhism and Shinto

The two major religious belief systems of both ancient and modern Japan are the import Buddhism and the native Shinto. Buddhism in Japan, as everywhere, proved capable of undergoing many mutations and adapting to local needs. The special Japanese versions are Zen, the Pure Land, and the Nichiren sects, which gradually developed after the introduction of the religion in the sixth century from Korea. Distinctions among the sects became clearer as time passed (see the discussion later in the chapter).

Buddhism gave Japanese religion a much broader and nobler intellectual content. Its insistence on ethical action and compassion for the weak and unfortunate was as beneficially transforming to Japanese life as it had been earlier in India and China. In Japan more than elsewhere in Asia, Buddhism emphasized meditation techniques. For the more intellectually demanding followers, Buddhist beliefs could be complex, but for most Japanese believers, the religion was relatively simple and joyful in its acceptance of things-as-they-are and in its anticipation of happiness in an eternal Heaven.

The **Shinto** (SHIHN-toh) religion is a native Japanese product, but it is fairly close to Chinese Daoism. The word *Shinto* means "the way of the gods," and the religion combines a simple animism, in which all kinds of natural objects possess a spirit, with a worship of great deities, such as the Sun Goddess, who are immortal and benevolent but not perceivable by the human senses. The Shinto legends with which all Japanese are familiar speak of a time when all things, even stones and trees, could speak and interact with humans, but they were forced into silence later and now must evidence their powers to humans through the *kami* (KAH-mee), or spirits, that inhabit them.

Shinto is a basically optimistic, guilt-free view of the world and personal ethics. It has no theology of the gods or sacred book, no heaven or hell or wrathful Yahweh, and no Fall of Adam. Shinto is supremely adaptable, however, and could serve as a sort of permanent underpinning to whatever more advanced, supernatural religion the individual Japanese might prefer. It persists to this day in that role.

Government and Administration

For the most part, Japan has a mountainous and broken terrain, which, as in the Greek example, helps explain why the process of creating a central government with effective controls was peculiarly slow and subject to reverses. The beginning of organized large-scale government occurred in the Yamato (yah-MAH-toh) Period in the fifth and sixth centuries CE. At that time the term *Japan* indicated a collection of noble clans, who ruled over the commoners by a combination of military and economic power familiar to students of feudal Europe. The Yamato, the biggest and most potent of these clans, ruled over a good-sized arable area in central Honshu near what is now the city of Osaka (oh-SAH-kah). The Yamato claimed direct descent from the Sun Goddess and founded what was to become the imperial family of the Japanese state. This family, or more precisely the dynasty that began with the Yamato clan leaders, has never been overturned. The present-day emperor is considered the direct descendant from the earliest Yamato, although he is no longer seen as a divinity.

During this early period, the relationship between Japan and Korea was important for both countries (see below).

HORYU-JI PAGODA. The massive Shinto temple is the world's oldest wooden building still in use. The 700-year-old structure stands in a park in the ancient Japanese capital of Nara. The pagoda style of architecture was brought to Japan from China and found new adaptations there.

Calmann & King, London, UK/Bridgeman Art Library

There appear to have been invasions as well as much commerce in both directions, and many Koreans lived among the Japanese until well into the first millennium CE. From Korea came several major cultural imports—most important, Buddhism, which arrived in Japan in the sixth century.

Buddhism soon became the favored viewpoint of the Yamato state's upper class, and by the beginning of the seventh century, it was used as the vehicle of a general strengthening and clarification of the role of the central government in Japan. In 604, Prince Shotoku (SHOH-toh-koo), a Yamato leader and a devout Buddhist, offered the *Seventeen Point Constitution,* which is the founding document of the Japanese state. It was not really a constitution in the modern sense but rather a list inspired by Buddhist and Confucian doctrine of what a government and a loyal citizenry *ought* to do. It has had great influence on both the theory and practice of political science in Japan ever since.

The way of affairs in China was the general model for the Seventeen Points, so to put his constitution into effect, Shotoku sent selected youths to China for a period of study and training under teachers, artists, and officials. In the seventh century, thousands of Japanese were thus prepared for governmental responsibilities and were also trained in the arts and techniques of Tang China. The Chinese model was particularly apparent in government. The village was the foundational unit of all civic affairs. The state's territory was divided into administrative units similar to the Chinese provinces and districts. Tax money was now to be paid to the central government by the peasantry, thus weakening the local lords who had previously been the tax collectors. A ministry of eight officials was created to advise and assist the emperor, whose position was greatly strengthened by the official adoption of the Sun Goddess myth. In all, this was one of the earliest and most impressive examples of deliberate cultural transfer from one people to another in history.

The Chinese example had a powerful influence in most public and many private spheres, but it was not overwhelming. The Japanese soon showed they were confident of their own abilities to distinguish what was useful and what was not. For example, they adopted the Tang equal field system, in which land was frequently redistributed among the peasants to attempt to ensure equity, but the Japanese soon changed this system to allow an individual to have transferable (salable) rights to a parcel of productive land no matter who actually tilled it. Another example was the Japanese approach to bureaucracy. Although they admired the efficiency of the Chinese bureaucracy, they did not imitate it. The concept of competitive meritocracy was and remained alien to Japanese thinking. Having competitive exams open to all threatened deep-rooted Japanese social values.

Government remained an aristocratic privilege in Japan; the lower classes were not allowed to attain high posts, regardless of their merit.

THE NARA AND HEIAN PERIODS, 710–1185

For seventy years after the death of Prince Shotoku in 622, the reforms he advocated were continued by members of the Fujiwara clan, which had intermarried with the Yamato and were to be the leading actors in Japanese government for the next couple of centuries. The first capital, Nara, was established in central Honshu, in 710. Buddhism was especially popular among the Nara clans, and when a Buddhist monk named Dokyo (DOH-kee-yoh) attempted to use his following in the numerous monasteries to usurp political power, there was a strong reaction. Dokyo also allegedly used his position as chaplain to the empress to further his political ambitions. When the empress died, Dokyo was driven into exile. This experience may explain why in all the remainder of Japanese history there have been only two other female rulers.

The reaction against the Buddhist monks and monasteries did not mean a rejection of the religion. In the early ninth century, Japanese visitors to the mainland became acquainted with the Tendai and Shingon sects of Buddhism and took them back to Japan. These sects, in contrast to the earlier version, featured magical elements and promises of salvation to all, which made them highly popular, and they spread quickly. During this period, Buddhism in Japan started a steady transformation from a narrow preoccupation of the court aristocrats into a vehicle of popular devotion.

In 794, the imperial court was moved to a new town called Heian (high-YAHN; modern **Kyoto**), where it remained until modern times. At this time, the aristocrats checked further Chinese influence by severing relations with the mainland—one of the several episodes of deliberate seclusion with which Japanese history is studded. For about a century, contacts with China and Korea were strictly limited, while the Japanese aristocracy devoted themselves to organizing the government and creating a cultural/artistic style that was uniquely their own. The process lasted several centuries and was more or less complete by about 1200.

Government during the Heian era quickly became a struggle—almost always concealed—between the Chinese model of an all-powerful emperor ruling through a bureaucracy and the kind of rough-and-ready decentralized feudalism that had marked the Yamato state before the reforms. The feudal aristocrats soon won out, as they proved more adept at securing the tax from rural peasant lands than the central government. Little by little, the

emperors were reduced to ceremonial figures, accorded great respect but essentially without means of imposing their will. A series of provincial noble families—above all, the **Fujiwara** (foo-jee-WAH-rah) **clan**—were able to make themselves the real powers. The Fujiwara ruled from behind the throne by arranging marriages between their daughters and the children of the monarchs and then having themselves nominated as regents. They remained content to dominate indirectly and did not try to displace the ruler.

This system of disguised rule by powerful families at court was to become a recurrent part of Japanese life under the name of the **shogunate** (SHOH-guh-nate). The true head of government was the *shogun,* or commander-in-chief of the imperial army. The shoguns stayed in the background but decided everything that mattered, while the divine emperors conducted the ceremonies.

After this system had worked fairly well for two centuries, it began to break down as rival clans finally found ways to break the Fujiwara monopoly. In the outlying provinces, and especially in eastern Japan, warriors known as *bushi* (BOO-shee) were experiencing a rise in power and prestige. The bushi, or **samurai**, as they are better known in the West, were the executors of the will of the large landholders and the enforcers of public order in a given locality. In their outlook, means of support, and demanding code of conduct (**bushido**; BOO-shee-doh), the bushi were similar to the medieval knights of western Europe. There were, however, some important differences: the samurai's code (see the Law and Government box) included no provision for chivalry toward women or for generosity toward a beaten opponent, who expected to die by ritual beheading. This made the samurai a more brutal and menacing figure to the ordinary man and woman.

Using their samurai effectively, the rival clans threw out the Fujiwara regents and then fought one another for supremacy. The house of Minamoto (mee-nah-MOH-toh) eventually won out and introduced the **Kamakura** (kah-mah-KOO-rah) **shogunate**.

THE KAMAKURA PERIOD, 1185–1333

The Kamakura Period of Japan's history (in most aspects, a Japanese version of European feudalism) was marked by the complete domination of the country by the samurai and their overlords in the clan aristocracy. The powers of the imperial court in Kyoto declined nearly to the vanishing point. Political leadership at any level depended on two factors: control of adequate numbers of fighting men and control of adequate *shoen* to support those fighting men.

The *shoen* (SHOH-ehn) were parcels of productive land, sometimes including villages. They had originally been created in the early Heian era as support for monasteries or rewards to servants of the emperor for outstanding service. Their critical feature was their exemption from the central government's taxing authority. Whereas most Japanese land was always considered the property of the emperor, lent out to his favored servants, the shoen and the rights to their use and income, called *shiki* (SHEE-kee), were strictly private and remained outside normal laws.

A monastery or official who owned shoen would often convey them to a more powerful person, who would allow the original owner to continue as tenant under his protection. Thus, the ownership and use system became ever more complex and eventually resembled the European system of feudal vassalage. It was not unusual for a shoen to have three to five "lords" who each had some special rights (*shiki*) to the land and its produce. Shoen and shiki were thus the currency used by the aristocrats to pay their samurai. In this sense and others we noted earlier, the samurai closely resembled the European knights, but there were enough differences that some authorities see the samurai as quite different from the knights and reject the idea that Japanese society in this era was basically the same as medieval European.

One of the chief differences was the **bakufu** (bah-KOO-foo), or military government under the shogun, which had no European equivalent. The shogun, always a member of the dominant clan controlling the emperor, was supposedly the executor of the emperor's will as head of the army. In fact, he was totally independent and the real ruler of Japan. The Kamakura Period derives its name from the small town of Kamakura where the shogun of the Minamoto clan resided—quite separate from the imperial court in Heian/Kyoto.

Perhaps the most dramatic demonstration of the way the shogun and his bakufu organization could lead the nation occurred in the late 1200s, when the feared Mongols under Kubilai Khan prepared to invade the islands (see Map 17.2). Having conquered China in its entirety and all of eastern Asia to Vietnam, the Mongols sought to do what the Chinese themselves had never attempted. Twice, the khan assembled armadas from his bases in Korea and landed on Kyushu, where the waiting samurai met his forces on the beach. The effectiveness of the Mongols' most potent weapon, their cavalry, was sharply limited by the terrain and by Japanese defenses, including a long wall along the coast that horses could not surmount. The Mongols called off the first invasion after fierce resistance led to a stalemate. The second attack in 1281 ended in a huge disaster when a typhoon (the *kamikaze,* or "divine wind") sank most of their ships and the 140,000 men on them. Mongol rule was thus never extended to the Japanese.

LAW AND GOVERNMENT

Samurai Honor

The samurai warriors were bound to a strict code of conduct that, among other things, told them that they were expected to die rather than surrender. Because it was commonplace for the victorious commander to order the execution of the captured enemy, the samurai usually had no choice in the matter. An expert in medieval Japanese affairs tells us:

> Those of the defeated who had not been killed in action often had recourse to suicide. We are in possession of many accounts of these suicides, whether the warrior cut open his abdomen with his dagger (*hari-kari* or *seppuku*), or threw himself onto his sword, or preferred to perish in his burning house with his most faithful servants and vassals (*junshi,* or collective suicide). When he was about to be taken prisoner, Yoshitsune "stabbed himself under the left breast, plunging the blade in so deeply it all but came out again in his back; then he made three further incisions, disemboweling himself and wiping the dagger on the sleeve of his robe." Thereupon his wife sought death at the hands of one of their vassals.

Some warriors' suicides were deliberately spectacular for the edification of their descendants:

> Yoshiteru climbed up on the watchtower of the second gate, from where he made sure that the Prince was now far away (for he had taken his place and his clothes in order to deceive

SAMURAI ARMOR. The expenses entailed in properly outfitting a samurai were sometimes borne by the daimyo, who was his lord and to whom he was pledged for lifelong service, but the two swords carried by the warrior were always his personal property. By the end of the Kamakura era in the 1300s, the samurai were a separate class in Japanese society, a position retained until the late nineteenth century.

Tower of London, London, UK/Bridgeman Art Library

the enemy and give his lord time to flee). When the time had come, he cut the handrail of the tower window so that he could be better seen, calling out his lord's name: "I am Son-un, prince of the blood of the first rank, Minister of Military Affairs and second son of Go-Daigo Tenno, ninety-fifth emperor since Jimmu Tenno. . . . Defeated by the rebels, I am taking my own life to avenge my wrongs in the Beyond.

> Learn from my example how a true warrior dies by his own hand when Fate plays him false!" Stripping off his armor, he threw it to the foot of the tower. Next he took off the jacket of his underdress with its tight fitting sleeves . . . and clad only in his brocaded breeches, he thrust a dagger into his white skin. He cut in a straight line from left to right, cast his entrails onto the handrail, placed the point of the sword in his mouth and flung himself headlong towards the ground.

> This kind of death was admired by the samurai and deemed heroic and worthy of praise by generations to come. Many put an end to their life in this way.

▶ *Analyze and Interpret*

How did this suicidal concept of military honor influence the medieval history of Japan? What does the threat of Yoshiteru to "avenge my wrongs in the Beyond" seem to say about the nature of the life to come?

Source: From L. Frederic, *Daily Life in Japan at the Time of the Samurai* (New York: Praeger, 1972), p. 190f.

THE ARTS AND CULTURE IN MEDIEVAL JAPAN

The partial severance of relations with China following the establishment of the capital in Heian allowed the Japanese full freedom to develop their own culture. Their language and literature show that they were vigorously imaginative. The Japanese and Chinese languages are radically different in both structure and vocabulary; the earliest Japanese writing was a close but necessarily clumsy adaptation of

MAP 17.2 Japan and the Mongol Invasion Routes in the Thirteenth Century

From their bases in Korea and northern China, the Mongols mounted two invasion attempts against Japan within a seven-year period.

MAP QUESTIONS
Considering that the Mongols were inexperienced at certain types of warfare, where were the likely weaknesses in their campaigns against Japan?

Chinese. This script was used in the eighth-century *Chronicles of Japan* and the *Records of Ancient Matters,* the first Japanese books. In the Heian Period, the language was simplified and brought into closer conformity with oral Japanese. The gradual withdrawal from Chinese vocabulary and modes of expression forced the court authors to invent literary models and expressions of their own. Japanese writers thus evolved two *syllabaries,* written signs that were based on phonetics, rather than being ideographs or pictographs like Chinese, and could therefore be used to match the syllables of the spoken language—in other words, the beginnings of an alphabet.

The world's first novel, the famous **Tale of Genji** (GEHN-jee) by the court lady Murasaki Shikibu (moo-rah-SAH-kee shee-KEE-boo; c. 976–1026), was written in the early eleventh century and tells us a great deal about the manners and customs of the Japanese aristocracy of the day (see the Arts and Culture box for an excerpt from Lady Murasaki). It reveals a culture of sensitive, perceptive people, who took intense pleasure in nature and in the company of other refined persons. The impressions left by the *Tale of Genji* are furthered by the other classic court tale of this era, Lady Sei Shonagon's (say shoh-NAH-guhn) *Pillow Book,* a collection of anecdotes and satirical essays centered on the art of love. Neither of these works owes anything to foreign models. The fact that their authors were women gives some indication of the high status of females among the educated class.

Poetry was the special strength of the early writers. Very early, the Japanese love of nature was evident. Prose was considered somewhat vulgar, and the domain of females, but poetry was for everyone—everyone, that is, in the tiny fraction of the population that partook of cultured recreations.

Japanese painting in the Heian era exhibited a marvelous sense of design and draftsmanship, following on the calligraphy practiced in the written word. Scenes from nature were preferred, but there was also a great deal of lively portraiture, much of it possessing the sense of amusement that marks many of Japan's arts. The wellborn were expected

ARTS AND CULTURE

Lady Murasaki

In the eleventh century, a Japanese noblewoman, whose name is uncertain, wrote the world's first work of literature that can be called a novel. The *Tale of Genji,* written between 1015 and 1025, is a long, fascinatingly detailed account of the life of a courtier at the Kyoto imperial palace and his relations with others there.

About the life of the author, we know only some fragments. She was born into an official's family, a member of the large and powerful Fujiwara clan that long occupied a major place in Japanese affairs. Shikibu, as she was named, probably received the minimal education customary for even high-class Japanese women.

Presumably, she did not know Chinese, which was the literary language of well-educated males in this epoch. She was married to another official at age twenty, but her husband died soon after, leaving his widow with a young daughter. For some years, Shikibu retired to a chaste widowhood in a provincial town. In 1004, her father received a long-sought appointment as governor of a province and used his influence to have his widowed daughter made lady-in-waiting to the empress Akiko in Kyoto.

From 1008 to 1010, Lady Murasaki (as she was now known at court) kept a diary, which was translated and published not long ago, but her major effort in her years with the empress in the extremely refined Kyoto palace was the *Tale of Genji.* In fifty-four books or chapters, which together are more than twice as long as Tolstoy's *War and Peace,* Lady Murasaki depicts the panorama of Japanese upper-class life in the ceremony-filled, ritualistic court of the emperor and his consort. She thus made a memorable, subtle outline of the traditions that guided the Japanese uppermost class and that would continue to be honored for most of the ensuing millennium.

PRINCE GENJI. The artful lover is shown here departing in the moonlight, in a nineteenth-century illustration for the famous novel. On one side is a courtly lady and her attendant watching the prince's departure.

Private Collection/Bridgeman Art Library

Prince Genji (Shining One) is a fictional character but presumably was drawn closely on an actual one. Stricken by the death of his mother, to whom he was greatly attached, the young man comes to court to forget his sorrow. Popular with both sexes for his gallantry and charm, he engages in a series of love affairs with the court women, in which he displays both his amorous character and his artistic refinement. In a setting where manners are everything, Genji reigns supreme, but his escapades with the ladies lead to trouble with jealous husbands and suitors, and Genji is banished from the court.

He soon obtains forgiveness and returns, only to fall deeply in love with the commoner Murasaki, whom he makes his wife. But she dies young and childless: heartbroken, Genji soon follows her in death.

The action now shifts to Genji's son and grandson by a former marriage. These two are in competition for the same girl, Ukifune, who feels committed to both in different ways. Depressed and ashamed, Ukifune attempts suicide but fails, and she decides to salvage her life by renouncing the world and entering a Buddhist monastery. The competing father and son are both deprived of what they want and are left in bewildered grief at their unconsummated love. The novel ends on a note of deep gloom.

The psychological intricacies of the story have fascinated Japanese readers for 900 years. The novel was first translated into English in the 1930s by Arthur Waley. Of Lady Murasaki's last years, we know nothing.

▶ *Analyze and Interpret*

Why do you think Murasaki chose this anything-but-happy ending to her novel? How much does it relate to what you understand as the ordinary lives of Japanese commoners in her day? Would that relationship be of concern to Lady Murasaki?

---

to be proficient in dance and music, and calligraphy was as revered as it was in China.

Great attention was given to the cultivation of beauty in all its manifestations: literary, visual, plastic, and psychic.

Men as well as women were expected to take pains with their appearance; both used cosmetics. (Blackened teeth were the rage among Heian court ladies!) A refined sense of color in dress was mandatory. Both sexes cried freely, and a sensitive

exclaim "Eat, drink, and be merry for tomorrow we die"; their message was more "Take pleasure now in the flight of the butterfly, for tomorrow neither it nor you will be with us."

Buddhist Evolution

Two Buddhist sects, the Pure Land and the Nichiren (NEE-chee-rehn), made many converts during the Kamakura Period. Both emphasized the salvationist aspect of the religion and the possibility of attaining nirvana through faith alone. The founder of the Pure Land sect, Honen (*c.* 1133–1212), insisted that the Buddha would save those souls who displayed their devotion to him by endlessly repeating his name. The Nichiren, who took their name from their thirteenth-century founder, held a similar belief in the mystical power of chanting devotional phrases and also emphasized the immortality of the soul. The Nichiren differed from all other Buddhists in being highly nationalistic and insisting that they alone had the power to lead the Japanese people on the righteous path.

Zen Buddhism, on the other hand, insisted on strenuous meditation exercises as the only way to purify the mind and prepare it for the experience of nirvana. Rising to prominence in the thirteenth century along with the Pure Land and Nichiren sects, Zen (derived from the Chinese *ch'an*) was to become the most influential of all forms of Buddhist worship in Japan. It was the preferred form for the samurai, who found that its emphases on self-reliance, rigorous discipline, and anti-intellectualism fit closely with their bushido code.

Interestingly, despite its popularity among warriors, Zen also underlay much of the Japanese interpretations of beauty and truth and remained a powerful influence on the visual arts. The famous rock gardens, for example, are a physical rendition of Zen principles of simplicity and restraint. Far outnumbered in adherents by both Pure Land and Nichiren, Zen became the favored belief among the upper class, and it has been the form of Buddhism peculiarly identified with Japan in foreign eyes.

THE ASHIKAGA SHOGUNATE, 1336–1573

The expenses of summoning a huge army to repel the Mongols in the 1280s proved fatal to the Minamoto clan. Despite their desperate efforts, they lost their hold on power. In 1336, the **Ashikaga** (ah-shee-KAH-gah) **clan** succeeded in establishing themselves in the shogunate, a position they continued to hold until the late sixteenth century.

The Ashikaga shoguns ruled from Kyoto as the head of an extended group of *daimyo* (DEYE-mee-oh), nobles who

Chinese and Japanese Special Fund, courtesy of Museum of Fine Arts, Boston

A JAPANESE LANDSCAPE. Japanese painting strives for a harmonious balance between the works of humanity and Nature, and this balance is revealed in this sixteenth-century work. Although natural objects are given much space by the artist, the painting's focal point is the house and the human figure within it.

sadness was cultivated. The Buddhist insistence on the transitory quality of all good things—the reminder that nothing is permanent—was at the heart of this aristocratic culture. Life was to be enjoyed, not to be worried about or reformed. The wise saw this instinctively and drew the proper conclusions. The Japanese would never have been so crude as to

much resembled the dukes and counts of feudal Europe in their lifestyle and powers. Some daimyo were much more powerful than others, and at times they were practically independent of the shogun. The most trusted vassals of the reigning shogun were entrusted with the estates surrounding Kyoto, whereas the outer provinces were rife with rebellion and conflicts among the daimyo.

The Ashikaga Period is the culmination of Japanese feudalism, one long and bloody tale of wars among the nobility and between groups of nobles and the shogun. For long periods all semblance of central authority seemed to have broken down in Japan. The imperial court was shoved still further into the background and did not play an independent political role at all during this era. All concerned gave verbal respect and honor to the reigning emperor, but these phrases were not accompanied by any devolution of power to him.

In the period embraced by the Kamakura and Ashikaga shogunates, 1200–1500, Japanese art forms turned definitively away from the emulation of Chinese models and became fully rooted in Japanese experience. Cultural institutions also reflect the increasing attention given to the warrior (samurai) in this age of constant war. The new forms of popular Buddhist worship and the literature of the Kamakura epoch glorified the simple, straightforward virtues of the soldier, in sharp contrast to the subtleties and introspection of the earlier *Tale of Genji* and other stories of the court society.

Contacts with China

Contacts with Song China were resumed and continued to be close throughout the Kamakura and Ashikaga shogunates, especially in trade. The Chinese especially desired the very fine Japanese steel for swords, which rivaled the "Damascus blades" for which European knights paid a fortune. Japan, in turn, received much from China, including the habit of tea drinking, which led to a whole subdivision of Japan's domestic culture, the tea ceremony. The coming of the Mongols briefly interrupted this commerce, but it soon resumed. Many goods were exchanged by force or illegally. Japanese pirates and smugglers gave the early Ming Dynasty (1378–1664) so much trouble that for a time, the Chinese rulers actually attempted to withdraw their coastal populations and make them live inland. Needless to say, this scheme was wholly impractical, and the smuggling went on unabated for another century, until Japan retired into voluntary seclusion (see Chapter 27).

Korea

As mentioned earlier, much of the commerce in goods and ideas between Japan and China was mediated through Korea. That country had already been a civilized society for several hundred years by the time the Japanese were organizing the Yamato (yah-MOH-toh) state. Korea in turn had been strongly affected by its proximity to China and had fallen into the Chinese orbit during the later Han and the Tang dynastic periods. At this time, the Korean peninsula was divided between three contesting kingdoms, all of which became tributary states of China under the powerful Tang Dynasty. Confucian ethics were widely adopted by the upper class, and the Chinese style of centralized government by bureaucracy was imposed after the unification of the country in the tenth century by one of the three contestants, the kingdom of Silla.

The rulers of Silla imitated the Tang governors in China but were not completely successful in their political strivings to rule as the "Son of Heaven." A feudal division of power between king and local lords continued. Fortunately for the dynasty, the collapse of the Tang in Beijing and the weakness of the Chinese thereafter allowed the Koreans a large degree of autonomy for the next several centuries. It was during this era that Korean national culture received its most important monuments, and the amalgam of Buddhist faith with Confucian ethics was deeply and permanently embedded in the educated class.

Only with the coming of the conquering Mongols in the thirteenth century did Korea again fall under strict alien controls. As in China, and for the same reasons, the era of Mongol rule was painful for the Koreans, and the Korean king became a mere Mongol agent. When the Mongols were driven out of China, they were also forced out of Korea, and a new period of quasi-independence under a new dynasty began.

THE EARLY SOUTHEAST ASIAN STATES

The term *Southeast Asia* is a recent invention, not coming into wide usage until after World War II. It denotes an enormous and varied area ranging from Burma in the northwest to Indonesia's islands in the southeast. By general consensus Vietnam, Cambodia, Laos, Malaysia, Thailand, and the Philippine Islands are included in this region as well (see Map 17.3).

Although all of these states but Thailand entered modern times as colonial possessions of European states, they all had a lengthy history of independent political organization previously. Their history was very much a factor in defining and segregating one people from others despite strong ethnic similarity. Most of the mainland Southeast Asians are descended from speakers of the

MAP 17.3 Southeast Asia, 500 CE–1200 CE

Through the Strait of Malacca at the tip of the Malaysian peninsula passed the largest volume of maritime trade in the world during this epoch and later.

MAP QUESTIONS
Where were the likely points of overland and oceanic passage for merchants trading between the Indian Ocean routes and China? What other factors facilitated the early development of trade and states in this region?

Turco-Mongolian language group, whereas most of the islanders are descended from speakers of Austronesian languages, with modern admixtures everywhere of Chinese and Indian immigrants. The original inhabitants of the mainland seem to have drifted slowly southward from southern China and eastward from India around 80,000 years ago, whereas most of the islanders came apparently from the mainland at some later dates. Archaeology has shown Neolithic farming sites dating to the fifth millennium BCE scattered throughout the region.

The earliest political-cultural units existed in the shadow of either imperial China or India, and these states were to have permanent influence on the Southeast Asians in many different spheres. As a general rule, China's influence was founded on military and diplomatic hegemony, whereas India's came via either a trading or a cultural-philosophical channel. The dividing line between the Chinese and the Indian spheres of culture was located in Vietnam, and there was little overlap.

Only in one Southeast Asian country—Vietnam—was the Chinese factor so powerful as to create at times an unwilling or coerced satellite. Elsewhere several influences conspired to make India the model and leading partner of Southeast Asia in cultural affairs: the activity of the Indians in the busy East–West Indian Ocean trade, the similarities in the Indian and Southeast Asian economies, and the extraordinary flexibility of the Hindu/Buddhist religious traditions (see Chapter 15).

Funan and Champa

The earliest mainland entities to be historically or archaeologically proven were Funan, in the Mekong River delta, and Champa (CHAHM-pah), in central Vietnam. Little is known for certain about ancient Champa and Funan (foo-NAHN). Both became empires of moderate extent during the early Christian era, and both were Hindu states, in the sense that the governing group was strongly influenced by Hindu Indian ideas and individuals. Funan succumbed to the Khmers (discussed later) in the sixth century and was wiped from the map. Champa managed to survive in some form all the way into the nineteenth century, when its Vietnamese neighbors finally overwhelmed it.

Kampuchea

In the seventh century, the conquerors of Funan moved into the politically dominant role that they would continue to occupy for the next several hundred years. These conquerors were the **Khmers** (kheh-MERS), ancestors of the present-day Cambodians. They built the great civilization centered on the city of Angkor and its surrounding villages.

Kampuchea (kahm-poo-CHEE-yah)—the original (and current) name of the Khmer state otherwise known as Cambodia—was the greatest of the ancient Southeast Asian mainland kingdoms. It remained so until its slow decline and fall to the invading Thais. Its wealth was based on a wet-rice agrarian economy that supported perhaps a million people in and close to Angkor (Chapter 15). The economy was based on hydrological engineering rivaling that of the Nile valley. These works modified the effects of the huge peaks and valleys of the monsoon weather pattern. They served some 12 million acres of paddies, which were capable of giving three harvests of rice per year.

Kampuchea began as another Hindu kingdom, with a semi-divine king, but in the twelfth and thirteenth centuries Hindu belief was supplanted by Hinayana Buddhism (see Chapter 5), with its emphasis on the equality of men and rejection of monarchic divinity. Not even the immense temple at Angkor Wat, built as a king's funeral monument like the pyramids of Egypt, could reestablish the prestige of the throne. Perhaps the temple contributed to its decline because of the heavy taxation its construction necessitated—another similarity to the Egyptian experience. The steady chipping away of Khmer territories by the Champa state on its east and the Thais on its north and west seems to have been as much a consequence as a cause of the decline of royal powers. By the late fourteenth century, Thais were taking over Angkor and much of the Khmer kingdom. The temple-city was abandoned in the early fifteenth century, not to be heard of again until French explorers, acting for the new colonial power, rediscovered it after a half-millennium's lapse.

Sri Vijaya

If Kampuchea was mainland Southeast Asia's primary power, the maritime empire of Sri Vijaya (sree vee-JAH-yah) held sway over much of the insular region during these same centuries. One of the most important sources for very early history, the diary of the Chinese Buddhist pilgrim I Jing (ee ching), written in the late seventh century, notes the abundance of shipping and mariners of all Asian nations in Sri Vijaya's harbors. It was common for ships to put up for months in these ports, waiting for the turn of the monsoon winds to enable them to return westward across the Indian Ocean.

Owing much to the initiatives and support of Indian colonists, the Sumatra-based Sri Vijayan kings gradually forced their way into the breach in intra-Asian trade left by the decline of Funan and Champa. Sri Vijaya sought little territory but focused instead on dominance in the busy straits of Malacca trade route, as well as supplying the South China ports with island spices and foodstuffs. It was a lucrative business, and the conquest of Sri Vijaya by the Chola buccaneers from India did not impede it. On the contrary, Indian conquest brought a higher degree of organization and expansion to trade. Chinese recognition of the rights of Sri Vijaya to monopolize the north-south trade along the Chinese coasts and down to Malacca was also a huge asset. When this recognition was withdrawn because of Chinese rivalry, the empire began to decline in earnest.

Majapahit

The Sri Vijaya **Majapahit** (mah-jah-pah-HIHT) rulers, centered on eastern Java, delivered the final blows against Sri Vijaya. They created the only indigenous (native to the area) empire to unify all of present-day Indonesia. Majapahit's success is supposedly attributable to the efforts of Indonesia's national hero, Gaja Mada (GAH-jah MAH-dah), the first minister of the king for a generation (1331–1364).

Gaja Mada supervised the conquest of the entire archipelago and possibly (accounts vary) of a considerable part of the mainland as well. Like its insular predecessors, Majapahit's empire was a trading and commercial venture, with command of the sea being far more important than landed possessions. The glory lasted for less than a century, however, before other challengers arose, led by the new city of Malacca on the straits that bear the identical name (see Map 17.3).

Majapahit was the last great Hindu kingdom in Southeast Asia, and its demise in the fifteenth century was caused largely by the coming of an aggressive Islam, again spearheaded by immigrants from the Indian peninsula. Where Hinayana Buddhism had replaced original Hindu belief in most of the mainland, Islam now replaced it in most of the islands. By the time of the arrival of the Portuguese, who

were the earliest Europeans in these latitudes, much of the population of the archipelago had been converted.

Burma and Thailand

After the fall of the Khmers, the mainland was gradually divided among three principal entities. In the far west, the Burmese kingdom centered on the religious shrines at **Pagan** (pah-GAHN). Founded as far back as the ninth century, it had gradually spread south and east to embrace several minority groups related to the majority Burmans. Originally Hindu, thanks to the region's common borders with India, the governing class adopted the Hinayana Buddhism brought to them from the centers of that faith in Sri Lanka during the tenth and eleventh centuries.

In the 1280s, the Mongol conquerors of China sent armies to the south, where they severely ravaged several Southeast Asian states. Chief among these victims were the Burmans, who saw their capital city of Pagan utterly destroyed and their political dominion wrecked as well. Burma disintegrated into several rival principalities during the next three centuries.

To the east of Burma, the Thai people, with their religious and political center at **Ayuthaya** (ah-yoo-THAH-yah), took advantage of the opportunity afforded by Kampuchea's weakening and the Mongol destruction of the Pagan kingdom. Although the Mongols militarily overwhelmed the Thais in their expeditions of the 1280s, they later favored them as tributaries rather than objects of exploitation. The rise of Thai power was closely linked to this favoritism.

Three great monarchs in the thirteenth, fourteenth, and fifteenth centuries assured the Thai kingdom of central importance in mainland Asia throughout early modern times. Their contributions ranged from adoption of Hinayana Buddhism, to a model land tenure system, an advanced and efficient code of law, and standardization of the language, both written and oral. Collectively, the Thai kings of the Chakri (CHAH-kree) Dynasty created the most stable and most administratively advanced state in the area.

Thailand (the name is a recent replacement for *Siam*) became the successor-through-conquest of Kampuchea in the fourteenth and early fifteenth centuries. By the fifteenth century, less than a century after its founding, the capital Ayuthaya had a population estimated at 150,000. Its temples and public gardens rivaled those of Angkor in its heyday and quite overshadowed the now-ruined Pagan.

Vietnam

Vietnam is the exception among the states we are now reviewing in its intense, love–hate relationship with China. For a thousand years, the Vietnamese were the oft-rebellious subjects of the emperor of the Middle Kingdom. When this "yoke" was finally thrown off in 939 CE, the educated people had been sinicized (made Chinese) to an extent not otherwise experienced anywhere, even in Korea and Tibet.

In 111 BCE, a Han ruler made *Nam viet* (nahm vee-YEHT; land of the Viets) into a province of the Chinese empire. For the next thousand years, imperial appointees who were schooled in Confucian principles and assisted by a cadre of Chinese officials governed it. Mahayana Buddhism, similar to China's version, was brought to the country by Chinese missionary monks. It soon became the dominant faith and remained so when the rest of Southeast Asia had turned to the Hinayana version. The pre-twentieth century Vietnamese script was the only Southeast Asian form of writing based on Chinese ideographs. In many different ways, then, China was the tutelary deity of Viet culture.

Yet this closeness inevitably brought forth a mirror image of rejection and dislike. Heavy-handedness and the serene presumption of superiority that so marked China's upper classes in their contacts with foreigners left their scars on the Vietnamese as deeply as on anyone else. The national heroes are two sisters, Trung Trac (truhng TRAHKH) and Trung Nhi (truhng NYEE), who as co-queens led an armed rebellion in 39 CE that resisted the Chinese for two years before being crushed. The sisters committed joint suicide and became the permanent focal point of anti-Chinese patriotism.

There followed 900 years of domination from the north, but the wish for independence never died out. After the weakening of the Tang Dynasty allowed successful revolt in 939, Vietnam (more precisely *Dai Viet,* the "kingdom of the Viets") became and remained a sovereign state for another millennium. Its relationship with its great neighbor to the north was always delicate, but the adoption of a tributary relationship, with certain advantages to both sides, allowed the Vietnamese effective sovereignty and maintained the peace. Even the Mongol conquerors of China came to accept the right of Dai Viet to exist as an independent entity. Their campaigns aimed at subduing the kingdom in both the 1250s and again in the 1280s were repelled by brilliantly led guerrilla warriors.

In the ensuing centuries, the Ly and the Tran dynasties ruled Dai Viet from the city eventually named Hanoi. They successfully expanded their territories against both the resurgent Champa kingdom to the south and the Khmers, later the Thais, to the west. In general, these dynasties followed the Chinese administrative style, backed up strongly by the official Confucian culture and the thorough sinicization of the educational system. The Le Dynasty was notably successful in organizing resistance against renewed Chinese invasion in the early 1400s, adding another chapter to the long Vietnamese saga of rejection of Chinese military hegemony coupled with admiration and pursuit of Chinese culture.

SUMMARY

THE EARLIEST PERIOD of Japan's history is shrouded in mist. The lack of written sources until the eighth century CE forces us to rely on archaeology and occasional references in Chinese travel accounts. Unlike many other peoples, the Japanese never experienced an alien military conquest that unified them under strong central control.

For most of Japanese history, the imperial court was essentially a symbol of national distinctiveness, based on religious mythology, rather than a government. Real power was exercised by feudal lords, organized loosely in clans, who dominated specific localities rather than nationally. In later times, the regent called the shogun was sometimes able to subdue these lords and create an effective military government parallel to that of the court.

Japan's relations with China and Korea were close through most of its early history but were punctuated with briefer periods of self-willed isolation. In the broadest senses, most of the models of Japanese culture can be traced to Chinese sources, which often came through Korea. Among Japan's notable borrowings from China were Buddhism, writing, and several art media and forms, but in each instance, the Japanese adapted these imports to create a peculiarly native product. They rejected entirely the Chinese style of imperial government and its accompanying bureaucracy, favoring instead a military feudalism.

The Southeast Asian societies experienced some type of extensive political organization beginning in the early Christian centuries, but little is known from historical sources until much later. The earliest mainland kingdoms seem to date from the fifth or sixth centuries CE, and those in the islands a good deal later as the Burman Pagan kingdom, the Khmer kingdom of Angkor, and the Thai kingdom of Ayuthaya exercised the greatest cultural and political influences in the first 1,400 years of our era. Although they originally subscribed to Hindu viewpoints carried by Indian traders, all of these and other mainland countries converted in time to Hinayana Buddhism.

Unlike its neighbors, all of which were under strong Indian cultural influence, Vietnam looked to the north and emulated Chinese Confucian values and practice for a lengthy period without surrendering its insistence on political sovereignty. Some of the mainland entities extended their domains into Malaya and the archipelago of Indonesia, but generally speaking, the islands brought forth their own imperial centers that rose and fell depending on control of the lucrative maritime trading routes. At the end of the period under discussion, a militant and proselytizing Islam was replacing both Hindu and Buddhist religions in most of the islands.

▶ Identification Terms

Test your knowledge of this chapter's key concepts by defining the following terms. If you can't recall the meaning of certain terms, refresh your memory by looking up the boldfaced term in the chapter, turning to the Glossary at the end of the book, or working with the flashcards that are available on the *World Civilizations* Companion Website: **academic.cengage.com/adler**

Ashikaga clan	*daimyo*	Majapahit	Shinto
Ayuthaya	Fujiwara clan	Pagan	*shoen*
bakufu	Kamakura shogunate	samurai	shogunate
bushido	Kampuchea	*shiki*	*Tale of Genji*

▶ Test Your Knowledge

Test your knowledge of this chapter by answering the following questions. Complete answers appear at the end of the book. You may find even more quiz questions in CengageNOW and on the *World Civilizations* Companion Website: **academic.cengage.com/adler**

1. Very early Japanese history is best summarized as
   a. a complete mystery until the Tang Dynasty in China.
   b. unknown except for sporadic Chinese reports.
   c. well documented from native sources.
   d. dependent on the reports of Japan's early invaders.
   e. extensively documented in Japan's early written language.
2. The first Japanese government we know of was organized by the
   a. Yamato clan.
   b. Shinto monasteries.
   c. Buddhist monks.

   d. Heian emperors.

   e. Chinese conquerors.

3. Shinto is best defined as

   a. a belief in the infallibility of the emperor.

   b. the original capital city of Japan.

   c. the native religion of the Japanese.

   d. the most important of the Buddhist sects in Japan.

   e. a strongly ritualistic religion.

4. The chief original contribution of the Japanese to world literature was the

   a. novel.

   b. epic.

   c. short story.

   d. essay.

   e. poem.

5. A shogun was

   a. the high priest of the Shinto temples.

   b. a samurai official.

   c. an illegal usurper of imperial authority.

   d. a general acting as political regent.

   e. a Japanese warrior.

6. In the Japanese feudal system, a shoen was

   a. an urban commercial concession.

   b. a property outside imperial taxation and controls.

   c. the preferred weapon of the samurai.

   d. land owned by a free peasant.

   e. land controlled by the state.

7. Which of the following best describes the relationship of China and Japan through 1400 CE?

   a. Japan was a willing student of Chinese culture.

   b. Japan selectively adopted Chinese models and ideas.

   c. Japan was forced to adopt Chinese models.

   d. Japan rejected Chinese pressures to conform.

   e. China made several cultural adjustments based on its interactions with Japan.

8. In Lady Murasaki's tale, Genji is

   a. a samurai warrior who has no time for love.

   b. a betrayed husband of a court beauty.

   c. a romantic lover of many court ladies.

   d. a wise peasant who avoids courtly snares.

   e. an elderly man recounting the adventures of his youth.

9. Which statement is correct about the early history of Southeast Asia?

   a. The mainland nations normally controlled the islands politically.

   b. The islands clung to their Hindu and animist beliefs throughout this period.

   c. The Hinayana Buddhists did not support the idea of divine kingship.

   d. The Khmer Empire was destroyed by the Chinese.

   e. When Portuguese merchants arrived in the region, most of its people were still Hindus.

10. Identify the false pairing of country/nation/empire with a geographic center:

   a. Kampuchea—Angkor

   b. Dai Viet—Hanoi

   c. Burma—Pagan

   d. Majapahit—Malacca

   e. Funan—Mekong River

Enter *CengageNOW* using the access card that is available with this text. *CengageNOW* will assist you in understanding the content in this chapter with lesson plans generated for your needs and provide you with a connection to the *Wadsworth World History Resource Center* (see description at right for details).

 ▶ **World History Resource Center**

Enter the Resource Center using either your *CengageNOW* access card or your standalone access card for the *Wadsworth World History Resource Center.* Organized by topic, this website includes quizzes; images; over 350 primary source documents; interactive simulations, maps, and timelines; movie explorations; and a wealth of other resources. You can read the following documents, and many more, at the *Wadsworth World History Resource Center:*

Shotoku, *Seventeen Point Constitution*
Ten Shinto Creation Stories

18 THE EUROPEAN MIDDLE AGES

500s	St. Benedict/Benedictine Rule
1066	William (the Conqueror) of Normandy conquers Anglo-Saxon England
c. 1075–1122	Investiture Controversy
1096	First Crusade
1100s	Gothic style begins
1152–1190	Emperor Frederick Barbarossa reigns
1179–1223	Philip II Augustus (France)
c. 1200	University of Paris founded
1212–1250	Emperor Frederick II

T HE FEUDAL EUROPEAN COMMUNITY that emerged from the trials and troubles of the Dark Age was built on personal status. Feudal law and custom assigned everyone to a place on the social ladder, but their specific rung depended on whether their function was to fight, to pray, or to work. The great majority, of course, fell into the third category, but they could occasionally leave it by entering one of the others. The church was open to entry from below and grew steadily more powerful in both the spiritual and the civil spheres. Its claims in worldly matters brought it into increasing conflict with the kings and emperors, a conflict that hurt both sides. Despite the resistance of both church and nobles, the royal courts gained increasingly more prestige and power. The Middle Ages (c. 1000–1300 CE) saw the faint beginnings of the modern European state and society.

THE WORKERS

Most people were peasants who worked on and with the land. Perhaps 90 percent of the population in western Europe, and more in eastern Europe, worked the fields, orchards, and woodlots for a (generally hard) living. Their lives were filled with sweaty labor, but this work was far from continuous. For six months of the year or so in North Europe, they were restricted by climate and habit to their huts and villages. Then they spent a great deal of time on farm and

 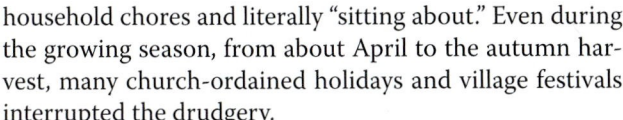

household chores and literally "sitting about." Even during the growing season, from about April to the autumn harvest, many church-ordained holidays and village festivals interrupted the drudgery.

What the modern world calls labor discipline—that is, the custom of reporting to a given place at a given time daily, prepared to do a given job in a specified manner—was almost unknown. Work was largely a communal responsibility; people worked with others in a rhythm dictated by the needs of the community and ancient traditions. These traditions left much room for rest and recreation.

The Feudal Serf

The work on the large manors, which (as we saw in Chapter 10) became dominant in western Europe, was performed by millions of serfs. By the year 1000, serfs had replaced slaves in most places in Europe. Slavery virtually disappeared because the Christian church was opposed to the enslavement of fellow Christians, and this viewpoint gradually prevailed. Because almost the entire continent had been converted to Christianity by 1100, few non-Christians were left who could be enslaved. Asiatics were sometimes encountered, and black slaves from Africa were occasionally purchased from Moorish traders, but they were so expensive that they were viewed as curiosities and kept in noble households rather than used for labor. In some places, particularly east of Germany, serfdom differed little from slavery in practice, and the following remarks apply more to the western region. Legally, however, a serf could not be bought or sold as a slave could, and no one questioned that a serf was a human being with God-given rights and a soul equal in the eyes of heaven to any other person.

Nevertheless, serfs were in important measure unfree. They were bound by law and tradition to a given place, normally a farm village, and to a given occupation, normally farmwork, under the loose supervision of their noble or clerical lord (*seigneur, Herr, suzerain*). Generally, the lord appointed a steward or other overseer to exercise the actual supervision. Beyond this general statement, it is difficult to give a specific description of serfdom because conditions varied so much by time and place. Conditions in, say, tenth-century France were not the same as in eleventh-century Spain or England. In general, however, serfs were bound to perform labor services for their lord and to pay certain "dues" and taxes to the lord, which were set by tradition and by sporadic negotiations.

Only rarely were these conditions written. The labor took myriad forms, but usually included work on the **demesne** (domain), the part of the agricultural land of the estate that belonged to the lord directly. The remainder of the estate's cultivable land (most of it, in most cases) was normally given out to the serfs for their own

Bridgeman-Giraudon/Art Resource, NY

SERFS AT WORK. Sheep shearing and harvesting the first crop of summer.

use (see Map 18.1). They did not own it outright, however, but had only a *usufruct* right (that is, a right to use the land, which was still owned by the lord). Serfs who fell into the lord's bad graces could lose their plots.

Serfdom usually became a hereditary condition. People usually had become serfs because they fell into debt or because they offered themselves and their land to a local strongman in exchange for his protection during a period of disorder. In bad times, it was always safer to be the ward of some powerful person than to try to stand alone. It was possible, however, for a serf to gain freedom. The most common way was simply to run away from the lord's manor and start a new life in freedom elsewhere, normally in a town. "Town air makes free" was an axiom of medieval lawyers. In western Europe, people who could prove they had resided in a town for a year and a day were considered legally free, whatever their previous condition may have been. Many other serfs gained their freedom with the lord's permission. Some were freed of further obligation by the lord's will; others were rewarded for good services; still others worked their way out of serfdom by paying off their debts. After the eleventh century, freedom could also be won by volunteering to open new lands, particularly in the Low Countries,

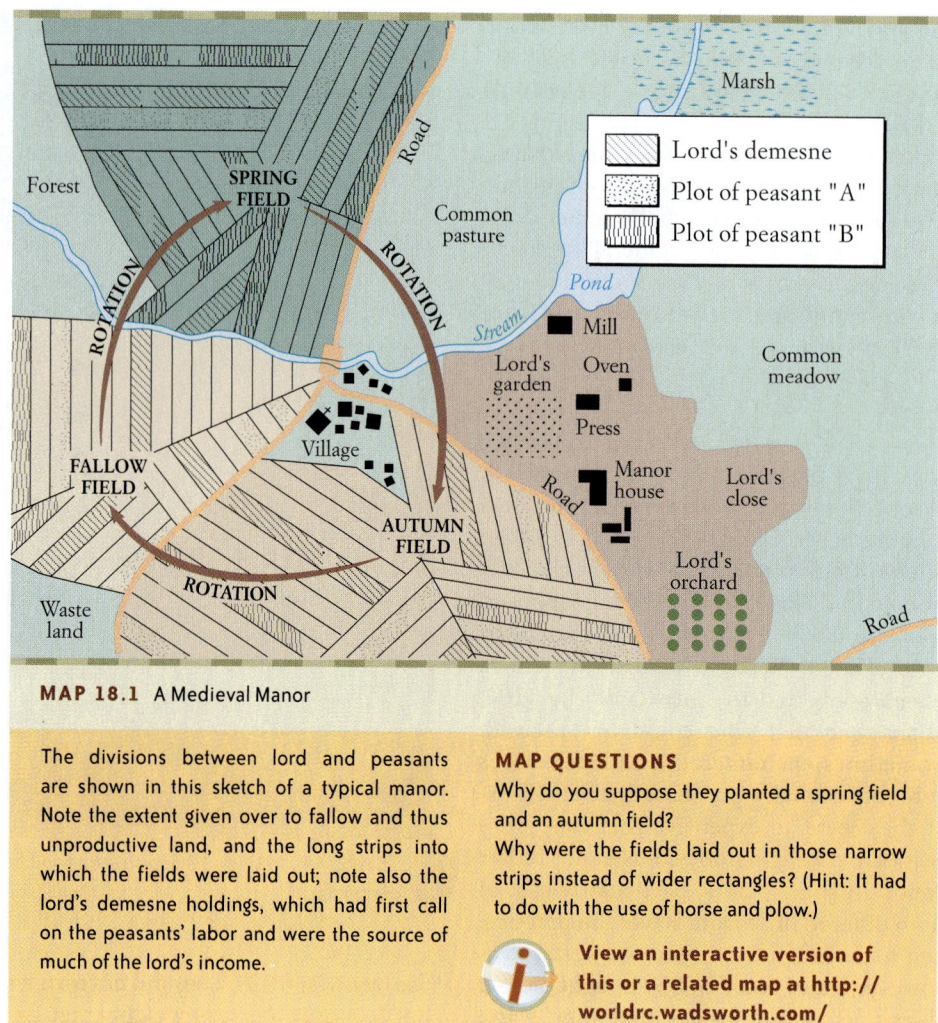

MAP 18.1 A Medieval Manor

The divisions between lord and peasants are shown in this sketch of a typical manor. Note the extent given over to fallow and thus unproductive land, and the long strips into which the fields were laid out; note also the lord's demesne holdings, which had first call on the peasants' labor and were the source of much of the lord's income.

MAP QUESTIONS

Why do you suppose they planted a spring field and an autumn field?

Why were the fields laid out in those narrow strips instead of wider rectangles? (Hint: It had to do with the use of horse and plow.)

View an interactive version of this or a related map at http://worldrc.wadsworth.com/

where dikes were constructed and land was reclaimed from the sea, and in eastern Europe, where much uncultivated land still existed and lords were anxious to gain new labor.

After the tremendous loss of life during the Black Death (see Chapter 20), the serfs who survived were in a strengthened bargaining position with their masters, and serfdom in western Europe became less onerous. Peasant tenants still had to meet certain feudal dues and minor obligations, but the old hardships and treatment like slaves were over.

Medieval Agriculture

Manorial agriculture made steady, although unspectacular, progress during the Middle Ages. Productivity, which was formerly very low (perhaps a 3:1 ratio for return of grain from seed), improved with the invention and introduction

of the iron-tipped plow in the twelfth century. Because it could till heavier soils, this implement opened up whole new regions to grain production. The introduction of the padded horse collar, which distributed the load so as to allow the horse to pull a much heavier burden, was another major advance. (It came almost a thousand years after its Chinese invention.) Horses were expensive and difficult to handle and keep fit, but they were so much more flexible and faster than oxen that their widespread use amounted to an agricultural innovation of the first importance—similar in impact to the introduction of tractors. The systematic use of animal manure as fertilizer also improved productivity, although this practice remained the exception.

The productivity of medieval agriculture was above all limited because one-third to one-half of the cultivated land was left **fallow** (unseeded) each year. This practice was necessary because it was the only way the land could

recover its nutrients in the absence of fertilizer. Every farmer had a piece or a strip of land in both the cultivated and the fallow segments of the manor, which were rotated from year to year.

Famines were common in years when the harvest was poor; reserves were at best sufficient for one bad harvest, and the miserable state of transportation and roads made it difficult to move foodstuffs. It was not unusual for people to starve in one area, while others had a surplus 100 or 150 miles away.

Urban Workers

The urban workers were not yet numerous and were sharply divided in income and social status. At the top were the craftsmen and shopkeepers. Some of them were highly skilled and enjoyed a solid economic livelihood; they could often afford to educate their children in the hope of advancing them still further. These people benefited from the guild system (see Chapter 20), which restricted competition and assured that their socioeconomic status would be secure.

Below these few fortunates were the semiskilled, unskilled, and casual laborers. These men and women worked for others and had few prospects of becoming independent. Many of them lived a hand-to-mouth existence that may have been harder than the lives of the bulk of the manorial peasants. They were often the victims of changed economic conditions (like a new trade route) or

local famines. A great many oscillated between seasonal agrarian jobs and town occupations.

Finally, the towns were filled with marginal people who never had steady work. They begged or moved on to more promising places, "living on air" in the meantime. Historians have estimated that as many as one-fourth of the population of seventeenth-century Paris fell into this category. The number in medieval days was smaller, because the towns were still relatively small and residence rights were restricted, but there must have been many then, too.

THE WARRIORS

The European nobility of the Middle Ages constituted perhaps 2 to 3 percent of the population on average, although their numbers varied from country to country and region to region. Their rights stemmed generally from **patents of nobility**, royal documents that granted them or their ancestors the status of noble and certain privileges that went with that status.

What type of preferences did they enjoy? The privileges could be almost anything imaginable: economic, political, or social, but above all, they were social. The nobles were thought to be of a different nature than the commoners. They spoke mostly to one another, married other nobles, held exclusive gatherings, and enjoyed an altogether different lifestyle than ordinary people, be they well-off or poor.

ELEVENTH-CENTURY KNIGHTS. From the Bayeux tapestry, a scene from the Battle of Hastings, 1066. These early Norman knights dressed in hauberks, leather tunics on which were sewn iron ringlets, and battle helmets fashioned out of hardened leather and iron strips. Note the distinctive Norman lance and shield. In later centuries, when powerful crossbows and even primitive guns came into use, plate armor replaced hauberks and chain mail.

Erich Lessing/Art Resource, NY

Like serfdom, noble status was hereditary; nobles were generally born noble. Nobility was thus a caste that was more or less closed to outsiders. In medieval times, it was rarely possible to buy one's way into the nobility by purchase of a patent, although the practice became common later. Women were equally as noble as men, if they were born into the caste. They could not become noble by marriage, however, whereas men occasionally could. In any event, it was unusual for either male or female nobles to marry beneath their position.

Also like serfdom, nobility varied so much that it is impossible to generalize accurately beyond a few facts. Not all nobles were wealthy, although many were. The only type of wealth that was meaningful was land. By the 1300s, it was not so unusual to find impoverished nobles who were anxious to have their sons marry rich commoners' daughters. Many once-noble families sank out of sight, pulled down by their ineptitude in business, their mortgages, or their hugely wasteful lifestyle. Their places were taken by newcomers from below, who had obtained a patent for themselves in some way or another (perhaps as a reward for distinguished military service).

Nobles were always free; they could not be bound as an inferior to another, but they were also normally **vassals** of some person of superior rank to whom they owed feudal loyalty and specific duties. In the early Middle Ages, these duties were military in nature. Later, they often changed into some sort of service. The superior person to whom service was owed was called the vassal's **suzerain** (SOO-zuhr-ane). He (or she) gave something of value to the vassal in return, perhaps political advantage, protection, or administration of justice. The details of a medieval noble's life were dictated by this system of mutual obligations.

The nobility were not only free but were also the sole political factor in medieval life. The king depended on his nobility to run the government and administration. In some countries, churchmen who were not noble by birth also held some offices, but the secular nobles were everywhere the decisive factor in government at all levels, from the royal court to the village.

A noble's rank more or less determined his job; there were basically five ranks of nobility, ranging downward from duke to count to marquis to baron to knight. Each country had its variations on this scheme. The knights only were seminoble in that their status was solely for their own lifetimes; their sons might be ennobled by the king, but they had no claim to nobility by birth. Knights were by far the most numerous of the nobility and the least prestigious.

The nobles originally claimed their preferred status by virtue of being professional soldiers, guardians, and judges. They supposedly protected the other members of society, upheld justice, ensured that the weak were not abused by the strong, and guarded public morals. That, at least, was the nobles' story! In fact, nobles were often noble because they or their ancestors were successful brutes and pirates who possessed stronger arms than their neighbors and intimidated them into submission. Alternatively, they bought or fought their way into the king's favor or married their way upward.

In any case, the nobles considered themselves as the defenders of society through the command of both God and king and their own sense of honor. Honor was a particularly important aspect of their lives, and every person was supremely conscious of its obligations. Honor meant spending a year's income on the marriage of a daughter or on a proper costume for a court function. Honor meant fighting duels over alleged insults from other nobles and refusing to fight them with commoners. Honor meant living as a nobleman should: as though he had a huge income, while holding money in contempt.

How did noblewomen fit into this pattern? Female nobles frequently held positions of some power in public life. Queens were generally considered to be a political misfortune, but this did not prevent a few women from attaining that rank. More frequently, widows of royal husbands served as regents, as did Blanche of Castile (see the Law and Government box). The widows were usually expected to seek another husband and defer to his advice. Some did, and some did not.

In private life, many noblewomen exerted a strong influence on their husbands or ran the extensive and complex household themselves, as we know from many historical records. They were responsible for the day-to-day management of the estates; when their husband was absent, which was frequent, they moved into his shoes in matters of commerce and even warfare. There are records of duchesses and abbesses who did not hesitate to resort to arms to defend their rights.

First and foremost, however, like all medieval women outside the convents, a noblewoman was expected to produce legitimate children to ensure the continuity of the (male) family name and wealth. A barren noble wife was in a highly unenviable position; sterility was automatically attributed to the woman, but divorce was next to impossible because of the church's opposition. Hence, sonless fathers sometimes turned to concubines in their search for posterity. A bastard so produced would have only very limited rights, even if he was acknowledged, but for some desperate fathers this was better than nothing. The legal ramifications of bastardy, especially the ability to inherit titles and property, were a preoccupation of medieval lawyers.

LAW AND GOVERNMENT

Blanche of Castile

In the violent and strongly patriarchal society of the Middle Ages, all women were under some constraints imposed by law and custom. Occasionally, an exception to the rule appeared, a woman who was in every way the equal of her male associates in terms of exercising public power. Blanche of Castile, queen of France, is a good example. She was also the medieval model of that perennial bugaboo of young wives, the possessive mother-in-law.

Blanche was a granddaughter of the most famous queen of the entire Middle Ages, Eleanor of Aquitaine, and the niece of the unfortunate John of England. Selected by her grandmother as a suitable match, she was married to the heir to the French throne, Louis, at the age of twelve. Her bridegroom was a ripe thirteen! This young age was not unusual for royal or noble marriages. The legal age of maturity was twelve for females, fourteen for males, conforming to current ideas on mental and moral development. For a time the wedded pair would live apart in their respective households. Such a marriage would not be consummated until later, when puberty had been reached at about sixteen for males, fourteen for females.

Blanche gave birth to her first child—of a total of twelve—when she was seventeen. Of the twelve, five lived to adulthood, which was a relatively high percentage for the time. The oldest surviving boy became King Louis IX, patron saint of the French kingdom. He and his mother remained extraordinarily close throughout their lives.

Blanche had a forceful temperament. At the age of twenty-eight, when her father-in-law, King Philip Augustus, refused to send money to her husband for one of the latter's feudal wars, Blanche swore that she would pawn her two children to get the needed cash. Philip decided to put up some funds after all.

Philip died in 1223, and Blanche's husband succeeded him as King Louis VIII. Only three years later, he also died, leaving his queen as regent and the guardian of his twelve-year-old heir, Louis IX. Blanche thus became not only queen but actual ruler. Although not unheard of in medieval Europe, it was unusual for a woman to exercise royal powers. Louis apparently knew and appreciated the qualities of his young wife; she did not disappoint his expectations.

Louis IX, a deeply pious person, was content to leave much of the task of governing to his mother even after he had attained his majority. Mother and son had a mutual appreciation that lasted until her death and was undisturbed by Louis's marriage in 1234. Blanche tried to make sure that this relationship would last by selecting Louis's bride, thirteen-year-old Marguerite of Provence. Joinville, Louis's contemporary biographer, tells us that despite Blanche's precautions, the mother-in-law was jealous of the young bride and took pains to assert her dominant position: "[Louis] acted on the advice of the good mother at his side, whose counsels he always followed."

Life at this court must have been difficult for young Marguerite, who found that the only way she could be with her husband without his mother was to accompany him on a crusade against the Muslims in the Holy Land in 1248. During the king's lengthy absence, Blanche again served as regent, and she was the reigning authority in France when she died, at age sixty-five, in 1252. Like her more famous grandmother Eleanor, she was a woman who knew how to handle the levers of power in a masculine age.

▶ Analyze and Interpret

Why was it considered to be a severe risk to the kingdom for a female to exercise actual governing duties? What might some of the positive, as well as negative, results be from marriage at the age of thirteen and fourteen into royal powers in the medieval age?

THE WORSHIPERS

The men and women who worshiped were less numerous than the warriors, but they filled a social niche that was just as important. In an age of faith, when no one doubted the reality of heaven, hell, or the Last Judgment, those who prayed for others were considered to be absolutely essential. They included both the parish clergy and the regular clergy, or monks, but because the monks were both more numerous and more important than the parish clergy, the following applies particularly to them. The chief visible difference between monks and parish priests was that the monks lived somewhat apart from the world in communities called *monasteries*. The monastery has had a long history in the Christian world. The first were founded in the fourth century in Egypt, but the most important monastic institutions were those founded by the Italian St. Benedict in the sixth century.

His **Benedictine Rule** for monastic life was the most widely observed, although several others were also in use during the Middle Ages (the Trappist and Cistercian rules, for example).

What was a Benedictine monastery like? The monks believed a mixture of manual and intellectual work was best for a pious and contemplative life. The monks operated extensive farms, which they sometimes leased out to peasants in part. They were also craftsmen, and the abbey house or main center of the monastery was a workshop filled with bustling activity, but the monks never forgot that their intercession with God on behalf of their fellows was at all times the center of their lives. From early morning to night, the Benedictines set aside hours for prayer and contemplation. They also usually ran schools for the more talented peasant youth, some of whom were invited to join them in the monastic life.

Monks and nuns (in the convents that were the close equivalent of the monasteries but designed for females) normally came from the aristocracy until the twelfth or thirteenth century, when they became increasingly middle class in origin. They were often the younger sons or daughters of a noble family, who had little hope of inheriting property sufficient to maintain them in proper style. Their parents therefore put them—with or without the agreement of the child—into a religious institution at the age of twelve or so. Sometimes, the child was miserable in the religious life and left it sooner or later without permission. More often, a compromise was arranged, and the unhappy monk or nun was allowed to leave without the scandal of an open rebellion.

The collective wealth of the monasteries was considerable. European Christians customarily remembered the church in their wills, if only to ensure that masses would be said for their souls in that way station en route to heaven called purgatory. Noble sinners often tried to escape their just desserts at the Last Judgment by leaving the local monastery or convent a large bequest on their deathbed. Because most of the charitable institutions of the Middle Ages were connected with and run by the clergy, it was natural to leave money or income-producing property to the church. In these ways, the property controlled by the church, and above all by the numerous monasteries, grew to tremendous figures. Historians reckon that, as late as the fifteenth century, the property controlled by the church institutions in western Europe outvalued that controlled by the Crown and nobles together.

This involvement with the business world and large amounts of money often had deleterious effects on the spiritual life of the monks and the nuns. Too often, monastic policy was made by those who oversaw the

Abbey of Montecassino/Bridgeman Art Library

THE INVESTITURE OF A BENEDICTINE MONK. Before being invested into a religious order, monks took vows swearing to lives of poverty, chastity, and obedience. Their purpose was to free monks from all worldly hindrances so they could devote their lives entirely to prayer, worship, and work.

investments and the rents, rather than the most pious and self-sacrificing individuals. The monasteries repeatedly fell into an atmosphere of corruption, fostered by the indifference of some of their leaders to religious affairs and their close attention to financial matters.

Despite this tendency, the monks and nuns did much good work and fulfilled the expectations of the rest of society by their devotions and their actions on behalf of the poor. We should remember that medieval government was primitive, and the social welfare services that we expect today from government did not exist. Instead, the church institutions—monasteries, convents, cathedrals, and parish churches—supplied most of the "welfare" for the aged, the poor, and the helpless. The clergy founded and managed the hospitals, orphanages, and hospices, asylums for the aged, and the shelters for the impoverished; provided scholarships for the deserving poor; and met a hundred other needs. In so doing, they were using funds contributed by the faithful or generated by the church business and rental income. Then as now, money was used for good ends as well as bad ones.

The New Clerical Orders

In the thirteenth century, for various reasons **heresies** became more widespread in the church than ever before. Regular armed crusades were even mounted against them at times. These crusades meant to stamp out heresy by killing or suppressing the heretics. Brutal force was their hallmark. To a pair of saintly young priests, this was not the Christian way, and they sought a different approach.

St. Francis of Assisi was a young Italian who practiced a life of total poverty and total service to his fellows (see the Patterns of Belief box). St. Dominic, a contemporary of Francis of Assisi, was a young Spaniard who wanted to reform the clergy in a different way. He wanted especially to convert the heretics back to the true faith by showing them the error of their ways calmly and peaceably. The Dominican Order was therefore an intellectual group, specializing in lawyerly disputation and preaching. Dominicans were the outstanding professors of law and theology in the early universities of Europe. To combat heresy, the Church instituted the **Inquisition**, a clerical court to bring individuals suspected of adhering to forbidden doctrines before a panel of Dominican friars who questioned their beliefs. Most were pardoned, but in its severest form, as it later became in Spain, the Inquisition sometimes employed brutal methods to extract confessions and then turned over the hardest cases to the secular officials for imprisonment or public burnings.

In their different ways, both Franciscans and Dominicans attempted to elevate the spiritual life of the clergy and, through them, the people of Europe. They attempted to bring about needed reforms in the church that the papal court was refusing to address. But their efforts were dulled with the passage of time and checked by a clerical hierarchy that did not want to hear of its failures and corruption or think about how to change.

THE ECONOMIC REVIVAL

Starting in the eleventh century, the towns of Europe, so long stagnant or semideserted, began a strong revival. Some entirely new cities were founded, for example, Berlin, Moscow, and Munich. Mostly, however, the eleventh- and twelfth-century revival saw the renaissance of older sites under the influence of three related factors: (1) increased trade, (2) a more peaceful environment, and (3) a higher degree of skills and entrepreneurial activity.

The basic reason for the resurgence of the towns was the rising volume of trade. After centuries of stagnation, Europe's merchants and moneylenders were again looking for new fields to conquer. The increasing ability of the royal governments to ensure a degree of law and order within their kingdoms was a key factor. Others included the steady rise in population, the ability of the townsmen to purchase their liberties from the feudal nobles (see the Society and Economy box), and the reappearance of clerical and professional people.

In western Europe, mercantile activity approached levels it had last reached a millennium earlier, in the fourth century. (In this context, "western" means Europe westward from midway across Germany, including Scandinavia and Italy.) Merchants found that a stable coinage and financial techniques such as letters of credit, which they learned from the Muslims, increased their commercial opportunities.

The obvious locations for markets were the strategic, protected places that had been market centers in Roman days. Old municipal centers, such as Cologne, Frankfurt, Innsbruck, Vienna, Lyon, and Paris, which had been almost abandoned in the sixth and seventh centuries, began to come back from the grave. They once again became what they had been under the Romans: commercial and crafts centers with some professionals and administrators, often in the employ of the church. Nevertheless, cities and towns were not yet large or numerous. By the twelfth century, for example, Cologne's population reached 30,000, which was a large city by medieval standards. The largest cities were Paris, Florence, and Venice, which had populations of somewhat less than 100,000 each in the twelfth century.

Several developments helped create a more peaceful setting for economic activity. One was the increased power of the church to enforce its condemnations of

PATTERNS OF BELIEF

St. Francis of Assisi

The man called Francis of Assisi has long been one of the most attractive of the medieval saints to modern eyes. His message was clear and simple: "Where there is hate, give love; where there is insult and wrongdoing, grant forgiveness and offer hope. Bestow happiness where there is sorrow, and give light where there is darkness." No one lived this high-minded creed better than its originator.

Francesco (Francis) de Bernadone was born the son of a wealthy cloth dealer in the prosperous town of Assisi in northern Italy. Although he apparently had no formal schooling, he was quick intellectually and was taken into his father's business early in life. He was a member of the "gilded youth" of the town, drinking heavily, getting involved with loose women, and generally enjoying himself as rich, carefree adolescents have always done. His life seems to have been an ongoing party.

But at age twenty, he opted to join the local freebooters (*condottieri*) and was taken prisoner during Assisi's squabble with the city-state of Perugia. He spent a year in captivity, which was surely a sobering experience. Two years later, ill with fever, he underwent a visionary experience that permanently changed his life. Faced with death, he came to believe that he had been spared for a purpose that he must discover. He renounced his family's wealth and began to dedicate his time to the service of God and the poor.

He visited the lepers and outcasts of the town and practiced a stringently simple life, begging his food. Wherever he was permitted, he preached to anyone who would listen a message of poverty, austerity, and, above all, love for every creature. Braving the inevitable ridicule, he called on his listeners to renounce their fortunes, sell their possessions, and give the proceeds to the poor around them. For his text, Francis took the word of Jesus to his apostles: "Take nothing for the journey, neither staff nor satchel, neither bread nor money." Trusting fully in the Lord, Francis demanded and practiced absolute poverty.

Some people were touched by the power and sincerity of his preaching and joined him. In a relatively brief time, he had a band of followers, the "Little Brothers of Francis," and came to the attention of Pope Innocent III. Although suspicious at first, Innocent eventually recognized Francis's sincerity and moral stature. His followers, called friars, were allowed to preach where they chose and to solicit the support of good Christians everywhere.

Francis died quite young, but not before he had almost single-handedly made substantial changes for the better in contemporary Christian practice. His example inspired many thousands to reject the materialism that had plagued the thirteenth-century clergy, especially the monastic orders. The Franciscans (who soon had a female auxiliary of nuns) always rejected the idea of the monastery, preferring to live and work among the people as helpmates and fellow sufferers.

Francis of Assisi felt a very strong bond between himself and all other beings. He addressed the birds and the beasts, the sun and the moon and the stars as his brothers and sisters. Once he preached a sermon to the birds, and the legend says that they responded by gathering around him. He did much to instill a love of God's natural world in his followers and should be called one of the Western world's first, and most attractive, ecologists.

▶ *Analyze and Interpret*
What effect on the Franciscan monks' attitude toward people might the founder's insistence that they beg for their food have? Do you know anyone whose lifestyle resembles that of Francis? What do you think of this person?

You can read more about St. Francis's life at the Wadsworth World History Resource Center.

those who fought their fellow Europeans or engaged in random violence. As the church became a major property holder, it began to use its influence against those who destroyed property through war and plunder. The Peace of God and the Truce of God were now enforced across most of the continent. Under the Peace of God, noncombatants, such as women, merchants, peasants,

and the clergy, were to be protected from violence. The Truce of God forbade fighting on Sundays and all holy feast days. Violators were subject to spiritual sanctions, including excommunication, and to civil penalties as well in most areas.

The **Crusades** also contributed to peace in Europe by giving ambitious young nobles an outlet to exercise their

SOCIETY AND ECONOMY

Liberties of Lorris

In the town charter of the small city of Lorris in northern France is the essence of the "liberties" that the medieval bourgeoisie gradually gained from a reluctant aristocracy, using the king as their protector. The charter of Lorris was granted by King Louis VII in 1155. By this time, the towns had fully recovered from the long centuries of decay and lawlessness after Rome's fall. Most of the rights deal with economic regulations and taxes because the feudal nobility were most likely to apply pressure in these areas. The eighteenth liberty is a good example of the rule that runaways would be free from serf status if they could remain in a town and out of trouble for a year and a day.

> The Charter of Lorris:
>
> 2. Let no inhabitant of the parish of Lorris pay a duty of entry nor any tax for his food, and let him not pay any duty of measurement for the corn [grain] which his labor, or that of his animals may procure him, and let him pay no duty for the wine which he shall get from his vines.
>
> 3. Let none of them go on a [military] expedition, on foot or horseback, from which he cannot return home the same day! ...

> 15. Let no man of Lorris do forced work for us, unless it be twice a year to take our wine to Orleans, and nowhere else ...
>
> 18. Whoever shall remain a year and a day in the parish of Lorris without any claim having pursued him thither, and without the right [of remaining] having been forbidden him by us or by our provost [equivalent of sheriff], he shall remain there free and tranquil ...
>
> 33. No man of Lorris shall pay any duty because of what he shall buy or sell for his own use on the territory of the parish, nor for what he shall buy on Wednesdays at the town market ...
>
> Given at Orleans, in the year of our Lord 1155.

▶ Analyze and Interpret

Who would be in the best position to take advantage of these liberties? Why would the local lords who fully controlled the peasants allow the townsmen these freedoms?

Source: As cited in O. Johnson, *World Civilization*, p. 364.

You can read all of the Liberties of Lorris at the *Wadsworth World History Resource Center*.

---

warlike impulses in a church-approved arena. Starting with the First Crusade in 1096, tens of thousands of aggressive younger sons of the nobility went off to Palestine or eastern Europe to fight the unbelievers, recover the long-lost Holy Land, and make their fortune (they hoped). Although the First Crusade was able to seize Jerusalem and briefly set up a Christian-ruled kingdom in Muslim Palestine, these exercises (there were eventually six, depending on how one counts) were usually destined to end in futility, or worse. One permanent effect was to refresh and deepen the animosity between Muslims and Christians, which had largely subsided since the Bedouin conquests had been completed centuries earlier. The terms *Crusade* and *crusader* have since then become the ultimate curse in Muslim countries, a counterweight to the jihad, directed by Satan rather than Allah.

The harmful aspects of the Crusades culminated in the fiasco of the Fourth Crusade (1204). In that, Western knights turned their belligerence and cupidity on their Greek hosts in Constantinople, rather than on the Muslims, and after much wanton plundering occupied the Christian city for the next sixty years. So great was the scandal that although several more attempts were made to organize feudal armies to regain the Holy Land for Christianity, none was successful and most were abortive. By the later 1200s, the Near East had reverted to uniform Muslim rule once again.

Finally, the renewed application of Roman law led to the use of legal procedures as a substitute for armed action in disputes. Interest in the corpus jurisprudentiae began in the law school founded at Bologna in the eleventh century. Roman law, which had always been retained to some slight degree in the church's administration of its internal matters, was now gradually reintroduced into secular affairs as well. The legal profession was already well-developed in the twelfth century.

In part, as a result of the first two factors, people began to develop greater skills and engage in more entrepreneurial activity. As trade and commerce increased and the threat of violence declined, it made sense for people to develop more skillful ways to make goods and provide services. As these skills became apparent to the potential users and buyers, entrepreneurs came into existence to bring the providers of skills and the users together. Along with entrepreneurs came real estate speculators (medieval towns were notoriously short on space), investment bankers (who usually started out as moneylenders), and a host of other commercial and financial occupations that we associate with doing business. Some of these people succeeded in becoming quite rich, and they displayed their success in fine townhouses and good living.

Bourgeoisie and Jews

Many people in the towns were what we now call the upper middle class: doctors, lawyers, royal and clerical officeholders, and, first and foremost, merchants. These were the **bourgeoisie**, the educated, status-conscious people who lived within the *bourg* or *burg*, which was a walled settlement meant to protect life and property.

The towns and their inhabitants were by now becoming a major feature of the political and social landscape, particularly in northwestern Europe and northern Italy. In the thirteenth and fourteenth centuries, kings discovered that their surest allies against feudal rebels were the propertied townsmen. The towns were the source of a growing majority of the royal tax revenue, even though they contained only a small fraction (perhaps 10 percent) of the European population. Whereas the agrarian villagers' taxes disappeared into the pockets of the nobles and their agents, the towns paid their taxes directly to the royal treasury.

By now, the townspeople were no longer dependents of the local lord; having purchased a charter from the throne, they had the privilege of electing their own government officials and levying taxes for local needs. Their defense costs (town walls were costly to build and maintain) were borne by the citizenry, not put into the devious hands of the nobles. The towns often had the privilege of deciding citizens' cases in their own municipal courts; appeal went to the king's officials, not to the local nobleman.

The residents of these reviving towns were not all Christians. A small Jewish population had come to western Europe from the Mediterranean Jewish colonies of the Diaspora. They lived completely segregated from the Christian majority in small urban areas of a block or two called **ghettos**. Initially, Jews provided several of the elementary financial services in medieval cities and in the countryside, but by the thirteenth century they were being rivaled by Christians, who no longer paid much attention to the church's official distaste for usury, or the taking of money for the use of money (interest). Most places prohibited Jews from

owning land or entering craft guilds, so they had little choice but to take up financial and mercantile pursuits.

Until the thirteenth century, outright attacks on the Jews were relatively rare, but in that century, the money-short kings of both England and France denounced and expelled the Jews on pretexts and seized their property, and the era of sporadic *pogroms,* or anti-Semitic mob actions, began. Fearful for their lives, the Jews began to migrate from western to eastern Europe. The eastern European states such as Poland and Hungary were more hospitable than the West at this juncture. These states, and especially their monarchic governments, badly needed the Jews' experience in trade and finance, which the native Christian populations were almost entirely lacking.

British Library/The Art Archive

MONEYLENDING. This manuscript illustration from fourteenth-century Italy shows the moneylender and his clients. Note the monks and other church officials, as well as the women who avail themselves of these forerunners of banks.

ROYAL KINGDOMS AND THE FORMATION OF STATES

The revival of the towns and the growth of urban populations were important factors in the steady strengthening of the royal governments against the nobles' claims for autonomy and feudal fragmentation. The foundations of the modern states of England, France, and Germany can be traced back to the thirteenth and fourteenth centuries.

What is a **state**? A state is a definite territory with generally recognized boundaries and a sovereign government. It recognizes no superior sovereignty within its own borders. It suppresses violence and maintains order among its subjects in the name of law and defends those subjects from outside oppressors and internal criminals. The state exercises its powers through a group of elected or appointed officials, courts, police forces, and an army.

England and France

England was a pioneer in creating a state. Since the fifth century, when the island was conquered by the barbarian Angles and Saxons, it had been divided among a series of tribal kingdoms that fought one another and the invading Vikings. The recently unified Anglo-Saxon kingdom of England had been invaded and conquered in 1066 by William (the Conqueror), the formidable duke of Normandy, who had a weak claim to the English throne that the English nobility had not recognized. By right of conquest of what he considered to be a collection of traitors, William proceeded to organize a new type of kingdom, in which the king alone was the source of final authority. Before this time, the kings of feudal Europe were always being reminded of their dependency on the voluntary collaboration of their nobles in national affairs. Now William could ignore these claims and establish a cadre of appointed noble officials who were all drawn from his supporters. A tangible sign of his power was the incredibly thorough and detailed **Domesday Book** (1086–1087), which was prepared as a royal census for tax purposes.

William's successors were not all so clever or determined as he, but by the middle of the twelfth century, the earmarks of a modern state were faintly visible in England. It had, among other things, a loyal corps of royal officials, a system of courts and laws that was more or less uniform from one end of the kingdom to the other, a royal army that looked only to the king, and a single national currency issued by the royal treasury.

France developed a little more slowly. In the early twelfth century, France was still a collection of nearly independent duchies and counties, whose feudal lords looked only reluctantly and occasionally to the king in Paris. Some of the French lords, such as the count of Anjou and the duke of Normandy, could figuratively buy and sell the French king; the royal territory around Paris was a fraction of the size of their lands. Furthermore, the king had no royal army worthy of the name.

This situation began to change in the late twelfth century, when the ambitious Philip II Augustus (1179–1223) came to the throne and started the process of unifying and strengthening the country. By the end of the thirteenth century, the king had become stronger than any of his nobles and was sufficiently in control of taxation and the military that he could intimidate any of them or even a combination of them. The Crown would experience many ups and downs from this time onward in France, but the outlines of the French state were in place by 1300.

A major difference between the English and French systems of government was that the English crown relied on unpaid local officials, who were rewarded for their service by customary fees, social privileges, and legislative powers (in the Parliament created in the thirteenth century). The French, on the other hand, created a royal bureaucracy, staffed by highly trained and highly paid officials, who were responsible only to the king and kept clear of local ties. The English system allowed for a maximum of local variations in administration and justice, although the entire kingdom conformed to the common law that the kings had gradually imposed. Each English county, for example, had its own methods of tax assessment, types and rates of taxes, and voting rights, as did the associated kingdoms of Scotland and Wales. The French royal bureaucrats carried out the same duties in the same fashion from one end of France to the other, but they were not able to overcome the large linguistic and customary differences that distinguished Brittany from Normandy or Provence from Anjou. Until the Revolution of 1789, France remained more a series of adjoining semiautonomous countries than a single nation. Thus, Parliament and the laws it created were the foundation of English unity, whereas the Crown and its loyal hierarchy of officials unified France.

The German Empire

The modern state that we know as Germany was created only in the late nineteenth century. For many hundreds of years before that, its territory was an agglomeration of petty principalities, kingdoms, and free cities. This had not always been the case, however. In the Early Middle Ages, Germans had lived under one powerful government headed by an emperor who claimed descent from Charlemagne, but this state failed and broke up. In the eleventh century, the emperor and the pope in Rome became embroiled in a long, bitter struggle over who should have the right to "invest" bishops in Germany—that is, to select the bishops and install them in office. This **Investiture Controversy** (from about 1075 to 1122) ripped the empire apart, as one noble after another took the opportunity to pull clear of the central government's controls.

Another factor weakening the empire was that emperors succeeded to the throne through election. Prospective candidates engaged in all sorts of maneuvering and conspiracy and were even willing to barter away much of their monarchic power to gain votes. Civil wars among the nobility were common at the death of each emperor.

In 1152, the noble electors finally tired of this exhausting sport and agreed on a strong leader in Frederick Barbarossa, who tried his best to reunify the Germans. However, Barbarossa's claims to rule in northern Italy—a claim going back to Charlemagne's empire—brought him into conflict with the Italian city-states and the pope in Rome, and he threw away what he had accomplished toward German unity by his costly and vain military expeditions into Italy.

Later, in 1212, Barbarossa's grandson Frederick II became the Holy Roman Emperor of the German Nation (the official title of the German king) and opted to settle in Sicily, which he made into one of the leading states in contemporary Europe. In the process, he ignored his possessions across the Alps, and the Germans looked on him as almost a foreigner rather than their rightful king. By the time Frederick died in 1250, imperial authority in Germany was severely weakened and would not recover. Instead of becoming the dominant state of late medieval Europe as its geographic and demographic destiny suggested it would be, the land of the Germans gradually broke up into several dozen competing feudal domains and independent cities. Not until the middle of the nineteenth century did Germany make up the political ground it had lost in the thirteenth.

MEDIEVAL CULTURE AND ARTS

What cultural changes accompanied this strengthening of central authority? The appearance of more effective central governments in parts of Europe during the twelfth century went hand in hand with the rising wealth of the urban population. Wealth meant a more lucrative base for taxes levied by the royal crown and by the church. To manage that wealth properly and to levy and collect the taxes, both institutions needed trained personnel who could plan and oversee the work of others. It is no accident that the first European universities appeared at this time.

The First Universities

The first universities were established in Italy. In the towns of Bologna and Salerno, specialized academies devoted to law and medicine, respectively, gradually expanded and attracted students from all over Europe. Slightly later, the University of Paris was founded by a royal charter; there students studied law, philosophy, and Christian theology.

Much of the university curriculum was devoted to commentaries on the semisacred books of the Greek Classical Age. Pagan authors such as Aristotle had long been forgotten in the Christian West, but they were now being recovered for study through the Muslims, especially in Spain, where the Christian majority had lived for centuries under Muslim rule. Unlike the West, the Muslims were quite aware of the value of the Greco-Roman classics and had preserved and studied them ever since conquering the Greek lands in the East (see Chapter 14).

The greatest Christian teacher of the twelfth and thirteenth centuries was St. Thomas Aquinas. In his *Summa Theologica,* he managed to use the arguments of Aristotle to prove the existence of God. Other great medieval teachers included Albertus Magnus and Peter Abelard, who used reason to teach the truths of faith in an age that was still ruled by universal belief in Christian doctrines.

The students at the universities were drawn from all strata of society, but most were apparently from the middle classes or the poor, who sacrificed much to pay their tuition charges (paid directly to the teachers, in this era). Many lived on the edge of starvation much of the time, but saw a university degree as a passport to a better social position and therefore worth the sacrifice. Many students supplemented their meager funds from home by serving as tutors to the children of the wealthy or as teachers in the "3 R" schools maintained in many towns.

Bibliothèque Nationale, Paris, France/Josse/The Art Archive

CRAFTSMEN AND THEIR TOOLS. This marvelously detailed miniature painting shows the crafts employed in sixteenth-century construction. Many of these techniques have not changed significantly since that time.

Females were unknown in medieval universities, as either students or teachers. Tension between town and gown was common. Students frequently rioted in protest against the greed of their landlords or the restrictions imposed by town officials. The course of study for a degree in theology (one of the favorites) usually lasted five years, law the same, and medicine somewhat longer. Lectures were the standard approach to teaching, with stiff oral examinations administered when the student felt ready. (It is remarkable how little the basic methods of university education have changed over 700 years!)

Gothic Architecture

The **Gothic style** of architecture and interior design came to be the norm in Europe during the thirteenth century. The first important example of Gothic architecture was the abbey church of St. Denis, which was built outside Paris in the mid-twelfth century. It was such an artistic success that the style spread rapidly throughout western Europe. The Gothic style's basic elements include a flood of illumination through windows and portals designed to throw the sunlight into every corner; an abundance of decoration, inside and out; and the use of arches, buttresses, and complex vaulting to support a sharply vertical, towering architecture.

The great Gothic cathedrals of the thirteenth and fourteenth centuries that were built from Italy north and west to England were expressions not only of building and artistic skills but also of the deep faith of those who constructed and used them. The cathedrals were also rich pictorial teaching devices, meant to instruct a still largely illiterate population in the mysteries and lessons of Christianity. Enormously expensive, they were built over generations of time with donations from all classes and the contributed labor of many hundreds of artisans. Each town strove to outdo its neighbors in the splendor of its cathedral. Many cathedrals were destroyed by fire at one time or another and were rebuilt. They could take 50 to 100 years to build or rebuild, and many were not completed until modern times.

Vernacular Literature

Until the end of the thirteenth century, all serious writing between educated people was normally conducted in Latin, the language of the church everywhere in western Europe and the most highly developed vocabulary and grammar of the day. In the fourteenth century, however, the common people's oral languages (the vernacular) began to be used for the first time as vehicles of literature such as poems, plays, and elementary readers for children.

The most important of these early works was Dante Alighieri's *Divine Comedy,* written in Italian, it is one of the great poetic epics of world literature. Somewhat later came the first important work in English: Geoffrey Chaucer's *Canterbury Tales,* which presented a panorama of English society. In the ensuing years, authors writing in the German, French, and Spanish vernaculars also scored artistic breakthroughs in literature. By the end of the fourteenth century, Latin was no longer the automatic choice of the educated for communicating what they held important.

SUMMARY

THE MIDDLE AGES were a period of substantial advances for the Europeans, who came back from the long centuries of instability, violence, and ignorance that followed the fall of the western Roman Empire. Three segments of society were recognized: the workers, the warriors, and the worshipers. The first were by far the most numerous, but the other two had important roles to fill in government and society. Town life revived after 1000 CE, especially in the western parts of the continent, where traders, bankers, and artisans of all types began to congregate in the former ghost towns left by the Romans. By the thirteenth century, towns and cities could be found with upward of 80,000 inhabitants. Cities such as Paris, Bologna, and Oxford had universities, and fine goods from the East were familiar, in part through the experiences of the crusaders, who sought to recover the Holy Land from its Muslim conquerors.

In the wake of growing population and increasing government stability, traders began to develop long-distance markets in basic goods. Peace was by no means universal, but the invasions had ceased and many of the riotous noblemen were diverted into the Crusades against the heathen in the Near East or in eastern Europe. The professions, particularly law, were also reviving, encouraged by the church and its strong interest in a law-abiding environment. Europe had finally emerged from the shadow of Rome's collapse and was developing a new culture. Noteworthy examples included the magnificent architecture and art of the Gothic style and the literary use of the vernacular languages.

▶ Identification Terms

Test your knowledge of this chapter's key concepts by defining the following terms. If you can't recall the meaning of certain terms, refresh your memory by looking up the boldfaced term in the chapter, turning to the Glossary at the end of the book, or working with the flashcards that are available on the *World Civilizations* Companion Website: **academic.cengage.com/adler**

Benedictine Rule	Domesday Book	heresies	state
bourgeoisie	fallow	Inquisition	suzerain
Crusades	ghettos	Investiture Controversy	vassals
demesne	Gothic style	patents of nobility	

▶ Test Your Knowledge

Test your knowledge of this chapter by answering the following questions. Complete answers appear at the end of the book. You may find even more quiz questions in CengageNOW and on the *World Civilizations* Companion Website: **academic.cengage.com/adler**

1. A social group ignored by the original medieval divisions of humanity was the
   a. peasantry.
   b. merchants.
   c. monks.
   d. soldiers.
   e. nobles.
2. A basic distinction between European slaves and serfs was that slaves
   a. could be sold to another person.
   b. could be severely beaten.
   c. had to work much harder.
   d. could be judged and punished by their master.
   e. usually gained their freedom upon their master's death.
3. Which of the following statements about a medieval manor is *false*?
   a. It was normally an economically self-sufficient unit.
   b. It was normally headed by an official of the church or a noble.
   c. It was normally dependent on the labor rendered by unfree peasants.
   d. It was normally a politically independent unit.
   e. It normally had a large part of its land lying fallow.
4. Members of the medieval nobility
   a. did not have any special legal status.
   b. were uninterested in military affairs.
   c. generally inherited their position.
   d. were limited to males only.
   e. could not be bound to others as vassals.
5. Noblewomen in the Middle Ages
   a. were strictly confined to domestic duties.
   b. generally married men younger than themselves.
   c. often carried large managerial responsibilities.
   d. played no role in political life.
   e. were often divorced by their husbands if they failed to produce heirs.
6. The usual path to becoming a monk was to
   a. be handed over by one's parent to a monastery's care.
   b. retire to a monastery in middle age.
   c. enter a monastery after being widowed.
   d. be conscripted into an order from a quota of recruits.
   e. voluntarily enter a monastery at about the age of seventeen.
7. The Dominican Order concentrated most of its efforts on
   a. total service to their fellow man.
   b. rooting out heretics in the country of France.
   c. practicing lives of total poverty.
   d. reforming the Church officialdom.
   e. scholarly discourse and preaching.
8. Most Jews in medieval Europe
   a. were prohibited from owning land.
   b. found themselves welcomed into craft guilds because of their skills.
   c. refused to lend money to non-Jews, making them unwelcome in many places.
   d. became more numerous than Christians in many towns.
   e. eventually migrated from eastern to western Europe in large numbers.

9. A major difference between England and France was
   a. England's insistence on a strong royal government.
   b. France's royal dependency on officials who volunteered their duties.
   c. France's use of a corps of royally appointed officials in the provinces.
   d. England's attempts to hold the king responsible for the defense of the whole realm.
   e. France's issuance of a single national currency.

10. Which of the following was not a vital ingredient in the making of medieval European culture?
    a. The Greco-Roman artistic heritage
    b. The Roman pre-Christian cult
    c. Christian theology
    d. Germanic customs
    e. The development of universities

Enter *CengageNOW* using the access card that is available with this text. *CengageNOW* will assist you in understanding the content in this chapter with lesson plans generated for your needs and provide you with a connection to the *Wadsworth World History Resource Center* (see description at right for details).

 **World History Resource Center**

Enter the Resource Center using either your *CengageNOW* access card or your standalone access card for the *Wadsworth World History Resource Center.* Organized by topic, this website includes quizzes; images; over 350 primary source documents; interactive simulations, maps, and timelines; movie explorations; and a wealth of other resources. You can read the following documents, and many more, at the *Wadsworth World History Resource Center:*

St. Benedict, *Rule*
Thomas of Celano, *First and Second Lives of Saint Francis*
Liberties of Lorris

. . . my greatest joy is in victory: to conquer enemies, to pursue them and steal their possessions, to make their women cry, to ride on fast horses and return to my wife and daughters.
—Attributed to Chinghis Khan

19 THE MONGOL INTRUSION

BACKGROUND
Pastoral Nomadism ◆ The West ◆ The East

THE MONGOLS
Chinghis Khan and the Rise of the Mongols ◆ The Conquests

THE MONGOL EMPIRE AND ITS SIGNIFICANCE
The Yuan Dynasty in China ◆ The Khanate of the Golden Horde in Russia ◆ The Dynasty of the Il Khans in the Middle East

FRAGMENTATION OF THE EMPIRE

THE ASIAN WORLD IN the period after the decline of the Abbasid caliphate in the West and the fall of the Tang Dynasty in the East was in a state of almost continuous upheaval. Waves of nomadic, pastoralist peoples emigrated out of the steppes of central Asia seeking new pasturelands for their flocks and wealth to plunder. In the lands of Islam, between the ninth and the early thirteenth centuries, this emigration was experienced as the relatively peaceful arrival of Turkish tribes. China, on the other hand, already had a long history of attacks by Turco-Mongolian "barbarians" from the North and West. For the most part, both of these great civilizations had found ways of dealing with such nomadic peoples: in the Islamic East, by converting them and, in China, by bribery and the building of a Great Wall to keep them out. In the thirteenth century these methods no longer worked. The civilizations of Asia, as well as eastern Europe, were about to experience an invasion at the hands of a new steppe land force—the Mongols.

BACKGROUND

Like the Berbers, Arabs, and the Turks of North Africa and Asia, the Mongols subsisted on a mode of living called **pastoral nomadism**. It differed in several significant ways from that of the early agrarian civilizations introduced in previous chapters.

Pastoral Nomadism

Throughout history, pastoral nomads existed on marginal desert or **steppe** land (prairie grasslands) that was unsuitable for agriculture. So rather than

depending on seasonal crops, as farmers did, they adapted to the more restrictive environments in which they lived by learning to breed and raise livestock, such as camels, dromedaries, goats, sheep, horses, and yaks, to satisfy their primary needs. These animals furnished milk, meat, and even blood for the food and fermented beverages on which they depended, as well as hides and hair from which they created clothing, carpets, and shelter for themselves. Generally speaking, pastoralists enjoyed secure ways of life and cultures that were as rich as those of their more settled neighbors. However, constant resource shortages obliged them to be continuously on the move in search of water, suitable grazing lands for their flocks, and alternative sources of food.

Because of their different ways of life, pastoralists' and farming peoples' dealings with each other often were tense and warlike. They depended on each other for products each of them needed: farmers for meat and livestock that pastoralists could provide, and pastoralists on cultivators for the products of field and farm. Trade was the predominant form of intercourse between herding and agriculturally based civilizations, but when severe want or shifts in the balance of power followed peaceful conditions, episodes of raiding or outright conquest typically broke out. Peoples like the Arabs, the Turks, and the Mongols were organized to be prepared constantly for raiding and warfare, so they wandered along the borders of the ancient civilizations of western and eastern Asia as constant threats to the peaceful existence that farming people's settled ways of life demanded.

Pastoral peoples usually were organized in tribes, which were subdivided into clans. Their usual form of military action involved raiding for livestock and slaves, but they sometimes conducted more prolonged campaigns to seize pastureland and water rights or to extend control over subject populations. They chose tribal leaders, whom Turco-Mongolians called *khans*, on the basis of their personal wealth and charisma, and above all for their military skills. Nearly always these were males.

Little evidence survives concerning the roles of women among the Mongols; however, women from the families of *khans* are thought to have participated in the management and negotiation of tribal affairs. Recent archaeological discoveries of burial mounds of western Asian Scythian nomads suggest that nomadic women sometimes fought as warriors alongside men. Grave mounds containing female remains accompanied by weapons, shields, and various symbols of wealth and honor lend support to this thesis. DNA taken from these skeletons has been found in samples taken from some Mongol women, providing evidence that the ancient Scythian "Amazons" were the direct ancestors of these women.

The West

Ethnically speaking, Islam's origins were Arabic and Persian. The Arab nomads who had conquered Persia in the 640s were quickly absorbed by the much more sophisticated and numerous Persians. Unlike the Arabs, the Persians had long been accustomed to serving as rulers and models for others, and they reasserted those talents after mass conversion to Islam. For two centuries, the message of the Qur'an came through an Arab-Persian filter. In the 900s, however, a new ethnic group, the Turkish peoples, began to dominate the religion and culture. In the next centuries, the Seljuk Turks (see Chapter 14), who initially assumed control over the Baghdad caliphate in the tenth century, and their Mongol successors gave Islam a Turco-Mongol cast that it retained for centuries. Conversion of these steppe peoples had proved to be an effective way of winning a potential enemy over to being a useful ally. The Seljuks, for example, were successful in their resumption of the jihads against the Byzantines. However, when a new threat appeared at Islam's doorstep in the early 1200s, the caliphs and sultans of Persia and Iraq were unable to contain it.

The East

As was seen in Chapter 16, China's Tang Dynasty had begun falling apart early in the tenth century as a result of internal conflicts. Another contributing factor to China's decline was the continual threats to its northern borders from steppe land tribes. The Tang rulers had tried to deal with this menace by allying themselves with one tribe to defeat others. First, it was a Turco-Mongolian tribe called the *Uigurs* (WEE-gers); after them, it was the *Kirghiz* (KEER-gihz). The latter proved to be unmanageable, however, and they eventually weakened Tang rule in China. The Song emperors who followed the Tang tried dealing with the problem in much the same fashion as their predecessors had, but their weakness could not stop the Kirghiz from raiding northern China. In addition, the Great Wall had fallen into a state of disrepair and was becoming ineffective at keeping the nomads out of the North. By the early 1200s, yet another tribe, the Jurchen, arose out of Manchuria to threaten Song rule. Faced with this new menace, the Song ruler once again turned to the old tactic of playing one nomadic tribe off against another. This time, however, the decision proved to be fatal. Their new allies from the Gobi Desert, the Mongols, slaughtered the Jurchen, but with the sweet taste of victory in his mouth, their leader, Chinghis Khan, had greater ambitions and moved to extend his control over China as well.

The Mongols

Before their conquests, the Mongols were a relatively small group of steppe nomads. Their sources of food were their herds of livestock and what they could obtain by hunting, while their small, but strong Mongol ponies served them as both a mode of transportation and food source. Being nomadic, they lived in felt, tentlike structures called **yurts,** made out of horsehair, and their highest level of leadership was the tribal warlord or *khan.*

Like other pastoral nomads, the prime advantage of the Mongols in war was their ability to cover long distances more rapidly than any of their settled enemies. Virtually living on their small, hardy ponies, Mongol warriors combined the tactic of surprise, an uncanny accuracy with the bow and arrow, and the ability to use massed cavalry against their mainly infantry opponents. They usually bypassed walled strongholds against which a cavalry charge would be ineffective and starved their enemies into submission through their control over the surrounding countryside.

Chinghis Khan and the Rise of the Mongols

If one measures greatness by the territorial extent of a person's conquests, then there can be no doubt at all that **Chinghis Khan** (CHING-his HAHN) was the greatest ruler in world history. He was originally named Temujin (teh-moo-jin) but was given the title Chinghis Khan

Dean Conger/Corbis

A MONGOL YURT. At the time of the Mongol conquests, these tentlike shelters were ideal for a nomadic, warlike people who were constantly on the move. The yurts were made from felt, which provided relatively good insulation against all kinds of temperature extremes.

("Great King") in later life. Before his death in 1227, he had come to rule a vast territory from the South Russian steppes to the China Sea. His sons and successors expanded the Mongol empire even farther, until it was easily the largest the world has ever seen.

Temujin was born about 1167 into a violent landscape and had to struggle almost from birth against harsh competitors. At the time of his birth, Mongolian life, typical of pastoralist nomads, centered around numerous tribes that warred against one another continuously, when they were not assaulting the richer lands of the Chinese and Koreans. Temujin enjoyed years of successful conquest in these tribal wars. Greatly feared for his ferocity and ruthlessness, by 1196 he had become powerful enough to assert personal control over all of the Mongol tribes. In 1206, at a meeting of the *Khuraltai* (HOO-ral-teye), the Grand Council of clan elders at the capital of Karakorum (KAH-rah-KOH-ruhm), he accepted the title of Great King (Chinghis Khan) of the Mongols and imposed tight military order on his hundreds of thousands of followers. For the first time in their history, the Mongols were united under one leader.

Chinghis Khan combined traditional Mongol fighting methods with propaganda and new forms of organization to forge his armies into a remarkably efficient war machine. First, he divided them into light and heavy cavalry. The light units relied purely on the swiftness of their horses and their light weapons of swords, bows, and arrows to make lightning strikes. The heavy cavalry units added Chinese-style armor to the usual light, Mongol weapons. To maintain both political and military unity, Chinghis never allowed his army to remain organized along traditional tribal lines, so he restructured it by mixing all of the tribal warriors into new units consisting of

Victoria and Albert Museum, London/Art Resource, NY

MONGOL ARCHER. Mongol soldiers typically traveled with as many as five ponies because they provided swift, sure transport as well as a food source. The Mongols' ability to carry out lightning attacks and to fire accurately from the backs of these mounts was the key to their military successes.

members from many different tribal and clan groups. The largest army unit, the *Tumen* (TOO-muhn), consisted of 10,000 men and was divided further into smaller tactical units of 1,000, 100, and 10.

Chinghis and his generals also learned to make use of Chinese inventions like gunpowder and primitive guns to improve their proficiency in the art of the siege. To keep the loss of life among his followers to a minimum, he deliberately encouraged the spread of rumors about Mongol blood thirst. The fears these instilled in demoralized opponents and the growing reputation of Mongol skills in battle and the siege won many battles and cities without a shot having to be fired. (For an example, see the apocryphal quote attributed to Chinghis at the head of this chapter.)

The Conquests

The Mongol conquests proceeded in three phases. The first lasted from 1206, when Chinghis and his army attacked China unsuccessfully, to his death in 1227. The initial

CHINGHIS KHAN. Chinghis united the Mongol clan leaders for the first time in their history and, as the first of the Great Khans, created a world empire that included much of the Eurasian landmass.

Bibliothèque Nationale, Paris, France/Bridgeman Art Library

failure in China forced Chinghis to direct his armies westward against the Turks and Persians. Proud cities such as Bokhara, Samarkand, and Herat, all centers of a rich Muslim civilization, were overwhelmed after desperate resistance, and their populations were massacred or led into slavery. Some cities never would recover their former wealth and importance. Mosques were turned into stables and libraries were burned. Never had such destruction been seen; word of an approaching Mongol army was sometimes enough to inspire wholesale flight. Everywhere, the invaders were feared for their reputed bloodthirstiness toward those who resisted (see the two Law and Government boxes), and despised as cultural inferiors. This was particularly true in China, but also in the Christian and Muslim lands they overran. Many of the conquered territories had been under Persian Muslim rule for centuries and had developed a highly civilized lifestyle.

Following these successes, Chinghis headed north. In 1222, he crossed the Caspian Sea and raided southern Russia. He and the Mongols attacked Novgorod, again striking so much fear into the Russians that they called the Mongols *Tartars*, "people from Hell." However, it was Chinghis's grandson, Batu (BAH-too), who completed the subjugation of Russia after 1238.

Sated by these victories, Chinghis and his followers returned to Mongolia and gave the peoples to the West a temporary reprieve. His stay in his homelands did not last very long, though, and in 1227 he was again on the road to more battles. Not to be denied a victory and having failed once, he launched a second invasion of northern China. Again, the selective use of terror was applied as his most effective propaganda weapon, and he massacred all Chinese in his path who resisted, sometimes including women and children (see Law and Government: A Muslim Describes the Mongol Invasion). The warlord finally had conquered the entire world that was known to him, which essentially included the grasslands of Mongolia, northern China, Turkistan, Afghanistan, Persia, and Russia. His success in China was short-lived, however, and his death in 1227 ended the first phase of the Mongol eruption.

By then, the Mongols believed that their great spirit-god, Tengri, had commanded them to conquer the entire world, and they came close to doing so in the second and third phases of their conquests. Chinghis's successors returned to Russia to add to the previous conquests and also defeated the Teutonic Knights of Germany along the way, driving their army back almost to the walls of Vienna. The sudden death in 1241 of another Great Khan, however, saved the city, as the Mongols hastily retreated to Mongolia to choose a new leader. Afterward, the Mongols under Chinghis's grandson, Hulegu (HOO-luh-goo), returned to Persia and Iraq in 1251, and in 1258 the great city of the caliphs, Baghdad, suffered the same fate as so many before it. What had been one of the greatest cities

LAW AND GOVERNMENT

The Mongol Army

Shortly after the devastating Mongol attack, a high-ranking Persian Muslim, Ala-ad-Din-Juvaini, wrote *The History of the World Conqueror.* Clearly impressed by the new overlords, he spoke of the discipline of the Mongol army:

> What army can equal the Mongol army? In time of action when attacking and assaulting, they are like trained wild beasts out after game, and in the days of peace and security they are like sheep, yielding milk, and wool and many other useful things. In misfortune and adversity they are free of dissension and opposition. It is an army after the fashion of a peasantry, being liable to all manner of contributions, and rendering without complaint what is enjoined upon it.... It is also a peasantry in the guise of an army, all of them, great and small, noble and base, in time of battle becoming swordsmen, archers and lancers in whatever manner the occasion requires....

> Their obedience and submissiveness is such that if there be a commander of a hundred thousand [men] between whom and the Khan there is a distance of sunrise and sunset, and if he but commit some fault, the Khan dispatches a single horseman to punish him after the manner prescribed; if his head has been demanded, he cuts it off, and if gold be required, he takes it from him.

▶ Analyze and Interpret

What reasons can you give to explain these apparent contradictions in the men who formed the Mongol army? Are they, in fact, contradictions? What does the Mongol army have in common with any good army?

Source: Ala-ad-Din Ata-Malik Juvaini, *Ghenghis Khan: The History of the World Conqueror,* trans. J. A. Boyle (Manchester: Manchester University Press, 1997), Vol. 1, p. 23; cited in *The Islamic World,* ed. W. H. McNeill and M. R. Waldman (Oxford: Oxford University Press, 1973).

---

in the world was severely plundered by Mongol troops; scholars have estimated that 80,000 of its citizens were killed. Among these was the last Baghdad caliph of the once proud and mighty Abbasid Dynasty, along with his son and heir. Some of the family managed to escape and flee westward to Egypt, where a much-reduced caliphate was maintained for 250 years in a humbler state under the protection of an Egyptian sultanate.

THE MONGOL EMPIRE AND ITS SIGNIFICANCE

It would be easy to assume, from their methods of waging war, that the intrusion of the Mongols into the great centers of civilization, like those of Islam and China, brought only destruction. While that often occurred during the initial conquests of new territories, once they settled down to governing their enormous empire, Mongol rule also opened new opportunities for the traders and merchants among the peoples they had conquered. For about a century, the so-called ***Pax Mongolica*** (Mongolian Peace) extended across many thousands of miles, all under the supervision of a single Great Khan at Karakoram or Beijing and the relatives and clan leaders he appointed as subordinates to represent him. Goods could be transported from as far away as China and Southeast Asia to the towns of the eastern Mediterranean with relative ease and safety, so long as a tribute or tax was paid to the Khan's agents.

The conquest reopened the old Silk Road after it effectively had been shut down during centuries of warfare among the Turkmen tribes of Central and Western Asia. Now for the first and only time, all of mainland Asia (except southern India) was under the rule of a single great power (see Map 19.1). The impact this had on world history was considerable indeed. Besides the transport of the usual goods, crucial new technologies passed from China to the West that paved the way to the early European modern age. The spinning wheel helped revolutionize textile making. The compass proved to be an invention of incalculable value to the bold navigators and sea captains, such as da Gama, Albuquerque, Magellan, and Columbus, of Europe's Age of Discovery. European and Turkish improvements on Chinese inventions like gunpowder, primitive guns, and rockets eventually gave them superior weapons that enabled the Europeans to conquer and to forge

LAW AND GOVERNMENT

A Muslim Describes the Mongol Invasion

The Mongols purposely used terrorism as one way to subdue their enemies, sometimes even without a fight. This description by Ibn al-Athir, a thirteenth-century Muslim, of the Mongol conquest of the Middle East reveals how effective a weapon this fear sometimes was.

. . . For even Antichrist will spare such as follow him, though he destroy those who oppose him, but these Tatars spared none, slaying women and men and children, ripping open pregnant women and killing unborn babes. Verily to God do we belong, and unto Him do we return, and there is no strength and no power save in God, the High, the Almighty, in face of this catastrophe, whereof the sparks flew far and wide, and the hurt was universal; and which passed over the lands like clouds driven by the wind. For these were a people who emerged from the confines of China. . . .

. . . Now this is a thing the like of which ear has not heard; for Alexander, concerning whom historians agree that he conquered the world, did not do so with such swiftness, but only in the space of about ten years; neither did he slay, but was satisfied that men should be subject to him. But these Tatars conquered most of the habitable globe, and the best, the most flourishing and most populous part thereof, and that whereof the inhabitants were the most advanced in character and conduct, in about a year; nor did any country escape their devastations which did not fearfully expect them and dread their arrival.

. . . It is now time for us to describe how they first burst forth into the lands. Stories have been related to me, which the hearer can scarcely credit, as to the terror of the Tatars, which God Almighty cast into men's hearts; so that it is said that a single one of them would enter a village or a quarter wherein were many people, and would continue to slay them one after another, none daring to stretch forth his hand against this horseman. And I have heard that one of them took a man captive, but had not with him any weapon wherewith to kill him; and he said to his prisoner, "Lay your head on the ground and do not move," and he did so, and the Tatar went and fetched his sword and slew him therewith. Another man related to me as follows: "I was going," said he, "with seventeen others along a road, and there met us a Tatar horseman, and bade us bind one another's arms.

My companions began to do as he bade them, but I said to them, 'He is but one man; wherefore, then, should we not kill him and flee?' They replied, 'We are afraid.' I said, 'This man intends to kill you immediately; let us therefore rather kill him, that perhaps God may deliver us.' But I swear by God that not one of them dared to do this, so I took a knife and slew him, and we fled and escaped." And such occurrences were many.

▶ Analyze and Interpret

Where does the author seem to have gotten this information? How much truth do you think there was in this report? Assuming some of it might be exaggeration, how do you suppose such stories originated? What sort of an impact did they have? Do you know of any other instances where terrorism was purposely employed in history as a weapon?

Source: Edward G. Browne, *A Literary History of Persia* (Cambridge: Cambridge University Press, 1902), Vol. II, pp. 427–431.
Scanned by Jerome S. Arkenberg, Cal. State Fullerton. The text has been modernized by Prof. Arkenberg.

You can read more of Ibn al-Athir's *On the Tatars* at the *Wadsworth World History Resource Center*.

commercial empires that spanned the globe for the first time in history (Chapter 22).

Yet, hidden dangers lurked as more people were placed into direct contact with each other over vast distances. Besides spices, silks, precious metals, and other luxuries, microbial agents and diseases were passed from region to region to deadly effect. In the late Middle Ages (Chapter 20), the Black Death—possibly a form of Bubonic Plague or anthrax—appeared first in Central Asia and then spread along the trade routes and devastated at least three great civilizations: those of China, Islamic Western Asia and North Africa, and Europe. Other regions that also might have been affected were Southeastern Asia and parts of sub-Saharan Africa. Later still, European and African diseases like smallpox and malaria destroyed most of the Native American civilizations of the New World.

MAP 19.1 The Mongol Empire in 1255

In the early 1200s, Chinghis Khan created the vastest empire ever seen. His sons and grandsons expanded and divided the empire after his death in 1227. Except for India and the far southeast, almost all of Asia and eastern Europe was under Mongol sway. The Yuan Dynasty in China was the host of Marco Polo. The map shows boundaries between various regions conquered by the Mongols.

MAP QUESTION

Despite these, what might have acted as an enduring connection between China and the West?

The Yuan Dynasty in China

To administer this great expanse of territory, Chinghis Khan installed members of his family in positions of command as he fought his way into western Asia. After his death, his sons and grandsons divided the huge empire among themselves. The richest part, China, went to the **Yuan Dynasty** (YOO-an), whose most illustrious member was Kubilai Khan (koo-buh-lee haan or koob'-lee haan), the host of Marco Polo. In 1279, Kubilai completed the conquests of China that had begun under Chinghis Khan. For half a century, the Chinese had made successful use of gunpowder to keep the Mongols at bay. They developed an early, primitive type of gun, called the *fire lance*, which permitted them to discharge several arrows at once against their fearsome attackers. This weapon had given them an edge for a while, but it figuratively backfired when the

Mongols learned the secrets of the new weapon and used it themselves.

Kubilai and his followers tried to transform China into their notion of what a land should be: one that resembled the grassy steppe-lands from whence they had come. Not fully understanding agriculture, they plowed up productive farmland to graze their horses and camels. One sage advisor to Kubilai, however, finally realized the wastefulness of such measures and convinced the Great Khan to abandon this behavior. After all, farmers who were allowed to cultivate could produce tribute; prevented from following their livelihood, they could produce nothing. Moreover, the Mongols soon learned to rely more on the Chinese and their institutions for help in governing.

China during the years of Yuan rule was divided into a hierarchy, with Mongol officials, called *stamp wielders*, at the top. The old Confucian examination system of earlier

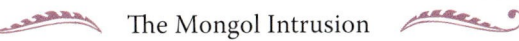

dynasties was discarded. The Mongols fought against assimilation. To find suitably educated people to staff government positions, they relied on foreigners more than on their Chinese subjects, and they accorded foreigners a higher status and supervisory authority over the old Mandarin elites. Many of these foreign recruits were Muslims, so Islam began making significant inroads into the eastern parts of China at this time, in addition to the Far West. The fact that Kubilai preferred foreigners over native Chinese explains why Marco Polo was given an important position when he visited the court of Kubilai Khan from 1275 to 1292.

The Mongols could not long remain entirely resistant to Chinese influences, however. Confucianism, while not encouraged, was at least tolerated. The universalism of Buddhism proved to be more appealing to the Mongols than native Chinese religions and philosophy, and even though the Mongols continued to segregate themselves from the Chinese, that faith found many converts among them.

The *Pax Mongolica* also meant that Yuan rule was a time of considerable prosperity for China, just as it was throughout the rest of the empire. It marked the end of further invasions from the North, a time of peace for a huge swath of territory, and the peaceful passage of merchants and caravans, which proved to be an enormous boon that helped offset the terrors of the initial invasions.

The Khanate of the Golden Horde in Russia

Once the Russians were subdued, the Mongols there proved to be unexpectedly tolerant of local ways. Called the **Khanate of the Golden Horde,** the Mongols settled down and converted to marginally more peaceful habits. For the most part, they remained content simply to extract tribute from their Russian subjects, otherwise leaving them to their traditions and Russian Orthodox Christianity. Eventually, too, most Mongols adopted Islam and its highly sophisticated culture. As in other regions over which they ruled, the Mongol Khans' ability to impose universal peace and stability went a long way toward assuring Russians under their rule a greater measure of peace than they had enjoyed previously. The Khanate of the Golden Horde proved to be the most durable of the four sub-khanates, lasting until 1480 before the Russians under the Muscovite principality finally ended the Mongols' regime.

The Dynasty of the Il Khans in the Middle East

Once Hulegu's hordes crushed Abbasid defenses and overran Baghdad, they continued their conquests to the West. Aleppo was sacked when it resisted, but Damascus surrendered and was spared. Neither Christians nor Hindus nor Buddhists had been able to stop them, and only their defeat in 1260 by the Egyptian sultanate's army **Ain Jalut** (AYN jah-LOOT), near Nazareth in Palestine,

saved the remaining Muslim lands from further destruction. Coming just two years after the Mongol conquest of Baghdad in 1258, this victory revived Muslim resistance and is one of the handful of truly decisive battles of world history.

Hulegu and his successors ruled the Islamic heartlands from Azerbaijan for the next ninety-one years as the dynasty of the **Il Khans** (il HAHNS). They were slow to convert to Islam, but as elsewhere the Mongols remained tolerant of their subjects' faith, and their rule was benign. This peaceful rule was terminated by a series of especially savage wars launched by another Turco-Mongolian warlord by the name of Timur-Lenk, or Tamarlane. Ironically, Tamarlane was a convert to Islam, but that did not prevent him from sweeping away everything in his path in a campaign of devastation upon entering eastern Iran in 1379. He went on to conquer virtually everything between northern India and Moscow, leaving behind him only death and ruin across the entire eastern Islamic world. His conquests seem to have served no purpose beyond conquest for its own sake. He made no real effort to create anything positive. He died in 1405, soon after defeating the Ottoman Sultan Bayezid in a Syrian battle, and left nothing behind. Under his sons, Tamarlane's so-called Timurid (TIH-muh-rid) Empire dissolved almost as quickly as it had appeared.

FRAGMENTATION OF THE EMPIRE

The Mongols had five Great Khans in the 1200s, beginning with Chinghis and ending with the death of Kubilai Khan in 1294 (see Table 19.1). After that, the ethnic segments of the huge empire went their separate ways. The nomadic culture and the Mongols' approach to government (exploitation through conquest) would have made it difficult to maintain their vast domain under a single center, even if much better communications and a much larger pool of loyal officials had been available. Because these resources were not available, the original unified conquest broke up within a century. First China, then Russia and the Middle Eastern lands separated from one another under sub-khanates with their own conflicting interests. Successive intra-Mongol fights for regional supremacy after 1280 further weakened the power of the dynasty.

The second and third generations of Mongol rulers were more sensitive to their subjects' needs and expectations and included some exceptionally able men. Their adoption of one or another of the competing religions of Asia also enhanced their prestige for a time at least. In China, Kubilai Khan favored Buddhism. One of the Middle Eastern Il Khan rulers adopted the Muslim faith in the 1290s and simultaneously began the revival of Persian power and prestige. The Russian-based Golden Horde khans also adopted Islam in the late 1200s, but their conversion had no influence on the Russian people, who remained steadfast in their Eastern Orthodox Christianity.

Gradually, the Mongols' far more numerous Christian (Russia, Near East), Muslim (Middle East, India), and Buddhist (China, Tibet) subjects began to make their presence felt, as they tamed and converted their conquerors. By the mid-1300s, the empire was disintegrating into its preconquest component parts, and rebellions against Mongol rulers were multiplying. In China and Persia first (late 1300s), then the Near East and Russia (1400s), Mongol rule became a bad memory. The former rulers were either absorbed into the subject populations or retired back into their desolate Central Asian homelands.

TABLE 19.1 The Great Khans of the Mongols

Chinghis Khan	1206–1227
Ogodei Khan	1229–1241
Guyuk Khan	1246–1248
Mongke Khan	1251–1259
Kubilai Khan	1260–1294

SUMMARY

THE TRIBES OF the central and eastern Asian steppe lands had long been a thorn in the side of their more settled neighbors to their west and south. The Chinese had been forced to build the Great Wall as a defense against the Mongols' continual depredations, and pressures against the Mongols' western neighbors forced the Germanic tribes and, in the ninth century, the Turks to migrate to the West, eventually contributing to the destruction of the western Roman Empire and the unsettling of the eastern Islamic Empire. The rise of the Mongols under their notorious warlord Chinghis Khan must be understood partly against this deep background. Yet, Chinghis's exceptional abilities as a leader unified the Mongols, and the formidable military talents of the mounted Mongol warriors accounted for their singular success as conquerors.

As always seems to be the case with the most successful conquerors in history, their victims saw them as exceptionally uncivilized. To some degree, the Mongols' reputation as particularly brutal conquerors can be attributed to this view. However, these accusations also seem to bear some truth, given that the Great Khans tried to spare their own blood and that of their soldiers through deliberate campaigns of terror tactics. Cities fell and, in many cases, peoples surrendered without a fight. Whatever the truth of the stories told about them, the Mongols undoubtedly created history's greatest empire, having conquered an unprecedented swath of territory that included most of the Eurasian landmass by the end of the thirteenth century. Once their invasions were completed, the Mongols settled down to a more peaceful existence and managed to create a zone of peace and prosperity that this enormous region had never before enjoyed.

▶ Identification Terms

Test your knowledge of this chapter's key concepts by defining the following terms. If you can't recall the meaning of certain terms, refresh your memory by looking up the boldfaced term in the chapter, turning to the Glossary at the end of the book, or working with the flashcards that are available on the *World Civilizations* Companion Website: **academic.cengage.com/adler**

Ain Jalut	Khanate of the	*Pax Mongolica*	Yuan Dynasty
Chinghis Khan	Golden Horde	steppe	yurts
Il Khans	pastoral nomadism		

▶ Test Your Knowledge

Test your knowledge of this chapter by answering the following questions. Complete answers appear at the end of the book. You may find even more quiz questions in CengageNOW and on the *World Civilizations* Companion Website: **academic.cengage.com/adler**

1. Judging by the previous strategies followed by the Tang and Song emperors of China in dealing with northern steppe peoples, when faced with the Mongol threat, one would have expected the Song to resort to
   a. seeking military assistance from the caliphs of Baghdad.
   b. recruiting a powerful army of mercenaries to defend their realm.
   c. relying on Japanese samurai to ward them off.
   d. playing off another steppe land ally against the Mongols.
   e. retreating farther south into China.

2. Before Chinghis was named as the Great Khan in 1206, it can be said that the Mongols
   a. were led by tribal warlords.
   b. already had seen the rise of previous Great Khans.
   c. were divided into numerous warring tribes.
   d. were attempting to invade China.
   e. were as described in both a and c.

3. The principal military advantage the Mongols enjoyed over their opponents lay in
   a. their ability to shoot bows and arrows accurately from horseback at full gallop.
   b. the genius of their war leaders in matters of strategy.
   c. their skillful use of military intelligence.
   d. their absolute belief in the power of their war god.
   e. both b and d.

4. Which of these is the correct sequence of Chinghis Khan's conquests?
   a. China, Mongolia, Afghanistan, Persia, and Russia
   b. Mongolia, Persia, Russia, China, and Afghanistan
   c. Mongolia, Turks, Persians, Russia, and northern China
   d. Mongolia, Persia, Turkistan, China, and Russia
   e. Mongolia, China, Turkistan, Persia, and Russia

5. Through the use of terror, the Mongols
   a. easily overran all enemies.
   b. often were able to cow enemies into surrender without a fight.
   c. sometimes frightened themselves.
   d. were so successful in defeating opponents that they no longer had to use weapons.
   e. frightened all of their enemies into thinking they were from hell.

6. After the Mongol conquests, the Abbasid caliphate
   a. was extinguished.
   b. continued to exist in a reduced state in Egypt.
   c. was relocated to Azerbaijan under the Il Khans.
   d. continued to exist in Baghdad under the domination of the Il Khans.
   e. was protected by the Khanate of the Golden Horde in Russia.

7. It appears that the principal difference between Mongol rule in China and in the Middle East is that the Mongols
   a. were more resistant to assimilation in Persia.
   b. preferred Islamic civilization.
   c. admired Abbasid rule.
   d. were more resistant to assimilation in China.
   e. resorted to the use of terror more frequently in governing China.

8. Russia was left to the Khanate called the
   a. Golden Horde.
   b. Abbasids.
   c. Il Khans.
   d. Timurids.
   e. Yuan.

9. The Timurids differed from the Il Khans in which respect?
   a. They were Buddhists.
   b. They were Christians.
   c. They were Muslims.
   d. They conquered the Muscovites.
   e. They left no lasting empire.

10. Which of the following can be said of the Mongol conquests as a whole?
    a. They were totally destructive.
    b. The Mongols were generally tolerant of their conquered subjects.
    c. They were good for long-distance trade.
    d. They usually resulted in a cultural decline wherever they happened.
    e. They were as described in both b and c.

Enter *CengageNOW* using the access card that is available with this text. *CengageNOW* will assist you in understanding the content in this chapter with lesson plans generated for your needs and provide you with a connection to the *Wadsworth World History Resource Center* (see description at right for details).

 **World History Resource Center**

Enter the Resource Center using either your *CengageNOW* access card or your standalone access card for the *Wadsworth World History Resource Center*. Organized by topic, this website includes quizzes; images; over 350 primary source documents; interactive simulations, maps, and timelines; movie explorations; and a wealth of other resources. You can read the following documents, and many more, at the *Wadsworth World History Resource Center*:

Marco Polo, *Prologue to Travels*
Ibn al-Athir, *On the Tatars*

20 LATE MEDIEVAL TROUBLES

Man proposes, and God disposes.
—Thomas A. Kempis

DISASTERS OF THE FOURTEENTH CENTURY
The Black Death ◆ The Hundred Years' War

PROBLEMS IN THE CHURCH
The Babylonian Captivity ◆ The Great Schism

SOCIETY AND WORK IN LATE MEDIEVAL EUROPE

MEDIEVAL SCIENCES

STARTING ABOUT 1000 CE, European civilization was revitalized and flourished during several centuries of expansion and consolidation. In the fourteenth century, however, a series of unprecedented disasters sharply reduced the population and caused a decline in the economy that continued for about 150 years. The feudal governing system and the agriculturally based economy reeled under great blows: the Black Death, the Hundred Years' War, and the labor shortage these events created.

The leaders of the Christian church became embroiled in one scandalous affair after another: the weakening of papal sovereignty during the Babylonian Captivity in France and then the Great Schism. Although the challenge to papal authority embodied in the Conciliar Movement was crushed, the popes never regained their previous moral authority, and the way was prepared for the eventual Protestant revolt against the Roman Church, the Reformation.

DISASTERS OF THE FOURTEENTH CENTURY

The problems that manifested themselves in fourteenth-century Europe had their origins in earlier days. By 1300, the population had been growing steadily for two centuries, aided by the new land that had been put into production, several major technical breakthroughs in agriculture, and the unusually benevolent climate, which brought warmer temperatures and appropriate amounts of rain to most of western and southern Europe for a century or longer.

These happy circumstances came to an end in the early fourteenth century. Most good land was by now already being used, and the technology to exploit the marginal lands (swamps, marshes, hillsides, and the like) did not exist. Worse still, this period experienced the beginnings of what climatologists call the **Little Ice Age**. This lasted for about 500 years and brought noticeably colder and wetter weather, hitting Europe especially hard in the first half of the fourteenth century with year after year of cold, rainy summers, shortened growing seasons, and frequent crop failures. Local famines became commonplace in parts of Europe; those who did not starve were often physically weakened as a consequence of poor nutrition over many years. Europe had too many mouths to feed, and the balance was about to be restored through the natural disasters of famine and disease and the man-made disaster of war.

The Black Death

The **Black Death** of the mid- and late fourteenth century is the most massive epidemic on record and by far the most lethal in the history of Europe, Asia, and parts of Africa. What was it, and why did it deal such a blow to Old World populations?

Until recently, scholars thought that it was a form of bubonic plague common in the Asian steppes but previously unknown to Europeans that was carried to the Mediterranean ports by Italian trading ships in 1346–1347. Most believed that fleas living on rats spread the plague bacillus, and the rats were then (as now) found everywhere humans lived. However, this theory has come under attack. Some now think that the Black Death was a form of anthrax or even an Ebola-like hemorrhagic fever. Whatever its precise nature, it reached Sicily in 1349, having traveled westward along the Silk Road from its place of origin in Central Asia. Within two years, this usually fatal disease had spread all over western Europe and North Africa; within two more, it had spread from Syria to Sweden and from Russia's western provinces to Spain (see Map 20.1). As in China, millions of people died in the first years of the plague. To make matters worse, it came back again to some parts of Europe during the 1360s and 1370s, sometimes killing one-third or even one-half of the populations of towns and cities within a few weeks.

No one had any idea of how the disease was spread or what countermeasures should be taken. Fourteenth-century European medicine lagged behind the medical practices in several other parts of the world. Even if the Europeans had been on the same level as the Muslims or the Chinese, though, they would have been unable to halt its spread. Because Europeans lacked any immunity to the disease, a high death toll was virtually inevitable: death came in about two out of three cases, with the highest mortality rates in the old and the young. City dwellers died in vast numbers because crowded conditions and primitive sanitation aided the spread of the disease. Those who had some place of refuge fled into the countryside, often carrying the highly infectious disease with them.

Italy, England, and the Low Countries were the most savagely hit, because these were the most urbanized areas. Debate continues on just how many Europeans died from the plague, but historians believe that as much as one-fourth of the English population succumbed over a period of a few years. Individual cities, such as Venice, Florence, and Antwerp, suffered even more; some were practically depopulated for a generation.

The economic consequences of the plague are not easily traced and do not lend themselves to generalizations. Government revenues were affected: with fewer taxpayers left alive, tax revenues declined sharply; public works such as the cathedrals had to be stopped for a generation or longer. Some places experienced a shortage of labor that was not relieved for at least two generations. In the towns, which had been overcrowded, the plague reduced the excess population, and the survivors enjoyed better health and work security. Wages for the surviving craftsmen and common laborers rose sharply despite vain attempts to impose wage and price controls. Merchants and traders found fewer consumers to buy their goods, however, and the volume of trade declined.

THE BLACK DEATH. A late medieval painter captures the dismay and despair of the victims of the plague. Note the swelling of the neck of the falling man, one of the most common signs of infection. Above, a devil and an angel battle in the sky, as St. Sebastian (with the arrow-pierced body) pleads for Christ's mercy on the sufferers. *Saint Sebastian Interceding for the Plague Stricken* by Josse Lieferinxe, c. 1500.

The Walters Art Museum, Baltimore (37.1995)

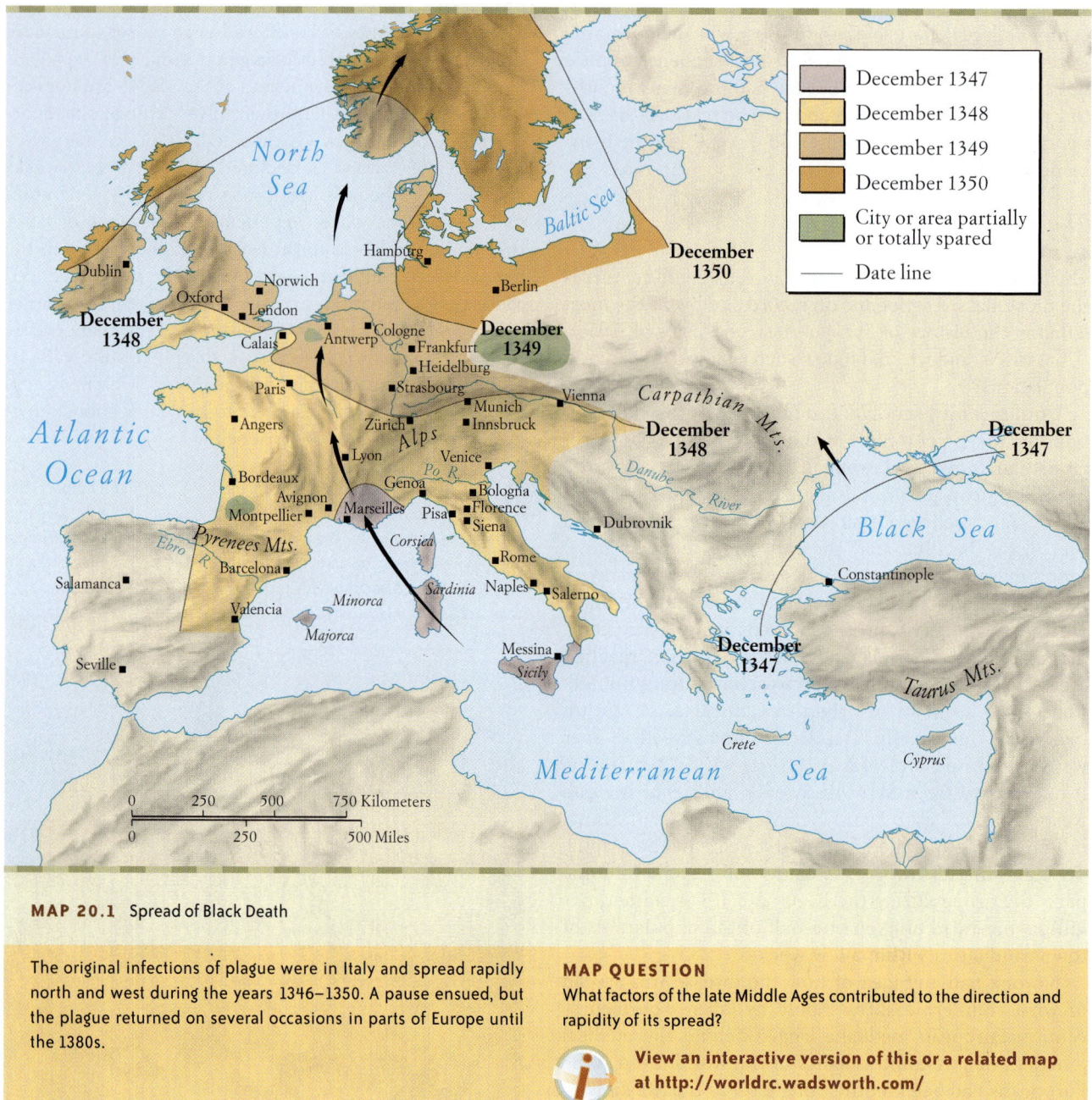

MAP 20.1   Spread of Black Death

The original infections of plague were in Italy and spread rapidly north and west during the years 1346–1350. A pause ensued, but the plague returned on several occasions in parts of Europe until the 1380s.

MAP QUESTION

What factors of the late Middle Ages contributed to the direction and rapidity of its spread?

View an interactive version of this or a related map at http://worldrc.wadsworth.com/

Peasants who were still bound in serfdom, those who had to pay high labor rents, and those who were otherwise dissatisfied with their lords took quick advantage of their strong bargaining position—or tried to. France, England, and Germany experienced peasant revolts against their lords. The peasants invariably lost these armed confrontations with the mounted and well-armed nobles, but in the longer run, the settlements made between lords and peasants favored the freedoms of the peasants. Serfdom of the near-slavery sort, which was already weak in western Europe, died as a result of the plague. The mobility of labor increased. Much land that had previously been worked had to be abandoned and reverted to waste.

What were the psychic consequences of the plague? These effects can be detected for the better part of a century after 1347. During the late fourteenth and fifteenth centuries, all types of European Christian art reveal a fascination with death. The figure of the Grim Reaper, the reminder of human mortality, and the waiting Last Judgment became major motifs in pictorial and sculptural art. The Dance of Death, a scene in which skeletons link arms with the living revelers, also appeared frequently. The grave is always present in the background, and morbidity is in the air.

Most Christians believed that a wrathful God had given earthly sinners a horrible warning about what awaited the world if morals and conduct were not improved. Many people joined penitential societies, while others chose more extreme measures to exorcise sin from their midst. Groups of flagellants traveled the countryside, whipping themselves to beat sin from their flesh. Others, blaming the Jews for the crucifixion of Jesus, believed that the plague was God's punishment for allowing Jews to live among them. These turned on Jewish minorities and thousands of innocent victims were publicly burned at the stake. It was at this time that Christianity took on much of the burden of guilt and shame, the consciousness of sin, and its consequences that distinguishes it from other major religions.

The Hundred Years' War

Even before the outbreak of the Black Death, another European disaster was under way: the Hundred Years' War. This conflict between England and France or, more accurately, between the kings and nobles of England and France, started because of a dynastic quarrel between the English Edward III and his French rival, Philip VI.

Recent interpretations of the causes of the war have stressed economic factors. English prosperity depended largely on trade with the towns of Flanders across the Channel, where most woolen cloth was produced using wool from English sheep. English control of the French duchy of Flanders would ensure the continuance of this prosperity and would be popular in both Flanders and England.

Questions of feudal allegiance also contributed to the conflict. The French kings had been trying for generations to increase their powers of taxation at the expense of their feudal vassals in the provinces. Many French nobles saw the English claim to Flanders as advantageous to themselves, because they thought an English king's control over the French provinces would inevitably be weaker than a French king's. So they fought with the English against their own monarch, saying that the English claim was better grounded in law than Philip's. The war turned out to be as much a civil war as a foreign invasion of France.

The course of the war was erratic. Several truces were signed, when one or both sides were exhausted. The conflict took place entirely on French soil, mostly in the provinces facing the English Channel or in the region of Paris. The major battles included **Crecy** in 1346, where the English archers used their new longbows effectively against the French (the English may have used a few of the just-introduced, gunpowder-charged cannon as well); Poitiers in 1356, where the English captured the French king and held him for ransom; and **Agincourt** in 1415, where the English routed the discouraged French a third time, but could not coerce a settlement.

By the 1420s, the war had long since lost its dynastic element. It had become a matter of national survival to the loyal French nobility, who were being pushed back to the walls of Paris (see Map 20.2). At this juncture appeared the patron saint of France, Joan of Arc. This peasant girl, who said she had been told by God to offer her services to the embattled (and ungrateful) Charles VII, routed the English and their French allies at Orleans in 1429 and changed the trend of the war, which now began to favor the French. In the ensuing twenty years, France recaptured almost all of the lands lost to the English invaders during the previous hundred. In 1453, the costly and sometimes bloody struggle finally ended with the English withdrawal from all of France except the port of Calais on the Channel.

Consequences of the Hundred Years' War. Although originally popular among the English, the war eventually came to be seen as a bottomless pit swallowing up taxes and manpower. The costs of maintaining a large army of mercenaries

MAP 20.2 The Hundred Years' War

Much of northern and eastern France, especially the rich duchy of Burgundy, joined with the English invaders in the attempt to escape the reach of the monarchs based in Paris.

MAP QUESTION

What reasons can you give that might explain why the English controlled the north of France?

 View an interactive version of this or a related map at http://worldrc.wadsworth.com/

in France for decades were enormous, and even the rich booty brought home from the captured French towns had not been enough to pay for the war. In addition, the war had disrupted England's commerce with continental markets.

The power and prestige of Parliament had increased, however. Since its origins in the thirteenth century, Parliament had met only sporadically. Now, in thirty-seven of the forty years between the beginning of the war in 1337 and Edward III's death in 1377, Parliament was in session. The king was always looking for money, and Parliament had to be consulted for the necessary new taxes. As a result, by the end of the war, Parliament was a determining voice in matters of taxation and other policy.

France did not experience a similar parliamentary development. The French kings allowed regional assemblies to meet in the major provinces, but they avoided holding a national assembly, which might have attempted to negotiate as equals with the Crown on national issues and policies.

This difference in parliamentary development between the two countries would become more significant and more visible as time wore on. France followed the path of most European monarchies in transferring power steadily *to the* royal officials and *away from* the nobles and burgesses of the towns, who would have been representatives to a parliament. England strengthened the powers of its parliament, while checking those of its king. In either case much depended on the personal traits of the king, the progress of wars, and sheer happenstance.

The Hundred Years' War effectively ended chivalric ideals of combat in Europe. The style of warfare changed dramatically during its course. No longer were the heavily armored horsemen the decisive weapon in battle. Cavalry would still play an important role in warfare for 400 years, but only as an auxiliary force, as it had been for the Romans. The infantry, supported by the earliest artillery and soon to be armed with muskets, were now what counted.

The longbow and cannon at Crecy had initiated a military revolution. With the introduction of gunpowder, war ceased to be a personal combat between equals. Now thanks to the cannon, you could kill your foe from a distance, even before you could see him plainly. The new tactics also proved to be great social levelers. Commoners armed with longbows could bring down mounted and armored knights. The noble horseman, who had been distinguished both physically (by being *above* the infantry) and economically (a horse was expensive to buy and maintain), was now brought down to the level of the infantryman, who could be equipped for a fraction of what it cost to equip a horseman. The infantryman could also be left to forage for himself at the expense of the local population as no horse could.

PROBLEMS IN THE CHURCH

The fourteenth century was also a disaster for the largest, most universal institution in the Christian world: the Roman Catholic Church. Whether a devout Christian or

©Giraudon/Art Resource, NY

JOAN OF ARC. This miniature of the patron saint of France is one of the few contemporary renditions that has survived. A peasant dressed in armor, she was an extraordinary female figure in this age of male warriors drawn from the nobility.

not, every person's life was touched more or less directly by the church. The church was represented at the community level by the parish church, and it was in every way the heart of community life throughout the Middle Age and into modern times. Whether in a village or a great city, the parish church was much more than a place of worship. Its bells rang out the news and announced emergencies. Popular festivities and the equivalents of town meetings were held there after the Mass. It was also an informal gathering point, a place for business dealings, and a social center. The three great events of ordinary lives were celebrated in the church: birth (baptism), marriage, and death (funeral).

Just as the church was the focal point of everyday life, the parish priest was an important man in the village community. Even if he was ignorant and illiterate, the priest was respected as the representative of an all-powerful, all-seeing lord and final judge. Few, indeed, would attempt to defy or even ignore him in the round of daily life. The church courts determined whether marriages were legal and proper, who was a bastard, whether orphans had rights, whether contracts were legitimate, and whether sexual crimes had been committed. In the church, the chief judge was the pope, and the papal court in Rome handled thousands of cases that were appealed to it each year. Most of the lawyers of Europe from the twelfth through the fourteenth centuries were employed and trained by the church.

As a result, the clergy came to have an increasingly legalistic, rather than a pedagogical or charitable, outlook.

Probably the greatest medieval pope, Innocent III, reigned from 1198 to 1216. He forced several kings of Europe to bow to his commands, including the unfortunate John of England, Philip II Augustus of France, and Frederick II, the German emperor. But in behaving much like a secular king with his armies and his threats of war, Innocent sacrificed much of the moral authority he had derived from his position as successor to St. Peter and deputy of Christ on Earth.

Later thirteenth-century popes attempted to emulate Innocent with varying success, but all depended on their legal expertise or threat of armed force (the papal treasury assured the supply of mercenaries). Finally, Pope Boniface VIII (1294–1303) overreached badly when he attempted to assert that the clergy were exempt from royal taxes in both France and England. In the struggle of wills that followed, the kings of both countries were able to make Boniface back down: the clergy paid the royal taxes. It was a severe blow to papal prestige.

Some years later, the French monarch actually arrested the aged Boniface for a few days, dramatically demonstrating who held the whip hand if it should come to a showdown. Boniface died of humiliation, it was said, just days after his release. His successor was handpicked by Philip, the French king, who controlled the votes of the numerous French bishops.

The Babylonian Captivity, 1305–1378

The new pope was a French bishop who took the name Clement V. Rather than residing in Rome, he was induced to stay in the city of Avignon in what is now southern France. This was the first time since St. Peter that the head of the church had not resided in the Holy City of Christendom, and, to make matters worse, Clement's successors—mostly French bishops—stayed in Avignon as well. The **Babylonian Captivity**, as the popes' stay in Avignon came to be called, created a great scandal. Everyone except the French viewed the popes as captives of the French crown and unworthy to lead the universal church or decide questions of international justice.

In 1377, one of Clement's papal successors finally returned to Rome but died soon thereafter. In the ensuing election, great pressure was put on the attending bishops to elect an Italian, and the one duly elected took the name Urban VI. Urban was a well-intentioned reformer, but he went about his business in such an arrogant fashion that he had alienated all of his fellow bishops within weeks of his election. Declaring his election invalid because of pressures placed on them, the bishops elected another Frenchman, who took the name Clement VII. He immediately returned to Avignon and took up residence once more under the benevolent eye of the French king, but the bullheaded Urban refused to step down. There were thus two popes and doubt as to which, if either, was the legitimate one.

The Great Schism, 1378–1417

The final episode in this demeaning decline of papal authority now began. For forty years, Christians were treated to the spectacle of two popes denouncing each other as an impostor and the Anti-Christ. Europeans divided along national lines: the French, Scots, and Iberians supported Clement; the English and Germans preferred Urban (largely because his sentiments were anti-French). Neither side would give an inch, even after the two original contestants had died.

The **Great Schism** hastened the realization of an idea that had long been discussed among pious and concerned people: the calling of a council, a universal conclave of bishops to combat growing problems within the structure and doctrines of the church. The **Conciliar Movement** was a serious challenge to papal authority. Its supporters wished to enact some important reforms and thought that the papal government was far too committed to maintaining the status quo. Its adherents, therefore, argued that the entire church community, not the pope, had supreme powers of doctrinal definition. Such definition would be expressed in the meetings of a council, whose members should include laypersons and not just clerics. These ideas fell on fertile ground and were eventually picked up by other fourteenth-century figures, such as the English theologian John Wyclif.

Wyclif believed that the clergy had become corrupt, that individual Christians should be able to read and interpret the word of the Lord for themselves, rather than depending on a perhaps biased clergy. His doctrines were popular with the English poor and were emblazoned on the banners of

Bibliothèque Nationale, Paris, France/Bridgeman Art Library

A MEDIEVAL COPYIST AT WORK. Thousands of monks labored at the tedious job of copying books for medieval libraries. This example comes from the thirteenth century.

the greatest popular uprising in English history, the revolt of 1381, which very nearly toppled the Crown. The rebels were called Wyclifites, or **Lollards**, and their ideas about the ability of ordinary people to interpret Scripture for themselves were to be spread to the Continent within a few years.

The scandal of the Schism aroused great resentment among Christians of all nations, and intense pressure was brought to bear on both papal courts to end their quarrel. Neither would, however, and finally a council was called at Pisa in Italy in 1409. The council declared both popes deposed and elected a new one, but neither of the deposed popes accepted the verdict, and so instead of two there were now three claimants!

A few years later, from 1414 to 1417, a bigger and more representative council met in the German city of Constance. The council had three objectives: (1) to end the Schism and return the papacy to Rome, (2) to condemn the Wyclifites and other heretics, and (3) to reform the church and clergy from top to bottom. The **Council of Constance** was successful in its first goal: a new pope was chosen, and the other three either stepped down voluntarily or were ignored. The council achieved some temporary success with its second goal of eliminating heresy, but the heresies it condemned simply went underground and emerged again a century later. As for the third objective, nothing was done; reforms were discussed, but the entrenched leaders made sure no real action was taken.

Additional councils were held over the next thirty years, but they achieved little or nothing in the vital areas of clerical corruption. The popes and other clerical officials who had resisted the whole idea of the council had triumphed, but their victory would come at a high price for their successors. The need for basic reform in the church continued to be ignored until the situation exploded with Martin Luther (see Chapter 23).

SOCIETY AND WORK IN LATER MEDIEVAL EUROPE

As we have noted, an upsurge in peasant rebellions followed the Black Death. All of them were crushed. Nevertheless, in the long run, the peasants did succeed in obtaining more freedoms and security. The *Jacquerie* of 1358 in France shocked the nobility, as the peasants raped and looted, burned castles, and even destroyed chapels. The nobles took a heavy revenge, but the French and Flemish peasants were by no means through. Revolts occurred repeatedly throughout the 1300s and early 1400s in parts of France.

In England, the Lollard rebellion of 1381 was an equal jolt to the upper classes and the king. One of its leaders was the priest John Ball. His famous couplet would be shouted or mumbled from now on: "When Adam delved and Eva span/Who was then the gentleman?" (*Delved* means plowed, and *span* is old English for spun.) (See the Patterns of Belief box "John Ball's Preaching" for more discussion.)

The causes of the Lollard rebellion were complex and varied from place to place, but almost all of England was involved, and in an unusual development, many artisans and laborers in the towns joined the peasants. These urban workers had been impoverished by a rigid guild system that prevented newcomers from competing with the established shops and kept pay rates low for all but the workers at the top.

The **guilds** were medieval urban organizations that controlled what was made, for what price, and by whom. First formed in urban areas in the 1200s, the guilds were very strong by the fourteenth and fifteenth centuries. Their scheme, in which a worker advanced from apprentice to journeyman to master as his skills developed, was almost universal. Most journeymen never took the final step upward, however, because the guild restricted the number of masters who could practice their trade in a given area.

The guilds aimed at ensuring economic security for their members, not competitive advantage. The members fixed prices and established conditions of labor for employees, length of apprenticeships, pay scales, examinations for proving skills, and many other things. The labor shortages caused by the Black Death actually prolonged and strengthened the monopoly aspects of the guild system. In some European cities, the guilds, which abhorred the free market, were the chief determinants of economic activity until the nineteenth century.

Bibliothèque Nationale, Paris /The Bridgeman Art Library

THE JACQUERIE. This brilliant illustration exemplifies the usual end of a peasant rebellion in the fourteenth century; the nobles massacre their challengers and throw them into the river, cheered on by the ladies in the left background.

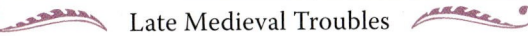
Urban areas had been terribly overcrowded, at least until the Black Death. The reduced populations that followed the plague enabled many towns to engage in the first instances of urban planning. Many medieval towns emerged from the crisis with open spaces, parks, and suburbs that made them more attractive. (*Suburb* originally meant a settlement outside the walls of the town.) Again and again, a cramped city found it necessary to tear down the old walls and build new ones farther out. This expanding series of defensive earthwork and masonry walls is still perceptible in the maps of some modern European cities.

Inside the town walls or just outside, many types of skilled and semiskilled workers plied their trades, generally in home workshops employing one or two workers besides the family members. Factories, or mass employment places of production, were still in the distant future. Machines of any type independent of human or animal energy were unknown. Even water- and wind-powered mechanisms, such as waterwheels and windmills, were relatively rare. (The Society and Economy box relates more about medieval life, specifically that of an Italian family.)

MEDIEVAL SCIENCES

In later medieval Europe, scientific studies improved somewhat from the elementary conditions of theory and practice in the earlier period. Europeans were becoming familiar with the Hindu/Arab invention of algebra, while the introduction of Arabic numbers made doing math faster and easier. With it, they became much more adept at dealing with unknown quantities. Some faint beginnings of chemistry can be detected. These took the form of alchemy, the search (begun by the Muslims) for the magical substance that would transform base metal into gold and silver.

Geography made considerable progress, borrowing heavily from Muslim cartography and knowledge of the seas. Most educated people already believed the world was a sphere, for instance, before Portuguese voyages proved that it was. But except in anatomy, medicine and surgery made little headway beyond what the Muslims and Greeks already knew. The main European medical center was at Salerno, which depended heavily on teachers

PATTERNS OF BELIEF

John Ball's Preaching

In the Lollard rebellion in fourteenth-century England, the peasantry responded violently to the question "When Adam delved and Eva span, who was then the gentleman?" In his *Chronicles*, the medieval author Froissart tells us of what happened:

A crazy priest in the county of Kent, called John Ball, who for his absurd preaching had thrice been confined to prison by the Archbishop of Canterbury, was greatly instrumental in exciting these rebellious ideas. Every Sunday after mass this John Ball was accustomed to assemble a crowd around him in the marketplace and preach to them. On such occasions he would say, "My good friends, matters cannot go on well in England until all things shall be in common; when there shall be neither vassals nor lords; when the lords shall be no more masters than ourselves. How ill they behave to us! For what reason do they thus hold us in bondage? Are we not all descended from the same parents, Adam and Eve? And what can they show, or what reason can they give, why they should be more masters than ourselves? They are clothed in velvet and rich stuffs, while we are forced to wear poor clothing. They have wines, spices, and fine bread, while we have only rye and the refuse of the straw; and when we drink, it must be water. They have handsome seats and manors, while we must brave the

wind and rain in our labours in the field, and it is by our labour they have wherewithal to support their pomp. We are called slaves, and if we do not perform our service we are beaten, and we have no sovereign to whom we can complain or who would be willing to hear us. Let us go to the king and remonstrate with him; he is young, and from him we may obtain a favorable answer, and if not we must seek to amend our condition."

Many in the city of London, envious of the rich and noble, having heard of John Ball's preaching, said among themselves that the country was badly governed, and that the nobility had seized upon all the gold and silver. These wicked Londoners began to assemble in parties and show signs of rebellion; they also invited all those who held like opinions in the adjoining counties to come to London: telling them that they would find the town open to them and the commonalty of the same way of thinking as themselves, and that they would so press the king, that there should no longer be a slave in England.

▶ **Analyze and Interpret**

What do you think was meant by the phrase "we must seek to amend our condition" in this statement? Why was it unusual that city dwellers would make common cause with the rural folk in something as dangerous as rebellion?

SOCIETY AND ECONOMY

Margherita Datini (1360–1423)

The discovery of hundreds of letters preserved by accident for 500 years in a residence in Prato, Italy, allows us to participate in many of the life events of a medieval Italian woman named Margherita Datini. She was the wife of a wealthy merchant, Francesco Datini, for more than thirty-five years, and during that time Francesco's frequent business trips made it necessary for the couple to communicate by letter.

The Datinis met in 1376, when he was almost forty and she was sixteen. Such an age difference was not uncommon in upper-class marriages of the period, although Datini was remarkable in not demanding a dowry from his bride's family. Margherita was an orphan, the daughter of a minor nobleman who had been executed in one of the incessant civil wars that wracked the northern Italian city-states. The winners had confiscated his property. Francesco was also an orphan, having lost both parents to the Black Plague, but he had been successful as a merchant in Avignon, serving the papacy of the Babylonian Captivity era. In 1382, the Datini household moved to the ancestral home in Prato, a textile town near Florence.

Datini decided to erect a real mansion on a lot he owned in the center of town, and he and Margherita lived out their long and generally happy lives there. The Datini house still stands. It is now a museum housing the archive they left. The Datinis experienced one great sadness: Margherita was unable to conceive, so they had no legitimate offspring. (Francesco had at least two illegitimate children and probably more.) Every classic remedy against barrenness was put into play, but nothing worked, not even the poultices of ghastly contents and the belts ornamented with prayers to St. Catherine.

Margherita's main tasks were the management of the large house and its several inhabitants. About eleven persons resided with the couple, four of whom were female slaves purchased at various times from Venetian merchants, who obtained them in Constantinople or in Venice's trading posts on the Black Sea. The others were servants, who were free to leave if they desired. All, slaves and servants, were treated well as members of the *famiglia*, the household. In addition to these live-in persons, several more servants came and went daily, so the lady of the house was constantly overseeing or instructing someone.

A few years after arriving back in Prato, Francesco's business as a cloth merchant and importer had grown so much that he opened a branch office in Pisa and a retail establishment in Florence. The separations these endeavors required persuaded Margherita to learn to read and write. In her frequent letters to her absent husband, she expresses many familiar concerns: he spends too much time away, he is probably unfaithful, and he gives his businesses more attention than his home. But good feeling is evidenced as well: Francesco clearly respected his wife's growing accomplishments as an educated woman; he was proud of her, while she was affectionate to him and wished she could see more of him. She even took care of his illegitimate daughter Ginevra as though the girl were her own.

When the plague returned in 1399, the Datinis pledged that they would endow a Prato charity if they survived. When Francesco died at the age of seventy-five in 1410, his wife was the executor of his will and followed his wishes by giving most of his large estate to the poor and orphans. The slaves were all freed and the servants well provided for, as were the surviving illegitimate children. Margherita survived thirteen more years, to age sixty-three, and is buried in Prato's St. Maria Novella churchyard, where the visitors to her former home can view her last resting place.

▶ *Analyze and Interpret*

What advantages can you see in an age difference so great as that of the Datinis at the time of marriage? Disadvantages? What do you think of the arrangement by which Margherita brought up the illegitimate daughter as her own, keeping in mind that she was childless and twenty-four years younger than her husband?

---

from the Muslim countries. Physics and astronomy would only advance after the 1400s. Biological sciences were still in their infancy, the social sciences were not yet heard of, and botany and zoology were basically where the third-century Greeks had left them.

Part of the problem in the lagging development of the sciences was the insistence of the universities that were then multiplying throughout Europe that scientific knowledge was less important than the arts and humanities. In places such as Oxford, Paris, Salamanca, and Heidelberg, the majority of the teachers specialized in theology, classical languages, and rhetoric, rather than biology, physics, or mathematics. The science that the modern world takes for granted as a major source of truth did not yet exist.

Perhaps the most important advances in science in the later medieval period are to be found not in the answers but in the questions posed by such scholars as Albertus Magnus and Roger Bacon, of Paris and Oxford, respectively. Both were seeking new ways to collect data about the natural world and pioneered what we now call the "experimental method" of ascertaining truth.

As we observed in Chapter 19, the teachings of Aristotle held pride of place in the humanities and natural sciences. Now familiar to Christians from his Muslim admirers in Spain and Sicily, he became almost as important in European thought as he had been in Muslim studies. His theories about the form of the cosmos, the revolution of the planets, and the nature of matter were considered the last word on the subject, even though they sometimes clashed with what could be observed. This reverence for authority was characteristic of the Middle Ages and was sometimes a severe obstacle to the introduction of new knowledge.

The clash between new and old was especially clear in the branch of philosophy called metaphysics. In the thirteenth century, the learned Thomas Aquinas had bridged the chasm between classical and Christian doctrines in his *Summa Theologica (The Highest Theology)*. This book became the standard work for Catholic theology into modern times. Its subtle and complex reasoning, however, was distorted by the "schoolmen," or *scholastics*, priests and university teachers who tried to ignore or undermine ideas that challenged tradition, especially church-approved tradition. Originally pioneers of a new rationalism that was very much needed in Western thought, the scholastics gradually became fossilized. By the 1400s, they had become a retarding force in education, committing themselves to verbal tricks and meaningless hairsplitting. By so doing they transformed the philosophy of the great Aquinas from the subtlest explanation of God's universe into an exercise for theology students.

SUMMARY

THE LATER MIDDLE Age (fourteenth and fifteenth centuries) was a mixed scene of cultural advances, social violence, economic and military disasters, and religious strife. The fourteenth century was a particularly disastrous epoch. The Black Death carried off perhaps one-fourth of the population to an early death, thereby creating a shortage of labor that impeded Europe's recovery for generations. Peasants seized the chance to escape serfdom, sometimes to the extent of rebelling openly against their lords. Such revolts were put down mercilessly, but the days of serfdom in the old sense were over from Germany westward.

In the towns, the new bourgeoisie continued to gain prestige and wealth at the expense of the nobility, while having to defend its position against the rising discontent of the urban workers. The guilds, which were originally intended to protect the livelihood of the master artisans, increasingly became closed castes of privilege.

The Hundred Years' War dealt a heavy blow to the French monarchy, which was rescued from disintegration only through Joan of Arc. The war also ended the domination of the field of battle by noble horsemen and signaled the coming of modern gunpowder war. The Babylonian Captivity and the Great Schism marked the onset of a decline in the papacy that was not to be reversed until after Luther's challenge. The major weapon in the papal arsenal, the moral authority of the Vicar of Christ, was rapidly being dulled as pope after pope gave more attention to politics and power than to matters of faith.

▶ Identification Terms

Test your knowledge of this chapter's key concepts by defining the following terms. If you can't recall the meaning of certain terms, refresh your memory by looking up the boldfaced term in the chapter, turning to the Glossary at the end of the book, or working with the flashcards that are available on the *World Civilizations* Companion Website: **academic.cengage.com/adler**

Agincourt	Conciliar Movement	Great Schism	Little Ice Age
Babylonian Captivity	Council of Constance	guilds	Lollards
Black Death	Crecy	*Jacquerie*	

▶ Test Your Knowledge

Test your knowledge of this chapter by answering the following questions. Complete answers appear at the end of the book. You may find even more quiz questions in CengageNOW and on the *World Civilizations* Companion Website: **academic.cengage.com/adler**

1. Which one of the following was *not* a consequence of the Black Death in European affairs?
   a. Severe labor shortage
   b. Preoccupation with death and guilt
   c. Heightened sensitivity to the natural world

d. Increased readiness to rebel against the peasants' lords

e. Declining tax revenues

2. Which of the following battles was a victory for the French in the Hundred Years' War?
   a. Crecy
   b. Orleans
   c. Agincourt
   d. Poitiers
   e. Calais

3. One consequence of the Hundred Years' War was
   a. an increase in the importance of France's parliament.
   b. an improvement in England's patterns of trade.
   c. an increasing acceptance of chivalry as a way of life.
   d. a more important role for the cavalry in battle.
   e. the development of a stronger parliament in England.

4. During the Babylonian Captivity, the pope became the satellite of the
   a. Holy Roman Emperor.
   b. Roman mob.
   c. French crown.
   d. German nobles.
   e. Swiss cantons.

5. One result of the Council of Constance was to
   a. elect a new pope in an attempt to end the Great Schism.
   b. end the idea of papal supremacy in the church.
   c. split the church into two halves.
   d. move the papacy from Rome to a new home in Avignon.
   e. initiate major reforms within the church.

6. The usual reaction of the nobles to peasant rebellions was to
   a. crush them and take bloody vengeance.
   b. blame the urban classes for inspiring them.

c. negotiate a compromise at the expense of the Crown.
d. free their remaining serfs and gain peace.
e. hire German mercenaries to crush the rebellions for them.

7. John Ball was the leader of
   a. a movement to strip the English upper classes of their privileges.
   b. the movement to make church councils superior to the papacy in defining doctrine.
   c. the Jacquerie in France.
   d. an English army in France that introduced gunpowder to warfare.
   e. a group of artisans who pushed for greater recognition of the guild system.

8. Which of the following did Margherita Datini *not* experience in her lifetime?
   a. Raising the illegitimate daughter of her husband
   b. Losing her father by execution
   c. Being frequently separated from her husband by business
   d. Raising two healthy sons
   e. Managing her rather large, prosperous household

9. Medieval universities emphasized the study of
   a. algebra.
   b. alchemy.
   c. surgery.
   d. biological science.
   e. theology.

10. A critically important figure for late medieval science was
    a. Aristotle.
    b. Euclid.
    c. Plato.
    d. Herodotus.
    e. Archimedes.

Enter *CengageNOW* using the access card that is available with this text. *CengageNOW* will assist you in understanding the content in this chapter with lesson plans generated for your needs and provide you with a connection to the *Wadsworth World History Resource Center* (see description at right for details).

 ### World History Resource Center

Enter the Resource Center using either your *CengageNOW* access card or your standalone access card for the *Wadsworth World History Resource Center*. Organized by topic, this website includes quizzes; images; over 350 primary source documents; interactive simulations, maps, and timelines; movie explorations; and a wealth of other resources. You can read the following documents, and many more, at the *Wadsworth World History Resource Center*:

Boccacio, description of the Black Death
Jean Froissart, *The Battle of Crecy*
Jean Froissart, *The Jacquerie*

21

THE EUROPEAN RENAISSANCE

Celui qui ne sait pas dissimuler ne sait pas regner. (He who doesn't know how to deceive doesn't know how to rule.)
—Louis XI of France

THE ITALIAN CITY-STATES

THE RENAISSANCE ATTITUDE

THE NORTHERN RENAISSANCE

THE POLITICAL ECONOMY OF RENAISSANCE EUROPE
The Theory of the State ◆ Royal Governments

ART AND ITS PATRONS

THE RENAISSANCE CHURCH

FAMILY LIFE AND EDUCATION OF CHILDREN

BEGINNING IN THE FOURTEENTH century, a new spirit manifested itself in Europe among the educated classes. Much later called the **Renaissance**, or "rebirth," it was mainly an urban phenomenon and restricted to the uppermost segments of society. There were in fact two distinct Renaissances: (1) a change in economic and social conditions and (2) an artistic and cultural movement that was founded on that change. The Renaissance also differed substantially south and north of the Alps. In the South (Italy), the intellectual spirit of the age was secular and anticlerical. In the North (German-speaking Europe), there was a more pronounced concern for religious reform and less emphasis on the assertion of individual excellence.

THE ITALIAN CITY-STATES

The Renaissance began in the northern Italian city-states, such as Florence, Venice, Milan, and Pisa. By counterbalancing the governance claims of the papacy against those of the Holy Roman Emperor, these cities had gradually succeeded in becoming independent of both (see Map 21.1).

Why did the first stirrings of the rebirth manifest themselves in this place and in this time? These cities were rich because of both trade advantage and financial genius. Genoa and Venice dominated the trade routes with the Mediterranean and North Africa; Florence was the center of the skilled metal and leather trades

MAP 21.1 Renaissance Centers

The Renaissance was limited to the confines of the old Roman Empire and left stronger traces in Italy and northwest Europe than elsewhere. Their absence in eastern Europe and weakness in the Iberian peninsula (Spain and Portugal) meant that the Renaissance was scarcely noticeable there.

MAP QUESTION

What major social and economic changes in late medieval Europe might have made these places the centers of the Renaissance?

and, with the Flemish, controlled the lucrative textile trade of much of Europe. In the fifteenth century, the huge wealth of the papal court made Rome once again—after a lapse of 1,000 years—a major center of culture and art.

But why specifically was Italy the leader? More and more in the late Middle Age, Italians were leading the way in innovations—scientific, artistic, and economic. Italians were the leading bankers, mariners, scientists,

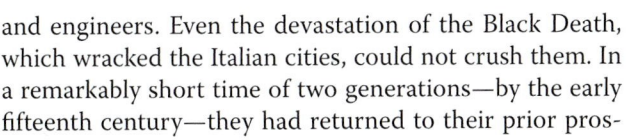

and engineers. Even the devastation of the Black Death, which wracked the Italian cities, could not crush them. In a remarkably short time of two generations—by the early fifteenth century—they had returned to their prior prosperity and positions of leadership.

The city-states of the fourteenth and fifteenth centuries were princely *oligarchies.* In other words, a small group of wealthy aristocrats, headed by a prince with despotic power, ran the government. No commoners, whether urban workers or peasants outside the city gates, enjoyed even a hint of power. In fact, a huge gap existed between the ruling group of aristocrats, merchants, bankers, and traders and the rest of the population, who were regarded with a detached contempt. It was possible to rise into the ruling clique, but difficult. The key to change was money.

THE RENAISSANCE ATTITUDE

The wealthy in an Italian city were highly educated and very much aware of and proud of their good taste in the arts. Led by the prince, the members of the oligarchy spared no pains or money to assert their claims to glory and sophistication in the supreme art of living well. What did "living well" mean to these individuals? Certain elements recur:

◆ *Individualism.* Wealthy men and women of the Italian Renaissance believed that the age-old Christian emphasis on personal humility was wrong. As wealthy and successful people, they did not fear to set themselves apart from the masses and were supremely confident that they could. Like the ancient Greeks and Romans they encouraged pride in human potential. A thirst for fame and a strong desire to put their own imprint on the contemporary world were at the heart of their psychology.

◆ *Secularism.* Increasing **secularism** in Italy meant that the focus of the upper classes' attention shifted steadily away from the eternal to worldly affairs. The life to come receded into the background as Renaissance men and women rediscovered the joys of life in the here and now. Increasingly, people viewed life as an opportunity for glory and pleasure, rather than as a transitory stage on the way to eternal bliss or everlasting damnation. *Man was the measure*—the ancient Greek motto—for what life had to offer.

◆ *Revival of classical values.* The ancient civilizations of the Greeks and especially the pagan Romans became the focus of artistic and cultural interest. Led by notable scholars such as Petrarch and Lorenzo Valla, the thinkers and writers of the fourteenth and fifteenth centuries looked back to pre-Christian Mediterranean culture for their values and standards. They were not anti-Christian so much as pro-humanity in their admiration for the achievements of Plato, Aristotle, Virgil, Terence, and countless other contributors to the pre-Christian intellectual world. The collection and careful editing of the ancient texts that had somehow survived (many through Muslim caretakers) became an obsession. What the modern world possesses of the Greco-Roman past is largely the work of medieval Islamic civilization and the European Renaissance.

There were, of course, variations of degree in these attitudes. Even in Italy, many people soberly upheld the medieval Christian viewpoint and insisted that humans were made for God and that the new emphasis on pleasure and self-fulfillment could lead only to disaster. Many of the scholars who paged through the Roman manuscripts were devout Christians, looking for holes in the arguments of their secular opponents or for proof of the earlier pagans' search for an all-knowing God.

In general, the Italian Renaissance was devoted to the *self*-realization of human beings whose earthly lives were the only sure ones they had. It rejected the devotional Middle Ages as a dark interlude, which had lasted all too long, between the light of the Greco-Roman Classical Age and the rebirth now beginning.

THE NORTHERN RENAISSANCE

North of the Alps, the Renaissance was also a powerful force, but with a rather different character than in Italy. Carried to Germany and the Low Countries by students returning from study with the great Italian artists and writers, the new spirit underwent a sort of sea change as it came northward. It became more pietist and less pagan, more reformist, and less self-centered.

The term **humanism** is often applied to the northern Renaissance and its leading figures. The humanists were scholars who were painfully aware of the corruption of church and society and wished to remedy it by gradualist means, through reforms grounded in ancient Christian teachings. The Renaissance in this context meant an attempt to return the church and lay society in general to a purer state; it was an attempt to reawaken a sense of Christians' duties and responsibilities toward themselves and their fellow humans.

In the North as well as in Italy, scholars put great confidence in the powers of the intellect to find the truth and employ it to bring about necessary reform. The use of reason, rather than dogma, was an important article of faith for humanists everywhere. They believed that if people could be brought to see the good, they would pursue it. The trouble with the world was that the good was everywhere obscured by bad habits, ignorance, or malice.

How did the reformers propose to achieve their aims? The English Thomas More's ***Utopia*** is an excellent example. The book was meant as a satire and a lesson for society. The people of Utopia (Greek for "no place") do not seek wealth because they see no rewards in it. They put their neighbors' welfare ahead of their own. Their education continues throughout their entire lives rather than being limited to a few childhood years. All individuals are absolutely equal in powers and status, and they live by reason rather than passion and ignorance.

It was a radical message: More was saying that a corrupt and ignorant society, not the individual sinner, was responsible for the sorry state of the world. Adam's sin was not enough to explain humans' plight. The way people lived with one another must be reformed—and by humans themselves.

The best known and most noble-minded of all the northern humanists was the Dutch Desiderius Erasmus, who lived in the late fifteenth and early sixteenth centuries;

by his death, his works were being read throughout Europe. His *Praise of Folly* was a scorching indictment of the so-called wisdom of the world and a plea for a return to simple virtues. Even more influential was his new, carefully researched edition of the New Testament, with his commentaries and introduction.

Erasmus's work has two basic themes: the inner nature of Christianity and the importance of education. By the inner nature of Christianity, he meant that the true follower of Christ should emulate Christ's life, not what the theologians have tried to make out of his gospels. Erasmus condemned the empty formalism that was so common in the church of his day. In so doing, he was one of the most important forerunners of the Protestant Reformation, although he absolutely rejected Protestantism for himself and condemned Luther's arrogance (see Chapter 23).

THE POLITICAL ECONOMY OF RENAISSANCE EUROPE

The political theory of the Middle Ages was based on a strong centralizing monarchy, which was blessed and seconded by a powerful and respected clergy. The favorite image for government was a man wearing a crown and holding a cross in his left hand and a sword in his right. But in the Hundred Years' War and other late medieval conflicts, that image suffered serious damage. In country after country, the feudal nobility were able to reassert themselves and again decentralize political power. This decentralization was then reversed in the fifteenth and sixteenth centuries. The monarchs, now armed with a new theory of authority, effectively denied the nobles' claims of autonomy and subdued their frequent attempts to rebel. The new basis of royal authority was not church and king in partnership, but the king as executive of the *secular* state.

The Theory of the State

The state in Renaissance thinking was a political organism that existed independently of the ruler or the subjects. It possessed three essential attributes: legitimacy, sovereignty, and territory.

◆ *Legitimacy* meant that the state possessed moral authority in the eyes of its subjects. It had a right to exist.
◆ *Sovereignty* meant that the state had an effective claim to equality with other states and that it acknowledged no higher earthly power over it.
◆ *Territory* is self-explanatory: the state possessed real estate that could be precisely bounded and contained certain human and material resources.

Francis G. Mayer/Corbis

THOMAS MORE. The force of character of Sir Thomas More, English statesman and humanist, comes through strongly in this great portrait by Hans Holbein the Younger. The chain of office worn by More shows that the painting was made between 1529 and 1533, when he was the lord chancellor of King Henry VIII before being executed for resisting Henry's divorce and remarriage to Anne Boleyn.

The royal personage was not the creator or owner, but only the servant, the executive agent, and protector of the state. He had every right and duty to use whatever means he deemed fit to ensure the state's welfare and expansion. In the fifteenth-century monarch's view, ensuring the welfare of the state was about the same as ensuring the welfare of the society in general. These so-called new monarchs were intent on one great goal: power. To be the proper servants of the state, they felt they must be the masters of all who might threaten it, and that meant being masters of intrigue, deceit, and intimidation. All of the Renaissance political theorists spent much time on the relationship between power and ethics, but none had the long-term impact of a young Italian with great ambitions, Niccoló Machiavelli. In his extraordinary treatise on politics entitled *The Prince* (1516), Machiavelli described power relations in government as he had experienced them—not as they *should* be, but as they were *in fact*. He thought that human beings are selfish by nature and must be restrained by the prince from doing evil to one another. In so doing, the prince could and should use all means open to him. He must be both the lion and the fox, the one who is feared and the one who is beloved. If it came to a choice between instilling fear and love, the wise prince will choose fear, which is more dependable (see the Law and Government box, which summarizes Machiavelli's position.)

Royal Governments

What Machiavelli was preaching was already being followed by the more aggressive throne-holders of Europe. In the fifteenth century the powers and prestige of various royal governments increased significantly, especially in France, England, and Russia (see Map 21.2).

France. France recovered much more rapidly than might have been expected from the devastation of the Hundred Years' War. The unpromising monarch who owed his throne to Joan of Arc's help, Charles VII (ruled 1422–1461), turned out to be one of the cleverest and most effective of kings. He created the first truly royal army and used it against those who tried to assert their independence. He also gained much stronger control over the French clergy, particularly the appointment of bishops.

Charles's policies were followed, with even greater cleverness, by his son Louis XI (ruled 1461–1483), the "Spider King," as he was called by his many enemies. Louis was especially effective at gaining middle-class support—and tax money—against the claims of the nobles. He also significantly expanded the size of the royal domain: that part of the country, centered on Paris, under the direct control of the Crown. Louis is credited with laying the foundation for the dimensions the French state attained under the great Bourbon kings of the seventeenth and eighteenth centuries.

Samuel H. Kress Collectio, © 1995 Board of Trustees, National Gallery, Washington, D.C.

DEATH AND THE MISER. The Dutchman Hieronymous Bosch was the sixteenth-century master of the grotesque and the damned. Here he shows what happens to the treasure of a miser. As Death comes for him—and the angel implores him to put his faith in the crucified Christ—monsters and thieves make off with his money.

MAP 21.2 Europe, the Near East, and North Africa in the Renaissance

The political divisions of the Mediterranean basin and Europe in the fifteenth century. Note the division of the western parts of the former Abbasid caliphate into several independent sultanates and the Ottoman Empire.

MAP QUESTIONS
In what parts of Europe does this map resemble modern Europe? What modern countries are missing?

England. England took more time to establish a centralized monarchy than had France and never proceeded as far. The strong rule of the early Norman kings ended with weak or unlucky individuals such as John the First (and Last!). In 1215, John (ruled 1199–1216) had had to accept the *Magna Carta* from his rebellious nobles. Over the centuries, this Great Charter was gradually transformed from a statement of noble privilege against an unloved king to a doctrine that held that the monarch, like all others, was bound to obey the laws.

The Hundred Years' War further weakened the royal powers and strengthened Parliament. By the mid-fifteenth century, Parliament had become the preserve of semi-independent barons and earls, who held the tax purse strings and drove hard bargains with the king in the wake

of the lost war. The nobility added to the turbulence by engaging in an obscure struggle over the succession to the throne. Called the **Wars of the Roses**, the conflict lasted fifteen years (1455–1471).

Three late-fifteenth-century kings (Edward IV, Richard III, and Henry VII) then gradually threw the balance of power in favor of the Crown. Of these, the most important was Henry VII (ruled 1485–1509), the founder of the Tudor Dynasty and a master of intimidation and intrigue. He enlisted the aid of the middle classes and the clergy, both of whom were exasperated by the squabbles of the nobles. Henry not only rebuilt the powers of the royal crown but also avoided foreign wars, which would have meant going back to the noble-dominated Parliament to beg for funds. By the time he died in 1509, the English royal government was in firm control of the state.

LAW AND GOVERNMENT

Machiavelli's *The Prince*

In the year 1513, the Florentine official and diplomat Niccoló Machiavelli (1469–1527) was arrested for treason and subjected to torture. Although he was soon released, his ambitions for power and wealth lay in ruins. Reluctantly retiring to his country estate, Machiavelli devoted much of his remaining life to writing a series of theoretical works on politics and the eventful history of his native Florence. But he is best remembered for his handbook on the art of governance, *The Prince,* the masterwork of Renaissance political literature. In it he elucidated a coldly realistic view—strongly reminiscent of the Chinese Legalists—of what law and lawgivers must do to preserve civic harmony.

Machiavelli's denial that common morality should influence a ruler's politics in any way and his insistence that violence and deceit can be justified in the name of good government have earned him a sinister reputation. To the present day, the adjective *Machiavellian* carries a cynical connotation. Yet the author, who had had every chance of observing what he wrote about, was just describing the actual practices of the Italian rulers of his day—and of many wielders of power since then.

I say that every prince ought to wish to be considered kind rather than cruel. Nevertheless, he must take care to avoid misusing his kindness. Caesar Borgia* was considered cruel, yet his cruelty restored Romagna, uniting it in peace and loyalty.... A prince must be indifferent to the charge of cruelty if he is to keep his subjects loyal and united.... Disorders harm the entire citizenry, while the executions ordered by a prince harm only a few. Indeed, of all princes, the newly established one can least of all escape the charge of cruelty, for new states are encumbered with dangers.

Here a question arises: whether it is better to be loved than feared, or the reverse. The answer is, of course, that it would be best to be both loved and feared. But since the two rarely come together, anyone compelled to choose will find greater security in being feared than in being loved.... Men are less concerned about offending someone they have cause to love than someone they have cause to fear. Love endures by a bond which men, being scoundrels, may break whenever it serves their advantage to do so; but fear is supported by the dread of pain, which is always present....

I conclude that since men will love what they themselves determine, but will fear as their ruler determines, a wise prince must rely upon what he, not others, can control. He need only strive to avoid being hated. Let the prince conquer his state, then, and preserve it; the methods employed will always be judged honorable, and everyone will praise him. For the mob of men is always impressed by appearances, and by results; and the world is composed of the mob.

How praiseworthy it is, that a prince keeps his word and governs by candor, rather than craft, everyone knows . . . yet, those princes who had little regard for their word, and had the craft to turn men's minds, have accomplished great things, and in the end, they have overcome those who suited their actions to their pledges.

▶ *Analyze and Interpret*

Do you agree that the wise ruler will choose fear over love from his subjects? How do Machiavelli's precepts translate into present-day politics? Can you give some examples from the news this week?

Source: Niccoló Machiavelli, *The Prince,* trans. Luigi Ricci, as revised by E. A. Vincent (New York: Oxford University Press, 1935). Used by permission.

You can read more of *The Prince* at the *Wadsworth World History Resource Center.*

*Caesar Borgia was the illegitimate son of Pope Alexander VI and one of the most ruthless Italian noblemen of the day.

The Holy Roman Empire (Germany). The great exception to the recovery of royal powers in the later fifteenth century was the German kingdom, technically still the Holy Roman Empire of the German Nation. Here there was no central power to recover; it had been utterly destroyed in the medieval struggles between emperor and pope and the struggles between emperor and nobles that then ensued.

Why couldn't the Germans recover from these eleventh and twelfth-century troubles by the fifteenth century? The critical weakness of the monarchy was that the emperor was elected, rather than succeeding by hereditary right. The seven electors, who were all German princes and bishops, could and did negotiate with the various candidates to strike deals aimed at preserving noble autonomy. As a result, Germany had no centralized government in the fifteenth century. The emperor was only the first among equals, and sometimes not even that. He did not have a bureaucracy, a royal army, a national parliament, or the power to tax his subjects. The Holy Roman Empire was really a loose confederation of principalities, dukedoms, and even free cities, some of which were almost always squabbling among themselves. All real power was in the hands of the local aristocrats and the churchmen.

Among the candidates for this weak throne, the Austrian **Habsburg Dynasty** had most often been successful. In the late fifteenth and early sixteenth centuries, a series of extraordinary events propelled them into great international prominence for the first time. Thanks to a series of marriages and the unexpected deaths of rivals, by 1527 the Habsburg territories had trebled in Europe and also included the huge overseas empire being rapidly conquered by Spain, which was now under a Habsburg ruler. It appeared that for the first time since the twelfth century, the Holy Roman Emperor would be able to assert real authority, but the prospects of establishing strong royal rule in Germany were not realized: the burgeoning division in religious affairs between Catholics and Protestants frustrated all efforts to unify the nation until the late nineteenth century.

Russia. Russia was a brand-new entrant—or rather a newly rediscovered entrant—on the European scene in the fifteenth century. The huge expanse of territory east of Christian Poland and Hungary was practically unknown to western Europeans after its conquest by the Mongols in the mid-1200s. The Asiatic tribesmen had severed almost all cultural contacts between Russians and both the Latin and Byzantine Christian worlds. The Mongols' adoption of Islam in the fourteenth century deepened the chasm that separated them from their Russian subjects.

The "Mongol Yoke" that lay on Russia for almost two and a half centuries (1240–1480) caused massive cultural decline. Before the Mongols came, the chief Russian state, the **Principality of Kiev**, had entertained close relations with Christian Europe and especially with the Orthodox Christian empire in Constantinople from which it had received its religion, literature, and law. Though situated on the extreme eastern periphery of the Christian world, Russia had felt itself to be a full member of the European family.

After the arrival of the Mongols, this situation changed radically. Ignorance and superstition became rife, even among the diminished number of the formally educated; the levels of technical and theoretical skills declined. Literacy all but disappeared among the laity.

In the absence of an independent Russian government, the Russian church came to play a particularly vital role in keeping the notion of a national community alive. The Church of Rome had been rejected as heretical ever since the split in 1054. After the Turks seized Constantinople in 1453, the belief grew in Moscow that this had been God's punishment for the Greeks' waverings in defense of Orthodoxy. Now, Russia was to become the fortress of right belief: the **Third Rome**. As a Russian monk wrote to his ruler in 1511: "Two Romes [that is, the Christian Rome of the fourth century, and Constantinople] have fallen, but the Third [Moscow] stands and there will be no fourth." Russia's government and church saw themselves as the implements of divine providence that would bring the peoples of Europe back to the true faith and defeat the infidels, wherever they might be.

By the late fifteenth century, the Mongols had been so weakened by internal conflicts that their former partner, the prince of Moscow, defied them successfully in 1480 and asserted his independence. Soon after the defeat of the Mongols, the prince of Moscow had extended his rule to all parts of the nation and had taken to calling himself *tsar* ("Caesar" in Slavic).

A tsar had far more power than any other European ruler of the day. His alleged powers were so impressive as to raise the question whether Russia was still a European state or whether, under the Mongols, it had become an Asiatic despotism in which the will of the ruler was automatically law of the land. Western European ambassadors and traders sent to Moscow in the sixteenth century felt that they had landed on truly foreign ground. They found themselves in a society that had no middle class and was untouched by the technical and psychological developments of the Renaissance. Its population's superstition and passivity were appalling, and its subservience toward its prince was striking to Western eyes.

ART AND ITS PATRONS

The most visible and historically appreciated form of Renaissance culture is its art, and Italy was the leader in every field. A tremendous creative outburst took place in Florence, Rome, Venice, Milan, and a dozen other city-states during the fifteenth and sixteenth centuries.

As in other widespread cultural phenomena, considerable variation existed from one locale to another. The spirit of North European painting and sculpture differed from that of the South. Northern art is more overtly religious and avoids the lush sensuousness that marks much Italian art. The outstanding exponents of the northern Renaissance in art were the Flemish portraitists of the fifteenth century, such as Van Eyck, Memmling, and Bosch. The Germans of the Rhine valley and Bavaria were also active in both painting and sculpture. Some of the most accomplished woodcarvings of any age were produced in southern Germany and Austria during this era. These, too, display little of the delight in the flesh or the interest in experimentation of the Italians. In general, architecture followed the same pattern. Variations on the Gothic style continued to be the standard in the North, and northern architects made no effort to imitate the revived classicism that was so popular in Italy.

The spirit of this art, wherever produced, was quite different from that of medieval art. The latter attempted to portray concretely the collective belief of a community, the Christian community. It subordinated the individual

and the particular to the group and the generic. Despite much technical innovation, medieval art was conservative and evolutionary in its spirit.

Renaissance art, in contrast, was intended to show the artist's mastery of technique and his newfound freedoms. It was experimental: new ideas were tried in all directions, and old ideas were put into new forms or media. The huge bronze doors of the Florentine cathedral cast by Ghiberti were something quite new: nothing like that had been attempted previously. With their twelve reliefs depicting the life of Christ, the doors were a brilliant success. Similarly, the enormous, architecturally unprecedented domes of the Florentine cathedral and St. Peter's in Rome were meant as a demonstration of what might be done by the bold human imagination, unfettered from its previous restrictions.

In painting, great talents such as Titian, da Vinci, Michelangelo, Botticelli, and Giotto led the way to an abundance of innovative compositions. All of them opened their studios to teach others, so that a wave of experimentation in the visual art forms swept across Italy and northward into Europe beyond the Alps. One of their great achievements was the mastery of perspective, which Giotto first accomplished in the early fourteenth century. He also led the way to a new realism in portraits.

In sculpture, the universal genius of Michelangelo was accompanied by Donatello, Cellini, and Bernini, to mention only some of the better-known names. Both Renaissance sculpture and painting broke sharply from their medieval forerunners. Artists now saw the human figure as a thing of superb animal beauty quite apart from its spiritual considerations or destiny.

Michelangelo was a leader in architecture as well. He designed much of the vast new St. Peter's Cathedral for one of the popes. Other leading architects included Bramante, da Vinci, and Brunelleschi. The basic architectural style of the Renaissance was an adaptation of the classical temple, with its balanced columns, magisterial domes, and lofty, symmetrical facades. The Gothic style was now dismissed as primitive and superstition-ridden in its striving toward a distant heaven.

The artist's position as a respected, powerful member of society was also a Renaissance novelty. Several of the leading figures of the art world were well rewarded in money and prestige. Leonardo da Vinci, for example, was one of the richest men of his time and lived accordingly. So did Michelangelo and Raphael, both of whom enjoyed papal esteem and commissions for the Vatican palaces and libraries.

Art was unashamedly used to display the wealth of the individual or group who had commissioned it, rather than their piety (as in medieval times). Artistic patronage was limited to a smaller group than had been true earlier. The princes and the oligarchies around them were a tiny fraction of Italian society, but they provided most of the artists' commissions. Only rarely would an artist work without a specific commission in the hope of finding a buyer later.

DOORS OF PARADISE. The beauty of these bronze doors (right) cast by Lorenzo Ghiberti for the cathedral in Florence was so overwhelming to his fellow citizens that they named them the Doors of Paradise. Ten panels show scenes from the Old Testament; the detail photo above shows the slaying of Goliath by David.

Baptistery, Florence, Italy/Bridgeman Art Library

Baptistery, Florence, Italy/Bridgeman Art Library

MICHELANGELO'S CREATION OF ADAM. This fresco was among many that the artist created for the Sistine Chapel in Rome between 1508 and 1512.

Vatican Museums and Galleries, Vatican City, Italy/ Bridgeman Art Library

Artists dealt with their patrons as equals. It was not at all unusual for a secure artist to refuse a lucrative commission because of a disagreement, and patrons respected talent and allowed the artists to execute their work much as they pleased. The idea of artistic genius came into currency at this time. Artists were thought to possess a "divine spark" or other quality that ordinary souls lacked, and therefore should be allowed to develop their talents without too much restriction.

THE RENAISSANCE CHURCH

Much Renaissance literature satirizes the Christian clergy and focuses attention on the corruption and indifference that had become common in the late medieval Church. These attacks are clearly directed at the personnel of the church, not its basic doctrines. Many village priests were still illiterate, and many monks had long since forgotten their vows of poverty and chastity. It was not at all unusual for a bishop never to set foot in his diocese because he preferred to live elsewhere. It was equally common for the abbot of a monastery to have produced a couple of illegitimate children with his "housekeeper." In any Italian town, the local clergy's political and financial interests often nullified their moral leadership. This embittered many of the leading figures of the Italian Renaissance and turned them into raging anti-clerics.

The example came from the top. Some of the fifteenth and sixteenth-century popes were distressingly ignorant of their religious duties and too mindful of their money and privileges. The Italian noble families who controlled the papacy and the papal court were involved in ongoing struggles for political domination of the peninsula and tended to treat the papacy and other high offices as their hereditary privilege. They regarded the increasing calls for reform as the mumblings of malcontents, which could be safely ignored. Only with the emergence of the Protestant challenge would they slowly realize their error (Chapter 23).

FAMILY LIFE AND EDUCATION OF CHILDREN

Our knowledge of family life in the Renaissance comes largely from the upper classes, as is usual for pre-modern history. Men continued to marry quite late, in their thirties and forties, after securing their inheritances. Women were normally much younger at marriage, so there were many middle-aged widows. Marriage to a rich or moderately well off widow who was still young enough to bear children was perceived as a desirable step for a man. Dowries were expected in every case, even among the poor in the countryside. A girl without a suitable dowry was practically unmarriageable.

Families were often large, especially among the well-to-do. The household might include children from a prior marriage, spinster sisters or elderly widows, servants, and perhaps the husband's illegitimate offspring. We know from surviving records that an Italian merchant's household might easily include as many as twenty persons, including servants. Wealthy households were of a similar size throughout most of the rest of Europe. (See the box on Margherita Datini in Chapter 20.)

The woman of such a house was expected to run this establishment with vigor and economy. If her husband was away (a business trip might last six months or longer), she was often entrusted with full authority. A woman had to be literate to handle these tasks, and all wealthy families had private tutors for their daughters as well as their sons.

In general, however, women did not fare well as a social group during the Renaissance. In fact, the position of upper-class women actually seems to have declined. They no longer enjoyed the political and economic liberties afforded to upper class women during the Middle Age. Middle-class women, on the other hand, probably had greater responsibility for the management of household and business affairs and played a role almost equal to that of their husbands.

As in the medieval period, the wives of artisans and merchants were often essential partners of the males, whose work could not be performed without their wives. Of working-class women, we as usual know relatively little, but we can assume that the male-dominated, patriarchal society went on without essential change. A particular crisis was the Europe-wide obsession with witchcraft, which appeared in the sixteenth century and took most of its

SOCIETY AND ECONOMY

Witchcraft

A special example of the relative decline in the social status of females during the Renaissance and early modern eras is the witchcraft mania that raged throughout Europe in the late sixteenth and seventeenth centuries. Although witches could be of either sex, women were by far the more commonly accused of evil deeds. The following are excerpts from seventeenth-century German sources.

> The woman either hates or loves; there is no third way. When she cries, be careful. There's two kinds of feminine tears: one sort for true pain, the other for deceitfulness.... There are three other reasons for the fact that more women than men are superstitious: the first is that women are easily swayed, and the Devil seeks them out because he wishes to destroy their faith . . . the second is because Nature has created them from less stable material, and so they are more susceptible to the implantation of evil thoughts and diversions. The third reason is that their tongues are loose, and so when they have learned how to make evil have to share it with others of their own ilk, and attempt to gain revenge by witchcraft, as they don't have the strength of men.
>
> Women's physical weakness was already indicated by her creation from a bent rib [of Adam], thus an imperfect creature from the start.

> It is a fact that woman has only a weaker faith [in God], as the very etymology of her name states: the word *femina* comes from *fe* and *minus* (*fe* = fides, faith; *minus* = less; therefore *femina* = one with less faith). . . . Therefore, the female is evil by Nature, because she is more prone to doubts, and loses her faith more easily, which are the main requisites for witchcraft.

This view of the female nature had bloody consequences: near the German town of Thann, a witch hunt commenced in 1572 that went on at intervals until 1629. In that period 152 witches were put to death, generally by hanging, sometimes by burning. Of that number, only eight were males. Sometimes, five to eight women were put to death at one time. Three hundred six persons, mostly women, were executed as witches in only six years in villages near Trier. In two of the villages, only two women were left alive.

▶ *Analyze and Interpret*

Where do you think the argument that women "are more easily swayed" originated, in a male view? Does this reflect your own view of female nature? Are women also of "less stable material"?

Source: Cited in *Frauen in der Geschichte*, vol. 2, eds. Annette Kuhn and Jorn Rusen (Dusseldorf: Pädigogischer Verlag Schwann, 1982), pp. 114 and 122.

victims from among the female population (see the Society and Economy box).

In both town and country, women had to do hard physical work as a matter of course. Spinning and weaving were the particular domain of the female, as was care of rural livestock. In the towns, records show that women performed just about every task that men did: butchering, baking, metalwork, dyeing cloth, and performing all of the handwork trades they had been doing throughout the medieval period. The separation of work by gender had not yet begun.

Education varied for the sexes, as had long been customary. In the towns, men were educated for an active career in commerce or a craft. Beginning at about age seven, they might attend a boarding school for a few years and then were apprenticed to an appropriate firm or craftsman. Literacy was common by this time among the urban population but still uncommon in the countryside, where most people lived. The peasant's son who received any education at all was still the exception, and the peasant bride who could spell out her name was a rare catch.

For girls of the upper and middle classes, education usually meant some study in the home under the supervision of a live-in or outside tutor, usually a seminary student who was trying to keep body and soul together until ordination. Their education focused on literacy in the vernacular with perhaps a bit of Latin, music making, and the domestic arts. Marriage was taken for granted as the fate of most young women. The alternative was a convent, which had little appeal, or spinsterhood, which had less. Intellectual women now had many more opportunities to express themselves in written forms, including history, poetry, religious tracts, and other formats, but their gender was still a severe obstacle to being taken seriously.

How were the earliest years passed? The treatment of young children was slowly changing among the upper classes, but not yet among the lower. Any family that could afford to do so—a minority, certainly—would send a newborn baby to a peasant wet nurse. She would keep the child until he or she was past the nursing stage—about two years (at times longer, and sometimes without any contact with the parents!). When the children returned to their parents' house, they were put under the exclusive care of the mother for the next several years. In wealthy homes, the father rarely had much to do with his children until they reached the "age of reason" (age seven), when he would take charge of their education.

The usual attitude among the upper classes was that very young children were of interest to adults only because they represented the continuation of the family line. After reaching age seven or so, they became more worthy of attention, not only because they had survived the most dangerous age but also because they were now becoming people with recognizable traits and personalities. By the Renaissance epoch, beating and other severe punishments were applied less often than in earlier centuries but were still common enough, as we know from many diaries.

We know less for certain about the lower classes because of the usual absence of sources. Probably, babies and very young children continued to get little love and cherishing by modern standards for the sensible reason that the parents could expect that about half of their offspring would die before reaching their seventh year. After that age, they were treated somewhat better, if only because they represented potential labor and "social security" for the aged parent.

SUMMARY

A REBIRTH OF secular learning derived from classical authors began in fourteenth-century Italy and spread north across the Alps in the ensuing years. Significant differences in mood and aims often existed between the two areas. The Renaissance produced the foundations of the modern state. That those foundations were laid along the lines of Machiavelli's *The Prince* rather than the lines of the northern Christian humanist tracts would prove fateful.

After the crisis of the Hundred Years' War had been surmounted, the fifteenth century saw a significant rise in monarchic powers and prestige. English and French kings fashioned effective controls over their unruly nobles. The Russian tsar also emerged as a strong ruler, but in Germany and Italy no progress was made in the consolidation of central government.

Individualism and secularism made strong advances among the educated, whereas the moral prestige of the clergy, and particularly the Roman papacy, continued to sink. The arts flourished under the stimuli of new wealth in the cities and a governing class that placed great store on patronage and fame. Painting and architecture witnessed notable experiments and successful new talents.

▶ Identification Terms

Test your knowledge of this chapter's key concepts by defining the following terms. If you can't recall the meaning of certain terms, refresh your memory by looking up the boldfaced term in the chapter, turning to the Glossary at the end of the book, or working with the flashcards that are available on the *World Civilizations* Companion Website: **academic.cengage.com/adler**

Habsburg Dynasty	Principality of Kiev	secularism	*Utopia*
humanism	Renaissance	Third Rome	Wars of the Roses

▶ Test Your Knowledge

Test your knowledge of this chapter by answering the following questions. Complete answers appear at the end of the book. You may find even more quiz questions in CengageNOW and on the *World Civilizations* Companion Website: **academic.cengage.com/adler**

1. During the fifteenth century, the territory now called Italy was
   a. under the firm control of the Holy Roman Emperor.
   b. broken into several political units centered on cities.
   c. finally brought under the monopolistic control of the papacy.
   d. split in allegiance between Rome and Florence.
   e. mostly agricultural, with few people residing in urban areas.
2. Which of the following attributes *least* fits the Renaissance worldview?
   a. Ambition
   b. Arrogance
   c. Confidence

d. Caution

e. Worldliness

3. Which of the following statements about Renaissance secularism is *false*?

a. It was vigorously opposed by Roman church leaders.

b. It was partially a by-product of a changing economy.

c. Most persons held to the basic tenets of Christian teaching.

d. It encouraged the acquisition of material things.

e. The upper class became more interested in worldly than spiritual matters.

4. The Renaissance in northern Europe differed from that of Italy by being

a. less secular.

b. more artistic.

c. less serious.

d. inferior in quality.

e. less intellectually stimulating.

5. The basic message of More's *Utopia* is that

a. personal wealth is the only sure path to social reforms.

b. education cannot reduce human sinfulness.

c. social institutions, not individuals, must be reformed first.

d. people are inherently evil and cannot really be changed.

e. to be happy, individuals must do what is best for their personal situations.

6. A new element in Renaissance city-state politics was

a. the preference for using fear rather than piety as a basis of government.

b. a professional army of mercenaries.

c. an absolute monarchy.

d. the organization of a taxation agency.

e. the concept of a secular state that existed independently of both ruler and ruled.

7. One of the peculiar features of Russian Orthodoxy was the belief that

a. Russians would be the political masters of all Europe.

b. all Russians would be saved eternally.

c. Moscow was destined to be the Third Rome.

d. the state was nonexistent.

e. the church should function independently of the state.

8. Titian and Van Eyck were both Renaissance

a. architects.

b. artists.

c. political theorists.

d. churchmen.

e. writers.

9. Which of the following was *not* a cause for scandal in the Christian church of the sixteenth and seventeenth centuries?

a. Illiteracy

b. Immorality

c. Thievery

d. Unconcern

e. Greed

10. The household of a wealthy sixteenth-century Italian could best be described as one in which

a. women had no control over everyday affairs.

b. husbands refused to travel outside the country because they did not trust their wives to run the households.

c. widowed women were relegated to an inferior, almost superfluous existence.

d. large numbers of variously related people sometimes resided together in one home.

e. women, though deemed important to the running of the household, remained illiterate.

Enter *CengageNOW* using the access card that is available with this text. *CengageNOW* will assist you in understanding the content in this chapter with lesson plans generated for your needs and provide you with a connection to the *Wadsworth World History Resource Center* (see description at right for details).

 **World History Resource Center**

Enter the Resource Center using either your *CengageNOW* access card or your standalone access card for the *Wadsworth World History Resource Center*. Organized by topic, this website includes quizzes; images; over 350 primary source documents; interactive simulations, maps, and timelines; movie explorations; and a wealth of other resources. You can read the following documents, and many more, at the *Wadsworth World History Resource Center*:

Machiavelli, selections from *The Prince*

Two Tractates from Vittorino da Feltre and other humanist educators

Worldview Three

EUROPEANS

Long struggle occurs between papacy and monarchs for supremacy within new kingdoms emerging from the imperial collapse. Law degenerates badly in early period, but begins comeback in medieval centuries. Beginnings of the modern state and rule by bureaucracy appear at end of period in western European kingdoms.

By the end of period, town-dwelling bourgeoisie significant in western Europe and challenging traditional noble–landlord social order. Feudal serfdom in West diminishes and becomes almost extinct after Black Death but is rejuvenated in the eastern countries. Long-distance trade resumes following establishment of stable governments in the West. Europeans seek new trade opportunities via ocean routes to eastern entrepôts as the fifteenth century ends.

Capitalism is promoted by developments in credit facilities for business and in new mobility of wealth and wealth producing production.

EAST ASIANS

Thousand-year-long golden age for China commences, which recovers in the late 500s from second period of disintegration and prospers during ensuing Tang and Song periods. Mongol conquest in the thirteenth century interrupts Chinese "mandate of heaven" monarchy, which resumes under vigorous Ming Dynasty in 1300s. Law and mandarin government operate to good effect for peace and stability, particularly in South, where nomads cannot reach. Japan emulates Chinese system, but imperial court never exerts control over nation in a like fashion to China; feudal nobility resists bureaucratic system and negates it in later part of this period by erecting shogunate as true locus of government powers.

Farming continues in both China and Japan as livelihood for huge majority, but in China cities' growth during Tang and Song eras is impressive. Towns with populations of more than 1 million are known. Trade in every type of good is active, but limited contacts are made with Western foreigners until arrival of Europeans in the 1500s. Travel and commerce over Silk Road stimulated by Mongol hegemony in thirteenth and fourteenth centuries; Chinese–Central Asian contacts multiply. Rise and fall of Chinese maritime expeditions in the fifteenth century demonstrate powers of government versus interests of mercantile class.

HINDUS

Written law is still exceptional in this oral civilization. Government exercised by minority of high caste warriors and confirmed by brahmin priests. Villages govern themselves with little contact with central or regional authorities except via taxation. Effective government is exception because of frequent nomadic invasions from north. Toward the end of period, invasions create ruling Muslim minority within Hindu mass.

Fieldwork as free or bonded laborers is norm throughout Indian history for majority. Domestic and external trade with Southeast Asia and Muslims to the west important in the cities. Colonial outreach to Southeast Asia and Pacific islanders strong in South India. Cotton cloth, spices, and precious metals exported.

EQUILIBRIUM AMONG POLYCENTRIC CIVILIZATIONS, 500–1500 CE

PATTERNS OF BELIEF

ARTS AND CULTURE

SCIENCE AND TECHNOLOGY

Eastern Europe and Russia brought into Orthodox orbit in 800s to 1000s. Political-religious divisions between East and West reach climax with schism between Constantinople and Rome in 1054. Eastern Orthodoxy closely associated with state and falls under royal or imperial dominion, especially Russia. Roman clergy often in conflict with Western kings after reform of the papacy in tenth and eleventh centuries. Clerical reform comes and goes throughout late medieval age as Christian church accumulates wealth and temptation for misuse.

Gothic architectural style spreads rapidly in twelfth and thirteenth centuries. In Italian Renaissance, Gothic style supplanted by neoclassical style. Vernacular languages replace Latin after 1300s in popular literature. Painting, sculpture, architecture, and metalwork profit from novel techniques and ideas. Secularism and individualism permeate Renaissance art and civic culture of ruling class.

After universities founded in 1200s, advances in humanities occur, but little in science. Technology attracts interest, especially after the Black Death and reduction of labor force. Few breakthroughs occur except in agriculture: three-field system, horse collar, use of animal manure, and better plows follow. New energy sources developed with introduction of windmills and watermills in northwestern Europe.

In China, Buddhism rivals and then blends with Confucian tenets among educated.
Peasantry continues ancestor worship and Daoism. In Japan, Buddhism enters from Korea in sixth century, subdivides into several noncompetitive sects, and strongly affects Shinto religion. Neither country produces clergy or much theology; ethics derived from nonsupernatural sources in both. Philosophy Buddhist-based in both and focuses on questions of daily life rather than abstract ideas. Warrior creeds increasingly dominant in Japan. Zen Buddhism particularly popular in Japan after 1100s.

Landscape painting, porcelain, bronzes, inlay work, silk weaving, and several forms of literature highly developed in China and Japan. Japanese take Chinese forms, but alter them to suit Japanese taste. Some art forms, such as Zen gardens and No drama for Japanese and jade sculpture and porcelain for Chinese, peculiar to each nation. Upper-class life allows more artistic freedom to Japanese women than to counterparts in wholly patriarchal China.

Technology highly developed in China throughout period.
Many inventions produced, including gunpowder, printing with movable type, paper made from wood pulp, navigational aids, water pump, and ship's rudder. Japanese are not so active and depend on Chinese importations but produce exceptional metal work.

Vedic Hinduism transformed in response to Buddhist challenge and recaptures almost all of Indians' allegiance. Both religions accept multiple nature of truth, in contrast with Christians and Muslims. Strong ethical tone dominates, as exemplified in the Upanishads, teachings of Mahavira among Jains, and Eightfold Path of Buddha. Near end of period, Muslim Turks establish rule in North India and dominate northern two-thirds of region via Delhi Sultanate. Muslim persecution accelerates Buddhist decline.

Art forms emphasize mutual dependency of gods and humans. Much art lost as result of climate and repeated invasions. Buddhist cave shrines and paintings are major repositories of extant art from early part of the period.
Much sculpture created in stone and metal of high quality. Indian artistic influence throughout Southeast Asian mainland and Indonesia. History and literature almost nonexistent.

Selective scientific advances made. Math particularly strong (e.g., zero concept, decimal system, much algebra). Pharmacy and medicine well-developed. Excellent metalwork. Technology dormant.

Worldview Three

 **LAW AND GOVERNMENT**

 **SOCIETY AND ECONOMY**

MUSLIMS

Law based on Qur'an as interpreted by ulama. Government also derived directly from doctrines of the Prophet and hadith tradition. Caliph is head of state and religion, as well as commander-in-chief, although the sultans supplant caliphs as de facto heads of state after tenth century. No separation between religion and state. Only Muslims full citizens; others usually excluded from office holding but not oppressed.

Mixed economy based on both urban and rural institutions. High levels of sophistication attained in trade and finance. Mercantile activity strongly developed, built on previous Eastern civilizations and extensive trading contacts. Agriculture organized along feudal lines. Wealth is open to all, Muslim and infidel, although non-Muslims required to pay additional taxes. Enormous variations in relative prosperity of Muslim groups, dependent on previous history and regional economy.

AFRICANS

Law almost always oral and customary until arrival of Muslim traders/ conquerors in North and East. Government based on ethnic affiliations, ranging from monarchs with cadres of officials to practically clan-level autonomy from all external authority. Large areas below Sahara never organize formal governments but remain stateless societies in which oral tradition and custom determine social behavior.

Lifestyles depend on changing climate and terrain. Nomadism prevalent among desert Berbers; agriculture important in rain forest zone, savanna grasslands, and coastal plains; additional livestock breeding in all regions except rain forest. Local trade in foodstuffs, salt, pottery, and metals. Long-distance trade across desert supports large-scale governments, beginning in Ghana of first millennium CE. Gold, salt, copper, iron, slaves, and animal by-products major trade items. Commerce occurs in collaboration with Arabs and Indians across Indian Ocean to Arabia and points east beginning in late first millennium CE.

AMERICANS

General absence of writing means reliance on customary law. Where states exist, government generally a divine monarchy of limited powers, with group of royal kin sharing in prestige and income from tribute. Priesthood always powerful, sometimes dominant. Conquest of neighbors the usual means of constructing imperial control over large areas. Causes of decline of states seldom known, although warfare, environmental degradation, and climatic change the most likely explanations.

These are the only ancient civilizations not located in river plains or valleys. Mesoamerican and Peruvian centers depend on surplus generated by new crops. Most subjects farmers, but a few urban areas (Tenochtitlán, Teotihuacan, Cuzco) appear in time. North of Rio Grande River, smaller-scale civilizations develop in Southwest (Puebloan) and east of Mississippi River (Cahokia and Iroquois). Considerable internal trade, but no contact made with extra-American civilizations.

CROSS-CULTURAL CONNECTIONS

Migrations
Europeans: Norse migration and settlement in Britain, Ireland, Normandy, Russia, Iceland, Greenland, and Newfoundland. Magyar migrations into Eastern Europe. Migrations of Europeans throughout globe in Age of Discovery.
Asians: Turkish migrations into northern China, western Asia, and southern Russia. Mongolian conquests and migrations into China, western Asia, Eastern Europe, and Russia.
Africans: Africans migrate or taken as slaves to southern and western Asia, the Mediterranean, Europe, and parts of the Americas (Brazil, Caribbean, and colonies in eastern America).
Americans: Migrations of Chichimec, Toltecs, and Aztecs from northern Mexico into Central Valley of Mexico. Puebloans abandon Four Corners area and migrate to Rio Grande region. Many Native American tribes migrate westward into Dakota Badlands and onto Great Plains.

Trade and Exchange Networks
Europe: Germans create the Hanseatic League network throughout Baltic region, Northwestern Russia, and Britain. Venice and Genoa establish near-total control over the Mediterranean end of trade with Asia and Africa. Portugal explores and establishes limited control over gold and pepper trade of West Africa; small-scale slave trade begun; all-water route to India discovered in 1497–1499. Spain explores and begins colonization of parts of the Caribbean. English King Henry VII sends Cabot to explore east coast of North America.
Asia: Silk Road and Indian Ocean networks link most of Asia, Africa, and Europe.
Africa: Persians, Arabs, Berbers, and Indians (Banyan) establish trade with parts of East and West Africa, making it part of westernmost extension of the Sahara and Indian Ocean networks.
America: North American network extends from American Southwest to Colombia. South American network extends from Peru and Ecuador throughout Western Andes and Amazon River basin

EQUILIBRIUM AMONG POLYCENTRIC CIVILIZATIONS, 500–1500 CE

PATTERNS OF BELIEF

ARTS AND CULTURE

SCIENCE AND TECHNOLOGY

Religious affiliation basic organizing principle of public life. Islam strongly exclusivistic and monopolistic in regard to truth. No pressure exerted on non-Muslims to convert, although many conquered peoples do. No formal priesthood, but ulama advise caliph and popularly regarded as principal experts on holy law. Muslim faith clashes with similar Christianity. Split between Sunni and Shi'a destroys Islamic unity and accentuates power struggles.

Art strongly influenced by Qur'anic prohibition of human portrayal. Architecture, interior decor, and landscaping strong points in plastic arts, as are poetry, storytelling, and history in literature. Respect for ancient achievements of Greeks in sciences and philosophy. Society strongly patriarchal.

Sciences initially and for a long time are promoted by Arab willingness to learn from Greeks and Persians. Major advances are made in math, chemistry, astronomy, and medicine, but by 1300, science is languishing in comparison with the West. Technology is selectively introduced, especially in maritime affairs and, for a time, in war. Muslims are frequently the first alien beneficiaries of earlier Hindu and Chinese breakthroughs.

Belief held in the power of nature and family spirits. Arrival of Muslims after about 700, and sub-Saharan peoples slowly converted, although veneration of spirits continues to be common even among Muslims.
Christianity isolated in Nubia and Ethiopia after seventh century.

Art devoted to religion or quasi-religious purposes. Fine bronzes and carvings in parts of sub-Saharan West and Southeast. Nok terra cotta work the oldest surviving art (seventh century).
Oral culture produced no written literature, although extensive oral traditions preserved rich traditions of history and verbal art.

Science stultified in contrast with other parts of the globe. Farm-based societies have complex systems of astronomy and astrology. Advanced methods of iron making and metals extraction. Extensive systems of irrigation used in some locations.

Religious belief unknown in detail. Gods are often fearful, demonic rulers of the afterworld. Faith strongly resembles aspects of Mesopotamia, with human sacrifice in some of the ruling groups (Aztec, Maya). No apparent connections exist between religion and ethics.

Much pre-Columbian plastic and pictorial artwork survives but little literature. Art serves theology and cosmology. Relief sculpture produced in Central America. Architecture highly developed in both Peru and Mexico.

Technology highly developed in engineering of large stone masses in buildings and fortifications. Mayan mathematics and accurate chronology other examples. Mastery of hydraulics at Tenochtitlán, massive stone structures in Mayan cities, and Incan road building over difficult mountain terrain demanded extensive science knowledge.

Spread of Foods, Diseases, Technologies and Ideas

Europe: Europeans invent basic elements of modern capitalism: double entry accounting, modern banking, and corporate business entities (e.g., chartered companies). *Asia:* Islamic civilization translates, preserves, and passes many works of classical Greece and Rome to Western Europe. Also invents and exports to Europe modern university as well as new tastes in cuisine, etiquette, and fashion; also new ideas about hunting (hawking), hydrography (windmills and watermills), horticulture, mathematics (place-value and algebra); and sailing (lateen sails and the astrolabe). Exports camel to North Africa. Central Asians export warhorses to China. Southeast Asians export spices and outrigger to Indian Ocean communities. India exports dyed cotton cloth and peppers; invents and exports place-value numeration to Islamic civilization and Europe. Koreans invent and export moveable type. China invents and exports gunpowder, paper, printing, stirrup, silk weaving, ship rudder, magnetism, and compass to Western Asia and Europe.
Africa: Early Iron Age spread of iron-making skills throughout subequatorial Africa. Methods for making high carbon iron developed; manufactured on East coast and exported to India, Persian Gulf, and Red Sea regions. Sheep and cattle introduced into southern Africa; some Khoisan-speakers adopt pastoral ways of life. Christianity briefly spreads through much of North and Northeast Africa. Islam enters North Africa in seventh century, then spreads into Sudanic belt after eleventh century; enters East Africa and spreads along the coast; spreads up Zambezi Valley into Mwenemutapa in fifteenth century.
America: Knowledge of metallurgy transmitted from South American civilizations to Central America; maize culture spreads from Mexico to Peru.

Part FOUR

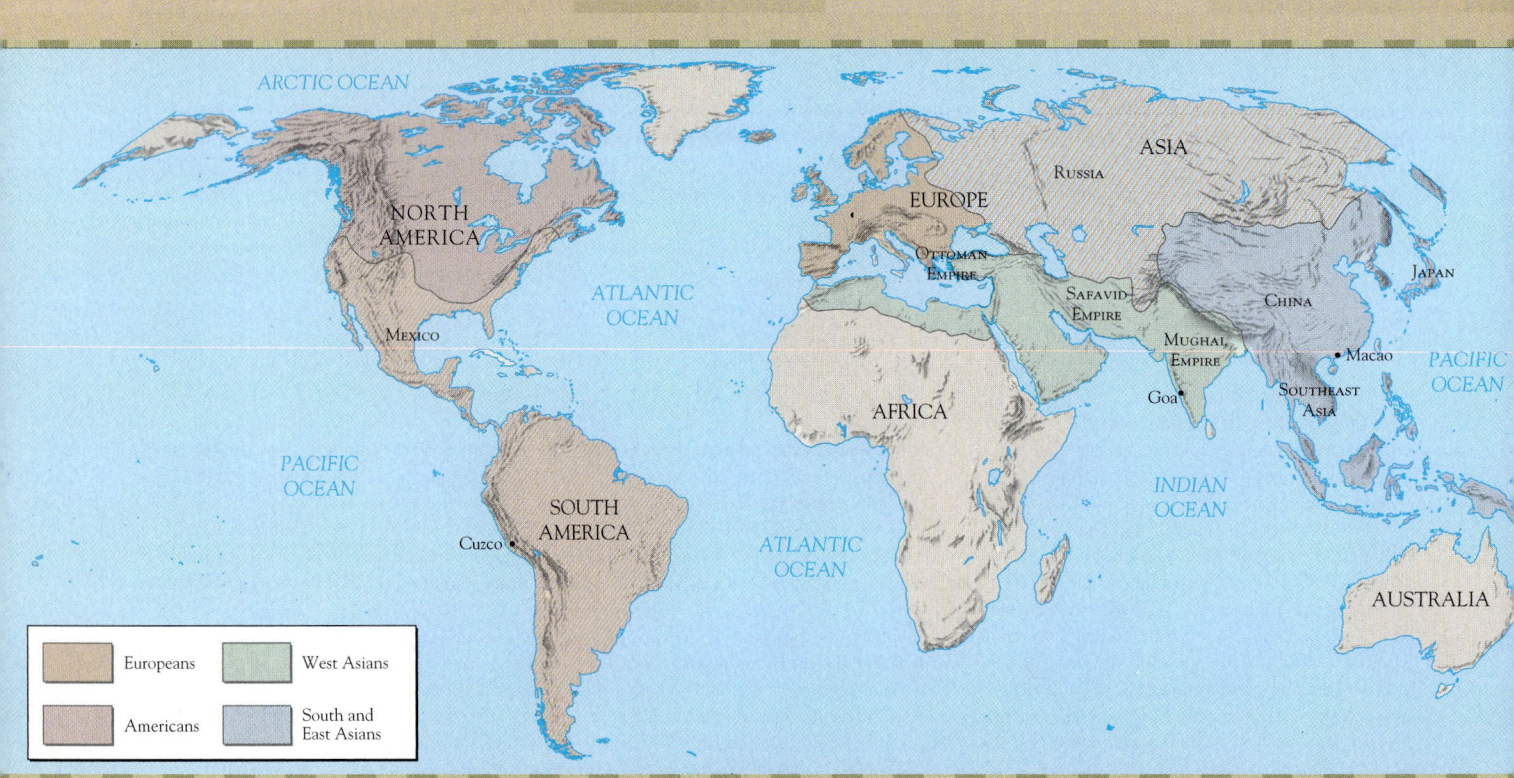

ARCTIC OCEAN

NORTH AMERICA

Mexico

ATLANTIC OCEAN

PACIFIC OCEAN

SOUTH AMERICA

Cuzco

ATLANTIC OCEAN

AFRICA

EUROPE

Ottoman Empire

Safavid Empire

Mughal Empire

Goa

RUSSIA

ASIA

CHINA

Macao

SOUTHEAST ASIA

JAPAN

PACIFIC OCEAN

INDIAN OCEAN

AUSTRALIA

	Europeans		West Asians
	Americans		South and East Asians

DISEQUILIBRIUM: THE WESTERN ENCOUNTER WITH THE NON-WESTERN WORLD, 1500–1700 CE

WITHIN FIFTY YEARS on either side of 1500 CE, a host of events or processes contributed to an atmosphere of rising confidence in the power of European governments and their supportive institutions. In the political and military realm, the Mongol yoke in Russia was lifted; the Turks, victorious at Constantinople, failed in an attempt to seize Vienna and central Europe; the Hundred Years' War had ended and the French recovery commenced. The economy finally recovered from the ravages of the Black Death, and maritime trade had increased significantly, as had the sophistication of commercial and financial instruments. The shameful derogation of the papal dignity brought about by the Babylonian Captivity and the Great Schism had ended. The worst of the peasant rebellions had been put down, and a peaceable transition from feudal agrarianism seemed possible, at least in the West.

But aside from these general developments, the epoch centered on 1500 is usually heralded as the beginning of the modern era because of two specific complexes of events: the questioning of traditional authority manifested in the Protestant Reformation and the voyages of discovery that revealed the possibilities of the globe to Europeans' imagination—and greed. Both of these complexes contributed, in very different ways, to the expansion of Europe's reach and authority that took place in the next 300 years, until Europeans began to claim a prerogative to decide the fates of others as almost a God-given right. This tendency was particularly striking in the American colonies, where the native Amerindians were either obliterated or virtually enslaved by their overlords, but it was also the case, although in a much more limited way, for eastern and southern Asia, the coast of Africa, and the island or Arctic peripheries of a world that was larger and more varied than anyone had formerly supposed.

The difference between 1500 and 1850 in this regard might well be illustrated by comparing the Aztecs' Tenochtitlán, which amazed the envious Cortés, with the sleepy, dusty villages to which Mexico's Indians were later confined. Similarly, one might compare the army of the Persian Safavid rulers of the early sixteenth century that reduced the mighty Mughals to supplicants for peace with the raggedy mob that attempted—in vain—to stop a handful of British from installing themselves on the Khyber Pass three centuries later. The West, whether represented by illiterate Spanish freebooters or Oxfordian British bureaucrats, seemed destined to surpass or be invincible against what one unrepentant imperialist called the "lesser breeds." Part Four examines the massive changes that were slowly evincing themselves during these three centuries of heightening interactions between the West and the rest of the world, interactions that by the end of the period had provoked a state of disequilibrium in a world that had existed in a state of harmony and balance since the early stages of the common era.

The voyages of discovery of the fifteenth and sixteenth centuries, the opening of maritime commerce across the Indian and Atlantic Oceans, and the resultant Columbian Exchange and the slave trade are the subject of Chapter 22. Chapter 23 considers in detail the successful Lutheran and Calvinist challenges to the papal church and their permanent effects on Western sensibilities. Chapter 24 briefly shifts the focus to Asia, where the rise and fall of the great Muslim empires of central Asia and India are discussed. Chapter 25 examines the absolutist idea, constitutionalism, and their expression in religious warfare and the desire for stability, all of which became the cornerstones of modern governments in Western and Central Europe, and to smaller degree in pre-revolutionary Russia as well. China's centuries of glory following the ejection of the Mongols through the early Qing Dynasty are analyzed in Chapter 26. The history of pre–Meiji Restoration Japan and Southeast Asia before 1700 follow in Chapter 27. Finally, the Iberian colonies of America and their struggle for independent existence are outlined in Chapter 28.

22 A LARGER WORLD OPENS

I have come to believe that this is a mighty continent which was hitherto unknown.
—Christopher Columbus

Mid-1400s	Portuguese begin voyages of exploration
1492	Christopher Columbus reaches Americas
1498	Vasco da Gama arrives in India
Early 1500s	Transatlantic slave trade begins
1519–1540	Spanish conquer Aztecs and Incans
1522	First circumnavigation of globe completed
1602	Dutch East India Company founded

MARITIME EXPLORATION IN THE 1400S

OVERSEAS EMPIRES AND THEIR EFFECTS
Portuguese Pioneers ◆ The Spanish Empire in the Americas ◆ The African Slave Trade Opens ◆ Dutch and English Merchant-Adventurers

MERCANTILISM

THE COLUMBIAN EXCHANGE

EUROPEAN IMPACTS AND VICE VERSA
The Fate of the Amerindians ◆ Racism's Beginnings

THE UNPARALLELED OVERSEAS EXPANSION of Europe in the later fifteenth and early sixteenth centuries opened a new era of intercontinental contacts. What were the motives for the rapid series of adventuresome voyages? They ranged from Christian missionary impulses to the common desire to get rich. Backed to varying degrees by their royal governments, Portuguese, Spanish, Dutch, French, and English seafarers opened the world to European commerce, settlement, and eventual dominion. Through the Columbian Exchange initiated in 1492, the New World entered European consciousness and was radically and permanently changed by European settlers. In most of the world, however, the presence of a relative handful of foreigners in coastal "factories" or as occasional traders meant little change in traditional activities and attitudes. Not until the later eighteenth century was the European presence a threat to the continuation of accustomed African, Asian, and Polynesian lifestyles.

MARITIME EXPLORATION IN THE 1400S

The Vikings in their graceful longboats had made voyages across the North Atlantic from Scandinavia to Greenland and on to North America as early as 1000 CE, but the northern voyages were too risky to serve as the channel for permanent European expansion, and Scandinavia's population base was too small. Four hundred years later, major advances in technology had transformed maritime commerce. The import of new sail rigging, the magnetic compass, and the astrolabe (an instrument used to determine the altitude of the sun or other celestial bodies) from Asia; a new hull design; and systematic navigational charts enabled Western seamen, led by the Portuguese, to conquer the world's oceans. Firearms of all sizes backed up their claims to dominion over their newly discovered territories. By the end of the fifteenth century, the map of the

Eastern Hemisphere was gradually becoming familiar to Europeans.

Knowledge of the high cultures of Asia was current by the early 1400s. Muslim traders long before had established an active commerce with Southern and Eastern Asia by their command of the Indian Ocean routes and the famous Silk Road through central Asia and had served as intermediaries to Europe (Chapter 14). Marco Polo's great adventure was well known even earlier, after the appearance of his book about his many years of service to Kubilai Khan.

Most of Europe's luxury imports had long come from Africa, China and India, while the Spice Islands (as they were called by Europeans) of Southeast Asia had been the source of the most valuable items in international exchange (see Map 22.1). In the fourteenth century, this trade was disrupted, first by the Ottoman Turkish conquest of the eastern Mediterranean and then by the breakup of the

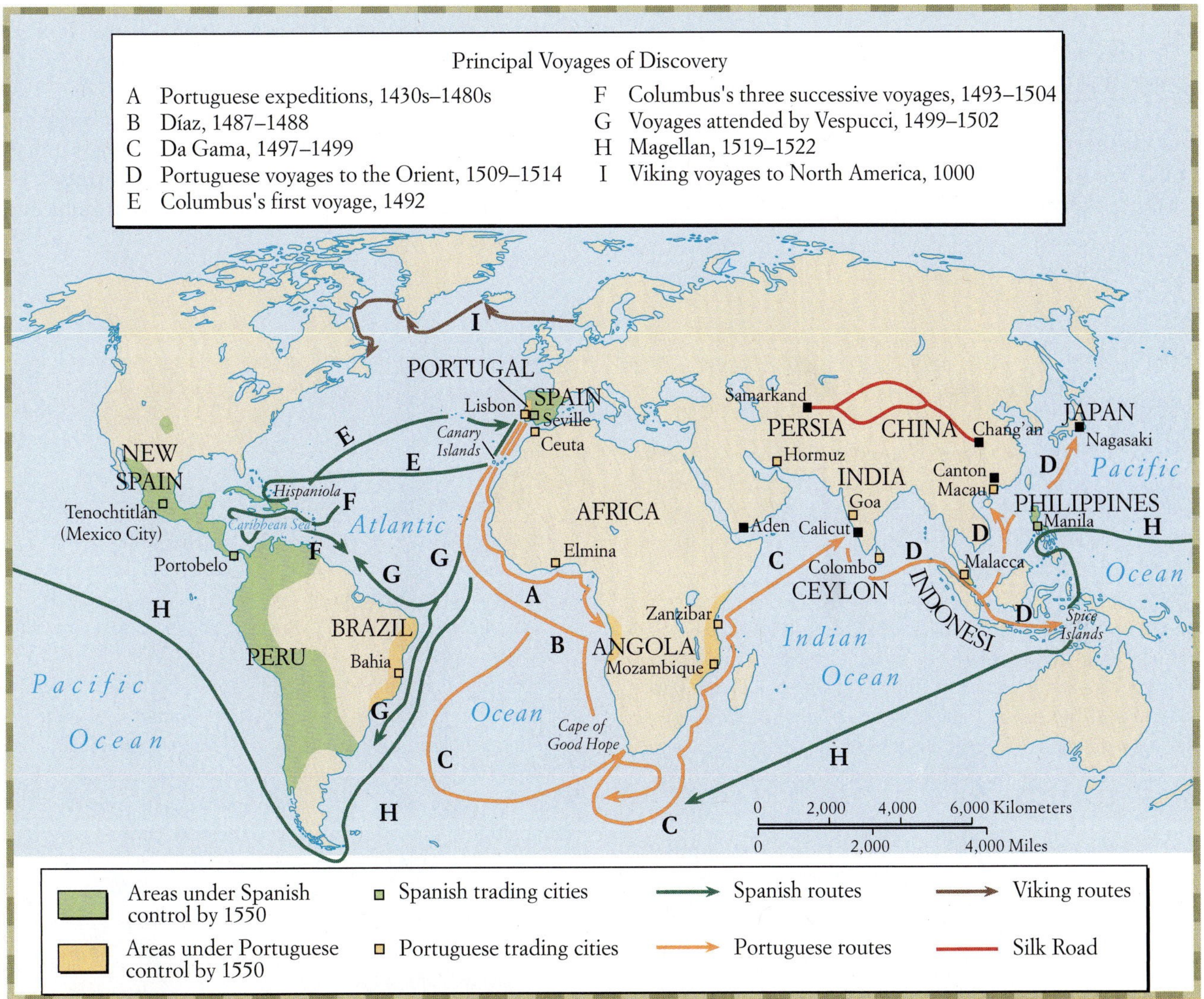

Principal Voyages of Discovery

A Portuguese expeditions, 1430s–1480s
B Díaz, 1487–1488
C Da Gama, 1497–1499
D Portuguese voyages to the Orient, 1509–1514
E Columbus's first voyage, 1492

F Columbus's three successive voyages, 1493–1504
G Voyages attended by Vespucci, 1499–1502
H Magellan, 1519–1522
I Viking voyages to North America, 1000

Areas under Spanish control by 1550	Spanish trading cities
Areas under Portuguese control by 1550	Portuguese trading cities
Spanish routes	Viking routes
Portuguese routes	Silk Road

WORLDVIEW MAP 22.1 Spanish and Portuguese Voyages in the Fifteenth and Sixteenth Centuries

The shaded areas indicate the portions of the newly explored regions that were mapped and settled. Unshaded areas indicate those that remained unexplored and relatively unknown.

MAP QUESTIONS
Using this map, can you trace the stages of expansion of global trade, from the earliest ones that linked southern and southwestern Asia to the beginnings of a world system? What does this map suggest about what might have prevented a truly global system of travel and trade in the early (fifteenth and sixteenth centuries') Age of Discovery?

View an interactive version of this or a related map at http://worldrc.wadsworth.com/

Mongol Empire, which had formed a single unit reaching from China to western Russia.

Security of transit across Asia was threatened, as was the Europeans' long-established and profitable interchange of goods with the Arabs and Persians. In 1453, the great depot of Eastern wares, Constantinople, fell into the hands of the Ottomans. With direct access to this old gateway to the East now lost, Europeans became more interested than ever in finding a direct sea route to the East by circumnavigating Africa and so allowing them to bypass the hostile Ottomans.

OVERSEAS EMPIRES AND THEIR EFFECTS

First the Portuguese and the Spanish and then the Dutch, English, and French created overseas empires that had far-reaching effects both at home and abroad.

Portuguese Pioneers

In the middle of the 1400s and under the guidance of the visionary **Prince Henry the Navigator** (1394–1460), tiny and impoverished Portugal sponsored a series of exploratory voyages down the west coast of Africa and out into the ocean as far as the Azores (about one-third the distance to the Caribbean) in a search for African gold and pepper. In 1488, the Portuguese captain Bartolomeo Diaz made a crucial advance by successfully rounding the Cape of Good Hope. Some years later, **Vasco da Gama** (VAHS-coh duh GAH-mah) sailed across the Indian Ocean to the west coast of India. (For a closer look at da Gama's exploits, see Science and Technology.) Trying to follow a new route around the southern tip of Africa that took him far to the west, Pedro Alvarez Cabral got blown all the way across the Atlantic, making landfall in Brazil, which he promptly claimed for Portugal. By 1510, Portuguese flags were flying over Goa in India and

SCIENCE AND TECHNOLOGY

Vasco da Gama's First Contacts in East Africa

One of the most daring of all the explorers sailing in the name of Portugal or Spain was Vasco da Gama, the first to round the tip of Africa and sail on to India. Da Gama made landfall on the Indian coast in 1498 before returning safely to Lisbon the following year. He kept a detailed diary of his epoch-making voyage, from which the following comments on the non-Muslim peoples of the East African littoral are taken.

These people are black, and the men are of good physique, they go about naked except that they wear small pieces of cotton cloth with which they cover their genitals, and the Senhores [chiefs] of the land wear larger cloths. The young women in this land look good; they have their lips pierced in three places and they wear some pieces of twisted tin. These people were very much at ease with us, and brought out to us in the vessels what they had, in dugout canoes....

After we had been here two or three days there came out two Senhores of this land to see us, they were so haughty that they did not value anything which was given to them. One of them was wearing a cap on his head with piping worked in silk, and the other a furry cap of green satin. There came in their company a youth who,

we gathered from gestures, came from another far country, and said that he had already seen great vessels like those that carried us. With these signs we rejoiced greatly, because it seemed to us that we were going to reach where we wanted to go....

This land, it seemed to us, is densely populated. There are in it many villages and towns. The women seemed to be more numerous than men, because when there came 20 men there came 40 women.... The arms of these people are very large bows and arrows, and assagais [spears] of iron. In this land there seemed to be much copper, which they wore on their legs and arms and in their kinky hair. Equally used is tin, which they place on the hilts of daggers, the sheaths are of iron. The people greatly prize linen cloth, and they gave us as much of this copper for as many shirts as we cared to give.

▶ Analyze and Interpret

What seems to have been the attitude of the East Africans toward these European strangers? To what do you attribute this view? From where do you suppose the previously seen "vessels" had come? To what kinds of material technology does it appear the Africans had access? Where do you think they got it?

Source: Harry Stephan, ed. *The Diary of Vasco da Gama (Travels through African Waters 1497–1499)* (Sydney: Phillips, 1998), pp. 32–33.

Macão on the coast of China (see Map 22.1). In 1511, the extraordinary admiral Afonso da Albuquerque seized the great port-depot of Malacca at the tip of the Malay peninsula. With the capital of their Indian Ocean empire in Goa, the Portuguese became the controllers of the most profitable sea trade in the world.

The Portuguese empire was really only a string of fortified stations called "factories," from which the Portuguese brought back shiploads of the much sought-after spices, gold, porcelain, and silk obtained from their trading partners in East Africa and the Southeast Asian mainland and islands. They paid for these imports initially with metal wares, cloth, and trinkets, and later with firearms and liquor. The Lisbon government was the initiator and main beneficiary of this trade, because Portugal's small upper and middle classes were unable to pay sufficiently to outfit ships for the expeditions.

The era of Portuguese leadership was brief. The country was too poor and its population too small to maintain this lucrative but thinly spread empire. By the late 1500s, the aggressively expanding Dutch merchants had already forced Portugal out of some of its overseas stations. Previously independent Portugal was incorporated into Catholic Spain in 1580, which gave the Dutch and English Protestants an excuse to attack the Portuguese everywhere. Eventually, by the end of the seventeenth century, Portugal was left with only Angola and the Kongo kingdom in West Africa, plus Mozambique, Macão, Goa, Brazil, and a few additional enclaves and scattered trading posts around the Indian Ocean rim.

How did a relative handful of European intruders establish themselves as regionally dominant authorities in these distant corners of the globe? In the Indian Ocean and Southeast Asia, the patterns established by the Portuguese were followed by all of their successors. The European outreach was seaborne, and control of the sea was the crucial element. Local populations that tried to resist quickly learned that it was not profitable to confront the European ships with arms, because the Europeans would generally win. Their naval cannon, more advanced methods of rigging, more maneuverable hulls, better battle discipline, and higher levels of training assured them of success in almost all engagements. The intruders avoided land warfare, unless and until mastery of the surrounding seas was assured, and in that case, land warfare was rarely necessary.

After an initial display of martial strength, the newcomers were usually content to deal with and through established local leaders in securing the spices, cotton cloth, silk, and other luxuries that they sought. In the normal course of events, the Europeans made treaties with paramount regional rulers that assured them a secure place in the export market. A kind of partnership thus evolved between the local chieftains and the new arrivals, in which both had sufficient reasons to maintain the status quo against those who might challenge it.

The Portuguese frequently made the mistake of alienating the local population by their brutality and their attempts to exclude all competition, but the Dutch and, later, the British were more circumspect. Unlike the Portuguese, they made no attempt until the nineteenth century

A PORTUGUESE GALLEON. In what kind of vessel did the early explorers set sail? Ships such as these opened the trade routes to the East and to Brazil and the Caribbean for the Lisbon government in the sixteenth and seventeenth centuries. In their later days, two or three rows of cannons gave them heavy firepower as well as cargo space.

Service Historique de la Marine, Vincennes, France/Lauros-Giraudon/Bridgeman Art Library

to bring Africans and Asians to Christianity. As a general rule, after the sixteenth-century Portuguese missionary efforts had subsided, the Europeans interfered little with existing laws, religion, and customs unless they felt compelled to do so to gain their commercial ends. Such interference was rare in both Asia and Africa. There, the European goal was to derive the maximum profit from trade, and they avoided anything that would threaten the smooth execution of that trade. The Spanish and Portuguese empires in the Americas were a different proposition, however.

The Spanish Empire in the Americas

By the dawn of the sixteenth century, a newly unified Spanish kingdom was close behind and in some areas competing with Portugal in the race for world empire. A larger domestic resource base and extraordinary finds of precious metals enabled Spain to achieve more permanent success than its neighbor. The Italian visionary Christopher Columbus was able to persuade King Ferdinand and Queen Isabella to support his dream of a shortcut to the "Indies" by heading *west* over the Atlantic, which he thought was only a few hundred miles wide. The first of Columbus's Spanish-financed voyages resulted in his discovery of the American continents. He made three more voyages before his death and was still convinced that China lay just over the horizon of the Caribbean Sea.

By then, the Spanish crown had engaged a series of other voyagers, including Amerigo Vespucci, who eventually gave his name to the New World that Columbus and others were exploring. In 1519–1521, the formidable Hernán Cortés conquered the Aztec Empire in Mexico. Soon Spanish explorers had penetrated north into what is now Florida, California, and Arizona. By the 1540s, Spain controlled most of northern South America as well as all of Central America, the larger Caribbean islands, and the South and Southwest of what is now the United States.

Perhaps the greatest of these ventures was the fantastic voyage of **Ferdinand Magellan**. Starting from Spain in 1519, his ships were the first to circumnavigate the world. A few survivors (not including the unlucky Magellan) limped back into Seville in 1522 and reported that the world was indeed round, as most educated people already had thought.

Like the Portuguese, the Spaniards' motives for exploration were mixed between a desire to convert non-Christians to the Roman Catholic Church and thus gain a strong advantage against the burgeoning Protestants (see Chapter 23) and the desire for wealth and social respectability. Land, too, was increasingly in short supply in Europe, especially for the younger offspring of the nobility and the landed gentry. Gold, God, glory, and acquiring land were the motives most frequently in play. By whatever motivation, however, the middle of the 1500s saw the Spanish adventurers creating an empire

that reached as far as the Philippine Islands. In the terms of the royal charters granted to Columbus and his successors, the Spanish crown claimed the lion's share of treasures found by the explorers. Indian gold and silver (*bullion*) thus poured into the royal treasury in Madrid. Those metals, in turn, allowed Spain to become the most powerful European state in the sixteenth and seventeenth centuries.

Unlike the Portuguese, the Spanish frequently came to stay at their overseas posts. Whereas the Portuguese were primarily interested in quick profits from the trade in luxury items from the East, the Spanish noble explorers were accompanied by priests, who set up missions among the Indians, and by a number of lowborn men (later women, also), who were prepared to get rich more slowly. They did so by taking land and workers from among the native population.

Finding that *El Dorado* and the much dreamed-of cities of gold and silver were mirages, the Spanish immigrants gradually created agricultural colonies in much of Middle and South America, using first Amerindian and then African slave labor. The Spanish colonies thus saw the growth of a multiracial society—Africans, Amerindians, and Europeans—in which the Europeans held the dominant political and social positions from the outset. The dominance of the whites was to assume increasing importance for the societies and economies of these lands both during their 300 years as colonies and later as independent states.

The African Slave Trade Opens

The European export of slaves from Africa commenced in the fifteenth century. When the Portuguese ventured down the West African coast, they quickly discovered that selling black house slaves to the European nobility could be a lucrative business, but the slave trade remained small in scale through the 1490s and began to grow only when slaves started to be shipped across the Atlantic. By the mid-1530s, Portugal had shipped moderate numbers of slaves to the Spanish Caribbean and to its own colony of Brazil, and the trans-Atlantic trade remained almost a Portuguese monopoly until into the next century. At that time, Dutch, French, and then English traders moved into the business and dominated it throughout its great expansion in the eighteenth century until its gradual abolition.

Few European women traveled to the Americas in the early years of colonization, so the Spaniards often married Amerindian or African women or kept them as concubines. As a result, *mestizos* (the offspring of Amerindians and whites) and *mulattos* (the children of Africans and whites) soon outnumbered Caucasians in many colonies. The same thing happened in Portuguese Brazil, where over time a huge number of African slaves were imported to till the sugarcane fields that provided that colony with its chief export. Here, the populace was commonly the offspring of Portuguese and African unions, rather than the Spanish-Indian mixture found to the north.

THE SLAVE SHIP. This engraving shows the usual arrangements for transport of black slaves in the Atlantic trade. Packed in close together with few or no sanitary facilities, death was common among the weakest. Occasionally, entire human cargoes were lost to outbreaks of contagious diseases.

Michael Graham-Stewart/Bridgeman Art Library

Dutch and English Merchant-Adventurers

Holland. When Portugal's grip on its Indian Ocean trade began to falter, the Dutch Protestant merchants combined a fine eye for profit with religious zeal to fill the vacuum. In the late sixteenth century, the Netherlands gained independence from Spain. Controlling their own affairs after that, the bourgeois ship owners and merchants of the Dutch and Flemish towns quickly moved into the forefront of the race for trade. By the opening of the seventeenth century, Amsterdam and Antwerp were the major destinations of Far Eastern shippers, and Lisbon had fallen into a secondary position.

Dutch interest in the eastern seas was straightforward and hard-edged. They wanted to accumulate wealth by creating a monopoly of demand, buying shiploads of Southeast Asian luxury goods at low prices and selling the goods at high prices in Europe. Many of the Asian suppliers were Muslims, and their relationship with the Catholic Portuguese had been strained or hostile. They preferred to deal with the Dutch Protestants, who were simply businessmen with no desire to be missionaries. If the suppliers were for one or another reason reluctant to sell, the Dutch persuaded them by various means, usually involving Dutch superiority in naval gunnery.

The Dutch focused on the East Indies spice and luxury trade, but they also established settler colonies at Cape Town in South Africa, in New Amsterdam across the Atlantic, and on several islands in the Caribbean. These colonies were less attractive to the Dutch and eventually surrendered to other powers, such as England. New Amsterdam became New York at the close of the first of two naval wars in the seventeenth century that made England the premier colonial power along the East Coast of the future United States.

How did such a small nation (Holland did not possess more than 2.5 million people at this juncture) carry out this vast overseas enterprise while it was struggling to free itself from its Spanish overlords? A chief reason for the Dutch success was the **Dutch East India Company**: a private firm chartered by the government in 1602, the company had a monopoly on Dutch trading in the Pacific. The company eventually took over the Portuguese spice and luxury trade in the East and proved to be an enormous bonanza for its stockholders. A partnership would be set up for one or more voyages, with both cost and profits split among the shareholders, while minimizing risks for all. The traders hired captains and crews who would be most likely to succeed in filling the ship's hold at minimal cost, whatever the means or consequences. Later in the seventeenth century, the focus of attention shifted from importing spices and luxury goods to the alluring profits to be made in the trans-Atlantic trade in African slaves.

England. The English colonial venture was slow in getting started. When the Portuguese and Spaniards were dividing up the newly discovered continent of America and the Far Eastern trade, England was just emerging from a lengthy struggle for dynastic power called the War of the Roses (see Chapter 21). Starting in the 1530s, the country was then preoccupied for a generation with the split from Rome under Henry VIII and its consequences (see Chapter 23). Then came the disappointing failure of Sir Walter Raleigh's "Lost Colony" on the Carolina coast in the 1580s and a war with Spain.

Only in the early 1600s did the English begin to enter the discovery and colonizing business in any systematic way. Like the Dutch, the English efforts were organized by private parties or groups and were not under the direction of the royal government. The London East India Company (often called the British East India Company), founded in 1600, is a good example. Similar to its Dutch counterpart, it was a private enterprise with wide political as well as commercial powers in dealing with foreigners and with its own military resources.

After two victorious wars against the Dutch in the 1650s and 1660s, the English were the world's leading naval power. The East Asian colonial trade was not important to them, however, and they soon gave up their attempts to penetrate the Dutch monopoly in East Indian luxuries, choosing to concentrate on India. (The only important English station in Southeast Asia was the great fortress port of Singapore, which was not acquired until the nineteenth century.)

English colonies in the seventeenth century were concentrated in North America and the Caribbean, and an odd mixture they were. The northern colonies were filled with Protestant dissidents who could not abide the Anglican Church regime: Puritans, Congregationalists, and Quakers. Maryland was a refuge for persecuted Catholics. Virginia and the Carolinas began as real estate speculations. They were essentially get-rich-quick schemes devised by nobles or wealthy commoners who thought they could sell off their American holdings to individual settlers at a fat profit. Georgia began as a noble experiment by a group of philanthropists who sought to give convicts a second chance.

Elsewhere, the English were less inclined to settle new lands than to make their fortunes pirating Spanish galleons or competing with the Dutch in the slave trade. What the Dutch had taken from the Portuguese, the English seized in part from the Dutch. This was equally true in the New World, where the English and French superseded the Dutch challenge to Portuguese and Spanish hegemony in the Caribbean in the eighteenth century.

France.　The colonial empire of France parallels that of England. While they were relatively late in entering the race, the French sought overseas possessions and/or trade factories throughout the world to support their prospering domestic economy. From Canada (as early as 1608) to the west coast of Africa (as early as 1639) and India (in the early eighteenth century), the servants of the Bourbon kings contested both their Catholic co-religionists (Portugal, Spain) and their Protestant rivals (Holland, Britain) for mercantile advantage and the extension of royal powers. Thus, the French, too, reflected the seventeenth-century trend of allowing state policies to be dictated more by secular interests than by religious adherences, a process we will examine in detail in Chapter 25.

Mercantilism

During this epoch, governments attempted to control their economies through a process later termed **mercantilism.** Under mercantilism, the chief goal of economic policy was a favorable balance of trade, with the value of a country's exports exceeding the cost of its imports. To achieve this goal, the royal government intervened in the market constantly and attempted to secure advantage to itself and the population at large by carefully supervising every aspect of commerce and investment. The practice reached its highest development in seventeenth- and eighteenth-century France, but it was subscribed to almost everywhere.

As for colonial policy, mercantilism held that only goods and services that originated in the home country could be (legally) exported to the colonies and that the colonies' exports must go to the home country for use there or re-export. Thus, the colonies' most essential functions were to serve as captive markets for home-country producers and to provide raw materials at low cost for home-country importers.

The Columbian Exchange

The coming of the Europeans to the New World resulted in important changes in the resources, habits, and values of both the Amerindians and the whites. Scholars call this the **Columbian Exchange**. Among the well-known introductions by the Europeans to the Western Hemisphere were horses, pigs, cattle, sheep, and goats; iron; firearms; sailing ships; and, less tangibly, the entire system of economics we call capitalism.

But the Columbian Exchange had another side: a reverse flow of products and influences from the Americas to Europe and through Europe to the other continents. Educated Europeans after about 1520 became aware of how huge and relatively unknown the Earth was and how varied the peoples inhabiting it were. This knowledge came as a surprise to many Europeans, and they were eager to learn more. The literature of discovery and exploration became extraordinarily popular during the sixteenth and seventeenth centuries.

From this literature, Europeans learned, among other things, that the Christian moral code was but one of several; that the natural sciences were not of overwhelming interest or importance to most of humanity; that an effective education could take myriad forms and have myriad goals; and that viewpoints formed by tradition and habit are not necessarily correct, useful, or the only conceivable ones. Initially just curious about the Earth's other inhabitants, upper class Europeans gradually began to develop a certain tolerance for other peoples' views and habits. This tolerance slowly deepened in the seventeenth and especially the eighteenth century as Europe emerged from its religious wars. The previously favored view of unknown peoples probably being "anthropophagi" (man eaters) began giving way to the concept of the "noble savage," whose unspoiled morality might put the sophisticated European to shame.

Contacts with the Americas also led to changes in Europe. Some crops such as sugarcane and coffee that were already known in Europe but could not be profitably grown there were found to prosper in the New World. Their cultivation formed the basis for the earliest plantations in the Caribbean basin and the introduction of slavery into the New World. In addition, a series of new crops were introduced to the European, Asian, and African diets. Tobacco, several varieties of beans and peas, potatoes, squashes, rice, maize, bananas, manioc, and other agricultural products stemmed originally from American or Far Eastern lands. First regarded as novelties—much like the occasional Indian or African visitor—these crops came to be used as food and fodder. The most important for Europe was the white or Irish potato, an Andean native, which was initially considered fit only for cattle and pigs but was gradually adopted by northern Europeans in the eighteenth century. By the end of that century, the potato had become the most important part of the peasants' diet in several countries. The potato was the chief reason European farms were able to feed the spectacular increase in population that started in the later 1700s.

So much additional coinage was put into circulation in Europe from the Mexican and Peruvian silver mines that it generated massive inflation. In the seventeenth century, the Spanish court used the silver to pay army suppliers, shipyards, and soldiers, and from their hands, it went on into the general economy. Spain suffered most in the long run from the inflation its bullion imports caused. Moreover, with its tiny middle class and ideological opposition to the new sciences, Spain resisted technological innovation and industrialization, so when the rest of Europe began industrializing, Spanish gold and silver went into the pockets of foreign suppliers, carriers, and artisans rather than into domestic investments or business. This situation would prove fateful in the next century.

In a period of inflation, when money becomes cheap and goods or services become dear, people who can convert their wealth quickly to goods and services are in an enviable position. Those whose wealth is illiquid and cannot be easily converted are at a disadvantage. As a result, the landholders—many of whom were nobles who thought it beneath them to pay attention to money matters—lost economic strength. The middle classes, who could sell their services and expertise at rising rates, did well. Best off were the merchants, who could buy cheap and sell at higher prices. But even the unskilled or skilled workers in the towns were in a relatively better position than the landlords: wages rose about as fast as prices in this century.

In many feudal remnant areas, where serfs paid token rents in return for small parcels of arable land, the landlord was dealt a heavy blow. Prices rose for everything the noble landlords needed and wanted, while their rents, sanctioned by centuries of custom, remained about the same. Many of them had been living beyond their means for generations, borrowing money wherever they could with land as security. Unaware of the reasons for the economic changes and unable to anticipate the results, many landlords faced disaster during the later sixteenth century and could not avoid bankruptcy when their long-established mortgages were called. Much land changed hands at this time, from impoverished nobles to peasants or to the newly rich from the towns. Serfdom in the traditional pattern became impractical or unprofitable. Already weakened by long-term changes in European society, serfdom was abolished in most of Western Europe.

EUROPEAN IMPACTS AND VICE VERSA

How strong was the European impact on the Amerindian cultures of the Western Hemisphere and on the peoples of the Far East, sub-Saharan Africa, and the Pacific Rim? Historians agree that it was enormous in some areas, but much less so in others. The Portuguese and others' trading factories on the African and Asian coasts had minimal impacts on the lives of the peoples of the interior. Only in exceptional circumstances was the presence of the Europeans a prominent factor in local people's consciousness. Even in the areas most directly affected by slaving such as Senegambia, the Nigerian Delta, and Angola, the consensus of recent scholarly opinion holds that there was considerable variation, largely depending on local traditions, demography, and political circumstances. In many cases, the slave trade undermined social and political structures and destroyed entire civilizations, such as Kongo and Ngola. In other locations like Dahomey and the tiny states of the Niger delta, new societies were created that depended on the trade. Almost everywhere, however, the commerce in human beings took away the youngest and most productive members of African societies, raised the frequency and level of violent conflict, and destroyed local craft production.

Spain's American settler colonies and Brazil were quite different in these respects. Here the intruders quickly and radically terminated existing Amerindian authority structures, replacing them with Spanish/Portuguese models. In the economy, the *encomienda* estates on which Amerindians were forced to live and toil replaced the villages with their free labor. Although the encomiendas were soon abolished, Spanish and Portuguese exploitation of helpless Amerindians and Africans continued on tobacco and sugar plantations, which replaced gold and silver mines.

As with the exchanges in agricultural products, the stream of external influences was not simply one way, from Europe to the rest of the world. In the Americas, a noticeable degree of change was wrought in the Spanish and Portuguese culture by prolonged exposure to Amerindian and African habits and attitudes. An example would be the adoption of maize culture by the mestizo and Spanish populations in Mexico. Another would be the incorporation of Amerindian irrigation technique.

In another part of the early imperial world created by the voyages of discovery, the architecture of the Dutch colonial town of Batavia (Jakarta) was soon converted from the trim and tight homes and warehouses of blustery Amsterdam to the different demands of the Javanese climate.

Perhaps it is most accurate to say that in the settler colonies of the Western Hemisphere and South Africa, the local peoples were extensively and sometimes disastrously affected by the arrival of the whites, but in the rest of the world, including most of sub-Saharan Africa, the Asian mainland,

and the South Pacific islands, the Europeans were less disruptive to the existing state of affairs. Sometimes local peoples even succeeded in manipulating the Europeans to their own advantage, as in West Africa and Mughal India. This would remain true until the nineteenth century. Promoted by industrialization at that time, the European impacts multiplied, became more profound, and changed in nature so as to subordinate the indigenous peoples in every sense.

The Fate of the Amerindians

By far the worst human consequences of the European expansion were the tragic fates imposed on the native Amerindians of the Caribbean and Hispanic America in the first century of Spanish conquest (see Evidence of the Past box). Although the Spanish crown imposed several regulatory measures to protect the Indians after 1540, little could be done to inhibit the spread of epidemic disease (measles and influenza, as well as the major killer, smallpox) in the Amerindian villages. As a general rule, because they had not been exposed to childhood diseases like measles and smallpox, the immune systems of the Amerindians were unable to cope with the diseases brought by the newcomers, whereas the Spaniards were much less affected by the Amerindian maladies. (Which ethnic group is responsible for the appearance of syphilis is much argued.)

Smallpox was a particular curse. The population of Mexico, which was perhaps as high as 20 million at the coming of Cortés, was reduced to 2 million only sixty years later, largely as a result of smallpox epidemics. On the Caribbean islands, few Amerindians survived into the seventeenth century in Cuba and the smaller islands. The same story repeated itself in the viceroyalty of Peru, where as many as 80 percent of the native population died in the sixteenth century. Only in modern times have the Amerindians recovered from this unprecedented disaster.

Racism's Beginnings

Africans came into European society for the first time in appreciable numbers during the fifteenth century. At that time the first faint signs of white racism appeared. The first slaves from Africa were introduced to Europe through Muslim channels. Their rich owners mostly regarded them as novelties, and they were kept as tokens of wealth or artistic taste. Some free black people lived in Mediterranean Europe, where they worked as sailors, musicians, and actors, but they were not numerous enough for the average European to have any firsthand contact.

Many Europeans thought of black people in terms dictated either by the Bible or by Muslim prejudices imbibed unconsciously over time. The biblical references were generally negative: black was the color of the sinful, the opposite of

Robert Frerck/Odyssey Productions, Inc.

THE NATIVE AMERICAN VOICE IN MEXICAN CATHOLICISM. This detail from the Church of Tonantzintla in Puebla, Mexico, illustrates another aspect of the Columbian Exchange. Indigenous peoples often interpreted European culture and religion through the filter of their own experiences. In this representation of various Roman Catholic saints, Native American artisans depicted their rain god, Tlaloc, in the upper, middle portion of the picture.

light in the world. "Blackhearted," "a black scoundrel," and "black intentions" are a few examples of the mental connection that was made between the color black and everything evil and contemptible. The Arab slave traders in both West and East Africa who supplied some of the European as well as the Asiatic markets were another source of prejudice. They were contemptuous of non-Muslim Africans of western Sudan or the East African coast in whose flesh they had dealt for centuries before the European trade began. These merchants' point of view was easily transferred to their Italian and Portuguese partners. However, once the European slave trade became big business in the seventeenth century, white racism became the mental cornerstone of a pervasive and viciously exploitative slave-based economy in many parts of the Western Hemisphere.

EVIDENCE OF THE PAST

Bartolomé de las Casas's Report on the Indies

Violence toward the conquered is a commonplace event in history, and nowhere is this more evident than in the history of the state religions. Using inhumane means to propagate Christianity was a cynical cover for some of the Spanish conquistadors in their obsessive search for Indian gold. They were resisted, however, in this bloodthirsty enterprise by one of their own number.

Bartolomé de las Casas (bahr-TAH-loh-may day-lahs-CAH-sahs: 1474–1567), a Dominican priest who had been a conquistador and slaveholder in the Caribbean in his youth, turned his back on his former life and devoted himself to protecting the Amerindians under Spanish rule. In his bold exposé entitled *Brief Relation of the Destruction of the Indies* (1522), he began an uncompromising campaign to show the horrendous treatment meted out by his fellow Spanish to the native populations of the New World. So graphic and terrible were his accounts that foreign powers hostile to Spain (notably, England) were able to use the records for centuries to perpetuate the so-called Black Legend of the viciousness of Spanish colonialism.

Glasgow University Library, Scotland/Bridgeman Art Library

PUNISHMENT FOR BACKSLIDERS. This pen-and-ink drawing from the "History of Tlaxcala," by the sixteenth-century artist Diego Munoz Camargo shows the brutal methods that some Spanish priests applied to Native Americans who abandoned Christianity for the religions of their ancestors.

Of the Island of Hispaniola

The Christians, with their horses and swords and lances, began to slaughter and practice strange cruelties among them. They penetrated into the country and spared neither children nor the aged, nor pregnant women, nor those in childbirth, all of whom they ran through the body and lacerated, as though they were assaulting so many lambs herded into the sheepfold.

They made bets as to who could slit a man in two, or cut off his head at one blow . . . they tore babes from their mothers' breasts by the feet, and dashed their heads against the rocks. Others, they seized by the shoulders and threw into the rivers, laughing and joking, and when they fell into the water they exclaimed, "boil the body of So-and-so! . . ."

They made a gallows just high enough for the feet to nearly touch the ground, and by thirteens, in honour and reverence of our Redeemer and the 12 Apostles, they put wood underneath and, with fire, they burned the Indians alive.

They wrapped the bodies of others entirely in dry straw, binding them in it and setting fire to it; and so they burned them. They cut off the hands of all they wished to take alive, made them carry them pinned on to their bodies, and said "Go and carry these letters," that is, take the news to those who have fled to the mountains. . . .

I once saw that they had four or five of the chief lords [Indians] stretched on a gridiron to burn them, and I think there were also two or three pairs of gridirons, where they were burning others. And because they cried aloud and

annoyed the Captain or prevented him from sleeping, he commanded that they should be strangled; the officer who was burning them was worse than a hangman and did not wish to suffocate them, but with his own hands he gagged them, so that they should not make themselves heard, and he stirred up the fire until they roasted slowly, according to his pleasure. I know this man's name, and knew his relations in Sevilla. I saw all the above things and numberless others.

And because all the [Indian] people who could flee, hid among the mountains and climbed the crags to escape from men so deprived of humanity . . . the Spaniards taught and trained the fiercest boarhounds to tear an Indian to pieces as soon as they saw him. . . . And because sometimes, though rarely, the Indians killed a few Christians for just cause, they made a law among themselves that for one Christian whom the Indians might kill, the Christians should kill a hundred Indians.

▶ Analyze and Interpret

Besides de las Casas, other Spanish priests tried to protect the Amerindians against cruelty, but usually in vain. What measures might have been taken by the clergy to diminish such cruelty? Was it logical to expect the priests or bishops to intervene effectively? What does the colonial record show?

Source: Bartolomé de las Casas, *A Very Brief Account of the Destruction of the Indies*, trans. F. A. McNutt (Cleveland: Clark, 1909), pp. 312–319.

SUMMARY

THE EXPLOSIVE WIDENING of Europe's horizons in the sixteenth century, in both the geographic sense and the psychological sense, was one side of the Columbian Exchange. First the Portuguese and the Spanish created their colonial empires, then the Dutch, the English, and the French after them. The original objective of the government-funded explorers was to find new, more secure trade routes to the East, but soon their motives changed to a mixture of enrichment, missionary activity, and prestige: gold, God, and glory.

The import of great quantities of precious metals created severe inflation and promoted the rise of the business/commercial classes. The discovery of customs and values that were different from those of Europeans gradually induced Europeans to adopt new attitudes of tolerance. The overseas expansion also added important new foods to the European diet.

For the non-Western hosts, this colonial and commercial outreach had mainly negative consequences, although circumstances varied from place to place. The most devastating effects were certainly in Spain's American colonies, where the indigenous peoples were almost wiped out by disease and oppression. In West Africa, East Africa, and the Asian mainland, the European trading presence had little overall effect on ordinary life at this time. Racism's beginnings, however, can be traced to its roots in the African slave trade commencing in this era.

▶ Identification Terms

Test your knowledge of this chapter's key concepts by defining the following terms. If you can't recall the meaning of certain terms, refresh your memory by looking up the boldfaced term in the chapter, turning to the Glossary at the end of the book, or working with the flashcards that are available on the *World Civilizations* Companion Website: **academic.cengage.com/adler**

Bartolomé de las Casas
Columbian Exchange

Dutch East India
Company

Ferdinand Magellan
mercantilism

Prince Henry the Navigator
Vasco da Gama

▶ Test Your Knowledge

Test your knowledge of this chapter by answering the following questions. Complete answers appear at the end of the book. You may find even more quiz questions in CengageNOW and on the *World Civilizations* Companion Website: **academic.cengage.com/adler**

1. The fifteenth- and sixteenth-century voyages of exploration were stimulated mainly by
   a. European curiosity about other peoples.
   b. the determination to obtain more farming land for a growing population.
   c. the individual explorers' hopes of enrichment.
   d. the discovery that the Earth was in fact a sphere without "ends."
   e. new technology.
2. Which of the following was *not* proved by Magellan's epic voyage?
   a. The globe was more compact than had been believed.
   b. The globe was indeed spherical.
   c. A sea passage existed south of the tip of South America.
   d. The islands called "Spice Lands" could be reached from the East.
   e. The journey was a long and difficult one.

3. Which of the following nations was most persistently committed to converting the natives of the newly discovered regions to Christianity?
   a. Spain
   b. Holland
   c. England
   d. Portugal
   e. France
4. What is the correct sequence of explorer-traders in the Far East?
   a. Spanish, English, French
   b. Spanish, Portuguese, Dutch
   c. Dutch, English, Spanish
   d. Portuguese, Dutch, English
   e. Spanish, Portuguese, English
5. The first to engage in the slave trade were the
   a. Dutch.
   b. Portuguese.
   c. Danes.
   d. English.
   e. Spanish.
6. Which of the following reasons was least likely to be the motive for a Dutch captain's voyage of discovery?
   a. A desire to deal the Roman church a blow

b. A search for personal enrichment
c. A quest to find another lifestyle for himself in a foreign land
d. The intention of establishing trade relations with a new partner
e. The desire to serve as a middleman between East Asia and Europe

7. Mercantilism aimed first of all at
   a. securing financial rewards for the entrepreneurs.
   b. allowing the impoverished a chance at rising in society.
   c. bringing maximum income to the royal throne.
   d. securing a favorable balance of foreign trade.
   e. developing a wide range of products for export.

8. Which proved to be the most important of the various new foods introduced into European diets by the voyages of discovery?
   a. Tomatoes
   b. Rice
   c. Potatoes
   d. Coffee
   e. Wheat

9. The sixteenth-century inflation affected which group most negatively?
   a. Landholding nobles
   b. Urban merchants
   c. Wage laborers
   d. Skilled white-collar workers
   e. Church officials

10. The most devastating effects on the native population brought about by European discovery occurred in
    a. India.
    b. Latin America.
    c. West Africa.
    d. Southeast Asia.
    e. North America.

Enter *CengageNOW* using the access card that is available with this text. *CengageNOW* will assist you in understanding the content in this chapter with lesson plans generated for your needs and provide you with a connection to the *Wadsworth World History Resource Center* (see description at right for details).

 World History Resource Center

Enter the Resource Center using either your *CengageNOW* access card or your standalone access card for the *Wadsworth World History Resource Center*. Organized by topic, this website includes quizzes; images; over 350 primary source documents; interactive simulations, maps, and timelines; movie explorations; and a wealth of other resources. You can read the following documents, and many more, at the *Wadsworth World History Resource Center*:

Prince Henry the Navigator, *Chronicle of the Discovery and Conquest of Guinea*
Selections from Christopher Columbus's Journal

> I have often been resolved to live uprightly, and to lead a true godly life, and to set everything aside that would hinder this, but it was far from being put in execution. I am not able to effect that good which I intend.
> —Martin Luther

23 THE PROTESTANT REFORMATION

LUTHER AND THE GERMAN NATIONAL CHURCH
Luther's Beliefs

CALVIN AND INTERNATIONAL PROTESTANTISM
Calvinism and Lutheranism Compared

OTHER EARLY PROTESTANT FAITHS
The Church of England

THE COUNTER-REFORMATION

RELIGIOUS WARS AND THEIR OUTCOMES TO 1600
France ◆ The Spanish Netherlands

THE LEGACY OF THE REFORMATION

THE SPLIT IN CHRISTIAN BELIEF and church organization that is termed the *Protestant Reformation* brought enormous consequences in its wake. Its beginning coincided with the high point of the Era of Discovery by Europeans. Taken together, these developments provide the basis for dividing Western civilization's history into the pre-modern and modern eras around 1500.

What the opening of the transatlantic and trans–Indian Ocean worlds did for the consciousness of physical geography in European minds, the Reformation did for the mental geography of all Christians. New continents of belief and identity emerged from the spiritual voyages of the early Protestants. Luther and Calvin worked not only a re-formation but also a trans-formation of the church and its members.

LUTHER AND THE GERMAN NATIONAL CHURCH

The upheaval called the **Reformation** of the early sixteenth century had its roots in political and social developments as much as in religious disputes. The longstanding arguments within the Christian community over various points of doctrine or practices had already led to rebellions against the Rome-led majority on several occasions. In the major instances in thirteenth-century France, fourteenth-century England, and fifteenth-century Bohemia, religious rebels (the official term is *heretics*, or "wrong thinkers") had battled the papal church. Eventually, all of them had been suppressed or driven underground. But now, in sixteenth-century Germany, **Martin Luther** (1483–1546) found an enthusiastic reception for his challenges to Rome among the majority of his fellow Germans.

Why was the church in the German lands particularly susceptible to the call for reform? The disintegration of the German medieval kingdom had been followed by the birth of dozens of separate, little principalities and city-states, such as Hamburg and Frankfurt, that could not well resist the encroachments of the powerful papacy in their internal affairs. Unlike the nations of centrally governed France, England, and Spain, whose monarchs jealously guarded their sources of revenue, the German populations were systematically milked by Rome and forced to pay taxes and involuntary donations. Many of the German rulers were angry at seeing the tax funds they needed going off to a foreign power and sometimes used for goals they did not support. These rulers were eagerly searching for some popular basis to challenge Rome. They found it in the teachings of Luther.

Luther was a monk who had briefly witnessed at first hand the corruption and crass commercialism of the sixteenth-century Roman *curia* (court). When he returned to the University of Wittenberg in Saxony, where he had been appointed chaplain, he used his powerful oratory to arouse the community against the abuses he had seen. He especially opposed the church's practice of selling *indulgences*—forgiveness of the spiritual guilt created by sins—rather than insisting that the faithful earn forgiveness by prayer and good works.

In 1517, a major indulgence sales campaign opened in Germany under even more scandalous pretexts than usual. Much of the money raised was destined to be used to pay off a debt incurred by an ambitious noble churchman, rather than for any ecclesiastical purpose. Observing what was happening, the chaplain at Wittenberg decided to take his stand. On October 31, 1517, Luther announced his discontent by posting the famous *Ninety-five Theses* on his church door. In these questions, Luther raised objections not only to many of the papacy's practices, such as indulgence campaigns, but also to the whole doctrine of papal supremacy. He contended that if the papacy had ever been intended by God to be the moral mentor of the Christian community, it had lost that claim through its present corruption.

Luther's Beliefs

Luther had more profound doubts about the righteousness of the papal church than merely its claims to universal leadership, however. His youth had been a long struggle against the conviction that he was damned to hell. Intensive study of the Bible eventually convinced him that only through the freely given grace of a merciful God might he, or any person, reach immortal salvation.

 **MARTIN LUTHER.** This contemporary portrait by Lucas V. Cranach is generally considered to be an accurate rendition of the great German church reformer in midlife. Both the strengths and weaknesses of Luther's peasant character are revealed.

Galleria degli Uffizi, Florence, Italy/Bridgeman Art Library

The Catholic Church, on the other hand, taught that men and women must manifest their Christian faith by doing good works and leading good lives. If they did so, they might be considered to have earned a heavenly future. Martin Luther rejected this notion. He believed that faith alone was the factor through which Christians might reach bliss in the afterlife and that faith was given by God and not in any way earned by naturally sinful man. It is this doctrine of **justification by faith** that most clearly marks off Lutheranism from the papal teachings.

As the meaning of Luther's statements penetrated into the clerical hierarchy, he was implored, then commanded, to cease. Instead, his confidence rose, and in a series of brilliantly forceful pamphlets written in the German vernacular, he explained his views to a rapidly increasing audience. By 1520, he was becoming a household word among educated people and even among the peasantry. He was excommunicated in 1521 by the pope for refusing to recant, and in the same year, Emperor Charles V declared him an outlaw.

The Catholic emperor was an ally of the pope, but the emperor had his hands full with myriad other problems, notably the assault of the Ottoman Turks. Charles had no desire to add an unnecessary civil war to the long list of tasks he faced. He took action against Luther only belatedly and halfheartedly, hoping that in some way an acceptable compromise might be reached.

Threatened by the imperial and papal officials, Luther sought and quickly found the protection of the ruler of Saxony, as well as much of the German princely class. They saw in his moral objections to Rome the excuse they had been seeking for advancing their political aspirations. They encouraged Luther to organize a national church free from papal overlords. With this protection and encouragement, Luther's teachings spread rapidly, aided by the newly invented printing press and by the power and conviction of his sermons and writings. By the mid-1520s, Lutheran congregations, rejecting the papal authority and condemning Rome as the fount of all evil, had sprung up throughout most of Germany and were appearing in Scandinavia as well. The unity of Western Christianity had been shattered.

CALVIN AND INTERNATIONAL PROTESTANTISM

It was not Luther, the German peasant's son, but **John Calvin** (1509–1564), the French lawyer, who made the Protestant movement an international theological rebellion against Rome. Luther always saw himself as a specifically German patriot, as well as a pious Christian, and his translations of the Scriptures were written in a powerful idiomatic German. (Luther's role in creating the modern German language is roughly the same as the role Shakespeare played in the development of English.) Calvin, on the contrary, detached himself from national feeling and saw himself as the emissary and servant of a God who ruled all nations. Luther wanted the German Christian body to be cleansed of papal corruption; Calvin wanted the entire Christian community to be made over into the image of what he thought God intended. When he was done, a good part of it had been.

Calvin was born into a middle-class family of church officeholders who educated him for a career in the law. When he was twenty-five, he became a Protestant, inspired by some Swiss sympathizers with Luther. For most of the rest of his life, Calvin was the leading figure in Geneva,

JOHN CALVIN. This Swiss portrait of the "pope of Geneva" in his younger days depicts Calvin in a fur neckpiece. This bit of bourgeois indulgence would probably not have been worn by an older Calvin.

IOANNES. CALVINVS.

Collection of Albert Rilliet, Geneva, Switzerland/Lauros-Giraudon/Bridgeman Art Library

laying down the law to that city's residents and having a major influence on much of the rest of Europe's religious development.

Calvin believed that the papal church was hopelessly distorted. It must be obliterated, and new forms and practices (which were supposedly a return to the practices of early Christianity) must be introduced. In *The Institutes of the Christian Religion* (1536), Calvin set out his beliefs and doctrines with the precision and clarity of a lawyer. From this work came much of the intellectual content of Protestantism for the next 200 years.

Calvin's single most dramatic change from both Rome and Luther was his insistence that God predestined souls. That is, a soul was meant either for heaven or hell for all eternity, but at the same time, the individual retained free will to choose good or evil. The soul destined for hell would inevitably choose evil—but did not have to! It was a harsh theology. Calvin believed that humanity had been eternally stained by Adam's sin and that most souls were destined for hellfire.

Despite its doctrinal fierceness, Calvin's message found a response throughout Europe. By the 1540s, Calvinists were appearing in Germany, the Netherlands, Scotland, England, and France, as well as Switzerland. Geneva had become the Protestant Rome, with Calvin serving as its priestly ruler until his death in 1564.

Calvinism and Lutheranism Compared

What were some of the similarities and differences between the beliefs of Luther and Calvin (who never met and had little affection for one another)? First, Luther believed that faith alone, which could not be earned, was the only prerequisite for salvation. Good works were encouraged, but they had little or no influence on the Last Judgment. Calvin demanded works as well as faith to indicate that a person was attempting to follow God's order on Earth.

Later, Calvinists saw their performance of good works as a sign that they were among **the Elect**, the souls predestined for heaven. The emphasis in some places and times shifted subtly from doing good works as a sign of serving God to believing that God would logically favor the members of the Elect. Therefore, those who were "doing well" in the earthly sense were probably among the Elect. From this concept, some later students of religion saw Calvinist beliefs as the basis for the triumph of the capitalist spirit in certain parts of Europe. In effect, a God worthy of man's love and worship could rationally be expected to smile on those who did his bidding in this life as well as the next.

Second, Luther saw the clergy as civic as well as spiritual guides for mankind. He believed in a definite hierarchy of authority within the church, and he retained bishops, who maintained their crucially important power to appoint priests. The bishops themselves had to pass inspection by the civil authorities, a subordination that was to prove fateful for the German Church. In time, the Lutheran pastors and bishops became fully dependent on the state that employed them, rarely defying it on moral grounds. Lutheranism became a state church, not only in Germany but also in Scandinavia, where it had become dominant by the mid-1500s. In contrast, Calvin insisted on the moral independence of the church from the state. He maintained that the clergy as well as laity had a duty to oppose any immoral acts of government, no matter what the cost to themselves. In conflicts between the will of God and the will of kings, the Calvinist must enlist on the side of God.

More than Lutherans, the Calvinists thought of the entire community, lay and clerical alike, as equal members of the church on Earth. Calvinists also insisted on the power of the congregation to select and discharge pastors at will, inspired by God's word. They never established a hierarchy of clerics. There were no Calvinist bishops but only presbyters, or elected elders, who spoke for their fellow parishioners in regional or national assemblies. The government of the church thus included both clerical and lay leaders. The combination gave the church's pronouncements great political as well as moral force.

By around 1570, Calvin's followers had gained control of the Christian community in several places: the Dutch-speaking Netherlands, Scotland, western France, and parts of northern Germany and Poland. In the rest of France, Austria, Hungary, and England, they were still a minority, but a growing one. Whereas Lutheranism was confined to the German-speaking countries and Scandinavia and

THE CALVINIST CHURCH. This painting is by a Dutch sixteenth-century master, Hendrik van Steenwyck, who portrays the "purified" interior of the Antwerp cathedral after it was taken over by Calvinists.

Private Collection/Bridgeman Art Library

did not spread much after 1550 or so, Calvinism was an international faith that appealed to all nations and identified with none. Carried on the ships of the Dutch and English explorers and emigrants of the seventeenth and eighteenth centuries, it continued to spread throughout the modern world.

OTHER EARLY PROTESTANT FAITHS

The followers of a radical sect called **Anabaptists** (Rebaptizers) were briefly a threat to both Catholics and Lutherans, but both put them down with extreme cruelty. The Anabaptists originated in Switzerland and spread rapidly throughout German Europe. They believed in adult baptism, a priesthood of all believers, and—most disturbingly—a primitive communism and sharing of worldly possessions. Both as radicals in religious affairs and as social revolutionaries, the Anabaptists were oppressed by all of their neighbors. After their efforts to establish a republic in the Rhineland city of Münster were bloodily suppressed, the Anabaptists were driven underground. Their beliefs continued to evolve, and they emerged much later in the New World as Mennonites, Amish, and similar groups.

Yet another Protestant creed emerged early in Switzerland (which was a hotbed of religious protest). Founded by **Ulrich Zwingli** (1484–1531), it was generally similar to Lutheran belief, although Zwingli claimed he had arrived at his doctrine independently. The inability of Zwingli's adherents and the Lutherans to cooperate left Zwingli's stronghold in Zurich open to attack by the Catholic Swiss. The Protestants were defeated in the battle, and Zwingli was killed. This use of bloody force to settle religious strife was an ominous note. It was to become increasingly common as Protestant beliefs spread and undermined the traditional religious structures.

The Church of England

As was often the case, England went its own way. The English Reformation differed from the Reformation on the Continent yet followed the general trend of European affairs. The English reformers were originally inspired by Lutheran ideas, but they adopted more Calvinist views as time went on. However, the Church of England, or Anglican Confession, came to be neither Lutheran nor Calvinist nor Catholic, but a hybrid of all three.

The reform movement in England had its origins in the widespread popular resentment against Rome and the higher clergy, who were viewed as more the tools of the pope than as good English patriots. As we have seen, already in the 1300s a group called the *Lollards* had rebelled against

A PROTESTANT VIEW OF THE POPE. Clothed in hellish splendor and hung about with the horrible symbols of Satan, the Roman pope is revealed for all to see in this sixteenth-century cartoon.

Ego fum Papa.

©Stock Montage, Inc.

the clerical claim to sole authority in interpreting the word of God and papal supremacy. The movement had been put down, but its memory persisted in many parts of England.

But it was the peculiar marital problems of **King Henry VIII** (1490–1547) that finally brought the church in England into conflict with Rome. Henry needed a male successor, but by the late 1520s, his chances of having one with his elderly Spanish wife Catherine were bleak. Therefore, he wanted to have the marriage annulled by the pope (who alone had that power), so he could marry some young Englishwoman who would presumably be able to produce the desired heir.

After trying to evade the issue for years, the pope refused the annulment because he did not wish to impair the close alliance of the Catholic Church with the Spanish monarchy. Between 1532 and 1534, Henry took the matter

into his own hands. Still believing himself to be a good Catholic, he intimidated Parliament into declaring him the "only supreme head of the church in England"—the **Act of Supremacy of 1534**. Now, as head of the church, Henry could dictate to the English bishops. He proceeded to put away his unwanted wife and marry the tragic Anne Boleyn, who was already pregnant with his child.

Much other legislation followed that asserted that the monarch, and not the Roman pope, was the determiner of what the church could and could not do in England. Those who resisted, such as the king's chancellor Thomas More, paid with their heads or were imprisoned. Henry went on to marry and divorce several more times before his death in 1547, but he did at least secure a son, the future King Edward VI, from one of these unhappy alliances. Two daughters also survived, the half-sisters Mary and Elizabeth.

Henry's Successors. Henry's actions changed English religious beliefs very little, although the Calvinist reformation was gaining ground in both England and Scotland. But under the sickly boy-king Edward (ruled 1547–1553), Protestant views became dominant among the English governing group, and the powerful oratory of John Knox led the Scots into Calvinism (the Presbyterian Church). At Edward's death, it seemed almost certain that some form of Protestant worship would become the official church under the succeeding ruler.

But popular support for Mary (ruled 1553–1558), the Catholic daughter of Henry VIII's first, Spanish Catholic wife, was too strong to be overridden by the Protestant party at court. Just as they had feared, Mary proved to be a single-minded adherent of the papal church, and she restored Catholicism to its official status during her brief reign. Protestant conspirators were put to death without hesitation (hence, she is called "Bloody Mary" in English Protestant mythology).

Finally, the confused state of English official religion was gradually cleared by the political skills of Mary's half-sister and successor, Elizabeth I (ruled 1558–1603). She ruled for half a century with great success while defying all royal traditions by remaining the Virgin Queen and dying childless (see the Law and Government box). She was able to arrive at a compromise between the Roman and Protestant doctrines, which was accepted by a steadily increasing majority and came to be termed the Church of England. In most respects, it retained the theology and doctrine of the Roman Church, including bishops, rituals, and sacraments, but its head was not the pope but the English monarch, who appointed the bishops and their chief, the archbishop of Canterbury. The strict Calvinists were not happy with this arrangement and wished to "purify" the church by removing all remnants of popery. These **Puritans** presented problems for the English rulers throughout the seventeenth century.

THE COUNTER-REFORMATION

Belatedly realizing what a momentous challenge was being mounted, the papacy finally came to grips with the problem of Protestantism in a positive fashion during the 1540s. Pope Paul III (served 1534–1549) moved to counter some of the excesses that had given the Roman authorities a bad name and set up a high-level commission to see what might be done to "clean up" the clergy. Eventually, the church decided to pursue two major lines of counterattack against the Protestants: a thorough examination of doctrines and practices, such as had not been attempted for more than 1,000 years, combined with an entirely novel emphasis on instruction of the young and education of all Christians in the precepts of their religion. These measures together are known as the **Counter-Reformation**.

The Council of Trent (1545–1563) was the first general attempt to examine the church's basic doctrines and goals since the days of the Roman Empire. Meeting for three lengthy sessions divided by years of preparatory work, the bishops and theologians decided that Protestant attacks could best be met by clearly and conclusively defining what Catholics believed. (Protestants were invited to attend, but only as observers; none did.) As a means of strengthening religious practice, this was a positive move, for the legitimacy and accuracy of many church doctrines had come increasingly into doubt since the 1300s. But the council's work had an unintended negative effect on the desired reunification of Christianity: the doctrinal lines separating Catholic and Protestant were now firmly drawn, and they could not be ignored or blurred by the many individuals in both camps who had been trying to arrange a compromise. Now one side or the other would have to give in on specific issues, a prospect neither side was prepared for.

The founding of the **Jesuit Order** was the most striking example of the second aspect of the Counter-Reformation. In 1540, Pope Paul III accorded to the Spanish nobleman **Ignatius of Loyola** (1491–1556) the right to organize an entirely new religious group, which he termed the Society of Jesus, or Jesuits. Their mission was to win, or win back, the minds and hearts of humanity for the Catholic Church through patient, careful instruction that would bring the word of God and of his deputy on Earth, the pope, to everyone. While the Jesuits were working to ensure that all Catholics learned correct doctrine, the *Index* of forbidden books was created and the Inquisition was revived to ensure that no Catholic deviated from that doctrine (Chapter 18). These institutions greatly expanded the church's powers to censor the writings and supervise the beliefs of its adherents. Both became steadily more important in Catholic countries during the next century, as what both sides regarded as a contest between ultimate Truth and abhorrent falsity intensified.

LAW AND GOVERNMENT

Elizabeth I of England (1533–1603)

In the late sixteenth century, England became for the first time a power to be reckoned with in world affairs. What had been an island kingdom with little direct influence on any other country except its immediate neighbors across the Channel gradually reached equality with the other major Western military and naval powers: France and Spain. But England's achievement was not just in military affairs. It also experienced a magnificent flowering of the arts and a solid advance in the economy, which finally lifted the nation out of the long depression that had followed the fourteenth-century plague and the long, losing war with France.

The guiding spirit for this comeback was Elizabeth I, queen of England from 1558 until her death in 1603. The daughter of Henry VIII and his second wife, the ill-fated Anne Boleyn, Elizabeth emerged from a heavily shadowed girlhood to become one of the most beloved of British lawgivers. Elizabeth was an intelligent, well-educated woman with gifts in several domains. One of her most remarkable achievements was that she managed to retain her powers without a husband, son, or father in the still very male-oriented world in which she moved.

Born in 1533, she was only three years old when her mother was executed. She was declared illegitimate by order of the disappointed Henry, who had wished for a son. But after her father's death, Parliament established her as third in line to the throne, behind her half-brother Edward and her Catholic half-sister Mary. During Mary's reign (1553–1558), Elizabeth was imprisoned for a time, but she was careful to stay clear of the hectic Protestant-Catholic struggles of the day. By so doing, she managed to stay alive until she could become ruler in her own right.

Her rule began amid many internal dangers. The Catholic party in England opposed her as a suspected Protestant. The Calvinists opposed her as being too much like her father Henry, who never accepted Protestant theology. The Scots were becoming rabid Calvinists who despised the English halfway measures in religious affairs. On top of this, the government was deeply in debt.

Elizabeth showed great insight in selecting her officials and maintained good relations with Parliament. She conducted diplomatic affairs with farsightedness and found she could use her status as an unmarried queen to definite advantage.

Philip of Spain, widower of her half-sister Mary, made several proposals of marriage and political unity that Elizabeth cleverly held off without ever quite saying no. She kept England out of the religious wars that were raging in various parts of Europe for most of her reign, but in one of these wars, against her ex-suitor Philip, the Virgin Queen led her people most memorably.

In 1588, after long negotiations failed, Philip sent the Spanish Armada to punish England for aiding the rebellious Dutch Calvinists across the Channel. The queen rallied her sailors in a stirring visit before the battle. The resulting defeat of the Armada not only signaled England's rise to naval equality with Spain but also made Elizabeth the most popular monarch England had ever seen.

A golden age of English literature coincided with Elizabeth's rule, thanks in some part to her active support of all the arts. Her well-known vanity induced her to spend large sums to ensure the splendor of her court despite her equally well-known miserliness. The Elizabethan Age produced Shakespeare, Marlowe, Spenser, and Bacon. By the end of the sixteenth century, English literature for the first time could hold a place of honor in any assembly of national arts.

Elizabeth's version of Protestant belief—the Church of England—proved acceptable to most of her subjects and finally settled the stormy waves of sixteenth-century English church affairs. By the end of her long reign, "Good Queen Bess" had become a stock phrase that most people believed, from barons to peasants.

ELIZABETH I OF ENGLAND. The Armada Portrait, perhaps the most famous, was painted by an anonymous artist in the late sixteenth century. Elizabeth was vain, despite being no beauty, and was always receptive to flattery, without in the least being influenced by it in matters of state.

Private Collection/Bridgeman Art Library

▶ Analyze and Interpret

Given that an unmarried queen was considered a political risk, what reasons of state could have impelled Elizabeth to remain "the Virgin Queen"? What political capital did she make out of creating the hybrid Church of England that otherwise would have been denied her?

RELIGIOUS WARS AND THEIR OUTCOMES TO 1600

The Counter-Reformation stiffened the Catholics' will to resist the Lutheran and Calvinist attacks, which had, at first, almost overwhelmed the unprepared and inflexible Roman authorities. By 1555, the **Peace of Augsburg** had concluded a ten-year civil war by dividing Germany into Catholic and Lutheran parcels, but it made no allowances for the growing number of Calvinists or other Protestants.

In the rest of Europe, the picture was mixed by the late 1500s (see Map 23.1). As we have just seen, England went through several changes of religious leadership, but it eventually emerged with a special sort of Protestant belief as its official religion. Scandinavia became Lutheran in its entirety, almost without violence. Austria, Hungary, and Poland remained mostly Catholic, but with large minorities of Calvinists and Lutherans, who received a degree of tolerance from the authorities. Spain and Italy had successfully repelled the Protestant challenge, and

the counter-reform was in full swing. Russia and southeastern Europe were almost unaffected by Protestantism, being either hostile to both varieties of Western Christianity (Russia) or under the political control of Muslims. In two countries, however, the issue of religious affiliation was in hot dispute and caused much bloodshed in the later 1500s.

France

France remained Catholic at the level of the throne but developed a large, important Calvinist minority, especially among the nobility and the urbanites. For a brief time the Catholic monarchs and the Calvinists attempted to live with one another, but religious wars began in the 1570s that threatened to wreck the country. The Evidence of the Past box on the St. Bartholomew's Day Massacre gives an eyewitness view of the violence.

After some years, the Calvinists found a politician of genius, Henry of Navarre, who profited from the assassination

MAP 23.1 Catholics, Protestants, and Orthodox Christians in Europe by 1550

The radical sects included Unitarians in eastern Europe, Anabaptists in Bohemia and Germany, and Waldensians in France. All of these rejected the idea of a privileged clergy and a priestly hierarchy, and all were vigorously persecuted by the authorities. Find the Ottoman Empire on the map.

MAP QUESTIONS

What was the official religion in this part of Europe? According to the map, what other faith was important in the part shown? Why do you suppose this was true?

 View an interactive version of this or a related map at http://worldrc. wadsworth.com/

of his Catholic rival to become King Henry IV of France. In 1593, he agreed to accept Catholicism to win the support of most French ("Paris is worth a mass," he is reported to have said). He became the most popular king in French history. His Protestant upbringing inspired the Calvinist minority to trust him, and he did not disappoint them.

In 1598, Henry made the first significant European attempt at religious toleration as state policy by issuing the **Edict of Nantes**. It gave the million or so French Calvinists—the Huguenots—freedom to worship without harassment in certain areas, to hold office, and to fortify their towns. This last provision demonstrates that the edict was more in the nature of a truce than a peace. It held, however, for the better part of a century. During that time, France rose to become the premier power in Europe.

The Spanish Netherlands

The Spanish Netherlands (modern Holland and Belgium) were ruled from Madrid by King Philip II, the most potent monarch of the second half of the sixteenth century. He had inherited an empire that included Spain, much of Italy, and the Low Countries in Europe, plus the enormous Spanish overseas empire begun by the voyages of Columbus.

But Philip was a man with a mission, or rather two missions: the reestablishment of Catholicism among the Protestant "heretics" and the defeat of the Muslim Turks in the Mediterranean and the Near East. These missions imposed heavy demands on Spanish resources, which even the flow of gold and silver out of the American colonies could not fully cover. Generally successful in his wars against the Ottomans, Philip could not handle a combined political-religious revolt in Spain's recently acquired province of the Netherlands that broke out in the 1560s. The Netherlands were a hotbed of both Lutheran and Calvinist doctrines, and the self-confident members of the large middle class were much disturbed at the Spanish aliens' attempt to enforce on them the Counter-Reformation and papal supremacy.

Thanks to Spanish overextension, the revolt of the Netherlanders succeeded in holding Philip's feared professional army at bay. The wars were fought with ferocity on both sides. While Philip saw himself as the agent of legitimacy and the Counter-Reformation, the English Protestants aided the Dutch rebels militarily and financially across the Channel. The English support was partly based on religious affinity, but even more on the traditional English dislike of a great power's control of England's closest trading partners.

In the mid-1580s, the friction came to a head. Philip (who had earlier tried to convince Elizabeth I to become his wife) became incensed at the execution of the Catholic Mary, Queen of Scots, by order of Elizabeth, who had imprisoned this possible competitor for England's throne. With the reluctant support of the pope, Philip prepared the vast Armada of 1588 to invade England and re-conquer that country for the "True Church."

The devastating defeat of the Armada—as much by a storm as by English ships—gave a great boost to the Protestant cause everywhere: It relieved the pressure on the Huguenots to accept Catholic over-lordship in France; it saved the Dutch Calvinists until they could gain full independence some decades later; and the defeat of the Armada marks the emergence of England as a major power, both in Europe and overseas.

Spain remained the premier military power long after the Armada disaster, but the country in a sense never recovered from this event. Other fleets were built, bullion from Mexican and Peruvian mines continued to pour into Madrid's treasury, and the Spanish infantry was still the best trained and equipped of all the European armies, but the other powers were able to keep Spain in check from now on, until its inherent economic weaknesses reduced it to a second-line nation by the end of the seventeenth century.

THE LEGACY OF THE REFORMATION

The Protestant movement made a deep impression on the general course of history in Europe for centuries. It is one of the chief reasons European history is conventionally divided into "modern" versus "medieval" around 1500. The religious unity of all western Europe under the Roman pope was irrevocably shattered, and with the end of such unity inevitably came political and cultural conflicts. For a century and a half after Luther's defiance of the papal command to be silent, much of Europe was engaged in internal acrimony that wracked the continent from the Netherlands to Hungary. In some countries, such as Italy, Spain, Sweden, and Scotland, one or the other faith was dominant and proceeded to harass and exile those who thought differently. In others, such as Austria, Germany, France, and the Netherlands, the question of religious supremacy was bitterly contested. Separation of church and state was not even dreamed of, nor was freedom of conscience. Even educated people did not seriously take up these strictly modern ideas until the eighteenth century.

In the Protestant societies, the abolition of the monasteries and convents and the emphasis on vernacular preaching helped integrate the clergy and the laity and thus blurred one of the chief class divisions that had been accepted in Europe since the opening of the Middle Age. Combined with the important roles of the middle-class Protestants in spreading and securing reform, this development provided new opportunities for the ambitious and hardworking to rise up the social ladder.

Some of the other long-term cultural changes that resulted from the Reformation included the following:

EVIDENCE OF THE PAST

The St. Bartholomew's Day Massacre

During the sixteenth-century religious wars in Europe, no battle-field was contested more ferociously by both sides than France. Not only did France contain Europe's largest population, but it lay between the Protestant North and the Catholic South. Although the bulk of the peasantry and the royal family remained Catholic, an influential and determined minority of nobles and bourgeoisie became Calvinists, or "Huguenots."

By 1572, because of the political astuteness of their leader, Gaspard de Coligny, the Huguenots were close to a takeover of the French government. However, the queen mother, Catherine de Medici, and the Catholic warlord Henry, duke de Guise, turned the weak-minded King Charles IX against Coligny. The result was a conspiracy that began with Coligny's assassination on August 24, 1572 (St. Bartholomew's Day), and quickly degenerated into a wholesale massacre of the entire Protestant population of Paris: men, women, and children. The death toll is estimated to have approached 10,000, and the streets and alleys reeked of the stench of decaying corpses for weeks afterward.

According to an anonymous Protestant eyewitness who was among the fortunate few to escape the carnage, vicious cruelties were committed without number, setting the scene for what would become twenty years of intermittent civil war in France:

> In an instant, the whole city was filled with dead bodies of every sex and age, and indeed amid such confusion and disorder that everyone was allowed to kill whoever he pleased, whether or not that person belonged to the [Protestant] religion, provided that he had something to be taken, or was an enemy. So it came about that many Papists themselves were slain, even several priests....
>
> No one can count the many cruelties that accompanied these murders.... Most of them were run through with daggers or poniards; their bodies were stabbed, their members mutilated, they were mocked and insulted with gibes sharper than pointed swords ... they knocked several old people senseless, banging their heads against the stones of the quay and then throwing them half dead into the water [the Seine River]. A little child in swaddling clothes was dragged through the streets with a belt round his neck by boys nine or ten years old. Another small child, carried by one of the butchers, played with the man's beard and smiled up at him, but instead of being moved to compassion, the barbarous fiend ran him through with his dagger, then threw him into the water so red with blood that it did not return to its original color for a long time.

▶ Analyze and Interpret

What event in your memory seems most similar to the St. Bartholomew's Day Massacre? What are the dissimiliarities?

Source: Excerpted from Julian Coudy, *The Huguenot Wars*, trans. Julie Kernon (Radnor, PA: Chilton, 1969).

You can read another eyewitness account of the St. Bartholomew's Day Massacre at the *Wadsworth World History Resource Center.*

---

1. *Higher literacy and start of mass education.* In much of Protestant Europe in particular, the exhortation to learn and obey Scripture provided an incentive to read that the common folk had never had before. The rapid spread of printing after 1520 was largely a result of Protestant tracts and the impact they were seen to have on their large audiences.

2. *Emphasis on individual moral responsibility.* Rejecting the Catholic assurance that the clergy knew best what was necessary and proper in the conduct of life, the Protestants underlined the responsibility of individual believers to determine through divine guidance and reading Scripture what they must do to attain salvation.

3. *Closer identification of the clergy with the people they served.* Both the Catholic and Protestant churches came to recognize that the church existed as much for the masses of faithful as it did for the clergy—a realization that was often absent previously—and that the belief of the faithful was the essence of the church on Earth.

4. *Increase in conflicts and intolerance.* Much of Europe fell into civil wars that were initially set off by religious disputes. These wars were often bloody and produced much needless destruction by both sides in the name of theological truth. Religious affiliation greatly exacerbated dynastic and the emergent national conflicts.

The Catholic-Protestant clashes led to intellectual arrogance and self-righteousness not only in religion but in general among those who wielded power. Open debate and discussion of contested matters became almost impossible between the two parts of Western Christianity for a century or more.

SUMMARY

AS MUCH AS the discovery of the New World, the Protestant movement gave birth to the modern era in the West. The protests of Luther, Calvin, and many others against what they saw as the unrighteous and distorted teachings of the Roman papacy had immense long-term reverberations in Western culture. The reformers combined a new emphasis on individual morality with assertions of the ability and duty of Christians to read the Gospels and take into their own hands the search for salvation.

Among Calvinists, the material welfare of the Elect on Earth was linked to their quality of being saved, a link that would gradually produce what later generations called the "Protestant ethic." The Catholic response was the Counter-Reformation, which, spearheaded by the Jesuits, eventually reclaimed much of the Protestant territories for the Roman Church at the cost of an alarming rise in religiously inspired conflict. Exceedingly bloody warfare broke out in the Netherlands and in France and Germany between groups asserting their possession of the only correct theology. Europe entered the Modern Age in a flurry of fierce antagonisms among Christians, some of which were to continue for generations and permanently split apart previous communities.

▶ Identification Terms

Test your knowledge of this chapter's key concepts by defining the following terms. If you can't recall the meaning of certain terms, refresh your memory by looking up the boldfaced term in the chapter, turning to the Glossary at the end of the book, or working with the flashcards that are available on the *World Civilizations* Companion Website: **academic.cengage.com/adler**

Act of Supremacy of 1534	Elect, The	justification by faith	Puritans
Anabaptists	Ignatius of Loyola	King Henry VIII	Reformation
John Calvin	*Institutes of the Christian*	Martin Luther	Ulrich Zwingli
Counter-Reformation	*Religion, The*	*Ninety-five Theses*	
Edict of Nantes	Jesuit Order	Peace of Augsburg	

▶ Test Your Knowledge

Test your knowledge of this chapter by answering the following questions. Complete answers appear at the end of the book. You may find even more quiz questions in CengageNOW and on the *World Civilizations* Companion Website: **academic.cengage.com/adler**

1. The posting of the *Ninety-five Theses* was immediately caused by
   a. Luther's outrage over the ignorance of the clergy.
   b. Luther's conviction that he must challenge papal domination.
   c. Luther's anger over the sale of indulgences.
   d. the tyranny of the local Roman Catholic bishop.
   e. Luther's anger that church tithes were being siphoned out of Germany to Rome.

2. Which of the following practices/beliefs is associated with Calvinism?
   a. The basic goodness of humans
   b. Predestination of souls
   c. Religious freedom for all
   d. Indulgences
   e. The rejection of good works as necessary for eternal salvation

3. Which of these men died fighting for his beliefs?
   a. John Calvin
   b. Martin Luther
   c. Ulrich Zwingli
   d. Henry VIII
   e. Henry IV

4. Henry VIII's reform of English religious organization occurred
   a. after study in the Holy Land.
   b. for primarily religious-doctrinal reasons.
   c. for primarily political-dynastic reasons.
   d. at the urging of the pope.
   e. after he experienced a vision from the Archangel Gabriel.

5. The term *Counter-Reformation* applies to
   a. a movement in Germany aimed at extinguishing the Lutherans.
   b. the strong resistance of the Roman clergy to real reforms.
   c. a Europe-wide campaign to win back the Protestants to Rome.
   d. the political and military efforts of the German emperor to crush the Protestants.
   e. the attempt by German princes to suppress Luther's ideas.

6. The Jesuit Order was founded specifically
   a. to train Catholic soldiers for battle.
   b. to oversee the activities of the Inquisition.
   c. to act as the pope's first-line troop in religious wars.
   d. to open a new type of monastery.
   e. to recover through education fallen-away Catholics.

7. The St. Bartholomew's Day bloodshed was
   a. the result of the Catholic fanatics' hatred of Protestants in France.
   b. the revenge of the English Calvinists on the English Catholics.
   c. the upshot of a failed attempt to overturn the Catholic dynasty in Spain.
   d. the slaughter of rebel peasantry in Flanders.
   e. the massacre of French Catholics by Huguenots.

8. The *Edict of Nantes*
   a. expelled all Protestants from Catholic France.
   b. gave Protestants in France a degree of official toleration.
   c. brought civic and legal equality to Protestants in France.
   d. ended the war between Catholic France and Protestant England.
   e. established religious tolerance between Spain and France.

9. Which of the provinces of King Philip of Spain caused him the most problems over religion?
   a. the American colonies
   b. the Netherlands
   c. the Italian provinces
   d. Spain
   e. the Caribbean

10. One of the chief negative effects of the Reformation on Europe was
    a. the lessening of educational opportunity.
    b. the loss of national identities.
    c. the diminished tolerance for variations from official doctrine.
    d. the decreased opportunities for social climbing.
    e. a loss of power for the clergy.

Enter *CengageNOW* using the access card that is available with this text. *CengageNOW* will assist you in understanding the content in this chapter with lesson plans generated for your needs and provide you with a connection to the *Wadsworth World History Resource Center* (see description at right for details).

 World History Resource Center

Enter the Resource Center using either your *CengageNOW* access card or your standalone access card for the *Wadsworth World History Resource Center*. Organized by topic, this website includes quizzes; images; over 350 primary source documents; interactive simulations, maps, and timelines; movie explorations; and a wealth of other resources. You can read the following documents, and many more, at the *Wadsworth World History Resource Center:*

Martin Luther, *Ninety-five Theses*
John Calvin, selections from *The Institutes of the Christian Religion*
King Henry IV, *Edict of Nantes*

He who cannot love another human being is ignorant of life's joy.

—Sa'adi

24 THE RISE AND FALL OF THE MUSLIM EMPIRES

THE OTTOMAN EMPIRE

Ottoman Government ◆ Non-Muslims under Ottoman Rule ◆ The Zenith of the Ottoman Empire: Suleiman and After

THE MUSLIM EMPIRES IN PERSIA AND INDIA

The Safavid Realm ◆ The Mughal Empire

AT THE TIME WHEN Europe slowly began finding its way out of centuries of feudal disintegration to early statehood and East Asian governments experienced challenges from both external and internal rivals, Islamic empires in Asia and Africa experienced seemingly endless upheavals. The Islamic world did not have a middle age of governmental evolution and consolidation. Instead, destructive wars that set Muslims against Muslims wracked the world of Islam and contributed much to its slow decline after 1600.

In Chapters 13, 14, and in parts of 15, we looked at how Islam expanded rapidly in the tropical zone between Spain and India. Within remarkably few decades, Arab Bedouin armies carried the message of Muhammad the Prophet from Mecca in all directions on the blades of their conquering swords. The civilization that sprang from this message and conquest was a mixture of Arab, Greek, Persian, Egyptian, Spanish, African, and Southeast Asian—the most cosmopolitan civilization in world history.

In the thirteenth century, the capital city of the Abbasid caliphs remained at Baghdad, but by then the Islamic world had become severely fractured into dozens of competing, quarreling states and sects. More devastating still, in that century the Mongols swept into the Islamic heartland in central and western Asia, destroying every sign of settled life in their path and establishing brief rule over half the world (see Chapter 19). After their disappearance, the Ottoman Turks gave Islam a new forward thrust. By the 1500s, the Ottomans had succeeded in capturing Constantinople and reigned over enormous territories reaching from Gibraltar to Iraq. Farther east and somewhat later, the Safavids in Persia and the Mughals in India established Muslim dynasties that endured into the early modern age.

THE OTTOMAN EMPIRE

The Mongols had smashed the Persian center of Islam in the 1250s, conquered Baghdad in 1258, and left the caliph as one of the corpses of those who had dared oppose them. At this time, the all-conquering intruders intended to wipe out the rest of the Islamic states that reached as far as Spain. One of these was the Ottoman principality in what is now Turkey, which took full advantage of the Mongols' defeat at Ain Jalut to maintain its independence.

The arrival of the Ottoman Dynasty in Asia Minor and their subsequent rise to the status of most powerful state in the Islamic world was the partial consequence of two developments that had preceded them. The first of these was the Turkification of the caliphate that had begun as early as the ninth century CE. The nomadic Turkish tribes began migrating from their homelands in the steppes of Central Asia early in that century, and soon large numbers of them inhabited the eastern lands of the Abbasid caliphate. Faced with increasing challenges to their authority from Kharijites (KAH-ri-jites) and Shi'ites (SHEE-ites), the Abbasid caliphs were forced to rely on the skills of these fearsome fighters to help quell revolts. Soon, Turkish troops under Turkish commanders were largely staffing the armies of the caliphate, but the real power resided in Baghdad under the Seljuk sultans (see Chapter14). Once in power in Baghdad, the Seljuks resumed the Muslim offensive against the rejuvenated Byzantine Empire in the eleventh century. In 1071, a crucial Seljuk victory over the Byzantines at the Battle of Manzikert gave the Turks direct access to Asia Minor for the first time. They established the Rum Sultanate in eastern Asia Minor and continued their *jihad* against the Christian enemies to the west.

The second important development was the growing importance of the **dervish**, or Sufi (SOO-fee), orders in Islam. As explained in Chapter 14, many Muslims embraced mystical forms of Islam after the death of al-Ghazzali (al-gah-ZAH-lee) in 1111 CE. Many dervishes/sufis formed religious associations or brotherhoods (*tariqas*; tah-REE-kahs). In most cases, these were organized around a central religious figure, or shaykh (shake), whom the dervishes believed possessed extraordinary spiritual authority and who was responsible for the spiritual and intellectual direction of his followers. Typically, too, the dervish order was organized into grades, much like a secret society (like the Masons in western Europe), and initiates graduated into higher levels of the order as they were allowed access to secret knowledge known only to members of these higher levels.

The Ottoman Empire began around 1250, when a Turkish chieftain named Osman (after whom the dynasty was named) and his group of followers entered into the service of the Rum sultans of eastern Asia Minor. Osman was given a small fiefdom in western Asia Minor to wage *jihad* (jee-HAHD) against the Byzantines. Thus, the empire began as a *ghazi* state; that is, one made up of **ghazis** (GAH-zees), or frontier warriors, whose express purpose was waging holy war against the Christians. Osman's tiny state was initially organized around two dervish orders, and besides being a warlord, the authority of Osman and his early successors appears to have come from their positions as shaykhs of one or both of these dervish orders.

Osman succeeded in becoming independent when the Mongols destroyed the Rum Sultanate soon after they overran Baghdad. By the time he died, Osman had established a core Ottoman state that included most of western Asia Minor through continual warfare against both his Muslim and non-Muslim neighbors. His son and successor, Orhan (ruled 1326–1359), continued this policy of expansion, and he began the conquest of what remained of the Byzantine Empire on the Balkan peninsula.

More important, as the Ottoman *ghazi* state continued to grow, Orhan reorganized it along feudal lines. Landed estates were parceled out among the commanders of the mounted army. Orhan was also noted for creating the system by which the growing numbers of various nationalities and religious groups were absorbed into the burgeoning Ottoman Empire. Each group was organized as a *millet*; that is, as a separate minority under the leadership of an appointed shaykh, who answered directly to the sultan and his officials. Each millet was allowed a degree of self-regulation under its shaykh, and its rights were protected.

 **MEHMED THE CONQUEROR.** The conqueror of Constantinople is portrayed in this Turkish miniature smelling a rose, symbolizing his cultural interests, as well as gripping a handkerchief, a symbol of his power.

Topkapi Palace Museum, Istanbul, Turkey/Giraudon/Bridgeman Art Library

By the 1450s, the empire had grown to include all of Asia Minor and most of the Balkans south of modern-day Hungary. Of the Byzantine Empire, only the great capital of Constantinople remained. After several failed attempts to capture the great fortress city of the Christians on the western side of the narrow waterway separating Europe from Asia, Sultan Mehmed the Conqueror (ruled 1451–1481) succeeded in taking this prize. A long siege weakened the Christians' resistance, and the sultan's new bronze cannon destroyed the walls. In 1453, the city finally surrendered. Under the new name of Istanbul, it became the capital of the Ottoman Empire from that time forward. By the reign of **Suleiman** (SOO-lay-man) **the Magnificent** (r. 1520–1566), Hungary, Romania, southern Poland, and southern Russia had been added to the sultan's domain, while in North Africa and the Middle East all of the Islamic states from Morocco to Persia had accepted his overlordship (see Map 24.1). At this stage, Ottoman military power was unmatched in the world.

Ottoman Government

Ottoman glory reached its apex during the reign of Suleiman the Magnificent, a sultan whose resources and abilities certainly matched any of his fellow rulers in an age of formidable women and men (Elizabeth I of England, Akbar the Great in India, and Ivan the Terrible in Russia). The government he presided over was divided into a secular bureaucracy; a religious bureaucracy; and a chancery called the **Sublime Porte,** after the gate in the sultan's palace near where it was located. At the head of both stood the sultan. The officials of the Sublime Porte were what we would call the civil government, and it was composed of many levels of officials from the **grand vizier** (vih-ZEER; prime minister) down to the lowliest copyists. Most members of the secular bureaucracy originally were non-Muslims who had converted to the Muslim faith.

The religious bureaucracy was parallel to the secular one. Its members were collectively the *ulama* (oo-la-MAH),

MAP 24.1 The Ottoman Empire's Growth

At its peak in the late 1500s, the domain of the sultan in Istanbul reached from the Persian Gulf to the Atlantic Ocean.

MAP QUESTION
As the Ottoman Empire expanded, what different groups came to be incorporated within it?

View an interactive version of this or a related map at http://worldrc. wadsworth.com/

or learned scholars of the law, the *Sharia*, which was derived from the holy book of Islam, the Qur'an. The sultan appointed a high official as the head of this vast bureaucracy called the **Shaykh al-Islam.** The religious bureaucracy lent its great moral authority to the work of the Sublime Porte. It was in effect a junior partner of the government. In the ordinary course of events, conflict between the two was unthinkable.

The army was an arm of the secular bureaucracy. The Ottoman army was far superior to European militaries by virtue of its professionalism and discipline. At its heart were the well-trained and well-armed **Janissaries,** an elite infantry corps. The Ottomans used a system called the **devshirme** (duv-SHEER-muh) to staff the Janissary units of the army and other high positions within the sultan's administration. Essentially this system was based on seizing Balkan Christian boys at a tender age, converting them to Islam, and giving them unlimited chances to advance themselves in both army and government. The system was designed to create new units of the army and the Sultan's palace, staffed by servants whose only loyalty was to the sultan. Some of the most brilliant leaders of the Ottoman state in the sixteenth through eighteenth centuries were these willing slaves of the sultan (as they proudly termed themselves), recruited from the infidel.

Through the *devshirme*, the Ottoman state for many years successfully avoided the weakening of the central authority that was inevitable with the kind of feudal system Orhan had created in the fourteenth century. Instead, by the time of Mehmed and Suleiman, the bulk of the standing army was a mobile, permanent corps that could be shifted about throughout the huge empire controlled by Istanbul. Therefore, aside from the cavalry corps, most soldiers came to depend on salaries paid directly to them by the central government. The Janissaries and other new infantry corpsmen remained loyal to the central government alone because of their lack of local connections and the fact that they rarely remained in one place very long.

As long as the Janissaries conformed to this ideal, the Ottoman governmental system operated smoothly and effectively. The provincial authorities obeyed the central government or were soon replaced and punished. But after about 1650, when the professional army was able to obtain land and develop the connections to purely local affairs that landholding entailed, a lengthy period of decline commenced.

Non-Muslims under Ottoman Rule

The treatment of non-Muslims varied over time. In the early centuries of Ottoman rule (1300–1600), official treatment of Christians and Jews was generally fair. These "People of the Book" were distinctly limited in what we would call civil rights, could not hold office, could not proselytize for converts or bear arms, and suffered many other disadvantages, but they were not forced to convert to Islam and could run their own civil and cultural affairs on the local and even provincial level. They were taxed, but not excessively. Until the seventeenth century, the public lives of minorities within the *millet* system seem to have assured them more security than most Jews or Muslims living under Christian rule could expect. On the other hand, the brutality with which the Ottomans treated defeated opponents and the forceful application of the *devshirme* proved the limits of Ottoman tolerance for the rights of subject populations.

The majority of the Balkan population was Orthodox Christian. Under Turkish rule, those peasants were almost always decently treated until the seventeenth century. They were allowed to elect their own headmen in their villages; go to Christian services; and otherwise baptize, marry, and bury their dead according to their traditions. Like other non-Muslims, they were more heavily taxed than Muslims, but they were allowed to own land and businesses and to move about freely.

In the course of the seventeenth century, however, the condition of the Balkan Christians deteriorated badly for several reasons, including the central government's increasing need for tax funds, the increasing hostility toward all infidels at Istanbul, and a moral breakdown in provincial and local government. "The fish stinks from the head," says an old Turkish proverb, and the bad example of the harem government in the capital was having effects in the villages.

During the eighteenth century, the condition of the Balkan Christians had become sufficiently oppressive that they began looking for liberation by their independent neighbors, Austria and Russia. From now on, the Ottomans had to treat their Christian subjects as potential or actual traitors, which made the tensions between the Sultan's government and his Christian subjects still worse. By the nineteenth and twentieth centuries, the treatment of Christian minorities, such as the Greeks, Armenians, and others, at times was about as bad in the Islamic Near East as any people have ever had to endure. Unfortunately for the Balkan states today, these old hatreds that Ottoman rule brought to the region remain the primary source of the ethnic and religious conflicts that continue to plague it.

The Zenith of the Ottoman Empire: Suleiman and After

The Ottoman Empire reached its peak during the reign of Suleiman the Magnificent in the sixteenth century. Many consider Suleiman to have been the empire's greatest ruler. Even in a dynasty that had many long-reigning sultans, the length of Suleiman's rule was remarkably long, from 1520 to 1566. His was an outstandingly stable rule in which it seemed that everything the sultan attempted to accomplish succeeded.

Immediately, when Suleiman came to the throne at 26 years of age, he was successful in extending control over all of North Africa. For many years, the Spanish and the Portuguese had attacked and occupied the port cities of Morocco and Algeria. To deal with them, Suleiman formed an alliance with a corsair by the name of Khair ad-Din Barbarossa. The attacks that followed by the combined fleets of Khair ad-Din and the well-armed Ottomans were effective in pushing the Iberians out of Tunis and Algiers. Suleiman also seized the island of Rhodes, which the Christian Knights of St. John hitherto had defended successfully against the Ottomans for centuries. With these victories, Suleiman came close to rivaling ancient Rome by winning complete control over the entire Mediterranean Sea. In southeastern Europe, the sultan's huge army seized the cities of Belgrade and Budapest. Suleiman's next and boldest move was against the capital of the Austrian Empire, Vienna. After a siege that lasted through the summer in 1529, autumn and colder weather finally obliged Suleiman to make an orderly withdrawal. Although the attack failed, it marked the crest of a long wave of Ottoman expansion in Europe.

As they had stacked conquest on top of conquest, the Ottoman sultans increasingly had come to be regarded by Muslims all over as the new caliphs of the Muslim *Umma* (see Chapter 13). With the golden age of the Abbasids long past, Muslims needed a powerful ruler who could assume the responsibilities of religious leadership that were essential to Islam. Ottomans such as Mehmed and Suleiman filled that need admirably. Besides his attacks on Christian Europe, for example, Suleiman defeated a powerful Safavid Shi'ite state in Iran (see following section) and managed to occupy Iraq. He also took charge of making the crucial arrangements for the annual pilgrimages to Mecca. In addition, he remodeled the Tomb of the Prophet Muhammad in Medina and the famous Dome of the Rock mosque in Jerusalem.

Despite the continued conquests and the unprecedented levels of prestige and influence achieved by the sultanate

EVIDENCE OF THE PAST

Harem Intrigue in the Death of Suleiman's Favorite Son

The following is an eyewitness account of a visit with Suleiman by Ogier Ghislain de Busbecq, who had been sent as the Austrian ambassador to the court of the Sultan near the end of his reign. As can be seen, Busbecq was impressed by the Sultan. However, take particular note of the hint of intrigue in the Sultan's harem with the account of the scheming of Roxilana, his favorite wife, to have Suleiman's favorite son, Mustapha, put to death.

> The Sultan was seated on a rather low sofa, no more than a foot from the ground and spread with many costly coverlets and cushions embroidered with exquisite work. Near him were his bows and arrows. His expression, as I have said, is anything but smiling, and has a sternness which, though sad is full of majesty . . .
>
> . . . He is beginning to feel the weight of years, but his dignity of demeanor and his general physical appearance are worthy of the ruler of so vast an empire. . . . Even in his earlier years he did not indulge in wine or in those unnatural vices to which the Turks are often addicted. Even his bitterest critics can find nothing more serious to allege against him than his undue submission to his wife [Roxilana] and its result in his somewhat [hasty] action in putting Mustapha . . . to death, which is generally [blamed on Roxilana's] employment of love potions and incantations. It is generally agreed that, ever since he promoted her to the rank of his lawful wife, he has possessed no [slave wives], although there is no law to prevent his doing so. He is a strict guardian of his religion and its ceremonies. . . . For his age—he has almost reached his sixtieth year—he enjoys quite good health, though his bad complexion may be due to some hidden malady; and indeed it is generally believed that he has an incurable ulcer or gangrene on his leg. The defect of complexion he remedies by painting his face with a coating of red powder.

▶ Analyze and Interpret

What effect did the death of Mustapha seem to have on the great sultan?

Source: From Edward Foster, trans. *The Turkish Letters of Ogier Ghiselin de Busbecq, Imperial Ambassador at Constantinople, 1554–1562* (Oxford: Clarendon Press, 1927), pp. 58–59, 65–66.

You can read about a visit to another of Suleiman's wives at the *Wadsworth World History Resource Center*.

under this monarch, already harbingers of future problems surfaced during Suleiman's reign. He introduced new practices that were followed by the sultans who came after him, all of which ultimately proved disadvantageous to the empire. For example, after the demoralizing losses of his favorite grand vizier and his son, Mustapha, to harem intrigues (see Evidence of the Past), Suleiman showed less and less interest in the day-to-day details of governing than had been the case beforehand. He withdrew from daily meetings of his *divan*, or royal council, allowing his new grand viziers to assume power, if not actual responsibility. The annual *jihads* and conquests continued, but Suleiman and his successors again deferred to their viziers and other military officials (who were given the title of *pasha*) for their execution.

The remainder of the sixteenth century and most of the seventeenth amounted to a stalemate between the Islamic East and the Christian West. This period saw growing difficulties for the Ottomans and the other great Muslim empires, especially in their dealings with the West. Yet, there was little or no actual loss of territory. In 1683, the Ottomans even managed again to muster sufficient resources for a second attack on Vienna. This assault failed, but unlike the failure of the first one in 1529, this one was followed by a disastrous defeat at the hands of a Habsburg army led by Eugen of Savoy. Finally, in 1699, the Ottomans were forced to sign the **Treaty of Karlowitz,** a momentous document that, after centuries of continuous expansion, forced the Ottoman sultan for the first time to cede territory to his European opponents.

THE MUSLIM EMPIRES IN PERSIA AND INDIA

In the sixteenth and seventeenth centuries, the Sufi and Shi'ite divisions, which had existed within the theology of Islam for many centuries, became noticeably stronger. The Sufi mystics sought a different path to God than orthodox Muslims (see Chapter 13). Some of the sufis of Central Asia adopted the historical views of the Shi'ites, who reject all of Muhammad's successors who were not related directly to him by blood or marriage. In the eighth century, as we saw in Chapter 14, this belief resulted in a major split between the Shi'ite minority and the Sunni majority, who believed that the caliph, or successor to the Prophet, could be anyone qualified by nobility of purpose and abilities. From that original dispute over succession gradually emerged a series of doctrinal differences. Much of Islamic history can be best conceived of within the framework of the rivalry between the Shi'ite and Sunni factions.

The Safavid Realm

Within the Islamic world, the greatest rival of the Ottoman Empire after the sixteenth century was the **Safavid Empire** of Persia. Therefore, it is ironic that they shared similar origins. The embryonic Safavid state began in the region of Tabriz, west of the Caspian Sea, and like the Ottoman ghazi state it was organized around a Turkish Sufi association. This brotherhood took its name from its founder, Safi ad-Din (shortened as "Safavid"), who claimed to be a descendant of Muhammad. By the fifteenth century, the Safavid state came to differ from the Ottoman orders in one important aspect, however: it converted to Shi'ite Islam. The Safavids became a major threat to the Ottomans when they evolved a militant theology that advocated the supremacy of Shi'ism through the force of arms. Spreading their views through propaganda, they converted many Turkish tribes in Iran, Syria, and eastern Asia Minor. These Shi'ites took over much of the Persian Muslim state, and from that base they waged frequent wars on their Sunni competitors to the west. In the early 1500s, a leader named Ismail, claiming to be a representative of the hidden Shi'a Imam, succeeded in capturing much of Persia and Iraq, including Baghdad, and made himself *shah* (king). With these successes, Ismail proclaimed Shi'ism to be the official cult of the Safavid state. Thus was founded the Safavid Empire, which lasted for two centuries and was a strong competitor to the Ottomans, who were Sunni Muslims (see Map 24.2). This doctrinal opposition to Sunni Islam and political rivalry with the Ottoman Empire became especially sharp by the early seventeenth century, and it reached its height during the reign of Shah Abbas I (ruled 1587–1629), the greatest of the Safavid rulers.

The European opponents of the Turks, who were then still established deep in central Europe, aided Shah Abbas in his conflicts with Istanbul. Several foreigners occupied high positions in his government, as Abbas strove to avoid favoring any one group within his multiethnic realm. His beautifully planned new capital at Isfahan was a center of exquisite art and crafts production, notably in textiles, rugs, ceramics, and paintings. The Safavid period is considered the cultural high point of the long history of Persia and the Iranian people. Just as in the case of Suleiman the Magnificent, the reign of Abbas represented the high point of Safavid rule in Persia. Following his reign, a gradual decline resulted from encroachments by highly independent Turco-Iranian tribesman. Making things even more complicated were the gradual and caustic influences of European imperialists. The empire slowly lost vigor and collapsed altogether in the 1720s under Turkish and Afghani attacks. It is worth noting that, like the European Christians, the various subdivisions within Islam fought as much against each other as against the infidel. A common

MAP 24.2 Safavid and Mughal empires

The Safavid Empire, shown at its maximal extent, about 1625 under Shah Abbas I, was crushed by Ottoman and Afghani attacks in the 1720s after two centuries of independent Shi'ite rule. The Mughal Empire, shown at its maximal extent, about 1700, included most of north and central India until the late eighteenth century, when losses to the Hindu Marathas and the British intensified.

MAP QUESTION

Can you locate the capitals of the Safavid and Mughal empires?

View an interactive version of this or a related map at http://worldrc.wadsworth.com/

religion is rarely able to counter the claims of territorial, economic, or military advantage in the choice between war and peace.

The Mughal Empire

When we last looked at the Indian subcontinent in Chapter 15, we commented on the gradual revival of Hindu culture under the Gupta Dynasty in the fourth and fifth centuries CE and the Golden Age that ensued. Very early in Islam's history, during the late 600s, Arabs and Persians had moved into the Indus valley and seized the province of Sind at its lower extremity. This was the beginning of a long, ongoing struggle between Hindu and Muslim in the northwest borderlands. Out of this struggle, 800 years after the province of Sind was captured, a branch of the Turks known as the **Mughals** (MOO-guls) created one of the most impressive Muslim empires in world history in northern India.

The word *Mughal* is a corruption of the name Mongol, to whom the Turks were distantly related. Muslims from Central Asia had raided and attempted to invade northern India since the 900s but had been repulsed by the dominant Hindus. As was seen in Chapter 15, in the early 1200s, the Delhi Sultanate was established by a Turkish slave army operating from their base at Ghazni in Afghanistan. Within a century, the sultanate controlled much of the Indian subcontinent, reaching down into the Deccan. Divorced from their Hindu subjects by every aspect of culture, language, and religion, the sultans and their courts attempted at first to convert the Hindus and then, failing that, to humiliate and exploit them.

The original dynasty was soon overthrown, but other Central Asian Muslims succeeded it, all of whom fought among themselves for mastery even as they extended their rule southward. Aided by continuing disunity among their Hindu opponents, Mongols, Turks, Persians, and Afghanis fought for control of the entire width of the Indian subcontinent from the Indus to the Ganges. At last, a leader, Babur, who was able to persuade his fellow princes to follow him, arose again from the Afghan base. Brilliantly successful battle tactics allowed him to conquer much of the

SEF/Art Resource, NY

MOSQUE OF SHAH ABBAS I (1611—1638). Persian architecture of the Safavid period differed significantly from that of the Ottomans. The heavier styles favored by the latter betray a significant Byzantine influence. The Safavid style, on the other hand, was characterized by its relative lightness, intricate surface work, extensive use of blue tiles, and *iwans*, the oversized *qibla*, seen in this mosque built by Shah Abbas the Great at Isfahan.

SEF/Art Resource, NY

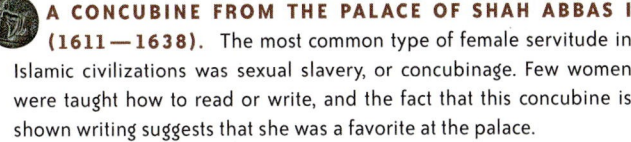

A CONCUBINE FROM THE PALACE OF SHAH ABBAS I (1611—1638). The most common type of female servitude in Islamic civilizations was sexual slavery, or concubinage. Few women were taught how to read or write, and the fact that this concubine is shown writing suggests that she was a favorite at the palace.

territory once ruled by the Delhi sultans. By the time of his death in 1530, he had established the Mughal Muslim Indian dynasty. This man's grandson and successor was Akbar the Great (ruled 1556–1605). Akbar was the most distinguished Indian ruler since Ashoka in the third century BCE. He was perhaps the greatest statesman Asia has ever produced.

Akbar earned his title "the Great" in several different ways. He splendidly fulfilled the usual demands made on a warrior-king to crush his enemies and enlarge his kingdom. Under his guidance and generalship, the Mughal Empire came to control most of the subcontinent—the first time a central government had accomplished this feat since the day of the Mauryan kings. Second, despite his own youthful illiteracy, he completely reorganized the central government, developed an efficient multinational bureaucracy to run it, and introduced many innovative reforms in society. Third and most strikingly, Akbar practiced a policy of religious and social toleration that was most unusual in the sixteenth century. He was at least formally a Muslim, ruling a Muslim-dominated empire, but he allowed all faiths including Christianity to flourish and to compete for converts in his lands.

Because most of his subjects were Hindus, Akbar thought it particularly important to heal the breach between them and the Muslim minority. His initiatives toward creating an ethnically equal society were remarkable. He married a Hindu princess, and Aurangzeb, one of his sons by a Hindu woman, eventually succeeded him. Hindus were given equal opportunities to obtain all but the highest government posts, and the Hindu warrior caste called Rajputs became his willing allies in governance. By repealing the odious poll tax (*jizya*) on non-Muslims, Akbar earned the lasting gratitude of most of his subjects. The sorrow that existed among both Muslims and non-Muslims at Akbar's death was the most sincere tribute to his character.

Midway in his long reign, around 1580, Akbar decided to build an entirely new capital at Fatehpur Sikri, some distance from the traditional royal cities of Delhi and Agra. This palace-city was soon abandoned and is now a ruin, but its beauty and magnificence were famous throughout the Muslim world. The court library reputedly possessed more than 24,000 volumes, making it easily the largest collection of books in the world at this time. Akbar's love of learning encouraged sages of all religions and all parts of the Asian world to come to his court at his expense as teachers and students. His cultivation of the official Persian language brought new dimensions to Indian literature. The ties with Persian culture enabled by the language contributed substantially to the revival of a sense of national unity among Hindus, which they had lacked since the Gupta era.

PATTERNS OF BELIEF

The *Rubaiyat* of Omar Khayyam

Perhaps the most-quoted poem in the English language is a nineteenth-century translation of a twelfth-century Persian philosopher, who may or may not have written the original. The *Rubaiyat* of Omar Khayyam is a collection of four-line verses that became associated with his name long after his death in 1122. Edward Fitzgerald, who had taught himself Persian while passing his days as a Victorian country gentleman, published them in 1859 in a very free translation. Instantly finding a public, the *Rubaiyat* was reprinted several times during Fitzgerald's life and many more since then.

The poem speaks in unforgettably lovely words of our common fate. Morality is all too often a negation of joy. Death comes all too soon: in wine is the only solace. The verse story, of which only a fragment is given here, opens with the poet watching the break of dawn after a night of revelry:

1

Awake! for Morning in the Bowl of Night
Has flung the Stone that puts the Stars to Flight
And lo! the Hunter of the East has caught
The Sultan's Turret in a Noose of Light.

2

Dreaming when Dawn's Left Hand was in the Sky
I heard a Voice within the Tavern cry,
"Awake, my Little ones, and fill the Cup
Before Life's Liquor in its Cup be dry."

7

Come, fill the Cup, and in the Fire of Spring
The winter Garment of Repentance fling
The Bird of Time has but a little way
To fly—and Lo! the Bird is on the Wing.

14

The Worldly Hope men set their Hearts upon
Turns Ashes—or it prospers; and anon,
Like Snow upon the Desert's dusty Face
Lighting a little Hour or two—is gone.

15

And those who husbanded the Golden Grain
And those who flung it to the Winds like Rain
Alike to no such aureate Earth are turn'd*
As, buried once, Men want dug up again.

16

I think that never blows† so red
The Rose as where some buried Caesar bled;
That every Hyacinth the Garden wears
Dropt in its Lap from some once lovely Head.

19

Ah, my Beloved, fill the Cup that clears
Today of past Regrets and future Fears—
Tomorrow?—Why, Tomorrow I may be
Myself with Yesterday's Sev'n Thousand Years.

20

Lo! some we loved, the loveliest and best
That Time and Fate of all their Vintage prest
Have drunk their Cup a Round or two before,
And one by one crept silently to Rest.

21

And we, that now make merry in the Room
They left, and Summer dresses in new Bloom,
Ourselves must we beneath the Couch of Earth
Descend, ourselves to make a Couch—for whom?

22

Ah, make the most of what we yet may spend,
Before we too into the Dust descend;
Dust into Dust, and under Dust, to lie,
Sans Wine, sans Song, sans Singer, and—sans End!

23

Alike for those who for TODAY prepare,
And those that after a TOMORROW stare,
A Muezzin from the Tower of Darkness cries
"Fools! your Reward is neither here nor there!"

24

Why, all the Saints and Sages who discuss'd
Of the Two Worlds so learnedly, are thrust
Like foolish Prophets forth; their
Words to Scorn Are scatter'd, and their Mouths are stop'd
with Dust.

25

Oh, come with old Khayyam, and leave the
Wise To talk; one thing is certain, that Life flies;
One thing is certain, and the Rest is Lies;
The Flower that once has blown for ever dies.

* "Aureate earth . . ." means once buried, the body is no golden treasure.
† The verb "to blow" here means "to bloom."

▶ Analyze and Interpret

Do you sympathize with the poetic point of view? Why or why not? Would a Sufi mystic or a Christian monk have agreed with it? Given the religious origins and foundation of Islamic societies, how do you suppose such a point of view would have been accommodated?

Source: *The Rubaiyat of Omar Khayyam*, trans. and ed. Edward Fitzgerald (New York: Dover, 1991).

You can read more of the Rubaiyat at the Wadsworth World History Resource Center.

Society and Culture. India under the Mughals remained a hodgepodge of different peoples, as well as different religions and languages. Besides those under Mughal rule, there were still many tribal groups, especially in the rain forest regions of the eastern coast, whom neither Hindu nor Muslims considered fully human and often enslaved.

The caste system continued to be refined in constant subdivisions among Hindus. Although the Muslims never acknowledged the caste system, it did serve as a useful wall to minimize frictions between subject and ruler. Despite extensive business and administrative dealings between the two religious communities, social intercourse was unusual at any level. Even among the majority Hindus, culturally based barriers existed that had nothing to do with caste.

A new religion, derived from the doctrines of both Hindu and Muslim, arose in the Far North during the seventeenth century. At first dedicated to finding a middle ground between the two dominant faiths, it eventually became a separate creed, called the religion of the **Sikhs** (seeks). Generally closer to Hindu belief (but rejecting caste), the Sikhs fought the last Mughal rulers and dominated the northwestern Punjab province. (They currently represent perhaps 5 percent of the total population of India and strive still for full autonomy on either side of the India-Pakistan border.)

After Emperor Aurangzeb (r. 1668–1707), the governing class was almost entirely Muslim again, and aspiring Hindus sometimes imitated their habits of dress and manners. Many foreigners, especially from the Middle East, came into the country to make their fortunes, often at the luxurious and free-spending courts of not only the emperor but also subsidiary officials. Prevented by imperial decrees from accumulating heritable land and office, the Muslim upper class took much pride in funding institutions of learning and supporting artists of all types.

In the fine arts, the Mughal rulers made a conscious and successful effort to introduce the great traditions of Persian culture into India, where they blended with the native forms in literature, drama, and architecture. The quatrains of Omar Khayyam's **Rubaiyat** (roo-BAY-yat), which have long been famous throughout the world, held a special appeal for Mughal poets, who attempted to imitate them (see the Patterns of Belief box for an excerpt from the *Rubaiyat*).

The **Taj Mahal** (tahj mah-HAAL), tomb of the much-loved wife of the seventeenth-century emperor Shah Jahan, is the most famous example of a Persian-Indian architectural style, but it is only one of many, as exemplified by the ruins of Fatehpur Sikri, the equally imposing Red Fort at Agra, as well as a whole series of mosques. Much painting of every type and format from book miniatures to frescos also survives from this era and shows traces of Arab and Chinese, as well as Persian, influence. By this time, Muslim artists ignored the ancient religious prohibition against reproducing the human form. The wonderful variety of portraits, court scenes, gardens, and townscapes is exceeded only by the precision and color sense of the artists.

The Muslims had an extensive system of religious schools (*madrasa*), while the local Brahmins took care of the minimal needs for literacy in the Hindu villages by acting as open-air schoolmasters. Increasingly, the Muslims used the newly created Urdu language (now the official language in Pakistan) rather than the Sanskrit of the Hindus.

Like the Safavid Persians to their west, the Mughals were an exceptionally cosmopolitan dynasty, well aware of cultural affairs in and outside of their own country and anxious to make a good impression in foreign eyes. They welcomed European travelers. Like Marco Polo's reports about Kubilai Khan's China, the sixteenth- and seventeenth-century tales of visitors to the Great Mughal were only belatedly and grudgingly believed. Such cultivation and display of luxury were still beyond Europeans' experience.

The Mughal Economy. The existing agrarian system was but slightly disturbed by the substitution of Muslim for Hindu authority. Beginning with the Delhi sultans, courtiers and officials were awarded a parcel of land consonant with their dignity and sufficient taxes to allow them to maintain a specified number of fighting men and their equipment. This system of rewarding individuals who rendered either civil or military duties to the state was called the *mansabdari* (mahn-sahb-DAH-ree). Some mansabdars maintained small armies of 5,000 or even 10,000 men. When the sultanate weakened, they established themselves as petty kings, joining the universal fray in northern India

THE TAJ MAHAL. This seventeenth-century tomb was designed in Indo-Persian style as the resting place of the beloved wife of Mughal emperor Shah Jahan. Building commenced in 1632 and was completed eleven years later. Four identical facades surround a central dome 240 feet high. Gardens and the river that flows beside it supplement the whole complex.

Bridgeman Art Library

for territory and prestige. This system was carried over into the Mughal period. Perhaps half of the mansabdars under Akbar were Hindus, creating a loyalty to the imperial government that continued even under Aurangzeb's determined Islamic regime.

The peasants on the mansabdar's domain were somewhat better off than their contemporary counterparts in Europe or China. Most of them were tenants rather than outright proprietors, but they were not yet haunted by the shortage of agrarian land that would arrive, as it did in China, during the later eighteenth century. Village tradition, the caste system, and government tax collectors restricted their freedoms. The latter were generally no worse than in other places, and their demand for one-third to one-half of the crop was bearable if the harvest was productive.

SUMMARY

THE THREE PRINCIPAL Muslim empires that occupied most of the Asian continent between 1250 and 1800 were able to hold their own militarily and culturally with their Chinese, Hindu, and Christian competitors. Often warring among themselves, they were still able to maintain their borders and prestige for 200 to 600 years. After the terrible destruction rendered by the Mongols, the Muslims of the Middle East absorbed their invaders and rebuilt their cities. Chief and most enduring among their states were those of the Ottoman Turks and the Indian Mughals. The Ottomans profited from the Mongol destruction of Baghdad and the Rum Sultanate by erecting their own powerful *ghazi* state and even eventually took Constantinople (Istanbul) for their capital. Under a series of warrior-sultans, the Ottoman leaders extended their power to the gates of Vienna before internal weakness drove them back in the 1700s. By the nineteenth century, the Ottomans had become so weak that they were sustained only by the rivalry of the major European powers. Thus, the dreaded sixteenth-century empire of Suleiman had been degraded to the sick man of Europe, so called by a British statesman.

For two centuries, the Shi'ite dynasty of the Safavids reclaimed grandeur for Persia and Iraq, where they ruled until they were brought down by the superior power of their Sunni rivals in Istanbul. The Mughals descended on Hindu India in the early sixteenth century and set up one of the few regimes in Indian history that managed to rule successfully most of this intensely varied subcontinent. Under the extraordinary Akbar the Great, this regime reached its apex, only to decline slowly during the following century.

▶ Identification Terms

Test your knowledge of this chapter's key concepts by defining the following terms. If you can't recall the meaning of certain terms, refresh your memory by looking up the boldfaced term in the chapter, turning to the Glossary at the end of the book, or working with the flashcards that are available on the *World Civilizations* Companion Website: **academic.cengage.com/adler**

dervish	grand vizier	*Rubaiyat*	Sublime Porte
devshirme	Janissaries	Safavid Empire	Suleiman the Magnificent
divan	Karlowitz, Treaty of	*Shaykh al-Islam*	Taj Mahal
ghazis	Mughals	Sikhs	

▶ Test Your Knowledge

Test your knowledge of this chapter by answering the following questions. Complete answers appear at the end of the book. You may find even more quiz questions in CengageNOW and on the *World Civilizations* Companion Website: **academic.cengage.com/adler**

1. Taken together at their height, the Ottoman, Mughal, and Safavid empires
   a. extended from the Atlantic Ocean to Australia.
   b. included all of Asia except the Japanese islands.
   c. could be termed a united political territory.
   d. extended from the Atlantic to the Ganges River valley.
   e. included such diverse areas as Iraq, India, and Italy.
2. The Ottoman Empire began
   a. as a Shia *dervish* order.
   b. as a *ghazi* frontier state.
   c. as a Byzantine state.

  d. subordinate to the Abbasid caliphs.
  e. as a combination of three formerly competing dynasties.
3. Which of the following was *not* accepted by Ottoman statecraft?
  a. The precepts and prescriptions of the Qur'an
  b. The function of the sultan as leader of the faithful
  c. The favored situation of the Muslims over the non-Muslim subjects
  d. The necessity to have at least one major Christian ally
  e. A grand vizier who served as the highest civil official
4. The treatment of non-Muslims in the Balkans under Ottoman rule
  a. deteriorated sharply in the seventeenth and eighteenth centuries.
  b. improved as the powers of the sultan diminished.
  c. tended to become better the farther away they were from the capital.
  d. depended entirely on the whims of the ruling sultan.
  e. deteriorated for a short time in the seventeenth century, but by 1900 was much improved.
5. Suleiman the Magnificent accomplished all of these *except*
  a. driving the Europeans out of North Africa.
  b. conquering Vienna.
  c. remodeling several monumental buildings.
  d. assuming leadership of the Islamic Empire.
  e. taking charge of the arrangements for the pilgrimage to Mecca.
6. Shi'ite Muslims
  a. believe the Qur'an is only partly correct.
  b. make up the largest single group of Islamic people.
  c. reject the prophetic vocation of Muhammad.

  d. believe the leader of Islam must be descended from the prophet Muhammad.
  e. refuse to admit Sufis into their sect.
7. The Ottoman and Safavid empires were similar in one respect: they both were
  a. governed by a sultan and a grand vizier.
  b. organized in their beginnings around a Sufi order.
  c. organized to fight as holy warriors against Christian infidels.
  d. weakened by the demoralizing effects of harem intrigues.
  e. based on the Sunni sect of Islam.
8. The Muslim rulers of the Safavid Dynasty were
  a. the conquerors of Constantinople.
  b. the allies of the Mughals in India.
  c. a Persian family that converted to Shi'ite Islam.
  d. the first conquerors of Persia for Islam.
  e. militant warriors who cared little for the arts.
9. The attitudes and policies of Akbar the Great regarding Hindus were that of
  a. tolerance.
  b. religious fanaticism.
  c. a desire to secularize them if he could not convert them.
  d. indifference.
  e. disdain.
10. The most universally revered of the Indian Mughal rulers was
  a. Aurangzeb.
  b. Akbar.
  c. Ashoka.
  d. Abbas.
  e. Babur.

Enter *CengageNOW* using the access card that is available with this text. *CengageNOW* will assist you in understanding the content in this chapter with lesson plans generated for your needs and provide you with a connection to the *Wadsworth World History Resource Center* (see description at right for details).

 World History Resource Center

Enter the Resource Center using either your *CengageNOW* access card or your standalone access card for the *Wadsworth World History Resource Center*. Organized by topic, this website includes quizzes; images; over 350 primary source documents; interactive simulations, maps, and timelines; movie explorations; and a wealth of other resources. You can read the following documents, and many more, at the *Wadsworth World History Resource Center*:

Sidi Ali Reis, *Mirat ul Memalik* (*The Mirror of Countries*)
Omar Khayyam, the *Rubaiyat*

25 FOUNDATIONS OF THE EUROPEAN STATES

> *The great and chief end of men's uniting into commonwealths, and putting themselves under governments, is the preservation of their property.*
> —John Locke

THE THIRTY YEARS' WAR

THEORY AND PRACTICE OF ROYAL ABSOLUTISM
French Government under Louis XIV ◆ Strengths and Weaknesses of French Absolutism

REVOLT AGAINST ROYAL ABSOLUTISM: SEVENTEENTH-CENTURY ENGLAND
Civil War: Cromwell's Commonwealth ◆ Restoration and Glorious Revolution of 1688

POLITICAL THEORY: HOBBES AND LOCKE

ABSOLUTISM EAST OF THE ELBE

PRUSSIA'S RISE

THE HABSBURG DOMAINS
The Struggle against the Ottomans

RUSSIA UNDER THE TSARS
Russia's Antipathies to the West ◆ Absolutism in Russia: Peter I

I
N EUROPE, THE SEVENTEENTH century saw the birth of the modern state as distinct from the domain of a ruling monarch. During this century, the powers attached to a governing office began to be separated from the person of the occupant of the office. This separation allowed the creation over time of a group of professional servants of the state, or bureaucrats, people who exercised authority not because of who they were, but because of the offices they held. Religious conflict between Protestant and Catholic continued but gave way to political-economic issues in state-to-state relations. The maritime countries of northwestern Europe became steadily more important thanks to overseas commerce, while the central and eastern European states suffered heavy reverses from wars, the Turkish menace, and commercial and technological stagnation.

Royal courts constantly sought ways to enhance their growing powers over all their subjects. These varied from west to east in both type and effectiveness. But by the early eighteenth century, some form of monarchic absolutism was in force in every major country except Britain. In this chapter, we focus primarily on France and England and somewhat less so on Russia and the German states of Austria and Prussia.

Kunsthistorisches Museum, Vienna, Austria/Bridgeman Art Library

THE THIRTY YEARS' WAR. In this panorama by Jan Brueghel, the horror of war in the seventeenth century is brought home. Turned loose on the hapless peasants and townspeople, the mercenaries who made up the professional armies of the day killed and stole as they pleased.

THE THIRTY YEARS' WAR

The Thirty Years' War, which wrecked the German states and was the most destructive conflict Europe had seen for centuries, arose from religious intolerance, but it quickly became a struggle for territory and worldly power on the part of the multiple contestants. The war began in 1618, when the Habsburg (HAPS-berg) Holy Roman Emperor attempted to check the spread of Protestant sentiments in part of his empire, the present-day Czech (check) Republic or Bohemia (boh-HEE-mee-ah), as it was then called.

By 1635, the war had become an international struggle beyond consideration of religion. The Protestant kings of Scandinavia and the Catholic French monarchy supported the Protestants, whereas the Spanish cousins of the Habsburgs assaulted the French.

For thirteen more years, France, Holland, Sweden, and the German Protestant states fought on against the Holy Roman Emperor and Spain. Most of the fighting was in Germany. But finally, a peace, the **Treaty of Westphalia**, was worked out in 1648 after five years of haggling. The big winners were France and Sweden, with the latter suddenly emerging as a major power in northern Europe. The losers were Spain and, to a lesser degree, the Austrian-based Habsburgs, who saw any chance of reuniting Germany under Catholic control fade. From 1648 on, Germany ceased to exist as a political concept and broke up into dozens, then hundreds of small kingdoms and principalities, some Catholic and some Protestant (see Map 25.1).

The Treaty of Westphalia was the first modern state treaty. From start to finish, its clauses underlined the

Louvre, Paris, France/Lauros/Giraudon/Bridgeman Art Library

HENRY IV AND HIS QUEEN. The great Flemish painter Peter Paul Rubens created this imaginary scene of the French king taking leave of his wife, Marie de Médici, to take command of the army fighting the Habsburg emperor. Between the royal figures is their little son who would grow up to be King Louis XIII and father of Louis XIV.

MAP 25.1 Europe in the Seventeenth Century

After the Thirty Years' War, the Holy Roman Empire was an empty phrase, with an emperor whose powers were nonexistent in the Protestant lands. The Catholic Habsburg emperors were consistently opposed by the equally Catholic French Bourbons, whose country lay between those of the Habsburgs and their Spanish cousins.

MAP QUESTION

Why did the Catholic kings of France oppose the Catholic Habsburgs?

View an interactive version of this or a related map at http://worldrc.wadsworth.com/

decisive importance of the sovereign state, rather than the dynasty that ruled it or the religion its population professed. Theological uniformity was replaced by secular control of territory and population as the supreme goal of the rival powers. This division negated any chance of German political unity for the next two centuries. For Spain, the ultimate results were almost as painful, although the war was not fought on Spanish territory. The Dutch Protestants gained full independence from Madrid, and Portugal, which had been under Spanish rule for sixty years, rebelled successfully in 1640. The

war with France was foolishly resumed until Spain was forced to make peace in 1659. By that date, the tremendous military and naval advantages that Spain's government had once possessed had all been used up. Spain's government was bankrupt, and its incoming shipments of overseas bullion were now much reduced. Worse, the domestic economy had seen little or no development for a century and a half. Despite much effort in the eighteenth century to regain its former status, Spain was now condemned to a second rank in European and world affairs.

THEORY AND PRACTICE OF ROYAL ABSOLUTISM

The theory of royal absolutism existed in the Middle Age, but the upheavals caused by the Hundred Years' War in France and England, the Black Death in the fourteenth century (see Chapter 20), and the wars of religion following Luther's revolt had distracted the rulers' attention and weakened their powers. Now, in the seventeenth century, they got back to the business of asserting their sacred rights.

The outstanding theorist of absolutism was a French lawyer, Jean Bodin (boh-DAN), who stated in a widely read book that "sovereignty consists in giving laws to the people without their consent." Sovereignty cannot be divided; it must remain in the hands of a single individual or one institution. For France, Bodin insisted that this person should be the French monarch, who had "absolute power" to give his people law. Another Frenchman, Bishop Bossuet (bos-SWAY), gave a theological gloss to Bodin's ideas by claiming that kings received their august powers from God. Bodin found his most potent and effective adherent in Cardinal Richelieu (rish-LYOU; 1585–1642), the prime minister for the young Louis (LOO-ee) XIII in the 1620s and 1630s. Richelieu was the real founder of absolute monarchy in France—and most of Europe soon imitated Paris. Despite being a prince of the church, Richelieu believed wholeheartedly in the primacy of the state over any other earthly institution. *Raison d'état* (ray-ZOHN day-TAH; reason of state) was sufficient to justify almost any action by government, he thought. The state represented order, the rule of law, and security for the citizenry. If it weakened or collapsed, general suffering would result. The government had a moral obligation to avoid that eventuality at all costs.

The cardinal set up a cadre of officials (***intendants***; ahn-tahn-DAHNTS) who kept a sharp eye on what was happening in the provinces and reported to the king's ministers. Thus, the faint outlines of a centralized and centralizing bureaucracy began to appear: these men were picked for their posts at least partially on merit, depended on the central authority for pay and prestige, and subordinated local loyalties and personal preferences to the demands and policies of the center. The cardinal-minister used them to check the independence of the provincial nobles, particularly the Huguenots. He used armed force on several occasions and summarily executed rebels.

Richelieu was the real ruler of France until he died in 1642, followed a bit later by his king. The cardinal had handpicked as his successor as chief minister another Catholic churchman, Cardinal Mazarin (mah-zah-REHN), who had the same values as his master. The new king, Louis XIV (ruled 1643–1715), was but five years old, so the government remained in Mazarin's hands for many years. The young Louis was brought up to believe that kingship was the highest calling on Earth and that its powers were complete and unlimited except by God—and perhaps not by him, either!

French Government under Louis XIV

Louis XIV had the longest reign of any monarch in European history. In the last fifty-four of those years, he was his own chief minister, totally dominating French government. He was the incarnation of absolute monarchy, believing in *divine right*, which said that the monarchy's powers flowed from God and that the king's subjects should regard him as God's representative in civil affairs.

The late seventeenth and eighteenth centuries were the Age of France or, more precisely, the Age of Louis XIV. Not only in government, but also in the arts, the lifestyle of the wealthy and the highborn, military affairs, and language and literature, France set the pace. What Florence had been to the Renaissance, Paris was to the European cultural and political world of the eighteenth century. King Louis allegedly once said, "I am the state," a statement he truly believed. He saw himself as not just a human being with immense powers and prestige but as the very flesh

Louvre, Paris, France/Giraudon/Bridgeman Art Library

LOUIS XIV. This masterful portrait by the court painter Rigaud shows Louis as he would have liked to appear to his subjects. The "well-turned leg" was considered to be an absolute essential for royal figures. Louis's wig and ermine cape were also necessities for a king.

propaganda against the monarch in the series of wars on which he now embarked.

Wars of Louis XIV. Although Louis kept the peace for the first thirty-five years of his reign, his overpowering thirst for glory led him to provoke four conflicts with England, Holland, and most of the German states, led by the Austrian Habsburgs, in the last twenty years. The most important was the final one, the War of the Spanish Succession (1700–1713), in which France tried to seize control of much-weakened Spain and its empire and was checked by a coalition led by England. The war bankrupted France and was extremely unpopular among the French people by its end. The signing of the **Treaty of Utrecht** in 1713 finally ended the hostilities. France succeeded only in placing a member of the Bourbon (boor-BOHN) family (the French dynasty) on the Spanish throne, but under the condition that Spain and France would never be joined together. England emerged as the chief winner, having gained control of part of French Canada and the key to the Mediterranean, Gibraltar. England's biggest prize, however, was Spain's concession of the rights to trade with her possessions in the Caribbean. The war began the worldwide struggle between England and France for mastery of Europe, but the Treaty of Utrecht helped vault England into a position that enabled her to become the world's greatest imperial and industrial power over the next 200 years.

Giraudon/Bridgeman Art Library

VERSAILLES. The view is from the garden side, with the grand fountain in the foreground. The palace lies a few miles outside Paris and is now one of the most visited tourist centers in Europe. Built by increments from the seventeenth through the eighteenth century, Versailles set the architectural and landscaping pace for the rest of the Western world's royalty.

and blood of France. It is to his credit that he took kingship very seriously, working twelve hours a day at the tedious, complex task of trying to govern a country that was still subdivided in many conflicting ways and notoriously difficult to govern. In this task he was greatly aided by a series of first-rate ministerial helpers—the marquis of Louvois (loo-VWAH), Jean-Baptiste Colbert (cohl-BAYR), Sebastien de Vauban (voh-BAHN), and others—each of whom made major contributions to the theory and practice of his chosen field.

Louis was steeped in Richelieu's concepts from childhood and was determined to establish the royal throne as the sole seat of sovereignty. To do so, he had to nullify the independent powers of the aristocrats in the provinces. He did this by forcing them to come to Versailles (vayr-SIGH), his magnificent palace outside Paris, where they vied for his favor and he could keep them under a watchful eye. He was generally successful at this effort. By his death, the previously potent nobles had been reduced to a decorative, parasitic fringe group, with few real powers and few responsibilities save those granted by the king.

Louis's revocation of the *Edict of Nantes* (nahnt) in 1685 was a mistake, which led to the loss of a valuable asset: the Huguenots (OO-geh-nose), who emigrated en masse in the following decade. By allowing them to do so, the king hoped to emphasize the unity of Catholic France. He mistakenly thought that most of the Calvinists had been reconverted anyway and that the edict was no longer needed. Welcomed to Protestant Europe, some 200,000 Huguenots served as bastions of anti-French activity and

Strengths and Weaknesses of French Absolutism

Louis XIV gave all of Europe a model of what could be accomplished by a strong king and a wealthy country. His well-paid officials were the most disciplined and most effective that any Western country had seen. Through them, the king kept a constant watch on the country as a whole. Anything that happened in the provinces was soon known at Versailles Palace and received a royal response whenever necessary. The palace was awe-inspiring, serving to reinforce Louis's prestige and power in visible fashion. Originally a mere hunting lodge for his father, Louis reconstructed it into the largest and most impressive secular structure in Europe. It was surrounded by hundreds of acres of manicured gardens and parks and was large enough to house the immense court and its servants. Its halls were the museums of

the Bourbon Dynasty and remained so until the French Revolution in 1789.

But problems also persisted. Finance was always the sore point for aspiring kings, and Louis spent huge amounts of cash in his quest for military and civil glory. A helter-skelter system of tax "farms," concessions for tax collection in the provinces, did not work well. Worse, with the government legally prevented from taxing the Church and the nobility, Louis's common subjects, particularly the peasants, were forced to bear most of the burden of his and his successors' extravagances. The financial problem of the monarchy was in fact never solved. The French peasants slowly became aware of the contrasts between the taxes they had to bear and the exemptions of various sorts enjoyed by the privileged orders of the clergy and nobility. When that discontent was later joined by the resentment of the much-enlarged group of middle-class townspeople during the course of the eighteenth century, the potential for revolution would exist.

REVOLT AGAINST ROYAL ABSOLUTISM: SEVENTEENTH-CENTURY ENGLAND

At the death of Queen Elizabeth in 1603, the English crown passed by prearrangement to Elizabeth's nearest male Protestant relative, the Stuart king James VI of Scotland, who became James I (ruled 1603–1625) of England. James was a great believer in absolutism and the divine right of kings and quickly alienated the English Parliament with his insistence that the Crown should have sole control over taxes and the budget. This plus his lack of respect for English customs and his arrogance combined to make him highly unpopular by the end of his reign. His greatest achievement was his selection of a committee of distinguished churchmen, who produced in short order the most influential English book ever written: the King James Version of the Bible.

The England that James ruled was fast developing into a society in which the commercial and professional classes had a great deal of political savvy and were becoming used to exercising local and regional power. The well-off merchants and municipal officials who were represented by Parliament's House of Commons now insisted on their rights to have final input on taxation and much else in national policy. They were armed with a tradition of parliamentary government that was already four centuries old. They could not be intimidated easily.

Another topic of acrid debate between the king and his subjects was the proper course in religious affairs. James had been brought up as a Scot Calvinist but had agreed to adopt Anglicanism (the Church of England) as king of England. In truth, many people believed he sympathized with Rome, which made the Anglicans nervous and appalled the growing number of Puritans.

It is impossible to say how numerous the Puritans were because Puritanism was more a state of mind than a formal affiliation. Puritans were inclined to accept the Calvinist social values: hard work, thrift, and a sober lifestyle that aimed at finding its true rewards in eternity. The capitalist ethic was rooted deeply in them, and they, in turn, were well represented in the business classes of England. In the House of Commons, they were now a majority.

Absolutist king and Puritan Parliament clashed repeatedly in the 1620s over taxation and religion. James died in 1625, and was succeeded by his son Charles I (ruled 1625–1649). The son turned out to be as difficult as his father. When the Commons attempted to impose limits on his taxing powers, he refused to honor the ancient custom of calling a Parliament at least every third year. He attempted to bring England into the Thirty Years' War against strong public opinion that held that England had no interest in that conflict. He appointed an archbishop of Canterbury who many people believed was a sympathizer with popery, and he was at least as provocatively stubborn as his father had been. Finding that Parliament would not cooperate with him, he sent it home in 1629 and ruled without its advice and consent.

Charles's marriage to a French Catholic princess had stirred up much resentment, and his high-handed attitude toward the Calvinist clergy finally offended his Scot subjects so badly that in 1640 they rose in revolt. Charles needed money—lots of it—to raise an army against them. That meant he had to impose new taxes, which in turn meant he had to summon Parliament.

By this time, Parliament had not met for eleven years, and when the representatives came together, they were in no mood to support an arrogant and unpopular king's demands. Instead, Parliament passed a series of restrictive laws on the royal powers, but the king maneuvered to bypass them in clear violation of English traditions. When the increasingly radical Puritans in Parliament insisted on direct control of military affairs, Charles raised an army of royalist supporters, and this action led directly to the beginning of civil war in 1642.

Civil War: Cromwell's Commonwealth

Britain divided about evenly between supporters of the king (the Anglican clergy, most of the nobility, and most peasants) and supporters of Parliament (most townspeople, the merchant and commercial classes, the Puritans, and the Scots). Regional and local economic interests often dictated political allegiance. After several years of intermittent struggle, the war ended with Charles's defeat. Parliament then tried the king for treason. After a rump trial, he was found guilty and beheaded in 1649.

After the king's execution, Parliament debated at length the question of where sovereignty lay, and it concluded by declaring that England was a *commonwealth*—that is, a republic with no monarch. Its executive was the chief organizer of the triumphant Puritan army, Oliver Cromwell, who had gained a deserved reputation as a man of iron will and fierce rectitude. During his turbulent tenure as Lord Protector (1653–1658), a comprehensive attempt was made to eliminate such vices as dancing, drinking, making merry on the Sabbath, and theatrical performances. Such efforts to limit human enjoyment had the predictable result: when Cromwell died, few people wanted to hear more about Puritan government. Cromwell's rule had also become unpopular because of the high taxes he levied to pay for frequent military expeditions. He put down rebellions against English rule in Catholic Ireland and Calvinist Scotland with much bloodshed, and forced them into the British Commonwealth. A maritime war with Holland in the 1650s brought England far along the road to control of the seven seas and in North America the rich prize of the former Dutch colony of New Amsterdam.

Three years before his death, the Lord Protector tired of parliamentary quibbling and instituted a forthright military dictatorship. When Cromwell's weak son attempted in vain to fill his father's shoes, parliamentary negotiations with the exiled son of Charles I were begun. After eighteen months, the **Restoration** was completed with the return of King Charles II (ruled 1660–1685) to his native land.

Restoration and Glorious Revolution of 1688

The pendulum of power in British government had swung decisively toward the House of Commons during the revolutionary era, and Charles made his peace with the Commons by establishing the beginnings of the ministerial system. The king appointed several of his trusted friends to carry out policy, but these men had to answer to parliamentary questioning. Gradually, this informal arrangement became a fundamental part of government and was formalized when the party system got under way in the eighteenth century. From it came the modern British cabinet, with its collective responsibility for policy and its reliance on parliamentary votes of confidence to continue its authority as a government.

Charles cared little about religion (his private life was a continual sexual scandal, and real or alleged royal bastards abounded), but one aspect of Charles's religious policy helped create problems for his successor. Under a secret arrangement with King Louis XIV of France, Charles was to receive a large annual monetary payment in exchange for returning England to Catholicism. Although nothing ever came of the rather absurd pact, the news inevitably leaked out in Britain and created a wave of anti-Catholicism that led to a virtual panic. Thus, when it became clear that the aging and (legitimately) childless Charles would be succeeded by his younger brother, James, who had become a practicing Catholic while in exile in France, the English viewed their new king with a great deal of suspicion from the outset.

James II (ruled 1685–1688) made things worse by flinging insult after insult at the Protestants in and out of Parliament. So long as the king had no Catholic children to succeed him, the English could grit their teeth and wait for the elderly man's death. But in 1688 his young second wife unexpectedly produced a healthy baby son who would be raised a Catholic and would presumably rule Britain for many years. To many, this prospect was too much to bear.

Practically all of England rebelled against King James in the **Glorious Revolution of 1688** that ended the Stuart male line on the English throne. James again went into French exile accompanied by his family, while parliamentary committees stepped into the vacuum in London. After brief negotiations to establish the boundaries of governing power, William of Orange, the Dutch Calvinist husband of James's daughter Mary, was invited to rule England jointly with his Protestant wife. So, as the guests of a self-confident Parliament, began the reign of William and Mary (1689–1702).

Significance of the Glorious Revolution. The revolution against James Stuart had been swift and almost bloodless; its significance was political and constitutional, not military or economic. Sovereignty shifted from the monarch to his or her subjects, as represented by their elected Parliament. From now on England was a constitutional state. The king or queen was the partner of Parliament in matters of high policy, both domestic and foreign. William and Mary had accepted the offer of the throne from a parliamentary delegation. What parliamentary committees had given, they could also legitimately take away. Although relations were generally cordial, the royal pair was never allowed to forget that.

The most concrete result of the Glorious Revolution was the **Bill of Rights**, which was adopted by Parliament in 1689. Its most important provisions spelled out the rights and powers of Parliament versus the Crown:

◆ Law was to be made only by Parliament and could not be suspended by the king.
◆ Members of Parliament were immune from prosecution when acting in their official capacities.
◆ The king could not impose taxes or raise an army without prior approval by Parliament.

In addition, the Bill of Rights ensured the independence of the judiciary from royal pressures, prohibited standing armies in peacetime, extended freedom of worship to non-Anglican Protestants, and stipulated that the throne should always be held by a Protestant.

With all it accomplished, however, the Glorious Revolution was *not* a democratic revolution. The great majority of the English and other Britons did not have the vote at any level beyond the village council. That right would have to wait until near the end of the nineteenth century. And women of any class would not have political equality in Britain until the twentieth century (see the Society and Economy box for a view of their status in guilds).

Mary's younger sister Anne succeeded William and Mary on the English throne. Like William and Mary, she died without surviving children. Parliament exercised its new powers by inviting the duke of Hanover, a distant German relative of King James I and the nearest male Protestant relation to the deceased queen, to become King George I (ruled 1714–1727). George thus introduced the **Hanoverian Dynasty** to Great Britain.

The first two Georges lived mostly in Hanover, could barely speak English, and showed little interest in the intricacies of English political life. Robert Walpole, the prime minister for more than twenty years (1721–1742), was the central figure in British government and the key developer of the ministerial government that had begun under King Charles II. Under Walpole, the parliamentary leadership manipulated the frequently absent monarchs more and more, so that Parliament became the more important force in most aspects of internal policy. While foreign affairs and the military still belonged primarily in the Crown's domain, Parliament was supreme in legislation and finance.

POLITICAL THEORY: HOBBES AND LOCKE

Two British political philosophers formed the basis of public debate on the nature of government during the tumultuous seventeenth century. In his book, *Leviathan*, Thomas Hobbes (1588–1679) thought that the pre-governmental "state of nature" had been a riotous anarchy, a "war of all against all." Recognizing the need to restrain violence, early societies soon gave birth to the idea of the state and to the state's living embodiment, the monarch. The state commanded absolute obedience from all. Those who rebelled should be crushed without mercy for the protection of the rest (see the Law and Government box). Most significant, however, was that Hobbes implied that

SOCIETY AND ECONOMY

Women and the Guilds

The change in females' economic status from the Middle Age to the early modern epoch was clearly downward. The near-equality that working women had enjoyed with males in the fifteenth century had deteriorated sharply by the late seventeenth, when this statement was made by a young German tradesman:

> Women are shut out from our guild and cannot be trained by a master. The reason is, they are given the leadership of the family, under the supervision of their husbands. Because it is impossible to know who will be their husband when girls are still children, it is better and more suitable to their sex to teach them the domestic arts, which any husband will appreciate. It is also better for everyone that each sex does what is proper for it, and doesn't attempt to butt into the other's affairs while ignoring or neglecting their own.
>
> I might add, that a woman who moves in male circles [namely, journeymen, who were almost always bachelors] puts herself in danger to her good reputation. . . . It is

certainly better that men, and not women, learn a trade, as not everything can be learned at home or during the apprenticeship, but must be picked up through experience and "wandering." From this comes the old saying of the journeymen: "what I haven't learned, I got from my wandering." But wandering doesn't suit women's place in the world, as they would return from their Wanderjahre [years of wandering] with their reputation in tatters, and therefore there is another axiom: "journeymen who haven't done their Wanderjahre, and maidens who have, are equally dubious." To lead, protect and command is the duty of a master, and is rightly given over to the male sex.

▶ *Analyze and Interpret*

What do you think of the defense of exclusion of women from the guilds? Given that females are often physically able to perform the same tasks as males, do you think that should be the primary consideration in job assignments?

Source: Dora Schuster, *Die Stellung der Frau in der Zunftverfassung* (Berlin: 1927).

the state and the monarch derived their sovereignty from *the people*, rather than from God.

Hobbes's uncompromising pessimism about human nature was countered at the end of the seventeenth century by the writings of John Locke (1632–1704). In his most famous work, the *Two Treatises of Civil Government*, Locke said that all men possess certain natural rights, derived from the fact that they were reasonable creatures. Some of those rights were voluntarily given up to form a government that would protect and enhance the remaining ones: the rights to life, liberty, and property. No prince might interfere with such rights or claim to have one-sided powers to define the citizenry's welfare. Insofar as the government fulfilled its duties, it should enjoy the citizens' support and loyal service. When it did not, it had no claim to their support, and they could righteously push it aside and form a new government.

Whereas Hobbes's words were harsh and shocking to most English people of his time, Locke's message fell on much more welcoming ground. His readers, like the author, were members of the middle and upper classes, who possessed properties and freedoms they were determined to protect from the claims of absolutist monarchs. The English Revolution of the 1640s and the events of the 1680s had given them confidence that their views were both correct and workable. Locke's arguments made good sense to them, and he was also to become the most important political philosopher for the English colonials in North America.

ABSOLUTISM EAST OF THE ELBE

East of Germany's Elbe River, absolute monarchy was able to develop more completely, largely because of the rural, farm-based economies that lingered there longer than in western Europe. Feudal monoculture estates lasted much longer than in France, England, and Sweden. The social cleavage between noble lord and peasant serf was enabled and perpetuated by the rising profits the landlords were able to wring from their large estates. The struggle between noble landowners and the royal government was resolved in eastern Europe by a silent compromise: the monarchs surrendered full control over the peasants to the landlords in return for the landlords' loyalty and service to the Crown. As time passed, the once-weak monarchs steadily gained power through control of the sole permitted armed forces, and the nobles became their servants, just as the peasants were servants to the nobles.

Moreover, no effective middle-class voice was ever heard in constitutional affairs east of the Elbe. Why? The towns were too few and too impoverished, and the small urban populations never gained self-government and

economic freedom as in the West. In part through actual use of armed force against the rebel nobles as in Russia and in part through its threat, as in Prussia and Austria, the royal dynasts were gradually able to subordinate all classes and interests to themselves.

The three states' political evolution was not identical, however. Russia became the most autocratic by far. The Romanov tsar (ROH-mah-noff zahr) was not beholden to any earthly power in Russian legal theory; his will was law. At the opposite extreme, the power of the Austrian emperor—always a member of the Habsburg Dynasty—was sharply limited by the high nobility until the later eighteenth century. The Prussian king—a Hohenzollern (HOH-hehn-zoh-lern)—originally had fewer supreme powers than the Romanovs but more than the Habsburgs. Eventually, the Prussian king was to become in fact the most powerful and successful of the three, and from Prussia came modern Germany.

PRUSSIA'S RISE

As we have seen, after the Thirty Years' War (1618–1648), much of Germany was in a state of economic decay and political confusion. The 300-odd German states and statelets were divided along religious lines: about half were Catholic and half Protestant. Neither accepted the other, and distrust and animosities were always present. The famines and epidemics that accompanied the war had led one-third of the population to an early death, and whole regions almost reverted to wasteland. From this unpromising situation, however, arose one of the major powers of modern Europe, Prussia-Germany.

The rise of the small and economically insignificant Prussia during the later seventeenth and eighteenth centuries was largely attributable to the Hohenzollern princes who occupied the Prussian throne from 1640 to 1786. Frederick William, the **Great Elector** (ruled 1640–1688), was a man of iron will and great talent. He united his previously separate family holdings of Prussia, Brandenburg, and some small areas in western Germany into a single government that was known thereafter simply as Prussia. During his reign, Berlin began its rise from a simple market town to a capital city. A sign of his strength was his victory over the powerful feudal lords in a constitutional struggle over who would have the final word regarding taxes.

Through such measures, the Great Elector tripled the government's revenues and then spent much of the increase on his prize: a new professional army. Every fourteenth male citizen was a member of the army on active service. No other European country even came close to this ratio. Its existence was enough to intimidate

LAW AND GOVERNMENT

Hobbes's *Leviathan*

Thomas Hobbes published *Leviathan* in 1651 to provide a philosophical basis for absolutist monarchy that went beyond the conventional idea of "divine right." Much influenced by the events of the day in England—the civil war was raging—Hobbes wished to demonstrate that strong control of the body politic by a monarch was a political necessity. Note how he bases all effective lawmaking on people's fear of punishment by a superior force, and not at all by the action of reason or compassion. He is interested in establishment of an effective governing authority, and not in the moral and/or reasonable basis for it. He had no illusions about the benign nature of mankind. The following excerpts come from the opening section of the second part of *Leviathan*, where the author summarizes his case:

> The final cause, end, or design of men (who naturally love liberty, and dominion over others) in the introduction of that restraint upon themselves . . . is the foresight of their own preservation, and of a more contented life thereby; that is to say, of getting themselves out of that miserable condition of war, when there is no visible power to keep them in awe, and tie them by fear of punishment to the performance of their covenants. For the laws of nature . . . without the terror of some power to cause them to be observed, are contrary to our natural passions. . . . And covenants without the sword are but words, and of no strength to secure a man at all. . . . And in all places where men have lived in small families, to rob and spoil one another has been a trade, and so far from being reputed against the law of nature, the greater spoils they gained, the greater was their honor. . . . And as small families did then; so now do cities and kingdoms, which are but greater families. . . .
>
> It is true that certain living creatures, as bees and ants, live sociably with one another. . . and therefore some man may perhaps desire to know, why mankind cannot do the same. To which I answer
>
> First, that men are continually in competition for honor and dignity, which these creatures are not. . . .
>
> Secondly, that amongst these creatures, the common good differs not from the private; and being by nature inclined to their private, they procure thereby the common benefit.

> Thirdly, that these creatures, having not [as man] the use of reason, do not see, nor think they see any fault, in the administration of their private business: whereas among men, there are very many that think themselves wiser, and abler to govern the public, better than the rest; and these strive to reform and innovate, one this way, another that way; and thereby bring it into distraction and civil war.
>
> Lastly, the agreement of these creatures is natural; that of men, is by covenant only, which is artificial; and therefore it is no wonder if there be somewhat else required to make their agreement constant and lasting; which is a common power, to keep them in awe, and to direct their action to the common benefit.
>
> The only way to erect such a common power . . . [is] to confer all their power and strength upon one man, or upon one assembly of men, that may reduce all their wills, by plurality of voices, unto one will . . . as if every man should say to every man, *I authorize and give up my right of governing myself to this man, or to this assembly of men, on this condition, that thou give up thy right to him, and authorize all his actions in like manner.* And he that carries this power is called *sovereign*, and said to have *sovereign power*, and everyone besides him is his *subject*.
>
> The attaining of this sovereign power is by two ways. One, by natural force . . . the other, is when men agree amongst themselves to submit to some man or assembly of men, voluntarily, in confidence to be protected by him against all others. This latter may be called a political Commonwealth.

▶ Analyze and Interpret

Do you believe Hobbes is wrong in his assumption that only fear of superior force keeps people in a more or less peaceable community? What might a devout Calvinist have to say about that assumption? How do *Leviathan* and *The Prince* by Machiavelli resemble or contradict one another?

Source: From *The English Works of Thomas Hobbes*, ed. Thomas Molesworth, vol. 3, chap. 17.

You can read further selections from Leviathan at the *Wadsworth World History Resource Center.*

his many opponents both inside and outside of Prussia's borders.

Frederick William also began the understanding between king and nobles that gradually came to characterize Prussian politics until the twentieth century. The Crown handed over the peasants to the noble landlords, who acted as their judge and jury and reduced most of them to a condition of misery as serfs. In return, the Crown was allowed almost total control over national policy, while the noble landlords' sons were expected to serve in the growing military and civil bureaucracy that Frederick William was creating.

As in the rest of eastern Europe, the Prussian urban middle classes did not play the crucial role they had in western Europe. They could not strike a "deal" with either king or nobles to guarantee their own rights. They had to pay the taxes from which the nobles' lands were exempt, and their social and political status remained much lower than that of the Prussian nobility, the *Junkers.*

After Frederick William's death, his son Frederick I and grandson Frederick William I ruled Prussia until 1740. By clever diplomacy in the War of the Spanish Succession, Frederick I was able to raise his rank from prince to the much loftier king of Prussia, while Frederick William I (ruled 1713–1740) was even more intent than his grandfather on building the finest army in Europe. During his reign, Prussia was aptly called "an army with a country." Military priorities and military discipline were enforced everywhere in government, and the most talented young men by now automatically entered state service. The officer corps became the highest social group in the nation, enjoying even its own legal code separate from the civil society.

The series of notable Hohenzollern monarchs culminated in the eighteenth century with Frederick II, the Great (ruled 1740–1786), who is generally seen as one of the most talented kings in modern history. His victories against Austria in Silesia (and later in the Seven Years' War) enabled Prussia to rise into the first rank of European powers. Under Frederick's rule, the Prussian economy prospered. The Prussian territorial gains in western Germany were brought together under the efficient bureaucracy that Frederick continued to develop. Frederick II cleverly associated the Prussian monarchy with a reviving German sense of national unity. With him began the "German dualism," the century-long contest between Austria and Prussia for leadership of the German-speaking people, the most numerous in Europe.

THE HABSBURG DOMAINS

Prussia's rival for eventual political supremacy over the fragmented Germans was Habsburg Austria. Based in Vienna, the **Habsburg Dynasty** (HAPS-berg) ruled over three quite different areas: Austria proper, Bohemia (the present-day Czech Republic), and Hungary (see Map 25.2). In addition, the Habsburgs found allies among the southern German Catholics, who sympathized with their Austrian cousins and had strong antipathies toward the Prussian Protestants.

The dynasty had acquired Hungary and Bohemia through lucky marriages in the sixteenth century. At that time, much of Hungary was still occupied by the Ottoman Turks (see the next section). Habsburg armies liberated it at the end of the seventeenth century. Although a potentially rich agricultural country, Hungary had been laid to waste by the Turks during their long occupation. By the end of the eighteenth century, it had been revivified and repopulated by Catholic Germans and others under the close control of the Vienna government.

The Struggle against the Ottomans

Toward the end of the seventeenth century, Austria was being threatened on several sides. Against its southern and eastern flanks, the Ottoman Turks were still a menacing foe, and they mounted an invasion that reached the outskirts of Vienna in 1683. In the west, the French monarch Louis XIV was readying the War of the Spanish Succession (1700–1715). The Ottomans' attack was beaten off, and the counterattack against the Ottomans went well at first, but then Austria's preparations for the imminent war with France allowed the Turks to recoup their strength temporarily. The Treaty of Karlowitz in 1699 (see Chapter 24) eliminated the threat of a Turkish invasion of Central Europe, and Austria became a leading power for the first time.

This new power, however, had a flaw that became apparent with time. Ethnically, the empire of Austria was the least integrated of all European countries. It included no fewer than ten different nationalities: Germans, Hungarians, Italians, Croats, Serbs, Slovenes, Poles, Czechs, Slovaks, and Ukrainians. In this historical epoch, few if any Europeans were conscious of their national affiliations in the modern, political sense and were thus not disturbed at being ruled by non-natives or being unable to use their native tongues in court proceedings or schools. Nevertheless, as late as the mid-eighteenth century, the Habsburg lands resembled a "salad" of nations and regions that had little in common except rule by the dynasty in Vienna.

Maria Theresa, the only surviving child of the previous emperor, became the first and only female to rule Austria (1740–1780). She and her son Joseph II (ruled 1780–1790) did much to modernize the Austrian armed forces and civil bureaucracy. She was also the first to introduce some coherence and uniformity to the Habsburg government. Despite losing Silesia to the Prussians in the *War of*

MAP 25.2   The Growth of the Austrian Empire, 1536–1795

By an extraordinary stroke of luck, the Vienna-based Habsburg family painlessly acquired the crowns of both Bohemia and Hungary when the last king of both those monarchies fell, childless, on the field of battle against invading Turks in 1526. The surviving widow and heir was a Habsburg princess.

MAP QUESTION

What happened that explains the success of Austria's expansion into the Balkans after 1600?

the Austrian Succession (1740–1748) at the outset of her reign, she slowly welded the various provinces and kingdoms into a single entity under a centralized government headquartered in the impressive royal city. Much later, in the mid-nineteenth century, when it gradually became clear that Austria was losing the battle over the future allegiance of the German-speaking people, the Austrians turned east and south to realize their version of colonial expansion. By so doing, they encountered the Turks, who had sunk into second-level status and would not have been a serious obstacle if they had been forced to stand alone. But in the nineteenth century, Europe's diplomats agreed to let the Turks continue to control southeastern Europe (the Balkans), so as to avoid the inevitable conflicts

British Library, London, UK/Bridgeman Art Library

THE BELVEDERE IN VIENNA. This palace was built by and for Prince Eugen of Savoy, greatest of the Habsburg generals in the wars of the late seventeenth and early eighteenth centuries. It is a perfect example of Austrian baroque architecture.

that would ensue if the Turks were pushed aside and replaced by others. Foremost among those contenders were the newly powerful Russians.

RUSSIA UNDER THE TSARS

Russia's government rose from centuries of retardation and near-disintegration to attain great power status in the eighteenth century (see Map 25.3). Until the 1200s, Russia had been an independent Christian principality based on the impressive city of Kiev (kee-YEV), with extensive trading and cultural contacts with both western and Mediterranean Europe through the Baltic and Black Seas. The Russians had been converted to Orthodox Christianity by Greek missionaries in the late 900s and had remained closely attached to Constantinople in secular, cultural, and religious doctrine for the next three centuries.

But in 1241, the fierce Mongols conquered the principality of Kiev and settled down to rule the Russians for the next 240 years (see Chapter 19). During that period, Russia's formerly numerous contacts with both eastern and western Europe were almost completely severed or neglected, and the Russians retrogressed in many differing fashions, ranging from literacy rates to peasant superstitions. Even their crafts and skills declined. Their governmental institutions also deteriorated. The Russian princes connived and maneuvered to serve as agents and intermediaries of the Mongol khan, who played them off against each other for almost two centuries. Moscow, one of the dozen or so principalities into which Russia was divided after the conquest, came through cunning, perseverance, and good luck to overshadow its rivals even

during the Mongol era. One Muscovite prince actually defeated the Mongol cavalry in 1380, but he could not follow up his victory.

The **Mongol Yoke**, as the Russians call it, was finally thrown off in a bloodless rebellion led by Moscow in 1480. The once-fearsome Golden Horde's remnant retired eastward into the Siberian steppe, and the Russians slowly reemerged into European view. In fact, as late as the 1600s, few western Europeans gave any thought to Russia or the Russians. Trade relations were eventually established with Britain through the Arctic seas and later with the Scandinavians and Germans through the Baltic. But beyond some raw materials available elsewhere and some exotic items such as ermine skins, there seemed little reason to confront the extraordinary challenges involved in trading with this alien society. Militarily and politically, it had nothing to offer the West, and whatever technical and cultural progress was made in Russia during these centuries almost always stemmed from Western sources.

Russia's Antipathies to the West

The Russians were in any case not inclined to welcome Western ideas and visitors except on a highly selective basis. The Orthodox church had been crucially important in keeping alive national identity during the Yoke, and most Russians responded with an uncompromising attachment to its doctrines and clergy. Their distrust of Western Christians was strong. The sporadic attempts of both papal and Protestant missionaries to convert the Russian "heretics" contributed, of course, to this distrust and dislike on the Russians' side.

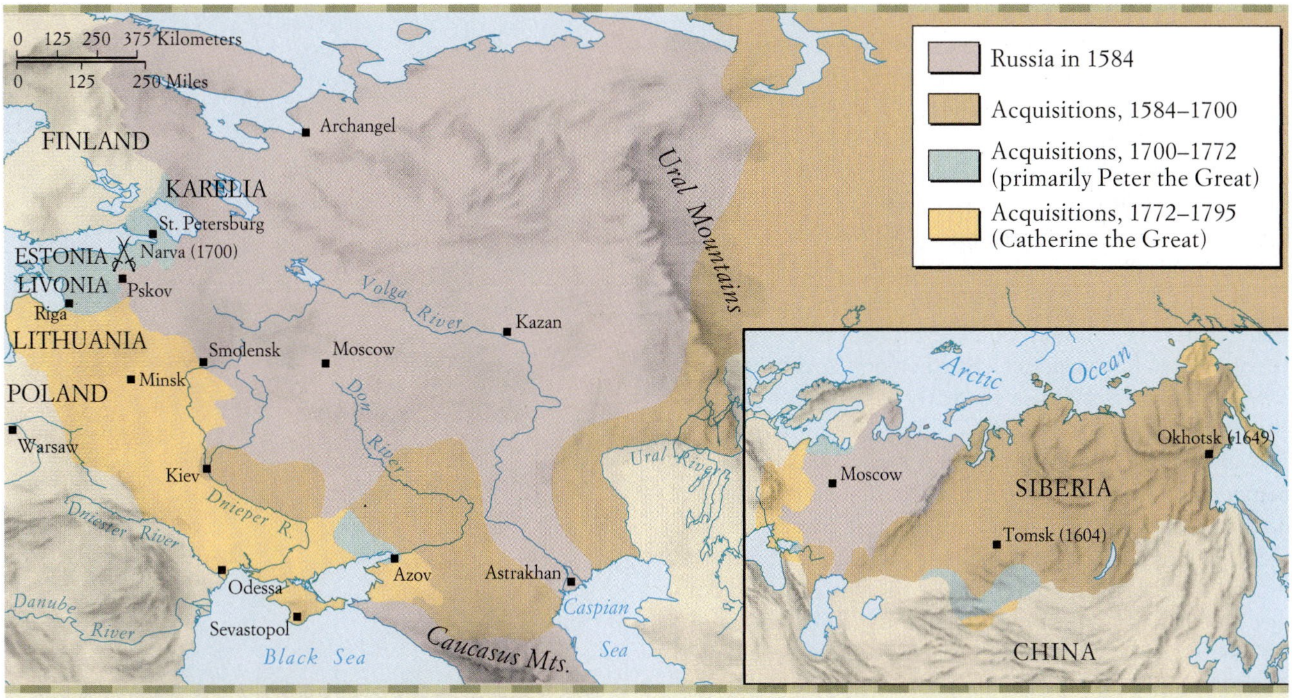

MAP 25.3 From Muscovy to Russia, 1584–1796

The "gathering of the Russian lands" by the Muscovite rulers was facilitated by their acting as the Mongols' agents for centuries and then by defeating them and the aggressive Lithuanians and Poles in the late 1400s. Later acquisitions were based on the alleged rights of Moscow to reclaim what had once been ruled.

MAP QUESTION

What changes helped enable the Russians to expand into the Black Sea and Caucasus regions under the Muscovites and the Romanovs?

View an interactive version of this or a related map at http://worldrc.wadsworth.com/

Culturally, Russia experienced almost nothing of the consequences of the Protestant revolt against Rome or the Renaissance, a situation that greatly heightened the differences between it and the rest of Europe. The Renaissance glorification of individuality, of examination of the human potential, of daring to oppose was to make no impact east of Poland. In religious affairs, the Russians either were ignorant of or rejected the changes Western Christianity had undergone, such as the enhanced role of the laity in the church, the emphasis on individual piety and Bible reading, and the restrictions on the clergy's power. Protestants were regarded either as negligible heretics with a basically erroneous Roman faith or—worse—Western surrender to the lures of a false rationalism that could only lead to eternal perdition.

Above all, from their Byzantine-inspired beginnings, the Russian clergy had accepted the role of partner of the civil government in maintaining good order on Earth. Unlike the papal or Protestant West, the Russian Christian establishment accorded the government full authority over the earthly concerns of the faithful. This tradition had been much strengthened by the church's close support of the Muscovite princes' struggle to free Russia from the Mongols. The high Orthodox clerics saw their role as helper and moral partner of the government in the mutual and interdependent tasks of saving Russian souls and preserving the Russian state.

Absolutism in Russia: Peter I

The expansion of the Muscovite principality into a major state picked up its pace during the sixteenth century. The tsar Ivan IV, or **Ivan the Terrible** (ruled 1533–1584), encouraged exploration and settlement of the vast and almost unpopulated Siberia. He brushed aside the Mongol remnants in a program of conquest that reached the Pacific shores as early as 1639–6,000 miles from Muscovy (muhs-COH-vee) proper. Soon after, Russia was brought into formal contacts with China for the first time—a fateful meeting and the onset of a difficult relationship along the longest land border in the world.

Like the countries of western Europe, Russia adopted a form of divine right monarchy in the seventeenth century. Already in the previous century, Ivan the Terrible had established a brutal model by persecuting all who dared question his rights. So fearful had been his harassment of his nobles (*boyars*) that many of them abandoned their lands and positions and fled. Those who chose to remain often paid with their lives for nonexistent "treason" or "betrayal." Whether Ivan became clinically paranoid is open to question. Mad or not, he bullied and terrified the Russian upper classes in a fashion that would have certainly led to revolt in other countries of the age, but in Russia, no such rebellion occurred in his day.

A Time of Troubles in the early seventeenth century threatened the state's existence. The ancient dynasty of Kievan princes died out, and various nobles vied with armed force for the vacant throne. A serf rebellion added to the turmoil, and the Poles and Swedes on the western borders took advantage of the confusion to annex huge slices of Russian territory. Nevertheless, recovery under the new **Romanov Dynasty** (ROH-mah-noff; 1613–1917) was fairly rapid. **Peter I, the Great** (ruled 1682–1724), is the outstanding example of Russian royal absolutism. Brutal he may have been, but there is no question of Peter's sanity. In fact, his foreign policy was one of the shrewdest of his age. Like Ivan IV, however, he was in no way inclined to share power with any group or institution and believed the fate of the country was solely his to decide. The impact of the human whirlwind called Peter on stolid, isolated, and conservative Russia is impossible to categorize. He was the first Russian ruler to set foot outside the country and to recognize how primitive Russia was in comparison with the leading countries of Europe. He brought thousands of foreign specialists, craftsmen, artists, and engineers to Russia on contract to practice their specialties while teaching the Russians. These individuals—many of whom eventually settled in Russia—acted as yeast in the Russian dough and had inordinate influence on the country's progress in the next century.

Peter was the driving force for an enormously ambitious, partly successful attempt to make Russia into a fully European-style society. He did westernize many Russian public institutions and even the private lives of the upper 2 to 3 percent of the society. This tiny minority of gentry or noble landowners/officials assisted the tsar in governing his vast country; they were swept up into lifelong service to the state, much against their will. In Peter's scheme, the peasants (five-sixths of the population) were to serve the nobility on their estates and feed the townspeople; the nobles were to serve the government as both military and civil bureaucrats at the beck and call of the tsar; and the tsar, in turn, saw himself as the chief servant of the state.

PETER THE GREAT. The great reformer/modernizer of backward Russia, painted in the early years of his reign.

Chateau de Versailles, France/Giraudon/Bridgeman Art Library

Defeating the Swedes and Poles, Peter established a new capital at St. Petersburg to be Russia's long-sought "window on the West," through which all sorts of Western ideas and values might flow. He began the slow, state-guided modernization of what had been a backward economy; he built a navy and made Russia a maritime power for the first time; he also encouraged such cultural breakthroughs as the first newspaper, the first learned journal, the Academy of Sciences, and the first technical schools.

But Peter also made Russian serfdom even more rigid and more comprehensive. He used his modernized, professional army not only against foreign enemies in his constant wars but also against his own peasant rebels. He discouraged any independent political activity and made the Orthodox clergy into mere agents of the civil government under a secular head. His cruelty bordered on sadism, and his personal life was filled with excess. Perhaps, as he himself said, it was impossible to avoid every evil in a country as difficult to govern as Russia. In any event, he remains the watershed figure of Russia's long history.

SUMMARY

THE THIRTY YEARS' War wrecked Germany while providing a forcible resolution to the question of religious conflict in post-Reformation Europe. The Treaty of Westphalia, which ended the war, was founded on state interests, rather than religious doctrine or dynastic claims. From the early seventeenth century on, doctrines of faith took an ever-decreasing role in forming state policy. The Catholic but anti-Habsburg French emerged as the chief beneficiaries of the conflict in Germany. France replaced Habsburg Spain as the prime force in military and political affairs and, under the guidance of Richelieu and the long-lived Louis XIV, became the role model for the rest of the aspiring absolutist monarchies on the Continent.

The English Revolution, sparked by the attempts of the Stuart kings to emulate Louis XIV, ended in clear victory for the anti-absolutist side. Led by the Puritan rebels against Charles I, the wealthier, educated segment of the English people successfully asserted their claims to be equal to the Crown in defining national policies and the rights of citizens. The Glorious Revolution of 1688 cemented these gains. The seeds thus planted would sprout continuously in the Western world for the next two centuries, especially in the British colonies in North America. Given a theoretical underpinning by philosophers such as John Locke and practical form by the 1689 Bill of Rights, the idea of a society that was contractual rather than authoritarian in its political basis began to emerge. Along with this came the ideal of a state that guaranteed liberty and legal equality for all its subjects.

The eastern European dynasties were able to grow and foil the occasional efforts to restrict their royal powers because neither of the two potential secular counterforces— the limited urban classes and the nobility—could find ways to substitute themselves for the throne. The clergy in all the eastern Christian empires were mainly a part of the machinery of government rather than an autonomous moral force that could challenge the government.

The rise of the Prussian Hohenzollern Kingdom began in earnest in the mid-1600s when the Great Elector cleverly made his petty state into a factor in the Thirty Years' War, while subordinating the nobility to a centralized government. Continued by his successors, the elector's policies culminated in the reign of his great-grandson Frederick II, one of the most effective monarchs of European history.

The Habsburgs of Austria, through fortunate marriage alliances, gradually came to rule a large empire based on Bohemia and Hungary as well as Austria proper. The weaknesses of this state were partially addressed by the efforts of Empress Maria Theresa, who brought a degree of centralization and uniformity to the government. But Austria's great problem—its potentially competing nationalities—remained.

After an obstacle-filled climb from obscurity under the Mongols, the Muscovite principality "gathered the Russian lands" in the 1500s and began to expand eastward. Its Polish, Turkish, and Swedish rivals in the West were gradually overcome by lengthy wars. The Russian nobility, once all-powerful, were reduced by the various devices of the tsars to more or less willing servants of the imperial throne. As in Prussia, this collaboration of throne and noble had been secured by giving the estate-owning nobility full powers over the unfortunate serfs and the sparse and insignificant urban residents.

▶ Identification Terms

Test your knowledge of this chapter's key concepts by defining the following terms. If you can't recall the meaning of certain terms, refresh your memory by looking up the boldfaced term in the chapter, turning to the Glossary at the end of the book, or working with the flashcards that are available on the *World Civilizations* Companion Website: **academic.cengage.com/adler**

Bill of Rights	Habsburg Dynasty	Mongol Yoke	Treaty of Utrecht
Glorious Revolution of 1688	Hanoverian Dynasty	Peter the Great	Treaty of Westphalia
Great Elector (Frederick William)	*intendants*	Restoration (English)	
	Ivan the Terrible	Romanov Dynasty	

▶ Test Your Knowledge

Test your knowledge of this chapter by answering the following questions. Complete answers appear at the end of the book. You may find even more quiz questions in CengageNOW and on the *World Civilizations* Companion Website: **academic.cengage.com/adler**

1. The Thirty Years' War began
   a. as a struggle for religious freedom for Protestant reformers in Bohemia.
   b. as a contest between Calvinists and Lutherans in Germany.
   c. as a political contest between Germans and French in the Rhineland.
   d. as an attempt by the French to re-Catholicize their nation.
   e. as none of these.

2. The founder of absolute monarchy in France was
   a. Jean Bodin.
   b. Louis XIV.
   c. Cardinal Richelieu.
   d. Cardinal Mazarin.
   e. Henry IV.

3. *Raison d'état* is most accurately translated as
   a. the power of a duly constituted government to do virtually anything to maintain internal order.
   b. a false reason given by a spokesperson to justify what the government desires.
   c. a pretext used by a government to justify illegal acts.
   d. the state's legal power to make war.
   e. the power of the state to choose its people's religion.

4. Which of the following characteristics was *not* true of the government of Louis XIV?
   a. It was based on parliamentary policy making.
   b. It was Catholic in religion.
   c. It was staffed by many members of the middle classes.
   d. It was highly concentrated in the person of the king.
   e. It succeeded in nullifying the actual powers of the aristocrats.

5. Which of the following seventeenth-century English monarchs was most successful in retaining the support of Parliament?
   a. James II
   b. Charles I
   c. James I
   d. Charles II
   e. William of Orange

6. The message conveyed by Hobbes's *Leviathan* was in brief that
   a. man would find his way to a better future.
   b. man could make more progress once religion was abolished.
   c. man was irredeemably stained by original sin.
   d. man needed a powerful government to avoid anarchy.
   e. man by nature would do good if taught to do so.

7. East of the Elbe, the feudal landlords of the fifteenth through seventeenth centuries
   a. maintained or increased their local powers and prestige.
   b. regularly overthrew the royal governments.
   c. suffered a general decline economically.
   d. practically became extinct with the rise of urban life.
   e. had little to do with the peasants under their control.

8. Maria Theresa's major achievement for Austria was
   a. to conquer more territories from the Turks.
   b. to bring order into the workings of government.
   c. to defeat the claims of the Prussians to Austrian lands.
   d. to clean up the corruption in society.
   e. to leave a strong son behind who would rule for thirty years after her death.

9. A great difference between Ivan IV, the Terrible, and Peter I, the Great, is
   a. the savagery of the first and the subtlety of the second.
   b. the minimal successes of Ivan and the tremendous ones of Peter.
   c. the tender consideration shown to the nobles by Peter.
   d. the degree to which they incorporated Western ideas into their country.
   e. their views about the concept of absolute rule.

10. The most striking difference between the absolutist governments in East and West was
    a. the almost complete lack of a middle class in the East.
    b. the ability of the peasants to express their political opinions to the central government.
    c. the coordination of the policies of the official church and the government.
    d. the degree to which constitutions restrained them in their policies.
    e. the development of professional armies in the East but not in the West.

 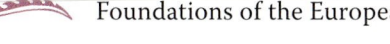

Enter *CengageNOW* using the access card that is available with this text. *CengageNOW* will assist you in understanding the content in this chapter with lesson plans generated for your needs, as well as provide you with a connection to the *Wadsworth World History Resource Center* (see description at right for details).

▶  **World History Resource Center**

Enter the Resource Center using either your *CengageNOW* access card or your standalone access card for the *Wadsworth World History Resource Center.* Organized by topic, this website includes quizzes; images; over 350 primary source documents; interactive simulations, maps, and timelines; movie explorations; and a wealth of other resources. You can read the following documents, and many more, at the *Wadsworth World History Resource Center:*

"The Secret History of the Reign of Jan Sobieski," 1683
The Treaty of Westphalia
Thomas Hobbes, selections from *Leviathan*
John Locke, "An Essay Concerning Human Understanding"

26 CHINA FROM THE MING THROUGH THE EARLY QING DYNASTY

Great wealth is from heaven; modest wealth is from diligence.
—Chinese Folk Saying

MING CHINA, 1368–1644

ECONOMIC PROGRESS
Urbanization and Technology

THE MING POLITICAL SYSTEM
The Bureaucracy

DEALING WITH FOREIGNERS

THE MANZHOU INVADERS: THE QING DYNASTY
Qing Government

QING CULTURE AND ECONOMY
Progress and Problems

THE AGES OF CHINA do not coincide with those of Europe. China had no Middle Age or Renaissance of the fourteenth century. The outstanding facts in China's development between 1000 CE and 1500 CE were the humiliating conquest by the Mongols and their overthrow by the rebellion that began the **Ming Dynasty.** For more than 200 years, the Ming rulers remained vigorous, providing the Chinese with a degree of stability and prosperity that contemporary Europeans would have envied. But the sustained creative advance in the sciences and basic technologies that had allowed China to overshadow all rivals during the thousand years between the beginning of the Song and the end of the Ming dynasties (600–1600) was slowly drawing to a close. The West was overtaking China in these areas, but as late as the eighteenth century, this was hardly evident to anyone. Possessed of an ancient and marvelous high culture, China was still convinced of its own superiority and was as yet far from being forced to admit its weaknesses.

MING CHINA, 1368–1644

The Ming was the last pure Chinese dynasty. It began with the overthrow of the hated Mongols, who had ruled China for 100 years. Founded by the peasant Zhu Yuanzhang (Choo yuwen-chahng), who had displayed masterful military talents in leading a motley band of rebel armies, the Ming would last 300 years. Zhu, who took the imperial title Hongwu (hoong-woo; ruled 1368–1398), was an individual of great talents and great cruelty. In many ways, his fierce ruthlessness was reminiscent of the First Emperor. He built the city of Nanjing (Nanking) as his capital near the coast on the Yangtze River. His son and successor, Yongle (yuhng-leh), was even more talented as a general and an administrator. During Yongle's twenty-two-year reign (1402–1424), China gained more or less its present heartlands, reaching from Korea to Vietnam and inward to Mongolia (see Map 26.1). The eastern half of the Great Wall was rebuilt, and the armies of China were everywhere triumphant against their Mongol and Turkish nomad opponents.

In the Ming era, China generally had an effective government. One sign of this was the sharp rise in population throughout the dynastic period. When the Ming took power, bubonic plague (the same epidemic that was

Map legend:
- Maximum extent of the Ming Empire
- Maximum extent of the Qing Empire
- The Great Wall
- The Grand Canal

MAP 26.1 The Empire under the Ming and Qing Dynasties

By the time of the Ming Dynasty, China had reached its modern territorial extent, with the exception only of Tibet and the far western deserts. Beijing and Nanjing alternated as the capital cities. At the height of the empire under the Qing Dynasty in the middle of the eighteenth century, both Tibet and the huge desert province of Sinkiang came under its control.

MAP QUESTIONS
Was the Great Wall as important during Ming times as it had been in earlier centuries? What does the map suggest about its continuing importance under the Qing dynasty?

simultaneously raging in Europe; see Chapter 20) and Mongol savagery had reduced the population to about 60 million, the same size it had been in the Tang period, 500 years earlier. The population rose to perhaps 150 million by 1600, the most dramatic rise yet experienced by any society.

This new population necessitated an equally dramatic rise in food supply. The old center of Chinese food production, the Yangtze basin in south-central China, was not able to meet the demand. A new area for rice cultivation in the extreme south near Vietnam was developed during the Ming, and some new crops from the Americas such as corn, squash, peanuts, and beans made their way into Chinese fields via the trans-Pacific trade with the Portuguese and Spanish. Interestingly, the Irish or white potato, which would become the staple food crop of northern European peasants in the eighteenth century, was introduced into China but did not catch on. Because rice has greater nutritional value than the potato, this turned out to be a boon for China.

ECONOMIC PROGRESS

Commercial activity steadily increased until it was probably more commonplace in China than in any other country of the world by the 1600s. A larger percentage of the labor force was directly engaged in buying, selling, and transporting goods than in any other land. The merchants remained quite low on the social ladder but were acquiring sufficient money to provide them with a comfortable and cultivated lifestyle.

Commercial contact with the Europeans started in the early 1500s with the coming of the Portuguese into the Indian and, soon, the Pacific oceans. Originally welcomed, the Portuguese behaved so badly that the Chinese quickly limited them to a single port, Macao (mah-COW). Here, in return for silver from the Americas, the Portuguese obtained luxurious and exotic goods that brought exorbitant prices from European nobles, who coveted them for the prestige they conveyed. A merchant who could take a few crates of first-class Chinese porcelain tableware back to Europe could make enough profit to start his own firm.

Urbanization and Technology

The Ming period also saw an enormous increase in the number of urban dwellers. Some Chinese cities, serving as marketplaces for the rural majority and as administrative and cultural centers, grew to have several hundred thousand inhabitants; one or two possibly had more than a million at a time when no European town had a population of even 100,000. In these Chinese metropolises, almost anything was available for money, and the kind of abject poverty that would arise later was probably still unknown.

Giraudon/Bridgeman Art Library

MING POTTERY MAKERS. The late Tang through the Ming eras saw significant developments in Chinese society. There were notable developments in the size and sophistication of its cities, technological innovation, and cultural efflorescence. A key to its manufacturing and commercial sectors was the organization of craftsmen, like these potters, into imperial workshops and guilds (*cohong*).

In general, the villagers and city dwellers of Ming China seem to have been decently housed and fed.

Historians have often asked why China with its large, financially sophisticated commercial class and a leadership role in so many ideas and techniques did not make the breakthrough into a mechanical mode of industry. Why, in other words, did the Chinese fail to make the leap from the "commercial revolution" of the later Ming period to an "industrial revolution" of the kind that began in the West a century later? Various answers have been proposed, but no single one is satisfactory. The Chinese esteem for artists and scholars and the tendency of such people to place little emphasis on accumulation of material goods must be part of the explanation. Engineers and inventors were never prominent in China's culture, even though Chinese science and technology led the world until at least the 1200s. Also, the Confucian ethos did not admire the capitalist entrepreneur or his activities. It was the retention of the old, not the invention of the new, that inspired properly educated Chinese. In the end, we can only attest that China did not experience an industrial-technical breakthrough. If it had, China and not western Europe would have been the dominant power of the world in the past three centuries.

THE MING POLITICAL SYSTEM

As always since Han times, the Chinese government culminated in the person of an all-powerful but not divine emperor, who ruled by the mandate of Heaven through a highly trained bureaucracy derived substantially from talented men of all classes and backgrounds. Hongwu, the peasant rebel commander, brought militaristic and authoritarian ways to the government he headed. The first Ming ruler divided China into fifteen provinces, subdivided into numerous counties, an arrangement that has survived almost intact into the present day. He made occupations hereditary and classified the population into three chief groups: peasants, soldiers, and workers. Supposedly, the class into which people were born would determine the course of their lives, but this was much truer on paper than in reality. China was far too vast and the bureaucracy far too small to allow this restrictive and non-traditional theory to be successfully put into practice.

But the emperor's powers during the early Ming were probably greater than ever before. Hongwu created a corps of palace eunuchs, men without families who had been raised since boyhood to be totally dedicated servants of the ruler. They served as his eyes and ears, and during periods of weak leadership, the eunuchs often exercised almost dictatorial powers over the regular officials, because they alone had direct access to the emperor. This practice, of course, led to much abuse, and the eunuchs were hated and feared by most Chinese. Curiously, the eunuchs never seem to have attempted to overthrow a legitimate ruler, although some Ming emperors practically turned the government over to them. The imperial corps of eunuchs lasted into the twentieth century, though their powers were much diminished by then.

After a brief sojourn in Nanjing during the rule of the first Ming emperor, the government was returned to the northern city of Beijing (bay-jing), which was originally built by the Mongols. In its center was the **Forbidden City**, a quarter-mile-square area of great palaces, offices, and living quarters for the higher officials. No ordinary person was ever permitted within its massive walls. The Forbidden City was expanded several times during the Ming, until it came to house more than 20,000 men and women, who served the emperor or his enormous official family. Its upkeep and the lavish entertainments and feasts that were regularly put on for thousands were a heavy burden on the whole country.

The Bureaucracy

The basis for entry and success in the bureaucracy remained the same as it had been for the last 1,500 years: mastery of the Confucian philosophy and ethics. Confucianism grew stronger than ever. Many schools were founded solely to prepare boys for the government service exams. These exams, which had been suspended by the Mongols, were immediately reinstated by the first Ming emperor. Their essentials would not change until the twentieth century. The exams were administered every other year at the lowest (county) level and every third year at the provincial capitals. Each candidate was assigned a tiny cubicle in which he slept and ate under constant surveillance when not writing his essays during the three to five days of the examination.

Only a tiny minority was successful in obtaining an official post even at the province level. The most distinguished of these would then compete for the central government posts every third year, and the successful ones were considered the most prestigious of all of the "men of Han." Unchanged for centuries, the exams influenced all Chinese education and kept what we now call the curriculum to a very narrow range. After basic reading, writing, and arithmetic, most Chinese schooling was aimed only at preparing students for the civil service examinations. It consisted of a good deal of rote memorization and required extensive knowledge of the various interpretations of Confucian thought. Imagination, creativity, and individuality were definitely not desired. Over the long term, this limited education put China's officials at a distinct disadvantage when confronted with situations that required flexibility and vision. On the other hand, the uniform preparation of all Chinese officials gave the country an especially cohesive governing class, the mandarins (see

EXAMINATIONS FOR GOVERNMENT POSTS. This seventeenth-century painting shows the examinations for government posts in progress. Despite years of preparation, very few candidates were successful at the higher levels.

©Giraudon/Art Resource, NY

Chapters 6 and 16), and conflicts generated by differing philosophies of government were rare or nonexistent. Until recently, civil upheaval and antagonism never occurred *within* the governing class, only *between* it and some outer group (usually foreigners, eunuchs, or provincial usurpers). This unity of view and the loyalty it engendered were valuable in preserving China from threatened disintegration on repeated occasions.

In the early Ming period, both the government and most of the educated population agreed on the vital principles of a good civic life and how to construct it. All officials, from the emperor down to the minor collector of customs in some obscure port, were accepted by the masses as their proper authorities. The ever-recurring question of how to meet the modest demands of the peasantry for survival without alienating the often rapacious landlord-officials was handled effectively. Unfortunately, this harmony declined in later years, as weak emperors ignored the examples set by the dynasty's founders.

DEALING WITH FOREIGNERS

The Mongols and other nomadic peoples on the northern and northwestern frontiers were still a constant menace after they had been expelled from China proper. Much of the large military budget of Ming China was spent on maintaining the 2,000 miles of the Great Wall, large sections of which had to be rebuilt to defend against potential invaders. To do this job, a huge army—well over a million strong—was kept in constant readiness. The main reason for moving the capital back to Beijing from Nanjing was to better direct the defense effort.

The rulers at Beijing followed the ancient stratagem of "use the barbarian against the barbarian" whenever they could, but twice they miscalculated, and the tribes were able to put aside their squabbles and unite in campaigns against the Chinese. The first time, the Mongols actually defeated and captured the emperor, liberating him only after payment of a tremendous ransom. The second time, they smashed a major Chinese army and overran Beijing itself in 1550. Eventually, both incursions were forced back, and the dynasty was reestablished.

With the Japanese, relations proceeded on two planes: that of hostility toward pirates and smugglers and that of legitimate and beneficial exchange. From the fourteenth century, pirate-traders (there was little distinction) from Japan had appeared in Korean and north Chinese waters. Gradually, they became bolder and often joined Chinese pirates to raid coastal ports well into the south. Because the Japanese could always flee out of reach in their islands, the Chinese could only try to improve their defenses, rather than exterminate the enemy fleets. During the sixteenth century, the Beijing government actually abandoned many coastal areas to the pirates, hoping this tactic would enable them to protect the rest.

Otherwise, the Ming period was a high point in cultural and commercial interchange between China and Japan. Direct Chinese-Japanese relations concentrated on trading between a few Japanese *daimyo* and Chinese merchants, a private business supervised by the respective governments. Several of the shoguns of Japan (see Chapter 27) were great admirers of Chinese culture and saw to it that Japan's doors were thrown widely open to Chinese ideas as well as artifacts.

The trading activity with the Japanese was exceptional, however. Generally speaking, China's rulers believed that the Empire of the Middle needed little from the outside world. A brief but significant excursion onto the Indian Ocean trade routes seemed to underline this conviction. The **Maritime Expeditions** of the early 1400s are a notable departure from the general course of Chinese expansionist policy, in that they were naval rather than land ventures. Between 1405 and 1433, huge fleets carrying as many as 30,000 sailors and soldiers traveled south to the East Indies, and as far west as the coast of Africa. The expeditions were sponsored by the government, and at the emperor's order, they stopped as suddenly as they had begun. Their purpose remains unclear, but it does not seem to have been commercial. The fleets made no attempt to plant colonies or to set up a network of trading posts. Nor did the expeditions leave a long-term mark on Chinese consciousness or awareness of the achievements and interests of the world outside.

The Maritime Expeditions were a striking demonstration of how advanced Chinese seamanship, ship design, and equipment were and how confident the Chinese were in their dealings with foreigners of all types. Although China certainly possessed the necessary technology (shipbuilding, compass, rudder, sails) to make a success of overseas exploration and commerce, the government decided not to use it. The government's refusal was the end of the matter. The large mercantile class had no alternative but to accept it because the merchants had neither the influence at court nor the high status in society that could have enabled the voyages to continue. In this sense, the failure to pursue the avenues opened by the expeditions reflects the differences between the Chinese and European governments and the relative importance of merchants and entrepreneurial vision in the two cultures.

Contacts with Westerners during the Ming era were limited to a few trading enterprises, mainly Portuguese or Dutch, and occasional missionaries, mainly Jesuits from Spain or Rome. The Portuguese, who arrived in 1514 before any other Europeans, made themselves so offensive to Chinese standards of behavior that they were expelled, then confined to the tiny port of Macao, near Guangzhou (gwong-choh). The missionaries got off to a considerably more favorable start. They made enormous efforts to

empathize with the Confucian mentalities of the upper-class Chinese officials and to adapt Christian doctrines to Chinese psyches. Several of the missionaries were well-trained natural scientists and were able to interest their hosts in their religious message via their demonstrations of Western mechanical and technical innovations.

Outstanding in this regard was Matteo Ricci (mah-TAY-yoh REE-chee; 1551–1610), a Jesuit who obtained access to the emperor thanks to his scientific expertise, adoption of Chinese ways of thought, and mastery of the difficult language. Ricci and his successors established a Christian bridgehead in the intellectual focal point of China that for a century or more looked as though it might be able to broaden its appeal and convert the masses. But this was not to be. (See the Science and Technology box for some of Ricci's remarks on Chinese technology and his insights into Chinese culture.)

SCIENCE AND TECHNOLOGY

Chinese Inventions

In the sixteenth century, an Italian priest named Matteo Ricci was invited by the emperor to reside at the court in Beijing in the capacity of court astronomer. Ricci had learned Chinese and drew on his learned background in the sciences to both instruct and entertain his hosts. His journals were published shortly after his death in 1610 and gave Europeans their first eyewitness glimpse of the Ming Dynasty civilization and the first knowledgeable insight into Chinese affairs since Marco Polo's report three centuries earlier.

All of the known metals without exception are to be found in China.... From molten iron they fashion many more things than we do, for example, cauldrons, pots, bells, gongs, mortars ... martial weapons, instruments of torture, and a great number of other things equal in workmanship to our own metalcraft.... The ordinary tableware of the Chinese is clay pottery. There is nothing like it in European pottery either from the standpoint of the material itself or its thin and fragile construction. The finest specimens of porcelain are made from clay found in the province of Kiam and these are shipped not only to every part of China but even to the remotest corners of Europe where they are highly prized.... This porcelain too will bear the heat of hot foods without cracking, and if it is broken and sewed with a brass wire it will hold liquids without any leakage....

Finally we should say something about the saltpeter, which is quite plentiful but which is not used extensively in the preparation of gunpowder, because the Chinese are not expert in the use of guns and artillery and make but little use of these in warfare. Saltpeter, however, is used in lavish quantities in making fireworks for display at public games and on festival days. The Chinese take great pleasure in such exhibitions and make them the chief attraction of all their festivities. Their skill in the manufacture of fireworks is really extraordinary and there is scarcely anything which they cannot cleverly imitate with them. They are especially adept at reproducing battles and in making rotating spheres of fire, fiery trees, fruit, and the like, and they seem to have no regard for expense where fireworks are concerned....

The art of printing was practiced in China at a date somewhat earlier than that assigned to the beginning of printing in Europe.... It is quite certain that the Chinese knew the art of printing at least five centuries ago, and some of them assert that printing was known to their people before the beginning of the Christian era....

Their method of making printed books is quite ingenious. The text is written in ink, with a brush made of very fine hair, on a sheet of paper which is inverted and pasted on a wooden tablet. When the paper has become thoroughly dry, its surface is scraped off quickly and with great skill, until nothing but a fine tissue bearing the characters remains on the wooden tablet. Then with a steel graver, the workman cuts away the surface following the outlines of the characters, until these alone stand out in low relief. From such a block a skilled printer can make copies with incredible speed, turning out as many as fifteen hundred copies in a single day. Chinese printers are so skilled at turning out these blocks that no more time is consumed in making one of them than would be required by one of our printers in setting up a form of [moveable metallic] type and making the necessary corrections....

The simplicity of Chinese printing is what accounts for the exceedingly large number of books in circulation here and the ridiculously low prices at which they are sold. Such facts as these would scarcely be believed by one who had not witnessed them.

▶ Analyze and Interpret

Why do you think the Chinese did not use gunpowder technology in war as in entertainments? In light of what Ricci reports, is contemporary European preference for metallic type justified?

Source: P. Stearns et al., eds. *Documents in World History: Vol. 2. The Modern Centuries* (New York: Harper & Row, 1988).

You can read further selections from Ricci's "The Art of Printing" at the *Wadsworth World History Resource Center*.

THE MANZHOU INVADERS: THE QING DYNASTY

The end of the Ming Dynasty came after a slow, painful decline in the mid-seventeenth century. A series of ineffective emperors had allowed government power to slip into the hands of corrupt and hated eunuchs, who made decisions on the basis of bribes, without responsibility for their consequences. Court cliques contended for supreme power. The costs of the multitude of imperial court officials and hangers-on were enormous and could be met only by squeezing taxes out of an already hard-pressed peasantry.

Peasant rebellions began to multiply as the government's ability to restrain rapacious landlords declined. The administrative apparatus, undermined by the eunuch cliques at court, ceased to function. Adding to the troubles was the popularity among the mandarins of an extreme version of scholarly Confucianism that rejected innovation.

The Manzhou (man-choo) tribesmen living north of the Great Wall in **Manchuria** had paid tribute to the Beijing emperor but had never accepted his overlordship. When the rebellions led to anarchy in several northern provinces, the Manzhou saw their chance. The Manzhou governing group admired Chinese culture and made it clear that if and when they were victorious, conservative Chinese would have nothing to fear from them. Presenting themselves as the alternative to banditry and even revolution, the Manzhou invaders gradually won the support of much of the mandarin class. One province after another went over to them rather than face continuous rebellion. The last Ming ruler, faced with certain defeat, committed suicide. Thus was founded the last dynasty of imperial China, the Manzhou or Qing (ching) dynasty (1664–1911). In its opening generations, it was to be one of the most successful as well.

Qing Government

When the **Qing Dynasty** was at the apex of its power and wealth, China had by far the largest population under one government and the largest territory of any country in the world (see Map 26.1). China reached its largest territorial extent at this time. The Qing had been close to Chinese civilization for many years and had become partially sinicized (adopted Chinese culture), so the transition from Ming to Qing rule was nothing like the upheaval that had followed the Mongol conquest in the 1200s. Many Ming officials and generals joined with the conquerors voluntarily from the start. Many others joined under pressure or as it became apparent that the Qing were not savages and were adopting Chinese traditions in government. High positions in the central and even the provincial governments were in fact occupied by two individuals: one Qing, one Chinese. Qing officials oversaw Chinese provincial

governors, and the army was sharply divided between the two ethnic groups, with the Qing having superior status as the so-called Bannermen, who occupied key garrisons.

Like most new dynasties, the Qing were strong reformers in their early years, bringing order and respect for authority, snapping the whip over insubordinate officials in the provinces, and attempting to ensure justice in the village. The two greatest Qing leaders were the emperors Kangxi (kang-shee; ruled 1662–1722) and his grandson Qienlong (chee-yen-loong; ruled 1736–1795). Their unusually long reigns allowed them to put their stamps on the bureaucracy and develop long-range policies. Both were strong personalities, intelligent and well-educated men who approached their duties with the greatest seriousness. Both attempted to keep the Manzhou tribesmen and the ethnic Chinese separate to some degree, although the Manzhou were always a tiny minority (perhaps 2 percent) of the population and were steadily sinicized after the early 1700s by intermarriage and free choice. (See the Law and Government box for more on Kangxi.)

Kangxi was the almost exact contemporary of Louis XIV of France and, like him, was the longest-lived ruler of his country's history. From all accounts, Kangxi was a remarkable man with a quick intellect and a fine gift for administration. He retained the traditional Chinese system of six ministries advising and implementing the decrees of the Son of Heaven in Beijing. He did much to improve the waterways, which were always of great importance for transportation in China. Rivers were dredged, and canals and dams built. He was particularly active in economic policy making, both domestically and toward the Western merchants whose vessels were now starting to appear regularly in Chinese ports. After decades of negotiations, Kangxi opened four ports to European traders and allowed them to set up small permanent enclaves there. This decision was to have fateful consequences in the mid-nineteenth century, when the Beijing government was in much weaker hands.

Kangxi's grandson, Qienlong, was a great warrior and perceptive administrator. He eradicated the persistent Mongol raiders on the western borders and brought Tibet under Chinese control for the first time (see Map 26.1). The peculiar fashion of dealing with neighboring independent kingdoms such as Korea as though they were voluntary satellites of China (tributaries) was extended to much of Southeast Asia at this time. Qienlong ruled through the last two-thirds of the eighteenth century, and we know a good deal about both him and his grandfather because Jesuit missionaries still resided in Beijing during this era. Their perceptive reports to Rome contributed to the interest in everything Chinese that was so manifest in late eighteenth-century Europe.

The early Qing emperors were unusually vigorous leaders, and the Chinese economy and society responded positively to their lengthy rule until the mid-nineteenth

LAW AND GOVERNMENT

Kangxi's Sacred Edict

Emperor Kangxi, the seventeenth-century Qing dynast, was perhaps the greatest of all the Chinese rulers, in part because of the extraordinary duration of his hold on the throne. In 1670, he issued a Sacred Edict to popularize Confucian values among the people.

1. Esteem most highly filial piety and brotherly submission, in order to give due importance to the social relations.
2. Behave with generosity toward your kindred, in order to illustrate harmony and benignity.
3. Cultivate peace and concord in your neighborhoods, in order to prevent quarrels and litigations.
4. Recognize the importance of husbandry and the culture of the mulberry tree, in order to ensure a sufficiency of clothing and food.
5. Show that you prize moderation and economy, in order to prevent the lavish waste of your means.
6. Give weight to colleges and schools, in order to make correct the practice of the scholar.
7. Extirpate strange principles, in order to exalt the correct doctrine.
8. Lecture on the laws, in order to warn the ignorant and obstinate.
9. Elucidate propriety and yielding courtesy, in order to make manners and customs good.
10. Labor diligently at your proper callings, in order to stabilize the will of the people.
11. Instruct sons and younger brothers, in order to prevent them from doing what is wrong.
12. Put a stop to false accusations, in order to preserve the honest and good.
13. Warn against sheltering deserters, in order to avoid being involved in their punishment.
14. Fully remit your taxes, in order to avoid being pressed for payment.
15. Unite in hundreds and tithing, in order to put an end to thefts and robbery.
16. Remove enmity and anger, in order to show the importance due to the person and life.

▶ *Analyze and Interpret*

What might Kangxi's motives have been in promoting such values to the common people?

Source: From *Popular Culture in Late Imperial China* by David Johnson et al. Copyright © 1985 The Regents of the University of California.

---

century, when the dynasty's power and prestige suffered under a combination of Western military intrusions and a growing population crisis. (This period is covered in Chapter 39.)

QING CULTURE AND ECONOMY

Although the Qing were looked on as foreign barbarians originally and they exerted themselves to remain separate from the Chinese masses, no break in fundamental cultural styles occurred between the Ming and Qing dynasties. As in earlier China, the most respected cultural activities were philosophy, history, calligraphy, poetry, and painting. In literature, a new form matured in the 1500s: the novel. Perhaps inspired by the Japanese example, a series of written stories about both gentry life and ordinary people appeared during the late Ming and Qing eras. Best known are the *Book of the Golden Lotus* and ***The Dream of the Red Chamber***, the latter a product of the eighteenth century. Most of the authors are unknown, and the books that have survived are probably only a small portion of those that actually had been produced. Some of the stories are pornographic, a variety of literature that the Chinese evidently enjoyed despite official disapproval.

Porcelain reached such artistry in the eighteenth century that it became a major form of Chinese aesthetic creation. Throughout the Western world, the wealthy sought fine "china" as tableware and *objets d'art* and were willing to pay nearly any price for the beautiful blue-and-white Ming wares brought back by the Dutch and English ships from the South China ports. Chinese painting on scrolls and screens was also imported in large amounts, as were silks and other luxury items for the households of the nobility and wealthy urbanites.

MING VASE. This superb example of Chinese porcelain was made in the seventeenth century, possibly for the developing export trade with Europe.

Musée Guimet, Paris, France/Bridgeman Art Library

The popular decorative style termed *chinoiserie* (shin-WAH-seh-ree) reflected late-eighteenth-century Europe's admiration for Chinese artifacts and good taste. The Clipper ships of New England made the long voyage around Cape Horn and across the Pacific in the first half of the nineteenth century to reap enormous profits carrying luxury goods in both directions: sea otter furs from Alaska and the Pacific Northwest and porcelain, tea, and jade from China.

During the Ming and Qing periods, far more people were participating in the creation and enjoyment of formal culture than ever before. By the 1700s, China had a large number of educated people who were able to purchase the tangible goods produced by a host of skilled artists. Schools and academies of higher learning educated the children of anyone who could afford the fees, generally members of the scholar-official class who had been governing China since the Han Dynasty.

In this era (from the 1500s on), however, China definitely lost to the West its lead in science and technology, which it had maintained for the previous thousand years. Developing a sensitivity to beauty, such as the art of calligraphy, was considered as essential to proper education in China as mastering literacy and basic math. Painting, poetry, and meditation were considered far more important than physics or accounting or chemistry. This ongoing downgrading of the quantitative sciences and the technical advances they spawned in the West was to be a massively negative turning point in international power relations for China. Aesthetic sensitivities and artistic excellence proved to be little aid when confronted by cannons and steam engines.

Progress and Problems

Among the outstanding achievements of the early Qing emperors were improvements in agriculture and engineering that benefited uncounted numbers of ordinary Chinese. Kangxi, for example, did much to ensure that the South China "rice bowl" was made even more productive and that the Grand Canal linking the Yellow River with the central coast ports and the Yangtze basin was kept in good order. New hybrid rice allowed rice culture to be extended and increased yields, which in turn supported an expansion in population.

Internal trade in the large cities and many market towns continued the upsurge that had begun during the Ming Dynasty and became ever more important in this era. Although most Chinese—perhaps 80 percent—remained villagers working the land, there were now large numbers of shopkeepers, market porters, carters, artisans, moneylenders, and all the other occupations of commercial life. Money circulated freely as both coin and paper, the coins being minted of Spanish silver brought from the South American colonies to Manila and Guangzhou to trade for silk and porcelain.

All in all, the Chinese in the early Qing period were probably living as well as any other people in the world and better than most Europeans. But this high standard of living worsened in later days, when for the first time the population's growth exceeded the ability of the agrarian economy to allow suitable productive work for it. By the nineteenth century, almost all of the land that had adequate precipitation or was easily irrigable for crops had already been brought under the plow. The major improvements possible in rice farming had already been made, and yields did not continue to rise as they had previously. Machine industry had not yet arrived in China (and would not for many years), and trade with the outside world was narrowly focused and on a relatively small scale that government policy refused to expand. (China wanted very few material things from the non-Chinese, in any case.) In the nineteenth century, rural China began to experience massive famines and endemic poverty that were the result of too-rapid growth in population in a technically backward society without the desire or means to shift to new production modes.

SUMMARY

THE OVERTHROW OF the Mongols introduced another of the great Chinese dynasties: the Ming. Blessed by exceptionally able emperors in the early decades, the Ming imitated their Tang Dynasty model and made notable improvements in agriculture and commerce. Urban life expanded, and the urban bourgeoisie of merchants became economically (but not politically) important. The borders were extended well to the west and north, and the barbarian nomads thrust once again behind the Great Wall for a couple of centuries.

In the classic pattern, however, the Ming's grip on government and people weakened, and the costs of a huge court and army pressed heavily on the overtaxed population. When rebellions began in the northern provinces, the people were encouraged by the promises of change offered by the invading Qing in the northeast. Triumphant,

the Qing leader began the final dynastic period in China's 3,000-year history, that of the Qing.

The two first Qing emperors were extraordinarily able men, who in the eighteenth century led China to one of the summits of its national existence. The economy prospered, and overpopulation was not yet a problem. In the arts there was extraordinary refinement and development of new literary forms. But in science and technology, China now lagged far behind the West, and the coming century would be filled with political and cultural humiliations. China entered the modern age unprepared to handle the type of problems that it faced on the eve of the European intrusion: growing impoverishment, military backwardness, and technical retardation. First the Europeans and then the Japanese would find ways to take advantage of these handicaps.

▶ Identification Terms

Test your knowledge of this chapter's key concepts by defining the following terms. If you can't recall the meaning of certain terms, refresh your memory by looking up the boldfaced term in the chapter, turning to the Glossary at

the end of the book, or working with the flashcards that are available on the *World Civilizations* Companion Website: **academic.cengage.com/adler**

The Dream of the Red Chamber

Forbidden City
Manchuria

Maritime Expeditions
Ming Dynasty

Qing Dynasty

▶ Test Your Knowledge

Test your knowledge of this chapter by answering the following questions. Complete answers appear at the end of the book. You may find even more quiz questions in CengageNOW and on the *World Civilizations* Companion Website: **academic.cengage.com/adler**

1. The most serious menace to China's stability during the 1300s and 1400s was
   a. the Japanese coastal pirates.
   b. the Mongol conquerors from the north.
   c. the conspiracies of the palace eunuchs.
   d. the invasions of the Vietnamese in the south.
   e. the isolation that caused the Chinese to fall behind the rest of the world.
2. The last dynasty to be of pure Chinese origin was the
   a. Qing.
   b. Song.
   c. Tang.
   d. Ming.
   e. Qin.

3. China's first commercial contact with Europeans was with the
   a. British.
   b. Dutch.
   c. Spanish.
   d. Greeks.
   e. Portuguese.
4. The emperor Hongwu initiated a period during which only the _____ had direct access to the emperor.
   a. royal family
   b. leading merchants
   c. government officials
   d. palace eunuchs
   e. military leaders
5. During the Ming/Qing era, China was ruled by a bureaucracy that was
   a. selected on the basis of aristocratic birth.
   b. controlled by a professional military establishment.
   c. dominated by the Buddhist priesthood.

d. selected on the basis of written examinations.

e. unconcerned about the Chinese peasantry.

6. During the Ming period, Chinese-Japanese contacts were

a. restricted to occasional commerce and raids by Japanese pirates.

b. thriving on a number of fronts, both commercial and cultural.

c. hostile and infrequent.

d. marked by the Japanese willingness to accept China's dominance.

e. exceptional, in that the Chinese adopted Japanese technology.

7. The Maritime Expeditions of the fifteenth century were

a. the product of contacts with Arab traders.

b. the result of Mongol invaders who had occupied China.

c. the government-sponsored explorations of the Indian Ocean.

d. begun at the initiative of private traders.

e. an opportunity for the Chinese to show the rest of the world their superiority.

8. The replacement of the Ming by the Qing Dynasty was

a. caused by a Japanese invasion of China and collapse of the Ming.

b. a gradual armed takeover from a demoralized government.

c. carried out by Westerners, who were anxious to install a "tame" government in Beijing.

d. caused by Western Christian missionaries hostile to the Ming.

e. the natural result of cultural interaction between the two groups.

9. The outstanding Qing emperors of the eighteenth century

a. learned much of political value to them from the West.

b. were cruel tyrants in their treatment of the common Chinese.

c. split governmental responsibility between Qing and Chinese.

d. tried hard to expand commerce between China and Europe.

e. rejected the traditional Chinese bureaucracy in favor of absolute rule.

10. Which of the following did *not* figure prominently in Qing cultural achievement?

a. Poetry

b. Landscape painting

c. Theology

d. Fictional narratives

e. Calligraphy

Enter *CengageNOW* using the access card that is available with this text. *CengageNOW* will assist you in understanding the content in this chapter with lesson plans generated for your needs and provide you with a connection to the *Wadsworth World History Resource Center* (see description at right for details).

 **World History Resource Center**

Enter the Resource Center using either your *CengageNOW* access card or your standalone access card for the *Wadsworth World History Resource Center.* Organized by topic, this website includes quizzes; images; over 350 primary source documents; interactive simulations, maps, and timelines; movie explorations; and a wealth of other resources. You can read the following documents, and many more, at the *Wadsworth World History Resource Center:*

Matteo Ricci, "The Art of Printing"
Pere du Halde, "The Chinese Educational System"
The Dream of the Red Chamber

27 JAPAN IN THE ERA OF EUROPEAN EXPANSION

*The white chrysanthemum
Even when lifted to the eye
Remains immaculate.*

—Basho

BEFORE THE 1500S, THE Japanese islands' contacts with the outer world were only with Korea and China. The arrival of Portuguese trader-explorers brought change to a substantial segment of society, which adopted Christian belief. But this trend was later reversed by government action, and in a remarkable turnabout, the Japanese entered a long period of self-imposed seclusion.

Southeast Asia also experienced the European outreach, but in a highly localized and restricted manner, linked to the exclusive interest of the newcomers in the spice trade. Only much later, in the nineteenth century, did Europeans begin to develop Southeast Asian colonies.

JAPAN

Although akin to China in some ways, Japan was very different in many others. The political power of the emperor in Kyoto was weak throughout early modern times, and Japan became a collection of feudal provinces controlled by clans. In the century between the 1460s and the 1570s, the warrior-nobles (**daimyo;** DEYE-myoh) had engaged in a frenzy of the "strong eating the weak." Finally, a series of military strongmen managed to restore order, culminating in the establishment of a type of centralized feudalism, the *Shogunate*.

The first European contacts occurred in the mid-1500s, when traders and missionaries were allowed to establish themselves on Japanese soil. One of the most important trade items brought by the Portuguese was firearms. Another was the Christian Bible. Contacts with Europe were complicated by Japanese distrust of the Christian faith and its hints of submission to an alien culture. The shogun eventually decided that this danger was intolerable. Within a generation's time, Japan withdrew behind a wall of enforced isolation from the world, from which it would not emerge until the nineteenth century.

FIRST EUROPEAN CONTACTS: CHRISTIANITY

The Portuguese arrived in Japanese ports for the first time in 1543, looking for additional opportunities to make money from their active trading with all the Eastern countries. They took Chinese silk to Japan and Japanese silver to China and used the profits from both to buy spices in the South Pacific islands to bring back to Portugal.

One of the first influences from the West to reach the thus-far isolated Japanese was Christianity, which arrived via the numerous Catholic missionaries sponsored by the Society of Jesus (Jesuits). The Jesuit order had been founded to fight Protestantism only a few years earlier, and its missionaries were well educated and highly motivated. For various reasons, a fair number of the daimyo were sympathetic to the Jesuit efforts and converted to Christianity during the 1550s and 1560s. By the year 1600, it is estimated that 300,000 Japanese had converted. That number would have constituted a far higher percentage of the population than do Christians in modern times.

At this time, most Japanese were adherents of either Shinto or one of the many varieties of Buddhism. Why did the ruling group allow the missionaries free access to the people? And why did the Japanese initially prove more receptive to Christianity than, for example, the Chinese or the Indians? It is impossible to say with certainty. One reason was the personal example of the Jesuits, led by St. Francis Xavier, who greatly impressed their hosts with their piety and learning.

Other changes were under way. In the later 1500s, a movement for Japanese national unity led by Oda Nobunaga (OH-dah noh-buh-NAH-gah; 1523–1582), a feudal lord who had fought his way to regional power, was getting under way. In the 1570s, the brutal Nobunaga succeeded in capturing Kyoto and most of the central island of Honshu, but he was

Museo Nacional de Soares dos Reis, Porto, Portugal/Giraudon/ Bridgeman Art Library

ARRIVAL OF THE PORTUGUESE. Note the black slave unloading the goods, showing that the Portuguese were already using black labor in their trans–Indian Ocean trade in the first half of the seventeenth century. The Japanese observer is possibly the merchant for whom the goods were consigned, and the monkey is the ship's mascot.

killed by one of his cohorts. Following Nobunaga's death, his lieutenant Toyotomi Hideyoshi (toh-yoh-TOH-mee hee-deh-YOH-shee) took over. Aided by the first large-scale use of firearms in Japan, Hideyoshi had visions of Asian, if not worldwide, supremacy. He invaded Korea with a well-equipped army of 150,000 as a first step toward the conquest of Ming China. Repulsed in 1592, he was in the midst of a second attempt when he died in 1598. After a couple of years of struggle among Hideyoshi's would-be successors, the formidable warrior and statesman Tokugawa Ieyasu (toh-koo-GAH-wah ee-eh-YAH-soo; ruled 1603–1616) seized the baton. (See the Law and Government box.)

Tokugawa ceased the abortive invasion of the mainland and by 1600 had beaten down his several internal rivals. Thus began the 250 years of the Tokugawa shogunate, a military regency exercised in the name of an emperor who had become largely a figurehead. Tokugawa "ate the pie that Nobunaga made and Hideyoshi baked" goes the schoolchildren's axiom in modern Japan. He was the decisive figure in premodern Japanese history, using a selective violence against the daimyo to permit a special form of centralized governance.

THE TOKUGAWA SHOGUNATE

Once in power, Tokugawa continued and expanded the changes that Hideyoshi had begun. By disarming the peasants, Tokugawa removed much of the source of the rebellions that had haunted Japan during the preceding century. From this time on, only the professional warrior class, the samurai, and their daimyo employers had the right to own weapons. The daimyo, who were roughly equivalent to the barons of Europe some centuries earlier, were expected to spend half their time at the court of the shogun, where they would be under the watchful eyes of the shogun and his network of informers.

In the early 1600s, the Tokugawa shoguns began to withdraw Japan into seclusion from outside influences. Earlier, Hideyoshi had had misgivings about the activities of the Jesuits within his domains, and in 1587 he had issued an order, which was later revoked, that they should leave. After newly arrived members of the Franciscan

Order attempted to meddle in the shogunate's internal affairs, Tokugawa acted. He evicted the Christian missionaries who had been in the country for half a century and put heavy pressure on the Christian Japanese to reconvert to Buddhism. After Christian peasants supported a revolt in 1637, pressure turned into outright persecution. Death became the standard penalty for Christian affiliation. In a few places, the Christians maintained their faith through

LAW AND GOVERNMENT

Tokugawa Ieyasu (1542–1616)

On March 8, 1616, the shogun Tokugawa Ieyasu died. According to his wish, he was buried in Nikko, a beautiful wood ninety miles north of Tokyo. His tomb stands at the end of a long avenue of great gardens. Posthumously, Tokugawa was given the title "Noble of the First Rank, Great Light of the East, Great Incarnation of the Buddha." He was already acknowledged as the individual who brought law to a lawless society.

Tokugawa Ieyasu (that is, Ieyasu of the Tokugawa clan) was born in 1542. During the last decades of the sixteenth century, he became an ally of Toyotomi Hideyoshi, the most powerful of all the feudal aristocrats who divided the country among themselves.

When Hideyoshi died unexpectedly in 1598, Ieyasu and another man were the prime candidates to succeed him. Tokugawa assembled a force of 80,000 feudal warriors, while his opponent led a coalition of 130,000. In the decisive battle of Sekigahara in 1600, the outnumbered Tokugawa forces claimed the field. In the next few years, Ieyasu destroyed the coalition's resistance and secured the shogun's office for himself and his second son. Ieyasu's victory was a turning point of great importance. For the next 250 years, the Japanese were forced to live in peace with one another. This "Era of Great Peace" was marked by the Tokugawa clan's uninterrupted control of the shogunate in Edo (Tokyo), while the semi-divine emperor resided in Kyoto and remained the symbolic center of Japanese patriotism.

Ieyasu was an extraordinarily gifted man. Coming out of the samurai tradition of military training, he was nevertheless

TOKUGAWA IEYASU. This portrait was done after the powerful warrior had assured his position as shogun in 1603.

Private Collection/ Bridgeman Art Library

able to appreciate the blessings of a permanent peace. He carefully redivided the feudal lords' domains throughout the islands to ensure his control over all of them. He established the daimyo as the officials of his kingdom. They were given considerable freedom to do as they pleased in their own backyards, so long as their loyalty to the shogun was not in doubt. Ieyasu and his successors in the 1600s did much to improve and nationalize Japan's economy, particularly among the peasant majority. The heimin or plain folk were divided into three basic groups: farmers, artisans, and traders, in that rank order. Farmers were generally regarded as honorable people, while traders were originally looked down upon, as in China. At the bottom of the social scale were the despised *hinin*, who were equivalent to the Indian untouchables. Unlike the untouchables, however, the hinin were able to rise in status.

In many ways, Tokugawa Ieyasu was the father of traditional Japan. The political institutions of the country did not change in any significant way after him until the late nineteenth century. He lives on in the pantheon of Japan's heroes as a model of military virtue, who reluctantly employed harsh and even brutal measures in order to bring about the rule of law in a lawless society.

▶ *Analyze and Interpret*

Would there have been many alternatives to Tokugawa's method of imposing order in sixteenth-century Japan? What problems may arise from having absolute powers supposedly in one man's (the emperor's) hands, while another actually exercises them? How might this arrangement be compared to similar situations throughout history (for example, the later Abbasid caliphate, as in Chapter 14)?

The Art Archive

HIDEYOSHI AS SAMURAI. This later illustration of General Hideyoshi allows close inspection of the traditional samurai costume and weapons.

century. It was a remarkable experiment with highly successful results so far as the ruling group was concerned. Japan went its own way and was ignored by the rest of the world.

Shogun, Emperor, and Daimyo

The Tokugawa shoguns continued the dual nature of Japanese government, whereby the shogunate was established at **Edo** (EH-doh; later Tokyo) while the emperor resided in the imperial palace at Kyoto and occupied himself with ritual and ceremony as the current holder of the lineage of the Sun Goddess who had created Japan eons earlier (see Chapter 17). True power in both a military and a political sense remained with the shogun, who now headed a council of state composed of daimyo aristocrats. An individual who was always a member of the Tokugawa clan acted in the name of the emperor while closely overseeing some twenty large and perhaps two hundred small land-holding daimyo, who acted both as his agents and as autonomous regents in their own domains. The shogun controlled about one-fourth of Japan as his own fiefdom. This system continued without important change until 1867.

The daimyo were the key players in governance and posed a constant potential threat to Tokugawa's arrangements. As the source of military power on the local level, they could tear down any shogun if they united against him. Therefore, to secure the center, the shogun had to play the daimyo against each other in the countryside. He did this by constant intervention and manipulation, setting one clan against another in the competition for imperial favor. The shogun controlled the domains near Edo or put them in the hands of dependable allies. Domains on the outlying islands went to rival daimyo clans, which would counterbalance one another. Meanwhile, the wives and children of the more important daimyo families were required to live permanently at Edo, where they served as hostages for loyal behavior. The whole system of supervision and surveillance much resembled Louis XIV's arrangements at Versailles in seventeenth-century France.

Economic Advances

Japan's society and economy changed markedly during these centuries of isolation. One of the most remarkable results of sakoku was the great growth of population and domestic trade. The population doubled in the seventeenth century and continued to increase gradually throughout the remainder of the Tokugawa period. Closing off trade with foreigners apparently stimulated internal production, rather than discouraged it, and domestic trade rose accordingly. The internal peace imposed by the powerful and respected government of the shogunate certainly helped.

"underground" churches and priests, but the majority gradually gave up their religion in the face of heavy state penalties and their neighbors' antagonism.

At the same time, Japan's extensive mercantile contacts with the Europeans and Chinese were almost entirely severed. Only a handful of Dutch and Portuguese traders/residents were allowed to remain in two ports (notably, Nagasaki, where two Dutch ships coming from the East Indies were allowed to land each year). (See Map 27.1.) The building of oceangoing ships by Japanese was forbidden. No foreigners could come to Japan, and no Japanese were allowed to reside abroad (with a few exceptions). Japanese who were living abroad were forbidden to return. The previously lively trade with China was sharply curtailed.

This isolation (called *sakoku* in Japanese history, pronounced SAH-koh-koo) lasted until the mid-nineteenth

MAP 27.1 Tokugawa Japan

The Japanese islands during the period of *sakoku*, which lasted until the mid-nineteenth century. Key cities, including the shogunate's capital, Edo, are shown.

MAP QUESTION
What features of Japan's physical geography might have made social and political unity difficult?

The daimyo aristocracy had an ever increasing appetite for fine wares such as silk and ceramics. Their fortress-palaces in Edo and on their domains reflected both their more refined taste and their increasing ability to satisfy it.

The merchants, who previously had occupied a rather low niche in Japanese society (as in China) and had never been important in government, now gradually gained a much more prominent place. Formerly, the mercantile and craft guilds had restricted access to the market, but the early shoguns forced them to dissolve, thereby allowing many new and creative actors to come onto the entrepreneurial stage.

Even so, the merchants as a class were still not as respected as were government officials, scholars, and especially the daimyo and their samurai. Nevertheless, the merchants' growing wealth, which they often lent—at high interest—to impoverished samurai, began to enhance their prestige. A money economy gradually replaced the universal reliance on barter in the villages.

Commercialization and distribution networks for artisans invaded the previously self-sufficient lifestyle of the country folk. Banks and the use of credit became more common during the later Tokugawa period. Some historians see the

SUNRISE. This wood cut by the famed engraver Hiroshige (1797–1858) shows a typical procession of laborers going to work in a seaside town, while the fishermen raise sail and the rice sellers ready their booths for the morning trade along the quay. The long net is presumably for capturing birds that will be put into the cages and sold.

growth of a specifically Japanese form of capitalism long before Japan's entry into the world economic system in the later nineteenth century.

Peasants and Urbanites

The condition of the peasants, who still made up the vast majority of the population, improved somewhat under the early Tokugawa regime. Since the beginnings of the shogunate under the Fujiwara (foo-jee-WAH-rah) clan, the peasantry had been sacrificed to keep the daimyo and their samurai retainers satisfied. In most of the Japanese lands, the peasant was no better than a serf and lived in misery. In the early Tokugawa era, the peasants received some protection from exploitation, and the shogun's government claimed that agriculture was the most honorable of ordinary occupations. But the government's taxes were heavy, taking up to 60 percent of the rice crop, which was by far the most important harvest. In later years, the increasing misery of some peasants led to many provincial rebellions, not against the shogun but against the local daimyo who were the peasants' landlords. These revolts, although numerous, were on a much smaller scale than those that would trouble Manzhou (or Manchu) China in the same nineteenth-century epoch.

Cities grew rapidly during the first half of the Tokugawa period but more slowly later. Both Osaka (oh-SAH-kah) and Kyoto were estimated to have more than 400,000 inhabitants in the eighteenth century, and Edo perhaps as many as 1 million. All three cities were bigger than any town in Europe at that date. The urban population ranged from wealthy daimyo and merchants at the top, through tens of thousands of less fortunate traders, shopkeepers, and officials of all types in the middle, and many hundreds

of thousands of skilled and unskilled workers, casual laborers, beggars, prostitutes, artists, and the unlucky samurai at the bottom. Most Japanese, however, still lived as before in small towns and villages. They depended on local farming, timbering, or fishing for their livelihood and had only occasional and superficial contact with the urban culture. Until the twentieth century, the rhythms of country life and rice culture were the dominant influence on the self-image and the lifestyle of the Japanese people.

TAMING THE SAMURAI

In the seventeenth and eighteenth centuries, the samurai caste, which had been the military servants of the wealthy daimyo and their "enforcers" with the peasants, lost most of its prestige in Japanese society. Estimated to make up as much as 7 percent of the population at the time of establishment of the Tokugawa regime, the samurai had now become superfluous.

With the creation of the lasting domestic peace, there was literally nothing for them to do in their traditional profession. They were not allowed to become merchants or to adopt another lifestyle, nor could they easily bring themselves to do so after centuries of proud segregation from the common herd. The Edo government encouraged the samurai to do what they naturally wished to do: enjoy themselves beyond their means. Borrowing from the merchants, the samurai tried to outdo one another in every sort of showy display. After a generation or two, the result was mass bankruptcies and social disgrace.

The fallen samurai were replaced in social status by newcomers, who were finding they could advance through commerce or through the civil bureaucracy. As in the West, this bureaucracy was slowly assuming the place of the feudal barons and becoming the day-to-day authority in governance. The samurai lost out to a new class of people: men who did not know how to wield a sword but were good with a pen. Trained only to make war and raised in the bushido (boo-SHEE-doh) code of the warrior, most of the samurai were ill equipped to transition from warrior to desk-sitting official of the shogun or a daimyo lord. Most samurai seem to have gradually sunk into poverty and loss of status as they reverted to the peasant life of their long-ago ancestors.

TOKUGAWA ARTS AND LEARNING

The almost 250 years of peace of the Tokugawa period produced a rich tapestry of new cultural ideas and practices in Japan. Some of the older ideas, originally imported from China, were now adapted to become almost entirely Japanese in form and content. The upper classes continued

to prefer Buddhism in one form or another, with a strong admixture of Confucian secular ethics. Among the people, Shinto and the less intellectual forms of Buddhism formed the matrix of belief about this world and the next. Japanese religious style tended to accept human nature as it is without the overtones of penitence and reform so prominent in Western thought. As before, a strong current of eclecticism blended Buddhism with other systems of belief and practice.

Literature and Its Audiences

Literacy rates were quite high in Japan and continued to increase in the later years of the Tokugawa period, when perhaps as many as 50 percent of the males could read and write the cheap product of wood-block printing presses. This percentage was at least equal to the literacy rate in central Europe of the day and was facilitated by the relative ease of learning the phonetic written language (in distinct contrast to Chinese, the original source of Japanese writing).

Literature aimed at popular entertainment began to appear in new forms that were a far cry from the elegant and restrained traditions of the past. Poetry, novels, social satires, and Kabuki plays were the foremost types of literature. By this era, all of these forms had been liberated from imitation of classical Chinese models, and several were entirely original to the Japanese.

Haiku (HEYE-koo) poems, especially in the hands of the revered seventeenth-century poet Basho, were extraordinarily compact revelations of profound thought. In three lines and seventeen syllables (always), the poet reflected the Zen Buddhist conviction that the greatest of mysteries can only be stated—never analyzed. Saikaku's contributions in fiction matched those of Basho in poetry, also during the late seventeenth century. His novels and stories about ordinary people are noteworthy for their passion and the underlying sense of comedy with which the characters are observed. Saikaku's stories, like Basho's verse, are read today in Japan with the same admiration afforded to them for centuries. (See Arts and Culture box.)

Kabuki (kah-BOO-kee) is a peculiarly Japanese form of drama. It is highly realistic, often humorous and satirical, and sometimes violent in both action and emotions. For its settings, it often used the "floating world," the unstable but attractive world of brothels, shady teahouses, and gambling dens. Kabuki was wildly popular among the upper classes in seventeenth- and eighteenth-century Japan. It was not unusual for a particularly successful actor (males played all parts) to become a pampered "star." Actors were often also male prostitutes, just as actresses in the West were often female prostitutes at this time. Homosexuality was strongly frowned on by the shogunate authorities, but it had already had a long tradition among the samurai and some branches of Buddhism.

Adaptation and Originality

In the fine arts, Japan may have drawn its initial inspiration from Chinese models, but it always turned those models into something different, something specifically Japanese. This pattern can be found in landscape painting, poetry, adventure and romance stories, gardens, and ceramics—in any art medium that both peoples have pursued.

The Japanese versions were often filled with a playful humor that was missing in the Chinese original and were almost always consciously close to nature, the soil, and the peasantry. The refined intellectualism common to Chinese arts appeared less frequently in Japan. As a random example, the rough-and-tumble of Kabuki and the pornographic jokes that the actors constantly employed were specifically Japanese and had no close equivalent in China.

The merchants who had prospered during the Tokugawa era were especially important as patrons of the arts. Again, a parallel can be drawn to the European experience, but with differences. The European bourgeoisie became important commissioners of art two centuries earlier than the Japanese merchants and did so in self-confident rivalry with the nobles and church. Japan had no established church, and the bourgeoisie never dared challenge the daimyo nobility for taste-setting primacy. Nevertheless, high-quality painting and wood-block prints displaying a tremendous variety of subjects and techniques came to adorn the homes and collections of the rich merchants. In fact, much of what the modern world knows of seventeenth- and eighteenth-century Japanese society is attributable to the knowing eye and talented hands of the artists rather than to historians. Unlike the Chinese, the Japanese never revered compilers of records. There are no Japanese equivalents of the great Chinese histories.

RESPONSE TO THE WESTERN CHALLENGE

In the later Tokugawa, the main emphasis of Japanese thought shifted from Buddhist to Confucian ideals, which is another way of saying that it changed from an otherworldly emphasis to an empirical concern with this world. The Japanese version of Confucianism was, as always, different from the Chinese. The secular, politically pragmatic nature of Confucius's doctrines comes through more emphatically in Japan. The Chinese mandarins of the nineteenth century had little tolerance for deviation from the prescribed version of the Master. But in Japan, several schools of thought contended and were unimpeded by an official prescription of right and wrong. Another difference was that whereas China had no room for a shogun, Japan had no room for the mandate of Heaven. Chinese tradition held that only

ARTS AND CULTURE

The Origins and Evolution of Haiku

Haiku is undoubtedly the most distinctive and well-known form of traditional Japanese poetry. Haiku has changed somewhat over the centuries since the time of Basho, and today it is typically a three-line, 17-syllable verse form consisting of three metrical units of 5, 7, and 5 syllables. Three related terms, *haiku*, *hokku*, and *haika*, have often caused considerable confusion. What we know today as haiku had its beginnings as hokku, a "starting verse" of a much longer chain of verses known as haika. The hokku was the most important part of a haika poem; therefore, it was an especially prestigious form of poetry from its inception. Before long, therefore, poets began composing hokkus by themselves. One nineteenth-century master in particular, Masaoka Shiki, formally established the haiku in the 1890s in the form in which it is now known. Here are a few samples of the poetry of Basho:

An old pond!
A frog jumps in—
The sound of water.

The first soft snow!
Enough to bend the leaves
Of the jonquil low.

In the cicada's cry
No sign can foretell
How soon it must die.

No one travels
Along this way but I,
This autumn evening.

In all the rains of May
there is one thing not hidden—
the bridge at Seta Bay.

The year's first day
thoughts and loneliness;
the autumn dusk is here.

Clouds appear
and bring to men a chance to rest
from looking at the moon.

Harvest moon:
around the pond I wander
and the night is gone.

Poverty's child—
he starts to grind the rice,
and gazes at the moon.

No blossoms and no moon,
and he is drinking sake
all alone!

Won't you come and see
loneliness? Just one leaf
from the *kiri* tree.

Temple bells die out.
The fragrant blossoms remain.
A perfect evening!

▶ *Analyze and Interpret*

To what do you attribute the appeal of this simple poetic form? What seems to be the poems' purpose, if any?

Source: From Haiku for People, http://www.toyomasu.com/haiku/#Basho.

China could be the Confucian "Empire of the Middle." The Japanese, on the other hand, although confident they were in that desirable position of centrality and balance, believed they need not ignore the achievements of other, less fortunate but not entirely misguided folk.

What was the significance of this pragmatic secularism for Japan? It helped prepare the ruling daimyo group for the invasion of Western ideas that came in the mid-nineteenth century. The Japanese elite were able to abandon their seclusion and investigate whatever Western technology could offer them with an open mind. In sharp contrast to China, when the Western avalanche could no longer be evaded, the Japanese governing class accepted it with little inherent resistance or cultural confusion.

At the outset of the Tokugawa shogunate, the Japanese educated classes were perhaps as familiar with science and technology as were the Westerners. Sakoku necessarily inhibited further progress. The Scientific Revolution and its accompanying technological advances were unknown in Japan, and the Enlightenment of the eighteenth century was equally foreign to the cultural landscape of even the most refined citizens (see Chapter 29). From the early 1800s, a few Japanese scholars and officials were aware that the West (including nearby Russia) was well ahead of them in certain areas, especially the natural sciences and medicine, and that much could be learned from the Westerners. These Japanese were in contact with the handful of Dutch merchants who had been allowed to stay in Japan, and they occasionally read Western science texts. "Dutch medicine," as Western anatomy, pharmacy, and surgery were called, was fairly well-known in upper-class Japan in the early nineteenth century although it did not yet have much prestige.

When the American naval commander Matthew Perry arrived with his "black ships" to forcibly open the country to foreign traders in 1853 and 1854, the Japanese were not as ill-prepared as one might assume after two centuries of isolation. Aided by the practical and secular Confucian philosophy they had imbibed, the sparse but important Western scientific books they had studied, and the carefully balanced government they had evolved by trial and error, the Edo government, the daimyo, and their subofficials were able to absorb Western ideas and techniques by choice rather than by force. Rather than looking down their cultured noses at what the "hairy barbarians" might be bringing, the Japanese were able to say, "If it works to our benefit (or can be made to), use it." Unlike China, the West decidedly did not overwhelm the Japanese. On the contrary, they were true to their nation's tradition by showing themselves to be confident and pragmatic adapters of what they thought could be useful to themselves, rejecting the rest.

Michael S. Yamashita/Corbis

HIMEJI CASTLE. This relatively late construction, known as the White Egret to the Japanese, stands today as a major tourist attraction. The massive stone walls successfully resisted all attackers.

SOUTHEAST ASIA

The territories in Southeast Asia that had succeeded in achieving political organization before the appearance of European traders and missionaries had little reason to take much notice of them until a much later era. Contacts were limited to coastal towns and were mainly commercial. In the 1600s, the Dutch had driven the Portuguese entirely out of the islands' spice trade, and they had established a loose partnership with the local Muslim sultans in Java and Sumatra to assure the continuance of that trade with Europe. After a brief contest with the Dutch, the British, in the form of the East India Company, had withdrawn from the Spice Islands to concentrate on Indian cotton goods. Only in the Spanish Philippines was a European presence pervasive and politically dominant over a sizable area.

Most of the insular Asians were by now converted to Islam, a process that began in the 1200s through contact with Arab and Indian Muslim traders. By the time the Portuguese arrived in 1511, Malacca had become a commercial crossroads of the Indian Ocean and East Asian networks, as well as the most important point of dissemination for Islam throughout the region. From Malacca the Portuguese extended their control over the Spice Islands. Except for the island of Bali, the original syncretistic blend of Hindu with animist beliefs that had been India's legacy had faded away. Only in the Philippines was there a Christian element.

If the islands were relatively untouched by the early European traders, the mainland populations were even less so. In the 1700s, the three states of Thailand, Burma, and Vietnam dominated the area. The first two were by then part of the *Hinayana* Buddhist world, while Vietnam under Chinese influence had remained with the *Mahayana* version of the faith. The once-potent Khmer state of Cambodia had been divided between the Thais and the Viets by stages during the fifteenth through seventeenth centuries. Nowhere was there a visible European influence so late as the end of the eighteenth century, but this was to change radically in the next century.

SUMMARY

AFTER A CENTURY of unchecked feudal warfare in Japan, three strongmen arose in the late sixteenth century to re-create effective centralized government. Last and most important was Tokugawa Ieyasu, who crushed or neutralized all opposition, including that of the Christian converts who were the product of the first European contacts with Japan in the mid-1500s.

By the 1630s, Japan was rapidly isolating itself from the world under the Tokugawa shogunate. The chief goal of the Tokugawa shoguns was a class-based political stability, which they successfully pursued for centuries. The shogun controlled all contacts with foreigners and gradually ended all interaction to isolate the island empire for more than 200 years. The daimyo nobility were carefully controlled by the shogun in Edo, who ruled from behind the imperial throne. Massive social changes took place at the same time the feudal political structure remained immobile. While urban merchants rose in the socioeconomic balance and peasants became wage laborers, the samurai slowly declined into obsolescence.

Population surged and the general economy prospered. The arts, particularly literature and painting, flourished. When Japan's solitude was finally broken, the governing elite were ready to deal with the challenge of Western science and technology constructively.

In Southeast Asia, the colonial period commenced with Dutch and Spanish presence in the Indonesian and Philippine Islands, respectively. But as late as the end of the eighteenth century, the Western traders and missionaries had had relatively little impact on the mass of the native inhabitants of the islands and even less on the mainland.

This situation changed gradually but with increasing rapidity. The nineteenth century saw both a transformation of the former subsistence economy of the peasantry and the introduction of direct European control of government both in the islands and on the mainland. By 1900, the entire region, except for Thailand, had become a European colony.

▶Identification Terms

Test your knowledge of this chapter's key concepts by defining the following terms. If you can't recall the meaning of certain terms, refresh your memory by looking up the boldfaced term in the chapter, turning to the Glossary at the end of the book, or working with the flashcards that are available on the *World Civilizations* Companion Website: **academic.cengage.com/adler**

daimyo   haiku   Kabuki   *sakoku*
Edo

▶Test Your Knowledge

Test your knowledge of this chapter by answering the following questions. Complete answers appear at the end of the book. You may find even more quiz questions in CengageNOW and on the *World Civilizations* Companion Website: **academic.cengage.com/adler**

1. The early Christian missionaries to Japan
   a. found a hostile reception.
   b. were mainly Protestants.
   c. made the mistake of trying to conquer the Buddhist natives.
   d. were welcomed and given a hearing.
   e. were evicted from the country within five years of their arrival.
2. The Shinto faith is best described as
   a. the native Japanese religion.
   b. the Japanese Holy Scripture.

   c. a mixture of Christianity and Japanese pagan belief.
   d. a variety of Buddhism imported from Korea.
   e. a reaction to the proselytizing of the Jesuits.
3. The Tokugawa shogun is best described as a
   a. military dictator.
   b. military adviser to the emperor.
   c. chief of government under the supposed supervision of the emperor.
   d. symbolic and religious leader under the emperor's supervision.
   e. feudal lord who first implemented shogunate rule.
4. The government system created by the shoguns in the 1600s
   a. allowed the local chieftains called *daimyo* to rule unchecked.
   b. was an imitation of the Chinese system of mandarin officials.

c. made the daimyo dependent on the shogun's favor.

d. used the emperor as military chief while the shoguns ruled all else.

e. provided imperial protection for the families of the daimyo.

5. Which of the following did *not* occur during the Tokugawa period?

a. Japanese elite thought shifted from Buddhist to Confucian patterns.

b. Japanese formal culture stagnated in its continued isolation from the world.

c. Trade and economic activity generally increased.

d. Internal peace and order were effectively maintained.

e. The elite samurai faded into obsolescence.

6. The reduction of the samurai's influence in public affairs was

a. carried out through government-ordered purges.

b. attempted but not achieved during the shogunate period.

c. achieved by eliminating internal warfare through a strong government.

d. achieved by encouraging them to become merchants and landlords.

e. opposed by the shoguns but supported by the emperor.

7. The Kabuki drama

a. specialized in dreamy romantic comedies.

b. was limited in appeal to the samurai and daimyo.

c. depicted drama in daily life in a realistic, humorous way.

d. was an import from China.

e. portrayed in realistic fashion the military exploits of the samurai.

8. Which of the following art forms was an original Japanese invention?

a. Wood-block printing

b. Haiku

c. Nature poetry

d. Weaving of silk tapestry

e. The epic poem

9. In general, it can be said of Japanese merchants that they

a. emigrated in large numbers and established wider trade networks under Tokugawa rule.

b. always enjoyed high status in Japanese society.

c. saw little change in their trade throughout the entire period of the Tokugawa shogunate.

d. gained in status after the imposition of sakoku.

e. saw an increase in trade with foreigners as a result of sakoku.

10. Which of the following was true of the *islands* of Southeast Asia by the 1600s?

a. The Portuguese established control over its trade.

b. The Dutch established control over its trade.

c. Most of its trade was lost to China.

d. Most of its inhabitants had converted to Islam.

e. Both b and d

Enter *CengageNOW* using the access card that is available with this text. *CengageNOW* will assist you in understanding the content in this chapter with lesson plans generated for your needs and provide you with a connection to the *Wadsworth World History Resource Center* (see description at right for details).

 World History Resource Center

Enter the Resource Center using either your *CengageNOW* access card or your standalone access card for the *Wadsworth World History Resource Center*. Organized by topic, this website includes quizzes; images; over 350 primary source documents; interactive simulations, maps, and timelines; movie explorations; and a wealth of other resources. You can read the following documents, and many more, at the *Wadsworth World History Resource Center*:

Honda Toshiaki, "A Secret Plan for Government"

Kaibara Ekken or Kaibara Token, "Greater Learning for Women"

FROM CONQUEST TO COLONIES IN HISPANIC AMERICA

> *[The conquest] was neither a victory nor a defeat.*
> *It was the dolorous birth of the mestizo people.*
> —Anonymous Inscription at the Site of Final Aztec Defeat

THE FALL OF THE AZTEC AND INCA EMPIRES

THE COLONIAL EXPERIENCE
Colonial Administration ◆ The Church in the Colonies

THE EARLY ECONOMIC STRUCTURE

STAGNATION AND REVIVAL IN THE EIGHTEENTH CENTURY

COLONIAL SOCIETY AND CULTURE

THE ARRIVAL OF THE Europeans in the New World started an enormous exchange of crops and commodities, modalities, and techniques. The beginning and most important phase of this exchange was conducted under the auspices of the Spanish conquistadores, who so rapidly conquered the Indian populations in the sixteenth century. For the next 300 years, most of the newly discovered lands were administered by a colonial system that superimposed Iberian Christian economic institutions, habits, and values on existing indigenous ones. The form of colonial lifestyle that gradually evolved in Latin America was the product of the native Indians and the imported black slaves, as much as of the whites.

THE FALL OF THE AZTEC AND INCA EMPIRES

We have seen (Chapter 22) that the initial phase of Spanish exploration in the Caribbean was dominated by the search for treasure. The "Indies" of Columbus were reputed to be lands of gold and spices, waiting to be exploited by the first individual who might happen upon them. Within a few years, however, this image was obliterated by the realities of the Caribbean islands, where gold was nonexistent. The search then shifted to the mainland, and the immediate result was the conquest of the Aztecs in Mexico and the Incas in Peru.

The Aztec capital fell in 1521 to conquistador Hernán Cortés, who began construction of Mexico City with stones from the leveled pyramids. Within a decade, Francisco Pizarro used the tactics of Cortés to conquer the Inca empire in South America. Pizarro, based in Panama, followed rumors of gold to the south, and by 1532 he had taken the Inca capital, Cuzco. Just as in Aztec Mexico, when the Spanish arrived in Peru, they found many allies to help them overthrow the Cuzco government, which was engaged in civil war. The viral pandemics (smallpox, measles, and influenza) carried by the Spaniards to Mexico and Peru decimated the Indians' ranks while hardly affecting the

Spaniards. The Native Americans perceived that their deities and leaders were powerless against the scourges of the conquistadores, while the apparently superior Catholic religion was able to protect its faithful. The generous social assistance programs of the Incas (see Chapter 11) were no longer enough to win the active loyalty of the Inca's subjects. Pizarro and his band, which was even smaller than that of Cortés in Mexico, were able to take the Inca king hostage and demolish the regime in a short time in the Peruvian lowlands and valleys. Some of the imperial family and their officials escaped to the high mountains and attempted to rule from there for another thirty years before being crushed.

Spain showed much less interest in colonizing the sparsely populated areas of northern Mexico and southern South America, where no gold or silver had been found. In these areas, recalcitrant Amerindian groups such as the Puebloans of New Mexico and the Mapuche (mah-POO-chay) of Patagonia, violently resisted Hispanization. The northernmost reaches of Spanish lands encompassed today's U.S. Southwest but were beyond the practical reach of the viceroyal capital, Mexico City. The effective northern borders of Spanish colonization were anchored by the fortified Franciscan mission towns of San Francisco and Santa Fe (see Map 28.1). The early Portuguese colonization of Brazil was similar to the Spanish colonization of Chile and the Argentine areas. Lacking the allure of precious metals and a ready-made Indian workforce, these regions were gradually colonized by merchants and farmers, rather than swiftly conquered by gold-seekers or would-be aristocrats. Brazil was named after the first natural resource exploited by the Portuguese: the valuable red dye, called *brazil*, extracted from the brazilwood tree. The (male) settlers in precarious areas, such as coastal Brazil, arrived without their wives and families. Iberian men freely mixed with indigenous women; their offspring in Brazil were called *mamelucos* (ma-muh-LOO-koez; the Portuguese version of Spanish-Indian *mestizos*). The societies were less class-conscious because everyone had to work together to survive.

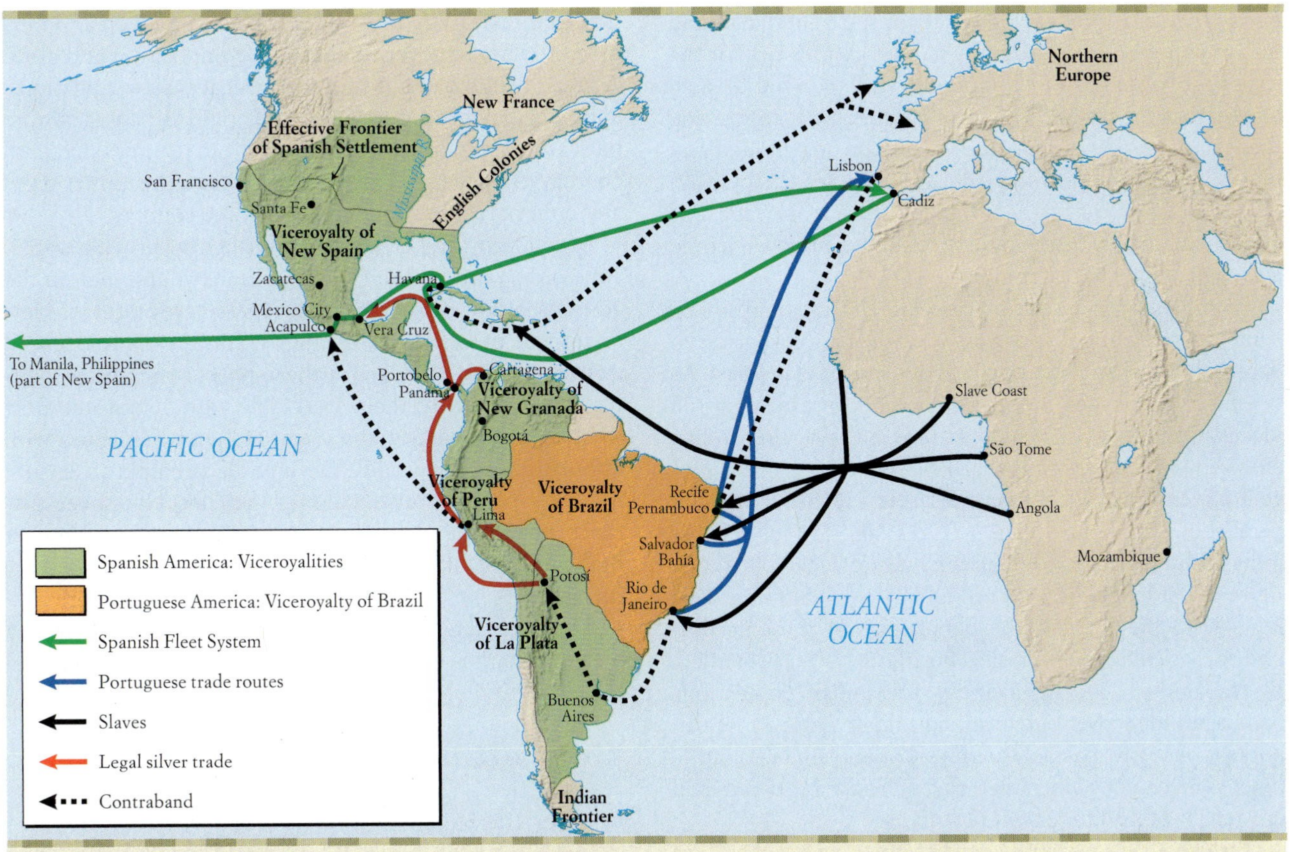

MAP 28.1 Colonial Latin America: Viceroyalties and Trade Connections

MAP QUESTION
How did commerce, both legal and contraband, connect colonial Latin America with the rest of the world?

THE COLONIAL EXPERIENCE

Spain's colonization of the New World focused on the conquered areas of the Aztec and Maya dominions (the colonial viceroyalty of New Spain) and the Inca empire (the viceroyalty of Peru). These areas had treasure in gratifying abundance, both in gold and, in even greater amounts, silver. Here Indian resistance was broken, and the small groups of Spaniards made themselves into feudal lords, each with his Spanish entourage and Indian servants. One-fifth (*quinto*) of what was discovered or stolen belonged to the royal government; the remainder could be divided up as the conquistadores saw fit. Agricultural production was greatly enriched by the introduction of draft animals and new crops (wheat, rice, sugar cane, citrus fruits). The survivors of the pre-Columbian empires furnished a ready-made free labor pool, which was accustomed to organized labor for tribute to a central authority.

In this earliest period, until about 1560, the Spanish crown, which in theory was the ultimate proprietor of all the new lands, allowed the conquerors of the Indians the **encomienda** (en-koh-MYEN-dah), or the right to demand uncompensated labor from the natives as a reward for the risks and hardships of exploration. This soon led to such abuses that the priests who were charged with converting the Indians to Christianity (especially the determined and brave Dominican Bartolomé de las Casas, see Chapter 22) protested vigorously to Madrid, and the encomienda was abolished midway through the sixteenth century on paper, although somewhat later in fact.

Prompted by protests from Father de las Casas and others, King Charles V and his advisors were the first Europeans to debate the legal and ethical status of conquered peoples. As a result of the debates, the Spanish home government passed idealistic reform laws, including a prohibition against Indian enslavement. However, no legalistic injunctions could prevent the ensuing demographic disaster, which was without parallel in history. Owing in part to a kind of soul sickness induced by their enslavement and subservience but much more to epidemic diseases brought by the whites and unfamiliar to the Indians, the populations of these accomplished, agricultural folk crashed horrifically (see Chapter 22). By the mid-seventeenth century, the Indian populations had begun to recover but never did so fully. Latin American populations only reached their pre-Columbian levels in the nineteenth century, when the influx of blacks and whites had created a wholly different ethnic mix.

African slaves were relegated to the lowest echelon of colonial society, with no protections from abusive "owners" (see Evidence of the Past). However, slavery in the Iberian colonies included the possibility of buying or otherwise earning one's freedom, creating a growing class of free African-Americans. The African cultural and religious influence is particularly strong in the plantation zone (the territory from the Caribbean area to southern Brazil), which was the destination of most slaves.

Colonial Administration

The Spanish administration in most of the Americas and the Portuguese system in Brazil were essentially similar. Under the auspices of the home government, an explorer/conqueror was originally allowed nearly unlimited proprietary powers in the new land. Soon, however, he was displaced by a royal council set up with exclusive powers over commerce, crafts, mining, and every type of foreign trade. Stringent controls were imposed through a viceroy or governor appointed by the Spanish government in Madrid and responsible solely to it. Judicial and military matters were also handled through the councils or the colonial *audiencia* (high court) in each province. The only hints of elective government were in the bottom ranks of the bureaucracy: the early Spanish town councils (*cabildos*) and the traditional communes of the Indian villages.

Iberian born nobles (*peninsulares*) dominated the colonial administration. It was highly bureaucratized and mirrored the home government in its composition and aims. A great deal of paper dealing with legal cases, regulations, appointment procedures, tax rolls, and censuses flowed back and forth across the Atlantic. From the mid-sixteenth century, the government's basic aim was to maximize fiscal and commercial revenues for the home country.

Secondarily, the government wished to provide an avenue of upward mobility for ambitious young men in the administration of the colonies. The viceroyalties of New Spain and of Peru were established in the mid-sixteenth century, and the holders of these posts were always peninsulares. A few of them were able administrators; most were court favorites being rewarded with a sinecure with opportunities for wealth. Despite all attempts to ensure Madrid's controls over colonial policies, the sheer distance involved and the insecurity of ocean travel meant that the local officials—normally **criollos** (cree-OH-yoz; native-born people of Iberian race in Latin America)—had considerable autonomy. Their care of their Indian and mestizo charges varied from blatant exploitation to admirable solicitude.

The Church in the Colonies

Another Iberian institution was a partner to the civil government in the colonies: the Catholic Church. Filled with the combative spirit and sense of high mission that were a legacy of the long *reconquista* struggle against the Moors, the missionaries were anxious to add the Central and South American Indians to the church's ranks. In this endeavor the government authorities supported

EVIDENCE OF THE PAST

Recovering Life Stories of the Voiceless: Testimonial Narratives by African Slaves

The oral histories of a handful of ex-slaves provide the only first-person accounts of life on the colonial plantations. Sympathetic editors have collected, edited, and published these accounts. The slaves in Cuba and Brazil worked mainly on cash-crop plantations in a variety of capacities. The following selection is from one of the few first-person slave narratives from Brazil. In about 1850, Mahommah G. Baquaqua told his story to one of the abolitionists who had freed him.

> [After being captured as a boy in Africa] I was then placed in that most horrible of places, the slave ship . . . [where] we became desperate through suffering and fatigue [as well as hunger and thirst]. . . . We arrived at Pernambuco [Recife, Brazil], South America, early in the morning. . . . We landed a few miles from the city, at a farmer's house, which was used as a kind of slave market. . . . I had not been there very long before I saw [the farmer] use the lash pretty freely on a boy, which made a deep impression on my mind. . . .
>
> When a slaver comes in, the news spreads like wild-fire, and down come all those that are interested in the arrival of the vessel with its cargo of living merchandise. . . . I was soon placed at hard labor [by my new master], such as none but slaves and horses are put to. [My master] was building a house, and had to fetch building stone from across the river, a considerable distance, and I was compelled to carry them that were so heavy it took three men to raise them upon my head, . . . for a quarter of a mile at least, down to where the boat lay. Sometimes the stone would press so hard upon my head that I was obliged to throw it down upon the ground, and then my master would be very angry indeed, and would say the [dog] had thrown the stone, when I thought in my heart that he was the worst dog; but . . . I dared not give utterance in words.

Source: Samuel Moore, ed. *Biography of Mahommah G. Baquaqua, A Native of Zoogao* [sic] *in the Interior of Africa*. Detroit: George E. Pomeroy and Co., 1854, pp. 34–50.

The Cuban ex-slave Esteban Montejo was 103 years old when he told his life story to an anthropologist, in 1963. The following passage begins with his birth on a sugar plantation.

> Like all children of slavery, the criollitos, as they were called, I was born in the infirmary where they took the pregnant

A BRAZILIAN PLANTATION IN 1830. A Portuguese colonist in Brazil planted the first sugar cane there in 1521. Sugar soon became Brazil's economic mainstay, and African slaves were imported to work on plantations like this one overlooking a harbor near Rio de Janeiro.

> black women to give birth. . . . Blacks were sold like piglets, and they sold me right off—that's why I don't remember anything about that place. . . . At all the plantations there was an infirmary near the [slave quarters]. It was a large wooden house where they took the pregnant women. Children were born there and stayed until they were six or seven years old when they went to live in the slave quarters and to work like everyone else. . . . If a little black boy was pretty and lively, they sent him inside, to the master's house. . . . [T]he little black boy had to spend his time shooing flies [with a large palm fan] because the masters ate a lot. And they put [him] at the head of the table. . . . And they told him: "Shoo, so those flies don't fall in the food!" If a fly fell on a plate, they scolded him severely and even whipped him. I never did this work because I never liked to be near the masters. I was a *cimarrón* [wild, runaway] from birth.

Source: Miguel Barnet, ed. *Biography of a Runaway Slave*. Translated by W. Nick Hill. New York: Pantheon Books, 1994, pp. 19–20, 22, 38.

▶ Analyze and Interpret

When Baquaqua and Montejo told their stories, they had lived many years as free men. Do you think that the intervening years might have affected their childhood memories of slavery in any way? What influence might the editors of their published stories have had on the narratives?

Bildarchiv Preussischer Kulturbesitz/Art Resource, NY

A HACENDADO AND HIS FAMILY. This nineteenth-century scene shows a Mexican hacendado, owner of a large plantation, with his wife and one of his overseers. The elaborate costumes were impractical but necessary in maintaining social distance from the peons.

The Granger Collection, New York

them. A church stood at the center of every town in the new lands; all other buildings were oriented around it. The bishops, nominated by the Crown, were as important in the administration of a given area as the civil governors; cultural and educational matters pertaining to both Europeans and Indians were in their hands. In its lavish baroque buildings and artworks, the church left a long-lasting physical imprint throughout the Spanish and Portuguese colonies. The spiritual imprint was even more profound, continuing to the present day.

THE EARLY ECONOMIC STRUCTURE

International commerce between the Iberian colonies and Europe and Asia connected the colonies to the nascent global economy (see Map 28.1). The major element in the economy of the early Spanish colonies was the mining of precious metals. Everything else served that end. (Brazil, the Portuguese colony, was originally a sugarcane plantation, but later it also emphasized mining.) The agricultural estates, which were first encomiendas and then *haciendas* (hah-see-EN-duhz)—rural plantation-villages with at least technically free wage labor—existed primarily to supply food for the mining communities. Handicraft industries made gloves and textiles, prepared foods, and provided blacksmithing services for the same market. There were few exports beyond the produce of the mines and a handful of cash crops such as sugar, tobacco, and indigo.

Rights to export goods to the Spanish colonies were limited to Spaniards; the goods could be carried only in Spanish ships, which left from one port, Seville (later also Cádiz), twice a year. From Latin America, another flotilla laden with the bullion mined the previous year left annually from the Mexican port of Vera Cruz. The restrictions on these flotillas were intended to protect the returning treasure from the Americas from pirates and to restrict what was sent to and taken from the colonies.

The great bonanza of the early years was the "mountain of silver" at Potosí (poh-tuh-SEE) in what is now Bolivia. Next to it came the Mexican mines north of Mexico City. The silver that flowed from the New World to Seville (and from Acapulco to Manila) from the 1540s to the 1640s far overshadowed the gold taken from Moctezuma and the Inca in the conquest period. When the volume declined drastically in the 1640s, the Madrid government experienced a crisis. Production stayed relatively low for a century, but thanks to new technology and increased incentives, it reached great heights in the later eighteenth century before declining again, this time for good.

The input of bullion did not produce lasting constructive results in Spain. Some of it flowed on through royal or private hands to enrich the western European shippers, financiers, merchants, and manufacturers who supplied Iberia with every type of good and service in the sixteenth and seventeenth centuries. Perhaps a third wound up in Chinese hands to pay for the Spanish version of the triangular trade across the Pacific: Spanish galleons left Acapulco, Mexico, loaded with silver and bound for Manila, where they met Chinese ships loaded with silk and porcelain, which, after transshipment across Mexico or Panama, wound up in Seville and might be reshipped back to the Caribbean. Less than half of the Spanish silver remained in Spanish hands, but this was enough to start an inflationary spiral there that seized all of Europe by the end of the sixteenth century and brought ruin to many landholding nobles (see Chapter 22).

STAGNATION AND REVIVAL IN THE EIGHTEENTH CENTURY

The later seventeenth century and the first decades of the eighteenth were a period of stagnation and decline in New Spain. The last Spanish Habsburg kings were so weak that local strongmen in Hispanic America were able to overshadow the high courts and municipal authorities of the viceroyal governments. The once-annual treasure fleets were sailing only sporadically, and the total supply of American bullion was down sharply from its high point. Several of the larger Caribbean islands were captured by the British, French, or Dutch or were taken over by buccaneers. The import/export controls imposed by the Madrid government were falling apart, because non-Spaniards were able to ignore the prohibitions against trading with the colonies, were granted exemptions, or collaborated with the criollos in smuggling in systematic fashion. By now the colonies could produce the bulk of their necessities and no longer had to import them.

At this juncture, the Spanish government experienced a revival when a new dynasty, an offshoot of the French Bourbons, took over in Madrid in 1701 as a result of the war of Spanish Succession (see Chapter 25). Especially under King Charles III (ruled 1759–1788), who figured among the most enlightened monarchs of the eighteenth century, thoroughgoing reform was applied to the Indies. A form of free trade was introduced, the navy and military were strengthened, and a new system of *intendants,* administrators responsible to the center on the French Bourbon model, was able to make Spanish colonial government much more effective. Taxes were collected as they had not been for years, and smuggling and corruption were reduced. The two Spanish American viceroyalties were subdivided into four: New Spain, Peru, New Granada (northern South America), and Rio de la Plata (Argentina and central South America). The officials for these new divisions continued to be drawn almost exclusively from the peninsula, an affront that the people in the colonies did not easily swallow. Another point of contention was that many criollo clergymen were among the Jesuit missionaries banished by the anticlerical Bourbons from the Iberian empire. Colonists throughout the Western Hemisphere rose up in protest against the expulsion of the Jesuits, who had won the hearts and minds of all, and who from their exile encouraged the emerging sense of Hispano-American identity among criollos and mestizos alike.

The reforms did not benefit the mass of Indian and mestizo inhabitants at all. Indian population increased (perhaps doubling) in the eighteenth century, creating an irresistible temptation to hacienda owners to press this defenseless and unskilled group into forced labor in the expanding plantation agriculture. The market for these products was not only the seemingly insatiable demand for sugar in Europe and North America but also the rapidly growing population in the colonies. The foreseeable result was an expansion of brutal serfdom, generating a series of Indian uprisings. Tupac Amaru, a descendant of the Inca, led the most notable of these in the 1780s. The viceroyal government of Peru was nearly toppled before the revolt was put down. A few years later in the Caribbean island of Haiti (then Saint Domingue), a black ex-slave named Toussaint L'Ouverture led an uprising of slaves that ended French dominion on that island. The Toussaint rebellion eventually succeeded in attaining complete independence for Haiti, and it made an indelible impression on both the friends and enemies of the daring idea of a general abolition of slavery.

The oppressed Indians and enslaved blacks were by no means the only Latin Americans who were discontented in the last years of the eighteenth century. Economic policy reforms, however needed, were also sometimes painful to the native-born criollos. With free trade, imports from Europe became considerably cheaper, hurting domestic producers. And the remarkable increase in silver production as a result of new mining techniques and new discoveries did not flow to the benefit of the locals but rather to what was more often now viewed as an alien government in Madrid. The loosening of the former restrictions on trade and manufactures had a distinctly stimulating effect on the intellectual atmosphere of the criollo urbanites. After decades of somnolence, there arose within a small but crucially important minority a spirit of criticism and inquiry, which reflected the stirring of European liberalism we shall examine in Chapter 30.

In the 1770s, the criollo elite witnessed the successful (North) American revolt against Britain, and a few years later, the radical French revolution doctrines seized their attention. In both of these foreign upheavals, they believed they saw many similarities with their own grievances against their government, similarities that were to be ultimately persuasive for their own rebellion.

COLONIAL SOCIETY AND CULTURE

The class system was based on the degree of "purity" of Spanish bloodlines. In a legal sense, both peninsulares and criollos were considered Spanish. However, the peninsulares considered themselves superior to their criollo cousins, whom they supposed were even physically inferior by virtue of their birth in the Americas. The peninsulares occupied the uppermost ranks of society, church, and government, and they excluded the criollos from positions of power to prevent the formation of a strong native-born elite that might threaten the dominance of the peninsulares. Yet the criollos (especially the descendants of the conquistadores), being owners of haciendas and mines, were often wealthier than the peninsulares. Both groups did their utmost to re-create Spanish life in the New World.

Social life was centered in the cities and towns, because the Spaniards preferred urban life. The elite lifestyle was slow-paced and leisurely, consisting of carriage rides and other outings to display their finery, religious ceremonies and festivals, and diversions such as gambling, bullfights, and the popular baroque poetry contests. It was said that the (mostly bad) colonial poets were a "flock of noisy magpies." For the men, there were cockfights, liaisons with the beautiful mixed-blood women, and other indulgences. The criollos, relegated to secondary status, cultivated intellectual and literary pursuits to enrich the limited cultural environment. Although the Inquisition prohibited reading novels and other heretical material, and the printing presses in Mexico and Lima produced mostly religious material, secular books were nonetheless widely available, and the criollo intellectuals kept abreast of Enlightenment thought and the latest European literary currents. Women were mainly limited to religious literature.

The monastery or convent were also options for the criollos. In the more lenient religious orders, the "cells" were more like suites of rooms.

In this strongly patriarchal society, women lacked independent legal status and were expected to obey their fathers, brothers, or husbands unconditionally. Spanish women were carefully protected because their family's honor depended on their irreproachable behavior. The daughters of criollos were married, if possible, to newly arrived peninsulares to ensure the family's prestige. Young men were sent to Spain or France for higher education. Young women were given a rudimentary education by tutors at home, and a few learned domestic and social arts at mission schools, but they were denied any higher education. In the final analysis, elite women had three alternatives: marriage, spinsterhood, or the convent. Widows of comfortable financial status were the most independent women in colonial times; they were free to make their own decisions, and they often ran the family businesses with great success.

The **mestizos** (mehs-TEE-sohz), or "mixed-blood," sons of Spanish men and Indian women, became adept at creating roles for themselves in a society that had originally despised them as mongrels. They served as intermediaries and interpreters among the elites, the Indians, and other categories of mixed-blood peoples. Mestizos were excluded from the universities and from positions in the church and the government. They could be soldiers but not officers, artisans' apprentices but not master craftsmen. Mestizos might also be tenant farmers or hacienda managers. The mestizo gaucho horsemen of the Argentine great plains area found their niche as providers of contraband cowhides and tallow. The mixed-blood *mamelucos* of Brazil were intrepid explorers of the western frontiers, who sometimes raided the Jesuit missions to capture Indian slaves.

The fifteen other categories of mixed-blood peoples were more severely restricted than the mestizos and were not

Museo de America, Madrid, Spain/Giraudon/Bridgeman Art Library

SISTER JUANA INÉS DE LA CRUZ. Sister Juana is revered as the finest poet of her time in New Spain (Mexico), an extraordinary achievement given the constraints on colonial women. Sister Juana's unique intellectual outlook made her the object of both admiration for her originality and severe criticism for her worldliness.

Method of throwing the Lasso.

Method of throwing the Bolas.

Private Collection/Bridgeman Art Library

GAUCHOS ON THE ARGENTINE PAMPAS. The gaucho, usually a mixed-blood mestizo, created a lifestyle that blended the cultures of Spanish and Native American horsemen. Gaucho contraband traders, frontiersmen, and soldiers helped shape the history of the River Plate region (today's Argentina and Uruguay).

permitted to bear firearms. African-Americans were at the bottom of the social pyramid. Along with the surviving Indians, they slaved from dawn to dusk in the mines, on haciendas and plantations, in sweatshops and mills, for little or no pay (see Society and Economy). Their only opportunities for rest were the Sunday mass and markets and the occasional festival. Non-Spanish women were less restricted because the Amerindian and African cultures were less patriarchal in origin. However, these women suffered sexual exploitation and abuse by their Iberian masters.

The subdued Amerindians lived in a variety of other settings besides haciendas and plantations. Communally run Indian towns, vestiges of the pre-Columbian empires, were remote from the Hispanic towns and were left intact. The only outsiders they saw were priests and the infamously corrupt tribute collectors. In areas where the Indians had dispersed and a demand arose for their labor in the mines, the Spanish rounded them up and settled them in newly established Spanish-run towns, where clergy saw to their instruction in the Catholic faith, and where they were readily accessible for tribute labor. Finally, the religious orders collected the Indians in missions, where they received the rudiments of religious indoctrination and were taught useful crafts. Treatment of the Indians in the missions ranged from exploitative to benevolent, but even in the best of cases, they were legally classified as minors and treated as children. Indians were exempt from some taxes, and because they were viewed as children in the eyes of the Church, they were beyond the reach of the Inquisition. The Jesuit missions in Paraguay and Brazil protected their Indian charges from capture by ruthless mameluco slave-hunters from Brazil.

SOCIETY AND ECONOMY

Forced Labor and Debt Peonage in the Spanish Colonies

The luxurious lifestyle of the colonial elites was supported by the labors of their inferiors in the social pyramid: Native Americans, Africans, and mestizos. They toiled in the textile mills and on the haciendas, where conditions (although wretched) were still preferable to working in the mines.

In the 1620s, a Spanish monk traveled through the Spanish colonies in the Americas, making careful observation of what he witnessed, including the workings of Mexican textile mills and how they got their labor.

"... To keep their [woolen] mills supplied with labor, they maintain individuals who are engaged and hired to snare poor innocents; seeing some Indian who is a stranger to the town, with some trickery or pretense, such as hiring him to carry something . . . and paying him cash, they get him into the mill; once inside, they drop the deception, and the poor fellow never again gets outside that prison until he dies and they carry him out for burial.

In this way they have gathered in and duped many married Indians with families, who have passed into oblivion here for 20 years, or longer, or their whole lives, without their wives and children knowing anything about them; for even if they want to get out, they cannot, thanks to the great watchfulness with which the doormen guard the exits. These Indians are occupied in carding, spinning, weaving, and the other operations of making cloth; and thus the owners make their profits by these unjust and unlawful means.

And although the Royal Council of the Indies, with the holy zeal which animates it in the service of God our Lord, of his Majesty, and of the Indians' welfare, has tried to remedy this evil . . . and the Viceroy of New Spain appoints mill inspectors to visit them and remedy such matters, nevertheless, since most of those who set out on such commissions aim rather at their own enrichment, . . . than at the relief of the Indians, and since the mill owners pay them well, they leave the wretched Indians in the same slavery; and even if some of them are fired with holy zeal to remedy such abuses when they visit the mills, the mill owners keep places provided in the mills in which they hide the wretched Indians against their will, so that they do not see or find them, and the poor fellows cannot complain against their wrongs."

Source: A. Vásquez de Espinosa, *Compendium and Description of the West Indies*, trans. C. Clark (Washington, DC: Smithsonian, 1942).

SLAVE LABORERS ON A CUBAN SUGAR CANE PLANTATION. Cuba's colonial economy, like Brazil's, depended on African slaves to work the sugar, tobacco, and cacao plantations.

Museo Nacional Palacio de Bellas Artes, Havana, Cuba/Index/Bridgeman Art Library

Spanish royal officials described the plight of the Indians in Peru, who not only paid the tribute tax, but also were condemned to the serfdom of debt peonage; that is, perpetually working off debts forced on them by their masters.

On farming haciendas, an Indian subject . . . earns from fourteen to eighteen pesos a year. . . . In addition, the hacendado assigns him a piece of land, about twenty to thirty yards square in size, to grow his food. In return the Indian must work three hundred days in the year, leaving him sixty-five days of rest for Sundays, other church holidays, illness, or some accident that may prevent him from working. The mayordomo [foreman] of the hacienda keeps careful record of the days worked by the Indian in order to settle accounts with him at the end of the year.

From his wage the master deducts the eight pesos of royal tribute that the Indian must pay; assuming that the Indian earns eighteen pesos, the most he can earn, he is left with ten pesos. From this amount the master deducts 2.25 pesos to pay for three yards of coarse cloth . . . [for] a cloak to cover his nakedness. He now has 7.75 pesos with which to feed and dress his wife and children, if he has a family, and to pay the church fees demanded by the parish priest. But . . . since he cannot raise on his little plot all the food he needs for his family, he must get from the hacendado each month two bushels of maize, [at] more than double the price if he could buy elsewhere, [an annual total of] nine pesos, which is 1.75 pesos more than the Indian has left. Thus the unhappy Indian, after working three hundred days of the year for his master and cultivating his little plot in his free time, and receiving only a coarse cloak and twelve bushels of maize, is in debt 1.75 pesos, and must continue to work for his master the following year. . . . [T]he poor Indian . . . remains a slave all his life and, contrary to [all] law . . . after his death his sons must continue to work to pay the debt of their father.

Source: Jorge Juan and Antonio de Ulloa, *Noticias secretas de América* (Madrid, 1918), 2 vols., I, pp. 290–292, as quoted in Benjamin Keen, ed., *Latin American Civilization*, 4th ed. (Boulder and London: Westview Press, 1986), pp. 75–76.

▶ *Analyze and Interpret*

When enslavement of Amerindians became illegal and obsolete, debt peonage replaced the *encomienda* system. Was debt peonage an improvement on the encomienda? Explain your answer.

The Indians throughout the colonies adopted Christianity, identifying particularly with the consoling figure of the Virgin Mary (similar to their earth goddesses) and with the crucified Christ (whose suffering paralleled their own traumatic conquest). To varying degrees, the Catholic saints were blended with pre-Columbian deities. A group of Indians devoutly praying at a saint's altar in a baroque cathedral might well be paying homage to the Inca or Aztec deity hidden under the statue's skirts. In the Caribbean areas, the Africans equated Catholic saints to Orisha deities, resulting in syncretic belief systems such as santería, which is still practiced by most Cubans.

SUMMARY

THE IBERIAN CONQUEST of Latin America was a clash of cultures that devastated the pre-Columbian civilizations but set the stage for the creation of a new society that blended contributions from Native Americans, Iberians, and later, Africans. As the conquerors and explorers became colonists, they replaced the Aztec and Inca masters at the top of the socioeconomic ladder. The conquerors' thirst for gold and elite status could be quenched only with the labor of the Indians. Some progressive missionaries tried in vain to protect their Indian charges in order to convert them humanely to Christianity. Unlike the Portuguese and other imperial powers, the Spanish monarchs grappled with the legal issues involved in the enslavement of their Indian subjects. However, few questioned the morality of importing African slaves to the great plantation zones of Brazil and the Caribbean islands.

The colonial experience in Latin America was quite different from that in Asia, North America, or Africa. Many Europeans eventually settled there but remained far outnumbered by the native Indians and the imported blacks. The church and government worked together to create a society that imitated that of the mother countries, while remaining different in many essentials. The unique melding of Iberian with Indian and African cultures proceeded at differing tempos in different places. After the flow of American bullion to the Old World tapered off in the mid-seventeenth century, a long period of stagnation and neglect ensued. A century later, the Spanish Bourbons supervised an economic and political revival in Latin America with mixed results. While the economies of the colonies were stimulated, so was resentment against continued foreign rule. By the early 1800s, armed rebellion against the mother country was imminent, inspired in part by the North American and French models.

▶ Identification Terms

Test your knowledge of this chapter's key concepts by defining the following terms. If you can't recall the meaning of certain terms, refresh your memory by looking up the boldfaced term in the chapter, turning to the Glossary at the end of the book, or working with the flashcards that are available on the *World Civilizations* Companion Website: **academic.cengage.com/adler**

criollos	*encomienda*	*haciendas*	*mestizos*

▶ Test Your Knowledge

Test your knowledge of this chapter by answering the following questions. Complete answers appear at the end of the book. You may find even more quiz questions in CengageNOW and on the *World Civilizations* Companion Website: **academic.cengage.com/adler**

1. Which of following Spanish terms does not apply to Hispanic American social or ethnic divisions?
   a. Criollo
   b. Menudo
   c. Mestizo
   d. Mameluco
   e. Mulatto

2. Which of the following factors helped bring about the rapid fall of both the Aztec and Inca empires?
   a. The Indians thought Cortés and Pizarro were devils.
   b. The conquistadores lost their Indian allies against the emperors.
   c. The conquistadores bribed Moctezuma and Atahualpa to betray their people.
   d. The Indians had steel weapons capable of killing an armored horseman.
   e. Masses of Indians died or were weakened by foreign diseases.

3. The following were introduced to the Americas by the Iberians:
   a. turkeys and tobacco.
   b. chocolate and maize.
   c. cattle, sugar cane, and wheat.
   d. pyramids and potatoes.
   e. tomatoes and tortillas.
4. Which of these were main features of the colonial system?
   a. Viceroyalties and cabildos
   b. Democratic elections
   c. Free trade among the viceroyalties
   d. The predominance of small farms owned by mulattos
   e. Separation of church and civil government
5. Of the following elements, which were important goals of the Spanish in the New World?
   a. Gold and silver
   b. Religious conversion of the Amerindians
   c. Establishment of new industries
   d. The Black Legend
   e. Both a and b
6. One result of the Bourbon reforms was
   a. decentralization of power and more autonomy for the colonies.
   b. vast improvements in the Indians' quality of life.
   c. mercantilism and trade monopolies.
   d. more efficient government and less corruption.
   e. mine closures and the breakup of huge haciendas.

7. The only successful rebellion by slaves in the Western Hemisphere occurred in
   a. Haiti.
   b. Cuba.
   c. Colombia.
   d. Brazil.
   e. Mexico.
8. Which factor led to the discontent of the criollos with colonial rule?
   a. The consolidation of two viceroyalties into one
   b. The peninsulares' exclusion of criollos from the upper echelons of government and society
   c. The expulsion of the Muslim Moors
   d. The Monroe Doctrine
   e. The Black Legend
9. Colonial Amerindians usually worked
   a. in the colonial government.
   b. in mines, mills, and religious missions.
   c. as foremen on the haciendas.
   d. for inflated wages and comfortable retirements.
   e. part-time as horsebreakers.
10. The colonial mestizos
   a. were exempt from taxation and the Inquisition.
   b. were never nomadic horsemen.
   c. served as links between the Indian and Spanish populations.
   d. were encouraged to attend university.
   e. could be military officers.

Enter *CengageNOW* using the access card that is available with this text. *CengageNOW* will assist you in understanding the content in this chapter with lesson plans generated for your needs, as well as provide you with a connection to the *Wadsworth World History Resource Center* (see description at right for details).

 **World History Resource Center**

Enter the Resource Center using either your *CengageNOW* access card or your standalone access card for the *Wadsworth World History Resource Center*. Organized by topic, this website includes quizzes; images; over 350 primary source documents; interactive simulations, maps, and timelines; movie explorations; and a wealth of other resources. You can read the following documents, and many more, at the *Wadsworth World History Resource Center*:

Aztec Accounts of the Conquest of Mexico
Hernán Cortés, "Second Letter to Charles V"

Worldview Four

LAW AND GOVERNMENT

SOCIETY AND ECONOMY

EUROPEANS

Law and government based on class, but effect of religious wars makes them increasingly secular. Absolutist monarchy the rule. Nobles and landlords rule free peasants in West, serfs in East. State and church still intertwined; religious tolerance considered dangerous to public order by most governments.

Economy continues to diversify, with strong capitalist character, especially in Protestant nations. Urban middle class prominent in business and commerce. Class divisions and number of impoverished increase, with serfdom common east of Elbe River. Machine industry begins in later eighteenth century.

WEST ASIANS

Government continues along traditional Qur'anic lines, and law follows *Sharia*. Ottomans bring Muslim empire to apex in sixteenth century, but cannot sustain momentum after 1700. Safavid Dynasty in Persia has 200 years of glory but exhausts itself between Ottoman and Mughal rivals.

Complex trade further evolves among Muslim countries as well as between them and non-Muslims. Slavery common, mainly from African sources. Wealth from gold mines in West Africa, spices from East Asia, and carrying trade between India/China and West.

SOUTH AND EAST ASIANS

Western presence not yet decisive but becoming more apparent. Many South Pacific territories under Western administration since 1500s. Japan originally welcomes Westerners but then shuts itself off in *sakoku*. China continues as imperial dynasty ruling through mandarin bureaucracy after Manzhou replace Ming in 1600s. India's north and center unified under Mughals in Delhi, with Europeans beginning to occupy coasts after 1700.

Japan prospers and advances while maintaining *sakoku* isolation. China has last great age under Qing before suffering humiliation from Europeans. Trade brings North and South together. Mughul India still well-organized country, with much commerce with Southeast Asia and islands. Merchants and craftsmen multiply, but everywhere agrarian village is mainstay of economy.

AMERICANS

By the mid-1500s, Spain and Portugal establish Iberian law and viceroyalties from Mexico to Argentina. Natives subordinated to minority of whites. Centralized colonial governments committed to mercantilist system and discouragement of autonomy. Reversal of policies occurs in later 1700s.

Mercantilism enforced until later 1700s, with colonial artisans and manufacturers obstructed by Madrid and London. Mining and plantation agriculture dominant large-scale economic activities in the Latin colonies. Most in both North and South live in agrarian subsistence economy.

CROSS-CULTURAL CONNECTIONS

Migrations and Population Changes
Europe: European migration and widespread colonization of Western hemisphere; fewer Europeans settle permanently in Asia and Africa.
Asia: SW Asians migrate and settle Asian and African lands on Indian Ocean; Chinese merchants migrate to SE Asia; Indians settle E. African coast.
Africa: Africans taken as slaves to Brazil, Caribbean Islands, New Spain, British colonies, Europe, India, and Middle East. Dutch settle Cape Colony.
America: Pandemics destroy up to 90% of Native Am. population; many cultures disappear. Ancestral Puebloans continue migrations to upper Rio Grande and Hopi Mesa.

Trade and Exchange Networks
Regional trade systems of the Old and New Worlds tied into global network for first time during era of European discovery and exploration. However, Europeans' creation of overseas empires and imposition of mercantilist trading rights adumbrate full potential of worldwide, free-market based system.

DISEQUILIBRIUM: THE WESTERN ENCOUNTER WITH THE NON-WESTERN WORLD, 1500–1700 CE

PATTERNS OF BELIEF

ARTS AND CULTURE

SCIENCE AND TECHNOLOGY

PATTERNS OF BELIEF	ARTS AND CULTURE	SCIENCE AND TECHNOLOGY
Protestant Reform breaks Christian unity. Papal church challenged, but regains some lost ground in seventeenth century. Churches become nationalistic, and theology more narrowly defined. Skepticism and secularism increase after 1700, leading to tolerance by end of eighteenth century. Enlightenment dominates intellectual affairs after c. 1750.	Renaissance continues in plastic arts; age of baroque architecture, sculpture, and painting in Catholic Europe. Neoclassicism of eighteenth century led by France. Vernacular literature flourishes in all countries. Western orchestral music begins. Authors become professionals, and arts begin to be democratized.	Physical, math-based sciences flourish in "scientific revolution" of seventeenth century. Science replaces scripture and tradition as source of truth for educated. Technology more important. Improved agriculture enables population explosion of eighteenth century. Beginnings of the Industrial Revolution in England.
Ulama and Islamic tradition resist evidence of Western economic and technical advances and refute it on doctrinal grounds. Orthodoxy severely challenged in parts of empire (e.g., Sufi, Shi'a) and becomes defensive. Expansion makes its last surge into Mughal India.	High point of Islamic art forms under Ottoman, Safavid, and Mughal aegis. Architecture, ceramics, miniature painting, and calligraphy particular strengths.	Sciences neglected; mental capital derived from Greek and Persian sources exhausted. Technology also lags, with all ideas coming from West rejected. By the end of period, Westerners moving into preferred posts in commerce of Ottoman and Mughal empires.
Religious beliefs undergo no changes from Buddhism (China, Japan, Southeast Asia); Hinduism (most of India, parts of Southeast Asia); Islam (North India, Afghanistan, East Indies); and Shinto (Japan). Christianity briefly flourishes in Japan until suppressed by Tokugawa shoguns in 1600s.	Superb paintings and drawings on porcelain, bamboo, and silk created in China and Japan. Calligraphy major art form. *Kabuki* and *No* plays invented in Japan, and novels in China. Poetry of nature admired. In India, Taj Mahal, frescoes, enamel work, and architecture are high points.	Sciences throughout Asia behind Europe by end of period. Exceptions in medicine and pharmacy. China adopts defensive seclusion from new ideas under mandarins. Technology lags, as overpopulation begins to be problem at end of period, further reducing need for laborsaving devices.
Catholicism makes impression on Latin American Indians, but religion remains mixed cult of pre-Christian and Christian beliefs, supervised by *criollo* priesthood and Spanish hierarchs.	Church in Latin America remains the sponsor of arts, but folk arts derived from pre-Columbian imagery remain universal. Little domestic literature written, but secular Enlightenment makes inroads into educated class by mid-eighteenth century.	Science and technology in Latin colonies dependent on stagnant mother country and have no importance to masses. Enlightened monarchs of later 1700s make improvements, but these are temporary and partial. In North America, Enlightenment finds acceptance.

Spread of Foods, Diseases, Technologies and Ideas

Europe: New World crops introduced to Europe; tobacco, potatoes, squashes, and maize have greatest impact. Bananas, yams, and coconuts introduced from Asia and Africa.

Asia: Some slaves exported to South Africa. Chinese migrations to regions of Southeast Asia. Some Southeast and South Asians convert to Christianity.

Africa: New World crops introduced, especially manioc and maize. Decline in population in regions of West Africa most heavily affected by the slave trade. Some states destroyed and others thrive because of slave trade. Christianity introduced in some regions, but survives in few areas beyond sixteenth century. Islam continues advances in West Africa.

America: New food crops brought from Old World: citrus fruits, beef, mutton, and spices. Wool textile weaving. European settlers and African slaves populate areas previously settled by Native Americans. New diseases imported from Europe and Africa. Christianity introduced and many Native Americans and Africans forced to convert.

Part FIVE

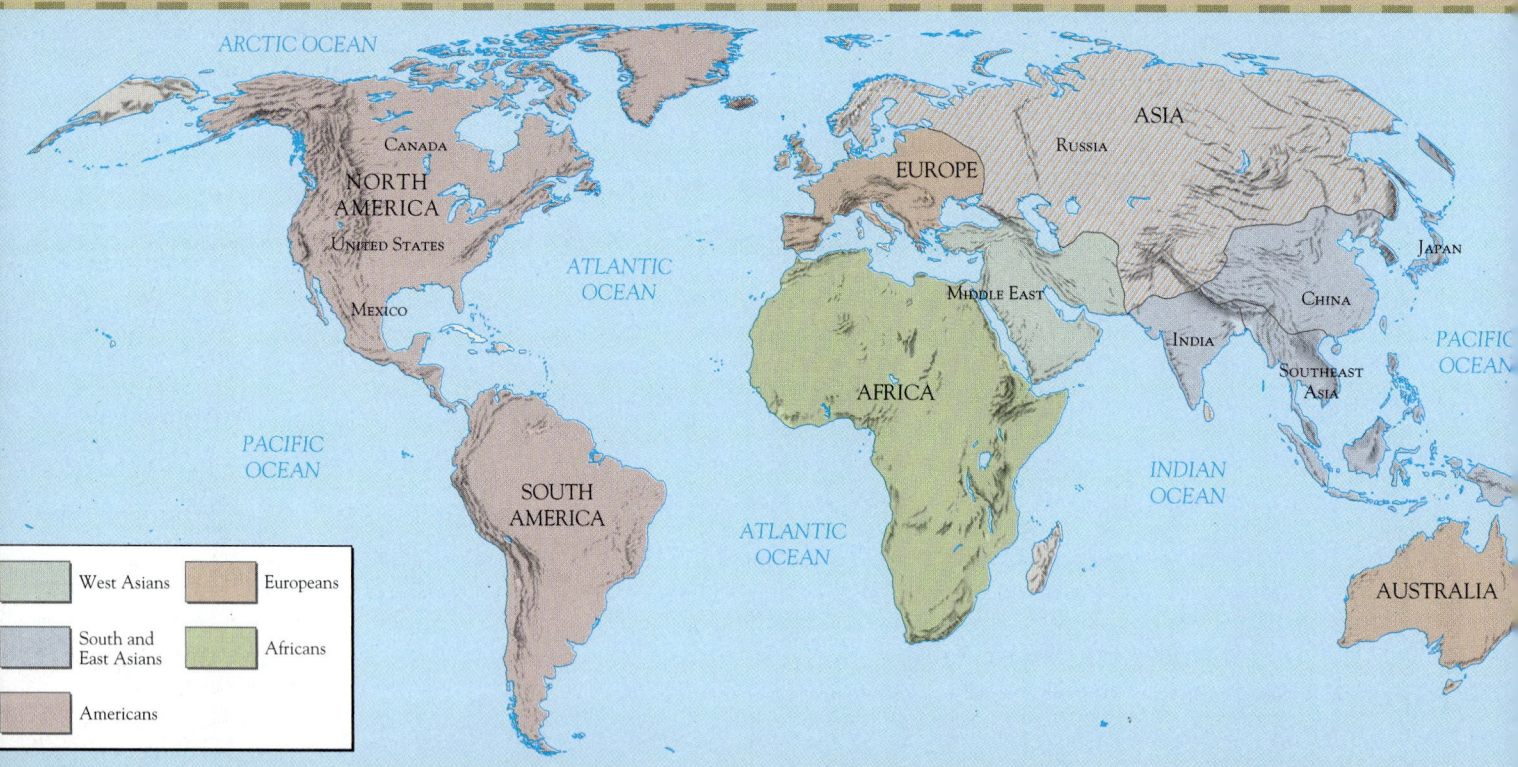

ARCTIC OCEAN

CANADA

NORTH
AMERICA

UNITED STATES

ATLANTIC
OCEAN

MEXICO

EUROPE

ASIA

RUSSIA

JAPAN

MIDDLE EAST

CHINA

PACIFIC
OCEAN

AFRICA

INDIA

SOUTHEAST
ASIA

PACIFIC
OCEAN

SOUTH
AMERICA

ATLANTIC
OCEAN

INDIAN
OCEAN

AUSTRALIA

	West Asians		Europeans
	South and East Asians		Africans
	Americans		

GLOSSARY

Abbas the Great See Shah Abbas the Great.

Abbasid Dynasty (Ah-BAH-sihd) The dynasty of caliphs who governed the Islamic Empire from the 750 until 1258 CE.

abbot/abbess The male/female head of a monastery/nunnery.

abstract expressionism A style of modern painting that does not seek to represent external reality but to convey emotional meaning through abstract shape and color.

abstractionism A twentieth-century school of painting that rejects traditional representation of external nature and objects.

Act of Supremacy of 1534 A law enacted by the English Parliament making the monarch the head of the Church of England.

Actium, Battle of The decisive 31 BCE battle in the struggle between Octavian Caesar and Mark Anthony, in which Octavian's victory paved the way for the Principate.

Age of the Barracks Emperors The period of the Roman Empire in the third century CE when the throne was repeatedly usurped by military men.

Agincourt (AH-zhin-cohr) The great victory of the English over the French in 1415, during the Hundred Years' War.

agrarian civilizations Civilizations that are based primarily on peasant farming.

Agricultural Revolution The substitution of farming for hunting-gathering as the primary source of food by a given people.

Ain Jalut (AYN Jah-LOOT) A decisive battle in 1260 during which an Egyptian Mamluk army turned back the Mongols and prevented them from invading North Africa.

Ajanta (Ah-JAHN-tah) Caves in central India that are the site of marvelous early frescoes inspired by Buddhism.

Akbar the Great (ACK-bar) Best-known of the Shahs of the Mughal Empire of India (r. 1556–1605). He was most famous for his policy of cooperation with his Hindu subjects.

Akhnaton (Ahk-NAH-tun) Name of a fourteenth century BCE Egyptian ruler who attempted to introduce monotheistic religious practice.

al-Afghani, Jamal al-Din (al-Af-GAH-nee: 1838–1897) Early leader of the Islamic reform movement.

Alexander the Great (356–323 BCE) Son of King Philip II of Macedon. Remembered for his conquest of the Persian Empire and most of the Near East, 336–323 BCE, from which the Hellenistic era began.

al-Ghazzali (al-Gah-ZAH-lee) (d. 1111) The "Renewer of Islam," he was an important figure in the development of sufism, Islamic mysticism.

Allah (Ahl-LAH) Arabic title of the one God.

Alliance for Progress The proposal by U.S. president John F. Kennedy in 1961 for large-scale economic assistance to Latin America.

Alliance of 1778 A diplomatic treaty under which France aided the American revolutionaries in their war against Britain.

al-Qaida A militant Islamist organization, formed by Osama bin Laden in the 1990s, that has adopted takfiri doctrines and has declared jihad against all Westerners and their Muslim supporters.

Amerindians Short for (Native) American Indians.

Amun-Ra (AH-mun-RAH) Originally, the Egyptian god of air and life, later he came to represent the sun and creation.

Amur River War 1976 sporadic shooting between Soviet and Chinese troops stationed along the Amur River following tensions that arose on the death of Mao Zedong.

Anabaptists Radical Protestant reformers who were condemned by both Lutherans and Catholics.

anarchism A political theory that sees all large-scale government as inherently evil and embraces small self-governing communities.

Anasazi (Ah-nah-SAH-zee) Term sometimes used to refer to Ancestral Puebloans.

Ancestral Puebloans These are the people native to the Four Corners area of the present United States. They built the Chaco Great Houses and cliff dwellings at Mesa Verde.

Anghor Wat (ANG-ghohr WAHT) A great Buddhist temple in central Cambodia, dating to the twelfth-century CE Khmer Empire.

Anglo-Egyptian Condominium Joint British and Egyptian control of the Sudan that followed British occupation of Egypt in 1882.

Anglo-French Entente The diplomatic agreement of 1904 that ended British-French enmity and was meant as a warning to Germany.

Anglo-Russian Agreement The equivalent to the Anglo-French Entente between Britain and Russia; signed in 1907.

Angola-to-Brazil trade A major portion of the trans-Atlantic slave trade.

animism A religious belief imputing spirits to natural forces and objects.

Anschluss (AHN-shluhs) The German term for the 1938 takeover of Austria by Nazi Germany.

anthropology The study of humankind as a particular species.

Antigonid Kingdom (An-TIH-goh-nihd) One of the Hellenistic successor kingdoms to Alexander the Great's empire. Included most of Greece and Asia Minor.

Anti-Slavery Movement Faction among mostly British evangelical Christians, which, beginning in the 1790s, was able to pressure Parliament with increasing effectiveness to ban slavery and the slave trade in Britain and throughout the British Empire.

apartheid (ah-PAHR-tide) The Afrikaans term for segregation of the races in South Africa.

appeasement The policy of trying to avoid war by giving Hitler what he demanded in the 1930s; supported by many in France and Britain.

Arabian Nights, The Also known as The 1001 Nights. Medieval collection of tales from the Islamic Middle East which greatly reflect life at the time of the Abbasid caliphs of Baghdad.

archaeology The study of cultures through the examination of artifacts.

Archaic Period 8000–2000 BCE in Native American history. Period when gathering slowly replaced large-game (megafauna) hunting.

aristocracy A social governing class based on birth.

Aristotle (384–322 BCE) One of the three greatest philosophers of Classical Greece. A student of Plato and teacher of Alexander the Great.

Ark of the Covenant The wooden container of the two tablets given to Moses by Yahweh on Mount Sinai (the Ten Commandments); the Jews' most sacred shrine, signifying the contract between God and the Chosen.

Arthashastra (Ahr-thah-SHAHS-trah) A compilation of hard-bitten governmental policies supposedly written by Kautilya to guide his master, Chandragupta Maurya, and one of the few literary sources of early India's history and culture.

Aryans A nomadic pastoral people from central Asia who invaded the Indus valley in about 1500 BCE.

Ashikaga clan (Ah-shih-KAH-gah) A noble Japanese family that controlled political power as shoguns from the 1330s to the late 1500s.

Ashoka (Ah-SHOH-kah) Greatest of the kings of ancient India. He greatly expanded the Mauryan kingdom through conquest. Later converted to Buddhism and encouraged its spread.

assimilation The acceptance of the culture and language of an alien majority by an ethnic minority to a degree that effectively blurs the distinctions between those groups.

assimilation and association French administrative policies applied to their colonies in Africa and Southeast Asia, whose objective was to acculturate their colonial subjects to French language, history, and civilization.

Assur The chief god of the Assyrian people.

Ataturk, Mustafa Kemal The "father of the Turks"; a World War I officer who led Turkey into the modern age and replaced the sultanate in the 1920s.

Atlantic Charter An agreement co-signed in 1941 by President Franklin D. Roosevelt and Prime Minister Winston Churchill outlining eight basic freedoms, which they proposed as essential for reconstructing the post-World War II world. It included the right of self-determination as one of those principles.

Audiencía (Auw-dee-EHN-see-yah) The colonial council that supervised military and civil government in Latin America.

August 1991 coup The attempt by hard-line communists to oust Mikhail Gorbachev and reinstate the Communist Party's monopoly on power in the Soviet Union.

Ausgleich of 1867 (AUWS-glike) The compromise between the Austro-Germans and Magyars that created the "Dual Monarchy" of Austria-Hungary.

Austro-Prussian War The conflict for mastery of the German national drive for political unification, won by the Bismarck-led Prussian Kingdom in 1866.

Avesta (Ah-VEHS-tah) The holy book of the Zoroastrian religion.

Avicenna (Ah-vih-SEHN-nah) See Ibn Sina.

Axis Pact The treaty establishing a military alliance between the governments of Hitler and Mussolini; signed in 1936.

Axum (AX-uhm) The center of the ancient Ethiopian Kingdom.

ayllu (Eye-YOO) Quechua name for the clan organization of the Peruvian Indians.

Ayuthaya The capital of the Thai Kingdom of early modern southeastern Asia.

Aztec Latest of a series of Indian masters of central Mexico before the arrival of the Spanish; developers of the great city of Tenochtitlán (Mexico City).

Babylon Most important of the later Mesopotamian urban centers.

Babylonian Captivity The transportation of many Jews to exile in Babylon as hostages for the good behavior of the remainder; occurred in the sixth century BCE.

Babylonian Captivity of the papacy See Great Schism.

Baghdad (Bag-DAD) Capital of the Islamic Empire under the Abbasid Dynasty. Built by the Caliph al-Mansur c. 763.

bakufu (Bah-KOO-foo) The military-style government of the Japanese shogun.

Balfour Declaration The 1917 public statement that Britain was committed to the formation of a "Jewish homeland" in Palestine after World War I.

banana republics A dismissive term referring to small Latin American states.

Bantu (BAN-too) Related peoples who speak languages that are part of the African language group called Bantu. They are spread through most of subequatorial Africa.

barbarian Greek for "incomprehensible speaker"; uncivilized.

Barracks Emperors The series of twenty Roman emperors between 235 and 284 who used troop command to force their way into power.

Battle of the Nations October 1813 at Leipzig in eastern Germany. Decisive defeat of the army of Napoleon by combined forces of Prussia, Austria, and Russia.

bedouin (BEH-doo-ihn) The nomadic inhabitants of interior Arabia and original converts to Islam.

Benedictine Rule The rules of conduct given to his monastic followers by the sixth-century Christian saint Benedict.

Berbers Indigenous people of North Africa and the Sahara Desert.

Beringia (Beh-RIHN-jee-ah) A land mass in the region of the Bering Strait over which Ancestral Native Americans migrated to the Western Hemisphere c. 30,000 to 10,000 BCE.

Berlin blockade The 1948–1949 attempt to squeeze the Western allies out of occupied Berlin by the USSR; it failed because of the successful Berlin Airlift of food and supplies.

Berlin Conference of 1884–1885 A conference called by Otto von Bismarck of all the major European powers to find a formula for adjudicating competing claims to foreign territory and to temper potential conflicts.

Berlin Wall The ten-foot-high concrete wall and "death zone" erected by the communist East Germans in 1961 to prevent further illegal emigration to the West.

Bhagavad-Gita (BAH-gah-vahd GEE-tah) The best-known part of the Mahabharata, detailing the proper relations between the castes and the triumph of the spirit over material creation.

big bang theory The theory that the cosmos was created by an enormous explosion of gases billions of years ago.

Bill of Rights of 1689 A law enacted by Parliament that established certain limits of royal powers and the specific rights of English citizens.

Bismarck, Otto von Chancellor of Prussia, then Germany under Kaiser William I. Unified Germany and built the Triple Alliance.

Black Death An epidemic of bubonic plague that ravaged most of Europe in the mid-fourteenth century.

Blackshirts/SS Hitler's bodyguard; later enlarged to be a subsidiary army and to provide the concentration camp guards.

Boers (Bohrs) The Dutch colonists who had been the initial European settlers of South Africa.

Boer War South African war between the Boers (people of Dutch descent) and Great Britain. Fought 1899–1902.

Bolsheviks (BOHL-sheh-vihks) The minority of Russian Marxists led by Lenin who seized dictatorial power in the October Revolution of 1917.

Boule (BOO-lay) The 500-member council that served as a legislature in ancient Athens.

bourgeoisie (BOOZH-wah-zee) The urban upper middle class; usually commercial or professional.

Boxer Rebellion A desperate revolt by superstitious peasants against the European "foreign devils" who were carving up China in the new imperialism of the 1890s; quickly suppressed.

Brahman (BRAH-muhn) The title of the impersonal spirit responsible for all creation in Hindu theology.

brahmin (BRAH-mihn) The caste of priests, originally limited to the Aryans and later allowed to the Indians, with whom they intermarried.

bread and circuses The social policy initiated by Augustus Caesar aimed at gaining the support of the Roman proletariat by freely supplying them with essential food and entertainments.

Brest-Litovsk Treaty of 1918 The separate peace between the Central Powers and Lenin's government in Russia.

Bronze Age The period when bronze tools and weapons replaced stone among a given people; generally about 3000–1000 BCE.

burning of the books China's Legalist first emperor attempted to eliminate Confucian ethic by destroying the Confucian writings and prohibiting its teaching.

bushido (BOO-shee-doh) The code of honor among the samurai.

Byzantine Empire The continuation of the Roman imperium in its eastern provinces until its fall to the Muslim Turks in 1453.

Caesaro-Papism A concept that applies when the supreme power of government is combined with supreme leadership of the Christian Church.

Cahokia (Cah-HOH-kee-ah) Large Native American settlement near East St. Louis, Illinois, c. 600–1300 CE. Note-worthy for its enormous ceremonial mounds.

caliph (Kah-LEEF) Arabic (Khalifa) for "deputy" to the Prophet Muhammad; leader of Islamic community.

Calpulli Aztec kinship groups.

Calvin, John (1509–1564) French theologian who developed the system of Christian theology called Calvinism, as delineated in his text, The Institutes of the Christian Religion.

Carthage Rival in the Mediterranean basin to Rome in the last centuries BCE before ultimate defeat.

cash crops Crops that are grown for sale rather than for consumption.

castas (CAHS-tas) In colonial Spanish America, mixed-blood people of color.

caste A socioeconomic group that is entered by birth and rarely exitable.

caudillo (Cow-DEE-yoh) A regional chieftain and usurping strongman who achieves national power in Latin America.

Cavour, Camillo (1810–1861) Prime Minister of Sardinia after 1852, he brought about the unification of the Italian states into the united Italy.

censors Officials with great powers of surveillance during the Roman republic.

Chaco phenomenon (CHA-coh) Ancestral Puebloan civilization that centered on the Great Houses of Chaco Canyon, c. 800–1150 BCE.

Chaeronea (Cay-roh-NEE-yah) The battle in 338 BCE when Philip of Macedon decisively defeated the Greeks and brought them under Macedonian rule.

Chartists A British working-class movement of the 1840s that attempted to obtain labor and political reform.

Chavin (Chah-VEEN) Early Peruvian Indian culture.

Cheka An abbreviation for the first version of the Soviet secret police.

Chiang Kai-shek (Chung Keye Shehk: 1887–1975) Early colleague of Sun Yat-sen who succeeded Sun as the leader of the Kuomintang. Opposed the rise of the Chinese Communist Party, but was defeated in 1949 and forced to flee to Taiwan.

Chichén Itzá (Chee-CHEHN Ee-TSAH) Site in the Yucatán of Mayan urban development in the tenth to thirteenth centuries.

Chinghis Khan (JENG-guhs KHAHN) Mongol conqueror, 1167–1227.

Civil Code of 1804 Napoleonic law code reforming and centralizing French legal theory and procedures.

Civil Constitution of the Clergy 1791 law in revolutionary France attempting to force French Catholics to support the new government and bring clergy into conformity with it.

civilization A complex, developed culture.

Cleisthenes (CLEYES-theh-nees) A sixth century BCE Athenian tyrant who laid the foundations of polis democracy.

Clovis culture (CLOH-vihs) The earliest Native American "culture" known to archaeologists. Dated c. 9500–8900 BCE, it was largely based on hunting very large game.

Coloureds South Africans of mixed European and African descent.

Columbian Exchange A term for the global changes in the resources, habits, and values of Amerindians, Europeans, Africans, and Asians that followed the "discovery" and settlement of the Americas by Europeans and Africans.

command economy The name given to communist economic planning in the Soviet version after 1929.

Committee of Public Safety The executive body of the Reign of Terror during the French Revolution.

Common Sense A pamphlet by Thomas Paine that was influential in hastening the American war of independence against Britain.

Commonwealth of Independent States (CIS) The loose confederation of eleven of the fifteen former Soviet republics that was formed after the breakup of the Soviet Union in 1991.

Communist Manifesto The 1948 pamphlet by Marx and Engels that announced the formation of a revolutionary party of the proletariat.

Community of discourse A group of people who share a common set of beliefs, symbols, and values.

Conciliar Movement The attempt to substitute councils of church leaders for papal authority in late medieval Christianity.

Confederation of Northern German States A confederation forged by Bismarck following the Prussian victory in the Austro-Prussian War of 1866.

Confucius (Cuhn-FYOO-shuhs) The fifth century BCE philosopher whose doctrines were permanently influential in Chinese education and culture.

conquistadores (Cahn-KEES-tah-dohrs) Title given to sixteenth-century Spanish explorers/colonizers in the Americas.

Constance, Council of The fifteenth century CE assembly of Christian officials called to settle the controversy over the papacy and to review and revise the basic doctrines of the church for the first time in a millennium.

consuls Chief executives of the Roman republic; chosen annually.

Coral Sea, Battle of the Naval engagement in the southwest Pacific during World War II, resulting in the removal of a Japanese invasion threat to Australia.

Corporation A company that the law bestows with the rights and liabilities of an individual. Generally, these are larger than partnerships and are highly capitalized through shares that are sold to the public.

Corpus Juris (COHR-puhs JOO-rihs) "Body of the law"; the Roman law code, produced under the emperor Justinian in the mid-500s CE.

Cortés, Hernan (Cohr-TEHZ) Spanish conquistador of the Aztec Empire, 1518–1521.

Counter-Reformation Series of measures that the Catholic Church took in the 1540s to counterattack against the Protestants, including a thorough examination of doctrines and practices and an emphasis on instruction of the young and of all Christians.

creationism A cosmology based on Christian tradition that holds that the universe was created by an intelligent Supreme Being.

Crecy (Cray-SEE) Battle in the Hundred Years' War won by the English in 1346.

Crimean War Conflict fought in the Crimea between Russia and Britain, France, and Turkey from 1853 to 1856; ended by the Peace of Paris with a severe loss in Russian prestige.

criollos (cree-OH-yohs) Creole; term used to refer to whites born in Latin America.

Crusades Medieval European wars waged principally to recover the Holy Lands (and Spain and Portugal) from Muslim control beginning in 1096.

Cuban Missile Crisis 1962 crisis created when Soviet Premier Nikita Khrushchev placed nuclear armed missiles in Cuba. America imposed a naval blockade, and a settlement was reached when the missiles were withdrawn in exchange for an American agreement to remove missiles from Turkey.

cultural relativism A belief common in the late twentiethcentury West that there are no absolute values to measure contrasting cultures.

culture The human-created physical and/or mental environment of a group.

culture system Dutch method of extracting wealth from Indonesian peasants by paying fixed (and often unfair) prices for their crops.

cuneiform (KYOO-nih-form) Mesopotamian wedge-shaped writing begun by the Sumerians.

Cuzco (COOS-coh) Capital city of the Inca Empire.

cynicism A Hellenistic philosophy stressing poverty and simplicity.

Dada A brief but influential European art movement in the early twentieth century that repudiated all obligations to communicate intelligibly to the general public.

da Gama, Vasco (duh GAH-mah, VAHS-coh: 1469–1524) First Portuguese to sail directly from Portugal to India and back, 1497–1499.

daimyo (DEYE-myoh) Japanese nobles who controlled feudal domains under the shogun.

Dao de Jing (DOW deh CHING) (Book of Changes) Daoism's major scripture; attributed to Lao Zi.

Daoism (Taoism) (DOW-ism) A nature-oriented philosophy/religion of China.

Dawes Plan A plan for a dollar loan and refinancing of post–World War I reparation payments that enabled recovery of the German economy.

D-day June 6, 1944; the invasion of France from the English Channel by combined British and American forces.

Declaration of the Rights of Man and Citizen The epoch-making manifesto issued by the French Third Estate delegates at Versailles in 1789.

decolonization The process by which Europeans withdrew from their colonies in Africa and Asia and restored self-rule.

deductive reasoning Arriving at truth by applying a general law or proposition to a specific case.

De Gaulle, Charles General who commanded the Free French forces during World War II. Became President of the Fifth Republic, 1958–1968.

De las Casas, Bartolomé (day-lahs-CAH-sahs, Bahr-TAH-loh-may) Spanish Dominican friar who wrote a scathing report in 1522 describing the devastation experienced by Native Americans at the hands of the Spanish.

Delhi sultanate (DEH-lee) The government and state erected by the conquering Afghani Muslims after 1500 in North India; immediate predecessor to the Mughal Empire.

Delian League An empire of satellite polei under Athens in the fifth century BCE.

deme The basic political subdivision of the Athenian polis.

demesne The arable land on a manor that belonged directly to the lord.

democracy A system of government in which the majority of voters decides issues and policy.

demographic transition The passage of a large group of people from traditional high birthrates to lower ones, induced by changing economic conditions and better survival chances of the children.

Deng Xiaoping (Dung Shau-ping: 1904–1997) Chairman of the Chinese Communist Party after the death of Mao Zedong; began the relaxation of CCP antipathy to capitalism, allowing limited free enterprise under liberalized CCP oversight.

dependency In the context of national development, the necessity to reckon with other states' powers and pressures in the domestic economy and foreign trade.

der Führer (dayr-FYOO-rehr) "The Leader" in Nazi Germany—specifically, Hitler.

dervish (DER-vihsh) A Turkish term for a sufi. See Sufi.

descamisados (des-cah-mee-SAH-dohs) "Shirtless ones"; the poor working classes in modern Argentina.

Descent of Man, The The 1871 publication by Charles Darwin that applied selective evolution theory to mankind.

détente (lit.) (day-tahnt) Relaxation; the term used for the toning down of diplomatic tensions between nations, specifically, the Cold War between the United States and the Soviet Union.

devshirme (duv-SHEER-muh) Ottoman system of recruiting young, Christian boys of the Balkan villages for the Janissary corps.

dharma (DAHR-mah) A code of morals and conduct prescribed for one's caste in Hinduism.

dhimmis (THIHM-mees) "People of the Book": Christians, Jews, and Zoroastrians living under Muslim rule and receiving privileged treatment over other non-Muslims.

Diaspora The scattering of the Jews from ancient Palestine.

Diaz, Bartolomeo (Dee-YAHS, Bahr-toh-loh-MAY-oh) Portuguese sea captain, the discoverer of the Cape of Good Hope at the southern tip of Africa, 1488.

diffusion theory The spread of ideas and technology through human contacts.

Directory The five-member executive organ that governed France from 1795 to 1799 after the overthrow of the Jacobins.

divan (dih-VAHN) A Turkish form of the Arabic word, diwan, meaning a Royal Council which advises the ruler.

divine right theory The idea that the legitimate holder of the Crown was designated by divine will to govern; personified by King Louis XIV of France in the seventeenth century.

Diwan (Dee-WAHN) A council of Islamic government ministers in Istanbul during the Ottoman Empire.

Domesday Book A complete census of landholdings in England ordained by William the Conqueror.

Dorians Legendary barbaric invaders of Mycenaean Greece in c. 1200 BCE.

Dream of the Red Chamber, The The best known of the eighteenth-century Chinese novels.

Duce, il (DOO-chay) "The Leader"; title of Mussolini, the Italian dictator.

Dutch East India Company A commercial company founded with government backing to trade with the East and Southeast Asians. The Dutch, English, and French governments sponsored such companies starting in the early seventeenth century.

economic nationalism A movement to assert national sovereignty in economic affairs, particularly by establishing freedom from the importation of foreign goods and technology on unfavorable terms.

Edo (EH-do) Name of Tokyo before the eighteenth century.

effective occupation One of the principles established during the Berlin Conference of 1884 for recognizing colonial claims. Essentially, it required that for a claim to be made, an effective administrative and police presence had to be established in the territory in question.

Eightfold Path The Buddha's teachings on attaining perfection.

Ekklesia (Ehk-KLAY-zee-yah) The general assembly of citizens in ancient Athens.

Elect, The A doctrine made famous by John Calvin that posits the notion that only a small minority (i.e. the "Elect") of the human race is predestined for salvation.

Emir (Eh-MEER) A provincial official with military duties in Muslim government.

empirical data Facts derived from observation of the external world.

empirical method Using empirical data to establish scientific truth.

Empiricist A school of Hellenistic Greek medical researchers.

Empress Dowager Cixi (1830–1908) Concubine of Qing Emperor, Xianfeng, she became the regent for her son, the emperor Tongxi. Exercising power for nearly fifty years, she encouraged the Taiping Rebellion and opposed badly needed reforms.

Enabling Act A law the German Reichstag passed in 1933 giving Hitler dictatorial power.

enclosure movement An eighteenth-century innovation in British agriculture by which formerly communal lands were enclosed by private landlords for their own benefit.

encomienda (en-koh-MYEN-dah) The right to organize unpaid native labor by the earliest Spanish colonists in Latin America; revoked in 1565.

Encyclopédie, The The first encyclopedia; produced in mid-eighteenth-century France by the philosophe Diderot.

Enlightenment The intellectual reform movement in eighteenth-century Europe that challenged traditional ideas and policies in many areas of theory and practice.

Epicureanism A Hellenistic philosophy advocating the pursuit of pleasure (mental) and avoidance of pain as the supreme good.

equal field system Agricultural reform favoring the peasants under the Tang Dynasty in China.

equity Fairness to contending parties.

Era of Stagnation The era of Brezhnev's government in the Soviet Union (1964–1982), when the Soviet society and economy faced increasing troubles.

Era of the Warring States The period of Chinese history between c. 500 and 220 BCE; characterized by the breakdown of the central government and feudal war.

Essay Concerning Human Understanding An important philosophical essay by John Locke that underpinned Enlightenment optimism.

Estates General The parliament of France; composed of delegates from three social orders: clergy, nobility, and commoners.

ethnic, ethnicity The racial, cultural, or linguistic affiliation of an individual or group of human beings.

Etruscans (Ee-TRUHNS-cuns) The pre-Roman rulers of most of northern and central Italy and cultural models for early Roman civilization.

European Economic Community An association of western European nations founded in 1957; now called the European Union, it embraces fifteen countries with several more in candidate status.

excommunication The act of being barred from the Roman Catholic community by decree of a bishop or the pope.

existentialism Twentieth-century philosophy that was popular after World War II in Europe; insists on the necessity to inject life with meaning by individual decisions.

Exodus The Hebrews' flight from the wrath of the Egyptian pharaoh in c. 1250 BCE.

extended family Parents and children plus several other kin group members such as in-laws, cousins, uncles, and aunts.

factories Fortified trading posts that Europeans established along the coast of (mostly West) Africa during the Age of Informal Empire.

Factory Acts Laws passed by Parliament in 1819 and 1833 that began the regulation of hours and working conditions in Britain.

factory system Massing of labor and material under one roof with a single proprietorship and management of production.

fallow Land left uncultivated for a period to recover fertility.

fascism A political movement in the twentieth century that embraced totalitarian government policies to achieve a unity of people and leader; first experienced in Mussolini's Italy.

Fathers of the Church Leading theologians and explainers of Christian doctrine in the fourth and early fifth centuries.

Fertile Crescent A belt of civilized settlements reaching from lower Mesopotamia across Syria, Lebanon, and Israel and into Egypt.

feudal system A mode of government based originally on mutual military obligations between lord and vassal; later often extended to civil affairs of all types; generally supported by landowning privileges.

Final Solution Name given by the Nazis to the wartime massacres of European Jews.

First Consul Title adopted by Napoleon after his coup d'état in 1799 that established him as the ruler of France.

First Emperor (Shi Huangdi) The founder of the short-lived Qin Dynasty (221–205 BCE) and creator of China as an imperial state.

First Five-Year Plan Introduced in 1929 at Stalin's command to collectivize agriculture and industrialize the economy of the Soviet Union.

First Industrial Revolution The initial introduction of machine powered production; began in late eighteenth-century Britain.

First International Title of original association of Marxist and other socialists, in 1860s Europe.

Five Pillars of Islam Popular term for the basic tenets of Muslim faith. Includes the profession of faith (shahada), prayer, fasting, pilgrimage, and giving alms.

floating world A term for ordinary human affairs popularized by the novels and stories of eighteenth-century Japan.

Folsom points Small, highly notched spear heads used for hunting by Paleoindians.

Forbidden City The center of Ming and Qing government in Beijing; entry was forbidden to ordinary citizens.

"four little tigers" Singapore, Taiwan, South Korea, and Hong Kong in the 1960s–1980s economic upsurge.

Four Noble Truths The Buddha's doctrine on human fate.

Fourteen Points The outline for a just peace proposed by Woodrow Wilson in 1918.

Franco-Prussian War The 1870–1871 conflict between these two powers resulting in German unification under Prussian leadership.

Frankfurt Assembly A German parliament held in 1848 that was unsuccessful in working out a liberal constitution for a united German state.

Frontier Wars Territorial wars that resulted when Trekboers (q.v.) encountered Bantu-speaking peoples in the region of the Fish River in the late 1700s.

Fujiwara clan (Foo-jee-WAH-rah) Daimyo noble clan controlling the shogunate in ninth- to twelfth-century Japan.

Gandhi, Indira Daughter of Jawaharlal Nehru who served as Prime Minister of India 1966–1975 and 1980–1984. Assassinated by Sikh religious extremists.

Gandhi, Mohandas (GAHN-dee, Moh-HAHN-dahs: 1869–1948) Advocate of non-violent protest against British rule and one of the founders of the modern state of India.

Gendarme of Europe Name given by liberals to the Russian imperial government under Tsar Nicholas I (1825–1855).

General Theory of Relativity Einstein's theory that introduced the modern era of physics in 1916.

Gentiles All non-Jews.

geocentric "Earth centered"; theory of the cosmos that erroneously held the Earth to be its center.

Ghana (GAH-nah) The earliest of the extensive empires in the western Sudan; also a modern West African country formed from the colony of Gold Coast when it won independence from Great Britain in 1957.

ghazis (GAH-zee) Muslim "crusaders," or holy warriors who fight against unbelievers.

ghetto Italian name for the quarter restricted to Jews.

Gilgamesh (GIHL-gah-mesh) One of the earliest epics in world literature, originating in prehistoric Mesopotamia.

glasnost (GLAS-nohnst) The Russian term for "openness"; along with perestroika, employed to describe the reforms instituted by Gorbachev in the late 1980s.

global warming The steady warming trend of the planet's temperature in the past century.

Glorious Revolution of 1688 The English revolt against the unpopular Catholic King James II and the subsequent introduction of certain civil rights restricting monarchic powers.

Golden Horde The Russia-based segment of the Mongol world empire.

golden mean Greek concept of avoiding the extremes; "truth lies in the middle."

Good Neighbor Policy President Franklin D. Roosevelt's attempt to reform previous U.S. policy and honor Latin American sovereignty.

Gothic style An artistic style, found notably in architecture, that came into general European usage during the thirteenth century.

Gracchi brothers Roman noble brothers who unsuccessfully attempted reform as consuls in the late republican era.

Grand Vizier (Vih-ZEER) Title of the Turkish prime minister during the Ottoman era.

Great Depression of the 1930s A depression that began in 1929 when the New York Stock Exchange collapsed, causing a severe crisis for banks and securities firms that spread around the world and created high levels of unemployment.

Great Elector Frederick William of Prussia (1640–1688); one of the princes who elected the Holy Roman Emperor.

Great Leap Forward Mao Zedong's misguided attempt in 1958–1960 to provide China with an instantaneous industrial base rivaling that of more advanced nations.

Great Proletarian Cultural Revolution The period from 1966 to 1976 when Mao Zedong inspired Chinese youth to rebel against all authority except his own; caused great damage to the Chinese economy and culture.

Great Purge The arrest and banishment of millions of Soviet Communist Party members and ordinary citizens at Stalin's orders in the mid-1930s for fictitious "crimes against the State and Party."

Great Reforms (Russia) Decrees affecting several areas of life issued by Tsar Alexander II between 1859 and 1874.

Great Schism A division in the Roman Catholic Church between 1378 and 1417, when two (and for a brief period, three) popes competed for the allegiance of European Christians; a consequence of the Babylonian Captivity of the papacy in Avignon, southern France.

Great Trek The march of the Boers, beginning in 1836, into the northeastern interior of South Africa where they founded the so-called Boer Republics.

Great Zimbabwe (Zim-BOB-way) The leading civilization of early southern Africa and exporter of gold to the East African coast.

Green Revolution The increased agricultural output in many Third World nations during the 1960s and 1970s that came from introducing high-yield crops and pesticides.

greenhouse gases Gases, such as carbon dioxide, that trap light radiation in the earth's atmosphere and produce a warming, greenhouse-like effect on world temperatures.

Gross Domestic Product (GDP) A measurement used by economists of the total wealth being produced by a country.

guild A medieval urban organization that controlled the production and sale prices of many goods and services.

Gupta Dynasty (GUHP-tah) The rulers of most of India in the 300–400s CE; the last native dynasty to unify the country.

Habsburg Dynasty The family that controlled the Holy Roman Empire after the thirteenth century; based in Vienna, they ruled Austria until 1918.

hacienda (hah-see-EHN-dah) A Spanish-owned plantation in Latin America that used native or slave labor to produce export crops.

Hagia Sophia (HAH-gee-yah Soh-FEE-yah) Greek name ("Holy Wisdom") of the cathedral in Constantinople, later made into a mosque by Ottoman Turkish conquerors.

Haiku (HEYE-koo) A type of Japanese poetry always three lines in length. The lines always have five, seven, and five syllables.

hajj (HAHJ) The pilgrimage to the sacred places of Islam.

Hammurabi (Ham-moo-RAH-bee: c. 1810–1750 BCE) Sixth king of Babylon; famous for his law code.

Han Dynasty The dynasty that ruled China from c. 200 BCE to 221 CE.

Hangzhou (Hahng-CHOH) Capital city of Song dynasty in China and probably the largest town in the contemporary world.

Hanoverian Dynasty The dynasty of British monarchs after 1714; from the German duchy of Hanover.

Han synthesis Ideology of the Han state that blended elements from Confucianism, Daoism, and Legalism.

harem Turkish name for the part of a dwelling reserved for women.

Harun al-Rashid (Hah-ROON al-RAH-shihd) Abbasid caliph of Baghdad, 786–809 CE.

heliocentrism Opposite of geocentrism; recognizes sun as center of solar system.

Hellenistic Kingdoms Kingdoms carved out of the empire conquered by Alexander the Great. Blended Greek and Asiatic cultures; extant in the Mediterranean basin and Middle East between 300 BCE and c. 200 CE.

helots (HEE-lots) Messenian semislaves of Spartan overlords.

Henry VIII, King (1491–1547) King of England 1509 until his death in 1547, Henry was a strong ruler and an important figure of the Protestant Reformation. He defied the Pope by signing the Act of Supremacy, which established the monarch as the supreme head of the Church of England.

Henry the Navigator, Prince (1394–1460) The third son of King João (John) I of Portugal, Henry played an important part in the early Portuguese exploration of the eastern Atlantic and the West African coast.

heresies Wrong belief in religious doctrines.

hetairai High-class female entertainer-prostitutes in ancient Greece.

hieroglyphics (high-roh-GLIH-fiks) Egyptian pictographs, beginning as far back as 3000 BCE, that could convey either an idea or a phonetic sound.

Hijra (HIHJ-rah) Literally, "flight"; Muhammad's forced flight from Mecca in 622 CE; it marks the first year of the Muslim calendar.

Hinayana Buddhism (Hih-nah-YAH-nah) A stricter, monastic form of Buddhism, claiming closer link with the Buddha's teaching; often called Theravada. Headquartered in Sri Lanka and strong in Southeast Asia.

historiography The writing of history so as to interpret it.

history Human actions in past time, as recorded and remembered.

Hittites (HIHT-tites) An Indo-European people who were prominent in the Near East around 1200 BCE.

Ho Chi Minh (Hoh-Chee-MIHN: 1890–1969) Communist and nationalist leader in French Indochina who fought against the Japanese in World War II. One of the principal founders of the modern nation of Vietnam, he fought to free his country from French rule, then from American invasion.

Hohenzollerns (HOH-ehn-ZOH-leh-rihns) The dynasty that ruled Prussia-Germany until 1918.

Homer Legendary author of the two epic poems of ancient Greece, the Iliad and the Odyssey.

hominid (HAH-mih-nihd) A humanlike creature.

Homo sapiens (HOH-moh SAY-pee-yehns) "Thinking man"; modern human beings.

Horus (HOH-ruhs) The falcon-headed god whose earthly, visible form was the reigning pharaoh in ancient Egypt.

hubris (HYOO-brihs) An unjustified confidence in one's abilities or powers leading to a tragic end.

Huguenots (OO-geh-nohs) French Calvinists, many of whom were forced to emigrate in the seventeenth century.

humanism The intellectual movement that sees humans as the sole valid arbiter of their values and purpose.

humanistic An adjective meaning something that emphasizes human qualities.

Hungarian Revolution The Hungarians' attempt to free themselves from Soviet control in October 1956; crushed by the Soviets.

Hussein, Saddam Iraqi dictator; an American invasion of Iraq in 2003 led to the overthrow of his government and widespread chaos.

Hyksos (HIHK-sohs) A people who invaded the Nile delta in Egypt and ruled it during the Second Intermediate Period (c. 1650–1570 BCE).

Ibn Sina (Ih-bihn SEE-nah) Well-known Islamic philosopher and physician (980–1037).

Ibn Taymiyya, Taqi al-Din (Ih-bihn Tie-MEE-yah) (1263–1328) Ultra-conservative Hanbali legal scholar whose writings are the foundation of the fundamentalist Wahhabi movement.

ideographs Written signs conveying entire ideas and not related to the spoken language; used by the Chinese from earliest times.

Ignatius of Loyola (1491–1556) Major figure of the Catholic Counter-Reformation who founded the Society of Jesus, or Jesuits.

Iliad The first of the two epics supposedly written by Homer in eighth-century Greece.

Il Khans (Il KHAHNS) One of the four major dynasties established from the empire of Chinghis Khan. Founded by Hulegu, Chinghis's grandson, after he destroyed Abbasid rule in Baghdad.

Imperator (Ihm-payr-RAH-tohr) Roman title of a temporary dictator given powers by the Senate; later, emperor.

Impressionists Members of a Paris-centered school of nineteenth century painting focusing on light and color.

Inca Title of the emperor of the Quechuan-speaking peoples of Peru before arrival of the Spanish.

indirect rule The British policy of governing their overseas colonies through "native rulers."

Indochina, Union of Official term for the French colonies in Indochina until their dissolution in the 1950s.

inductive reasoning Arriving at truth by reasoning from specific cases to a general law or proposition.

Indus Valley civilization Earliest known civilization of India; flourished c. 3000–1500 BCE. Largely known from archaeological discoveries at Mohenjo Daro and Harappa.

infamia (ihn-fah-MEE-yah) Roman term for immoral but not illegal acts.

Informal Empire The era in African history that lasted from the 1400s to about 1880, when Europeans remained content to restrict their dealings with Africa primarily to trade.

Inquisition Roman Catholic agency that was responsible for censorship of doctrines and books; mainly active in Iberian lands in the fifteenth through seventeenth centuries.

Institutes of the Christian Religion, The John Calvin's major work that established the theology and doctrine of the Calvinist churches; first published in 1536.

intelligentsia Russian term for a social group that actively influences the beliefs and actions of others, seeking reforms; generally connected with the professions and media.

intendants (ahn-tahn-DAHNTS) The traveling officials appointed originally by Cardinal Richelieu to monitor the honesty and efficiency of provincial French authorities.

Investiture Controversy A dispute between the Holy Roman Emperor and the pope in the eleventh and early twelfth centuries about which authority should appoint German bishops.

Iranian Revolution The fundamentalist and anti-Western movement led by the Ayatollah Khomeini that seized power from the shah of Iran through massive demonstrations in 1979.

irredentism The attempt by members of a nation living outside the national state to link themselves to it politically and/or territorially.

Islamism The modern, militant reassertion of basic Islamic values and principles by many Muslims.

Ivan the Terrible (Ivan IV: 1530–1584) The first ruler of Russia to assume the title of tsar. He overcame Mongol resistance to extend the Russian empire into Siberia.

Jacobins Radical revolutionaries during the French Revolution; organized in clubs headquartered in Paris.

Jacquerie (ZHAH-cuh-ree) A French peasant rebellion against noble landlords during the fourteenth century.

Janissaries (JA-nih-sayr-rees) From Turkish yeni cheri, meaning "new troops"; an elite troop in the Ottoman army; consisted of Christian boys from the Balkans.

Jesuits Members of the Society of Jesus, a Catholic religious order founded in 1547 to combat Protestantism.

Jewish War A rebellion of Jewish Zealots against Rome in 66–70 CE.

jihad (Jee-HAHD) Holy war on behalf of the Muslim faith.

Jihad of Abd al-Qadir (Abd Al-KAH-deer) Jihad led by the marabout, Abd al-Qadir, in the 1840s, against the French invasion of Algeria.

Jihad of al-Hajj Umar (al-HAJJ OO-mahr) Jihad of the 1840s–1870s which was led by the sufi shaykh, al-Hajj Umar Tal.

Jihad of Usman dan Fodio (OOS-man dan FOH-dee-oh) Jihad that took place between 1804 and 1817 in the north of what now is Nigeria. It began as a revolt against the "heretical" practices of the Hausa kings, but resulted in the establishment of a Muslim caliphate.

Judea One of the two Jewish kingdoms emerging after the death of Solomon when his kingdom was split in two; the other was Samaria.

July Monarchy The reign of King Louis Philippe in France (1830–1848); so called because he came to power in July 1830.

Junkers (YOONG-kers) The landowning nobility of Prussia.

jus gentium (YOOS-GEHN-tee-yum) "Law of peoples"; Roman law governing relations between Romans and others.

justification by faith Doctrine held by Martin Luther whereby Christian faith alone, and not good works, could be the path to heavenly bliss.

ka (kah) The immortal soul in the religion of ancient Egypt.

Ka'ba (KAH-bah) The original shrine of pagan Arabic religion in Mecca containing the Black Stone; now one of the holiest places of Islam.

Kabuki (Kah-BOO-kee) A type of popular Japanese drama depicting heroic and romantic themes and stories.

Kalidasa (Kah-lih-DAH-sah) Hindu philosopher and playwright of the Gupta period; influenced the development of Sanskrit literature.

Kamakura shogunate (Kah-mah-KOO-rah) Government by members of a noble Japanese family from the late twelfth to the mid-fourteenth century in the name of the emperor, who was their puppet.

kami (KAH-mee) Shinto spirits in nature.

Kampuchea (Kahm-poo-CHEE-yah) Native name of Cambodia, a state of Southeast Asia bordered by Thailand and Vietnam.

Karlowitz, Treaty of (1699) Treaty in which, for the first time, the Ottoman Empire had to cede territory in the Balkans to its Austrian opponent.

karma (KAHR-mah) The balance of good and evil done in a given incarnation in Hindu belief.

Karnak (KAHR-nack) The site of a great temple complex along the Nile River in Egypt.

Kashmir (Kazh-MEER) A province in northwestern India, largely populated by Muslims, that Pakistan also claims.

Kellogg-Briand Pact A formal disavowal of war by sixty nations in 1928.

KGB An abbreviation for the Soviet secret police; used after Cheka and NKVD had been discarded.

Khanate of the Golden Horde Sub-khanate of the Mongol Empire located in eastern and central Russia.

Kharijites (KHAH-rih-jites) Like Shi'ites, these are one of the two religious minorities in Islam. Basically, they reject the caliphate, and believe that leadership of the Umma (q.v.) rightfully belongs to the most pious, and that authority comes from the community itself.

Khmers (KAY-mers) The inhabitants of Cambodia; founders of a large empire in ancient Southeast Asia.

Khomeini, Ayatollah Ruholla (1900–1989) Iranian Shi'ite cleric who led the 1979 Iranian revolt against the Shah.

Khrushchev, Nikita Succeeded Stalin as First Secretary of the Soviet Communist Party, 1955–1964. Utterly convinced of the eventual triumph of communism in the world, he followed policies that generally were more conciliatory towards the West.

Kilwa (KILL-wah) A Swahili city-state that dominated the gold and ivory trade from East Africa, c. 1300–1450 CE.

King of Kings The title of the Persian emperor.

Kivas (KEE-vahs) Underground ceremonial chambers among Puebloan Native Americans.

Kleindeutsch (KLEYN-doitsh) "Small German"; adjective describing a form of German unification that excluded the multinational Austria; opposite of grossdeutsch.

knights Type of feudal noble who held title and landed domain only for his lifetime; generally based originally on military service to his overlord.

Korean War 1950–1953 war between United Nations, led by the United States, and North Korea; precipitated by the invasion of South Korea.

Kubilai Khan (KOOB-lay KHAHN) Mongol Great Khan and founder of the Yuan Dynasty of China.

Kuomintang (KMT) The political movement headed by Chiang Kai-shek during the 1930s and 1940s in China.

Kush (Kuhsh) Kingdom in northeast Africa that had close relations with Egypt for several centuries in the pre-Christian epoch.

Kwame Nkrumah (KWAH-may Ng-KROO-mah: 1909–1972) In 1957, led the Gold Coast—renamed Ghana—as the first nation among the colonial states of Africa to achieve independence. Fierce advocate of African socialism and Pan-Africanism.

Kyoto (KEE-o-to) Ancient capital of the Japanese Empire and seat of the emperor.

Labour Party Political party founded in 1906 by British labor unions and others for representation of the working classes.

l'ancien régime (LAHN-syahn ray-ZHEEM) "The old government"; the pre-Revolutionary style of government and society in eighteenth-century France.

Lao Zi (Lau-TSUH) Mythical author of the Dao de Jing, or Book of Changes, which has served as the text for various versions of Daoist folklore and philosophy for many centuries in China.

Late Manzhou Restoration An attempt by Chinese reformers in the 1870s to restore the power of the central government after the suppression of the Taiping rebellion.

League of Nations An international organization founded after World War I to maintain peace and promote amity among nations; the United States did not join.

Left The reforming or revolutionary wing of the political spectrum; associated originally with the ideals of the radical French Revolution.

legalism A Chinese philosophy of government emphasizing strong authority.

Legislative Assembly The second law-making body created during the French Revolution; dominated by the Jacobins, it gave way to the radical Convention.

Legitimacy A term adopted by the victors at the Congress of Vienna in 1815 to explain the reimposition of former monarchs and regimes after the Napoleonic wars.

Levantine Corridor Region that included most of present-day Israel-Palestine, Lebanon, Syria and northern Iraq. Archaeologists have discovered the earliest evidence of agriculture here.

levée en masse (leh-VAY ahn-MAHS) General conscription for the army; first occurred in 1793 during the French Revolution.

Leviathan A book by Thomas Hobbes that supported the necessity of the state and, by inference, royal absolutism.

liberum veto (LEE-bay-rum) Latin for "free veto"; used by Polish nobles to nullify majority will in the Polish parliaments of the eighteenth century.

lineage (LIHN-ee-age) A technical term for family or clan association.

Little Ice Age A period of global cooling that lasted from the late thirteenth century to the seventeenth century.

little red book Contained the thoughts of Chairman Mao Zedong on various topics; used as a talisman during the Cultural Revolution by young Chinese.

Livingstone, David Medical missionary, explorer, and humanitarian who explored much of sub-equatorial Africa during the period of the 1840s–1860s. He especially advocated "legitimate trade" as a substitute for the slave trade in Africa.

Locarno Pact An agreement between France and Germany in 1925.

Lollards Name of unknown origin given to the English religious rebels of the 1380s who later protested against the privileges of the clergy and were vigorously persecuted.

Long March The 6,000-mile fighting retreat of the Chinese communists under Mao Zedong to Shensi province in 1934–1935.

Luther, Martin (1483–1546) Began the Protestant Reformation with his famous Ninety-Five theses. Also noted for his translation of the Bible into German.

Lyric poetry Poetry that celebrates the poet's emotions.

Maastricht Treaty (MAHS-trict) Signed in 1991 by members of the European Community; committed them to closer political-economic ties.

Maat (MAHT) Egyptian goddess of universal order and balance.

Machtergreifung "Seizure of power;" Nazi term for Hitler's rise to dictatorial powers in Germany.

Machu Picchu (MAH-choo PEE-choo) Incan city in the high Andes Mountains.

Magellan, Ferdinand (Ma-JEL-lan) First man to sail completely around the world, 1519–1522.

Maghrib or **Maghreb** (Mah-GREEB) Northwest Africa, north of the Atlas Mountains. Usually includes Morocco, Algeria, and Tunisia.

Mahabharata (Mah-hahb-hah-RAH-tah) A Hindu epic poem; a favorite in India.

Mahayana Buddhism (Mah-hah-YAH-nah) A more liberal, looser form of Buddhism; originating soon after the Buddha's death, it deemphasized the monastic life and abstruse philosophy in favor of prayer to the eternal Buddha and the bodhisattvas who succeeded him.

Mahdi, The (MAH-dee) A charismatic Islamic mystic, Muhammad Ahmad, who led a serious rebellion against Egyptian rule in the Sudan, 1881–1885.

Majapahit (Mah-JAH-pah-hit)The main town of a maritime empire in fourteenth century Indonesia.

Mali (MAH-lee) The West African empire that was the successor to Ghana in the 1300s and 1400s.

Manchester liberalism The economic practice of exploiting the laboring poor in the name of the free market.

Manchuria Large province of northeastern China, seized in the nineteenth century by Russia and Japan before being retaken by the Maoist government.

mandarins (MAN-dah-rihns) Chinese scholar-officials who had been trained in Confucian principles. Usually associated with the landed elite.

mandate of heaven A theory of rule originated by the Zhou Dynasty in China emphasizing the connection between imperial government's rectitude and its right to govern.

mandates Britain and France governed several Asian and African peoples after World War I, supposedly as agents of the League of Nations.

manor An agricultural estate of varying size normally owned by a noble or the clergy and worked by free and unfree peasants/serfs.

Mansa Musa (MAHN-sah MOO-sah) King of Mali, early fourteenth century.

Manu (MAH-noo) Legendary lawgiver in India.

Manus (MAH-nuhs) "Hand"; Latin term for the legal power of a person over another.

Manzhou (Man-CHOO) Originally nomadic tribes living in Manchuria who eventually overcame Ming resistance and established the Qing Dynasty in seventeenth-century China.

Manzikert, Battle of (MAN-zih-kert) Battle fought in 1071, which gave victory to the Seljuk Turks over the Byzantines. Made Turkish Muslim entry to Asia Minor possible.

Mao Zedong (Mau Tseh-duhng: 1893–1976) Joined the Communist Party in the 1920s and became its principal leader. Later defeated the Kuomintang, and, as Chairman of the CCP, ruled China until his death in 1976.

marabout (MAH-rah-boot) A leader of a radical sufi brotherhood in North Africa and the Sahara Desert.

Marathon The battle in 490 BCE in which the Greeks defeated the Persians, ending the first Persian War.

March on Rome A fascist demonstration in 1922 orchestrated by Mussolini as a preliminary step to dictatorship in Italy.

March Revolution of 1917 The abdication of Tsar Nicholas II and the establishment of the Provisional Government in Russia.

Maritime Expeditions (China's) Early fifteenth-century explorations of the Indian and South Pacific Oceans ordered by the Chinese emperor.

Marshall Plan A program proposed by the U.S. secretary of state George Marshall and implemented from 1947 to 1951 to aid western Europe's recovery from World War II.

Massacre on Tienanmen Square See Tienanmen Square, massacre on.

Masscult The banal culture that some think replaced the traditional elite culture in the twentieth-century West.

matriarchy A society in which females are dominant socially and politically.

matrilineal descent Attribution of name and inheritance to children via the maternal line.

Maya The most advanced of the Amerindian peoples who lived in southern Mexico and Guatemala and created a high urban civilization in the pre-Columbian era.

May Fourth Movement A reform movement of young Chinese students and intellectuals in the post–World War I era; Mao Zedong was a member prior to his conversion to Marxism.

McMahon Letter British correspondence in 1916 which promised support for the creation of an Arab state in the Middle East in exchange for an Arab alliance in driving Turkey out of the region.

Medes An early Indo-European people who, with the Persians, settled in Iran.

Meiji Restoration (Mei-JEE) The overthrow of the Tokugawa shogunate and restoration of the emperor to nominal power in Japan in 1867.

Mein Kampf (Meye-n KAHMF) "My Struggle"; Hitler's credo, written while serving a prison term in 1924.

mercantilism A theory of national economics popular in the seventeenth and eighteenth centuries; aimed at establishing a favorable trade balance through government control of exports and imports as well as domestic industry.

meritocracy The rule of the meritorious (usually determined by examinations).

Mesopotamia Literally, "the land between the rivers;" the fertile lands between the Tigris and Euphrates Rivers where the earliest known civilizations appeared in the fourth millennium BCE.

Messenian Wars Conflicts between the neighbors Sparta and Messenia that resulted in Messenia's conquest by Sparta in about 600 BCE.

messiah A savior-king who would someday lead the Jews to glory.

mestizo (mes-TEE-so) A person of mixed Amerindian and European blood.

metaphor of the cave Plato's explanation of the difficulties encountered by those who seek philosophical truth and the necessity of a hierarchy of leadership.

Mexica (Meh-SHEE- cah) Warlike nomadic Native Americans who invaded Central Mexico around the eighth century CE. Some called Aztecs.

Mexican Revolution The armed struggle that occurred in Mexico between 1910 and 1920 to install a more socially progressive and populist government.

Middle Kingdom The period in Egyptian history from 2100 to 1600 BCE; followed the First Intermediate Period.

Midway Island, Battle of (1942) Naval victory won by the Americans that put them on the offensive in the Pacific war against the Japanese.

Milan, Edict of A decree issued by the emperor Constantine in 313 CE that legalized Christianity and made it the favored religion in the Roman Empire.

Ming Dynasty Ruling dynasty of China, 1368 to 1644.

Minoan (Mih-NOH-wan) An ancient civilization that was centered on Crete between c. 2000 and c. 1400 BCE.

missi dominici (MEE-see Doh-MEH-nih-chee) Agents of Charlemagne in the provinces of his empire.

modernism A philosophy of art of the late nineteenth and early twentieth centuries that rejected classical models and values and sought new expressions and aesthetics.

Mohenjo-Daro (Moh-HEHN-joh DAH-roh) Site of one of the two chief towns of the ancient Indus valley civilization.

moksha (MOHK-shah) The final liberation from bodily existence and reincarnation in Hinduism.

monarchy Rule by a single individual, who often claims divine inspiration and protection.

Mongols Name for collection of nomadic, savage warriors of Central Asia who conquered most of Eurasia in the thirteenth century.

Mongol Yoke A Russian term for the Mongol occupation of Russia, 1240–1480.

monoculture Overreliance on one or two crops in a region; an economically precarious system.

monoeconomies Economies very narrowly based on the production of just one commodity (or a very few) produced for export.

monotheism A religion having only one god.

Monroe Doctrine The announcement in 1823 by U.S. president James Monroe that no European interference in Latin America would be tolerated.

Mughals (MOO-guls) A corruption of "Mongol"; refers to the period of Muslim rule in India.

Muhammad (Moo-HAH-mahd) The prophet of Islam.

Muhammad Abduh (Muhammad AHB-doo) (1849–1905) Leading intellectual of the Salafiyya Islamic reform movement in Egypt.

Muhammad Ali Pasha (1769–1849) Viceroy of Egypt, 1803–1849, he introduced important reforms to reorganize Egypt and its army and navy along European lines.

Muhammad Reza Shah Pahlavi (Muhammad RAY-zah PAH-lah-vee: 1919–1980) Son of Shah Reza Pahlavi, he was the Shah of Iran from 1941 until his overthrow by the Iranian Revolution in 1979.

mulatto (muh-LOT-to) A person of mixed African and European blood.

Munich Agreements The 1938 meetings between Hitler and the British and French prime ministers that allowed Germany to take much of Czechoslovakia; the agreement confirmed Hitler's belief that the democratic governments would not fight German aggression.

Munich putsch The failed attempt by Hitler to seize power by armed force in 1923.

municipia (myoo-nih-KIH-pee-yah) The basic unit of Roman local government; similar to a present-day municipality.

Muslim Brotherhood, the A militant association of Muslims formed during the British occupation of Egypt. Its goals were to drive out the "infidels" and to restore Egypt to a Muslim government. For many years, it engaged in attacks and assassinations, but more recently most members have become more moderate, preferring politics over violence.

Muslim Brotherhoods Associations of Islamic groups that have strong fundamentalist leanings and practice mutual aid among members.

Mussolini, Benito Fascist dictator of Italy during the 1920s and 1930s. One of the three Axis allies during World War II.

Mycenaean (Meye-seh-NEE-yan) Referring to the history and culture of the earliest known Indo-European inhabitants of the Greek peninsula, between c. 1600 and c. 1100 BCE.

mystery religions One of various Hellenistic cults promising immortal salvation of the individual.

Nantes, Edict of A law granting toleration to French Calvinists that was issued in 1598 by King Henry IV to end the religious civil war.

Napoleonic Settlement A collective name for the decrees and actions by Napoleon between 1800 and 1808 that legalized and systematized many elements of the French Revolution.

Nasser, Colonel Gamal Abdel (1918–1970) Egyptian nationalist leader who was the President of Egypt from 1952. Remembered best for seizing the Suez Canal from Anglo-French control in 1956.

National Assembly The first law-making body during the French Revolution; created a moderate constitutional monarchy.

nationalism A form of allegiance in which people owe their loyalty and devotion to the state or nation in which they live.

natural law The idea, originated by Romans, that all humans, by virtue of their humanity, possess certain rights and duties that all courts must recognize.

natural selection The Darwinian doctrine in biology that change in species derives from mechanistic changes induced by the environment.

Navigation Acts Laws regulating commerce with the British colonies in North America in favor of Britain.

Nazism The German variant of fascism created by Hitler.

Neanderthal Man A species of Homo sapiens flourishing between 100,000 and 300,000 years ago and that mysteriously died out; the name comes from the German valley where the first remains were found.

Negritude A literary term referring to the self-conscious awareness of African cultural values; popular in areas of Africa formerly under French control.

Nehru, Jawaharlal (NAY-roo) (1889–1964) Close associate of Mahatma Gandhi who became Prime Minister of India following Gandhi's death and served in that office for fifteen years until his death in 1964.

neocolonialism Literally, "new" colonialism, meaning the control, primarily economic, which the former colonial powers continue to exert over their former colonies in Asia, Africa, and Latin America.

Neo-Confucianism An eleventh- and twelfth-century CE revival of Confucian thought with special emphasis on love and responsibility toward others.

Neolithic Age The period from c. 7000 BCE to the development of metals by a given people.

New China Movement An intellectual reform movement in the 1890s that attempted to change and modernize China by modernizing the government.

New Economic Policy (NEP) A policy introduced at the conclusion of the civil war that allowed for limited capitalism and private enterprise in the Soviet Union.

New Imperialism, the The late nineteenth-century worldwide colonialism of European powers interested in strategic and market advantage.

New Kingdom or Empire The period from c. 1550 to 700 BCE in Egyptian history; followed the Second Intermediate Period. The period from 1550 to c. 1200 BCE was the Empire.

Nicaea, Council of (Neye-SEE-yah) A fourth-century conclave of bishops that defined essential doctrines of Christianity under the supervision of the emperor Constantine.

Niger River (NEYE-jer) The great river draining most of the African bulge.

Ninety-five Theses The challenge to church authority publicized by Martin Luther, October 31, 1517.

Nineveh (NIH-neh-vay) The main city and later capital of the Assyrian Empire.

nirvana (ner-VAH-nah) The Buddhist equivalent of the Hindu moksha; the final liberation from suffering and reincarnation.

NKVD An abbreviation for the Soviet secret police; used after Cheka but before KGB.

Nonaggression Pact of 1939 The treaty between Hitler and Stalin in which each agreed to maintain neutrality in any forthcoming war involving the other party.

North American Free Trade Agreement (NAFTA) An agreement signed by the United States, Canada, and Mexico in 1993 that provides for much liberalized trade among these nations.

North Atlantic Treaty Organization (NATO) An organization founded in 1949 under U.S. aegis as a defense against threatened communist aggression in Europe.

nuclear family Composed of parents and children only.

Nuclear Test Ban The voluntary cessation of aboveground testing of nuclear weapons by the United States and the Soviet Union; in existence from 1963 to the present.

Nuremberg Laws Laws defining racial identity that were aimed against Jews; adopted in 1935 by the German government.

October Revolution of 1917 The Bolshevik coup d'état in St. Petersburg that ousted the Provisional Government and established a communist state in Russia.

Odyssey (AH-dehs-see) Second of the two Homeric epic poems, detailing the adventures of the homeward-bound Ulysses coming from the siege of Troy; see also Iliad.

Oedipus Rex (OY-dih-pus REHKS) Part of a triad of tragedies written by the classical Greek playwright Sophocles concerning the life and death of Oedipus and his daughter, Antigone.

Oil boycott of 1973 The temporary withholding of oil exports by OPEC members to Western governments friendly to Israel; led to a massive rise in the price of oil and economic dislocation in many countries.

Old Kingdom The period of Egyptian history from 3100 to 2200 BCE.

Old Testament The first portion of the Judeo-Christian Bible; the holy books of the Jews.

oligarchy Rule by a few.

Olmec The earliest Amerindian civilization in Mexico.

1001 Nights, The See Arabian Nights, The.

Operation Barbarossa Code name for German invasion of the Soviet Union in 1941.

Opium Wars Conflicts that occurred in 1840–1842 on the Chinese coast between the British and the Chinese over the importation of opium into China. The Chinese defeat began eighty years of subordination to foreigners.

Orange Free State One of the two political organisms founded after the Boer Great Trek in southern Africa.

Organization of African Unity (OAU) The association of sub-Saharan African nations founded in 1963 for mutual aid and, it was hoped, eventually the creation of a "United States of Africa."

Organization of American States (OAS) An organization founded in 1948 under U.S. auspices to provide mutual defense and aid; now embraces all countries on the American continents except Cuba.

Organization of Petroleum Exporting Countries (OPEC) Oil cartel founded in 1961 by Arab governments and later expanded to include several Latin American and African members.

Origin of Species, The Charles Darwin's book that first enunciated the evolutionary theory in biology; published in 1859.

Osama bin Laden (Oh-SAH-mah bihn LAH-dihn: 1957–present) Saudi-born Arab who organized the al-Qaida terrorist organization to wage Islamic jihad against the Western nations.

Osiris (Oh-SEYE-rihs) A chief Egyptian god, ruler of the underworld.

Ostpolitik (OHST-poh-lih-tihk) German term for Chancellor Brandt's 1960s policy of pursuing normalized relations with West Germany's neighbors to the east.

Ostracism (AH-strah-sihzm) In ancient Greece, the expulsion of a citizen from a polis for a given period.

Pagan Ancient capital of the Burmese Kingdom in southeastern Asia. Destroyed by the invading Mongol army in the thirteenth century CE.

Paleoindian Period 9500–8900 BCE in Native American history.

Paleolithic Age The period from the earliest appearance of Homo sapiens to c. 7000 BCE, though exact dates vary by area; the Old Stone Age.

paleontology The study of prehistoric things.

Palestine Liberation Organization (PLO) An organization founded in the 1960s by Palestinians expelled from Israel; until 1994 it aimed at destruction of the state of Israel by any means. Superseded by the autonomous Palestinian Authority created in 1997.

Pan-Africanism Movement begun in the early twentieth century among African- and Caribbean-Americans to create unity among black people around the world. In the 1960s, became a movement to create a politically unified Africa.

Pan-Arabism A movement after World War I to assert supranational Arab unity, aimed eventually at securing a unified Arab state.

pantheism A belief that God exists in all things, living and inanimate.

Paragraph 231 of the Versailles Treaty The "war guilt" paragraph, imputing sole responsibility for reparation of all World War I damages to Germany.

pariah An outcast; a person having no acknowledged status.

Paris Commune A leftist revolt against the national government after France was defeated by Prussia in 1871; crushed by the conservatives with much bloodshed.

Parthenon The classic Greek temple to Athena on the Acropolis in Athens's center.

Pastoral nomadism A way of life prevalent in most steppelands. Characterized by nomadism and dependence on livestock breeding rather than on agriculture.

patents of nobility Royal documents conferring nobility.

patria potestas (PAH-tree-yah poh-TEHS-tahs) The power of the father over his family in ancient Rome.

patriarchy A society in which males have social and political dominance.

patricians (patres) The upper governing class in ancient Rome.

patrilineal descent Attribution of name and inheritance to children via the paternal line.

Pax Mongolica (PAHKS Mon-GOH-lih-cah) The "Mongol peace"; between c. 1250 and c. 1350 in most of Eurasia.

Pax Romana (PAHKS Roh-MAH-nah) The "Roman peace"; the era of Roman control over the Mediterranean basin and much of Europe between c. 31 BCE and 180 CE or later.

peaceful coexistence The declared policy of Soviet leader Nikita Khrushchev in dealing with the capitalist West after 1956.

Peace of Augsburg Pact ending the German religious wars in 1555, dividing the country between Lutheran and Catholic hegemony.

Peloponnesian War (pehl-luh-puh-NEE-zhan) The great civil war between Athens and Sparta and their respective allies in ancient Greece; fought between 429 and 404 BCE and eventually won by Sparta.

peonage (PEE-on-ihj) In Latin America, a type of serfdom that tied peasant workers to a hacienda through alleged debts owed to the employer.

perestroika (payr-rihs-TROY-kah) The Russian term for "restructuring," which, with glasnost, was used to describe the reforms instituted by Gorbachev in the late 1980s USSR.

Pericles (PAYR-rih-clees) The Athenian democratic leader and spokesman who died in the midst of the Peloponnesian War in the fifth century BCE.

Persepolis (Per-SEH-poh-lihs) With Ecbatana, one of the twin capitals of the Persian Empire in the 500s BCE; destroyed by Alexander the Great.

Persians An early Indo-European tribe that, along with the Medes, settled in Iran.

Persian Wars The conflict between the Greeks and the Persian Empire in the fifth century BCE, fought in two installments and ending with Greek victory.

Peter the Great, Ruler of Russia (1682–1725) Peter I is noteworthy for his absolutist style of rule and as a great innovator who tried to modernize his country along European lines.

Petrine succession The doctrine of the Roman Catholic Church by which the pope, the bishop of Rome, is the direct successor of St. Peter.

Pharaoh (FAYR-roh) The title of the god-king of ancient Egypt.

philosophes A French term used to refer to the writers and activist intellectuals during the Enlightenment.

Phonetic alphabet A system of writing that matches signs with the sounds of the oral language.

Piedmont "Foot of the mountains"; the north Italian kingdom that led the unification of Italy in the mid-nineteenth century.

plastic arts Those arts that have three dimensions.

Platea The land battle that, along with the naval battle of Salamis, ended the second Persian War with a Greek victory over the Persians.

Plato (427–347 BCE) Student of Socrates and teacher of Aristotle. Recorded Socrates' dialogues. Wrote the Metaphor of the Cave and The Republic.

plebeians (plebs) The common people of ancient Rome.

pogrom (POH-grum) Mob violence against local Jews.

polis (PAH-lihs) The political and social community of citizens in ancient Greece.

Political Islam The assertion that Islam must serve both as a guide to life and as the basis of modern government in parts of the world where Muslims are the majority.

polytheism A religion having many gods.

Popular Front The coordinated policy of all antifascist parties; inspired by the Soviets in the mid-1930s against Hitler.

Porte, The A name for the Ottoman government in Istanbul.

post-Impressionist A term for late nineteenth-century painting that emphasizes color and line in a then-revolutionary fashion.

Postmodernism Philosophy of the late twentieth century that emphasized the significance of language as text in signifying power relationships in societies.

Praetorian Guard (Pree-TOH-ree-yan) The imperial bodyguard in the Roman Empire and the only armed force in Italy.

Precedent What has previously been accepted in the application of law.

Pre-Socratics Greek philosophers prior to Socrates who focused on the nature of the material world.

primary resistance A term applied by some historians for the initial, largely local form of resistance that usually followed soon after European occupation of territory in Africa.

primogeniture A system of inheritance in which the estate passes to the eldest legitimate son.

Princeps (PRIHN-keps) "The First" or "the Leader" in Latin; title taken by Augustus Caesar.

Principality of Kiev The first Russian state; flourished from c. 800 to 1240 when it fell to Mongols.

Principate The reign of Augustus Caesar from 27 BCE to 14 CE.

proconsuls Provincial governors and military commanders in ancient Rome.

proletariat Poverty-stricken people without skills; also, a Marxist term for the propertyless working classes.

Provisional Government A self-appointed parliamentary group exercising power in republican Russia from March to October 1917.

Psychoanalysis A psychological technique that employs free associations in the attempt to determine the cause of mental illness.

Ptah (pu-TAH) Egyptian god or rebirth, renewal.

Ptolemaic Kingdom of Egypt (Tah-luh-MAY-ihk) Egyptian state created by Ptolemy, one of Alexander the Great's generals, in the Hellenistic era.

Pueblo culture (PWEH-bloh) Name given to the Native American culture that has flourished in the Four Corners region of the U.S., c. 400–present.

Punic Wars (PYOO-nihk) The three conflicts between Rome and Carthage that ended with the destruction of the Carthaginian Empire and the extension of Roman control throughout the western Mediterranean.

Punt To ancient Egyptians, the lands that probably included southwest Arabia and the Horn of Africa.

purdah (PURR-dah) The segregation of females in Hindu and Muslim society.

Purgatory In Catholic belief, the place where the soul is purged after death for past sins and thus becomes fit for Heaven.

Puritans The English Calvinists who were dissatisfied by the theology of the Church of England and wished to "purify" it.

Putsch A coup d'état, the overthrow of an existing government.

putting-out system An economic arrangement between individuals or small producers for production of handwork at home and payment by the piece; it was replaced by the factory beginning in late eighteenth-century Britain.

Pyramid of Khufu (Cheops) The largest pyramid; stands outside Cairo.

Qadi (KAA-dee) An Islamic judge, learned in Islamic theology and law.

Qing Dynasty (Ching) The last Chinese dynasty, which ruled from 1644 until 1911; established by Manzhou invaders after they defeated the Ming rulers.

Quadruple Alliance The diplomatic pact to maintain the peace established by the Big Four victors of the Napoleonic Wars (Austria, Britain, Prussia, and Russia); lasted for a decade.

quanta (KWAHN-tah) A concept in physics indicating the expenditure of energy.

Quechua (KETCH-wah) The spoken language of the Incas of Peru.

Qur'an (Koor-AHN) The holy scripture of Islam, thought to be (lit.) the word of God.

raison d'état (RAY-zohn day-TAH) The idea that the welfare of the state should be supreme in government policy.

Raja Turkish for "cattle"; used to refer to non-Muslims.

Realpolitik (Ree-AL-poh-lih-tik) Political policies that are based on practical considerations rather than on ideology.

Red Guards The youthful militants who carried out the Cultural Revolution in China during the 1960s.

Red International See Third International.

Reform Act of 1832 Brought about a reform of British parliamentary voting and representation that strengthened the middle class and the urbanites.

Reformation The sixteenth-century upheaval led by Martin Luther and John Calvin that modified or in some cases rejected altogether some

Catholic doctrine and practices; led to the establishment of Protestant churches.

Reign of Terror The period (1793–1794) of extreme Jacobin radicalism during the French Revolution.

Renaissance The social, artistic, and cultural "rebirth" that arose in Europe in the fourteenth century.

reparations question Money and goods that Germany was to pay to the victorious Allies after World War I under the Versailles Treaty.

Republican government A form of governing that imitates the Roman res publica in its rejection of monarchy.

Rerum novarum (REHR-rum Noh-VAHR-rum) An encyclical issued by Pope Leo XIII in 1890 that committed the Roman Catholic church to attempting to achieve social justice for the poor.

Restoration (English) The period of the 1660s–1680s when Charles II was called by Parliament to take his throne and was thus restored to power.

revanchism (ray-VAHNSH-ism) Wounded national pride and the desire to compensate for a loss in other ways.

revisionism (Marxism) The late-nineteenth-century adaptation of Marxist socialism that aimed to introduce basic reform through parliamentary acts rather than through revolution.

Revolution of 1989 The throwing out of the communist governments in eastern Europe by popular demand and/or armed uprising.

Rigveda (Rihg VAY-dah) The most ancient of the four Vedas, or Hindi religious epics, brought into India by the Aryans.

Romanov Dynasty (ROH-mah-noff) Ruled Russia from 1613 until 1917.

Romantic movement The generic name for the trend in literature and the arts of early nineteenth-century Europe away from rationalism and social improvement and toward a celebration of the emotions and individualistic views.

Rome, Treaty of The pact signed by six western European nations in 1957 that is the founding document of the European Union.

Rose Chamber Rescript of 1839 A major component of the Tanzimat; it called for the full equality of all Ottoman subjects, regardless of religion or ethnicity.

Rubaiyat (Roo-BAY-yaht) The verses attributed to the twelfth-century Persian poet Omar Khayyam.

Safavid Empire (SAH-fah-vihd) The dynasty of Shi'ite Muslims that ruled Persia from the 1500s to the 1700s.

Sahel The arid belt extending across Africa south of the Sahara; also called the Sudan.

sakoku (SAH-koh-koo) Japan's self-imposed isolation from the outer world that lasted two centuries until 1854.

Salafi movement (Sah-lah-FEE-yah) Intellectual movement begun by Muhammad Abduh to try to modernize Islamic law. More recently, the term has come to be associated with Islamism and a repudiation of the West.

Salamis The naval battle that, with the battle of Platea, ended the second Persian War with a Greek victory.

Samaria One of the two kingdoms into which the Hebrew Kingdom was split after Solomon's death; the other was Judea.

Samsara (Sahm-SAH-rah) The recurrent reincarnation of the soul; a concept shared by Hinduism and Buddhism.

samurai (Sa-muh-REYE) Japanese warrior-aristocrats of medieval and early modern times.

Sanhedrin (San-HEH-drihn) The Jewish governing council under the overlordship of Rome.

Sanskrit The sacred language of ancient India; came originally from the Aryans.

Sardinia-Piedmont See Piedmont.

sati (Sah-TEE) In India, the practice in which a widow committed suicide at the death of her husband.

Satrapy (SA-tra-pee) A province under a governor or satrap in the ancient Persian Empire.

Savanna The semiarid grasslands where most African civilizations developed.

scientific method The method of observation and experiment by which the physical sciences proceed to new knowledge.

Scramble for Africa The sudden race for colonies in Africa amoing the major European nations that occurred between about 1882 and 1914.

secondary resistance A term some historians apply to the more delayed, regional, and supra-ethnic forms of armed resistance that occurred after European occupation of territories in Africa during the first few decades of the colonial era.

Second Front The reopening of a war front in the west against the Axis powers in World War II; eventually accomplished by the invasion of Normandy in June 1944.

Second Industrial Revolution The second phase of industrialization that occurred in the late 1800s after the introduction of electric power and the internal combustion engine.

Second International Association of socialist parties founded in 1889; after the Russian Revolution in 1917, the Second International split into democratic and communist segments.

secret speech Premier Nikita Khrushchev of the USSR gave an account in February 1956 of the crimes of Joseph Stalin against his own people that was supposed to remain secret but was soon known internationally.

secularism The rejection of supernatural religion as the arbiter of earthly action; emphasis on worldly and humanistic affairs.

Seleucid Kingdom of Persia One of the three Hellenistic Kingdoms. The successor state to the empire of Alexander the Great in most of the Middle East.

Self-strengthening The late nineteenth-century attempt by Chinese officials to bring China into the modern world by instituting reforms; failed to achieve its goal.

Selim III, Sultan (Seh-LEEM) Ottoman sultan, 1792–1807. He introduced the first reforms of the Ottoman Empire, which later became the Tanzimat.

Seljuks (Sel-JUCKS) Turkish converts to Islam who seized the Baghdad government from the Abbasids in the eleventh century.

Semitic Adjective describing a person or language belonging to one of the most widespread of the western Asian groups; among many others, it embraces Hebrew and Arabic.

serfdom Restriction of personal and economic freedoms associated with medieval European agricultural society.

Seven Years' War Fought between France and England, with their allies, around the world, 1756–1763; won by England, with major accessions of territory to the British Empire.

Shah Abbas the Great (SHAH Ahb-BAHS) Greatest of the Safavid Shahs of Persia (r. 1587–1629). He extended the boundaries of the Safavid Empire to their greatest extent.

Shaka (SHAH-kah) King of the Zulu people of South Africa. During the 1810s, he united the Zulu into a powerful, militaristic state in the region of Natal.

Shang Dynasty The first historical rulers of China; ruled from c. 1500 to c. 1100 BCE.

Sharia (Shah-REE-yah) The sacred law of Islam; based on the Qur'an and the oral traditions (Sunna) of the Prophet Muhammad.

Shaykh (Shake) An Arabic honorific form of address for a respected elder, leader, or a scholar.

Shaykh al-Islam (Shake al-Is-LAHM) Highest religious official of the Ottoman Empire.

Shi'ites (SHEE-ites) A minority sect of Islam; adherents believe that kinship with Muhammad is necessary to qualify for the caliphate.

shiki (SHEE-kee) Rights attached to parcels of land (shoen) in Japan.

Shinto (SHIHN-toh) Native Japanese animism.

Shiva (SHEE-vah) A member of the high trinity of Hindu gods; lord of destruction but also of procreation; often pictured dancing.

shoen (SHOH-ehn) Parcels of land in Japan with shiki (rights) attached to them; could take many forms and have various possessors.

shogunate (SHOH-guh-nate) The government of medieval Japan in which the shogun, a military and civil regent, served as the actual leader, while the emperor was the symbolic head of the state and religion.

show trials First used for the staged trials of alleged traitors to the Soviet system in 1936–1937; generically, a political trial in which the conviction of the accused is a foregone conclusion.

Siddhartha Gautama (Sih-DAHR-thah Gau-TAH-mah) The proper name of the Buddha.

Sikhs (SEEKS) Members of a cult founded in the sixteenth century CE who seek a middle way between Islam and Hindu belief; centered on the Punjab region in northern India.

Sino-Soviet conflict Differences in the interpretation of Marxism that were accentuated by conflict over proper policy vis-à-vis the United States in the 1950s and 1960s in Moscow and Beijing.

Sino-Tibetan languages The family of languages spoken by the Chinese and Tibetan peoples.

Social Darwinism The adaptation of Darwinian biology to apply to human society in simplistic terms.

Social Democrats Noncommunist socialists who refused to join the Third International and founded independent parties.

Socrates (470–399 BCE) First of the three great philosophers of the Greek Classical age. Questioned the nature of knowledge and ethical conduct. Athenian court tried and executed him for "corrupting" the youth of the city.

Solidarity The umbrella organization founded by Lech Walesa and other anticommunist Poles in 1981 to recover Polish freedom; triumphed with new government in 1989.

Song Dynasty (Sung) The dynasty that ruled China from c. 1127 until 1279, when the last ruler was overthrown by the Mongol invaders.

Songhay (Song-GEYE) A West African state, centered on the bend of the Niger River, which reached its fullest extent in the sixteenth century before collapsing.

spinning jenny A fundamental mechanical improvement over hand-spinning of cotton thread, developed by an English engineer in the 1780s.

Spirit of the Laws One of the basic tracts of the eighteenthcentury Enlightenment, written by Baron Montesquieu and adopted by many reformers of government throughout Europe.

Springtime of the Peoples The spring and summer of 1848 when popular revolutions in Europe temporarily succeeded.

Stalingrad The battle in 1942 that marked the turning point of World War II in Europe.

Stalinist economy Involved the transformation of a retarded agrarian economy to an industrialized one through massive reallocation of human and material resources directed by a central plan; imposed on the Soviet Union and then, in the first years after World War II, on eastern Europe.

Stamp Act of 1765 A law enacted by the British Parliament in 1765 that imposed a fee on legal documents of all types and on all books and newspapers sold in the American colonies.

state The term for a territorial, sovereign entity of government.

steppes In physical geography, steppes generally are characterized by relatively low levels of rainfall and growths of short grasses. Usually suitable only for livestock.

Stoicism A Hellenistic philosophy that emphasized human brotherhood and natural law as guiding principles.

Storm Troopers/SA The street-fighting "bully boys" of the Nazi Party; suppressed after 1934 by Hitler's orders.

Structural Adjustment Programs (SAPs) Programs designed by the World Bank to achieve economic improvement in developing countries; frequently failures.

stuprum (STOO-prum) A Roman legal term denoting acts that were both immoral and illegal; contrast with infamia, which was an immoral but not illegal action.

Sublime Porte A term that came to be applied to the Chancery and diplomatic corps of the Ottoman bureaucracy.

Successor states Usual term for the several eastern European states that emerged from the Paris treaties of 1919 as successors to the Russian, German, and Austro-Hungarian Empires.

Sudan (Soo-DAN) Lit. Arabic for "Blacks," from the Bilad al-Sudan, the "Land of the Blacks" in the arid belt extending across Africa south of the Sahara.

Sufi (SOO-fee) Arabic term for a popular form of Islam that emphasizes emotional union with God and mystical powers.

Sui Dynasty (Soo-wee) Ruled China from c. 580 to c. 620 CE; ended the disintegration of central government that had existed for the previous 130 years.

sui juris (SOO-wee JOO-rihs) "Of his own law"; Roman term for an individual, especially a female, who was not restricted by the usual laws or customs.

Suleiman the Magnificent (SOO-lay-man) Ottoman Sultan, 1520–1566 CE. Greatest of the Ottoman sultans, his long reign was the high-water mark of the Ottoman Empire.

Sumerians The creators of Mesopotamian urban civilization.

Sunna (SOO-nah) Literally, the "way" or example set by the Prophet Muhammad. It is the oral tradition that Muslim legal scholars rely upon to supplement the Qur'an as another source of the Sharia.

Sunnis (SOO-nees) The majority group in Islam; adherents believe that the caliphate should go to the most qualified individual and should not necessarily pass to the kin of Muhammad.

Sun Yat-sen (Soon Yaht-sehn: 1866–1925) Educated in Western schools, Sun helped overthrow the Qing monarchy and became one of the founders of the Kuomintang Party and of the Chinese Republic.

Supremacy, Act of A law enacted in 1534 by the English Parliament that made the monarch the head of the Church of England.

suzerain The superior of a vassal to whom the vassal owed feudal duties.

Swahili (Swah-HEE-lee) A hybrid language based on Bantu and Arabic; used extensively in East Africa. Often used to refer to the people and civilization of the East African coast.

Syndicalism A doctrine of government that advocates a society organized on the basis of syndicates or unions.

Taipings Anti-Manzhou rebels in China in the 1860s.

Taj Mahal (TAHJ Mah-HAL) The beautiful tomb built by the seventeenth-century Mughal emperor Jahan for his wife.

takfiri A radically Islamist doctrine that declares all moderate Muslims who refuse to engage in jihad against the West to be themselves unbelievers, and therefore under a sentence of death.

Tale of Genji (GEHN-jee) First known novel in Asian, if not world, history; authored by a female courtier about life in the Japanese medieval court.

Taliban (Ar. Students) Islamic fundamentalist militants who came to power in Afghanistan in 1995 and were expelled from the country a few years later by American and native forces.

Tamarlane (TAA-mahr-lane) Turco-Mongolian conqueror and founder of the short-lived Timurid state in the Middle and Near East during the late fourteenth century.

Tang Dynasty Ruled China from c. 620 to c. 900 CE and began the great age of Chinese artistic and technical advances.

Tanzimat reforms (TAN-zih-maht) Lit. "New Order" in Turkish. The state-directed reforms of the Ottoman Empire that lasted from 1839 to 1876.

tariqa (tah-REE-kah) Muslim sufi (popular mystic) brotherhoods, generally all-male.

Tartars (TAR-tars) Russian name for the Mongols.

Tel el Amarna The site of great temple complexes along the Nile River in Egypt.

Tenochtitlán (Teh-noch-tiht-LAHN) Chief city of the Aztec civilization. It probably was built c. 1325, and was conquered by Cortes in 1521. It was renamed Mexico City, and served as the capital of colonial Mexico.

Teotihuacan (TAY-oh-tee-WAH-kahn) One of the Classical Native American civilizations of Mexico, dated 300 BCE to 800 CE.

Test Act Seventeenth-century English law barring non-Anglican Church members from government and university positions.

Tetrarchy "Rule of four"; a system of monarchic rule established by Roman emperor Diocletian at the end of the third century CE; failed to achieve its goals.

theocracy The rule by gods or their priests.

Theravada Buddhism (Thayr-rah-VAH-dah) A stricter, monastic form of Buddhism entrenched in Southeast Asia; same as Hinayana Buddhism.

Thermidorean reaction The conservative reaction to the Reign of Terror during the French Revolution.

Third Estate The great majority of Frenchmen: those neither clerical nor noble.

Third International An association of Marxist parties in many nations; inspired by Russian communists and headquartered in Moscow until its dissolution in 1943.

Third Republic of France The government of France after the exile of Emperor Napoleon III; lasted from 1871 until 1940.

Third Rome A Russian myth that Moscow was ordained to succeed Rome and Constantinople as the center of true Christianity.

Third World A term in use after World War II to denote countries and peoples in underdeveloped, formerly colonial areas of Asia, Africa, and Latin America; the First World was the West under U.S. leadership, and the Second World was the communist states under Soviet leadership.

Tienanmen Square, massacre on The shooting down of perhaps thousands of Chinese who were peacefully demonstrating for relaxation of political censorship by the communist leaders; occurred in 1989 in Beijing.

Tilsit, Treaty of A treaty concluded in 1807 after the French under Napoleon had defeated the Russians; divided Europe/Asia into French and Russian spheres.

timar (Tih-MAR) An Ottoman feudal estate held by a member of the Ottoman cavalry.

Timbuktu (Tim-buck-TOO) City located on the Niger River in West Africa. One of the principal staging centers of the trans-Saharan caravan trade in the Middle Ages.

Time of Troubles A fifteen-year period at the beginning of the seventeenth century in Russia when the state was nearly destroyed by revolts and wars.

Titoism The policy of neutrality in foreign policy combined with continued dedication to socialism in domestic policy that was followed by the Yugoslav Marxist leader Tito after his expulsion from the Soviet camp in 1948.

Toltec (TOHL-tehc) An Amerindian civilization centered in the Valley of Mexico; succeeded by the Aztecs.

Torah (TOH-rah) The first five books of the Old Testament; the Jews' fundamental law code.

Tories A nickname for British nineteenth-century conservatives; opposite of Whigs.

totalitarianism The attempt by a dictatorial government to achieve total control over a society's life and ideas.

Total war The modern form of warfare that first appeared in the twentieth century that involved the recruitment of entire civilian populations, in addition to the troops in the field, in support of the war effort.

Trans-Saharan trade Ancient trade between Mediterranean and Red Sea regions and Sub-Saharan regions of Africa: primarily linked the Maghrib with the western and central Sudan.

Transvaal (Trans-VAWL) Second of the two independent states set up by the Boer Great Trek in the early nineteenth century in South Africa.

Trekboers (TREHK-bohrs) South African Boer "pioneers" who trekked away from Cape Colony and civilization to settle deep inland on the South African frontier.

tribunes The chief representatives of the plebeians during the Roman republic.

Triple Alliance A pact concluded in 1882 that united Germany, Austria-Hungary, and Italy against possible attackers; the members were called the Central Powers.

Triumvirate "Three-man rule"; the First Triumvirate existed during the 50s BCE. and the Second in the 30s BCE during the last decades of the Roman republic.

Truman Doctrine The commitment of the U.S. government in 1947 to defend any noncommunist state against attempted communist takeover; proposed by President Harry Truman.

Tula (TOO-lah) Chief city of the Toltec civilization, built around 800 CE and located to the northeast of today's Mexico City.

Tutankamen (too-TAHNK-ah-men) Boy pharaoh who ruled Egypt 1347–1339 BCE.

Twelve Tables The first written Roman law code; established c. 450 BCE.

ulama (oo-lah-MAH) Muslim religious scholars, usually specialists in Holy Law (see Sharia); sometimes called "mullahs."

Umayyad Dynasty (Oo-MAHY-yad) The caliphs resident in Damascus from 661 to 750 CE.

Umma (OO-mah) The entire Muslim community, meaning something like the Christian concept of the "Church."

Uncertainty principle The modern theory in physics that denies absolute causal relationships of matter and, hence, predictability.

unequal treaties Chinese name for the diplomatic and territorial arrangements foisted on the weak Qing Dynasty by European powers in the nineteenth century; also, the commercial treaties forced on just-opened Japan by the same powers and the United States.

Union of Indochina Sometimes referred to simply as Indochina. This was the official French name for their colony that included Vietnam, Laos, and Cambodia.

Upanishads (Oo-PAH-ni-shads) The ancient Hindu holy epics dealing with morals and philosophy.

urban migration A term for the widespread demographic event beginning in Europe in the early nineteenth century that saw millions of people moving into the towns and cities from the countryside.

Utopia "Nowhere"; Greek term used to denote an ideal place or society.

Utopian socialism The dismissive label given by Marx to previous theories that aimed at establishing a more just and benevolent society.

Utrecht, Treaty of Treaty signed in 1713 that ended the War of the Spanish Succession. A defeat for King Louis XIV of France, it gave Britain access to the valuable trade of the Spanish Caribbean Islands.

vassal In medieval Europe, a person, usually a noble, who owed feudal duties to a superior, called a suzerain.

Vedas (VAY-dahs) The four oral epics of the Aryans brought into ancient India.

Verdun, Treaty of A treaty concluded in 843 that divided Charlemagne's empire among his three grandsons; established what became the permanent dividing lines between the French and Germans.

vernacular The native oral language of a given people.

Vespucci, Amerigo (Vehs-POO-chee, Ah-meh-REE-goh) Italian geographer who helped map the early discoveries in the New World, and after whom it was named ("America").

villa The country estate of a Roman patrician or other wealthy Roman.

Vishnu (VISH-noo) One of the high Hindu trinity of gods, the god who preserves the universe and karma.

vizier (Vih-ZEER) An official of Muslim government, especially a high Turkish official equivalent to prime minister.

Wahhabism (Wah-HAHB-ism) Movement begun by Muhammad Abd al-Wahhab in the mid-1700s to impose a fundamentalist, Islamic law on Arabia. It became the foundation of Saudi Arabia as well as contemporary, radical—and sometimes violent—Islamic fundamentalism.

wandering of peoples A term referring to the migrations of various Germanic and Asiatic tribes in the third and fourth centuries CE that brought them into conflict with Rome.

Wannsee Conference The 1942 meeting of Nazi leaders that determined the "final solution" for the Jews.

waqf (WAHK-f) An Islamic trust established by the devout to benefit a particular group of people or institution (a mosque, for example). Usually, the ulama administer these foundations much as lawyers oversee trusts today.

Warsaw Pact An organization of the Soviet satellite states in Europe; founded under Russian aegis in 1954 to serve as a counterweight to NATO.

Wars of the Austrian Succession Two 1740s wars between Prussia and Austria that resulted in important advantages to Prussia and its king, Frederick the Great.

Wars of the Roses An English civil war between noble factions over the succession to the throne in the fifteenth century.

Waterloo The final defeat of Napoleon in 1815 after his return from Elban exile.

Wealth of Nations, The The short title of the pathbreaking work on national economy by Adam Smith; published in 1776.

weapons of mass destruction (WMDs) Deadly nuclear, chemical, or biological weapons.

Weimar Republic (VEYE-mahr) The popular name for Germany's democratic government between 1919 and the Nazi takeover.

wergeld (VAYR-gehld) Under early Germanic law, a fine paid to an injured party or his or her family or lord that was equivalent to the value of the injured individual.

Westphalia, Treaty of The treaty that ended the Thirty Years' War in 1648; the first modern peace treaty in that it established strategic and territorial gains as more important than religious or dynastic ones.

Whigs A nickname for British nineteenth-century liberals; opposite of Tories.

white man's burden A phrase coined by Rudyard Kipling to refer to what he considered the necessity of bringing European civilization to non-Europeans.

white settler colonies African colonies that experienced relatively large amounts of white, European immigration during the colonial period, primarily Algeria, Kenya, (Southern) Rhodesia, Angola, Mozambique, and South Africa.

women's liberation Movement, begun in the 1960s, to improve the economic and social status of women.

World Bank A monetary institution founded after World War II by Western nations to assist in the recovery effort and to aid the Third World's economic development.

Yalta Conference Conference in 1945 in southern Prussia where Franklin D. Roosevelt, Joseph Stalin, and Winston Churchill (the "Big Three") met to attempt to settle postwar questions, particularly those affecting the future of Europe.

Yamato state (Yah-MAH-toh) The earliest known government of Japan; divided into feudal subdivisions ruled by clans and headed by the Yamato family.

yin/yang East Asian philosophical distinction between the male and female characters in terms of active versus passive, warm versus cold, and the like.

Yom Kippur War (YAHM kih-POOR) A name for the 1973 conflict between Israel and its Arab neighbors.

Young Ottomans A group of Western-educated Turkish intellectuals and journalists who, in the 1870s, supported the transformation of the Ottoman sultanate into a constitutional monarchy.

Yuan Dynasty (YOO-an) Official term for the Mongol dynasty of the Great Khans in China, 1279–1368.

yurts (YERTS) Tent-like, Mongol dwellings usually made of felt.

Zama, Battle of Decisive battle of the Second Punic War; Roman victory in 202 was followed by absorption of most of the Carthaginian Empire in the Mediterranean.

Zambo (SAAM-bo) Term for mulattos in Brazil; in colonial Spanish America, offspring of Spanish and Indian.

Zanzibar Sultanate Sultanate (Arab government) established in 1832 on the East African island of Zanzibar by the former Sultan of Oman, Sayyid Said bin Sultan al-Busaidi.

Zarathustra (ZAY-rah THROOS-trah) The mythical founder and chief prophet of the ancient Persian religion known as Zoroastrianism, which influenced Jewish and later Christian belief.

Zealots (ZEH-luhts) Jewish religious extremists at the time of Jesus who opposed Roman occupation and used guerilla methods and assassination against them to drive them out of Israel and Judea.

Zhou Dynasty (Choh) The second historical Chinese dynasty; ruled from c. 1100 to c. 400 BCE.

ziggurat (ZIHG-goo-raht) The stepped and elevated temple structures that the ancient Mesopotamian civilization erected in honor of its gods.

Zionism (ZEYE-yuh-nism) A movement founded by Theodor Herzl in 1896 to establish a Jewish national homeland and to revive the study of Hebrew as a spoken language.

Zulu War South African war fought in 1879 between Britain and the Zulu peole. Its cause was Afrikaner expansion during the Great Trek and a British desire to defeat Africans who stood in the way of white settlement.

Zwingli, Ulrich (1484–1531) Theologian of the early Protestant Reformation who was influential in establishing Protestantism in his native Switzerland.

ANSWERS TO TEST YOUR KNOWLEDGE

CHAPTER 1
1. b, 2. e, 3. d, 4. a, 5. c, 6. c, 7. b, 8. b, 9. e, 10. c

CHAPTER 2
1. a, 2. b, 3. b, 4. d, 5. b, 6. b, 7. d, 8. c, 9. b, 10. a

CHAPTER 3
1. c, 2. c, 3. c, 4. a, 5. e, 6. c, 7. b, 8. a, 9. a, 10. e

CHAPTER 4
1. b, 2. d, 3. b, 4. b, 5. c, 6. c, 7. b, 8. a, 9. c, 10. a

CHAPTER 5
1. a, 2. b, 3. a, 4. d, 5. d, 6. a, 7. a, 8. c, 9. e, 10. c

CHAPTER 6
1. a, 2. b, 3. b, 4. b, 5. a, 6. e, 7. b, 8. d, 9. d, 10. b

CHAPTER 7
1. a, 2. b, 3. b, 4. c, 5. b, 6. b, 7. a, 8. e, 9. a, 10. b

CHAPTER 8
1. c, 2. c, 3. c, 4. a, 5. e, 6. a, 7. a, 8. a, 9. d, 10. e

CHAPTER 9
1. c, 2. b, 3. d, 4. c, 5. a, 6. d, 7. d, 8. a, 9. a, 10. e

CHAPTER 10
1. c, 2. a, 3. b, 4. b, 5. e, 6. c, 7. b, 8. d, 9. d, 10. c

CHAPTER 11
1. e, 2. c, 3. a, 4. b, 5. e, 6. e, 7. e, 8. d, 9. c, 10. a

CHAPTER 12
1. b, 2. a, 3. a, 4. c, 5. b, 6. b, 7. a, 8. d, 9. b, 10. a

CHAPTER 13
1. b, 2. c, 3. e, 4. d, 5. b, 6. d, 7. a, 8. e, 9. c, 10. a

CHAPTER 14
1. b, 2. b, 3. c, 4. b, 5. b, 6. b, 7. c, 8. c, 9. d, 10. e

CHAPTER 15
1. a, 2. c, 3. c, 4. d, 5. b, 6. c, 7. a, 8. a, 9. c, 10. e

CHAPTER 16
1. d, 2. d, 3. c, 4. a, 5. a, 6. b, 7. c, 8. a, 9. e, 10. c

CHAPTER 17
1. b, 2. a, 3. c, 4. a, 5. d, 6. b, 7. b, 8. c, 9. c, 10. d

CHAPTER 18
1. b, 2. a, 3. d, 4. c, 5. c, 6. a, 7. e, 8. a, 9. c, 10. b

CHAPTER 19
1. d, 2. e, 3. a, 4. c, 5. b, 6. b, 7. d, 8. a, 9. e, 10. e

CHAPTER 20
1. c, 2. b, 3. e, 4. c, 5. a, 6. a, 7. a, 8. d, 9. e, 10. a

CHAPTER 21
1. b, 2. d, 3. a, 4. a, 5. c, 6. e, 7. c, 8. b, 9. c, 10. d

CHAPTER 22
1. c, 2. a, 3. a, 4. d, 5. b, 6. c, 7. d, 8. c, 9. a, 10. b

CHAPTER 23
1. c, 2. b, 3. c, 4. c, 5. c, 6. e, 7. a, 8. b, 9. b, 10. c

CHAPTER 24
1. d, 2. b, 3. d, 4. a, 5. b, 6. d, 7. b, 8. c, 9. a, 10. b

CHAPTER 25
1. a, 2. c, 3. a, 4. a, 5. d, 6. d, 7. a, 8. b, 9. d, 10. d

CHAPTER 26
1. b, 2. d, 3. e, 4. d, 5. d, 6. b, 7. c, 8. b, 9. c, 10. c

CHAPTER 27
1. d, 2. a, 3. c, 4. c, 5. b, 6. c, 7. c, 8. b, 9. d, 10. e

CHAPTER 28
1. b, 2. e, 3. c, 4. a, 5. e, 6. d, 7. a, 8. b, 9. b, 10. c

CREDITS

This page constitutes an extension of the copyright page. We have made every effort to trace the ownership of all copyrighted material and to secure permission from copyright holders. In the event of any question arising as to the use of any material, we will be pleased to make the necessary corrections in future printings. Thanks are due to the following authors, publishers, and agents for permission to use the material indicated.

Chapter 1. **8:** top, Musée National du Bardo, Tunis, Tunisia/©Werner Forman/Art Resource, NY. **8:** bottom, Kenneth Garrett/National Geographic Image Collection/Getty Images. **10:** left, French Ministry of Culture and Communication, Regional Direction for Cultural Affairs, Rhone-Alps region, Regional Department of Archaeology. **10:** right, Joy Tessman/National Geographic Image Collection/Getty Images. **11:** Naturhistorisches Museum, Vienna, Austria/Ali Meyer/The Bridgeman Art Library.

Chapter 2. **18:** © Israel Ancient Art and Architecture Collection Ltd./The Bridgeman Art Library. **21:** top, Georg Gerster/Photo Researchers, Inc. **21:** bottom, © Gianni Dagli Orti/Corbis. **22:** Monastery, Goettweig, Austria/©Erich Lessing/Art Resource, NY. **23:** © Iraq Museum, Baghdad/Photo © Held Collection/The Bridgeman Art Library. **25:** top, Kunsthistorisches Museum, Vienna, Austria/©Erich Lessing/Art Resource, NY. **25:** bottom, Louvre, Paris, France/The Bridgeman Art Library.

Chapter 3. **31:** © Erich Lessing/Art Resource, NY. **32:** © Erich Lessing/Art Resource, NY. **35:** left, © Erich Lessing/Art Resource, NY. **35:** right, © Werner Forman/Art Resource, NY. **36:** © Giza (El Gizeh), Cairo, Egypt/Bildarchiv Steffens/The Bridgeman Art Library. **37:** The British Museum, London, UK/The Bridgeman Art Library. **38:** © Egyptian National Museum, Cairo, Egypt/Giraudon/The Bridgeman Art Library. **39:** © Réunion des Musées Nationaux/Art Resource, NY.

Chapter 4. **44:** © British Museum, London, UK/Photo © Boltin Picture Library/The Bridgeman Art Library. **45:** top, © Persepolis, Iran/The Bridgeman Art Library. **45:** bottom, © Persepolis, Iran/The Bridgeman Art Library. **48:** © Israel Images/Alamy. **49:** Private Collection/Christie's Images/The Bridgeman Art Library. **52:** © Israel Museum, Jerusalem, Israel/Ancient Art and Architecture Collection, Ltd./The Bridgeman Art Library.

Chapter 5. **57:** left, National Museum of India, New Delhi, India/The Bridgeman Art Library. **57:** right, Robert Harding Picture Library. **59:** National Maritime Museum, Haifa, Israel/©Erich Lessing/Art Resource, NY. **60:** © Government Museum and National Art Gallery, Madras, India/Lauros-Giraudon/The Bridgeman Art Library. **61:** © Polonnaruwa, Sri Lanka/The Bridgeman Art Library. **62:** © Government Museum and National Art Gallery, Madras, India/Lauros-Giraudon/The Bridgeman Art Library. **63:** © Borromeo/Art Resource, NY.

Chapter 6. **70:** British Museum, London, UK/The Bridgeman Art Library. **71:** © China Newsphoto/Reuters/Corbis. **72:** left, © Giraudon/Art Resource, NY. **72:** right, © Eastern Asian Collection, Brandenburg, Berlin, Germany/The Bridgeman Art Library. **73:** © SEF/Art Resource, NY. **74:** © FPG/Getty Images.

Chapter 7. **85:** © Ashmolean Museum, University of Oxford, UK/The Bridgeman Art Library. **88:** left, Musée d'Art et d'Histoire du Judaisme/©Réunion des Musées Nationaux/Art Resource, NY. **88:** right, © Nimatallah/Art Resource, NY. **90:** © American School of Classical Studies at Athens: Agora Excavations. **91:** © Erich Lessing/Art Resource, NY. **92:** British Museum, London, UK/The Bridgeman Art Library. **93:** Pinacoteca Capitolina, Palazzo Conservatori, Rome, Italy/Index/The Bridgeman Art Library.

Chapter 8. **99:** Museo Archeologico Nazionale, Naples, Italy/Alinari/The Bridgeman Art Library. **102:** Museum fuer Islamische Kunst, Staatliche Museum zu Berlin, Berlin, Germany/©Bildarchiv Preussischer Kulturbesitz/Art Resource, NY. **105:** Acropolis, Athens/Alinari/ The Bridgeman Art Library. **106:** left, Scala/Art Resource, NY. **106:** right, Casa di Lucrezi Frontone, Pompeii, Italy/Roger-Viollet, Paris/The Bridgeman Art Library.

Chapter 9. **112:** Museo Etrusco, Lazio, Rome, Italy/Bernard Cox/The Bridgeman Art Library. **115:** British Museum, London, UK/photo © Michael Holford, London. **118:** Segovia, Spain/Ken Welsh/The Bridgeman Art Library. **121:** Louvre, Paris, France/Lauros-Giraudon/The Bridgeman Art Library. **124:** © Scala/Art Resource, NY. **125:** Museo e Gallerie Nazionali di Capodimonte, Naples, Italy/Lauros-Giraudon/The Bridgeman Art Library.

Chapter 10. **131:** The Bridgeman Art Library. **132:** San Apollinare Nuovo, Revenna, Italy/Dagli Orti/The Art Archive. **134:**

AKG, London. **136:** Bibliothèque Municipale, Laon, France/ The Bridgeman Art Library. **138:** Musée Condé, Chantilly, France/Giraudon/The Bridgeman Art Library. **140:** Louvre, Paris, France/Peter Willi/The Bridgeman Art Library. **142:** San Vitale, Ravenna/Giraudon/The Bridgeman Art Library.

Chapter 11. 152: Jake Page, *In the Hands of the Great Spirit* (New York: Free Press, 2003), p.23. **153:** Werner Forman/Art Resource, NY. **155:** Werner Forman/Art Resource, NY. **156:** Sean Sprague/Mexicolore/The Bridgeman Art Library. **162:** Richard A. Cooke/Corbis.

Chapter 12. 171: Darryl Plowes. **173:** Images&Stories/Alamy. **175:** © The Granger Collection. **176:** Peter Garlake, *The Making of the Past: The Kingdoms of Africa.* Elsevier/Phaidon, (1990) p. 101. **177:** left, Images of Africa Photobank/Alamy. **177:** right, © Heini Schneebeli/The Bridgeman Art Library.

Chapter 13. 184: Bibliothèque Nationale, Paris, France. **187:** Mecca, Saudi Arabia/Bildarchiv Steffens/The Bridgeman Art Library. **188:** The Bridgeman Art Library.

Chapter 14. 195: left, Victoria and Albert Museum, London, UK/The Stapleton Collection, UK/The Bridgeman Art Library. **195:** right, Bodleian Library, University of Oxford, MS. Bodl. 360, fol. 26v. **197:** left, © Mark Shenley/Alamy. **197:** right, The Metropolitan Museum of Art, Rogers Fund, 1942 (42.63) Photograph, all rights reserved, The Metropolitan Museum of Art. **198:** Ken Welsh/The Bridgeman Art Library.

Chapter 15. 206: © John Elk/Stock Boston. **207:** © The Bridgeman Art Library. **208:** Private Collection/Ann & Bury Peerless Picture Library/The Bridgeman Art Library. **210:** Ellora, Bombay, India/The Bridgeman Art Library. **212:** © Robert Harding Picture Library Ltd/Alamy.

Chapter 16. 216: left, The Bridgeman Art Library. **216:** right, Ian McKinnell/Alamy **217:** British Library, London, UK/The Bridgeman Art Library. **219:** Corbis Collection/Alamy. **222:** Werner Forman/Art Resource, NY.

Chapter 17. 229: Calmann & King, London, UK/The Bridgeman Art Library. **232:** Tower of London, London, UK/The Bridgeman Art Library. **234:** Private Collection/The Bridgeman Art Library. **235:** Chinese and Japanese Special Fund, courtesy of Museum of Fine Arts, Boston.

Chapter 18. 243: Bridgeman-Giraudon/Art Resource, NY. **245:** Erich Lessing/Art Resource, NY. **248:** Abbey of Montecassino, Italy/The Bridgeman Art Library. **252:** British Library, London, UK/The Art Archive. **254:** Bibliothèque Nationale, Paris, France/Josse/The Art Archive.

Chapter 19. 260: left, Victoria and Albert Museum, London, UK/Art Resource, NY. **260:** right, Dean Conger/Corbis. **261:** Bibliothèque Nationale, Paris, France/The Bridgeman Art Library.

Chapter 20. 269: Saint Sebastian *Interceding for the Plague Stricken* by Josse Lieferinxe, ca. 1500. The Walters Art Museum, Baltimore (37.1995). **272:** © Giraudon/Art Resource, NY. **273:** Bibliothèque Nationale, Paris, France/The Bridgeman Art Library. **274:** Bibliothèque Nationale, Paris, France/The Bridgeman Art Library.

Chapter 21. 282: Francis G. Mayer/Corbis. **283:** Samuel H. Kress Collection, © 1995 Board of Trustees National Gallery, Washington, D.C. **287:** left, Baptistery, Florence, Italy/The Bridgeman Art Library. **287:** right, Baptistery, Florence, Italy/ The Bridgeman Art Library. **288:** Vatican Museums and Galleries, Vatican City, Italy/The Bridgeman Art Library.

Chapter 22. 301: Service Historique de la Marine, Vincennes, France/Lauros-Giraudon/The Bridgeman Art Library. **303:** Michael Graham-Stewart/The Bridgeman Art Library. **306:** Robert Frerck/Odyssey Productions, Inc. **307:** Glasgow University Library, Scotland/The Bridgeman Art Library.

Chapter 23. 311: Galleria degli Uffizi, Florence, Italy/The Bridgeman Art Library. **312:** Collection of Albert Rilliet, Geneva, Switzerland/Lauros-Giraudon/The Bridgeman Art Library. **313:** Private Collection/The Bridgeman Art Library. **314:** © Stock Montage, Inc. **316:** Private Collection/The Bridgeman Art Library.

Chapter 24. 323: Topkapi Palace Museum, Istanbul, Turkey/ Giraudon/The Bridgeman Art Library, London. **329:** left, SEF/Art Resource, NY. **329:** right, SEF/Art Resource, NY. **331:** The Bridgeman Art Library, London.

Chapter 25. 335: left, Kunsthistorisches Museum, Vienna, Austria/©Erich Lessing/Art Resource, NY. **335:** right, Louvre, Paris, France/Lauros-Giraudon/The Bridgeman Art Library. **337:** Louvre, Paris, France/Giraudon/The Bridgeman Art Library. **338:** Giraudon/The Bridgeman Art Library. **346:** British Library, London, UK/The Bridgeman Art Library. **348:** Chateau de Versailles, France/Giraudon/The Bridgeman Art Library.

Chapter 26. 354: Giraudon/The Bridgeman Art Library. **355:** © Giraudon/Art Resource, NY. **360:** Musée Guimet, Paris, France/The Bridgeman Art Library, London.

Chapter 27. 364: Museo Nacional de Soares dos Reis, Porto, Portugal/Giraudon/The Bridgeman Art Library. **365:** Private Collection/The Bridgeman Art Library. **366:** The Art Archive. **368:** Musées des Beaux-Arts, Angers, France/Giraudon/The Bridgeman Art Library. **371:** Michael S. Yamashita/Corbis.

Chapter 28. 377: Bildarchiv Preussischer Kulturbesitz/Art Resource, NY. **378:** The Granger Collection, New York. **380:** top, Museo de America, Madrid, Spain/Giraudon/The Bridgeman Art Library. **380:** bottom, Private Collection/The Bridgeman Art Library. **381:** Museo Nacional Palacio de Bellas Artes, Havana, Cuba/Index/The Bridgeman Art Library.

INDEX

St. Francis Xavier, 364
Franks, 135, 139
Frederick Barbarossa, 254
Frederick I, 344
Frederick II, 254, 273
Frederick the Great, 344
Frederick William
 civil bureaucracy created by, 344
 professional army of, 342, 344
 reign of, 342
Frederick William I, 344
Fujiwara clan, 231, 368
Funan, 238

Gaja Mada, 238
Gama, Vasco da, 300
Ganges River, 58
Gao, 174–175
Gauchos, *380*
Gauls, 116
Genesis, 21, 22
Geneva, 313
Genoa, 279
Gentiles, 50, 131
Geocentric universe, 101
Geography
 of Africa, *168*
 of Greece, 85
 during Han Dynasty, 217
 important figures in, 101–102
 Islamic, 196
 of Japan, 229
 progress made in, 275
King George I, 341
Germanic people, early. *See also* Germany
 conversion to Christianity of, 136–137
 customs and society of, 136–138
 invasion of Roman Empire by, 135–136
 law of, 137
 women in, 137
Germany. *See also* Germanic people, early;
  Holy Roman Empire
 defeat of Teutonic Knights of, 261
 effect of Thirty Years' War on, 335
 evolution of modern, 342
 Investiture Controversy in, 253–254
 and Protestant Reformation, 310–312
Ghana, 172
 Ibn Khaldun's account of decline of, 174
Ghazis, 323
Ghazzali, Abu Hamid Muhammad al-, 195,
  323
Ghiberti, Lorenzo, 287
 bronze doors of, *287*
Gilgamesh, 21, 22
Giotto, 287
Glorious Revolution of 1688, 340
 significance of, 340–341
Gobi Desert, 259
Gods/Goddesses/Spirits. *See also* Yahweh
 anthropomorphic Greek, 103, 104
 of Aryans, 58
 of Assyrians, 42
 of Aztecs, 156
 of early Germanic people, 136
 of Egypt, 31, 33, 37
 Hindu, 60, 206
 Inca, 160
 of India, 63, 207
 in Mesoamerican civilizations,
   153, 155
 of Mongols, 261

in Neolithic Age, 11, 13
Persian, 46
Roman, 118, 120, 121–122
of Shang Dynasty, 68
of Sumerians, 19–21
of Zhou Dynasty, 70–71
Gold
 in Africa, 172, 177
 from Americas, 302
 taxes on, in Africa, 173
Golden mean, 104
Gothic architecture, 255
Grand Canal, of China, 221, 360
Grand vizier, 324, 327
Great Elector, 342, 344
Great Houses, 162
Great Palace at Knossos, 85
Great Pyramid of Khufu, 35–36, *36*
Great Schism, 273–274
Great Wall, *216*
 disrepair of, 259
 during Ming Dynasty, 353, 356
 Qin construction of, 215, 219
Great Zimbabwe, 177, 177–178
 decline and abandonment of, 178
Greece
 Classical Age of, 87
 craftsmanship of ancient, 105
 Dark Age, 87
 effect on Roman civilization of, 111, 112
 epochs of ancient, 84
 final act in Classical, 91
 geography and political development of, 85
 Hellenic, 86–91
 Hellenistic, 91, 93–96
 humanism in (800–100 bce), 98–107
 legacy of, 108
 map of early, 86
 origins of civilization in, 85–87
 patterns of belief in Classical, 100
 Peloponnesian War, 91
 periods of philosophy in, 99
 religion in, 103–104
 rise of, 44
 science during Hellenistic Period of,
   101–103
 types of government in, 87
Pope Gregory I, *136*
Guilds
 benefits of, 245
 Chinese, 354
 in Japan, 367
 power of, 274
 women and, 341
Gunpowder, 222, 262, 272
Gupta Dynasty, 203–204, 328
 economic and cultural progress under, 204
 and its trading partners, 205

Habsburg Dynasty, 286, 342, 344
 areas ruled by, 345
Habsburg Holy Roman Emperor, 335
Haciendas, 378
Hadrian, 120
Hagia Sophia, 142
Haiku, 369
 origins and evolution of, 370
Haiti, 379
Hajj, 183, 184
Hammurabi
 law and government under, 25
 women under reign of, 24

Han Dynasty, 216–220
 arts and sciences under, 217
 economy, government, and
   foreign affairs under, 217–219
 end of, 220
 expansion during, 216
Hangzhou, 222
Hannibal, 114
Hanoverian Dynasty, 341
Han synthesis, 216–217
Harappa, 56–58
 abandonment of, 57
Harem, 199
Hari-kari, 232
Caliph Harun al-Rashid, 199, 207
Hebrews, 47–48. *See also* Jews; Judaism
 Babylonian captivity of, 48, 51
 Bible of. See Old Testament
 capital of, 48
 economic change and social customs of,
   50–51
 economy of, 80
 education in culture of, 51
 Exodus of, 47
 law and government of, 49
 Old Testament of, 22
 prophets of, 50
 religion and patterns of belief of, 50. See
   also Judaism
 self-segregation of, 50
 trade of, 48
Heian era, 230–231
Heliocentrism, 101
Hellenic culture, 84, 98
 art and literature in, 104–105
 culture in, 88
 early, 87
 humanism in, 103–104
 women in, 108
Hellenistic civilization, 84
 art and literature in, 105–106
 hereditary nature of slavery in, 108
 importance of Alexandria to, 102
 law and government in, 92
 mystery religions of, 101
 philosophies of, 101
 science and technology in, 102
 scientists of, 102
 society and economy during,
   93, 106
 women in, 108
Hellenistic kingdoms, 94
 Greeks and Easterners in, 95
 Rome's defeat of, 115
the Hellespont, 87
Helots, 89, 90
Henry (Duke de Guise), 319
King Henry IV, 318
Henry of Navarre, 317–318
Prince Henry the Navigator, 300
Henry VII, 284
Henry VIII, 303, 316
 Act of Supremacy of 1534 of, 315
 dispute with pope of, 314–315
 successors to, 315
 Heresies, 249
 condemned, go underground, 274
Heretics, 310, 318
 Russian, 346, 347
Hesiod, 105
Hideyoshi, Toyotomi, 364, 365
 as samurai, *366*

Suetonius, 120
Sufis, 194–195, 323
Sufism, 194–195
    tariqas of, 195, 196
    verses of al-Rumi, 196
Sui Dynasty, 221
Sui juris, 125
Suleiman the Magnificent
    army under, 325
    domain of, 324
    eyewitness account of visit
        with, 326
    harbingers of future problems
        and, 327
    Ottoman Empire under, 325–327
Sulla, 116
Sumerian civilization, 18–24
    accomplishments of, 18–19
    cities in, 27
    mathematics and chronology
        in, 23
    religion and the afterlife in, 19–22
    successors to, 27
    writing in, 23–24
Summa Theologica (Thomas Aquinas), 254
    distortion of, 277
Sundiata, 173
Sunna, 194
Sunni Muslims, 188
    split between Shi'ite Muslims and,
        327
Susa, 46
Suzerain, 246
Swahili
    city-states, 175–177
    ivory and gold work of, 178
    religious architecture, 176
    trade, 175
Syllabaries, 233
Syncretism, 211, 382

Tacitus, 120
Taj Mahal, 197, 331
Tale of Genji (Murasaki), 233, 234
Taliban, 194
Talmud, 51
Tamarlane, 265
Tang Dynasty, *220*, 220–222
    foreign affairs during, 221
    formal culture in, 225
    reforms of, 221
    threat from steppe land tribes to, 259
Taoism, 75
Tariqas, 195, 196, 323
Tartars, 261. *See also* Mongols
Taxes
    collected by emirs, 194
    collected from non-Muslim subject
        peoples, 188, 190, 191
    in early English counties, 253
    in Egypt, 171
    imposed on Saharan traders, 173
    Inca, 160
    James I wants Crown control over, 339
    paid to Rome by Germans, 311
    Parliament and new, 272
    poll, on non-Muslims, 329
    in Roman Empire, 129
    under Shih Huang-di, 216
    under Prince Shotoku, 230
Technology

in Americas, 152
    Arab, 195
    Chinese, 354
    Egyptian, 81
    in Hellenistic civilization, 102
    Indian, 81
    Mesopotamian, 81
    metal, in China, 81
    during Ming Dynasty, 357
    passed from China to West, 262
    Roman engineering and construction, 147
    spread of ideas and, 147, 295
Tel el Amarna, 36
Temple of Jerusalem, 48
    last remnant of, *49*
    second destruction of, 52
Temujin. *See* Chinghis Khan
Ten Commandments, 50
Tengri, 261
Tenochtitlán, 156
Teotihuacan, 155–156
    Avenue of the Dead at, *156*
Terence, 120, 281
Territory, of state, 282
Tetrarchy, 129
Thailand, 239
the Elect, 313
Theocracy, 24
    in early Peruvian kingdoms, 159
    Indus Valley civilization as
        possible, 57
    Islamic, 188
    polytheistic, 153
    in Teotihuacan, 155
Emperor Theodosius, 134
Theravada Buddhism, 62
Thermopylae, battle of, 90
Thirty Years' War, 335–336
    famines and epidemics accompanying, 342
St. Thomas Aquinas, 254, 277
The 1001 Nights, 197
Tiberius, 119
    arts under, 120
Tiber River, 110
Tibet, 266, *353*
Tiglath-Pileser, 43–44
Tigris and Euphrates rivers, 18, 27, 28
    unpredictable flooding of, 30
Timbuktu, 173
    Sankore mosque in, 174
Time of Troubles, 348
Timurid Empire, 265
Timur-Lenk. *See* Tamarlane
Titian, 287
Tokugawa, Ieyasu, 364. *See also* Tokugawa
        shogunate
    background of, 365
Tokugawa shogunate
    arts and learning during, 368–369
    Christianity during, 365–366
    economic advances during, 366–368
    law and government during, 365
    main emphasis of Japanese thought during
        later, 369–371
    peasants and urbanites in, 368
    shogun, emperor, and daimyo under, 366
Tower of Babel, 20
Towns, 17
    engage in first urban planning, 275
    Hebrews make transition to, 50
    resurgence of, during Middle Ages, 249, 252

Trade
    among pastoral peoples, 259
    between China and Japan, 236
    Chinese, 216
    decline of, due to plague, 269
    disease spread through, 263, 269
    disruption of Roman, 129
    East African, 175
    Egyptian, 39–40
    and exchange networks, 80, 146
    and expansion of scale in Mesopotamia, 27
    export, of Athenian population, 105
    favorable balance of. See Mercantilism
    of Gupta Dynasty, 205
    of Hebrews, 48
    Indian Ocean–Red Sea, 172
    Indus Valley civilization and early, 55–58
    Islamic community and
        (c. 1200 ce), 199
    in Kush, 171
    luxury, of India, 211
    maritime exploration and, 301–302
    in Mesoamerican civilizations, 154
    in Muslim world, 199
    Pax Mongolica and, 262
    Persian, 45
    Phoenician maritime, 44
    relations under tsarist Russia, 346
    and Renaissance, 279–280
    in Roman Empire, 123
    silk, of China, 73
    during Song Dynasty, 224
    spice, 363, 364, 371
    and spread of Buddhism, 63–64
    trans-Pacific, to China, 354
    trans-Saharan, and kingdoms of the Sudan,
        172–175
Trans-Saharan trade, 172
    Gao and, 174–175
Treaty of Karlowitz, 327, 344
Treaty of Utrecht, 338
Treaty of Verdun, 139
Treaty of Westphalia, 335–336
Tribes, 259
Tribunes, 113
Trojan War, 86–87, 88, 112
Troy, 86–87, 88, 112, 120
Truce of God, 250
Trung Nhi, 239
Trung Trac, 239
Tsars, 286
    Romanov, 342
    Russia under, 346–348
Tse-tse fly, 167
Tudor Dynasty, 284
Tumen, 261
Turks
    coming of, 200–201
    Ottoman. See Ottoman Empire
King Tut. *See* Tutankhamen
Tutankhamen, 36
    death mask of, *38*
    discovery of tomb of, 38
Twelve Tribes of the Hebrews, 47
    nomadic background of, 50
Two Treatises of Civil Government (Locke), 342
Tyranny, 88, 89

Uigurs, 259
Ulama, 175, 324–325
    power of, 194

Umar, 188
Umayyad Dynasty, 188–189
  conversion under, 190
  overthrow of, 189
Umma, 187, 326
Universe
  geocentric, 101
  heliocentric model of, 101
University
  during Middle Ages, 254–255
  Muslim creation of first, 195
  started under Han, 221
Upanishads, 81, 207
Upper Egypt, 33
Urbanization, 245
  in China, 354
  in Middle Ages, 252
Urban VI, 273
Urdu, 331
Uthman, 189
Utopia (More), 282

Valla, Lorenzo, 281
Vandals, 129, 136
Van Eyck, Jan, 286
Vassals, 246
Vauban, Sebastien de, 338
Vedas, 58, 81, 207
Vedic Epoch, 58–59
Venice, 279
Versailles Palace, 338–339
Vespasian, 52
Vespucci, Amerigo, 302
Lake Victoria, 169
Vietnam, 239, 353
  autonomy of, 224
Vikings, 139, 141, 253, 298
Virgil, 120, 281
Virgin Queen. *See* Elizabeth I
Vishnu, 60, 207, *208*
Visigoths, 136
Viziers, 194

Walpole, Robert, 341
Wandering of the Peoples, 129
Wang Wei, 221, 223
Waqf, 198, 199
Warfare. *See also specific wars*
  Aryan, 58
  Assyrian, 42–43
  of Aztecs, 156–157
  conducted by pharaohs, 40
  horse and chariot in, 43
  between Israel and Judea, 50

Mongol, 260
in Paleolithic Age, 8–9
Roman, 113, 115
siege, 43, 261
slavery and, 26, 33, 43–44, 173
Spartan, 89–90. See also specific wars
War of the Austrian Succession, 344–345
War of the Spanish Succession, 338, 344, 379
Wars of the Roses, 284, 303
Waters, Frank, 163
Way of Nature, 75
The Way of the Dao, 75
  excerpt from, 76
Well-field reform, 221
Wergeld, 137
West Goths, 136
Whirling Dervishes, 194, 195
William and Mary, 340–341
William of Orange, 340. *See also* William and Mary
William (the Conqueror), 253
Witchcraft, during Renaissance, 289
Women
  in African society, 170
  attitude of Laws of Manu toward, 59
  Aztec, 158
  under Confucian philosophy, 73, 75
  in early Japan, 233–234
  from families of khans, 259
  and guilds, 341
  under Hammurabi, 24
  in Hellenic culture, 87, 108
  in Hellenistic civilization, 108
  in Hinduism, 210
  in Hispanic America, 380
  Judaism and, 50
  in Maya culture, 155
  medieval, 246, 247
  in Muslim world, 198–199
  in Neolithic societies, 11
  nomadic, 259
  position of, in early India, 62–63
  in pre-Christian Germanic society, 137
  in pre-Muslim Arabia, 185
  during Renaissance, 288–289
  in Rome, 124–125
  status of, in Mesopotamia, 26–27
Writing
  in China, 69–70
  cuneiform, 23, 24
  Egyptian, 36–37
  evolution of, 23–24

humans before invention of, 5
in Kush, 171
in Mesoamerican civilizations, 153
in Sumerian civilization, 19
Wu, 218
Wu-di, 216
Wyclifites, 274
Wyclif, John, 273–274

Xerxes, 46
  Second Persian War, 90
Emperor Xuanzong, 221, 223

Yahweh, 48
  becomes sole deity of Jerusalem's Jews, 50
  changing conception of, 51–52
  laws of, 50
Yamato Period, 229–230
Yangtze River, 224
Yayoi culture, 228
Yellow River, 68, 224
Yin-yang principles, 73, 76, 223
Yongle, 353
Younger Dryas Event, 17–18
Yuan Dynasty, 224, 264–265
Yurts, 260

al-Zahrawi, 196
Zama, battle of, 114
Zanj, 175. *See also* Swahili
Zarathustra, 46. *See also* Zoroaster
  dualism doctrine of, 50
  similarity between Judaism and doctrines of, 46
  teachings of, 47
Zealots, 52, 131
Zen Buddhism, 229, 235, 369
Zeno, 101
Zhou Dynasty, 68, 70–73
  cir perdue bronze casting during, 72
  culture and daily life in, 71
  disintegration of, 74
  last years of, 214
  literature in, 70
  rival philosophies during, 75
  Sima Qian's anecdotes about, 218
Zhu Yuanzhang. *See* Hongwu
Ziggurats, 20, 21
Zoroaster, 46. *See also* Zarathustra
  followers of, Muslims and, 190
Zwingli, Ulrich, 314